Review of Biblical Literature

2012

Society of Biblical Literature

Review of Biblical Literature

Editor
Jan G. van der Watt (The Netherlands)

Managing Editor
Bob Buller (U.S.A.)

Editorial Board
Athalya Brenner (The Netherlands)
James Alfred Loader (Austria)
Stephen J. Patterson (U.S.A.)
Joseph Verheyden (Belgium)
Jürgen K. Zangenberg (The Netherlands)

Volume 14 (2012)
ISSN 1099-0046

Society of Biblical Literature
825 Houston Mill Road, Suite 350
Atlanta, GA 30329
http://www.sbl-site.org

© 2012 Society of Biblical Literature

All rights reserved. No part of this publication may be reproduced in whole or in part, in any form, including electronically, except in the following instances: (1) brief quotations embodied in critical articles and reviews; (2) classroom or reserve-library use on a not-for-profit basis, where 10 percent or less of the entire text, or a single chapter/article, may be duplicated to create up to fifty copies without charge or permission; and (3) authors may republish their own articles, chapters, or reviews in scholarly publications, provided that proper credit is given to the original place of publication. Permission must be obtained in instances where an author wishes to republish more than 20 percent of an entire monograph.

Typesetting by Lindsay Lingo, The Project Company, Loveland, Colorado

Contents

Editor's Foreword	v

Book Reviews

Reference Works	1
Biblical Themes	7
Ancient Near East	21
Languages	39
Archaeology and History	53
Hebrew Bible/Old Testament: General	68
Pentateuch	83
Former Prophets	104
Latter Prophets	126
Writings	149
Apocryphal/Deuterocanonical and Other Jewish Writings	176
Septuagint	186
Hebrew Bible/Old Testament Theology	193
Judaism: General	199
Judaism: Dead Sea Scrolls	208
Judaism: Rabbinic and Medieval	219
Judaism and Christianity	240
Greco-Roman World and Hellenism	244
New Testament: General	254
New Testament and Christian Origins	261
Jesus	268
Synoptic Gospels	282
John	315
Acts	327
Paul and the Pauline Epistles	337
General Epistles and Hebrews	382
Revelation	402
New Testament and Biblical Theology	411
Early Christianity and Early Christian Literature	417
History of Interpretation	440
Hermeneutics and Methods	451
Textual Criticism and Translation	468
Bible and Culture	488

Indexes

Authors and Editors	505
Reviewers	507
Publishers	508

Editor's Foreword

The *Review of Biblical Literature* has established itself internationally as one of the leading review organs for biblical literature and related fields. It has become especially known for being comprehensive, international, timely, and authoritative:

- *RBL* reviews a wide and comprehensive spectrum of books from publishers large and small across the entire range of biblical studies and its cognate disciplines. To broaden our offerings, *RBL* publishes multiple and contrasting reviews as often as possible.
- Not only does *RBL* review books written in various languages (e.g., English, German, French, Italian, Spanish, Hebrew); it also invites scholars from a variety of language groups to review for *RBL*. Further, the editorial board overseeing this process consists of leading academics from Australia to America.
- *RBL* reviews are published in a timely fashion. As a rule, we attempt to review books within two years of their publication, and we try to place the review within a few months of receiving a book. Finally, we typically publish each review within two to three months of receiving it.
- *RBL* reviews are written by the most qualified scholars available, whether a member of the Society of Biblical Literature or the broader scholarly guild. In addition, all *RBL* reviews are vetted to ensure their quality by a member of our editorial board.

During the past twelve months, thanks to the cooperative efforts of our reviewers, editors, and staff, *RBL* has published 390 reviews. With an average of 3.5 pages per review, the past year's output would fill nearly 1,400 published pages. To take this a step further, the 6,700 reviews published since the beginning of *RBL* through the end of September 2012 would require more than 23,400 printed pages. This is truly a monumental accomplishment, not least because it has been achieved almost entirely through the contributions of volunteers

As is well known, *RBL* announces the publication of new reviews in a weekly newsletter. That newsletter is distributed to over 9,000 subscribers, many of whom have no other contact with the Society than *RBL*. The *RBL* newsletter plays a significant role in leading scholars, students, and interested laypersons to the *RBL* website (www.bookreviews.org), where they can read the latest reviews or search for books reviewed since *RBL*'s creation thirteen years ago. The *RBL* website records over two million visits each year. Taking all these data into account, it is no stretch to conclude that *RBL* indeed leads the way in providing reviews of biblical studies publications.

But there is even more to the story than the number of reviews *RBL* publishes and the number of visitors to the website. *RBL* also leads the way in building bridges between biblical scholarship from every region of the world. Not only do we provide free access to scholarly reviews to anyone with access to the Internet, but over the last twelve months we have published reviews by scholars from thirty different countries, which underscores our international scope. These countries include: Argentina, Australia, Austria, Belgium, Canada, Colombia, Denmark, Ethiopia, France, Germany, Greece, India, Ireland, Israel, Italy, Japan, Lebanon, Malaysia, Mexico, the Netherlands, New Zealand, Nigeria, Norway, Romania, Singapore, South Africa, Sweden, Switzerland, the United Kingdom, and the United States. Somewhat surprisingly, more *RBL* reviews were authored by scholars outside the U.S. than by scholars within the U.S.: 54 percent non-U.S. versus 46 percent U.S.

Obviously, our success depends not only on the publishers supplying books but also on hundreds of academics who are willing to share their time and expertise with the readership of *RBL*. We would like to thank them all. *RBL* is a group effort in the true sense of the word, with so many SBL members joining together to make it the success it is.

Thus with gratitude and pride we present this print publication, a selection of 153 reviews published on our website during the latter half of 2011 and the first half of 2012. We hope that what we present here will stimulate readers to make even more use of the website as we foster biblical scholarship together.

Jan van der Watt
RBL General Editor
Radboud University Nijmegen
Nijmegen, The Netherlands

REFERENCE WORKS

The Cambridge Dictionary of Christianity, edited by Daniel Patte. Cambridge: Cambridge University Press, 2010. Pp. lxvii + 1343. Paper. $39.99. ISBN 9780521820967.

James D. G. Dunn, Durham University, Durham, United Kingdom

This is certainly an impressive tool with a number of features that make it stand out among similar dictionaries or encyclopedias. It covers what may simply be described as the full range of Christianity, beginning with the broadest definition of Christianity: "a Christian is anyone who claims to be a follower of Jesus Christ" (xlv). So its "ecumenical openness" is more open than most ecumenists, including not only the main traditional groupings (denominations), but also "independent Christians," many of whom are "charismatic," and so-called "marginal Christians."

It recognizes the need for specialist articles on the history of Christianity in specific geographical areas. "The length of an article on a given nation reflects the approximate number of Christians who reside in that country today" (xlvii). It has made special efforts to provide articles that give an insider's perspective, providing insights into aspects of a culture that outsiders often miss and that clarify the distinctive features of Christianity in these countries. So, for example, there are entries not only on the Orthodox Church but on the Eastern Orthodox and on the Oriental Orthodox, with individual entries on the different national bodies under these names. This is of particular importance in reflecting the "inculturated" character of the charismatic and Pentecostal movements in many parts of the world.

The dictionary aims to clarify plurality of understandings. On Scripture it refers to the different ways in which believers relate a scriptural text to their lives, including the recognition that for many believers "Scripture is a Word-to-live-by." It has more than twenty columns on "Bible Interpretation," sampling different cultural contexts. On religious experience and worship, it observes the distinction between inculturation and syncretism and includes descriptions of how Christianity is seen from the perspective of another religion. Its treatment of Christian ethics does not ignore such negatives as "anti-Semitism," "Crusades," and "Inquisition," and it includes a cluster on "Poverty" and entries on "Preferential Option for the Poor" and "Pregnancy."

An interesting feature of the more than 3,500 articles and entries is the technique of splitting a large theme into a cluster of more specific themes. For example, the "Eschatology" cluster samples contextual views and practices on "Eschatology and Apocalypticism" in Africa, in Eastern Orthodox Europe, in Mexico, and in

North America, including "Feminist Perspectives." The "Mission" cluster includes a sampling of contextual views and practices on "Anti-slavery," "Emigration or Colonization," "Imperialism," and "Race" and provides studies on various regions of mission, including "Catholic Mission in China, 16th–18th Centuries," "Mission in Post-Communist Eastern Europe," and "Mission in North America: Mission as Conquest." The "Women's Ordination" cluster is broken down to "the Early Church," "the Orthodox Church," "the Roman Catholic Church," "in Africa," "in Asia," "in North America," and "in Western Europe," each written by different (women) authors.

Since the other principal university press in the United Kingdom has also produced a one-volume dictionary (*The Oxford Dictionary of the Christian Church* [Oxford University Press, 1997]) an obvious reviewer's tactic is to compare the two. I will use the abbreviations OUP and CUP. The most obvious comparison is in terms of size: with OUP at xxxvii + 1786 pages and CUP at lxvii + 1343 pages, both two-column pages. This is misleading, however, since CUP uses a bigger font and the columns are narrower. Consequently, the OUP columns have about twice as many words as the CUP columns, though with the larger font CUP is easier on the eyes. Other differences are the relatively brief introduction of the OUP, with ten pages of abbreviations, whereas CUP has a twenty-page preface explaining the editorial policy and structure of the dictionary but only three pages of abbreviations.

CUP is also much more U.S.A.-oriented, with entries for "John Adams," "Thomas Jefferson," and "George Washington" (also "Booker T. Washington'), whereas OUP is more U.K.- and Europe-oriented, with entries on "St Alban," "St Cuthbert," "Edward the Confessor," and many popes. But then the CUP address is given as New York. Characteristic of the different orientations of the two dictionaries is that CUP's focus on geographical entries means that there are only two entries on united churches ("United Church of Christ in the Philippines," "United Church of Christ"), plus two extensive articles on "United Kingdom" (7 columns) and "United States" (more than 18 columns), whereas OUP has entries on "United Church of Christ," "United Free Church of Scotland," "United Methodist Church," "United Methodist Free Churches," "United Presbyterian Church," "United Reformed Church," "United Secession Church," "United Society for the Propagation of the Gospel," as well as "United States of America, Christianity in" (10 columns).

The most striking difference, however, is that OUP includes a sometimes substantial bibliography (in smaller font) at the end of most entries, whereas CUP has no bibliographies. To meet the obvious obligation, the contents page concludes with the note: "For a comprehensive bibliography, see http://hdl.handle.net/1803/3906." Of course, that assumes that users of the dictionary will have ready Internet access, and even so use of the bibliography is rather inconvenient, and "comprehensive" is a too generous description. For a test case I checked the "Aristotle and Christianity" entry and was disappointed to find only six general studies, whereas the OUP "Aristotle" bibliography has nearly two smallish-font columns on text, translations, and studies. Bibliography for "Justin Martyr': CUP, two on texts and one general; OUP, more than half a column (smallish font). In contrast, "Secularism" has only a few lines and no bibliography in OUP, whereas "Secularism/Secularization and Desecularization" in CUP has nearly five columns and eight entries in the bibliography. I think I would have preferred a smaller font for the CUP *Dictionary* and at least a basic bibliography attached to the often rather brief and sparse entries—though truly comprehensive bibliographies available through the web would also be more than welcome.

Some other sample comparisons from entries under A: "Adoptionism" (CUP 3 lines; OUP full column); "Adventism/ists" (CUP more than 2 columns; OUP less than half a column); "Advowson" (CUP 4 lines; OUP full column); "Africa" (CUP 8.5 pages; OUP 2 pages); "Agape" (CUP 7 lines; OUP 1.5 columns); Alcuin (CUP 7 lines; OUP more than 1 column); "Alleluia" (CUP 3 lines; OUP 1 column); Angola (CUP 3 columns; OUP more than 1 column); Argentina (CUP nearly 7 columns; OUP more than half a column); "Armagh" (CUP 2 lines; OUP less than 1 column); "Arminianism" (CUP half a column; OUP 1.5 columns); "Ascension" (CUP 9 lines; OUP 1 column); "Assumption" (CUP 10 lines; OUP 2 columns).

Entries distinctive to each are also indicative of the different orientations of the two dictionaries. In CUP we find entries on "Abuse," "Acculturation," "Jane Addams," "African American" cluster (nearly 6 columns), "Michael Agricola," "Alcoholics Anonymous," "Alternative Trading," "American Literature and Christianity," "Ancestor Veneration and Christianity Cluster (8 columns), "Androcentrism," "Susan Anthony," "Anthropology Cluster" (13.5 columns), "Anti-Semitism," "Anxious Bench" (5 lines), "Apocalypticism Cluster" (more than 4 columns), "Arts and Theology," and "Asian American Theologies." In OUP we find entries on "Mme Acarie," "accidie," "accommodation," "John Acton," "Karl Adam," "Patrick Adamson," "Aelfric," "St. Aidan," "St. Ailred," "Albertus Magnus," "Alogi," "Alternative Services," "Lancelot Andrewes," "Fra Angelico," "Archaeology, Christian," "Aristides," "Matthew Arnold" and "Thomas Arnold," "ars praedicandi," "Assyrian Christians," and "Athenagoras."

I suspect for historical information, including influential Christian thinkers and leaders in the past, I will turn at once to the OUP *Dictionary*, but for a North American perspective on contemporary issues I will certainly not neglect the CUP *Dictionary*.

The Eerdmans Dictionary of Early Judaism, edited by John J. Collins, and Daniel C. Harlow. Grand Rapids: Eerdmans, 2010. Pp. xxxvii + 1360. Hardcover. $95.00. ISBN 9780802825490.

Siam Bhayro, University of Exeter, Exeter, United Kingdom

It gives me great pleasure to review this excellent resource. The *Eerdmans Dictionary of Early Judaism* (hereafter *EDEJ*) bills itself as "the first reference work ever on Judaism in the Greco-Roman age" (back sleeve). The question before us is not so much the veracity of that claim but more whether *EDEJ* has any advantages over its multivolume predecessors, such as *The Cambridge History of Judaism* and Compendia Rerum Iudaicarum ad Novum Testamentum. *EDEJ* has two main advantages: first, it is a single, very affordable volume; second, it is up to date. Despite the corollary that the level of coverage is not as detailed as those older, multivolume works, *EDEJ*'s quality of scholarship and well-organized structure means it is likely to become the first point of reference for all those interested in early Judaism.

EDEJ opens with thirteen major essays by leading specialists that provide an excellent synthesis of current scholarship: "Early Judaism in Modern Scholarship," by John J. Collins; "Jewish History from Alexander to Hadrian," by Chris Seeman ("From Alexander to Pompey") and Adam Kolman Marshak ("From Pompey to Hadrian"); "Judaism in the Land of Israel," by James C. VanderKam; "Judaism in the Diaspora," by Erich S. Gruen; "The Jewish Scriptures: Texts, Versions, Canons," by Eugene Ulrich; "Early Jewish Biblical Interpretation," by James L. Kugel; "Apocrypha and Pseudepigrapha," by Loren T. Stuckenbruck; "The Dead Sea Scrolls," by Eibert Tigchelaar; "Early Jewish Literature Written in Greek," by Katell Berthelot; "Archaeology, Papyri, and Inscriptions," by Jürgen K. Zangenberg; "Jews among Greeks and Romans," by Miriam Pucci Ben Zeev; "Early Judaism and Early Christianity," by Daniel C. Harlow; and, finally, "Early Judaism and Rabbinic Judaism," by Lawrence H. Schiffman. At 290 pages, this substantial opening section showcases all that is excellent in the field and in itself makes owning *EDEJ* worthwhile.

EDEJ then continues with the dictionary section proper—over one thousand pages containing 520 entries covering a rich range of subjects from "Aaron" to "Zerubbabel." The primary focus is on the period from Alexander the Great to Hadrian, although relevant aspects of the Persian period and early rabbinic Judaism are also included. The entries fall into the following broad topics (number of entries): Apocrypha (16), archaeological sites (10) and artifacts (24), Bibles (6), daily life (28), Dead Sea Scrolls (60), Greco-Roman writers (7), Hebrew Bible (17), historical figures (22), Jewish revolts (4), Josephus (4), languages (8), literary genres (19), modern scholars (12), mythical motifs (26), nations and other groups (32), New Testament (10), Philo (6), places (37), practices (34), Pseudepigrapha (44), rabbinic literature (7), reception of biblical figures (19), religious beliefs (60) and institutions (4), and social groups (4).

In addition to the opening essays and the dictionary entries, the editors have been careful to provide a series of features that further enhance the utility of *EDEJ*. The system of cross-references employed throughout is extremely helpful, and the provision of both an alphabetical and a topical list of entries shows that the editors have very much taken a user-orientated approach to assembling *EDEJ*. There are twenty-four maps, a chronological outline (538 B.C.E.–200 C.E.), numerous clear black and white photographs, and some other rather nice surprises (e.g., the chart of Philo's works on 1066–67).

There is no doubt that the publication of *EDEJ* is a really big moment in the hitherto short history of early Jewish studies. One particularly gratifying aspect of

EDEJ is the number of comparatively young scholars who have contributed to it, thus demonstrating that the field is vibrant and has a bright future. In addition to its excellent production quality, high scholarly standard, and thoughtful design, there is one more reason to praise this volume: its price. For what it is, the official price is certainly modest. Also, a certain popular Internet shopping outlet has it listed for around two-thirds of the publisher's price, making it a realistic acquisition for every graduate student—I hope that future editions maintain this feature.

Given how vibrantly the field is developing, it will probably be necessary for a second edition to be produced in the not-too-distant future. With this in mind, I offer the following remarks. (1) The entry on "Ethiopic" opens with the following statement (609): "Ethiopic is a Semitic language formally spoken in Ethiopia and still used in the liturgy of the Christian church in Ethiopia. The language has two principle dialects: North Ethiopic and South Ethiopic. The oldest northern dialect is Ge'ez, which is regarded as Classic Ethiopic. Among early Jewish writings preserved in Ethiopic are...." It should read "Geʿez" rather than "Geʾez" (i.e., with ʿayin rather than ʾaleph), and "Classical" rather than "Classic," and, given the imprecise use of the term "Ethiopic," would be best corrected to something along the following lines (compare, e.g., W. Leslau, *Comparative Dictionary of Geʿez [Classical Ethiopic]* [Wiesbaden: Harrassowitz, 1991], ix):

> Ethiopic is a subgroup of languages within the Semitic language family whose northern forms include Tigre and Tigrinya and whose southern forms are Amharic, Argobba, Harari, Gafat, and Gurage. Classical Ethiopic, referred to as Geʿez, is a member of the northern branch and was the official language of the Aksumite Empire that adopted Christianity in the fourth century. Among early Jewish writings preserved in Geʿez are....

(2) The entry on "Targum" states (1278): "The term 'targûm' is based on the quadriliteral verbal root *trgm*, which has cognates in other Semitic languages but is likely to have had an Indo-European origin." This seems to be based on Rabin's attempt to derive the term from the Hittite verb *tarkummāi-* "to announce, report" (see Ch. Rabin, "Hittite Words in Hebrew," *Orientalia* 32 [1963]: 135). This suggestion, however, is not widely accepted (see, e.g., M. E. J. Richardson, trans. and ed., *The Hebrew and Aramaic Lexicon of the Old Testament* [Leiden: Brill, 1994–2000], 1787, which states "but that is further removed from Heb. than the Akk. and as such is not really to be accepted"). It is likely that the root RGM is Common Semitic, with a wide semantic development across the various languages (e.g., Akkadian "to cry out, bring an accusation"; Arabic and Geʿez, "to curse"; Aramaic and Ugaritic, "to speak"), with a t-stem having the meaning "to translate."

(3) The problematic use of the term "Job Targum" to refer to 4Q157 and 11Q10 (e.g., 362 and 816) is at odds with Tigchelaar's correct statement that "it has few, if any, of the features typical of the later rabbinic targumic tradition, so it should be classified as a translation rather than as a precursor of the rabbinic targums" (817). In view of this, I would suggest two things: we should use a term along the lines of "Aramaic Job from Qumran"; and, despite Tigchelaar's state-

ment, with which I am in complete agreement, some reference should be made to the fine paper by Sally Gold that attempts to argue a contrary view and, in the process, broadens our understanding of this text (see S. L. Gold, "Targum or Translation: New Light on the Character of Qumran Job (11Q10) from a Synoptic Approach," *Journal for the Aramaic Bible* 3 [2001]: 101–20).

(4) The entry on "Satan and Related Figures" (1196–1200), includes a discussion on "Belial," which also has its own entry (435–36). The former should probably be cross-referenced to the latter. Similarly, I think the entry on "Art" (381–86) should be cross-referenced to the entry on "Synagogues" (1260–71), as the latter discusses art at some length.

(5) Unfortunately, the entry "Parthians" (1027–29) is entirely focused on the political and military history of the Parthians in respect of the Seleucids and the Romans—information that is readily available elsewhere. Readers of *EDEJ* would certainly expect the entry to discuss the relationship between the Parthians and the very important Jewish communities that fell under their control. Turning to the entry on "Mesopotamia, Media, and Babylonia" (935–37), I was disappointed once again. The section on "Jews under Persian and Parthian Rule" (935–36) has nothing about the Jews under the Parthians, save for the following observation: "During the Second Temple period the Jews in Mesopotamia were under Parthian rule much of the time." The rest of the section deals with the evidence for exiled Jews under the Achaemenids. Given the importance of the Jewish communities under Parthian control and the significance of the period, this omission needs to be resolved. As it stands, both entries are flawed, and the title of the second entry is very misleading in that the entry neglects to discuss Media altogether. Furthermore, given that Babylonia is part of southern Mesopotamia, it should simply be titled "Mesopotamia."

(6) As noted above, *EDEJ* includes twelve entries on important modern scholars (such as Robert Henry Charles, Martin Hengel, and Emil Schürer), including two who are still alive (Jacob Neusner and E. P. Sanders). Obviously, this is one aspect that will require constant updating. I think it would be useful to have entries for Daniel Boyarin, Gershom Scholem, and Geza Vermes, who, in quite different ways, have made extremely important contributions to the study of early Judaism.

(7) Similarly, the scope of *EDEJ* will naturally expand as successive reviewers and users suggest other subjects for entries. Two that come to mind immediately are the second-century B.C.E. sage "Joshua bar Perahia," for whom the most recent treatments are either unpublished (M. J. Geller, "Joshua b. Perahia and Jesus of Nazareth: Two Rabbinic Magicians" [Ph.D. diss., Brandeis University, 1974]) or in Hebrew (M. D. Herr, "Joshua ben Peraḥya," *Encyclopaedia Hebraica* [1968] 19:245–46), and the first-century C.E. rabbi "Hanina ben Dosa" (see G. Vermes, "Hanina ben Dosa," *JJS* 23 [1972]: 28–50; 24 [1973]: 51–64).

(8) Finally, I do not think that a reference work such as *EDEJ* should serve as a platform for an individual to grind a particular axe. In this regard, the section on "Neo-Babylonian History in the Book of Daniel" (412) is not suitable. It

ignores a large body of scholarship that addresses this subject, leaving the uninitiated reader with the impression that contrary or more-balanced views do not exist. Unfortunately, the same contributor is responsible for the entries criticized above in number 5.

On the whole, the quality of scholarship on display in *EDEJ* is excellent, although, as number 5 above demonstrates, the treatment of matters Mesopotamian and further east could be strengthened. This is probably indicative of the current state of early Jewish studies, so it would be unfair to criticize *EDEJ* for simply reflecting its field. As I mentioned at the start of this review, *EDEJ* bills itself as covering "Judaism in the Greco-Roman age." Actually, it does much more than this, but the use of the term "Greco-Roman" betrays the Western bias that often pervades the field. At some point we shall have to look eastward much more seriously. In the meantime, I am very pleased to have *EDEJ* in my library.

BIBLICAL THEMES

Hermeneutics of Holiness: Ancient Jewish and Christian Notions of Sexuality and Religious Community, by Naomi Koltun-Fromm. Oxford: Oxford University Press, 2010. Pp. xii + 309. Hardcover. $74.00. ISBN 9780199736485.

Michael L. Satlow, Brown University, Providence, Rhode Island

As the Israelites stood at Mount Sinai ready to receive the Torah, Moses (partially at God's behest) commands them to sanctify themselves, wash their clothes, and "do not go near a woman" (Exod 19:14–15). These commands were as puzzling to ancient readers as they remain to modern ones. What does it mean for the people to "sanctify" themselves, and what does this have to do with clean clothes and sexual abstention?

In this fine study, Koltun-Fromm tries to untangle the ancient discursive web that in large part was generated by or tied to this biblical pericope. Koltun-Fromm traces the ways in which the Hebrew Bible and some of its earliest interpreters (down to the Babylonian rabbis of the fifth-sixth centuries C.E.) linked their understandings of holiness (i.e., sanctification), sexuality, and ritual purity. Each of these topics individually has received extensive scholarly treatment, but Koltun-Fromm's distinctive contribution is to show the relationships between them.

Koltun-Fromm develops a simple but effective heuristic (or "patterns," as she calls them) to help understand these discursive strands: "holiness ascribed, holiness achieved, and holiness acquired through the avoidance of semen pollution" (239). Holiness ascribed is the notion that Israel is intrinsically holy (referring back to Exod 19:6), whereas "holiness achieved" means that holiness is something to be gained through proper behavior and thus also lost through improper actions. Holiness through avoidance of semen pollution, while perhaps a bit clumsily phrased, means to convey the link between one particular kind of ritual purity and holiness. Most early biblical commentators, that is, read Moses' commands to wash clothes and avoid women as concerned with ritual purity caused by contact with semen.

Chapter 1, "In the Beginning," elaborates the different stances toward holiness and sexuality found in the Hebrew Bible. Here Koltun-Fromm locates and develops her three patterns of holiness. E and D, she argues, posit that all members of Israel are holy; P ascribes holiness only to priests; and H allows for the achievement of holiness by all Israelites. The avoidance of semen pollution is found in various biblical strands as well.

Chapter 2, "Holy Seed or Holy Deed," traces these biblical ideas in some Second Temple–period literature. Hence, for Jubilees all of Israel has ascribed holiness, but "[k]eeping the positive commandments and avoiding profaning or defiling behavior is key to keeping and protecting their holy status" (55–56). By contrast (and surprising in light of the importance of Jubilees for the authors of the Dead Sea scrolls), the Dead Sea scrolls subscribe to a model of "holiness achieved." Koltun-Fromm here could have engaged more directly the many Dead Sea texts that suggest predestination.

Chapter 3, "Holiness Perfected," focuses on Paul. Paul ascribes holiness to Israel, but it is a weak kind of holiness in comparison to the achieved holiness open to all through faith. "Paul falls in line with the H hermeneutic that promotes holiness as achievable through obedience to the law," the "law" here, of course, being faith in Christ (78). Pure sexual behavior "functions as a protective barrier around one's faith" (83). Achieved holiness is always vulnerable and must be protected through proper sexual behavior.

Chapter 4, "Mother-City of All Evils," closely reads the Acts of Judah Thomas and the Odes of Solomon, the earliest Christian works composed in Syriac that discuss ascetic practices, primarily focusing on the former. The Acts of Judah Thomas collapses all sexual activity—forbidden or not—into a general category of unholy activity. Monogamy is tolerated, but renunciation is better. "Behaving in a holy manner, befitting a member of the holy community, translates to sexual renunciation because sexuality represents everything that is nonheavenly and, hence, unholy" (124). The Acts thus serves as a bridge in Eastern Christianity between Paul's advice to avoid sexual activity as a way to protect faith and Aphrahat's full-blown defense of sexual asceticism.

Chapter 5, "Wedding Garments and Holy Yokes," turns to the fourth-century Christian sage Aphrahat. Aphrahat creates a hierarchy of holiness that is based on sexual behavior. At the top of this hierarchy are the *bnay qyama*, an elitist Christian group (132: "spiritual nobility") set aside by virtue of their avoidance of semen pollution. Aphrahat links his promotion of celibacy to a material conception of the practitioner's "marriage" to God alone. Moses is a particularly important figure for Aphrahat. In Aphrahat's reading (paralleling that of some contemporary rabbis) of the biblical account, Moses left his wife for a life of celibacy at Mount Sinai, thus remaining always pure (i.e., free of semen pollution) and ready to receive God. Aphrahat thus attempts to rebut Jewish claims (so he says) that sexual renunciation is a perversion of God's will. The *bnay qyama*, like Moses, achieve holiness through their restraint.

Chapter 6, "Zipporah's Complaint: Moses Is Not Conscientious in the Deed!" puts (primarily) rabbinic traditions about Moses' celibacy into dialogue with Aphrahat. All more or less agree that Moses was celibate after Mount Sinai. Aphrahat and the rabbis all tell variations on a common theme, which Koltun-Fromm attributes to their common milieu and dependence on a common "library."

Chapter 7, "Sanctify Yourself," turns more broadly to the rabbis of late antiquity. Koltun-Fromm's focus here is on "holy achievement—status gained particularly through certain sexual practices" (213). The rabbis see sexual restraint, she claims, as a supererogatory practice that solidifies their holiness and thereby also their authority. That is, like Aphrahat's *bnay qyama*, the rabbis use sexual renunciation to help create their own distinctive and elitist group identity. The "sanctify yourself" of Exod 19 is thus read as, if not total asceticism, sexual self-control, even in permitted relationships.

Koltun-Fromm's book makes a distinctive and valuable contribution to the already-extensive scholarship on Jewish and Christian sexuality in antiquity. She joins Eliezer Diamond in arguing that asceticism was a far more important practice for the rabbis than is normally acknowledged. As with Syriac-speaking Christians, celibacy (even temporary) and sexual self-control were seen as virtues that increased holiness, if for no other reason than it avoided semen pollution. The rabbis developed this approach in dialogue with both their biblical heritage and their larger cultural milieu. The extent of this claim is open to debate—it may be less prominent than Koltun-Fromm claims. In any case, though, she forces scholars to engage more directly with the late antique claims of both Jews and Christians that link "proper" sexual practice (or its absence) to holiness.

Further attention to some larger issues would have further strengthened the book. This is primarily a history of ideas; there is almost no attention to the material reality of the producers of these texts. As such, I would have liked to have seen more discussion of how her conclusions fit into scholarly treatments of the body, particularly among early Christians. (More use could have been made of Peter Brown's work here.) At the same time, the lack of development of a historical context makes it difficult for the reader to see why the authors or communities under consideration made the exegetical decisions that they did. It also creates some uncertainty—apparently for Koltun-Fromm herself—about how to explain similarities between Aphrahat and the rabbis. She posits that "Aphrahat and his contemporaneous rabbis had access to similar biblical interpretive collections and 'libraries' that they depended upon equally to develop their exegesis and theology" (25). Who wrote the texts contained in these libraries, and who collected and administered the libraries themselves? Koltun-Fromm does not give these critical questions the attention that they would need to support her explanatory model.

This book clearly should be read alongside the work of her primary conversation partners: Daniel Boyarin, Eliezer Diamond, Isaiah Gafni, Christine Hayes, Jonathan Klawans, and my own work. In an area that has become somewhat stagnant over the last five years, *Hermeneutics of Holiness* opens several new and exciting research possibilities.

Circumcision as a Malleable Symbol, by Nina E. Livesey. Wissenschaftliche Untersuchungen zum Neuen Testament 2/295. Tübingen: Mohr Siebeck, 2010. Pp. x + 198. Paper. €49.00. ISBN 9783161506284.

Matthew Thiessen, College of Emmanuel and St. Chad, Saskatoon, Saskatchewan, Canada

Livesey's monograph is a revision of her 2007 doctoral dissertation written under Jouette Bassler at Southern Methodist University. She argues that scholarly treatments of circumcision in early Judaism fail to do justice to the variety of meanings Jews attributed to the rite. She claims that, while most reference works, particularly Andreas Blaschke's *Beschneidung: Zeugnisse der Bibel und verwandter Texte* (TANZ 28; Tübingen: Francke, 1998), "acknowledge the differences in understandings of circumcision, rarely is that same degree of variety reflected in the analytical discussions" (1). She contends that scholars fail to synthesize an ancient author's statements on circumcision. Livesey attempts to provide a thorough treatment of early Jewish perceptions of circumcision.

In chapter 1 Livesey discusses the literary function of the rite of circumcision in 1, 2, and 4 Maccabees, as well as in Jubilees. First Maccabees portrays the conflict between not only law-observant Jews and the hellenizing policies of Antiochus IV but also between law-observant Jews and hellenizing Jews. Following Steven Weitzman ("Forced Circumcision and the Shifting Role of Gentiles in Hasmonean Ideology," *HTR* 92 [1999]: 37–59), she concludes that in 1 Maccabees circumcision functions as a sign of allegiance to the Hasmoneans: "To accept circumcision is to identify with the Hasmoneans" (11). In her treatment of circumcision in Jubilees, Livesey recognizes the author's halakic strictness with regard to the rite: eighth-day circumcision alone is the sign of the covenant, thereby excluding non-Jews from the covenantal community. Her treatments of 2 and 4 Maccabees demonstrate that the same stories of circumcision can function differently. For 2 Maccabees, Jewish women who faithfully circumcise their sons suffer death. Thus, circumcision functions in this narrative as a sacrifice. This accords with the book's view that martyrs are pivotal figures during this period of Israel's history. In contrast, 4 Maccabees believes law and reason as weapons with which to combat the passions. Law observance serves to overcome the passions; consequently, circumcision is a sign of reason and, by extension, a way of controlling passion.

Chapter 2 provides a brief account of circumcision in the writings of Josephus. Livesey focuses on the narrative of Izates' adoption of Jewish customs. The story contains two perspectives on the advisability of his undergoing circumcision. Ananias claims that Izates need not be circumcised in order to please God, while Eleazar argues that Izates should not only read God's law but also obey it by undergoing circumcision. Livesey demonstrates that the narrative supports Eleazar's position, since God protects Izates after his circumcision. She concludes that, "according to the Adiabene narrative, circumcision is a decisive mark of commitment to Judaism" (40).

Chapter 3 examines Philo's understanding of circumcision in *Spec.* 1.2–11, *QG* 3.46–62, and *Migr.* 89–93. Livesey argues that circumcision functions differently in each of these passages. In *Special Laws*, Philo notes six reasons for circumcision, four that he has inherited and two that he claims are his own. The common thread throughout is that the rite serves "as a benefit for health, the promotion of health, life itself and well-being" (58). In *Quaestiones et Solutiones in Genesim*, circumcision draws the mind closer to God. In *Migration*, Philo demonstrates his commitment to the physical rite, in spite of his penchant for allegorizing. Again, circumcision benefits the mind and strengthens participation in the political body of the Jews, something that the allegorizers fail to do.

In chapter 4 Livesey examines Galatians, Philippians, and Romans. In Gal 2, Paul uses περιτομή to refer to Jews. The term is used neutrally to describe Jews, in contrast to ἀκροβυστία, which refers to Gentiles. In contrast, in Gal 4–5 Paul portrays Gentile circumcision as a sign of slavery. In Philippians, Paul uses περιτομή to refer to believers in Jesus who do not put their confidence in literal circumcision (Phil 3:3). If Livesey is correct, Paul here uses περιτομή to refer to Jewish and Gentile believers. This passage contrasts sharply with Gal 2, where Paul uses the term to refer only to Jews, and Gal 4–5, where circumcision functions negatively. Similarly, in Rom 2 Paul uses circumcision to refer to those who keep God's commandments, and in Rom 4 he uses it as an "allegory" for the righteousness of faithfulness (113). Despite the varying ways in which Paul uses circumcision language, the constant is that he is "opposed to the notion of Gentiles becoming circumcised" (121).

The first half of chapter 5 surveys circumcision in Justin Martyr, Augustine, Aquinas, and Luther. For Justin, circumcision separates Jews from others so that they might more easily suffer for their rejection of the Christ. Although Augustine and Aquinas also thought circumcision was a sign before Christ, Augustine believes it to be a sign of salvation, while Aquinas views it as a sign of faith. According to Livesey, it is with Luther that a shift occurred: "While treatments of circumcision prior to this point dealt principally with the ways in which circumcision itself did not actually save a person ... Luther focused on the circumcised person. After Luther, circumcision became associated with Jews, those who performed works to save themselves or to become righteous" (140). Her final section of this chapter deals with modern interpretations of circumcision. She summarizes the finds of chapter 5 as follows: "The history of interpretation of circumcision demonstrates that distortions in the meaning of circumcision occur as secondary interpreters remove statements from their context and then modify them to suit their own purposes" (155).

Livesey provides a careful treatment of the roles circumcision plays in the writings of the late Second Temple period, one that undermines simplistic portrayals of the rite's function. But, having criticized others for not taking into account the full spectrum of an author's portrayal of circumcision, she falls into the same methodological problems. For instance, in her treatment of Jubilees, she discusses only Jub. 15 at length. To be sure, this passage, with its expansive commentary on Gen 17, is central to the author's view of circumcision, yet her argument could have been further nuanced by a discussion of God's promise to circumcise Israel's heart (1:23), the reworking of Isaac's circumcision (16:14; cf. Gen 21:4), the portrayal of circumcision as one of Abraham's tests (17:17), Abraham's command that all his sons circumcise their sons (20:3), and the author's reworking of Gen 34 (30:12). Additionally, precisely because the author is reworking Genesis and the first third of Exodus, she should deal with omissions from biblical accounts that contain circumcision (i.e., Moses' near death on his way to Egypt [48:1–4; cf. Exod 4:24–26], and the Passover legislation [Jub. 49; cf. Exod 12:43–49]). Her treatment of Jubilees would also have been strengthened had she taken into account Michael Segal's recent treatment of circumcision (*The Book of Jubilees: Rewritten Bible, Redaction, Ideology and Theology* [JSJSupp 117; Leiden: Brill, 2007], 229–45), which argues that Jubilees' emphasis on eighth-day circumcision is a response to perceived Pharisaic halakic laxity.

Additionally, given that Livesey examines treatments of circumcision between 200 B.C.E. and 100 C.E., I wondered at her selection of early Christian texts. Many scholars argue for a first-century dating for Luke-Acts, John, and the Gospel of Thomas. Consequently, these works might be relevant to her discussion. After all, Luke is the only Gospel that mentions the circumcision of John the baptizer and Jesus (1:59; 2:21), and Acts narrates the controversies over circumcision in the early church (7:8, 52; 11:1–3; 15:1–5; 16:1–3; 21:21). Likewise, John and Thomas are the only two Gospels that portray Jesus speaking about circumcision (John 7:23; Thomas 53). If Livesey is convinced that these works date to the second-century C.E., she should mention this in a note or, better yet, discuss them in her fifth chapter along with Justin Martyr.

This raises important questions about the content of her fifth chapter: Why has Livesey chosen these particular writers, and how does such a selection affect her argument? Why Justin and Augustine but not Origen or Chrysostom? Why Luther but not Calvin? For that matter, why treat only Christian interpreters? Why not examine differing conceptions of circumcision among rabbinic Jews or Samaritans? I would not expect Livesey to survey all of these various authors, but I would like to know the reason why she chose to treat some authors and not others.

These criticisms aside, Livesey has helpfully demonstrated that any discussion of a rite or aspect of early Judaism must do justice to the wide variety of perspectives held regarding that rite. Her monograph shows that scholarship has too often settled for sweeping statements about the function of circumcision without taking into account the diverse views held by Jews.

Mother Goose, Mother Jones, Mommie Dearest: Biblical Mothers and Their Children edited by Cheryl A. Kirk-Duggan and Tina Pippin. Semeia Studies 61. Atlanta: Society of Biblical Literature, 2009. Pp. x + 232. Paper. $30.95. ISBN 9781589834415.

Melanie Howard, Princeton Theological Seminary, Princeton, New Jersey

In *Mother Goose, Mother Jones, Mommie Dearest: Biblical Mothers and Their Children*, editors Cheryl A. Kirk-Duggan and Tina Pippin draw together a delightfully diverse collection of essays devoted to the exploration of "the role, place, and politics of identity of biblical mothers and their relationships with their daughters and their sons" (5). This volume brings attention to the important, if oft neglected, role of mothers within the biblical narrative and the connections between that role and the constructions of motherhood that are prevalent today.

The three-pronged paradigm of motherhood, simplified by the witty shorthand titles of Mother Goose, Mother Jones, and Mommie Dearest, provides a loose but cohesive framework for the book's heterogeneous forays into a variety of issues surrounding motherhood. Mother Goose, the archetypal "good mother," stands as a contrast to Mommie Dearest, the mother whose excessive self-interests lead to her abusive and manipulative behavior toward her children. Mother Jones, a model based on the early twentieth-century fighter for fair labor practices, serves as an illustration of assertive risk-takers. Together, these exemplar mother figures hold together the diverse perspectives on mothers and mothering in this volume.

Engaging the sensitive topic of father-daughter incest in both Lev 18 and contemporary churches, Madeline McClenney-Sadler advocates for a restructuring of family dynamics in which mothers cease to view fathers as the sole head of household. Illustrating her essay with a poignant tale from her own experiences counseling a survivor of incest, McClenney-Sadler highlights the dangers of assuming male authority in the household for mothers who keep silent in the face of their husband's abuse of their children.

The next two essays take on the book of Ruth as a conversation partner. Wil Gafney provocatively suggests that Naomi plays a key role in the abduction of her daughters-in-law for marriage to her sons and in the "sexploitation" of Ruth in order to procure a grandson. While Gafney admits that Ruth need not have been an unwilling pawn in this scheme, she nonetheless finds it "troubling" that Naomi would make such use of "the sexual and reproductive services of another woman" (35). A different reading of Ruth by Brian Britt juxtaposes the biblical text alongside J. M. Coetzee's 1999 novel *Disgrace* in order to highlight the sacrificial roles into which mothers can be forced in situations of rival group conflict. Britt observes that, while the female protagonists of both texts adopt a self-sacrificial role of sorts, they simultaneously resist the imposition of the role of sacrificial victim by external forces.

In another unique juxtaposition of modern culture with the biblical text, Frank M. Yamada explores the virtuous mother–wayward son configuration as it is exemplified in the popular television show *The Simpsons* (between characters Marge and Bart) and in Judges (between Samson and his unnamed mother). In both cases, Yamada observes that chaos is the result of characters stepping out of their expected roles, and resolution is only possible by the reinstitution of predictable behavior.

Mignon R. Jacobs takes up the question of how mothers function when they parent not only sons but kings. Because of the inevitable overlap between the private and public domains, Jacobs suggests that queen mothers such as Bathsheba can have unexpected but considerable power over their sons. Thus, such a queen mother, like Mother Goose, may appear "unassuming" while nonetheless serving as a "model of wisdom" (82).

In a unique exploration of the history of interpretation of Gen 3:16a in Anglo-American medical and theological communities of the last two centuries, Linda S. Schearing highlights the ways in which exegesis of this verse figured prominently in medical literature concerning the use of anesthesia during child birth. This very interdisciplinary approach sketches how a discussion of female piety and the experience of pain in child birth were connected in medical literature from the eighteenth to the twentieth centuries.

Cheryl A. Kirk-Duggan explores the portrait of the mother in Prov 31 as a composite of Mother Goose, Mother Jones, and Mommie Dearest. Challenging the assumption that Prov 31 describes the quintessential mother, Kirk-Duggan suggests instead that the attributes of this fictional woman are "neurotic, pathological, and impossible to achieve—then and now" (107). Such dismantling of "useless, perfect mothers' paradigms" (103) can have a liberating effect for mothers today.

The connection to contemporary mothers is extended in the essay by Mark Roncace and Deborah Whitehead in which they trace the "messy entanglement" (113) of sexual desire and desire for God both within biblical texts and contemporary devotional literature aimed at evangelical women. Roncace and Whitehead compare the suggestion of divine paternity in the Bible to contemporary devotional texts that, while drawing on a similar association between sexuality and spirituality, nonetheless "are tempered by a heavy-handed stress on gender essentialism and a naturalized theology of gender roles" (126).

As the first of several essays devoted to the exploration of mothers in the New Testament, Andrew M. Mbuvi's examination of Jesus' mother reads Mary as a Mother Jones prototype for African women and widows. Advocating for the position that Mary herself was a widow, Mbuvi suggests that Mary's subversive refusal to be smothered by cultural norms makes her an empowering example for African widows today.

Turning to Mary's son Jesus, Tina Pippin problematizes the notion that Jesus' casting of himself as a mother hen in Matt 23:37–39 is a comforting and maternal image. Rather, drawing on cultural relics as diverse as Mother Goose rhymes and Alfred Hitchcock's *The Birds*, Pippin paints a portrait of Jesus as a Mother Goose turned Mommie Dearest.

Stephanie Buckhanon Crowder continues the conversation on the relationship between Mother Goose and Mommie Dearest as it relates to the Canaanite woman in Matt 15:21–28 and to mothers in an African Diasporan context. Buckhanon Crowder navigates the tricky terrain between working when it is pursued for the benefit of family and working that becomes wrecking that is detrimental to a mother's children.

Drawing attention to the Mother Jones paradigm, Brenda Wallace examines the widow of Luke 18:1–8 as an archetype for mothers of justice movements. Wallace invites an allegorical reading of the parable that envisions God as the persistent widow, and she proposes the development of a hermeneutic of the marginalized based on the "similarities between the need for prayer and the need for justice in the parable and in the prayers of the marginalized" (181).

Margaret Aymer's essay on Paul's casting of himself as a mother invokes the Mother Goose paradigm. Aymer suggests that an examination of ancient motherhood reveals that mothers do not have the all-powerful authority of fathers and that Paul, in recognizing a similar balance of power in his relationship with early churches, relies on his powers of persuasion in much the same way a Roman mother might use rhetorical power to make up for the limits of her authority.

The responses by Tat-siong Benny Liew and Alison Jasper provide a fitting conclusion to this volume by offering some summarizing comments and directions for future conversations on the topic of mothers and mothering in the biblical text and beyond. Jasper's call for a heterologous reading that challenges "oppressive political ideology" (212) and Liew's suggestion for expanding the tropes of motherhood to include that of Mother-City and Mother-Land (204) are particularly worthy of consideration. Liew suggests only a limited expansion of these tropes, but it may be worth questioning the validity of even using such a restrictive list of paradigms by which to categorize biblical mothers. As many of the volume's contributors note, fitting both biblical and contemporary mothers into one or another of these models is particularly challenging, given the diversity of mothers and mothering practices. Furthermore, it is rather surprising that, despite the prevalence of the barren-woman motif in biblical texts, only a handful of essays (Gafney, Yamada, Roncace and Whitehead) touch on this topic, and none of them delves further into issues of infertility, conception, or miscarriage.

Overall, the quality of essays in *Mother Goose* is of the highest caliber, and Kirk-Duggan and Pippin have brilliantly arranged this collection so as to highlight points of continuity between otherwise very disparate pieces. In spite of the potentially confining limits of the Mother Goose, Mother Jones, Mommie Dearest paradigm, this model provides a helpful framework for the volume as a whole. This book will well serve the interests of anyone concerned about the role and function of mothers in the biblical text and beyond.

Images of Zion: Biblical Antecedents for the New Jerusalem, by Lois K. Fuller Dow. New Testament Monographs 26. Sheffield: Sheffield Phoenix, 2010. Pp. x + 286, Hardcover, $95.00, ISBN 9781906055950.

Nils Neumann, Institut für Evangelische Theologie, Universität Kassel, Kassel, Deutschland

Lois K. Fuller Dow ist Dozentin für Neues Testament am McMaster Divinity College in Hamilton. In ihrer Monographie „Images of Zion" unternimmt sie eine kanonische Untersuchung zur Bedeutung der Motive „Jerusalem" und „Zion" in den biblischen Schriften, die letztlich in die Frage einmündet, wie sich vor diesem kanonischen Hintergrund die Schilderung vom „neuen Jerusalem" in Offb 21–22 erklären lässt.

Ein ausführlicher Einleitungsteil (1–42) klärt zunächst die Zielsetzung und die in der Studie verfolgte Herangehensweise an die biblischen Texte: Für ein angemessenes Verständnis der Aussagen über das „neue Jerusalem" in der Johannesoffenbarung ist ein intertextuelles Werkzeug vonnöten, da diese Aussagen auf Vorstellungen aufbauen, die durch die Tradition bereits vorgegeben sind. Entsprechend kann die Darstellung im letzten Buch der Bibel als „Neu-Interpretation" („reinterpretation") von schon vorhandenen Gedanken aufgefasst werden (2). Um dieser Gegebenheit gerecht zu werden, wählt die Verfasserin für ihre Studie einen kanonischen Ansatz. Von der Warte der Johannesoffenbarung aus betrachtet ist ein solcher Ansatz deswegen angemessen, weil der Text sich an eine dezidiert christliche Leserschaft richtet und dabei die autoritative Geltung des alttestamentlichen Kanons voraussetzt (7). Ausdrücklich umfasst der kanonische Ansatz in Verlängerung dieses Grundsatzes auch die Annahme, dass der Bibel normative Bedeutung für das christliche Leben und den christlichen Glauben zukommt (11). Um die Vorstellung vom neuen Jerusalem in der Johannesoffenbarung klären zu können, behandelt die Verfasserin die Aussagen zu Zion und Jerusalem erstens im Alten Testament, zweitens in einigen außerkanonischen jüdischen Schriften, drittens im Neuen Testament unter Absehung von der Johannesoffenbarung und viertens schließlich in der Johannesoffenbarung selbst (41–42). Es geht ihr darum, herauszufinden, wie die Lehre vom neuen Jerusalem im letzten Buch der Bibel („what the book of Revelation teaches") beschaffen ist (19). Um dies zu verwirklichen, ist die Kenntnis der anderen Schriften vonnöten; doch eine etwaige diachrone Beschreibung von der Fortentwicklung bestimmter Motive liegt explizit nicht auf der Linie des kanonischen Ansatzes (22). Im Anschluss an eine Skizze zur Forschungsgeschichte des Zions- und Jerusalem-Motivs innerhalb der verschiedenen Textcorpora wendet sich die Verfasserin dann ihren eigenen Beobachtungen an den Schriften zu.

Das Kapitel über Zion und Jerusalem im Alten Testament (43–110) trägt den Titel „Die Tradition wird etabliert" („The Tradition Established") und setzt am Anfang des Kanons an, d.h. es beginnt mit einer Analyse des Pentateuch. Dort fällt auf, dass der Pentateuch eine Reihe von abweichenden Bezeichnungen kennt, die sich auf den Zion beziehen, wenn sie im kanonischen Zusammenhang

Biblical Themes 17

gelesen werden; zu diesen gehören u.a. „Salem", „Tal des Königs" und „Berg des Herrn" (50). All diese Größen bezeichnen einen Ort der Begegnung zwischen Gott und den Menschen, wo die Menschen Gott anbeten und ihm Opfer darbringen können, und wo sie Gottes Weisung und seinen Segen erhalten. In den sog. „Geschichtsbüchern" (Jos–2Kön) kommt dem Zion vor allem die Funktion zu, dass er den Zielpunkt des Exodus darstellt (67). Dort wird der Tempel errichtet, in dem das Volk zu Gott beten und Vergebung finden kann. Gleichzeitig fungiert die Stadt Jerusalem als heiliger Ort Gottes und auch als Hauptstadt eines Volks, das sich regelmäßig gegen seinen Gott versündigt. In den Büchern der Chronik, Esra und Nehemia festigt der Zion die Identität des Gottesvolks, das aus dem Exil zurückkehrt. Der Ort repräsentiert die neu aufkeimende Hoffnung und ist gleichwohl auch wieder der Platz, an dem sich die Treue des Volks zu seinem Gott aufs Neue bewähren muss (75). Eine komplexe Sichtweise auf den Zion liegt in den Psalmen vor: Er ist Gottes Wohnstätte und insofern auch Ort der Freude, da hier die Begegnung zwischen Gott und Mensch intensiv stattfinden kann. Mit der Erfahrung des Exils zeigt sich aber auch die Verletzlichkeit dieses Platzes. Deswegen sprechen die Psalmen ebenso die Hoffnung darauf aus, dass Gott seine Wohnstätte wieder aufrichten werde (82). Innerhalb der prophetischen Schriften (Jes–Mal) liegt schließlich eine zweifache Akzentuierung in der Rede vom Zion vor. Am Berg Gottes kristallisiert sich für die Propheten einerseits Gottes Gericht an seinem Volk und andererseits auch sein rettendes Handeln (103). Beides gehört sachlich zusammen, da sich in dieser Dualität die Beschaffenheit der Beziehung zwischen Gott und seinem Volk ausdrückt. Es ergibt sich insgesamt im Alten Testament ein Bild vom Zion, nach dem dieser Ort einen Punkt darstellt, an welchem die Gegenwart Gottes sich mit der menschlichen Welt berührt (107).

Unter der Überschrift „Die Tradition wird erweitert" („The Tradition Expanded") setzt sich das zweite Kapitel der Studie (111–38) mit der Präsentation des Zion in einer Reihe von außerkanonischen Schriften auseinander. Anders als im vorigen Kapitel geht die Studie hier aber nicht an den einzelnen Texten entlang sondern bündelt diese von vorn herein nach den verschiedenen Phasen der Geschichte Israels, wie der alttestamentliche Kanon sie präsentiert. Die Stationen auf diesem Weg der Geschichte Gottes mit seinem Volk nehmen ihren Ausgang bei der Erwählung Jerusalems durch Gott als Wohnstätte und verlaufen dann über die Erlebnisse Abrahams, den Aufbau Jerusalems mit seinem Tempel durch David und Salomo, die Zerstörung und das Exil und weitere Stadien bis hin zu eschatologischen Vorstellungen über die Bedeutung Jerusalems am Ende der Zeit. Dabei zeigt sich, dass die außerkanonischen Texte die Tradition des Alten Testaments weiterdenken und auf ihre Weise akzentuieren. Besonders die überzeitliche Relevanz von Zion und Jerusalem wird dabei fokussiert: Nicht nur hat Gott schon von Beginn an den Zion als Wohnstätte für sich ausersehen, sondern er hat den Zion auch zu dem Platz bestimmt, an dem die endzeitliche Aufrichtung seiner Herrschaft sich durchsetzen wird (136–38).

„Die verschobene Tradition" („The Tradition Shifted") lautet die Überschrift zum dritten Kapitel der Untersuchung (139–79), das sich mit dem Motiv von Zion und Jerusalem im Neuen Testament auseinandersetzt. Im Matthäusevangelium nimmt die Jesusfigur den Platz ein, der bislang Zion als Kontaktpunkt zwischen Gott und der Menschheit zukam (146). Auch das Markusevangelium kritisiert die irdische Stadt Jerusalem aufgrund ihrer Ablehnung Jesu (148). Im lukanischen Doppelwerk kommt Jerusalem eine Schlüsselstellung zu, denn es fungiert als Ausgangspunkt sowohl für die Geschichte Jesu (153) als auch für die Verbreitung des Christusglaubens nach der Himmelfahrt (159). Das Johannesevangelium schenkt dem Tempel besondere Beachtung und überträgt die traditionell vorgegebene Zions-Theologie auf ihre Jesus-Figur. Die paulinischen Schriften stellen die Gemeinschaft der Christusgläubigen als Erben der Verheißungen dar, die sich für sie mit einem himmlischen Jerusalem und dem Zion verbinden (172). Nur vorübergehende Bedeutung besitzt das irdische Jerusalem auch nach dem Hebräerbrief. Durch das Kommen Christi verschiebt sich der Akzent hin zu einem himmlischen Jerusalem. Wer an Christus glaubt, ist in gewissem Sinne schon am Zion angelangt, aber die endgültige Ankunft als vollständige Gemeinschaft zwischen Christus und dem Glaubenden steht noch aus (177). Schlussendlich spiegeln die neutestamentlichen Schriften somit—ähnlich den außerkanonischen—eine Akzentverschiebung vom irdischen Zion hin zu einer durch Jesus Christus bestimmten Größe wider, die sie als himmlisches Jerusalem begreifen (178).

Die Darstellung des Motivs von Zion bzw. Jerusalem in der Johannesoffenbarung benennt die Verfasserin mit dem vierten Kapitel (180–221) als „Die erfüllte Tradition" („The Tradition Fulfilled"). Ein sorgfältiger Durchgang durch die relevanten Textpassagen führt zu dem Ergebnis, dass (das himmlische) Jerusalem in der Johannesoffenbarung primär für die Nähe zwischen Gott und den Menschen („intimacy between God and his people") steht (197). Das himmlische Jerusalem verkörpert Gemeinschaft und Leben (207), Gottes Herrschaft und Gegenwart realisieren sich hier letztgültig im Eschaton (214).

Das abschließende und kurze fünfte Kapitel des Buchs (222–34) schlägt einen Bogen vom Jerusalem- bzw. Zions-Motiv der Johannesoffenbarung hinein in die Glaubenswirklichkeit heutiger Christinnen und Christen. Es weist darauf hin, wie der biblische Text auch heutigen Lesenden noch eine Motivation bieten kann, sich auf die Begegnung mit Gott einzulassen (228–29). Einige Schlussbemerkungen (235–42) runden zusammen mit einem Literaturverzeichnis und ausführlichen Registern das schöne Buch ab.

Insgesamt legt die Verfasserin mit ihrer Studie eine überzeugende Darstellung des Zions-Motivs in den biblischen Schriften vor. Notgedrungen kann manch interessanter Aspekt dabei nur in äußerster Kürze angesprochen werden. Der gebotenen Kürze verdankt sich auch die merkwürdige Inkongruenz des zweiten Hauptkapitels im Vergleich zu den Kapiteln 1, 3 und 4: Denn innerhalb des gegebenen Rahmens können die Texte der außerkanonischen Literatur schlechterdings nicht einzeln und vollumfänglich besprochen werden, so dass dieser Teil der Studie besonders gerafft wirkt.

Trotzdem ist die Erwähnung der nicht-kanonischen Schriften sehr begrüßenswert. Dieser Teil zeigt, dass die Verfasserin trotz ihrer kanonischen Herangehensweise nicht die Existenz weiterer Schriften negiert sondern sie zum Verständnis der biblischen Texte beitragen lässt. So tritt schlussendlich eine Entwicklung zutage, die sich anhand des Motivs vom Zion durch den biblischen Kanon hindurchzieht: Jerusalem und der Zion bilden den Kristallisationspunkt für die Begegnung zwischen Gott und seinem Volk, der sich im Verlauf des Kanons aufgrund des Erscheinens Jesu Christi von der irdischen Sphäre hin zu einer eschatologisch-himmlischen Dimension verlagert. Von den einzelnen Erkenntnissen, die im Verlauf der Untersuchung vorgetragen werden, können daher auch motivgeschichtlich denkende Forscherinnen und Forscher profitieren.

Einige zentrale Stärken und Schwächen teilt die vorliegende Studie mit dem Genre der „biblischen Theologie": Der kanonische Ansatz lässt den roten Faden innerhalb der biblischen Texte deutlich hervortreten, während wünschenswerte Differenzierungen oftmals zu knapp ausfallen. Doch die Verfasserin reitet wacker auf diesem theologischen Pferd, von dessen Rücken man zu beiden Seiten herunterfallen kann.

Risking Truth: Reshaping the World through Prayers of Lament, by Scott A. Ellington. Eugene, Ore.: Pickwick, 2008. Pp. xiv + 200. Paper. $24.00. ISBN 9781556352638.

Philip E. Satterthwaite, Biblical Graduate School of Theology, Singapore

This is an impressive book, a study of biblical prayers of lament that takes in the lament psalms, Job, Jeremiah, Lamentations, and parts of the New Testament, integrating a reading of the biblical text with a number of contemporary concerns. Ellington develops a wide-ranging, rich, and suggestive argument, but without a sense of undue haste or compression, and always in an accessible style. He draws on much previous research, but creatively, and in the service of a coherent and illuminating argument. There are worthwhile insights on every page.

Chapter 1 ("Why Should We Cry Out?") surveys biblical prayers of lament in the Bible. Lament arises out of times of disappointment, rejection, grief, and catastrophe; out of a conflict between belief and experience; out of an unwillingness to abandon trust in God alongside a refusal to pretend that facts are other than they are. Lament is thus an expression of faith, but one that involves a risk, for what if God does not respond and turn lament into praise? Large issues are at stake in lament prayers: God's activity in history; God's commitment to his people. It is surely significant that there is so little lament in the contemporary Western church.

Are texts that speak of God feeling anger and pain, "repenting" of a former decision, and so on "mere anthropomorphisms"? Chapter 2 ("Risking an Imperfect God") documents a shift in Jewish and Christian thinking on this point in the twentieth century. Certainly the Bible depicts God as relational from Genesis on, and even for God relationship involves risk and the possibility of rejection and pain. The book of Hosea, in which God responds to Israel's covenant violation with fierce threats of judgment, but also with sadness and even anguish, naturally figures in this part of Ellington's argument. On the human side, too, lament can be a response to what seems like a betrayal of trust, to what seems like an inexplicable hostility on God's part. But one of the things driving lament is the trust that the one addressed is not really an enemy and will not continue to be hostile.

Chapter 3 ("Is the Story Still True?") focuses on the Psalms. Lament psalms (communal and individual) make up perhaps one third of the Psalter. More than that, many of the praise psalms have their roots in situations that originally gave rise to lament. If the Psalter as a whole begins with lament and ends in praise (as many have noted), some individual psalms clearly go in the other direction. Lament psalms express disorientation and isolation. In particular, many laments (e.g., Pss 44; 77; 89) begin by retelling parts of Israel's story but go on to express a sense of being cut off from that story: Has God forgotten how to save? Ellington traces a three-stage movement in some psalms (e.g., Pss 22; 51; 71) from *reality* (a present experience of divine rejection) to *remembrance* of God's past dealings (exodus and conquest, creation, previous personal experiences of God's deliverance) to *response* (testifying to God's deliverance); from disorientation to reorientation and a renewed sense of being part of Israel's story. But again there is the risk: If God does not answer by bringing deliverance, what does that imply for the truth of the story and the lamenter's part in it?In the book of Job, God brings disaster into the life of an innocent man. In chapter 4 ("Risking the World in Job") Ellington notes how much of Job's speeches is taken up with lament: Job's friends talk *about* God, treating what has happened to Job as a theological problem; Job addresses laments *to* God, in the hope of restoring a relationship over which a shadow has inexplicably fallen. Ellington is not the first to have seen this, but focusing on Job's speeches as laments sharpens the point greatly. For Ellington, the book of Job "raises the intriguing possibility that *right speech* may, in certain contexts, include *wrong content* from a theological perspective" (118). Job's orthodox friends are condemned in spite of their orthodox theology, showing that "theology that has been severed from its existential roots can become at best irrelevant and at worst blasphemous in the face of suffering," whereas Job "demonstrates that, in the face of overwhelming suffering and loss, lament is faithful speech" (118). It thus makes sense that God should both accuse him of talking about things he did not understand (38:2) and commend him for having spoken rightly (42:7).

Chapter 5 ("Jeremiah and the Vocation of Shared Suffering") focuses on a prophet called to mediate between God and Israel at a time when the covenant relationship was close to rupture and suffering because of his dual role as God's representative and people's representative. Jeremiah's laments often reflect an anguish in God's own heart, as God contemplates, but for a long time cannot finally enact, judgment against his people. Lamentations presents the other side of the coin: the pleas of a people who feel they have suffered enough at God's hand.

Chapter 6 ("Can Messiah Come without a Cry?") considers the New Testament. Would we not expect the dominant note of the New Testament to be one of praise to God for sending Jesus in fulfillment of prophecy (see Luke 1–2)? And when those who follow Christ suffer, does not a theology of the cross help them to see those sufferings from a very different perspective (Acts 4:24–30; 5:40–41)? Certainly the New Testament contains no extended prayers of lament like those in the Old Testament. Instead, there are brief petitions that seem to act as summaries for much more extended prayers: "Jesus, Son of David, have mercy on me!" (Mark 10:47). At times the summary takes the form of an Old Testament citation: "Rachel weeping for her children" (Matt 2:18). Nonetheless, lament supplies an important part of the framework of Revelation (Rev 6:10; 16:5–7; 19:1–2). It also plays an important role in Matthew's Gospel, where it is those who lament and plead persistently who drive Jesus to extend his ministry beyond the lost sheep of Israel (e.g., Matt. 15:21–28)

A short concluding chapter pulls together some of the main ideas running through the book.

This is a creative and fruitful study. By focusing on the theme of lament, Ellington is able to cast new light on familiar issues. Thus, the solution to Job's seemingly contradictory speeches in chapters 24–27 is perhaps not to reallocate parts of them to Bildad or Zophar but to draw a comparison with the psalms of lament in which the "repeated shifting back and forth between complaint and expressions of trust" seems to reflect "the emotional state of the one praying" (125). In Jeremiah, lament plays a key role in the move from old covenant to new covenant: "the laments of Jeremiah … center on the recognition of God's pathos…. This acknowledgement of God's suffering provokes in the prophet a re-visioning of the nature of covenant that exceeds the limits placed on the relationship by the Sinai covenant" (135).

I have few criticisms. There are about fifteen cases where the text seems to contain the wrong word (e.g., "fundament insight" on 40, instead of "fundamental insight"). These minor blemishes are a pity in a book that is generally so lucidly and eloquently written. In the chapter on the New Testament, I was surprised to find no reference to Rom 8:22ff., particularly in a section that includes the statement that "there is also a continued need for cries and protests in the in-between time, in the now-but-not-yet of the unfolding Kingdom of God" (181). But perhaps Ellington expected his readers to make that connection for themselves.

I heartily commend this book.

ANCIENT NEAR EAST

Mythos und Mythologie: Studien zur Religionsgeschichte und Theologie, by Manfred Görg. Ägypten und Altes Testament 70. Wiesbaden: Harrassowitz, 2010. Pp. 337, Hardcover, €63.80, ISBN 9783447058957.

Mark W. Hamilton, Abilene Christian University, Abilene, Texas

As its name implies, this volume examines the instantiations of Israel's underlying views of the world (*Mythos*) in specific cultural narratives and practices

(*Mythologie*). As Görg puts it in one of several statements of the relationships of the macroscopic and the microscopic, "Vielleicht hilft hier eine unprätentiöse Unterscheidung von 'Mythos' und 'Mythologie', die den 'Mythos' auf eine elementare 'Äußerung' oder 'Ur-Sprache' bezieht, in die sich eine Gottesprädikation hüllt, um dann in der 'Mythologie' al seiner 'Arbeit am Mythos' … eine vielseitig verzweigte Reflexion zu finden" (69). The twenty-five essays collected here, each published between 1993 and 2009, explore five large-scale themes (Gottesbilder, Schöpfungsbilder, Menschenbilder, Geschichtsbilder, and Glaubensbilder), thus sketching the author's views of major aspects of Israelite thought as preserved in the Bible and in other artifacts. The articles show a remarkable degree of cohesion, given their origins in journals and other volumes of collected essays, with the first two and last essays laying out the major themes of the rest of the book. Görg writes in a clear and readable German style that should not unduly tax Anglophone readers and thus should make his work accessible to a wider audience of scholars and students.

Section 1's (13–93) investigation of deity begins with theoretical discussion of Menschenwort and Gotteswort, playing on the multivalent meanings of "word" and the intimate connections of biblical theology with philology. Then follows a closely related article on the divine name as the signifier of a history ("Der JHWH-Verehrung in Israel wohnt so von Anfang an ein soteriologischer Aspekt inne" [36]). The next three essays take up, in turn, the issues surrounding the identification of Y-H-W-H (or Y-H-W-Y-W) as a place name (related to the Shasu-land) in Egyptian texts, the interlinking images of Yhwh as husband and lion (in Hosea and Egyptian glyptic), and the crucial issue of "Gott als König: Die Bedeutung einer komplexen Metapher für das Gottesverständnis in den Psalmen" (65–93). In the last, Görg argues that Israel's notion of divine enthronement did not originally include the ark but resembled Egyptian ideas of a throne resting above the cosmos, founded in *ma'at* (transposed into צדקה), with the old epithet יהוה צבאות being a calque of Egyptian *Db3.tj* ("enthroned" [78]). Whatever the merits of the last point, the overall case that Israelite understandings of divine kingship both derive from Egyptian antecedents and go their own way deserves careful consideration, especially for those of us who focus more on Syrian, Anatolian, or Mesopotamian parallels.

The second section of the book (97–155) similarly contains five essays, these considering "Chaos und Chaosmächte im Alten Testament," "Vorwelt–Raum–Zeit: Schöpfungsvorstellungen im ersten Kapitel der Bible" (both on Gen 1:1–2:4a), "Das Übersetzungsproblem in Gen 2,1," "Der Granatapfel in der Bildsprache des Hohenliedes," and "'Gegenwelten'—biblisch und religionsgeschichtlich betrachtet." The first draws close comparisons between the P creation story and the cosmology of Hermopolis, helpfully describing the former's notion of chaos as "Ziel- und Stillosigkeit" (105), while the second nicely connects to it when laying out the threefold schema of creation that appears in both Israelite and Egyptian texts (and the latter culture's art, well-represented in line drawings here). Again, Görg carefully both compares and contrasts surviving material from the two cultures, showing both dependencies and new directions. The same approach informs his treatment of the erotics of the pomegranate imagery in Song of Songs and his treatment of the paradise imagery in the Hebrew Bible.

Section 3 explores biblical anthropology. As so often throughout the volume, Görg's work reflects his broad humanistic education as he locates the discussion within the context of modern Western thought. Thus his opening essay on the divine image within humankind ("'Ebenbild Gottes': Ein biblisches Menschenbild zwischen Anspruch und Realität" [159–71]) connects the P creation story both to Egyptian royal ideology and ideas of human relationships to animals and to the modified modernism of Moses Mendelssohn's *Jerusalem*, with its response to Lessing and his contemporaries. A similarly multilayered approach animates his study of temple imagery in Gen 2:4b–3:24, whose mix of garden/paradise, birth, and creation images he situates in an Egyptian environment (for which he also posits a connection to the Solomonic temple [173–94], a view that might trouble some American scholars). Görg then turns to two examples of literary prosopography, studies of the stories of Abraham (seven type-scenes in JE [195–207]) and Moses (comparing him to known enemies of Egypt during Dynasty XIX: Amenmesse, By/Beya, Ramsesperre [209–28]). The section concludes with a study of theriomorphic imagery in Ps 91, again locating the menagerie in the context of Egyptian ideas as seen in glyptic (229–39).

Section 4 (243–90) consists of five essays on historical problems in the Pentateuch: "Abraham und die Philister," "Israel in Hieroglyphen," "Der sogenannte Exodus zwichen Erinnerung und Polemik," "Mose und die Gaben der Unterscheidung" (a response to Assmann's *Moses the Egyptian*), and "Der Dämon im Ritualgesetz des Yom Kippur" (defending the possibility of an Egyptian connection while locating the ritual's overarching theology in a firmly Israelite setting). The heterogeneous nature of this section of the book means that scholars interested in the particular topics of Israel's origins and connections to Egypt throughout its history will take up the articles seriatim rather than as an overarching whole. But such is the nature of books such as this one.

Section 5 includes the most free-ranging (and, arguably, least persuasive) essays, treating the development of ideas from ancient Egypt, via Israel, to the New Testament. Topics include "Vom Wehen des Pneuma" (293–96), "Die 'Heilige Familie': Zum mythischen Glaubensgrund eines christlichen Topos" (which compares and contrasts Coptic and other Eastern Christian, and latterly Roman Catholic, notions of Joseph, Mary, and Jesus with those centering around Osiris, Isis, and Horus, without, however, assuming a simple baptism of polytheism [297–305]), "Die Göttin Isis und die Heilige Maria" as mother of God, protector, and virgin (though affirming that Mary is "immer Mensch gewesen und neimals Göttin geworden" [307–16]), and "Gottes Sohn und Gottes Kind" (317–23). These more popular essays are highly provocative, though ultimately unsatisfying because they raise issues that they cannot fully develop in such a limited scope (but see Görg's full-length treatments of Egyptian and Israelite religions). "Offenbarung als Mythos?" (325–34) closes the book by returning to key theological questions central to the German context as influenced by Bultmann and his students and opponents. Görg's point that Bultmann sought the elimination of *Mythologie* rather than *Mythos* and that the latter need not be played off against logos or the key elements of Christian theology serves those of us interested in such questions as a helpful clarification of the much-vexed relationship between religio-historical and theological approaches to our material (for Görg, the two intertwine).

To conclude, how is one to assess *Mythos und Mythologie*? The book shows both minor faults such as a number of typographic errors (e.g., Ch. Westermann for Cl. Westermann [98], Pierre Ricoeur for Paul Ricoeur [53 n. 1], or "zewifelsfrei" for "zweifelsfrei" [290]) and a more serious one of failing to engage with Anglophone scholarship (especially egregious for studies of the exodus traditions or, say, the Azazel material in Milgrom's major commentary), so that one must sometimes struggle to connect his research with the agendas current in American, Israeli, and British circles. Still, the collection deserves serious attention from scholars around the world because Görg has rightly reminded us that Egypt played a major role in the intellectual and aesthetic, not to mention political, life of Israel and thus that Egyptian religion lives on, often in disguise, in Judaism and Christianity mediated through the biblical traditions. For those of us whose interests habitually focus further north and east, much less those who try to understand Israel's texts solely "on their own terms" (whatever that would mean), this collection provides a healthy corrective. However compelling individual arguments are, Görg demonstrates the imagination and care for evidence marking any good scholar. This volume, therefore, makes a useful contribution to our discipline as it seeks to integrate historical, literary, and theological concerns.

Die aramäischen Achikar-Sprüche aus Elephantine und die alttestamentliche Weisheitsliteratur, by Michael Weigl. Beihefte zur Zeitschrift für die alttestamentliche Wissenschaft 399. Berlin: de Gruyter, 2010. Pp. xvi + 880 + 14 plates. Cloth. $210.00. ISBN 9783110212082.

Mark W. Hamilton, Abilene Christian University, Abilene, Texas

The Elephantine manuscript of Ahiqar has long deserved fuller treatment, both as a witness to the intellectual life of a small border town of the Achaemenid Empire and as a legacy of the early stages of a larger Aramaic literary culture that still persists in its Syriac guise. The fact that the Ahiqar legend survived in Jewish and, later, Christian circles and that its development owed relatively little directly to the text fortuitously preserved uniquely in southern Egypt presents a fascinating historical conundrum worth exploring. Professor Weigl's massive study of the sapiential material in the Elephantine text marks a significant step in that direction.

This volume opens with an extended discussion of the history and current state of research on Ahiqar in its various recensions (1–59), including the text's potential connections to Judaism. The heart of the book begins, however, in chapter 2 and continues through chapter 10 (61–542), with each chapter considering a column of text in the Elephantine manuscript (following the arrangement in *TADAE* rather than those of Kottsieper or Lindenberger). The saying-by-saying commentary identifies structures and points of contact linking the various proverbs and draws on a range of comparative material, both predating the Ahiqar collection (especially Mesopotamian and, arguably, some biblical material) and postdating it (such as Second Temple Jewish sapiential literature). Weigl's attention to philological and thematic issues is admirably exhaustive in scope.

Chapter 11 (543–636) examines "Stylistik und ornamentale Form," a category that embraces aspects of literary typology (for Weigl, Aussageworte, Wünsche, and Aufforderungen/Warnungen/Mahnworte), stock formulas or syntagmata, and themes (e.g., the nature of human beings, justice and law, government, war and death, nature and living things). Weigl carefully distinguishes between the Ahiqar and biblical traditions, describing the first as less abstract and less focused on piety and theology than the second (611–16), while still noting numerous points of contact in theme and style. (One might dispute this characterization in part, since the biblical wisdom texts fall on different parts of a spectrum from the particularity of Prov 10–31 to the more sophisticated dialogues of Job 3:1–42:6.) Not surprisingly, some sayings seem to blur category boundaries. For example, Weigl includes among his literary types both animal sayings and disputations, most of which involve anthropomorphized animals. On the whole, this chapter helpfully summarizes Ahiqar's ways of deploying themes widespread in many wisdom traditions (ancient and not) for its own purposes.

Chapter 12 (637–764) draws together the results previously set forth and considers the coherence of Elephantine Ahiqar as a "book" and places its proverbs in some sort of historical setting. Situating the text in northern Syria at the crossroads of Aramaic-, Canaanite-, and Akkadian-speaking cultures, Weigl posits a plausible setting for the Ahiqar legend (which, after all, took other forms in Armenian and Syriac guise [684 n. 150]), while leaving open the literary history of the so-called Egyptian recension. He persuasively shows that, while the sayings take several forms and perhaps arose in different places, the editor of the work has "ein redaktionelles Konzept vor Augen" (696). The ancient work is thus comparable to a range of literature from through the ancient Near East, notably including the biblical book of Proverbs. Weigl concludes, finally, with a forty-nine-page bibliography and extensive indices, as well as a full transcription of the Elephantine text arranged by sayings. In short, then, this volume seeks (without saying so overtly) to address definitively the key issues for this text in sufficient detail that all subsequence research will need to deal with the conclusions set forth here. To my mind, Weigl has written a magisterial and praiseworthy treatment of Ahiqar. Let me comment, then, on a number of issues that his work raises and offer a few suggestions for future studies.

First, the sequence and organization of units in the papyrus are debatable, given the text's state of preservation. The sequence in *TADAE*, followed here, makes sense of the whole, with the opening lines of column 6 providing a fitting entrance to a collection, though even this much is uncertain. Weigl is right, then, to avoid arguing for a large-scale structure in the sayings (instead treating each column in turn, without prejudice), except in such isolated units as sayings 42–45 (568) or his postulating of sayings 1 and 14–15 as an inclusio. On the other hand, the manuscript itself tends to group sayings in three to five long lines alternating with shorter ones and occasionally uses scribal sigla (especially a + mark), apparently indicating some interest in clustering related sayings. As has often been noted in the study of biblical manuscripts (note the recent interest in the exegetical use of *setumah* and *petuchah*), such clues sometimes reveal how an ancient scribe understood the material with which he was working. Perhaps there is more work to be done here, however tentatively we must proceed.

Second, Weigl rightly pays attention to the linguistic profile of this text, noting both that it differs from that of the prose tale preceding it in the Elephantine manuscript and that the dialect of Aramaic used in the sayings section seems most like early texts in Imperial Aramaic (dissimilation of ק and ב around velars; nonassimilation of נ; loosening of germination with נ; quiescent א). However his broader evidence for a northwestern location also presents countervailing data, since the telltale signs cited come from Old Aramaic texts (Tel Fekheriye, Zençirli). In other words, the Elephantine dialect shows conservative features, and thus its date as "early Imperial Aramaic" (e.g., 659) may be correct (it does not fit Old Aramaic as well as Lindenberger argued, for example; cf. Degen), but it is also possible that the collection derives from several locales not now recoverable (a view to which Weigl sometimes seems to subscribe [e.g., 756]). He also argues, however, that the long list of thematic (not verbal) parallels between Ahiqar and Prov 10–22, 25–29 (the latter of which he, like Fox, dates to the Neo-Assyrian period following Prov 25:1) point to a similar date for the earliest layers (Vorstufen) of the former, or at least the broad conception of the work. The evidence is thus not entirely clear.

Third, Weigl acknowledges the problems with the hypothesis that the Ahiqar tradition began to harden in the late Neo-Assyrian period (i.e., that the time of the story relates closely to the time of its composition), noting repeatedly that the Elephantine text seems to have developed in a complex way not now fully recoverable and that the connection between the opening narrative and real events or even courtly practices is unclear. This caution is reasonable, since, for example, the statements about kings and courts in the sayings collection seem sufficiently general as to be learned commonplaces while the presentation of the monarch in the prose tale criticizes royalty astringently. Arguably, Ahiqar served as a "literarischer 'Typus'" (704–9), yet one is left wondering why the redactor/author of the text decided to attribute the sayings to the displaced wise man and how the assignation functioned rhetorically (an admittedly difficult question in view of the text's state of preservation).

To conclude, then, this volume should take its place as a definitive study of a major text. It lays foundations for further rhetorical and sociocultural studies of the Ahiqar proverbs that could move from Weigl's sketching of some such issues to more full-blown studies. Students of ancient Near Eastern wisdom traditions thus owe the author a significant debt.

The Aramaic and Egyptian Legal Traditions at Elephantine: An Egyptological Approach, by Alejandro F. Botta. Library of Second Temple Studies 64. New York: T&T Clark, 2009. Pp. xvii + 237. Hardcover. $130.00. ISBN 9780567045331.

Aaron Koller, Yeshiva University, New York, New York

The book under review is an important monograph about the law within the Aramaic texts from Elephantine. These texts have fascinated scholars since their discovery, some more than a century ago. They have also remained in the public eye, and in 2004 the Brooklyn Museum published a small volume on the texts written by Edward Bleiberg, to accompany the traveling exhibition "Jewish Life in Ancient Egypt." In terms of academic publications, however, the golden age of Elephantine studies to this point was decades ago. In the middle of the twentieth century, in the wake of the publication of another cache of texts, there was a spate of studies of lasting value. Aramaists and legal scholars, notably Yechezkel Kutscher, Reuven Yaron, J. J. Rabinowitz, and Yochanan Muffs, published thorough studies of the language and legal traditions in the texts. Bezalel Porten published the most important book on the texts in 1968, which synthesized all that was known about the texts and moved the field forward significantly.

Since then, Porten has continued to publish studies of individual texts as well as more synthetic studies. He has also recruited excellent scholars with other specialties, so that we now have from Porten new editions of all the texts, done in collaboration with paleographer Ada Yardeni, a grammar of Imperial Aramaic as found in these texts, written together with Semitist Takamitsu Muraoka, and legal studies, published together with legal scholar Zvi Henri Szubin. The language was also studied thoroughly and insightfully by Margaretha Folmer in her long study of Imperial Aramaic.

Other scholars have discussed the texts within the Aramaic legal traditions becoming more and more visible to us with the discoveries of the papyri from Wadi ed-Daliyeh and the various texts from the Judean Desert. Andrew Gross wrote an important book on the Aramaic legal traditions, and studies by Baruch Levine and Doug Gropp have tackled related problems as well.[1] Also worthy of

---

1. For some representative examples, see Andrew D. Gross, *Continuity and Innovation in the Aramaic Legal Tradition* (JSJSup 128; Leiden: Brill, 2008); Douglas M. Gropp, "The Wadi Daliyeh Documents Compared to the Elephantine Documents," in *The Dead Sea Scrolls Fifty Years after Their Discovery: Proceedings of the Jerusalem Congress, July 1997* (ed. Lawrence H. Schiffman, Emanuel Tov, and James C. VanderKam; Jerusalem: Israel Exploration Society and the Israel Museum, 2000), 826–35; Baruch A. Levine, "Prolegom-

note is the book by Anke Joisten-Pruschke on the religious life of the Jews at Elephantine.[2]

There have not, however, been any monographs regarding the law of the papyri themselves in many years. Summary statements have been written, by Porten, for example (in *A History of Ancient Near Eastern Law* [ed. Raymond Westbrook; Leiden, 2003]). Innovative studies of the law in the papyri, however, have been written in recent years only by Hélène Nutkowicz and by Alejandro Botta.[3] One may argue that the dearth of recent publications attests to the thoroughness with which the earlier scholars did their work and to the lack of any need to revisit issues discussed so well decades ago. According to Botta, however, there is such a need, because the earlier scholars saw the law at Elephantine through the prism of the Semitic world, earlier (Mesopotamian) or later. Botta argues that a reevaluation of the legal traditions in light of Egyptian texts shows that, in fact, "Egypt" is not just the geographical setting of these texts but the cultural and legal world from which they emerge, as well.

To begin where Botta begins, however, it should be emphasized that the book under review is the first full-length monograph on the law of the texts from Elephantine in decades and should be applauded for that reason alone. Indeed, Botta does not disappoint in this respect: the first section of the book (8–71) is a detailed study on the legal formulae in the papyri. Botta is acutely aware throughout of variation within the corpus—and thus one might say that this chapter does for the legal traditions what Folmer's book does for the language. Botta is able to show diachronic change within the corpus (e.g., with regard to how dates are written [45–49]) and synchronic variation (35–44, e.g., in the way property boundaries are enumerated). This chapter is an important reading for anyone interested in the texts from Elephantine.

What follow this discussion are two case studies of legal formulae in the Aramaic texts, which Botta argues should be seen as reflexes of older Egyptian formulae rather than as native to Aramaic or borrowed from Mesopotamian traditions. This section, which comprises the central argument of the book, has to be read against the background of a question asked by Porten two decades ago. In a paper published in 1992, Porten listed thirty-five parallels between the formular-

---

enon," in the reprint edition of Yochanan Muffs, *Studies in the Aramaic Legal Papyri from Elephantine* (HOS 1: The Near East 66; Leiden: Brill, 2003), xii–xli.

2. Anke Joisten-Pruschke, *Das religiöse Leben der Juden von Elephantine in der Achämenidenzeit* (Wiesbaden: Harrassowitz, 2008).

3. See, e.g., Nutkowicz, "Concerning the Verb *śnʾ* in Judaeo-Aramaic Contracts from Elephantine," *JSS* 52 (2007): 211–25. For Botta's publications not included in the present book, see also "A Reevaluation of the Use of זבן and יהב in Elephantine," *Antiguo Oriente* 6 (2008): 99–108, and "How Long Does an Eternal Covenant Last? עולם in the Light of Aramaic-Egyptian Legal Documents," *Bible Translator* 59 (2008): 158–63.

ies found in Aramaic and Demotic legal texts of the Achaemenid period. In his conclusion, he wrote:

> There are at least four explanations for any or all of these equivalents: (1) the Aramaic borrowed from the Demotic; (2) the Demotic borrowed from the Aramaic; (3) both borrowed from a third source; (4) both evolved independently if coincidentally. While preliminary investigation suggests that some Demotic terms may be of eastern origin, as maintained by Kutscher, Muffs, Rabinowitz, and (in part) Yaron, the data are not adequate to assert that other Aramaic terms, by chance attested in the fifth century B.C.E., derive from the Demotic. To pursue the investigation requires the joint effort of the Assyriologist, the Aramaist, and the Egyptologist. … It is certainly a real desideratum to unravel the mutual influence on the macro-level, that of legal systems.[4]

In response to Porten, Egyptologist Robert Ritner wrote an important article arguing that, in twenty-four of the thirty-five examples Porten pointed to, there is Egyptian evidence for the formulae centuries before any plausible contact with Aramaic speakers. Therefore, he argued, in these cases and no doubt more, the clauses and formulae must be seen as Egyptian in origin.[5] Botta's work is also an answer to the question posed by Porten (his dissertation advisor). The two studies in the center of the book, on the שליט clause and the withdrawal (רחק) clause, are his attempt to resolve the question in favor of an Egyptian origin of the Elephantine legal formulary as a whole.

The first example is a brief discussion of the שליט clause (81–95). This clause, which gives or denies "control" of some type to someone, has parallels in Akkadian texts and was studied by many; Rabinowitz and Kaufman argued that the Aramaic influenced the Akkadian texts, whereas Muffs suggested the opposite. Gropp argued that the clause is an Aramaic innovation that draws on earlier (but different) Mesopotamian traditions. Botta shows that there are different scribal traditions preserved within the Elephantine corpus regarding the use of the שליט clause, which injects a measure of nuance into the discussion.

As for the origin of the clause, he points to the use of *sḥm* "to exercise authority" in Egyptian *nonlegal* texts from as early as the Old Kingdom. "The evidence provided above strongly supports the native Egyptian origins of the Aramaic שליט clause and suggests that the Aramaic clause was patterned after the Egyp-

---

4. Bezalel Porten, "Aramaic-Demotic Equivalents: Who Is the Borrower and Who Is the Lender?" in *Life in a Multi-cultural Society: Egypt from Cambyses to Constantine and Beyond* (ed. Janet H. Johnson; SAOC 51; Chicago: University of Chicago Oriental Institute, 1992), 259–64 (quotation from 264).

5. Ritner published his important paper, "Third Intermediate Period Antecedents of Demotic Legal Terminology," in *Acts of the Seventh International Conference of Demotic Studies* (ed. Kim Ryholt; Copenhagen: University of Copenhagen, Museum Tusculanum, 2002), 343–59. Aramaists, on the whole, have therefore not taken notice.

tian" (95). This is an overstatement: the evidence shows that both Akkadian and Egyptian have words for "to have authority," which is not surprising; neither shows evidence of a legal formula comparable to the Aramaic one. Rather than seeing the Aramaic as borrowing from the Egyptian in this case, it seems best the שליט clause as native to the Aramaic traditions.

The discussion of the withdrawal (רחק) clause is longer, covering chapters 5–7 (96–198). Here the lack of Egyptian legal documents becomes a serious problem. Since Egypt's dry climate does not distinguish between texts based on their genres, but tends to preserve indiscriminately (if not as pervasively as we would like), the fact that there are no documentary legal texts from before the middle of the first millennium B.C.E. has generally been taken to mean that such texts did not exist in earlier Egypt. If this is the case, the whole idea of looking for the origins of the Aramaic legal formulary is misguided. But Ritner, and now Botta, can point to expressions in nonlegal texts that seem to serve legal purposes, granting privileges, delineating borders, allocating responsibilities, and so on.

Again, the greatest strength of Botta's discussion is the sensitive and nuanced discussion of the formularies found in the Aramaic texts themselves. These chapters are filled with charts displaying clearly the ways in which the various contracts and structured, and the accompanying analysis discusses the differences between the various structures and the purpose of the individual clauses, especially the "withdrawal" clause.

To compensate for the lack of documentary texts, Botta turns to other types of texts, such as Middle Kingdom coffin texts and a suspect's opening statement as recorded in the proceedings in the trial of an accused tomb robber. One wonders, however, whether such texts can even bear the burden here placed upon them: demonstrating the Egyptian origins of the Aramaic *legal formulary*. Indeed, Botta nicely shows that Egyptian has multiple terms for the concepts of "distance, relinquish claims," not only the adjective *w3y* (in the expression *di w3y* "cause to be distant") but also *nʿ* "to be clear"; the two seem to be interchangeable (141–42). To my mind, this shows that there was no Egyptian formulary in the normal sense of the term: there was no set phrase with legal import, only common words pressed into ad hoc service. This may be the first step on the way to the development of a legal formulary, but it does not show one already in existence. The same point seems to emerge from Botta's demonstration that Abnormal Hieratic (contemporary with Demotic but found in Thebes and Upper Egypt) uses *ḥ3ʿ* in the same way that Demotic uses *w(3)y* (167–68).

Botta also points out that the *marzeaḥ* papyrus, said to be from the seventh century, shows that Aramaic scribes would not need Egyptian help to invent the "withdrawal" clause, since it is attested there already. It should be at least mentioned that, according to Rollston, this text is a forgery.[6] (I would add that,

---

6. Christopher A. Rollston, "Non-provenanced Epigraphs I: Pillaged Antiquities, Northwest Semitic Forgeries, and Protocols for Laboratory Tests," *Maarav* 10 (2003): 135–

although elsewhere Botta argued that רחק in Ezekiel is *not* modeled on the withdrawal clause, taking it as such still seems to me to be a very persuasive reading, especially if the text of Ezek 11:15 is left unemended and the form רַחֲקוּ is understood to be an imperative, "forfeit all claims!"[7]) Ritner suggested in his paper that Egyptian influence on the Aramaic formulary may go back to the Late Bronze Age, when the Egyptians controlled much of the Levant, but this is a suggestion Botta does not seem to follow.

Where, then, does this all leave us? Unfortunately, it is not entirely clear. Botta concludes that "the Jewish/Aramaic arrived in Egypt with a solid background of legal terminology and legal formulae. ... But the need to produce legal documents that would be valid within the Egyptian context compelled them to modify/adapt their own formulae/ formulary to the Egyptian tradition" (203). It appears that the Egyptian origins of the Aramaic legal formulary cannot be demonstrated, after all.

This book is quite valuable for anyone studying the texts from Elephantine, however. All students of the texts should make Ritner's article and Botta's monograph required reading, since they complicate the Mesopotamian-centric view that dominated the study of these texts for decades. Botta's studies do not upend the conventional wisdom and locate the origins of the formulary in Egypt rather than Mesopotamia, but instead complicate matters. One emerges with a picture of a full-blown Aramaic tradition that has long been in contact with Mesopotamian traditions now coming into contact with Egyptian law. The latter did not have a long tradition, but the Egyptian language certainly did, and plausibly certain expressions were calqued from Egyptian into Aramaic in the emerging symbiosis.

Of God and Gods: Egypt, Israel, and the Rise of Monotheism, by Jan Assmann. George L. Mosse Series in Modern European Cultural and Intellectual History Madison: University of Wisconsin Press, 2008. Pp. x + 196. Paper. $26.95. ISBN 9780299225544.

James K. Hoffmeier, Trinity International University, Deerfield, Illinois

Jan Assmann is a senior Egyptologist who has produced important scholarly contributions to the study of ancient Egyptian religion and is especially known

---

93, and "Non-provenanced Epigraphs II: The Status of Non-provenanced Epigraphs within the Broader Corpus of Northwest Semitic," *Maarav* 11 (2004): 57–79. This is not to endorse any or all of Rollston's views, only to bring them to the reader's attention.

7. Cf. Botta, "רחק in the Bible, A Re-evaluation," *Bib* 87 (2006): 418–20, responding to Frank Moore Cross, "A Papyrus Recording a Divine Legal Decision and the Root רחק in Biblical and Near Eastern Legal Usage," in *Texts, Temples, and Traditions: A Tribute to Menahem Haran* (ed. Michael V. Fox et al.; Winona Lake, Ind.: Eisenbrauns, 1996), 311–20, reprinted in Cross, *Leaves from an Epigrapher's Notebook: Collected Papers in Hebrew and West Semitic Palaeography and Epigraphy* (Winona Lake, Ind.: Eisenbrauns, 2003).

for his work on solar religion (e.g., *Re und Amun: Die Krise des polythestischen Weltbilds im Ägypten der 18.–20. Dynastie* [OBO 51; Fribourg: Universitätsverlag, 1983]; *Sonnenhymnen in Thebanischen Grabern* (Mainz: von Zabern, 1983]). In recent years he has ventured into the arena of the religion of ancient Israel (e.g., *Moses the Egyptian* [Cambridge; Harvard University Press, 1997]). His latest contribution deals with the complex question of the "Rise of Monotheism." This is an important book that will have a significant impact on the study of Near Eastern religions in general and the religion of Egypt and Israel in particular.

His entry into the arena of biblical studies stems from his conviction that "Egyptology can contribute directly to the study of monotheism" (8). He begins by offering an understanding of polytheism based on the Egyptian system (ch. 1). He rightly recognizes that the "Egyptian pantheon was anything but a random accumulation of deities" (13). Many of the deities can be traced to specific locales that were brought together as a result of political unification of what had been a mosaic of local polities.

On myth, Assmann contends that it is "not merely as story about the gods but a form of thought, a way of world-making, a deep-structural generator of stories" (19), but, he observes, Egypt lacks a myth "about a god that does not mention other gods" (20). He further defines this type of mythology as "*historia divina*," a history taking place in the divine world" (20). In ancient Israel, *historia sacra* functions in the place of myth. I concur with his observation that a fundamental difference between Egypt and Israel is that Hebrew *historia sacra* deals with God's relationship with humans (hence the focus on historiography), while in Egypt this is not the case. The gods rarely have direct interaction with humans in Egypt.

Assmann is concerned about the role that violence plays both in polytheism and in monotheism, although he rightly recognizes that their purpose is different. By its inclusivistic nature, polytheism does not force conversions or punish dissenters (if there was such a thing!). The distinction lies in the fact that "pagan violence stems from the distinctions between state and religion," whereas "monotheistic violence … is directed against paganism" (29). In Egypt, Akhenaten's persecution of Amun and Amun-Re (at least the Amun part of the hybrid deity) are well known and will be taken up again later. One gets the impression that violence in monotheism is truly troubling to Assmann, as he takes up this theme when defining monotheism and again in chapter 6, which is titled "No God by God: Exclusive Monotheism and the Language of Violence."

In Egypt, the god Seth was "the personification of death and violence" (33). He committed fratricide against Osiris and dueled Horus for control of Egypt, gashing out his eye in the process. His violent tendencies are turned against Apophis, who nightly does combat with Re in the solar bark. His association with the Canaanite storm-god Baal is discussed, but Assmann does not investigate the Hebrew and Christian figure of Satan, the epitome of evil and violence; this might have been an interesting line of inquiry. It is not clear how Seth's violence operating within a polytheistic system should be understood. Assmann suggests that it might be to explain the violence associated with sacrifices.

Like most historians of religion, Assmann rightly rejects the notion still held by many *Altstestamentler*s that "there is an evolutionary line that leads from polytheism to biblical monotheism" (74). He resonates, rather, with C. S. Lewis's notion that "behind the gods arises the One" (53) and hence uses the title "All Gods are One" for chapter 3. This view runs counter to that staked out by Erik Hornung's 1971 study, *Der Eine und die Vielen*, the English edition of which in 1982 explicitly mentions Assmann's earlier works that questioned the classical understanding of Egyptian polytheism. Assmann does not consider the "hyphenating of Gods" (e.g., Amun-Re or Path-Sokar-Osiris) as evidence for combining deities to point to "the One"; rather, this practice is indicative of "the idea of a kind of deep-structural identity" (58).

"Hierarchy" within a pantheon does isolate the creator god as the uncreated deity who logically stands at the pinnacle and thus might lend itself to people in polytheistic cultures elevating such a deity to an almost "God" status (58–62). While Assmann does not explicitly state it, there is the implication that the creator-god is the One behind the many, and this becomes clearer in what he calls "Explicit Theology" that he finds in the "Instructions for King Merikare," where it is said for the creator, "God knows every name" (62–63). He attributes this seemingly monotheistic understanding to the wisdom genre and labels it "henotheism," which while silent on other gods because they "do not exist," co-exists with many cults and lacks the exclusivity of fully developed monotheism. Monolatry is different from henotheism, for Assmann, in that only one deity is worshiped, but there is no denial of the existence of other gods. This is a helpful distinction, but for Assmann it serves as an important philosophical understanding for the later post-Amarna practice of all the gods are three, Amun, Re, and Ptah, and in essence, these three are one and the same (64).

In chapter 4 Assmann addresses the issue of "Monotheism as an Axial Movement" (this is the subtitle of this chapter). The Zoroastrian eighteenth-century scholar A. H. Anquetil-Duperron had advanced the theory that around 500 B.C. there was a convergence of charismatic leaders, Zoroaster, Buddha, the Hebrew prophets, and Greek philosophers, across Asia to Europe that led to "a great revolution for humankind" (77). The *Achsenzeit* (Axial Age) theory was further advanced by Karl Jaspers (who actually coined the term *Achsenzeit*) and others who saw a breakthrough in this era occurring from which monotheism emerged.

With regard to Egypt, Assmann observes that "ancient Egyptian evidence invites us to modify the Axial Age theory in two respects that are of some importance to our general search for the roots of monotheism" (78). He suggests that one needs to consider "smaller-scaled transformations" as influential on a culture rather than major movements and the role that "breakdown and breakthrough" play in cultural and religious transformation to monotheism.

Personal piety, which has its roots prior to the Amarna Age, as Posener demonstrated, is especially prominent in the Amarna and Ramesside eras; it is viewed as an important development on the road to monotheism because the worshiper can have a direct relationship with the deity outside the confines of the official cult. Such movements, Assmann suggests, were the outcome of "the breakdown of the political system, which had stressed the religious monopoly of the state" (83). In a sense, Akhenaten tapped into this sentiment by establishing himself as the sole mediator who in turn would represent the people to the Aten. But one must ask if this "breakdown" gives sufficient cause to explain Atenism. The lengthy, glorious reign of Akhenaten's father, Amenhotep III, does not seem like a traumatic period. Historians often consider his thirty-eight-year reign to represent the apex of the Egypt's grandeur in the New Kingdom, the *pax agyptiaca*.

Assmann believes that Atenism was monotheistic because of its exclusive nature and because of the way it persecuted other deities, closed temples, and fired entire priesthoods. In the history of religion, Atenism is the first religious system to distinguish between true and false religion, which when it appears in Israel later in history Assmann labels the "Mosaic distinction" (even though this development does not coincide with the Mosaic period; see below). Consequently, Akhenaten's religious revolution predates the Axial Age by more than eight centuries. Although implied in Assmann's study—he does not explicitly state it—Atenism deals a deathblow to the nineteenth- and early twentieth-century understanding of religious evolution toward monotheism, the pinnacle of religious development. While he is prepared to accept the Amarna interlude as a genuine expression of monotheism in Egypt, he falls in line with biblical scholars who believe that monotheism in Israel began at the end of the divided monarchy (Josiah) and climaxed in the exilic period (Deutero-Isaiah). It would be helpful were Assmann to address more thoroughly this seeming inconsistency.

"Trauma and Reorientation," for Assmann, were instrumental in "the rise of biblical monotheism and covenant theology" (83). The trauma began with the Assyrian dominance of Israel, the fall of Samaria (722 B.C.), followed by the destruction of Jerusalem and the exile. The loss of kingship and temple were especially traumatic and created the impetus for the emergence of the Mosaic distinction "between true and false[, which] meant the distinction between religion and politics, or church and state" (85). This latter distinction is one that Assmann continues to make, and in Israel, he maintains, this "was not achieved until the sixth and fifth centuries BCE" (86).

This chapter raises several questions to me. First, if covenant theology and monotheism were achieved in the seventh–fifth centuries, why did Jeremiah writing when addressing the Judeans in Babylonian captivity through the "Book of Consolations" speak of a "new covenant," specifically: "Behold, the days are coming, says the LORD, when I will make a *new covenant* with the house of Israel and the house of Judah, *not like the covenant which I made with their fathers when I took them by the hand to bring them out of the land of Egypt*, my covenant which they broke" (Jer 31:31–32 RSV)? Assmann speaks of Moses and the exodus in terms of mnemohistory, that is, how earlier events are remembered, not "what really happened" (157 n. 33). So if Jeremiah has a memory of an earlier covenant and can speak of a new covenant, this was not a novelty of the seventh–sixth centuries.

Another question is that Assmann's concept of the separation between "church and state" strikes me as a very modern and Western concept that seems totally alien to the ancient world. The Judean returnees to Jerusalem had "separation" forced on them by their Persian overlords and later by Greek and Roman powers. Thus it was accidental separation, and in contrast the messianic ideal was one in which the Davidic kingship was somehow reconstituted and no separation would exist (Jer 23:5-7; 33:14-21; Ezek 34:23-24; 37:24-28). The ideal apparently was for God to reign over Israel in Zion through the medium of his anointed ruler, who was his son (Ps 2:6-7).

Finally, if Akhenaten's monotheistic Atenism defied the Axial Age theory in the fourteenth century B.C., why in theory could Yahwistic monotheism not have originated in the same general period?

The role of a written sacred canon and monotheism is addressed in chapter 5. Assmann rightly sees a close relationship between the two and observes that "there is not a single monotheistic religion that is not based on a canon of holy writ" (90). Assmann has written widely on the subject of "cultural memory" and "mnemohistory." It is within the canonized texts of the various monotheistic traditions that such memory is preserved to the point that "monotheism, therefore, is primarily a matter of memory" (92). Once again, the author follows the traditional biblical scholarly theory that the time of Josiah is when the codification of the law began (94).

Having argued for the importance of canonical scriptures to monotheism, he does not address its apparent absence in Egypt, unless the Hymn to Aten with its long and short version reflects the existence of such authoritative dogma. It would have been interesting for him to discuss this matter.

In chapter 6 Assmann returns to "Exclusive Monotheism and the Language of Violence" (subtitle, 106). As stated previously, the "violent" tendencies of monotheistic religions is troubling to Assmann, and thus he asks, "are violence and intolerance, rigor and zealotry the price that exclusive monotheism has had to pay for sticking to the notion of a very personal and passionate God while stressing the idea of Oneness?" (109). He answers his own query, saying that there is nothing "inherently or structurally violent and intolerant" about monotheism. He traces the language of violence toward pagans and paganism within Israel to the cruel language found in "Assyrian loyalty oaths," which in turn left its imprint on Deuteronomic laws (113). Here he seems to take his cues from D. J. McCarthy and Moshe Weinfeld, who desperately tried to make Wellhausen's dating of D square with contemporary comparative data, that is, Assyrian, and thus they artificially excluded the oaths and curses in earlier legal materials from the ancient Near East.[1] It is essential if one is seeking to investigate the history of ideas, that all ancient Near Eastern materials from all periods be included in the investigation.

---

1. On this point, see my discussion in *Ancient Israel in Sinai* (New York: Oxford University Press, 2005), 183-92. The curses and oaths of Hittite treaties of the latter half of

The Bible, like other ancient Near Eastern texts, has its own history of transmission and challenges of interpretation, but need it be limited a priori to the eighth century and later?

Following Othmar Keel's lead, Assmann concurs that monotheism undergoes a maturing process that becomes "true monotheism" (126) when it parts ways with zealotry and violent ways. I suggest another factor might be considered. Rather than the separation of church and state, which Assmann sees as necessary for monotheism to flourish, it is their union that creates the problem. By that I mean that when a nation, kingdom, empire, or caliphate operates under the banner of exclusive monotheism, there exists the rationale to be coercive and forceful. Second Temple Judaism operated under the constraints of foreign rulers. Diaspora Judaism, like the Christians that 1 Pet 1:1 described as "exiles of the dispersion" across Anatolia, were not in a position to impose religious preferences on the polytheistic majority, so they rested their hopes in an apocalyptic vision of God's reign over the earth (e.g., Zech. 14). Similarly the Pilgrims and Puritans in the Americas initially thought they could create a Christian state. Some today would see "political Islam" from this perspective. The Mormons had a similar vision for their community in Utah in the 1840s. Violence is a vehicle used by some monotheistic communities that wish to enforce their vision of purity and "truth."

Jan Assmann has written a thoughtful and insightful book that must be read by serious students of biblical and Near Eastern religions. This study is an important contribution to the ongoing discussion on the origins and history of monotheism. The questions raised in this review are intended to keep the dialogue going.

Ludlul Bēl Nēmeqi: The Standard Babylonian Poem of the Righteous Sufferer, by Amar Annus and Alan Lenzi. State Archives of Assyria Cuneiform Texts 7. Helsinki: Neo-Assyrian Text Corpus Project, 2010. Pp. lvi + 72. Paper. $35.00. ISBN 9789521013348.

Christopher A. Rollston, Emmanuel School of Religion, Johnson City, Tennessee

Ludlul Bēl Nēmeqi ("Let Us Praise the Lord of Wisdom") seems to have consisted in antiquity of four tablets (or "segments") of approximately 120 lines each (xix). Naturally, the entire poem (written in Akkadian) has not been preserved. However, some fifty "manuscripts" of Ludlul are known at this time and have been employed within this volume (many of these manuscripts are, of course, quite fragmentary). Several decades ago W. G. Lambert published a superb critical edition of Ludlul Bēl Nēmeqi in his volume entitled *Babylonian Wisdom Literature*

---

the second millennium B.C. are replete with violent language (see Gary Beckman, *Hittite Diplomatic Texts* [2nd ed.; Atlanta: Scholars Press, 1999]).

(Oxford: Clarendon, 1960). That edition has served the field very well for a long time. During recent years, however, there have been some new tablet discoveries, and some of these discoveries have been particularly useful in filling lacunae. For example, Annus and Lenzi note that "Lambert's edition lacked about two-thirds of the opening hymn and knew the last ten lines of Tablet I only fragmentarily," but (especially) because of discoveries from Nimrud and Sippar, all of the lines (i.e., all 120 lines) of tablet 1 are now known (xi). Furthermore, there have been some significant joins that have been most useful as well. For example, Lambert's MS j and MS k have been joined to a number of fragments (x). Because of this sort of progress (i.e., more tablets, new joins), a new edition became necessary, hence, the volume herein reviewed.

This volume presents the text, transliteration, and translation of Ludlul Bēl Nēmeqi. As for the cuneiform script used within the volume, the authors state that it has been "generated automatically from the composite transliteration provided by the authors, using programs and fonts created by the State Archives of Assyria Project" (xxxvii). That is to say, the cuneiform texts in this volume are not to be misconstrued as "handcopies" made from the tablets. Rather, the cuneiform is a standardized "typeset" version of the cuneiform script. Thus, the authors note (quite rationally) that "the primary purpose of the cuneiform text is pedagogic," that is, for those who wish to use the volume in the classroom or for self-study (xxxvii). Along those lines, it should be emphasized that there is a (fairly) schematic means in this volume of signifying restorations and partial restorations. Thus, "solid black characters represent text preserved in at least one manuscript and outline characters stand for restored text and correspond to items within square brackets or angels brackets in the transliteration." Signs that are totally reconstructed (i.e., no traces present) are "covered by shading" (i.e., printed in a shaded rectangle), signifying the fact that the signs are in a "destroyed area" of the tablet (xxxvii). For these sorts of reasons, the authors candidly note that those wishing to conduct research on the cuneiform text must collate the original tablets or consult the *editio princeps* of the various tablets or tablet fragments. That is, they state that "the cuneiform text provided here is not adequate" for research purposes (xxxvii). Someone might wish to critique this project (SAA) for the use of a standardized typeset cuneiform script, and one can arguably understand the reason for such a criticism (e.g., it lulls a student into thinking that reading tablets is easier than it is, or it does not force the student to appreciate the multifaceted complexities of reading actual tablets), but it must also be conceded that there are pedagogical benefits (e.g., easier reading for beginning and intermediate students) to the use of a typeset script. The cuneiform text (3–14) is followed by the transliteration (15–30) and the translation (31–44). A normalization of the text is not provided. Regarding the translation, Annus and Lenzi note that the vocabulary of Ludlul is of a "high literary register and bears witness to the poet's rich poetic artistry." They suggest that it might have been fitting for them to have produced a translation that captured "this ancient literary panache." However, because of the pedagogical thrust of the SAACT series, they decided that a translation that "tended toward the literal" would serve better the present volume's users" (xxxviii). I should note in this connection that readers will find the English translation to be a fine, idiomatic translation, another commendable feature of this volume.

Lambert's system for manuscript sigla is used in this volume (with modest modifications). Thus, in terms of formatting and presentation, "sources in Assyrian script from the library of Assurbanipal are in uppercase letters. Other Assyrian sources are indicated with lower case, italicized letters (not in bold, as Lambert used). Sources in Babylonian script are designated with lower case, roman letters" (xli). Moreover, although the authors state that "this is not a full critical edition," they also note that "all known textual variants, including orthographical variants, are indicated in the critical apparatus." Furthermore, they note that the critical (i.e., textual) apparatus "also presents the Akkadian explanatory glosses from the [ancient] commentary text (MS G), preceded by the word explained" (xxxviii). Readers will find the critical apparatus of this volume to be clear and lucid. Moreover, the ancient commentary text (often consisting basically of glosses of the most difficult vocabulary of the gifted poet of Ludlul) is something that readers will find very useful, and interesting, at a number of levels.

This volume contains brief but very useful discussions on various aspects of the content of *Ludlul*. For example, it has often been suggested that Šubši-mešrê-Šakkan (the major protagonist of the work) was also the author, but Annus and Lenzi demur on this subject. They do note that this name (Šubši-mešrê-Šakkan) means "create wealth, O Šakkan," and that this personal name (although rare) is attested in the epigraphic record. However, they state that they believe it is not likely that the sufferer of this poem was also the author of it (xvii). Someone might contest and state that the first-person is used within this poem, but Annus and Lenzi note that scribes often wrote works in the name of the monarch (and thus in the first person), and they also note, of course, that pseudonymous (or fictional) royal autobiographies are attested. Thus, they contend that the presence of the first-person in this poem does not necessarily reveal anything about authorship. Regarding the date of the composition of Ludlul, they state that the poem was arguably composed "during the last few centuries of the second millennium BCE, that is, sometime during the late Kassite period, between the reign of Nazimurutaš and the mid-twelfth century BCE" (xviii). Contained within this slender volume is also a very nice summary of the contents poem itself, a discussion of some of its philological and poetic features (e.g., lexical sophistication, use of parallelism), and also a most useful (if perforce brief) discussion of the classification of Ludlul as "wisdom literature" (xix–xxxvi).

This volume contains a sign list (61–68), consisting of every sign that is printed in this volume. Naturally, next to each sign is a number, corresponding to the number of that sign in Borger's *Assyrisch-babylonische Zeichenliste*. Furthermore, there is also a glossary of every word that occurs in this volume, accompanied by an English translation (47–56). This glossary also functions as a concordance for the volume as well, as the tablet number and line number for these words are provided. It should also be noted that the volume contains a list of personal names (there are very few in Ludlul), a list of place names, and a list of divine names (57).

Ultimately, this volume is a *sine qua non* for various fields and subfields of ancient Near Eastern studies. That is, Assyriologists will find this volume to be a very useful contribution, but the audience for this volume certainly includes those who work in fields such as Northwest Semitic, Hebrew Bible, Egyptology, Hittite, literary criticism, and the history of religions. No library should be without it.

LANGUAGES

Modality and the Biblical Hebrew Infinitive Absolute, by Scott N. Callaham. Abhandlungen für die Kunde des Morgenlandes 71. Wiesbaden: Harrassowitz, 2010. Pp. xv + 343. Paper. $117.00. ISBN 9783447061582.

Jeremy M. Hutton, University of Wisconsin-Madison, Madison, Wisconsin

Grammars of Biblical Hebrew often attribute significantly different nuances to infinitives absolute, depending on whether they precede a finite verb of the same root ("used … to *strengthen* the verbal idea"; GKC §113n), follow a finite verb of the same root ("sometimes to express the long *continuance* of the action"; GKC §113r), or appear independently (in which case the infinitive absolute "appears as *a substitute for the finite verb*"; GKC §113y). Although most grammarians would acknowledge the schematic nature of these categories, allowing that patterns of actual usage in the Hebrew Bible are much more complex, the positional analysis of the infinitive absolute has remained infrequently challenged. With this study, Callaham scrutinizes the status quo, proposing an alternative interpretation of the infinitive absolute's semantic function. Shortly stated, Callaham argues that, "Since the paronomastic infinitive construction [i.e., Callaham's term for both the *qātōl* + finite form and finite form + *qātōl* syntagmata] duplicates a verbal idea with a semantically minimalist verb form that contributes nothing to the construction other than the verbal idea itself, it is likely that its primary function is narrowed predicate focus or verb focus" (42). Specifically, Callaham traces this focus to the *modal* features and context of the verbal form, and *not* to the verbal idea.

Callaham begins his study with a concise and well-written introduction (ch. 1, pp. 1–56). After laying out the problems surrounding interpretation of the infinitive absolute in Biblical Hebrew (1–16), he briefly surveys models of verbal modality in general linguistics (17–31), as well as the modes of research that have typically been employed in studies of mood and modality in Biblical Hebrew (mostly morphologically based; 31–38). After summarizing a few more recent studies of the effects of the order of constituents in verbal clauses on modality (39–43), Callaham addresses the book's linguistic method (43–56): he claims that, "the … study justifies its assertion of verb focus through inductive observation of available data in Biblical Hebrew rather than through appeal to cross-linguistic predicate cleft research" (43). The infinitive absolute has typically evaded thorough (or, at least, sufficient) examination in recent studies of the Biblical Hebrew verbal system, according to Callaham (43–46). In order to remedy this situation, he categorizes the entire Biblical Hebrew corpus of *verbal* infinitives absolute in three successive chapters. (The process of examining the *verbal* instances of the infinitive absolute means that the 197 nonverbal, adverbial usages of the form are omitted from the inductive study—although they are dutifully recorded in the appendix.) First, however, Callaham examines the morphological particularities whereby the infinitives absolute may be recognized and collected (46–52) and provides a concise overview of the study's methodology (53–56).

The instances of the infinitive absolute have been arranged in three categories derived from F. R. Palmer's typology of modality (*Mood and Modality* [Cambridge Textbooks in Linguistics; Cambridge: Cambridge University Press, 1986; 2nd ed., 2001]): propositional modality (ch. 2, pp. 57–122), event modality (ch. 3, pp. 123–88), and nonmodal usages (ch. 4, pp. 189–208). Within each chapter Callaham differentiates between the various subcategories of each type of modality and, within each of these subcategories, between prose and poetic usages. Finally, within the prose sections, a further distinction can be drawn between appearances of the infinitive absolute in narrative and in discursive contexts (53), although this distinction is not represented in the texts' arrangement. The study is synchronic (54) and deals primarily with the Qere reading tradition of the text. For the most part, Callaham's arrangement of the texts is straightforward and intuitive (with the exception of providing texts in the Christian canonical ordering rather than in the standard order of the Hebrew textual editions). The individual data chapters of the book thus require little additional description, and critique will be withheld until below.

Callaham summarizes his findings in the book's fifth chapter (209–30). Here he provides several large, statistically based conclusions concerning the data he has gathered and processed. Although it would be difficult to list all the noteworthy conclusions that he has reached, a few salient observations may be listed here:

- The verbal usage of the infinitive absolute in Biblical Hebrew occurs in preponderantly modal contexts, although indicative usages represent a solid minority (this is my own interpretation of Callaham's data and graphs; his own description is in general agreement with this assertion, but since his goal is to emphasize the *modal* appearances of the infinitive absolute, the indicative use of that verbal form is played down somewhat).

- "Biblical Hebrew rarely employs the infinitive absolute to communicate jussive modality" (210).

- "Paronomastic infinitive constructions more frequently express a broader range of modalities than independent infinitives absolute" (210).

- "[W]hen Biblical Hebrew employs independent verbal infinitives absolute in modal contexts, the language uses the infinitives differently in prose than in poetry"—this observation *may* be linked to the differences in genre manifested in the variant styles (213).

- "[N]arrative and discourse employ the independent infinitive absolute in radically different modal contexts.... [The] collected data strongly support the contention that the paronomastic infinitive construction is a characteristic of 'spoken' Biblical Hebrew" (215).

- "[S]ocial relationships partially govern the expression of modality in speech acts" (217).

- "In neither prose nor poetry does Biblical Hebrew significantly differentiate the use of pre- and postpositive paronomastic infinitive constructions according to modal context" (220). (In short, the commonly held distinction between, e.g., *qātōl* + *yiqtōl* and *yiqtōl* + *qātōl*, with which we began, is contradicted by Callaham's research).

- "[I]n both prose and poetry, paronomastic infinitives absolute in subject-initial verbal clauses are highly modal ... [but] not all passages with leading paronomastic infinitive constructions and *yiqtol* verbs in prose are ... modal" (222).

- "[I]t is entirely plausible that biblical authors may employ paronomastic infinitive constructions in such contexts to accent any modality that the cognate verb conveys" (225; see also 229).

Finally, Callaham ends his conclusion by reflecting on the ways that his study has in some ways confirmed claims concerning the use of the infinitive absolute in Biblical Hebrew and in other ways refuted such claims (227–30). There follow two appendices; the first (231–323) displays in a single, easily consulted chart Callaham's complete data set (including the nonverbal appearances of the infinitive absolute). Appendix I essentially doubles as the citation index, although the reader will not find pages listed for each citation but instead will be directed to the appropriate section of the book. The second appendix (324–26) provides a brief introduction to the "Chi square test of independence," the statistical tool whereby the validity of Callaham's results is tested. A bibliography concludes the study (327–43).

Callaham's book is an important one for Biblical Hebrew studies, since it challenges a long-established paradigm and largely succeeds in its critique. By testing the function of the infinitive absolute in every verbal usage and demonstrating the form's strong correlation with modal contexts, Callaham has helped to broaden our understanding of its function in Biblical Hebrew. In this regard, Callaham joins the recently developing discussion between scholars such as Ahouva Shulman ("The Use of Modal Verbal Forms in Biblical Hebrew Prose" [Ph.D. diss., University of Toronto, 1996]), Hélène Marie Dallaire ("The Syntax of Volitives in Northwest Semitic Prose" [Ph.D. diss., Hebrew Union College, 2002]), and John A. Cook ("The Biblical Hebrew Verbal System: A Grammaticalization Approach" [Ph.D. diss., University of Wisconsin-Madison, 2002]), all of whom he engages in this study. In light of this generally positive impression of Callaham's book, most of the comments below are perhaps to be seen as directions for further study; nonetheless, they point to areas of inchoate analysis in the broader study of the infinitive absolute.

The most obvious point from which to deepen Callaham's study would be an analysis of the (purportedly) "nonverbal" occurrences of the infinitive absolute. One wonders, for example, how the decision was made to exclude these examples from the present study (although, to be sure, Callaham has dutifully collected them in his database). This point is especially curious in light of the fact that infinitives absolute are forms built on productive verbal roots and operate in tandem with other verbs (and verbal forms) to emphasize or otherwise augment the verbal idea. For example, the common word הַרְבֵּה (√רבה, *hiphil*) is most easily glossed with the English adverbs "many" or "great(ly)":

Gen 15:1bβ: שְׂכָרְךָ הַרְבֵּה מְאֹד
NRSV and JPS: "your reward shall be very great."
KJV: "[I am ...] thy exceeding great reward."

But given the propensity of the infinitive absolute to take the place of inflected finite verbal forms (as Callaham capably confirms), it is conceivable that הַרְבֵּה could be read as a verbal instance of the infinitive absolute, continuing the verbless clause in verse 1bα2 (אָנֹכִי מָגֵן לָךְ "I am a shield to you"). If the syntagma [verbless clause] + [verbal infinitive absolute] is nonproductive (i.e., not otherwise attested), then having the data handy to demonstrate this point would have bolstered the validity of Callaham's argument. A similar criticism might be applied to Callaham's decision to relegate the infinitives absolute of Judg 14:9 to his nonverbal category (260). There two infinitives absolute appear following a *wayyiqtōl*: וַיֵּלֶךְ הָלוֹךְ וְאָכֹל. This is one of the classic examples employed by proponents of the older paradigm, in which a paronomastic infinitive absolute following a finite verb of the same root occasions translation as an imperfect, continuous verb (e.g., NRSV translates: "and [he] went on, eating as he went"). Thanks in part to Callaham's research, we might approach this nuance a bit more tentatively with the caveat that *wayyiqtōl*s are by their very nature constrained to clause-initial positions; infinitival accentuation—regardless of whether it is accentuation of the verbal idea *or* modal context—must therefore occur postpositively in such circumstances. But this realization does not prevent us from questioning why both הָלוֹךְ and אָכֹל should be categorized as "nonverbal" here, especially since the latter conveys new (verbal!) information. An additional study accounting for the identification of 197 infinitives as nonverbal would have been in its own right a much-desired collation of data. Unfortunately, not having analyzed these 197 cases of "nonverbal" infinitives absolute myself, I am unable to say how the instances of reanalysis suggested above might affect Callaham's statistical conclusions. Presumably, the first instance (הַרְבֵּה in Gen 15:1) might qualify as an example of future or commissive modality (translating as, e.g., "[I will] make great your reward"). The second instance (וְאָכֹל הָלוֹךְ in Judg 14:9) would qualify as an indicative, nonmodal usage. Whether a "verbal" reanalysis of all the claimed "nonverbal" appearances of the infinitive absolute would change Callaham's findings appreciably cannot be predicted with confidence.

A subsidiary point of critique is the subclassification of certain forms of modal infinitives absolute. Callaham's analysis is careful and for the most part intuitive, if not at times fully explained. But some instances resist easy classification, and the reader's interpretive matrices may not align fully with Callaham's. For example, Callaham translates 2 Kgs 4:43:

> But his servant said, "How can I give this to a hundred men?" So he said, "Give to the people and let them eat, for Yahweh says this: 'They *will* **eat** and **have more than enough**.'" (Hebrew: 83; ... כִּי כֹה אָמַר יְהוָה אָכֹל וְהוֹתֵר, emphasis original)

The classification of הוֹתֵר as a modal future ("[they will] have more than enough") is logical. But the modality of אָכֹל could, in my estimation, be interpreted according to a number of modal categories: conditional ("[Even if] they eat..."), deontic-permissive ("They may eat, [because]..."), deontic-obligative ("they must eat..."), deontic-imperative ("Eat!—[and you will have more than enough]"), and dynamic-abilitive ("they are [now] able to eat..."). All seem plausible, if somewhat forced, alternative interpretations, when left unconstrained by a more attentive consideration of syntactic markers (e.g., frequent presence of אִם in conditional contexts and the like). Although Callaham does make several observations concerning such syntactic constraints and cues, they usually receive only passing and fairly general scrutiny.

A related consideration is the application of the categorical descriptions themselves, particularly the epistemic-assumptive subcategory of propositional modality. This category encompasses those occurrences in which "People make judgments based on facts they assume to be correct.... A common means of expressing ... inner knowledge is through the use of the verb יָדַע ('know') and the particle כִּי (in this case, 'that')" (58). These cues for the identification of epistemic-assumptive modality are valuable, but the group of collected texts could have been broken down into two constituent subgroups: one in which the paronomastic infinitive absolute appears in the epistemic statement (e.g., the sequence יָדֹעַ + *ידע* כִּי found in 1 Sam 20:3, 9; Jer 13:12; Jer 40:14), and one in which it appears in the actual proposition, for example:

1 Sam 22:22 (excerpt): ... יָדַעְתִּי... כִּי־הַגֵּד יַגִּיד לְשָׁאוּל
Callaham (60): "I knew...that he would tell Saul...."

Although in both cases the infinitive absolute occurs in the *context* of modality ("context" broadly construed), its participation in that modality assumes two clearly distinct roles. In the second set, it clearly augments (or, more properly, accentuates?) a finite verb that *must* be understood as modal, since it appears in a proposition, the facticity of which is determined by the speaker's viewpoint (i.e., David *knows* this proposition to be the case) rather than by the occurrence of the actual event.[1] Conversely, in the first set the infinitive absolute augments the verb *introducing* the proposition and thus seems to verge closer to an indicative, nonmodal usage. In short, additional studies focusing more specifically on the syntactic structures of certain modal subcategorizations would complement Callaham's broader topic nicely.

Despite these caveats, Callaham's study is a helpful analysis of the (often nebulous) role played by infinitives absolute in Biblical Hebrew. It calls into question a number of well-worn assumptions and proposes a more linguistically sophisticated interpretive framework through which analysis of the biblical (and, for that matter, epigraphic and postbiblical) texts might proceed. Most importantly, it comprises an early and essential step toward a fuller understanding of modality in Biblical Hebrew by gathering much of the necessary data in a single, easily consulted volume. The linguistic study of Biblical Hebrew has profited greatly from Callaham's work.

An Akkadian Lexical Companion for Biblical Hebrew: Etymological-Semantic and Idiomatic Equivalents with Supplement on Biblical Aramaic, by Hayim Tawil. Jersey City, N.J.: Ktav, 2009. Pp. xxiv + 503. Paper. $79.50. ISBN 9781602801141.

Aaron D. Rubin, Pennsylvania State University, University Park, Pennsylvania

As the oldest attested Semitic language and the only well-attested member of the Eastern branch of the Semitic family tree, Akkadian is clearly important for the comparative study of the Semitic languages. Add to this the fact that Akkadian has a long and diverse literary tradition that has clearly had some influence on biblical literature, and it is evident why Akkadian is important for the study of Biblical Hebrew. The volume under review by Hayim Tawil is focused specifically on the comparison of Biblical Hebrew/Aramaic and Akkadian, using cognates

---

1. I use here the convenient distinction made by John A. Cook between "the actuality of the event ... with respect to the speaker's viewpoint" over against "the ontology of the event itself" ("The Biblical Hebrew Verbal System: A Grammaticalization Approach" [Ph.D. diss., University of Wisconsin-Madison, 2002], 64–65; see also 71–72 for additional discussion).

and semantic/idiomatic parallels. Since the study of Akkadian has become quite widespread among biblical scholars—at the expense of Arabic, Ethiopic, and even Aramaic—there will surely be an audience for this book in the field.

Tawil's work is arranged like a Hebrew dictionary, with a supplement for biblical Aramaic. Under each Hebrew (or Aramaic) entry is an Akkadian cognate, followed by some notes (more on these below). At first glance this looks something like an etymological dictionary. Although etymological dictionaries are in short supply for the Semitic languages, the scholar of Hebrew has a decent amount of resources at his or her disposal. For Biblical Hebrew, the popular dictionaries of Brown-Driver-Briggs (BDB) and Koehler-Baumgartner (*HALOT*) both contain etymologies, though these are sometimes unreliable. BDB is especially weak when it comes to Akkadian, since Assyriology was still in its early years when that lexicon was published over a hundred years ago. (Ugaritic was yet undiscovered when its authors wrote.) The comprehensive Hebrew-Hebrew dictionary of Even-Shoshan, covering all periods of Hebrew, also contains (very brief) etymological notes. The dedicated etymological dictionary of Ernest Klein (*A Comprehensive Etymological Dictionary of the Hebrew Language for Readers of English*) is generally pretty good and probably the most useful reference tool for Hebrew etymologies, though (as with Even-Shoshan's dictionary) comparative data is most often limited to Arabic, Akkadian, and Ugaritic.

For Akkadian, the only real resource for etymologies is W. von Soden's *Akkadisches Handwörterbuch* (*AHw*). The most comprehensive lexicon of Akkadian, the *Chicago Assyrian Dictionary*, includes no etymological information whatsoever, nor do other, smaller dictionaries of Akkadian. When searching for an Akkadian root, the Hebrew resources mentioned above can often be helpful, as can Wolf Leslau's *Comparative Dictionary of Ge'ez*, which is the closest thing there is to a comparative Semitic dictionary. The *Dictionnaire des racines sémitiques*, edited by David Cohen et al., can also be useful, though to date it only covers from ' to ḥ (using the order of the Hebrew alphabet).

Tawil's book can certainly be used with profit for the cognates it provides, though it is not intended as an etymological dictionary. The lack of other Semitic cognates and any reference to Proto-Semitic make this clear. Still, finding Akkadian cognates to Hebrew words will certainly be a popular use for this volume, so I was curious to see how it compared in this capacity to some of the reference works mentioned above. I chose ten Hebrew entries at random from Tawil and checked those same Hebrew lexemes in BDB, *HALOT*, and Klein. Of the ten words that I checked (שנה, רכב, צמד, פלג, נאד, חבורה, זרק, דשא, דרדר, and תקן), *HALOT* and Klein provided Akkadian cognates for nine out of the ten, while BDB had cognates for eight. Only the rare word דרדר 'thistle' was lacking a cognate in all three, while חבורה 'wound, blow' was also lacking a cognate in BDB.

Tawil also includes an Akkadian index (with about 1,300 words), meaning that it can also be used to find Hebrew cognates to some Akkadian words. Therefore I also checked the ten corresponding Akkadian cognates in *AHw*. I found etymological information for all ten: five of the words had a note about the

Semitic root (or simply an indication that the root was common Semitic), and five gave an explicit Hebrew cognate.

The real strength in Tawil's lexicon is in the citations it provides and the contextual and semantic notes that accompany each entry. These show places in which Hebrew and Akkadian cognates are used in similar contexts or share a special semantic development or idiomatic usage. For example, if we look up the root יתר in BDB, *HALOT*, or Klein's dictionary, we find in all three places the Akkadian cognate verb (*w*)*atāru*, with no further comment. Both roots have the same general meaning 'be in excess'. In the Bible, we find once the expression שפת יתר (Prov 17:7), which is usually taken to mean something like 'fine speech' or 'eloquent speech'. In his entry for the noun יֶתֶר (152), Tawil, following a 1976 article by N. Waldman, notes that the cognate Akkadian noun (*w*)*atartu* can have the meaning 'falsehood' (though I think that 'exaggeration' is a more precise translation), providing a nice parallel, then, with the phrase שפת שקר 'lying speech' in the second half of this verse. If Waldman and Tawil are correct, then this is a semantic development common to Hebrew and Akkadian ('excess' → 'exaggeration, falsehood'), presumably one that took place already at some proto-Semitic stage. So an Akkadian cognate is not given by Tawil just for the sake of etymology, but rather to help illuminate the nuance of meaning or idiomatic usages in the Hebrew text.

Another example can be found in the entry for the root כבד 'be heavy' (153). Here we learn that both Hebrew and Akkadian use this root in conjunction with the nouns 'ear' and 'eye' to indicate, respectively, poor hearing and poor eyesight, as in עיני ישראל כבדו 'Israel's eyes were dim' (Gen 48:10). Parallel idioms could undoubtedly be found in other languages around the world, but here there is still a good chance these idioms are common Semitic. Data from other Semitic languages would certainly strengthen the case.

Sometimes a semantic parallel from Akkadian may be accepted a little too readily. For example, the Akkadian word *daddaru* is described in one Akkadian text as having a bad stench. Tawil, therefore, assumes that the Hebrew cognate דרדר must be understood as 'ill-smelling plant' in Hos 10:8. However, there is no reason to think that the context warrants this meaning in the fixed expression קוץ ודרדר, which occurs also in Gen 3:18. It also seems likely that the use of the expression in Hosea is an intentional echoing of its use in Genesis, where the meaning 'ill-smelling plant' certainly does not fit.

Among the words included in Tawil's lexicon, alongside true cognates, are loanwords from Akkadian into Hebrew, as well as loans from West Semitic into Akkadian. This is appreciated, since it could be interesting to see if a borrowing is used differently than in the source language. Tawil usually indicates that a word is a borrowing in his notes (cf. the entries for סריס, אגרת, or תלמיד) but occasionally fails to note this fact (e.g., שוק 'street'). Some borrowings (or alleged borrowings) are omitted completely (e.g., סם 'incense').

It is a bit disappointing that, for the sake of thoroughness, Tawil does not include words with Akkadian cognates or sources from postbiblical Hebrew, for example, the root זוז 'move' (cognate with Akkadian *izuzzum*) or the noun ארדיכל/אדריכל 'architect, artisan' (< Akkadian *ar[a]d ekall-*).¹ However, such words are few, and Tawil's aims are explicitly toward biblical studies, not the history of the Hebrew language.

Following the entries and notes, Tawil sometimes points out relevant work in the secondary literature, which is a very helpful feature. These references are usually quite clear, though occasionally a note is ambiguous. For example, at the end of the entry for 265) ספד), there is a reference to "Gruber, 449–55," but there are two possible matches in the bibliography.

At the end of the lexicon, before the index, Tawil provides a very brief (six-page) overview of the history and structure of Akkadian. His overview of Akkadian dialects is quite useful, and I was pleased to see in his chart of consonant correspondences (468) that Tawil has followed the latest scholarship, for example, reconstructing Proto-Semitic *ts in place of more traditional *s. I disagree, however, with Tawil's equation of the Akkadian relative *ša* and Hebrew relative -שׁ (470), which despite their similar appearance are almost certainly unrelated. Akkadian *ša* is cognate with the rare biblical Hebrew relative זו/זה, while -שׁ is a reduced form of אשר.² I know that many will side with Tawil on this contentious issue.

Unfortunately, parts of the book are riddled with minor typographical errors. I happened to look at the bibliography first and within five minutes had found almost twenty errors (misspelled and wrong names, missing diacritics, wrong years, and the like). I mention this not to find fault with this work, which has great value. I only mean to point out that after seeing the errors in the bibliography, I was a bit wary of trusting the Akkadian and Hebrew forms in the lexicon, where a missing macron or dot beneath a letter can make a difference. Of course, it is easy to double-check these forms in other dictionaries, but one does want to have confidence in the lexicographer's eye for detail.

In sum, Tawil's lexicon is a very useful tool for finding Akkadian cognates to biblical Hebrew words, as well as the reverse, and is a bit more thorough and up-to-date in scholarship than existing biblical Hebrew dictionaries. The semantic parallels listed provide an excellent resource for illuminating the nuances of the biblical text. The book can also be easily used by those with little or no knowledge of Akkadian.

---

1. On Akkadian *izuzzum*, see John Huehnergard, "*izuzzum* and *itūlum*," in *Riches Hidden in Secret Places: Ancient Near Eastern Studies in Memory of Thorkild Jacobsen* (ed. Tzvi Abusch; Winona Lake, Ind.: Eisenbrauns, 2002), 161–85.

2. See John Huehnergard, "On the Etymology of the Hebrew Relative *šɛ-*," in *Biblical Hebrew in Its Northwest Semitic Setting: Typological and Historical Perspectives* (ed. Steven E. Fassberg and Avi Hurvitz; (Winona Lake, Ind.: Eisenbrauns, 2006), 103–25.

Oath Formulas in Biblical Hebrew, by Blane Conklin. Linguistic Studies in Ancient West Semitic 5. Winona Lake, Ind.: Eisenbrauns, 2011. Pp. xii + 106, Hardcover, $34.50, ISBN 9781575062037.

Yael Ziegler, Herzog College, Alon Shevut, Israel

Blane Conklin's study is a systematic analysis of the various individual constituents of biblical oath formulae. He examines the authenticating elements, the function of several particles that introduce the content of an oath, and oaths that are introduced with no marker. Conklin appends a schematic overview of oath formulae in Semitic languages other than Hebrew after the conclusion of his book.

Prompted by an oath passage in the book of Ruth that produced contradictory translations, Conklin sets out to demonstrate that the problem of this passage is of a linguistic nature and consequently has a linguistic solution, one that is to be found specifically by examining the morphosyntax of oath formulae. He proposes to gather oath formulae together so that their patterns and tendencies may be seen within a larger matrix and thereby better understood.

In his introductory chapter, certainly the most accessible and least technical one in the book, Conklin tackles some basic concepts in oath scholarship. This includes a brief foray into the linguistic field of pragmatics and specifically speech act theory, which is fundamental to elucidating the manner in which an oath is used in communication. Conklin then offers some introductory observations about oaths, which are beneficial for the reader. Cogent explanation of matters such as the connection between sacred and vulgar language and the subsequent correlation between formal oaths and profane "oaths" (4), together with his succinct survey of the wider cultural and linguistic world of oaths (especially what he terms their authenticating element, 5–7) are helpful introductions to the general topic. It may have been more pertinent to include at this point Conklin's appendix, which examines coeval oath formulae in other Semitic languages. Certainly these oaths are much more closely related to biblical oaths than those in Bantu dialects or contemporary English. More important for the purposes of this study, Conklin discerns a bipartite structure of the oath formula in biblical Hebrew, one that contains what he terms an authenticating element, followed by the content of the oath (4). It is regrettable that Conklin's all too concise survey of these introductory topics omits nearly any references to the extant scholarship on oaths. The bulk of Conklin's review of oath scholarship focuses on previous grammatical studies of oath formulae (8–12). Conklin notes the shortcomings of these studies in their discussion of oath formulae, particularly in their discussion of clauses introduced by the particle *ky*. The lack of any detailed study focusing on the morphosyntax of oath clauses and the nonoath usages of these formulae leads him to propose a systematic analysis of the morphosyntax of the particles in oaths, while relating to the larger morphosyntactic content of those particles in Biblical Hebrew.

Conklin proceeds to examine in detail the individual elements that constitute oath formulae, devoting his first analytic chapter to the authenticating element in the biblical Hebrew oaths (ch. 2). Dividing the authenticating elements into five, including the raising of the hand, invocation of witnesses, the verb for swearing, and two oath phrases, Conklin usefully illustrates the different ways in which the oath-taker indicates that his oath is binding. He maintains that the common purpose of these five elements has gone unnoticed in biblical scholarship, resulting in an atomistic approach to the discussion of oaths. Several possible indicators have been omitted in this chapter, leaving open the question as to whether Conklin rejected them as oath indicators or simply disregarded them. One notable omission is the word *halilah*, often translated as a profanation. While this word remains controversial among scholars with regard to its use in conjunction with oath-taking (Ziegler, 128–33), its exclusion from the entire book is, in my view, a lacuna. It is, moreover, curious that Conklin did not relate to the placing of the hand under the thigh as an oath indicator, perhaps even as a subset of his category of the raising of one's hand. Finally, Conklin fails to introduce any discussion of curses into his examination of authenticating elements (with the exception of a brief reference in his conclusion that suggests this as a further avenue of research [77]). This is peculiar, inasmuch as many scholars regard the oath simply as a self-imprecation. This may be the case specifically with regard to the formula of "thus will God do," but it is generally supported by the use of the word '*rur* in several unambiguous oath formulations (e.g., Josh 6:26; Judg 21:18). Moreover the word '*lah*, which often connotes an oath, may properly mean curse (Brichto, 34). Omitting any discussion of the role of the curse in an examination of oath authenticators represents a serious lapse.

Chapter 3 inspects oath content formulated as a conditional clause. After a brief summary of previous scholarship on conditional-clause syntax, Conklin conducts his own examination to see if conditionally formulated oaths correlate with regular biblical conditional clause syntax, using 1 Samuel as a sample study. After a particularly technical discussion, heavily weighted by grammatical and syntactic terminology (but helpfully summarized in four tables), Conklin deduces that conditionally framed oaths correlate closely to regular conditional clause protases. Conklin concludes that conditionally formulated oaths should be seen as conditional protases of conditional sentences in which an apodosis that would have expressed a negative has been elided. While this is certainly a compelling comparative survey, it neglects to ask the fundamental question as to why the apodosis should be elided. Conklin's brief explanation of the phenomenon of oath ellipsis in his introduction (4) does not satisfy the need to address the idea at the conclusion of this chapter, at the very least in a footnote. This omission correlates with my general impression that this study, while successful in its comparative surveys and catalogues, falls short in its analysis of the phenomena that it establishes.

Chapter 4, which is devoted to oaths marked with the word *ky*, is in many ways similar to the previous one. After summarizing the secondary literature on the function of this particle in biblical Hebrew, Conklin employs 1 Samuel as a baseline for investigating the use of the particle itself and then its appearance as part of an oath. His argument against the consensus view that the particle *ky* in biblical oaths is emphatic or asseverative in function is well-founded. Instead, he suggests that *ky* functions in oaths as a complementizer of the predicate, namely, "I swear that...." In the cases where the verb is not present, Conklin hypothesizes that the verb was elided, leaving the complementizer to stand for it. In this chapter, Conklin does not shy away from the complex syntax of these clauses, providing an analysis of the difficult *ky* clauses as well.

Chapter 5 appears to be the most innovative chapter in the book. This chapter examines fourteen oaths that do not use a conditional protasis or *ky* to introduce an oath. These oaths use, variably, the word *'šr* as a complementizer, the word *mah* (which appears in only one verse, making it difficult to regard as a "category" of its own), and ten cases of oath content that lack all markers. Conklin's final discussion of the compound particle *ky-'m* is, in my mind, his most convincing. His argument that this phrase does not have the meaning of an asseverative and should instead be treated as two distinct particles is persuasive.

Conklin's study successfully gathers together data that is helpful in addressing the various markers that introduce biblical oaths. In doing so, he has elucidated the meaning and morphosyntactic function of these oath markers and illustrated the way in which certain oath particles mirror the use of these particles in biblical Hebrew. This undoubtedly helps us to understand better the actual meaning of various oaths. While the conclusions reached fulfill the stated goal of improving our ability to interpret certain difficult biblical verses, it would have been valuable if this study had taken the next step and illustrated the way in which Conklin's insights can shed light on the broader biblical narratives. Generally, it appears that Conklin's study is more concerned with pointing out phenomena rather than explaining their significance. Interesting observations such as "in each of the texts in this section [that in which the raising of the hand is the authenticating element], the essential content of the oath is spelled out in an infinitival construct phrase" (15), leaves the reader wondering whether there is any meaning to this correlation. Moreover, Conklin's bid to extrapolate a correlation between the type of authenticating formula and the type of oath content bears no fruit in his own estimation (65), thereby raising the question (which is not addressed) of the value of this direction of research. Nevertheless, there is little doubt that this study represents an original linguistic contribution to the study of oaths and contains some important new understandings of various oath formulae and the particles that introduce them.

Writing and Literacy in the World of Ancient Israel: Epigraphic Evidence from the Iron Age, by Christopher Rollston. Society of Biblical Literature Archaeology and Biblical Studies 11. Atlanta: Society of Biblical Literature, 2010. Pp. xix + 171. Paper. $21.95. ISBN 9781589831070.

Ian Young, University of Sydney, Sydney, Australia

In this volume Christopher A. Rollston provides an introduction to Northwest Semitic, particularly Hebrew, epigraphy. It is written in a manner accessible both to those early in the study of the Old Hebrew inscriptions and to more experienced scholars who wish a deeper acquaintance with this field. It presents in one volume both an introduction to Rollston's important previous work in this field, as well as developing a number of significant new proposals.

In his "Introduction" Rollston discusses "The Importance of Archaeological Context for Analyses of Inscriptions." Here he emphasizes the benefits of knowledge of the provenance and archaeological context for enabling study of such issues as the history of specific sites and regional language and script variations. He then lays the basic groundwork for the study of the inscriptions, dealing with such issues as the differences between lapidary and cursive scripts.

Chapters 1–3 form "Part 1: The Epigraphic Record: The Broad Tableau." In chapter 1, "The Origins of Alphabetic Writing: A Summary of the Salient Features," Rollston gives a basic but informative account of issues related to the origins and early history of the alphabet. He describes the evidence for a date of origin in the early second millennium B.C.E. There is a good introduction to the acrophonic principle whereby the first sound of the object pictured (such as *mym* "water") was what the letter signified. The chapter concludes with an introduction to the cuneiform alphabet at Ugarit, variant orders of the alphabet, and the consonant mergers leading to the twenty-two-letter alphabet of Iron Age Northwest Semitic.

Chapter 2 is "The Use of the Phoenician Script during the Iron Age and the Rise of the Levantine National Scripts." It begins by describing the developments at the end of the second millennium B.C.E. in regard to the stabilization and standardization of the stance of the letters of the alphabet and the direction of writing, as well as the previously mentioned consonant mergers that led to the twenty-two-consonant "Phoenician" alphabet. The chapter traces the dominance of the Phoenician script in the early first millennium and the subsequent branching off of the distinct Hebrew and Aramaic national scripts. Discussion of significant developments in the script is consistently tied to the excellent hand copies of the texts discussed. Rollston succinctly but clearly outlines various major issues relating to these scripts, such as the dating of the early Byblian inscriptions, the absence of non-Phoenician features in early inscriptions from Israel such as the Gezer Calendar and Tel Zayit abecedary, the archaic script of the Tel Fakhariyeh inscription, and others beside. Throughout this, and the description of the national scripts, Rollston gives clear, expert guidance to important distinctive features of letter typology.

Chapter 3, "The Nature of the Northwest Semitic Epigraphic Record Form and Function," is aimed at illustrating the diversity of the epigraphic record during the Iron Age, in order to provide a window into the nature and function of writing in the Iron Age. It does this by giving mini-portraits of varying lengths of important inscriptions illustrative of particular types and genres. This chapter provides a brief but accurate introduction that gives a sense of the range and diversity of epigraphic remains from the Iron Age.

Chapters 4–8 form "Part 2: The Scribe and Literacy." In chapter 4, "The Status of the Scribe and the Tools of the Trade," Rollston describes the respected status of the ancient Near Eastern scribe as a member of the elite class. He cites Egyptian and Mesopotamian texts lauding the scribal profession. A similar text is found in the second century B.C.E. Jewish book of Ben Sira, chapter 38. For earlier biblical times, Rollston points to the regular association between the scribe and the royal court.

Chapter 5 is "Scribal Education in Ancient Israel: The Old Hebrew Epigraphic Evidence." Here Rollston enters into the long-standing discussion of the existence of "schools" in ancient Israel and argues that "the Old Hebrew epigraphic evidence demonstrates that there was a formal, standardized scribal education in ancient Israel" (91). This chapter builds a very impressive case, based on numerous types of evidence, that would need to be addressed by anyone discussing this question in the future. Rollston begins by arguing that, far from being easy, proficiency in even a relatively simple script such as the Old Hebrew alphabet would have required some time. He then gathers evidence for a standardized education mechanism. He points to a clear development of the Hebrew script in the eighth to sixth centuries B.C.E., which yet exhibits consistency in any one period; he uses the *samek-pe* sequence as evidence of standardized education about the relative position of letters to other letters; he notes discernable diagnostic differences between the contemporary Hebrew, Aramaic, and Phoenician scripts; consistent orthographic practices; and the common use of hieratic numerals. One other argument that he uses is that "two dialects of Hebrew are reflected in the Old Hebrew epigraphic record, but random dialect variation does not occur" (109). However, he does show awareness of just how tenuous is our evidence for a distinct "northern Hebrew" in many features. For example, the classic "example" of the reduction of the diphthong $ay > \bar{e}$, *yn* "wine" in the Samaria Ostraca (for southern *yyn*), is pretty much the *only* example, with counterexamples such as *byt* at Tell Qasile and Beth-shean. Nevertheless, this is only a minor plank in a very well constructed argument.

As the title suggests, chapter 6, "Monumental Buildings for Education, Scribal Practice Texts, and Print Exposure in the Scribal Home," deals with three topics. In response to the suggestion that we should expect evidence of monumental school buildings, Rollston argues that, as in the rest of the ancient Near East, we should expect scribal education in ancient Israel to have taken place mostly in a domestic context. Rollston then explores the fascinating suggestion that we have an actual educational text in a seventh-century B.C.E. inscription from the City of David. This contains the same name written twice, once by a trained hand, the other by an unpracticed one, which can plausibly be explained as a student copying the text of his (almost certainly *his* [126]) teacher. The differences between the practiced and unpracticed hands are explained in detail with reference to some more superb hand copies of the text. Finally, Rollston draws on recent research on literacy to suggest that sons of scribes would have been environmentally predisposed to higher literacy due to "print exposure" at home and that sons of scribes commonly entered their father's profession.

Chapter 7, "The Extent of Literacy in Ancient Israel," argues that "the Old Hebrew epigraphic data and the biblical data align and reveal that trained elites were literate and there is a distinct dearth of evidence suggesting that non-elites could write and read" (134). Rollston surveys the Old Hebrew epigraphic evidence and shows how tenuous are arguments that it provides any evidence of nonelite literacy. As Rollston notes, this dovetails with the fact that in the biblical texts it is scribes, priests, and government officials who are described as reading and writing, in relation to which he cites my 1998 articles. I have seen no reason to change my mind about the conclusions of those studies, and Rollston has added here to the strength of the case.

Chapter 8, "Inscriptions from the Market: A Precarious Basis for Statements about the Nature of the Epigraphic Record, Scribal Practices and Literacy," is a call for more methodological discrimination between provenanced and nonprovenenced inscriptions. The volume concludes with a very useful four-page glossary, a bibliography, and subject, Scripture, and author Indexes.

This volume is a very useful, not-too-technical introduction to Northwest Semitic epigraphy. Its relatively small size is deceptive of the amount of information packed into it. The superb hand copies of inscriptions, mostly by the author, are worth the price of the book on their own. But they achieve even greater value when used as a visual reference for the detailed descriptions of script developments provided throughout the book. Together these features allow the reader to get a grasp on the detailed but important differences between various types of Northwest Semitic scripts. My one small criticism is that sometimes specific letters are discussed with reference to the hand copy of longer inscriptions. I imagine it would be difficult for less-experienced readers of these inscriptions to easily pick out the letters in question (e.g., 21, on the Ahiram inscription).

In conclusion, I would not hesitate to recommend this book to anyone who wished a reliable introduction to, and overview of, the current state of scholarship on the Northwest Semitic scripts of the Iron Age.

ARCHAEOLOGY AND HISTORY

Lahav II: Households and the Use of Domestic Space at Iron II Tell Halif: An Archaeology of Destruction, by James W. Hardin. Lahav: Reports of the Lahav Research Project / Excavations at Tell Halif, Israel 2. Winona Lake, Ind.: Eisenbrauns, 2010. Pp. xviii + 286, Hardcover, $69.50, ISBN 9781575061634.

Raz Kletter, University of Helsinki, Tallinn, Estonia

Lahav II is the second report in a series of planned reports on the excavations at Tell Halif/Lahav in the northern Negev of Israel, headed by J. D. Seger. The excavations lasted for twelve seasons (1976–1999; it was renewed under Oded Borowski in 2007). The present report discusses mainly ceramic finds from three seasons (1992, 1993, 1999) in dwelling unit F7, Stratum VIb, Field IV; dated to the late eighth century B.C.E. This study originated as a doctoral dissertation in the University of Arizona in 2001. The stated goal (1) is "to use the spatial data obtained from destruction deposits at Tell Halif to shed light on the Iron II household's activities and organization."

The book includes eight chapters. A general introduction (ch. 1, 1–6) is preceded by a short glossary. In chapter 2, "Studying the Household" (7–34), Hardin treats theories concerning domestic space in archaeology and defines the "archaeological household" of Judah in the eighth century B.C.E. with the common "pillared buildings" (called by others "four-room houses").

Chapter 3, "Household Archaeology in the Southern Levant" (35–83), explains why destruction layers in the area and at Tell Halif are useful for studying domestic space and how the material finds of the F7 dwelling were treated in order to facilitate the study. Here Hardin reviews also "pillared dwellings" and the study of ceramics as a source for analysis of households.

Chapter 4, "Tell Halif: Its History and Remains" (84–123) is mainly a review of the tell, its stratigraphy, and its remains. This part would perhaps fit better the general introduction (ch. 1). Chapter 4 also offers a discussion of formation processes and concludes that the impact of postdestruction processes on the F7 assemblage was minimal.

Chapter 5, "Investigating the F7 Dwelling: The De Facto Assemblage" (124–60) is the core of the work, where the finds are presented and analyzed. The F7 dwelling has five rooms. Hardin defines thirteen "activity areas" in them and tries to identify the various activities based on the nature and distribution of the finds.

Chapter 6 offers a short review on "Houses and Social Structure: Ethnographic and Ethnoarchaeological Data" (161–73). It uses data from nineteenth- and twentieth-century C.E. Arab villages in Palestine/Israel and from villages in Iran.

Chapter 7, "Biblical Texts, the Dwelling, and Social Structure" (174–94) compares the archaeological and ethnographic data with the biblical sources. The basis for understanding the latter is the three-tier structure suggested for the Iron I period by Gottwald and by Stager (177–78) and the identification of the *bet-'ab* (extended family) as the basic family unit in the Bible (178–82). Hardin supports the view that the biblical texts can and should be used for reconstruction of Iron Age realities (e.g., 175).

Chapter 8, "Conclusion" (186–94), summarizes the results of the study. Hardin suggests that the F7 dwelling and pillared/four-room houses in general were dwelling houses of small, extended families (the biblical *bet 'ab*) throughout the entire Iron Age period. The Iron I pillared houses are identical to those of the Iron II, except by size.

There are two excursuses: "A History of Destruction Strata" (74–83) lists destruction strata in sites in Palestine/Israel from the Early Bronze to the Neo-Babylonian period, while "Biblical Texts, Historical Reconstructions, and Revisionist Trends" (186–94) reviews and criticizes the "minimalist" attitude.

Here it is impossible to discuss details of the many finds and their analysis that lie at the core of the work. Praise to the meticulous work of Hardin and the Lahav team on the finds; perhaps only archaeologists can appreciate how great an effort is required for such a spatial analysis, explaining "why" only one dwelling unit is treated. Much work and thought are invested here.

Three issues seem to deserve comment. First, while the archaeological analysis of the finds is sound, it involves many interpretations. A few examples will suffice. There are different views about the entrance to room 1. Was it blocked, indicating different temporal stages (thus Seger), or not (thus Hardin, 127–30)? The decision here affects the conclusions later. Determining "activity areas" is again open to interpretation. For example, activity area C is separated from B mainly by lack of finds, not by clear building features (fig. 5.2 and p. 134). Area G is very arbitrary, determined mainly by the limits of the excavation and by later pits. It is not certain if the house had two stores (159–60); if so, the nature of the upper store is unclear, and finds from it are probably mixed with those of the lower floor. Similarly, activities are interpreted soundly, but often one cannot reach conclusive results. Are twelve wine jars, a funnel, a strainer, several stoppers, and two *broken* bullae (area M, 156–57) evidence of wine production or only of wine storage and consumption? If activity area B is cultic, why do we have only the broken-off head of a figurine rather than an entire or restorable one? (See fig. 5.9 and the restoration as a whole figurine in fig. 5.12.) There are questions of interpretation of specific finds. Fragment Pl. 3:1 is identified as an upper torso of a female pillar figurine with breakage areas of breasts, but it is quite flat and has no sign of arms on the sides/below the broken areas. It seems to be part of an animal body, or a "bed model." Of course, similar difficulties exist for almost any archaeological study.

A second issue is the identification of social reality from the archaeological remains. This problem is apparent from the beginning: the tension between the social definition of "household" and the so-called "archaeological household" (glossary, xvii). If the latter is "simply a pedagogical term used by scholars to refer to the individuals who generally occupied pillared dwellings until scholars can determine whether these individuals were an extended household (the *bet 'av*?), a nuclear family, or another unit," then it is not a well-defined term nor something simple. The "archaeological household" does not pinpoint the inhabitants but the physical space, the house or dwelling; identifying what is the "unit" here is complex. Hardin refers to some "ideological" studies of Faust on Iron Age houses, but not to his suggestions about various houses and differences between periods and urban/rural sites (e.g., A. Faust, "Differences in Family Structures between Cities and Villages in Iron Age II," *Tel Aviv* 26 [1999]: 233–51). There is no consensus yet as to who lived in each "pillared/four-room" house: the nuclear family, the extended family, or both (varying with time/between types of sites).

A third issue is the biblical sources and their comparison with the archaeological (and ethnographic) ones. A source often quoted for the composition of the family is the story of Micah (Judg 17–18), but even here the details are scanty. In addition to our inability to date this story clearly and the usual questions of historical reliability and aims, one must stress its extremely exceptional nature. This story pictures the very opposite of a "normal" Judean family: a fatherless family with a nameless mother, completely disinterested in daily life and agriculture, obsessed with allegedly pious but probably very wrong cultic acts, leading to eternal shame. Can we identify the accidental details in such a highly articulated and enigmatic story and reconstruct from them Iron Age social realities? The "model" of three-tiers in Iron Age Judah/Israel is far from certain; the biblical terms are often difficult or more vague than what is often presumed (see H. G. M. Williamson, "The Family in Persian Judah: Some Textual Reflections," in *Symbiosis, Symbolism and the Power of the Past* [ed. W. G. Dever and S. Gitin; Winona Lake, Ind.: Eisenbrauns, 2003], 469–86). The issue is not "minimalism" per se but rather the very limited nature of the biblical data about social structure(s), which leaves various interpretations possible.

The book is well-edited and clearly written. Some finds will have to be treated again in forthcoming reports, since they are not fully published here (e.g., weights and bullae), but this does not detract from the present analysis. I did not find statistical tables listing the numbers of each item from each activity area/room, though they would not have changed the conclusions. The book is a worthy addition for the study of houses and families in Iron Age Israel/Palestine. If more scholars follow with detailed studies for other houses and sites, a large archaeological database would accumulate, hopefully elucidating some of the issues mentioned above.

From Roman to Early Christian Thessalonikē: Studies in Religion and Archaeology, edited by Laura Nasrallah, Charalambos Bakirtzis, and Steven J. Friesen. Harvard Theological Studies 64. Cambridge: Harvard University Press, 2010. Pp. xiv + 437. Paper. $40.00. ISBN 9780674053229.

Karl P. Donfried, Smith College, Northampton, Massachusetts

This diverse, comprehensive, and rich volume deals with various aspects of the history, archaeology, and religion of Thessalonikē from 100 B.C.E. to 700 C.E. The fact that such a significant volume could be produced is a tribute to the outstanding initiatives and contributions that have been undertaken by long-time Harvard professor Helmut Koester, a mentor to so many, including myself. The volume contains fourteen chapters and is evenly divided into two major parts: "The Early Roman Empire" and "The Later Roman Empire and the Early Byzantine Period." Since all of the essays in the first half deal with or are closely related to Roman Thessalonikē, a concentration on these is natural, given the readership of *RBL*, and since the introduction to the volume by Laura Nasrallah summarizes all fourteen contributions.

Pantelis Nigdelis's opening essay on "Voluntary Associations in Roman Thessalonikē: In Search of Identity and Support in a Cosmopolitan Society," reviews some forty-four inscriptions, many funerary, representing the second and third centuries and revealing four types of associations: religious, professional, household, and one composed of arena/theater devotees. The religious associations are primarily Dionysiac and those that represent the Egyptian gods as well as a group of others. There are considerably fewer professional associations than religious, although four are documented. Nigelis finds limited participation of women in most associations, although women are in fact attested, often as cultic officials, in the Dionysiac associations of the second and third centuries C.E. Among the several assets of participating in the activities of such an association was to gain "a new collective identity, thereby adopting the political behavior of their era" (36). Richard Ascough's "Of Memories and Meals: Greco-Roman Associations," dealing with a similar topic, is richly provocative. That the Dionysian associations allow us to understand the references to drinking and drunkenness in 1 Thess 5:5–8 is evident, but that Paul persuaded a preexisting workers' association to worship Jesus is less persuasive, especially given the brevity of his stay in Thessalonica. Since many of the associations in the city are preoccupied with eating, Ascough's suggestion that Paul's injunction in 2 Thess 3:10 ("Let him not eat"), as well as the broader context in 2 Thess 3:6–14, may have reference to disorderly behavior at meals and the necessary exclusion of such persons from "ritualized commensality" (66).

Melanie Johnson-DeBaufre's contribution about the "elusive" women of 1 Thessalonians ("'Gazing Upon the Invisible': Archaeology, Historiography, and the Elise Wo/men of 1 Thessalonians") is both enigmatic and puzzling, filled with what appear to be a wide range of unsupported generalizations. As the argument progresses, it appears that Johnson-DeBaufre's concern is more with questionable secondary interpretations of 1 Thessalonians (see the discussion of Lone Fatum [80–81]) than with the text itself. In referring to my own linguistic remarks with regard to the use of *skeuos* in 1 Thess 4:3, the argument is skewed by her own ideological reading of these verses, as, for example, her assertion that the remarks in *The Cults of Thessalonica and the Thessalonian Correspondence* invites only "a series of erotic/exotic wo/men to saunter into the reader's historical imagination" (84). Further, where, one must ask, is there in 1 Thessalonians a discussion of "an egalitarian social movement" (86)? Here as well nondocumented, bold conjectures dealing with "empire studies" and "postcolonial criticism" are substituted for critical analysis of the texts at hand. When the author states that "gender may also be a site of resistance to empire that goes beyond attempting to rein in the reign of the phallus through marriage" (92), she blatantly misunderstands the linguistic analysis of 1 Thess 4:3! What reputable scholars argue that in 1 Thess 4:3–8 "women were not actually *there* or not *really Christians*" (98), and, how, specifically, does a shift to the question of "creation and contestation of spaces and identities" (98) lead to a more precise and critical exegesis based on the text of 1 Thessalonians? To argue that Acts 17:5–7 is instructive not because it may refer to a historical situation but rather because the "story 'think's spatially" (100) is arbitrary at best.

Christine M. Thomas appropriately emphasizes the "somatization" of the sacred in her essay on 1 Thessalonians, "Locating Purity: Temples, Sexual Prohibitions and 'Making a Difference' in *Thessalonikē*," and this is accurately acknowledged as a key theme in 1 Thess 4:3–5. As with Paul, so the sectarians at Qumran did not distinguish between cultic and moral impurity; *both* revealed the moral state of the individual. However, this essay seems to categorically reject the evidence for the presence of Judaism in Thessalonica found in Acts 17 as well as failing to understand that at his core Paul is a Jew using very specifically Jewish terminology 1 Thessalonians. The New Testament *hapax* "compatriot" can, of course, refer to fellow Thessalonians very broadly, but its specific placement in the context of verses 14–16 as a parallel to the "Jews" suggests that suffering being endured by the believers in Christ in that city are at the hands of non-Christ-believing Jews. That "tribes" are "epigraphically attested at Thessalonikē" (115), while accurate, still does not define the meaning of the term within a specific context such as we have in 1 Thess 2. Further, can one agree with Thomas that the "individual, or her physical body, is where the holy is located" in 1 Thessalonians? Is not the "somatization" of the sacred given ultimate meaning because they are "in Christ" (1 Thess 4:16), "who died for us, so that whether we are awake or asleep we may live with him" (1 Thess 5:10)? Finally, one other item must be added to Thomas's quite correct observation, namely, that the holy is not located only in the believer but in the believing community, the church. For this very reason Paul can write to the Corinthians as he does in 1 Cor 3:16–17.

Helmut Koester's "Egyptian Religion in Thessalonikē: Regulation for the Cult" is characteristic of the creative, pioneering, and enormous contributions that he has had made to New Testament and early Christian studies. In so many ways his archaeological work and observations have transformed these studies in dramatic and foundational ways, and his scholarship is characterized by prudent analysis of artifacts and texts. Further, he urges that, while discoveries can often be related to limited areas, they must always be considered and viewed in relationship to the culture, politics, and religion of the larger areas to which they are connected. Further, he is quite correct in reminding us with regard to 1 Thessalonians that it is Paul's broader eschatological message that determines his proclamation in Thessalonikē, not necessarily the local Thessalonian conventions, although, I would add, these local conventions allowed Paul to shape and actualize his broader message about redemption in Jesus Christ to the local situation as we find, for example, in his unique shaping of his opening verse: "To the church of the Thessalonians in God the Father and the Lord Jesus Christ." Another essay shaped by detailed archaeological examination within the Roman period is that of Thea Stefanidou-Tiverious, "Social Status and Family Origin in the Sarcophagi of Thessalonikē." Following careful examination of locally made Roman sarcophagi, she concludes that a significant and economically strong part of the population of the city came from Asia Minor, that the city maintained an "eastern-style public and private life" (184), and that close cultic relationships existed between the cities of Macedonia and Asia Minor. These conclusions, together with the discussion regarding the connection between garland sarcophagi, religious practice, and the cult of the dead require careful reflection as one attempts to understand Thessalonikē as the cultural matrix within which 1 Thessalonians was shaped.

Steven Friesen in his "Second Thessalonians, the Ideology of Epistles, and the Construction of Authority: Our Debt to the Forger" argues that 2 Thessalonians is most accurately described as a forgery and understands the development of Pauline pseudepigrapha to have developed in five stages: "1) personal presence; 2) oral traditions surviving in the community after Paul's departure; 3) a letter that substitutes for Paul's personal presence; 4) competition between letter and oral tradition; and finally 5) the epistle as authoritative document" (191). For such a paradigm, 2 Thessalonians represents stage 4 and 3 Corinthians stage 5. Although Friesen raises significant points, his suggested trajectory omits both a discussion of the sociology of the Pauline mission, including its geography and chronology, as well as the motivations and methods involved in the Pauline letter collection. One must recognize that within key cities throughout the Roman Empire there existed a broad network of missionary centers that embraced over eighty-six co-workers and associates. To map the growth and development of this trajectory requires that several key issues be reexamined including the process and purposes for letter writing in missionary situations for which there is little, if any, evidence prior to Paul. Were letters, for example, that bore the name of Paul written only by the apostle alone or jointly (i.e., 1 Thessalonians, "Paul, Silvanus, and Timothy"; 1 Corinthians, "Sosthenes") or by such authorized delegates as Titus? How often and to what degree was an amanuensis employed? Further, will the results of such investigations be able to maintain the currently fashionable scholarly distinction between "Pauline" and "non-Pauline," and are these categories not much more fluid than many acknowledge? To recognize Paul not as a solitary charismatic leader charging through the Roman Empire essentially on his own but rather as the leader of a missionary movement involving multiple vibrant centers linked to a team of almost one-hundred will of necessity change images, perceptions, and scholarly methods of analysis. Thus, for many of Friesen's arguments to be persuasive, including that "we do the letter and the author an injustice if we do not recognize this accomplishment" of forgery (207) or that Paul did not understand all of his "letters as authoritative statements of divine truth" (207), the entire topic of Pauline letter writing needs to be viewed against a far broader and more fluid background than is considered in this essay.

Finally, for those wishing to probe the splendid essays written by a wide range of prominent experts found in the final section, "The Later Roman Empire and the Early Byzantine Period," it will be useful to indicate the authors with titles. They include: Slobodan Ćurčić, "Christianization of Thessalonikē: The Making of Christian 'Urban Iconography'"; James Skedros, "Civic and Ecclesiastical Identity in Christian Thessalonikē"; Anastassios C. Antonaras, "Glassware in Late Antique Thessalonikē (Third to Seventh Centuries C.E.)"; Aristotelos Mentzos, "Reflections on the Architectural History of the Tetrarchic Palace Complex at Thessalonikē"; Laura Nasrallah, "Early Christian Interpretation in Image and Word: Canon, Sacred Text, and the Mosaic of Moni Latomou"; Charalambos Bakirtzis, "Late Antiquity and Christianity in Thessalonikē: Aspects of a Transformation." Each contains carefully articulated dimensions of the continuing transformation of ancient Thessalonikē.

Israel in Transition 2: From Late Bronze II to Iron IIA (c. 1250–850 BCE): The Texts, edited by Lester L. Grabbe. Library of Hebrew Bible/Old Testament Studies 521. New York: T&T Clark, 2010. Pp. x + 260. Hardcover. $120.00. ISBN 9780567649485.

Friedrich Schipper, University of Vienna, Vienna, Austria

Der vorliegende Band ist der zweite eines zweibändigen Sammelwerkes über die Zeitperiode von 1250 bis 850 v.Chr. in Israel, dessen Essays aus den Beiträgen der beiden Tagungen des European Seminar in Historical Methodology in Verbindung mit der European Association of Biblical Studies in Budapest im Jahr 2006 und in Wien im Jahr 2007 hervorgegangen sind. Der Herausgeber, Lester L. Grabbe, Professor für Hebräische Bibel und Frühjudentum an der Universität Hull (England), ist durch seine Tätigkeit als Organisator solch biblisch-historiographischer Tagungen und Herausgeber der Tagungsbände wohlbekannt. Der erste Band, ebenfalls von Grabbe herausgegeben und bereits im Jahr 2008 im selben Verlag erschienen, liegt dem Rezensenten trotz Nachfrage beim Verlag nicht vor, so bleibt diese Bewertung auf den zweiten Band beschränkt und daher Teilwerk. Dies ist insofern relevant, da das ursprüngliche Konzept der wissenschaftlichen Auseinandersetzung mit dem Thema in den beiden Tagungen ein interdisziplinäres gewesen ist. So ging es den Organisatoren darum, die Geschichte Israels von der ausgehenden Bronzezeit bis in die Eisenzeit aus dem jeweiligen Blickwinkel der Archäologie wie auch der Textwissenschaft zu beleuchten und so die verschiedenen Gesichtspunkte der Vertreter der verschiedenen Fachdisziplinen herausarbeiten zu können. Dabei war es bei einigen Teilnehmern durchaus umstritten, ob vor allem die biblische Textwissenschaft überhaupt etwas zu historischen Fragestellungen beitragen kann und ob derartige Auseinandersetzungen eigentlich Sinn machen. Die Ergebnisse dieses interdisziplinären Diskurses in zwei Bänden—einen zur Archäologie und einen zur Textwissenschaft—getrennt voneinander vorzulegen, ist eine zu hinterfragende redaktionelle Entscheidung, so scheint doch der interdisziplinäre Ertrag rein formal wieder aufgehoben. Eine andere Gliederung des Gesamtwerkes wäre eventuell sinnvoller gewesen. Diese Kritik soll aber dem vorliegenden Einzelband als solches keinerlei Abbruch tun. So ist es Grabbe gelungen, wichtige Vertreter der Textwissenschaft zu versammeln, die mit ihren Beiträgen die grundlegenden und teils eben divergierenden Positionen in der Forschung darstellen. Darüber hinaus schließt Grabbe den Band selbst mit einem Beitrag ab, in dem er die Gesamtdiskussion der Tagungen reflektiert und damit die Aufspaltung des Stoffes in die beiden fachlich getrennten Teilbände gleichsam zu kompensieren sucht.

Mit seiner Einleitung bietet der Herausgeber eine Reihe von Zusammenfassungen (Abstracts) aller Essays von zumeist etwa 1 Seite. Es folgen 9 Essays und die erwähnte Zusammenfassung des Herausgebers sowie ein Essay als Appendix, das nicht auf einen Beitrag bei den Tagungen zurückgeht, sondern eine Übersetzung eines bereits a.O. publizierten Beitrags darstellt. Der Band schließt mit einem Index von Schriftstellen sowie von modernen Autoren.

In seiner Analyse über „Samuel, Sources, and Historiography" stellt A. Graeme Auld, emeritierter Professor für Hebräische Bibel an der Universität Edinburgh, eingangs zur Diskussion, ob die Frage nach der Datierung der Quellen und der Komposition der Samuelbücher in der Sache überhaupt weiterführt. So unterscheiden sich die LXX- und MT-Versionen der Geschichte von David und Goliath wesentlich, wobei dies konventionell auf verschiedene Vorlagen zurückgeführt wird. Auld votiert für eine alternative Sicht, die impliziert, dass die Unterschiede der Versionen nicht auf rivalisierende Quellen zurückgehen, sondern schlicht auf das natürliche Wachstum von Texten, im konkreten Fall schreibt er von einem Midrasch-artigen Wachstum, bei dem nicht andere, eventuell früh datierende Quellen eingearbeitet, sondern eher Lücken im Text mit vorhandenem Material gefüllt wurden. Bei seinen Ausführungen baut Auld auf seine früheren Studien zum Thema auf—„The Making of David and Goliath" (1992), sowie „The Story of David and Goliath: a Test Case for Synchrony Plus Diachrony" (2004)— und führt sie hier nun weiter.

Mit einem Überblick zu den gegenwärtigen Strömungen in der Historiographie beginnt Marc Zvi Brettler, Professor für Bibelwissenschaft an der Brandeis University, seinen Beitrag „The David Tradition", und befindet, dass sich aktuell ein Konsens entwickelt, der die Extreme des Postmodernismus und Skeptizismus zurückweist als auch jene, die der biblischen Tradition unkritisch den Vorzug geben und den gebräuchlichen Kanon der kritischen Historiographie ignorieren. Der einzige gangbare Weg ist jener der literarkritischen Analyse, die nicht a priori voraussetzt, ob ein Text nun historisch ist oder nicht. Eine Untersuchung der parallelen Traditionen in 1. Sam 24 und 26 über Davids Flucht vor Saul bietet eine ideale Gelegenheit, um die Entwicklung der davidischen Tradition verstehen und damit entscheiden zu können, ob diese Tradition Potential zur Rekonstruktion der frühen Monarchie hat. Brettler verneint dies schließlich, da sich aus literarkritischer Sicht beim gegenwärtigen Forschungsstand noch viel zu wenig über den Ursprung bzw. den ursprünglichen Kontext dieser beiden Kapitel sagen lässt.

Philip R. Davies, emeritierter Professor für Bibelwissenschaft an der Universität von Sheffield, untersucht in seinem Beitrag „The Beginnings of the Kingdom of Judah" die Konsequenzen der Entdeckung der Tel-Dan-Inschrift für die biblische Historiographie und geht den verschiedenen Interpretation von *bytdwd* nach. Da seiner Meinung nach die Fragmente der Stele verschiedentlich zusammengesetzt werden können, ergeben sich, ausgehend von der Übersetzung als *Haus Davids*, mehrere Möglichkeiten. Basierend auf der Bedeutung des Terminus im Alten Testament votiert Davies für eine Lesung als *Familie Davids* und lehnt eine Interpretation als direkten Nachweis für ein Königreich Juda ab, dessen historische Existenz er grundsätzlich in Frage stellt. Vielmehr, so spekuliert Davies, könnte das *bytdwd* der Tel-Dan-Inschrift ein Nachweis für ein Stammesfürstentum sein, das in einem Abhängigkeitsverhältnis zu Königreich Israel stand.

Der Herausgeber des Bandes, Lester L. Grabbe, stellt in seinem Beitrag „From Merenptah to Shoshenq: If We Had Only the Bible ..." eben jene Frage, die er auch in seinen vorangegangenen vergleichbaren Studien gestellt hat: Was würden wir über Israel und seine Geschichte wissen, wenn wir nur die Bibel hätten? Zwar steht für die Zeit ab Mitte des 9. Jhs. epigraphisches Material zur Rekonstruktion der Geschichte Israels zur Verfügung. Doch für jene Zeitperiode, die das Thema dieses Bandes ist (1250–850 v.Chr.), gibt es kaum außerbiblisches schriftliches Quellenmaterial zu Israel. Das macht eine Abgleichung des biblischen Befundes schwierig. Grabbes frühere Schlussfolgerungen bestätigt er schließlich durch seine hier vorgelegte Studie: Je später in der Geschichte der Monarchie, desto zuverlässiger sind die literarischen Information.

Ernst Axel Knauf, Professor für Altes Testament und Biblische Archäologie an der Universität Bern, bietet in drei zusammenhängenden Beiträgen zur vorstaatlichen Zeit Israels seine Überlegungen zur Frage der Historizität der biblischen Texte. In den ersten beiden Beiträgen, „History in Joshua" und „History in Judges", wertet er einzelne Stellen aus und stellt die Ergebnisse in Überblickstabellen dar. Die meisten Texte, die sich auf datierbare Ereignisse beziehen, sind „post-Iron IIa" und verteilen sich gleichermaßen auf die vorexilische und die persische Zeit, nur wenige weisen in die hellenistische Zeit. Er folgert, dass die einzelnen Stellen zwar historische Elemente enthalten, die Erzählungen als Ganzes aber nicht mit der historischen Realität der vorstaatlichen Zeit korrespondieren. Als Appendix enthält der Band auch Knaufs Beitrag „Exodus and Settlement", ursprünglich Abschnitt 3 der Einleitung zu seinem Buch „Josua" (ZBKAT 6, 2008). Dabei führt er zunächst aus, dass zwar die Tradition vom Exodus von Anfang an Teil der biblischen Tradition gewesen ist, die Tradition vom verheißenen Land jedoch in das 7. bzw. 6. Jh. datiert. Diese Tradition sei erst mit dem Verlust der Staatlichkeit Israels wichtig geworden. Auch Elemente assyrischer Theologie seien in dieser Phase in die biblische Tradition eingeflossen. So gehören die *hrm*-Texte in diese Zeit und nicht zu den ursprünglichen Erzählungen.

Niels Peter Lemche, Professor für Theologie an der Universität Kopenhagen, drückt in seinem Beitrag „How to Deal with 'Early Israel'" zunächst seine Zweifel aus, dass eine Erforschung der Geschichte der Eisen-I bis IIa-Zeit überhaupt irgendetwas Neues zu Tage fördern würde und stellt 5 Fragen, die er in seinem Beitrag abarbeitet: 1. Was hat sich in den letzten Jahren in der (biblischen) Geschichtswissenschaft getan? 2. Was hat sich in den letzten Jahren in der (biblischen bzw. palästinischen) Archäologie getan? 3. Welchen Einfluss hat mittlerweile die Sozialanthropologie auf die (biblische) Geschichtswissenschaft? 4. Inwiefern hat sich die Methodik geändert, mit der die Geschichtswissenschaft an biblische Texte herangeht? 5. Was für eine Geschichte Israels kann heute geschrieben werden? —Insofern untersucht er gleichsam die jüngere Forschungsgeschichte und prüft vor allem inwiefern seine eigenen Thesen und Ansätze sowie die seiner Mitstreiter Thompson et al. in der etablierten Forschung rezipiert worden sind. Der Befund fällt verhalten aus und Lemches Urteil daher eindeutig: Es wären kaum Fortschritte zu verzeichnen und man stünde heute immer noch dort wo man vor 10 oder 20 Jahren war. Doch ohne eine radikale Umkehr in der Hermeneutik wäre das Unterfangen einer Geschichte des frühen Israels hoffnungslos.

Robert D. Miller II, Professor für Altes Testament an der Catholic University of America in Washington DC, diskutiert „A 'New Cultural History' of Early Israel". Im ersten Teil seines Beitrags fasst er systematisch verschiedene Positionen einer Kulturgeschichte Israels zusammen. Dabei fokussiert er auf vergleichende Architekturforschung, Siedlungsmuster und Keramiktypologien. Darauf basierend hinterfragt er grundsätzlich die typlogische Methodik in der syro-palästinischen Archäologie. Er kommt jedoch zum Schluss, dass das biblische Bild der frühisraelitischen Religion zutreffend ist, was bedeutet, dass die religiösen Praktiken nicht mit späteren jüdischen religiösen Standards im Einklang stehen.

In seinem Beitrag „David the Mercenary" weist John van Seters, emeritierter Professor an der University of North Carolina at Chapel Hill, darauf hin, dass David in der davidischen Erzählung für die Ausübung seiner militärischen Macht im Wesentlichen auf Söldner zurückgreifen muss, während dies für die ihm nachfolgenden Könige kaum bzw. gar nicht der Fall ist. Das legt nahe, dass dieser Umstand ein Indikator für die Entstehungszeit jener Stellen der Daviderzählung ist, in denen von Söldnern die Rede ist. Van Seters untersucht daraufhin das Söldnerwesen des 1. Jts. im ostmediterranen Raum und im Vorderen Orient und kommt zum Schluss, dass der „Sitz im Leben" der „Kreti und Pleti" das persische Militär des 5. Jhs. gewesen sein muss. Somit wurde die davidische Erzählung im 5. und 4. Jh. entsprechend ausgestaltet und der Erzähler hat David nach dem militärischen Vorbild persischer Könige oder Satrapen seiner eigenen Zeit modelliert. Demnach sind diese Stellen anachronistisch und haben keinerlei Wert für eine Rekonstruktion der Geschichte der frühen Monarchie.

In seinen „Reflections on the Discussion: Text and Archaeology" fasst der Herausgeber des vorliegenden Bandes bzw. des Doppelbandes, Lester L. Grabbe, noch einmal alles zusammen, verweist dabei auch auf seinen abschließenden Beitrag des 1. Bandes (2008) und nützt im Wesentlichen die Gelegenheit, um sich selbst als Historiker noch einmal in der Mitte zwischen Maximalisten und Minimalisten zu positionieren, der versucht, die groben Grundlinien einer Geschichte Israels auf der Basis archäologischer Daten und anderer zeitgenössischer Quellen (Inschriften etc.) zu rekonstruieren, in einem zweiten Schritt jedoch sehr wohl die biblischen Erzählungen prüft und so gewonnene Daten in das historische Gesamtbild integriert. Dabei schließt Grabbe jedoch, dass für den zur Diskussion stehenden Zeitraum (1250–850 v.Chr.) eben kaum historisch zuverlässiges, biblisches Quellenmaterial zur Verfügung steht—ein Umstand, der sich für die Folgeperioden ganz anders darstellt.

Biblical History and Israel's Past: The Changing Study of the Bible and History, by Megan Bishop Moore and Brad E. Kelle. Grand Rapids: Eerdmans, 2011. xvii + 518. Paper. $46.00. ISBN 9780802862600.

Bob Becking, Utrecht University, Utrecht, The Netherlands

This is an important book. The authors report how the study of the history of ancient Israel has lost its naïveté. They correctly detect a change from the form of history writing that can be labeled as basically a retelling of the biblical story in the middle of the twentieth century to the contemporary elaborated evidence-based approach of the past. They are doing this by telling the story of the development of the scholarly knowledge on the various periods on ancient Israelite history.

In the introduction (1–42) they give a broad outlook on the general developments in the field. A few basic observations are made that can be summarized in three movements. (1) Concerning the text of the Hebrew Bible. The historical-critical approach to the emergence of the Hebrew Bible has functioned as a distortion of the traditional view on Israel's past. The statement of Wellhausen that any given text reflects more the circumstances of the period in which it was written down than the period it presumably describes is of course fundamental for every historical approach. Moore and Kelle make clear that the truth of this adagium has only slowly been integrated in the mindset of the historians of ancient Israel. Its truth is also basic for the controversy between minimalists, who bring Wellhausen's view to a maximum, and maximalists, who still believe that there exists some minimum of historicity in later texts (the often-mentioned kernels). (2) Archaeology. The "archive in the field" has given a great variety of new insights. Problematic, however, is the way this information is treated. For too long, archaeology has been "biblical" archaeology: digging with the Bible in one hand and hoping that finds will corroborate the biblical story. (3) Social sciences. The so-called "new archaeology" has revived the importance of the social-science approach in the study of the past. If anything, ancient Israel was a community of people with all sorts of interhuman actions. The authors make clear that the introduction of models from the field of ethnology has helped us to understand movements of the past. They correctly warn that these models always are limited and biased. In my opinion, a fourth dimension would be necessary; I will come back to that later.

The second chapter discusses the historicity of the patriarchs and matriarchs (43–76). The authors make clear how and why the claim of historical kernels in the stories and Israel's ancestors has disappeared. For scholars such as Albright, the patriarchs were real historical persons. Due to the work of, for example, Van Seters and Thompson, the arguments for that claim are now no longer seen as valuable. The biblical narratives are generally seen as late and therefore not containing correct memories of the past. The use of archaeology and ethnographic parallels by Albright is shown to be to bibliocentric. Next to that, the parallels are often not restricted to the "patriarchal age." The motif of "the wife as sister" has been a more general ancient Near Eastern *topos* than had been assumed.

Chapter 3 reflects on the search for Israel's beginning (77–143). This is a very interesting part, since it discusses important themes from Israel's national memory. These themes—sojourn in Egypt; exodus; wilderness wandering; occupation of the central hill areas—are in a way interrelated but are better discussed separately. As for the sojourn in Egypt, Moore and Kelle accept the importance of the reports on the Hyksos, the Shasu, and the Hapiru, but they make clear that these sources are too haphazard for a construction of the past that goes beyond "somewhere in the Bronze Age Asians dwelled in Egypt." A connection with a Joseph-group cannot be established. As for the exodus, a comparable view needs to be defended. The traditional identifications of Moses and Pharaoh with historical figures from Egyptian history remain weak. It is a pity that they overlooked the proposal by Johannes C. de Moor (*The Rise of Yahwism: The Roots of Israelite Monotheism* [2nd ed.; Leuven: Peeters, 1997]), who unconvincingly argued for an identification of Moses with a person Beya known from some sources.

The emergence of "Israel" in the central hill area of the Levant is one of the most intriguing aspects of the history of ancient Israel. The authors should be praised for the fact that they have summarized the difficult discussion on these matters in a brilliantly clear way. They present the well-known theories such as invasion from outside, peasant revolt, and reemergence of a Middle Bronze Age community in a very readable way. They make clear that the loss of confidence in the historiographical trustworthiness of the biblical record was instrumental for the loss of traditional view. The existing models, however, are not without flaws. The Nothian concept of an amphictyony is a clear example of transposing a concept from a relatively similar culture without, however, looking at the differences. Although they do not express the idea in such words, the authors tend to a view that the main flaw in all models is the concept of mono-causality. I would applaud the idea that ancient Israel emerged from a variety of groups with different social and religious backgrounds who merged into one ethnicity as a result of the demographic expansion in the early Iron Age.

Chapter 4 (145–99) discusses the monarchical period in such a way that the outlines, the presuppositions, and the implications of the various approaches are presented. As for the Hebrew Bible, the Deuteronomistic History hypothesis is outlined in its origin (Noth) and development into a multilayer theory. Unfortunately, the authors did not consider the position of Thomas Römer, whose 2005 monograph (*The So-Called Deuteronomistic History: A Sociological, Historical and Literary Introduction* [London: T&T Clark, 2005]) is, in my opinion, very informative. As for the historiographical value of the Deuteronomistic History, the authors make clear that, despite its relatively late date, some scholars still argue for the trustworthiness of various details even in cases when no corroborating extrabiblical evidence is present. Correctly, they argue that 1 and 2 Chronicles cannot be seen as historical evidence for preexilic events, although the heirs of the Albright school still plead for such a position. In regard of the extrabiblical evidence, they correctly claim the Mesopotamian and West-Semitic evidence has often been uncritically and Bible-centrically evaluated.

The fifth chapter (200–265) is dedicated to the period of the beginnings of permanent governance. In the middle of the twentieth century, the stories about Israel's first three kings were construed as first-hand authentic documents (Rost). This position and its implication, that we know quite a lot about the fate of the first kings, has disappeared. This is partly due to a better understanding of the character of the reports in 1 and 2 Samuel as highly ideological texts and partly to the discoveries—or better: the lack of—in the field of archaeology. These discoveries make clear that the concept of a united monarchy should be assessed as an historical construct with no clear basis in the evidence. Interestingly, the authors argue for the historicity of Saul, albeit in the role of the last Labayu; in other words, Saul should be construed as comparable to the Canaanite kings who governed city-states and are mentioned in the Amarna correspondence. As for David, they discuss the proposal by McKenzie and Halpern, who argue for some historicity. Unfortunately, they have overlooked a recent book by John Van Seters on David that argues that the stories in1 and 2 Samuel need to be connected to the perils of the period of Ezra and Nehemiah (*The Biblical Saga of King David* [Winona Lake, Ind.: Eisenbrauns, 2009]). It would be interesting to know how Moore and Kelle would react to Van Seters's statement: "We now know with a high degree of confidence that the sociohistorical context in the Court History of David simply cannot be supported by the archaeological for the 10th century and must belong to a much later age" (xii). As for Solomon, the discussion on "high and low chronology" is of great importance.

In chapter 6 the Iron Age kingdoms of Judah and Israel are highlighted (266–333). The authors clearly lay out the pitfall that is given by the fact that there are so many contemporary sources to that period. Here an interesting shift is detectable with regard to the use of, for instance, Assyrian royal inscriptions. Earlier generations construed these texts as trustworthy and primary sources and hence isolated those fragments that could be connected to the history of ancient Israel. Nowadays it has become clear that these inscriptions are drenched in the royal ideology and only present the perspective of the Mesopotamian court.

Chapter 7 is dedicated to the exilic, or, more precisely, the Neo-Babylonian, period (334–95). The shift in the label is very significant. "Exile" is a primarily biblical concept, a construct based on the views of a specific group in ancient Israel who claimed that their ancestors had been in Babylon. On the basis of that claim, they pretended to be the real Israel. This ideology is distorted by recent research. Important is the unmasking of the myth of the empty land and the myth of the mass return. As Hans Barstad has convincingly argued, the area around Jerusalem was not uninhabited in the Neo-Babylonian period. Next to that, the idea that, after Cyrus's conquest of Babylon in 539, the exiles massively and in one movement returned to Yehud is now abandoned for the view that in a process of more than a century various groups returned from Babylonia, sometimes supported by the Persian power. As for the life in "exile," it is a pity that Moore and Kelle do not pay attention to a group of cuneiform inscriptions that inform on the deeds and doing of a group of West Semites in newly reclaimed agricultural areas in southern Babylonia, especially in the cities URU ša ᴾna-šar, "the City-of-Nashar; "Eagleton," and *al Ya-hu-du*, "the city of Judah/Yehud," most probably in the vicinity of Borsippa. The texts are dated from the early years of Nebuchadnezzar II until deep into the Persian period. They make clear that the "exiles" lived in relatively good conditions and were able to organize themselves in some sort of ethnic guild.[1]

The postexilic or, better, Persian period (396–464) has recently been debated quite heavily. The authors make clear that scholars have not yet reached the beginning of a consensus on that period. Joe Blenkinsopp's magnificent book appeared apparently too late to be incorporated by them (*Judaism, the First Phase: The Place of Ezra and Nehemiah in the Origins of Judaism* [Grand Rapids: Eerdmans, 2009]). The section on the "parting of the ways" between Judaism and Samaritanism could have been better informed. I would be interested in the view of the authors on the existence of a Persian period sanctuary at Mount Gerizim.

I appreciate this book very much. It is informative and clearly written, and it summarizes complex discussions in digestible formats. Nevertheless, I have a few questions that are all connected to the absence of a fourth dimension as referred to above. In my view, the quality of this book could have been improved by connecting the trends in the approaches on the history of ancient Israel with movements in the field of theoretical historiography. I am fully aware of the fact that developments in the field of theoretical historiography only reach our field with some delay, but nevertheless it would have been interesting to look for such albeit delayed connections. I will not make them, but only a few remarks. Moore and Kelle sometimes refer to longer trends in history, such as their interpretation of the reign of Saul as a continuation of the Canaanite kingship system from the Bronze Age. They, however, do not refer to the important methodological work of Fernand Braudel, who distinguished three paces in historical movements. Peter Burke's *What Is Cultural History?* (2004) could have helped, in my view, to better understand the epistemological difference between the minimalists and the maximalists, since they present at least two different schools. Remarkable is the constant use of the concept "source" throughout this book. This concept, especially with distinction between primary and secondary sources, the latter being of no great historical relevance, is out-dated. Next to that, they quite often argue or refer to an argument that can be summarized as "late source has no value." This argument is a late reflex of Thucydides, who thought that the eyewitness was the only trustworthy source. I dare to go a different direction in which

---

1. See L. Pearce, "New Evidence for Judaeans in Babylonia," in *Judah and the Judaeans in the Persian Period* (ed. O. Lipschits and M. Oeming; Winona Lake, Ind.: Eisenbrauns, 2006), 399–411; idem, "'Judean': A Special Status in Neo-Babylonian and Achemenid Babylonia?" in *Judah and the Judaeans in the Achaemenid Period: Negotiating Identities in an International Context* (ed. O. Lipschits, G. N. Knoppers, and M. Oeming; Winona Lake, Ind.: Eisenbrauns, 2011), 267–77.

I construe a given text as a narrative on the past. As such, this narrative mirrors the ideology of its author(s). The narrative, however, contains a set of propositions at the level of the history of an event that could be correct. This implies that the lateness of a text is not a compelling argument against the historicity of all the elements in that narrative. I would like to conclude with a minor detail of criticism. On page 206 it is suggested that Lemche's *Ancient Israel* (1988) was first published in Dutch. As far as I can see, the book was first published in a more northern branch of the Germanic languages (*Det gamle Israel: En skildring af det israelitiske samfund fra sammenbruddet af broncealderkulturen til hellenistisk tid* [Aarhus: ANIS, 1984]).

I hope that this book will find an abundance of readers.

HEBREW BIBLE/OLD TESTAMENT: GENERAL

A Compendium of Musical Instruments and Instrumental Terminology in the Bible, by Yelena Kolyada. London: Equinox, 2009. Pp. xviii + 304. Hardcover. $140.00. ISBN 9781845534097.

Helen Leneman, Bethesda, Maryland

This book, adapted from Kolyada's PhD thesis published in Russian (Kompozitor, Moscow, 2003) is the first compendium of musical instruments and instrumental terminology in the Bible. There are other books that deal with music in the Bible in a general way. But this compendium, defined as a collection of concise yet detailed information about a subject, is unique. Kolyada considers it "both a reference book and a piece of serious scholarly research based on historical facts, comparative linguistic analysis, and careful musical study" (introduction, 1). This is an accurate description of the book, which includes an astounding amount of information from a wide range of sources in many languages. The depth and breadth of research are both impressive. The goal, in Kolyada's words, is "to give much up to date information about the instruments mentioned in the Bible, and thus to form a contribution to the discipline of biblical musicology" (23). She succeeds admirably in meeting this goal.

There are seven chapters, of which the first and last are historical surveys. The first chapter describes the historical background of Hebrew (Kolyada's term) instrumental music, including its origins, links with neighboring cultures, and the role of music in ancient Israel. Kolyada also discusses the most recent research findings by musicologists and organologists (organology is the science of musical instruments and their classification) working in biblical studies together with archaeologists and philologists. The final chapter traces the ongoing discussion of "Hebrew" musical instruments in postbiblical times, including in the writings of the church fathers and of medieval and Renaissance commentators.

Chapters 2–6 are a systematic analysis of each instrument mentioned in the Bible. Chapters 2–4 are organized based on the type of instrument discussed, while instruments whose identification is ambivalent are discussed in a separate chapter (5), as are generic or unclear musical terms (6).

The three main classes of instruments are strings, winds, and percussion. These are subdivided into horns and woodwinds, membranophones and idiophones. Physical descriptions of the instruments based on texts of different periods and archaeological finds are followed by a discussion of all the biblical mentions of the instrument, in a wide variety of translations (which are all analyzed). Extensive discussion of etymology of the names of the instruments follows. Theories about the origins of the instrument are discussed, as well as influences on later iconography and hymnography. The modern Hebrew meaning of the word is given at the end of each chapter, and illustrations of the instruments are provided. A bibliographical list of writers and which instrument they wrote about follows each chapter. This makes it easy for the reader interested in further researching any particular instrument.

The book also includes an enormous amount of well-organized material in two appendices, with several charts, indices of terms and personal names, glossaries, lists of historical and literary sources, in addition to a rich bibliography. Among the many valuable supplements is a complete list of every reference to musical instruments in the Bible, plus a table of instrumental ensembles and their names as found in different versions of the Bible—thirty-six versions in twenty languages. The large majority of references is to the Hebrew Bible (primarily Psalms), though there are also several apocryphal and New Testament references. All this supplementary material is an invaluable asset for the researcher studying instruments mentioned in the Bible.

Each page of this volume is densely packed with information. However, Kolyada occasionally deviates from the straight description of instruments to theories of their place and use. For example, in chapter 1 she discusses the phenomenon of a system of musical education in ancient Israel. She considers the *nayyot*, which she translates as "schools of prophets" (lit. "huts"), to be the first step. It is impossible to understand what word she is translating here, without Hebrew letters or a biblical citation. She states that those with either a prophetic gift or musical talent came here to be taught music with which they would accompany sacrifices (7; citing 1 Sam 9:12; 10:5; 1 Kgs 3:2; and others). She also states that these schools of music came to replace the schools of prophets. The Levites supposedly received thorough training in professional performance, especially in liturgy (7). Kolyada's rather modern concept of musical education in the ancient world seems to have no textual basis. The rest of the chapter explores music's social function in the biblical world.

Among the fascinating tidbits to be found in this chapter's endnotes are a discussion of why the lute was probably the only instrument popular in Egypt that never became popular among the Israelites (26 n. 17) and the legend of Job as a patron of musicians that originated in the apocryphal Testament of Job (26 n. 22).

Every chapter is densely packed with an amazing amount of fascinating information, though much of it is highly technical. The inclusion of modern Hebrew words that derive from biblical terminology is particularly interesting. One example in chapter 2 of a word derivation not commonly known is the instrument פסנטרין mentioned in the book of Daniel, where it is one of the string instruments (50). It has been translated numerous ways, since no one knows what it really was. But the word jumped out for this reviewer, since the modern Hebrew word for piano, פסנטר, is clearly derived from פסנטרין.

The history of shofar blasts in chapter 3 is very well outlined and includes numerous interesting musical examples. Kolyada even cites two British oratorios (of 1873 and 1903) that include the shofar (72). The author might have been interested to know of a much more recent inclusion. American composer George Crumb, in his 2001 collection of Appalachian songs, includes the shofar in the song "Joshua Fit the Battle of Jericho," a very appropriate use.

Kolyada frequently discusses other cultures' use of various instruments mentioned in the Bible. This is particularly interesting in her discussion in chapter 4 of פעמנים (tinkling bells) attached to clothes, a usage that goes back to very ancient times (Assyria, Egypt, and India). This practice is still found today in shamanic cultures, where as in the past the bells function to keep away evil spirits. The usage in the Bible could well reflect "a remnant of pagan magic" (119).

Chapters 5 and 6 are a discussion of the etymology of ambivalent, generic, and uncertain musical terms. Words are included that may not necessarily even be instruments. Kolyada even discusses words (נחילות and שלשים) that appear in the Bible only one time (137–38), an impressive degree of thoroughness. The discussion of the puzzling word סלה (162) is very complete and enlightening.

The final chapter delves into the discussion of biblical instruments found in the Talmud. Kolyada explains how the appearance of these instruments in talmudic literature "are both a witness to and a bearer of the developing musical practices of many centuries" (175). Instruments described in later literature, both medieval and Renaissance, are transformed in various ways due to these cultures' temporal and geographical distance from the Bible (183). These transformations are also due in large part to the discrepancies in translations over the centuries. Each culture replaced unfamiliar names with more familiar ones, so that contemporary readers would better relate to the musical descriptions (196). One of the most amusing examples is an eighteenth-century illuminated Bible in which the court ensemble accompanying King David's anointing ceremony is a band of Russian folk instruments (206 n. 67).

Kolyada has done an admirable job of bringing together a vast body of research in this field into one volume, where previously much of the information was not very accessible. This is particularly true of the many Russian sources she used that have probably never before been translated into English.

In spite of the thoroughness and preciseness manifested in this volume, there are inaccuracies throughout the book reflecting gaps in Kolyada's knowledge or understanding of Hebrew and Jewish culture. Though none of these errors is connected to music, they nonetheless could have been avoided with more editorial attention.

Kolyada occasionally uses terms without defining them. For example, she discusses "some Jewish haggadahs" (39), which could confuse the reader into thinking she is talking about a Passover haggadah. The more correct term would have been *midrash haggadah* or simply rabbinic legend from the Talmud. She is sometimes inconsistent with her identification of sources. Abraham Ibn Ezra is identified variously as a Jewish philosopher (34), rabbinic scholar (53), talmudic teacher (54, 133), talmudic exegete (161), and Jewish exegete (162). While it may be argued that he was all of the above, the inconsistency could be confusing for the reader unfamiliar with his name.

In her discussion of the horn or קרן, Kolyada attributes the images of Moses with horns in western European Renaissance art to be a reflection of the "power, might and supernatural strength of the horn" (67). This is a significant mistake. The images of Moses with horns are due to the mistranslation of the original Hebrew text. The word קָרַן in Exod 34:29 is a verb meaning "radiated," but Jerome in his Vulgate translation vocalized it as קֶרֶן, which led to its incorrect translation as "horns." Far from reflecting strength, these horns on Moses were later used in anti-Semitic diatribes and caricatures that demonized Jews.

Strange usage of a word is found in the sentence discussing a talmudic passage about the need to hire at least two חליל (flute) players: "The performers, when necessary, could even be goyim" (92). Kolyada has clearly translated the passage straight from the Talmud without understanding that the word *goyim*, though meaning Gentiles in both ancient and modern Hebrew, has an entirely different sense today. It is widely used as a Yiddish word and has a disparaging and slangy tone. It would have been more appropriate to say "Gentiles" or "non-Jews."

Her etymology of the Hebrew שופר as deriving from the two words שוא (hollow, empty) and פר (*par*, bull) (68) is very unconvincing. Her assertion that the seven blasts of "seven shofars [*sic*]" described in Josh 6:3-6 "may well be considered a historical fact" (70) is completely unfounded. She even repeats this claim later in the chapter, saying that the possibility of this event having occurred "has been confirmed in modern times by a scholarly experiment" (80), but in her endnote, no such experiment is described. Instead, she offers several examples from ancient cultures that ascribe supernatural qualities to musical instruments (102 n. 31).

The most serious errors are in the area of liturgy. The statement "Modern shofars, for instance, in American Jewish communities since the 1940s, also have removable metal mouthpieces which make blowing them a lot easier" (70) is inaccurate and misleading. Use of this mouthpiece is by no means a common practice; it would have been acceptable to say that modern shofars *may* have removable mouthpieces. Kolyada gives no citations for this unfounded statement. She also writes that on the second day of Rosh Hashannah, when the story of the Akedah is read from the Torah, it is read "to the accompaniment of shofar blasts" (76). Dramatic as that would be, no Torah reading is ever accompanied. The blowing of the shofar occurs at a different point in the service.

Another error related to liturgical practice is in the glossary at the beginning of the book, where Kolyada describes the holiday of Shavuot as the holiday commemorating God's giving the Torah to Israel, which in ancient times "also" signified the bringing of the first fruits to the temple. This definition is backwards: as is the case for many Jewish holidays, the origins lay in agriculture, with the religious overlay added much later by the rabbis.

A more serious error is in chapter 6, where Kolyada connects the ancient Hebrew root מן (mn) to modern Hebrew words meaning melody, such as מנגן (menaggen; 162). The root of this word is נגנ (ngn), and the מ at the head of the word is part of its conjugation. Though this is the only significant Hebrew error in the book, it should have been caught.

As to the format of the book, though it is a matter of personal preference, for me the use of endnotes instead of footnotes is a serious distraction. Most of the numerous endnotes are lengthy and complex, and the continual flipping back and forth makes it difficult to retain any sense of continuity. Another technical quibble is with the illustrations. Presumably for cost-cutting motives, all illustrations (over sixty) are line drawings done by the author's husband, Anatoly Morozov. The only original illustration is the one that adorns the cover of the book, and it highlights how much is lost in the reduction to simple black-and-white drawings. These drawings are accurate representations of the wide variety of ancient instruments discussed and are valuable contributions for this reason. Nonetheless, the book would have been richer with even a few color plates or at least photographs of the original sources.

In spite of these flaws, this book is highly recommended for biblical scholars or musicologists interested in exploring a little-known area of music history and the role of music in the Bible. This excellently researched book will be a welcome addition to many libraries.

Men and Masculinity in the Hebrew Bible and Beyond, edited by Ovidiu Creangă. Bible in the Modern World 33. Sheffield: Sheffield Phoenix, 2010. Pp. xiv + 273. Hardcover. $95.00. ISBN 9781907534096.

Stuart Macwilliam, University of Exeter, Exeter, United Kingdom

It is handy for a reviewer of this impressive volume of essays that it already contains two reviews of its own contents. The first, by David Clines, is even more valuable than his own contribution to the main text; in it he reflects on—and not without criticism—his fellow essayists and ends by detailing omissions and suggestions for further research. Stephen D. Moore's virtuosic review contextualizes the volume with regard to masculinity studies both in general and to biblical studies in particular, carefully articulating the rather complicated relationship between masculinity studies and its far more established feminist (?) sibling.

Moore is right to characterize the underlying theoretical stance of the volume as a "'structuralist' endeavor" (245), an exercise in creating a "grammar" of biblical masculinity, a detailing of "rules, codes and conventions that enable and determine the production, the construction, the performance of biblical masculinity" (245). But equally correctly he notes a parallel tendency of the contributors to utilize a poststructuralist approach, with an emphasis on destabilizing normative concepts of masculinity.

Susan Haddox's paper on Genesis is a good example of this dualism. Her anthropological model of four criteria of masculinity is one that is used with variations by other contributors and owes much to Clines's earlier work on the masculinity of David,[1] the four being avoidance of women/feminization; virility (including violence); honor (including maintaining one's family); and wisdom/persuasiveness. She also uses the concept of hegemonic masculinity, according to which a dominant ideal emerges from competing versions. She competently applies this concept to Abraham, his sons, and his grandsons and concludes that none of them matches up to hegemonic masculinity and that Yhwh surprisingly favors those whose masculinity is subordinate.

This clear hint that masculinity in the Hebrew Bible is not as straightforward as one may suppose is taken up with gusto by Roland Boer in a paper on Chronicles that bears some similarities to his contribution to the *Queer Bible Commentary*.[2] Boer sees in Chronicles a male utopia, complete with phallic temple,[3] but it is a shaky utopia undermined by such oddities as men giving birth (the verb *yld* being the culprit) and a predisposition to campness (evidenced by, among other things, an exaggerated interest in interior design).

With the contributions by Brian DiPalma, David Clines, and Mark George, we are back safely, if unadventurously, with anthropology. Taking three of the four criteria of masculinity as outlined by Haddox, DiPalma compares the portrayal of Pharaoh with that of Moses. Pharaoh's failure in all three presents no challenge to biblical assumptions about masculinity and indeed reinscribes it. On the other hand, the tension between Moses' central importance as a biblical character and his ambiguous relationship to the three criteria leaves their meaning and value compromised.

The most interesting feature of Clines's chapter on the Sinai account is his discussion of beauty as a criterion of masculinity, but, although he makes some fascinating remarks about the shining of Moses' face as a sign of beauty, more could be said about masculine beauty: how, for instance it signals status and power or how it contrasts (or not) with the depiction of female beauty.

---

1. David J. A. Clines, "David the Man: the Construction of Masculinity in the Hebrew Bible," in his *Interested Parties: The Ideology of Writers and Readers of the Hebrew Bible* (JSOTSup 205; Sheffield: Sheffield Academic Press, 2005): 212–43.

2. Roland Boer, "1 and 2 Chronicles," in *The Queer Bible Commentary* (ed. Deryn Guest et al.; London: SCM, 2006), 251–67.

3. I rather agree with Clines (235) that to equate the excessive height of the temple with the phallic is perhaps to strain credulity.

Deuteronomy's formidable array of regulations is read by Mark George as a detailed definition of masculinity: the ideal (male) Israelite is defined by what he must or, more particularly, most not do. In other words, masculinity is taboo-driven, though how far this takes us in an understanding of how Israelite masculinity worked is unclear.

The central essays in the volume are the most stimulating. Ovidiu Creangă presents a subtle discussion of Joshua mapped against the contrasts of both the literary sources and the development of Joshua's career. He compares Joshua as warrior with Joshua as a student of Moses' law. Both roles exhibit qualities that by this stage in the volume we may recognize as criteria of ideal masculinity: as warrior he displays virility; as student of the law, wisdom/persuasiveness. But both roles are compromised: the warrior by a dubious portrayal of his sexuality (invisible wife and children) and the student of the law by his subordinate role to Moses and his questionable relationship with him. Creangă joins Cheryl Strimple in offering perhaps the most interesting essay in the volume. In their account of Naaman's leprosy (2 Kgs 5) they read disability as a metaphorical device that underscores the precariousness of masculinity. For the first time in this volume we are presented with a vivid picture of masculinity as a *process*, with ups and downs, winners and losers. The significance of Maria Haralambakis's essay on the Testament of Job is that she shows how masculinity studies both derive from and react to previous feminist scholarship. The presence of women in the text has led some scholars to see it as presenting a "positive portrayal of women" (128). Haralambakis argues that through all his misfortunes Job maintains a dominant position as a man. Indeed, the relatively slender contribution to the narrative made by his two wives allows Haralambakis to maintain that Jeremiah is fulfilling one of Clines's criteria of masculinity by being a womanless male. A similar pessimism about the inescapable embeddedness of masculinity in the Hebrew Bible is evidenced by Sandra Jacobs. In her essay on the rainbow imagery of the Noachic covenant she employs non-Israelite ancient Near Eastern sources to show that the bow is a symbol of virility, and she sees the association between the covenant and circumcision as another reference to male virility. To top it all, Jacobs links the mention of "every male" (*zkr*) in the Abrahamic covenant (Gen 17:10) to the mention of remembrance (the verb *zkr*) in the Noachic covenant (9:16) and concludes that in subsequent rabbinic texts the "most valued recollections remain only those that are inherently male" (163).

Of the four criteria of masculinity, Ela Lazarewicz-Wyrzykowska focuses on just one, that of honor, and in line with anthropological studies in the Middle East and the Mediterranean, in which honor is associated with the maintenance of sexual virility, she cogently reads the Samson narratives (Judg 13–16) as a fluctuating and violent struggle to maintain honor. For her, masculinity is "constantly endangered" (184) and "undermines the popular perception of biblical masculinity as a uniform, secure and stable feature of biblical men" (185).

C. J. Patrick Davis takes the traditional perception of Jeremiah as a lamenting prophet and gives it a good shake. He traces its development from Second

Temple literature onwards, then turning back to the text of Jeremiah itself makes some convincing suggestions: that Jeremiah's call to communal lament is made to men in such aggressive terms as to feminize his audience; further, that Jeremiah's depiction of ritual lamentation on the part of women in 9:17–19 is in keeping with his customary masculine contempt for women. The explicit mention of women is a means of depicting the shaming and death of the (male) covenant community. Although I have argued elsewhere that Jeremiah's use of female imagery is not entirely negative and that his own masculinity is questionable,[1] I am impressed by Davis's powerful reading.

A first reading of Andrew Todd's report on how discussion of Dan 7 in a number of Bible study groups played out along gender lines comes as a curious conclusion to a set of close readings of the biblical texts. But perhaps it does give us pause to reflect on the extent to which all readers of (biblical) texts are prone to fall into our allotted roles as gendered readers (and reviewers!).

Shadow on the Steps: Time Measurement in Ancient Israel, by David Miano. Society of Biblical Literature Resources for Biblical Study 64. Atlanta: Society of Biblical Literature, 2010. Pp. xx + 267. Paper. $34.95. ISBN 9781589834781.

Spencer L. Allen, John Brown University, Siloam Springs, Arkansas

In this work, a revised version of his dissertation, David Miano contends, contrary to a wave of recent scholarship, that the time-measuring systems employed by scribes of the First Temple period can be meaningfully reconstructed from biblical texts. In order to make this case, Miano first defines the various units of time on the basis of philological and source analysis and then applies these definitions to the numerous genealogical lists, king lists, and chronicles contained in the Primary History (PH; Genesis–2 Kings). In addition to demonstrating that the primary sources used by the Priestly and Deuteronomic History (DH) editors were each written in regular, recoverable formulaic patterns, Miano also proposes new solutions to problems posed by chronological irregularities and variant textual witnesses that have long troubled biblical scholars. Moreover, because he aims to uncover these primary sources rather than establish a new, wholly reliable, biblical chronology, Miano concedes that the chronological data from the different sources often cannot be reconciled; instead, he attempts to evaluate the historical reliability of each source with the hope that other scholars will use these individual sources to reconstruct the history of Judah and Israel in the first half of the first millennium. On the whole, Miano's treatment of the various units of time, proposed primary sources, textual emendations, chronological corrections, and treatment of 2 Kgs 18–19 are well-argued and generally convincing.

---

1. Stuart Macwilliam, "Queering Jeremiah," in idem, *Queer Theory and the Prophetic Marriage Metaphor in the Hebrew Bible* (BibleWorld; London: Equinox, 2011), 84–96.

The book takes its name from the episode about "the steps of Ahaz" mentioned in 2 Kgs 20:8–11 (= Isa 38:7–8, 22). Miano suggests that these steps belonged to a solar clock that Ahaz had installed on the roof of the palace (14–15). In that episode, an ailing Hezekiah asks Isaiah for a sign that Yahweh will heal him, and Isaiah delivers the sign: the clock's shadow will fall down the ten steps when the sun goes backwards in the sky. Just as Yahweh would extend the day by transforming that evening into midday, so would he extend Hezekiah's life. Basing his conception of Ahaz's clock on both the Cairo shadow clock and earlier proposals by Yigael Yadin and William Propp, his dissertation advisor, Miano suggests that the clock was designed with two sets of ten steps to designate twenty distinct units of daylight, each approximately 36 minutes in length (18). Because a 36-minute time unit would represent a chronometric anomaly in the ancient world, Miano also entertains alternative clock designs that would posit twenty-four distinct daily time units, which would correspond to the 12 hours of daylight in the Egyptian and Babylonian time-keeping systems.

The introduction provides a list of the major preexilic chronometric sources that he examines throughout the book. Miano divides this list into two categories, early classical prophets and the PH. The prophets surveyed include Amos, Hosea, Micah, Isaiah, Zephaniah, and Jeremiah, but the PH receives substantially more attention because it contains much more chronological data than do the prophets. The PH also receives more attention in the introduction due to the lack of scholarly consensus on either the divisions of the material into its various sources or the relative dates of those sources, particularly the Pentateuch. Miano provides virtually no discussion of the long-standing debates surrounding the pre/postexilic nature of the Priestly material, and he completely ignores the newer arguments suggesting the Yahwist source is a postexilic work. Instead, he follows the source divisions and dates laid out by R. E. Friedman, a member of his dissertation committee, and several other prominent North American and Israeli scholars. Thus, the Yahwist material includes the Pentateuchal J material and the so-called Court History of David, and the Priestly material includes both the P material and the material produced by the Holiness School. The first edition of the DH is dated to Josiah's reign, and the Elohist source and several narratives found in Samuel and Kings are collectively referred to as "northern materials" and are dated to the period of the divided monarchy. Finally, Miano carefully differentiates the chronological additions of postexilic editors and redactors from their preexilic sources, such as the Priestly redactor R and the school responsible for the second edition of the DH. This differentiation allows him to provide more accurate chronometric definitions used by each source and more consistently apply those definitions to their chronological frameworks throughout the remainder of the book.

Chapters 1 and 2 make up the book's first of two main sections and deal with units of time. Chapter 1, "Calendars," revolves around the cyclical and natural units of astronomical time. "Day" (*yôm*) is the first unit discussed and defined. As one might expect, when used as a quantitative measure, a "day" is a 24-hour period, but Miano is less interested in how long each day lasted than in when each day was thought to begin. Because each source *could* have its own understanding of when a day begins, he examines the treatment of "day" in each source and argues that J, E, DH, and P all generally conceive of the civil day as beginning at sunrise. Miano rejects verses often used as evidence for the day beginning at sunset in preexilic Israel. Regarding the DH, the Passover begins at sunset in Deut 16:6 not because the day begins then but because the exodus and original Passover meal themselves took place at night (11). Regarding P, the creation account in Gen 1 presents a sequence of daily events that occur during one 24-hour period, as indicated by the consecutive *waw* in the refrain. Each day consisted of a creative act, an evening, and a morning that signals the transition from one day to the next. Finally, the Sabbath and other holy days are explicitly said to run "from evening to evening" (e.g., Lev 23:32; Exod 12:18–19) precisely because P's liturgical/cultic day differed from the civil day. Miano's analysis of "months" also benefits from source analysis. Both P and DH use month numbers to identify the twelve months of the year, but P only identifies the months by their numbers in order to indicate the correct dates for rituals and holy days on the liturgical calendar. When historical dates with numbered months appear in P material, such as the crossing of the Jordan in Josh 4:19, these dates are considered the work of R (22–23). The chapter finishes with a discussion of the various year-reckoning systems at work in ancient Israel.

In contrast to the natural units in chapter 1, chapter 2, "Long-Time Reckoning," focuses on the ancient Israelite interpretation of linear time as it relates to the building of a historical narrative. The first of the three topics discussed in the chapter is the counting system of time units in ancient Israel, especially the difference between the biblical use of ordinal and cardinal numbers. Whereas the biblical use of ordinal numbers resembles our modern use, none of the biblical sources use cardinal numbers the same way we do. "According to their point of view, exactly one week from now would be eight days, while for us it would be only seven days" (51). The biblical authors included the current day, whereas we exclude it. Recognizing this difference is essential for properly understanding the genealogies and other chronologies that Miano examines in subsequent chapters. The second topic treated is the biblical concept of *era*, which Miano observes was not nearly as important to the biblical authors as they are to biblical scholars. The famous 480 years, which he argues is 479 in our modern counting system, that elapsed between the exodus and Solomon's building projects is only mentioned in 2 Kgs 6:1 (56), though the groundwork for 480 is set by the DH in the book of Judges (104–5). The third time unit considered is the generation (*dôr*), which generally represents 40 years in the DH (59). Miano rejects suggestions that "generation" can also mean "life span" or a unit as large as 100 years, which are interpretations that have been offered to reconcile the 400 years in Gen 15:13 with the four generations mentioned in verse 16. He maintains that the four generations should represent 160 years and acknowledges that the tension between these two verses was not intended by the author (61). Finally, he notes that generations are counted differently in the biblical sources than are other time units; children are counted the first generation and grandchildren are counted as the second generation (62). Thus, the fourth generation that is mentioned in Gen 15:16 refers to the great-great-grandchildren of those first oppressed in Egypt. Taken together, chapters 1 and 2 provide an excellent foundation for the chronological reexaminations undertaken in chapters 3 and 4.

Chapter 3, "Genealogical Chronologies," begins the second and lengthier of the book's two main sections as it explores P's genealogies in Gen 5 and 11. According to Miano, the two chronologies in Gen 5 and 11 are Priestly products that resulted from the combination of two unrelated, written primary sources that listed the generations from Adam to Jacob (see table 3.3 on 95–96). One source listed the father's age when his son was born (e.g., "Seth lived 105 years and begot Enosh," Gen 5:6 [MT]), and the other listed the number of years each man lived (e.g., "And all the days of Seth were 912, and he died," 5:8). Because these lists were unrelated, their data provided divergent information when combined into one narrative. The Priestly author(s) responsible for combing the two primary sources into the genealogies made some adjustments in order to harmonize the data and calculated the intervals between the birth of each man's son and his death (e.g., "Seth lived after he begot Enosh 807 years," 5:7). However, an assortment of discrepancies remained, and later scribes developed their own tactics to correct the data, which explains the numerous variants that appear in the three main textual witnesses: the Masoretic Text (MT), the Samaritan Pentateuch (SP), and the Greek Septuagint (LXX). Following the work of Ralph Klein, Ronald Hendel, and others, Miano uncovers the ideological issues driving each variant, recognizes the systematic methods used by each witness, and proposes a reliable reconstruction for the archetypal text (see table 3.1 on 70–71). Furthermore, by reconstructing P's original chronological data and recognizing the nature of P's structure, style, and interests, Miano can distinguish the original P material from later R additions and R's more precise interest in calendrical dates. For instance, in P's work, the flood came and went while Noah was 600 years old, whereas the flood lasted an entire year in R's revision (85). Numerous other numerical and chronological oddities or perceived irregularities are satisfactorily explained as a result of Miano's treatments of the genealogies in Gen 5 and 11.

Chapter 4, "Rulership Chronologies," deals with the recording of history in light of king/judge lists and royal chronicles. Miano proposes that the chronology for the six minor judges was obtained from one annal-like source that lacked narrative interests (102), and he reconstructs its contents in appendix A (217–18). In contrast, he suggests that the periods of oppression by Israel's enemies (e.g., the 18-year Moabite oppression in Judg 3:14), the regularity of the 40-year periods of peace, and other chronological additions (e.g., 9:22) are the DH editors' own innovations. The remainder of the chapter focuses on the chronologies in the book of Kings: uncovering the different primary sources available to the DH editors and examining the accuracy of these sources against known extrabiblical chronological data. Miano claims that previous examinations of the chronology in Kings failed because they did not distinguish between data provided by the Josianic editor of the DH and the exilic reviser (106). Rather than treat the material as a homogeneous mix, he separates it into its primary sources and attributes the use of these sources to either the Josianic editor or the exilic reviser. For example, the Josianic editor had Judahite king lists available to him that included each king's age at his accession to the throne, the length of his reign, his capital (Jerusalem), and biographical information about the queen mother (reconstructed in appendix A on 218–20). The synchronism that accompanies each Judahite accession from Abijam to Hezekiah, however, was likely taken from Israelite annals and added by the exilic reviser. Miano's argument for the gradual integration of additional primary sources in different editions of the DH is convincing both because each reconstructed primary source is internally consistent with its use of formulary and because his proposed, variant primary sources often contain chronological data that cannot be mutually reconciled.

Miano's study also simplifies the use of variant textual witnesses to reconstruct the history of ancient Judah and Israel. To be sure, he examines the chronological data from the Old Greek (OG) tradition and compares it with the MT, upon which he based his initial study of the various primary sources, but as with the genealogies in Gen 5 and 11, Miano recognizes the methods that both the OG and MT scribes employed to correct the conflicting data found within the exilic reviser's edition. Numerous tables compare OG and MT chronological and synchronic data to provide a quick glimpse into his reconstructed archetypal text for the DH.

With the primary sources separated and the archetypal DH texts reconstructed, Miano can finally evaluate the historical reliability of each primary source and each DH edition. He does so by comparing each primary source's synchronisms with foreign kings against the generally accepted dates, beginning with the destruction of Jerusalem in 586 and working backwards. Again, numerous tables and charts are provided to help the reader process the data before accessing the historical reliability of each primary source. In short, the chronicles (i.e., "the scrolls of the affairs of the days for the kings of Judah/Israel") that were added by the exilic reviser align better with our presumed chronology of the ancient Near East than do the king lists that were added elsewhere by the same reviser. According to Miano's reconstruction of the Judahite king list, Rehoboam accessed the throne in Judah in 973, whereas the accession took place in 934 in the Judahite chronicle. The latter is deemed more historically reliable because the synchronism in 1 Kgs 14:25 places Shishak of Egypt's campaign against Judah in Rehoboam's fifth regnal year, which corresponds well with the generally accepted dates for this king's reign in reconstructed Egyptian chronologies (ca. 945–925).

Chapter 5, "Conclusions and Implications," provides a thorough summary of the conclusions reached in chapters 1–4 and offers a reasonable explanation for the obvious interest in history displayed by the exilic reviser of the DH and for his inclusion of chronological data not available to the Josianic editor. Like the Josianic editor, the reviser imagined Israel's history as beginning with the exodus, but as someone living in exile, the reviser feared that his fellow expatriates were doomed to forget their national history unless that history were fixed in time.

Miano suggests that a history without any firm dates connecting it to the present is less likely to connect with its audience and is vulnerable to becoming mythology. In contrast, the histories of P and R include fixed dates that occurred before the exodus (see P's timeline on 214–15). The exilic reviser feared this transformation from history to mythology, so he supplemented the original DH, which included few dates, with new primary sources. Fortunately for us, this new material provides more reliable chronological data for the monarchic period, which Miano hopes will serve as a jumping point for future research.

Two appendices complete the book. Appendix A includes Miano's reconstructed primary sources concerning the six minor judges and Judahite king list (see above). In appendix B, a revision of an article published in 2007, Miano presents a compelling argument in which the so-called B1 narrative (2 Kgs 18:13a and 18:17–19:8; A = 18:13b–16 and B2 = 19:9–37; p. 241) of the Assyrian invasion into Judah is shown to have originally told the story of Sargon's campaign to Judah in 712 rather than Sennacherib's in 701, as is commonly accepted.

By recovering the primary sources that the editors of the DH and PH used to collect their chronological data and then accessing their historical reliability on a case-by-case basis, Miano has demonstrated that the conflicting data and dates in the Bible's historical narratives cannot and should not be reconciled. As a result, the father-son co-regencies in Jerusalem that Edwin Thiele and others have proposed to tidy up the synchronisms between the Israelite and Judahite kingdoms can finally be abandoned in our pursuit of a reconstructed Israelite history. Miano's approach also minimizes the primacy of textual emendations—which bogged down M. Christine Tetley's 2005 book—in establishing our primeval and preexilic timelines. Variant textual witnesses often disagree in Genesis and Kings, and Miano offers several reconstructed archetypal texts; however, the focus of the proposed emendations is not establishing an Ur-text and re-creating the perfect timeline. Rather, he offers the emendations to explain the methodologies employed by various scribes (P, R, both the DH editor and reviser, and later copyists) to make sense of the already contradictory material they inherited.

The charts, tables, and timelines located throughout the book are extremely helpful, and they will surely play a large role in establishing this book as a handy reference work for those interested in exploring Israelite history. Indeed, the charts and tables often relay Miano's arguments faster and more smoothly than does his prose. However, there are a few tables whose alignment and spacing could be improved to facilitate comprehension even further (e.g., table 4.5 on 134; cf. the better use of alignment in table 4.7 on 136). There also appears to be a mathematical error on page 149, in which a certain discrepancy is said to have been "seventeen years" rather than "twenty-seven years." Finally, I anticipate that scholars who disagree with the "standard Documentary Theory" that Miano uses "as a point of departure" (3) will find many of Miano's assumptions problematic and reflexively challenge his findings in chapters 1 and 2. However, many of Miano's findings (e.g., that the day started at sunrise in ancient Israel) should hold up regardless of when and how each pentateuchal source was written. Still, whatever minor grievances or concerns his work may stir, Miano successfully demonstrates that there never was an ideal set of chronological data available to any biblical author or editor, and he appropriately advises scholars to pursue other aspects of preexilic Israelite history and scribal techniques, rather than "invent an elaborate and complicated theory to make the numbers conform to one another" (106). Miano's book will surely be a useful tool in these future pursuits.

Gottes Körper: Zur alttestamentlichen Vorstellung der Menschengestaltigkeit Gottes, by Andreas Wagner. Gütersloh: Gütersloher Verlagshaus, 2010. Pp. 208. Paper. £19.95. ISBN 9783579080956.

Mark W. Hamilton, Abilene Christian University, Abilene, Texas

In this eminently readable and engaging work, Professor Wagner offers to a wide audience an informed overview of Israelite reflections on divine embodiment within the context of the history of ancient Near Eastern religions. In a nontechnical yet learned way, he examines texts and art portraying deities and humans in order to understand the literary portrayals of Yhwh in the Hebrew Bible. The fifty-five figures (mostly photographs) in the book allow readers to gain a clear sense of how Wagner contextualizes literary presentations within the history of ancient Near Eastern (mostly Egyptian and, to a lesser extent, Mesopotamian) art.

Wagner opens with three methodological chapters that develop his case in a way reminiscent of a detective story, in which the reader learns bit by bit where the tale is going. Chapter 1 thus offers a brief discussion of method, acknowledging the complexity of ideas such as anthropomorphism and noting that the study of a body in texts and graphic art is a matter of the study of parts of the body (13–20). The commonsensical approach to method is pursued throughout the book, which carefully catalogues the biblical references to various body parts (see 135–58) and their signification. Wagner deepens it in chapter 2 (21–39) by considering the Pentateuch's prohibition of divine images, which, as he notes, both forecloses certain religious expressions and opens the door to others, and in particular to the textualization of reflections on divine embodiment. He then moves, innovatively, in my view, to try to link textual and visual material (especially from Kuntillet 'Ajrud, though his later discussion also considers several seals, all of which reflect Assyrian or Egyptian influence, however). The significance of this move does not become fully clear until later in the book, where Wagner connects the picture of the Israelite persons on the Kuntillet 'Ajrud pithos to biblical texts, on one side, and to Egyptian conventions of multiperspectival portraiture, on the other. Chapter 3 (40–51) returns to the nature of anthropomorphism, noting the theological complexity of the idea and the ways in which scholars have changed from denigration to appreciation of the phenomenon.

The book's second movement, chapters 4 (53–100) and 5 (101–66), lays out the evidence for Israel's understanding of human (especially male) and divine bodies. Wagner points out that Egyptian and, to some extent, Mesopotamian art self-consciously used multiple perspectives in depiction as a way of attempting to represent three-dimensional objects in two-dimensional space (not having developed methods for portraying perspective). He then traces literary imagery comparing bodies to physical objects ("your neck is a tower" or "your eyes are doves"), drawing heavily on Song of Songs. He further catalogues the body parts mentioned for human beings and delineates the ways in which the extant texts refer to them. This methodical approach makes it clear that the Bible mostly talks about a few parts and considers them in terms of how, and how well, they function and how they figure in communication (though the boundaries between these two categories seem more porous than Wagner allows for).

Having set forth Israel's basic understandings of the human body in chapter 4, Wagner turns in chapter 5 to the body of God. Here again the body parts named in the text are chiefly occupied either in activity in the human sphere (e.g., hands that save) or in bilateral communication (a mouth that speaks, ears that either do or do not hear). As the author puts it,

> Eine erste "systematische/theologische" Aussage, die mit den Anthropomorphismus im AT über den Weg des anschaulichen Darstellens der Körperhaftigkeit Gottes erzielt wird, kann man daher folgendermaßen zuspitzen: Gott ist gegenüber dem Menschen ein Macht ausübender und ein (in der Welt) handelnder Gott, ein Gott, der kommunikationsfähig ist wie ein Mensch, der daher als "Kommunikationspartner" des Menschen erscheint. Beide Charakteristika zeigen: der alttestamentliche Gott ist kein ferner, weltabgewandter Gott, sondern ein mit dem Menschen kommunizierender und in der Welt handelnder Gott. (156)

The book concludes with a brief look at the human body as a copy of the divine (ch. 6 [166–81]), which one hopes lays the groundwork for subsequent study, and then with a summary chapter (ch. 7 [183–88]) and a useful bibliography.

To reiterate, this work offers the reader an accurate and easily readable guide to an important, if neglected, topic. Much of the evidence presented is well-known to specialists, and on a number of points, especially relating to the glyptic material, much more can be said. One may also object to some of Wagner's claims, as, for example, when he argues "[i]m AT ist Gott durchweg menschengestaltig, er nimmt keine Tiergestaltigkeit an und schon gar keine Mischgestaltigkeit" (162). Such a claim flies in the face of a number of metaphors for the Israelite deity, who has wings, roars like a lion, and so on. It would thus need more defense than the cursory treatment it receives here. The same is true of the blanket statement that ancient Near Eastern art does not differentiate among individuals (80); though generally true, exceptions to the rule exist (e.g., note the different crowns on Assyrian rulers or the famous bust of Nefertiti).

The primary questions facing the scholarly study of divine embodiment, however, relate to method. Wagner's commonsensical approach, which has the already-lauded merit of clarity and empirical verifiability, can blind us to the larger semiotic patterns of bodily signification. Put crassly, bodies are more than their parts. Body parts signify within networks of signs and sign-users. Wagner acknowledges this point early in his treatment of anthroporphism but does not return to it throughout his analysis. In other words, his study furnishes the raw material for future research, not the end point.

Consider an example. Psalms of lament often enjoin God to hear and see as the psalmist speaks. Body parts of both conversation partners are involved, and their proper use in communication (thus their rhetorical function) becomes a key issue. Improper use of the body by either partner results in continued tragedy. Yet deeply interrelated with the body images are other semiotic planes such as kingship and subalternity. The patterns of bodily display are strongly conditioned by other understandings of social relationships. One hopes for further research along such lines.

In sum, then, Wagner's book should stimulate much discussion in the future. It deserves an English translation to make it available to a wider audience, and one may hope for much more work along these lines, all of which will owe the book at hand a debt.

PENTATEUCH

Methods for Exodus, edited by Thomas B. Dozeman. Methods in Biblical Interpretation. Cambridge: Cambridge University Press, 2010. Pp. xiv + 254. Paper. $24.99. ISBN 9780521710015.

Danny Mathews, Pepperdine University, Malibu, California

A daunting obstacle confronts students who seek to become acquainted with the field of biblical studies—a diverse discipline that is immense, bewildering, and fluid, with no consensus on method. The current publishing market appears to be saturated with an abundance of resources that purport to provide an orientation to the task of biblical interpretation and an overview of the variety of methods in biblical studies (recent publications range from the massive *Methods Matter: Essays on the Interpretation of the Hebrew Bible* [ed. Joel M. LeMon and Kent Harold Richards, Society of Biblical Literature, 2009] to the slim *A Pathway of Interpretation: The Old Testament for Pastors and Students*, by Walter Brueggemann [Cascade, 2008], not to mention the older, standard resources provided by Fee, Stuart, Hayes/Holladay, and Gorman that continue to be updated and revised).

Yet the new series Methods in Biblical Interpretation somehow manages to find and fill a niche in a saturated market through its inclusion of only a limited selection of both newer and traditional methods and a demonstration of the application of these methods to the same segments of texts from a single book of the Bible (selected books so far include Exodus, Psalms, Matthew, and Luke). By refusing to *cover* every method, the result is *uncovering* a few methods that, along with a supplementary bibliography for each chapter and a concluding glossary, serve as a basic point of orientation to help the student hit the ground running in becoming well-versed in basic methods used by biblical scholars. These observations, along with the availability of the series in an e-book format, allows for the use of this book in a variety of individual and classroom settings.

Exodus is an apt selection from the Old Testament, given the variety of genres represented in the book, which continues to be the subject of a vast and varied interpretive literature. The six essays in this book are authored by specialists and are roughly arranged with traditional, text-based methods (chs. 1–3) followed by newer ideological approaches (chs. 4–6; with the exception of ch. 1; see below). Each chapter strives to follow a modular format that gives attention to the definition and history of the method and an application of the method broadly to the entire book of Exodus and specifically to a close study of Exod 1–2 and 19–20. This format, along with a fair assessment of the strengths and shortcomings of each method, places the student into a good position to acquire a broad, critical familiarity with some of the major approaches used in the study of Exodus. A major oversight in this book, however, is the lack of a concluding annotated bibliography arranged by method despite the claim of its existence in the introduction to the book (xiii). However, each chapter generally has a good bibliography of standard resources, with two chapters including a separate section on resources related to the study of Exodus.

Since the beginning student will typically begin interpretive work by focusing on the received text, the essay on literary and rhetorical criticism by Dennis T. Olson is a particularly appropriate introduction to the book. Olson provides an excellent overview of the variety of approaches associated with study of the final form of the text organized in three categories: constructive, deconstructive, and dialogical/rhetorical. These are three heuristically useful categories that embrace a variety of approaches, such as rhetorical and narrative criticism, structuralism, deconstruction, poststructuralism, and the dialogic approach of Mikhail Bakhtin. Olson's preference is clearly with the rhetorical approach through his adapted presentation of Phylis Trible's nine steps of a rhetorical study of a text and a detailed demonstration of these steps in action in a close study of the nature and interrelationship of the three scenes of Exod 2:1–22. This aspect of Olson's essay promises to provide a useful way for students to begin working with the biblical text. Given the emphasis on persuasion in rhetorical criticism, it is suggested that step nine receive a minor modification by asking students to articulate the persuasion or claim made by the text. For example, an observation of the absence of any mention of God in Exod 2:1–22 juxtaposed with a rapid-fire mention of God five times in Exod 2:23–25 might result in a claim that God is indeed concerned about injustice and is already at work behind the scenes (through the birth and identification of Israel's future savior) despite the appearance of God's absence. Of course, this observation raises questions about limiting the boundary of the text to verse 22. Olson's essay alone is worth the price of this book. It provides a quality, integrative approach that balances well both theory and practice and is clearly the result of years of experience in the classroom.

Unfortunately, the remaining essays fail to meet the high standard set by Olson, focusing too much on theory and appearing to be written to scholars instead of students. Kenton L. Sparks's essay on genre criticism presents a fascinating tour of the generic diversity of Exodus on the macro-level (describing Exodus as a "charter myth") and the various mixture of genre throughout the book (such as international treaties, legal codes, and temple construction narratives for Exod 25–40). Yet this chapter could have been more student-friendly by a considerable condensation of a three-page discussion of source/redaction criticism and a streamlined simplification of the highly abstract and theoretical presentation that occupies the first ten pages. It would be more helpful to include a clearer and sharper differentiation between genre and form criticism. A more effective pedagogical strategy might involve beginning the chapter with a concrete example of genre criticism, perhaps by moving the fine discussion of Exod 1–2 to the beginning that will form the basis for the theoretical and abstract discussion of genre criticism. It must also be mentioned that an overview of genre studies on Exodus should highlight the watershed work of Hugo Gressmann and take serious account of the contributions of George Coats.

After presenting a clear and concise definition and the interrelatedness of source and redaction criticism, Suzanne Boorer identifies briefly the basic criteria of both methods, provides a ten-page review of the history of these methods, and demonstrates these methods in action in Exod 1–2 (focusing more on source criticism) and 19–20 (focusing more on redaction criticism). The application of the methods is done in context of newer approaches in pentateuchal scholarship, with the assumption of P and non-P layers along with a greater role given to a Deuteronomistic redaction. Unfortunately, the essay is mostly inaccessible to the novice and presupposes a good grasp of the Documentary Hypothesis through the detailed discussion of the various documents (J, E, E1, E2, D, P, RJEP, etc) without providing clear definitions and discrete examples of each source. It would have been more effective, perhaps, to begin with a close study of the two versions of the call of Moses in Exod 3 and 6, especially since these texts have played a crucial role in the history of source and redaction criticism. Before reading this essay, the beginning student would find it helpful to study the color-coded text and interpretive commentary provided by Richard Elliot Friedman in *The Bible with Sources Revealed* (HarperSanFrancisco, 2003).

The final three chapters, on ideological approaches ("Liberation Criticism," by Jorge Pixley; "Feminist Criticism," by Naomi Steinberg; "Postcolonial Biblical Criticism," by Gale A. Yee), all provide an illuminating treatment that highlights the thickness and multivalent character of Exod 1–2 and 19–20 as well as the urgent and relevant contemporary issues at stake in reading and interpreting biblical texts. Of these essays, I found Steinberg to be the most helpful through a clear and nuanced overview of the contours of feminist criticism and particularly through a close attention to the rich variety of feminist approaches to Exod 1–2. The final essay by Yee provides an extended postcolonial reading of Exod 1–2 with the argument that the received text is an amalgam of voices of both oppression and liberation. Since the Bible "can be used to inspire liberation, but also legitimate oppression," the interpretive task should be done with great care. However, Yee's essay departs from the book's format through an omission of an extended study of Exod 19–20, focusing instead on the conquest narratives in Joshua. Also, despite her correct observation that Exodus is "a compilation of a long traditioning process," she limits the object of her investigation to the Persian period and assumes that Egypt serves as a cipher for Persia. It might also be appropriate to inquire about the anticolonial nature of the text in other stages of development, such as the portrayal of Moses in Exod 2 as an anti-Sargon figure in the Neo-Assyrian period. In spite of these minor quibbles, the interaction with feminist and liberation approaches makes Yee's essay a fine conclusion that will aid the student in thinking about the interrelationships of these newer ideological approaches.

Given the potential of this series of books to provide a versatile and accessible resource on methods in biblical interpretation, it is hoped that this book will be revised into a more student-friendly format. To achieve this goal, it is suggested that the essays take seriously student feedback in the revision process. One suggestion from this reviewer is to consider highlighting the glossary terms in bold whenever they occur throughout the book.

These Are the Generations: Identity, Covenant, and the 'toledot' Formula, by Matthew A. Thomas. Library of Hebrew Bible/Old Testament Studies 551. New York: T&T Clark, 2011. Pp. xvii + 148. Hardcover. $110.00.ISBN 9780567151414.

Mark McEntire, Belmont University, Nashville, Tennessee

Discussion of the *toledoth* formula has long been common in works on the book of Genesis or the entire Pentateuch. Note, for example, the important role it plays in Joseph Blenkinsopp's influential introduction to the Pentateuch (*The Pentateuch: An Introduction to the First Five Books of the Bible* [New York: Doubleday, 1992], 58–59, 99–100). This revised dissertation (Claremont) by Matthew A. Thomas is the first book-length study of the phenomenon. Not only does it give more attention to the appearances of this formula, but it also uses the resulting observations as a means of interpreting Genesis and the Pentateuch on a "macrostructure" level.

The introduction of this work identifies "two primary questions." The first of these concerns "the nature and purpose of the *toledoth* formula in the final form of the book of Genesis." The second question deals with one particular type of answer to the first, the "narrowing" function of the *toledoth*, which moves from Adam (Gen 5:1), representing all of humanity, to Jacob (37:2), representing all of Israel, to Aaron and Moses (Num 3), representing the religious leadership of Israel (2–3).

Chapter 1 defines the *toledoth* formula, especially to distinguish it from the similar שמות formula. The remainder of the introduction addresses methodology. Thomas's study relies primarily on methods related to linguistics, beginning with a study of the "surface structure of the final form of the book of Genesis and the Pentateuch," examining the "syntax, semantics, and function" of the *toledoth* formula (18). The key phrase, אלה תלדות, appears ten times in the book of Genesis. It has been customary in studies of Genesis to include the similar phrase at 5:1, זה ספר תלדות, and combine the double occurrence of אלה תלדות in reference to Esau (36:1 and 36:9) to produce a ten-*toledoth* structure for the book of Genesis. This scheme also has the advantage of placing five of those headings within the "primeval" material (1:1–11:26) and five within the "ancestral" material (11:27–50:26). Thomas completes chapter 1 by listing and briefly discussing all of these occurrences, along with the one in Num 3:1 (the *toledoth* of Moses and Aaron), and the subsequent sections into which they divide the text.

Between chapters 1 and 2, Thomas includes a significant excursus on the fascinating question, "Why is there no *toledoth* heading for Abraham?" This excursus includes a discussion of six proposals offered by a variety of scholars, including Thomas's own. What is missing from the discussion is a clear statement of where such a heading would appear in the current book of Genesis and thus from where it might be missing. Thomas argues that a *toledoth* of Abraham would have destroyed the "literary suspense" of Genesis, that "the tension in the text regarding the provision of an heir for Abraham and Sarah would have been undermined from the beginning" (50–51). This would be true if such a *toledoth* was placed in Gen 12, but it seems to me that the more likely placement is in Gen 25, where such suspense has already been resolved by the narrative.

One of the most valuable features of this study is the way it often moves in a very different direction from prior studies and proposes new possibilities. In chapter 2 Thomas focuses on variation in the *toledoth* formula and distinguishes, on carefully established syntactical grounds, between the occurrences of אלה תלדות that begin with ו (coordinate) and those that do not (independent). He classifies all occurrences of the phrase as "verbless clauses" in Hebrew and builds on the work of Francis Anderson on this general feature to establish the *toledoth* formula as a "heading," then argues that the five occurrences without ו begin new sections of Genesis. These five are at 2:4, 5:1, 6:9, 11:10, and 37:2. The remaining six *toledoth* formulae in Genesis, those with ו, begin subheadings under these main headings. This creates a very uneven kind of structure in terms of length, but so does the more common "ten *toledoth*" organization described above. The five primary sections vary in length from little more than one chapter (5:1–6:8) to about twenty-six chapters (11:10–37:1). Thomas's most significant conclusion is that the independent formulae occur at points in the text where the story is being "narrowed," while the coordinate formulae occur at places where there is not narrowing. This explains well, for example, the double appearance of Shem in the *toledoth* of Genesis. He appears with his brothers, Ham and Japheth, in a coordinate formula in 10:1 and by himself in an independent formula at 11:10. The former begins a "segmented" genealogy, the latter a "linear" one, a difference treated extensively in the next chapter.

The primary subject of chapter 3 is the genealogies to which the *toledoth* formulae point. In Genesis, Thomas identifies two types of genealogies, linear and segmented, each of which has a particular function in the book. The linear genealogies, such as 5:1–31, move the story along rapidly, while segmented genealogies "function to record and preserve those family lines that will not be of major interest to the ongoing story" (104). There is nothing particularly new here, but the extension of this idea to the *toledoth* of Moses and Aaron in 3:1 offers a provocative thesis. Drawing on the repeated use of the term *toledoth* in the census of Num 1:17–46 (eleven times) and parallels between Num 1–4 and Gen 11:10–32, Thomas argues that the first few chapters of Numbers function both to shift the focus of the Pentateuch onto the "civil and cultic leadership of Israel, as shown in Moses, Aaron, and their successors," and preserve the presence of Israel in the census lists (102–3). Thomas does not connect this analogy, which could be understood to indicate a rejection of the Israelite people, with YHWH's stated desire to kill the Israelites (e.g., Num 14:12) and start building a new people with Moses.

In chapter 4 Thomas uses his observations about *toledoth* formulae and the narrowing of the story to identify three key points in the Pentateuch, which are revealed by *toledoth* elements identified as inconsistent at the end of chapter 3. Among these inconsistencies are the destruction of the world and almost all of its people in the flood in order to narrow the story rather than simply choosing one brother, the inclusion of a genealogy for a rejected brother like Ishmael, when not all such brothers (e.g., Nahor) are given such attention, and the inclusion of all Israel as a "rejected" element when the story narrows its focus to the civil and cultic leadership. The three turning points are the promise after the flood, the promise to Abraham, and Sinai. The patterns observed in *toledoth* formulae and the breaks in the pattern have led Thomas to focus on covenants as the basis for the narrowing of the story.

Readers are likely to have different responses to the realization that the most innovative line of argumentation in this study has led back to such an old and familiar conclusion. The idea that covenants are the most important feature of Genesis has occurred to readers who paid little or no attention to the genealogies. The greatest value of this work lies not in this conclusion but in the compilation and analysis of data that leads up to it. Of the various functions of genealogies, including increasing the pace of the story, narrowing the focus of the story, and preserving the presence of unselected family lines in the text, the last may be the most intriguing. Why do we get the *toledoth* of Ham, Japheth, Ishmael, and Esau? The focus of this book specifically on the *toledoth* formulae, unfortunately, serves to omit the genealogy of Cain in Gen 4:17–22 from the discussion. This family, filled with the most creative and innovative humans in the Bible, is effectively drowned in the flood. Thomas describes the genealogies of the rejected brothers as "life preservers," and the writer of Genesis has thrown one to this family, but why? Does covenant answer this question?

This is a well-produced, well-researched volume, in the great tradition of the JSOTSup series. It gives careful attention to a feature of Genesis and the Pentateuch that has received more use than rigorous analysis in the past. Thomas's work deserves the attention of everyone working on the book of Genesis.

The Captivity of Innocence: Babel and the Yahwist, by André LaCocque. Eugene, Ore.: Cascade, 2010. Pp. xvi + 190. Cloth. $23.00. ISBN 9781608993536.

Richard S. Briggs, Cranmer Hall, St. John's College, Durham University, Durham, United Kingdom

The text of Gen 11:1–9 is short enough to be laid out elegantly in chiastic form as a one-page chapter on page 127 of LaCocque's study. But what an extraordinary text it is, and what a tower of commentary and critique it has brought forth—reaching even to the very heavens. As the pivotal moment at which the book of Genesis swings from mythic history toward the specificity of the call of Abram, naming Babylon as it does so, it attracts massive interest from critics with historical concerns. It is a gem of a literary artwork, concise but beautifully sprung in its way with language, thus always available for close literary readings. But then it is also a story of human yearning on a cosmic scale and of being put in place in a world-defining divine response, to which the anthropologists will flock in their numbers. Then it is also a moment of phallic symbolism irresistible to the psychoanalytic concerns of others, all the while being a narrative of *construction* and *deconstruction* to which postmodernists of all stripes are invited. There can be few biblical scholars who could not find something resonant to say about Babel, from whichever angle they approach it across the plains of modern academic discourse.

What André LaCocque has done is basically gather together all these rubrics and take them one at a time in—one cannot resist the pun—a *tour de force* of sustained attention to this most fecund of texts. The book arrives as the third and final panel in his "triptych" of studies of the work of the Yahwist in Gen 1–11, following on from accounts of Eden and of Cain and Abel. If ever evidence were needed that there are more searching ways of writing about stretches of biblical narrative than in the mode of straightforward commentary, LaCocque has certainly provided it. On this occasion especially he is able to show with ease that these early Genesis texts are patient of multiple layers of reading and rereading. Taken together, the trilogy that this book completes will stand as a major biblical-theological landmark in treatments of the Yahwist as a voice to be heard today.

The book begins with a lengthy prologue that effectively rehearses standard biblical studies criteria for reading Babel. There is much on J and P as they are interwoven through the primeval history. LaCocque suggests, rightly in my judgment, that the tale that we have is probably not capable of being peeled apart into earlier layers but is rather the singular work of one who is watching the ways of God and God's people among the Babylonian ziggurats of the exile. Several reading lenses are paraded before the reader. The opening analysis grabs the reader with this well-observed comment: "At the level of imagination, no translation is necessary. The readership of the tale is immediately universal and timeless" (1). If there is a slight oddity about this prologue, it is that most of it makes better sense after one has wrestled with the text itself, which is delayed to the next chapter. Perhaps there was no obvious place to gather this kind of review of scholarship.

Part 1 of the book then pursues a range of approaches loosely gathered under the rubric of "construction." A forty-four-page chapter pursues a twice-over reading of the text in detail: once with a view to lexical and grammatical detail, then again with what LaCocque calls "close reading." This is a fine exercise of sustained attention to detail and will reward any student of the passage, being perhaps closest to the traditional mode of commentary that increasingly fades from view as the book progresses.

There follows a study of the work of J as myth. LaCocque is careful to explore what sorts of questions might be thrown into relief by this slippery term. Particularly helpful are his reflections on time as the enemy of myth: time is the obstacle to the work of the Babelians, he suggests, who are themselves trying to construct a timeless barrier to the experience of human existence. Evil, too, is opened up by the mythic account. It is parsed here as the fundamental human desire to be like God, "the human pretension to be autonomous" (84).

The next chapter offers a psychoanalytic approach. This reader must confess that here the range of concerns seemed to outstrip the textual resources available for reflecting on them. True, LaCocque offers his perspective as "only one ring of the textual 'onion,'" (104), and he is content to suggest that none of what he says here need have been in the conscious mind of the Yahwist, but he does think it may (or must?) have been *subconsciously* present. For example, to pick the example that seemed most illuminating, it is striking to the psychoanalytically minded reader that in this narrative of speech amidst reaching for the sky, the Babelians are conspicuously quiet as they go about their work: "Words are not center stage—the Babelians are oddly silent while building; technique is central" (97). The Yahwist was perhaps not making this point as such, but there it is for us to see as we ponder this myth among myths. Elsewhere it is a little more debatable whether the conclusion of the Babel story is really "an amazing precursor of modern astronomy" (101), and as for the reflections on "The Tower as Phallus" (118–20), these may be of interest to those for whom sentences such as "the tower of Babel is thrust up toward the sky and challenges God as impregnator" are more profound than simply bizarre.

Looming over the horizon, as we pass into the single chapter that makes up part 2, is Jacques Derrida, for whom Gen 11:1–9 was that rare thing, a biblical text that paraded the rupture of language between heaven and earth right on the surface of the text. And so we have "Deconstruction," inevitably. Bakhtinian chronotopes jostle for space with Freud's destructively present and absent mother of the child. We are in the territory of statements such as, "The divine violence in Gen 11:8–9 shatters the implicit violence of monoglossic ideology" (137–38), wherein the serious point seems to me to be lost beneath the uneasy co-opting of a heavily theorized vocabulary for talking about what language can (and does) do to people. Derrida, on the other hand, was a serious thinker who never seemed to be able to get over how much fun he could have dismantling social constructs. It is mildly exhausting trying to peel away the layers of the interpretive onion by this point, and LaCocque does not on the whole seem to be having as much fun as Derrida, so that the fizz is gone when we arrive at, "The Babel tower *is* a tower and *is not* what towers generally are; in that sense, it *is not* a tower, as the height of this one is in heaven" (153–54). So that's "is and is not," check. Without denying that there is much food for thought in this part 2, I could not escape the conclusion that the average reader who would benefit from it would be better off simply searching out Derrida's original piece on the text ("Des Tours de Babel," which the reader of LaCocque would not know was once in *Semeia* 54 [1991]: 3–34).

Genesis 11:1–9 is an endlessly fascinating text, and André LaCocque has written a probing and thoughtful book on it, which in part because it does cover so many angles of approach will not keep most readers happy all the way through. Nevertheless, his trilogy of studies of the Yahwist in Gen 1–11 succeeds admirably in showing how the ancient text still speaks, in myriad voices, today. One misses, in this case, some reflection of the interpretive trajectory followed by Christian readings of the Babel story. Ibn Ezra gets a page, along with the rabbis, and a fascinating page it is, hinting at the possibility that there is blessing in amongst the narrative's judgment, which I have elsewhere argued may be an angle worthy of much more exploration. But there's the rub. A review that suggests that a monograph that possibly goes on too long in relation to its very short generating text, then wishes that more might have been said, is—like the book under review—living in the shadow of Babel. André LaCocque's study is to be welcomed for shining several refractions of light through that shadow, which is not quite the same as describing how light might overcome the darkness.

Festive Meals in Ancient Israel: Deuteronomy's Identity Politics in Their Ancient Near Eastern Context, by Peter Altmann. Beihefte zur Zeitschrift für die alttestamentliche Wissenschaft 424. Berlin: de Gruyter, 2011. Pp. xii + 299. Hardcover. $150.00. ISBN 9783110255362.

Stephen A. Reed, Jamestown College, Jamestown, North Dakota

This monograph is a revised version of the author's 2010 dissertation. The first two chapters provide an overview of the history of scholarship of the book of Deuteronomy, the treatment of Deuteronomic cultic meals, and methods for the study of food. Each of the three major chapters is devoted to a particular meal text in Deuteronomy (12:13–27; 16:1–17; 14:22–29). The book also includes a short introduction and conclusion, a bibliography, and an index of biblical texts, extrabiblical texts, and iconography. Throughout the work there are lengthy footnotes with many technical details and interaction with different scholars.

In the introduction Altmann expresses his basic thesis: "Food in centralized festive celebrations, as well as in localized meals, is a literary *topos* for the construction and maintenance of the common Israelite story and shared identity in Deuteronomy" (2). In order to explain how Deuteronomic meals serve this rhetorical purpose, Altmann draws on parallels with "iconographic and literary portrayals of banquets" in the ancient Near East. He also uses insights from other studies of food, including the sociology of food, ritual studies, and the biology of eating.

In the first chapter, "Overview of the History of Scholarship of Deuteronomy," most attention is given to the controversies of the composition of the book and to its relationship to other legal codes in the Bible. Altmann agrees with those who propose a preexilic Deuteronomic code for some materials in Deuteronomy. He thinks that the ideas of covenant and loyalty oaths, feasting language, and iconography of meal scenes from Neo-Assyrian times provide the best background for early forms of three meal texts of Deuteronomy.

In the second chapter, "Treatment of the Deuteronomic Cultic Meals," Altmann discusses the exegetical work of Nathan MacDonald, Georg Braulik, and Walter Houston on the cultic meals of Deuteronomy and summarizes sociological and anthropological perspectives of Jack Goody, David Sutton, and Massimo Montanari and studies related to the biology of smell and taste as well as ritual theory. He summarizes key points from researchers that are useful for the study of meal texts of Deuteronomy. He concludes the chapter by explaining the approaches he will use for each of the three major chapters of his book.

In chapter 3, "Material Culture and the Symbolic Meaning of Meat in Deuteronomy 12," Altmann begins with a brief treatment of meat as a symbol in the biblical corpus. This is followed by two lengthy sections on "Iconography and Records of Meat and Banquets in the Ancient Near East" and "Diet and Archaeology." After this there is a section on the composition of Deut 12 and a conclusion of the significance of meat from a socio-political background. Altmann argues that meat was highly valued and was probably rare during Assyrian control. Meat eaten at festivals was to be distributed equitably to all and shared in community, which helped unify the people. The festival meal honored Yahweh as the giver of food, not the king of the ruling Assyrians. Some meat was shared in a common place, while other meat was eaten in the homes of families.

The treatment of meat in the Hebrew Bible seems rather brief here (less than five pages) and, surprisingly, makes no mention of issues of clean and unclean food (Deut 14:3–21) or issues of the eating of blood. Altmann seems to agree with the view that the issue of blood in Deut 12 is a secondary addition responding to concerns of Lev 17 and is not a central issue for the Deuteronomic program (116). Not all scholars agree that dietary issues and the prohibition of eating of blood are simply later additions to the Deuteronomic law code. Nathan McDonald, for instance, entitles his chapter on food in Deuteronomy as "Chewing the Cud: Food and Memory in Deuteronomy" (*Not Bread Alone: The Uses of Food in the Old Testament* [Oxford: Oxford University Press, 2010], 88 n. 51).

In chapter 4, "The Cultic Meals of the Deuteronomic Cultic Calendar (16:1–17) in Light of Comparative Ancient Near Eastern Texts," most of the attention is given to ritual and narrative texts from Emar, Assyria, and Ugarit to illustrate the divine banquet motif, which often included such details as "beginning with preparation of the meal (first meat and then wine), followed by the invitation, and finally the consumption (again first meat and then wine)" (170). Altmann gives some attention to innerbiblical antecedent texts related to festivals from Exod 12:1–13:16; 23.

While ritual and narrative texts from the ancient Near East are useful for explaining the meaning of meal texts in Deuteronomy, treatments of these texts seem too extensive in this chapter. About fifty pages are devoted to these texts, and only twelve pages are devoted to innerbiblical parallels. Altmann does not address Priestly texts such as Num 28–29 and Lev 23 because he thinks that their understanding of meals is quite different than in Deuteronomy (see 186 n. 217). Thus he thinks the texts from the ancient Near East explain the meal texts of Deuteronomy better than other biblical texts.

Earlier Altmann said that "it is not of necessary importance to trace the origins of the festivals in order to determine their meaning in Deuteronomy" (167 n. 144). He contrasts his approach to that of Rolf Rendtorff, who explains the "festivals in terms of their origin and long-term development" (167 n. 144). Certainly meanings of festivals can change over time, but one might argue that inner biblical parallels are more valid than ancient Near Eastern parallels.

Chapter 5, "Deuteronomy 14:22–29 in Light of Ancient Near Eastern Tribute and Modern Anthropology," is the shortest chapter (thirty pages as compared to chapter 3's sixty-one pages and chapter 4's seventy-eight pages). Altmann begins with a history of scholarship of the text that includes comparison with other Pentateuchal texts, then contains a relatively short treatment of ancient near Eastern and Israelite background and concludes with a section of a reading of Deut 14:22–29.

While tribute and tithes usually benefit either the temple or palace, in the Deuteronomic code they are brought to Yhwh and are consumed by all members of the community. In Altmann's words, "Instead of sending their produce to the central—and only—temple for Assur in this period in Assyria, the DC suggests communal consumption of the tithe at Yhwh's temple" (225).

Chapter 5 ends with a synthesis of exegesis and social-scientific and biological evidence that applies to all three of the meal texts treated in the book. Altmann concludes: "Deuteronomy creates a system that entices and encourages people to throw their allegiance to the Israelite group imagined in the DC, especially because their taxes and gifts are returned to them" (p. 238). "Yhwh plays liberal host to tasty banquets through his regular blessings for those who are willing to come in order to consume food and drink at his banquets and to become part of the Deuteronomic 'Israelite community'" (239), and "They [The food items consumed during the banquets] are given as gifts from the deity when the people take on Yhwh's yoke in place of the Assyrian or other possible 'foreign' options" (239).

Chapter 6 concludes the book. The three cultic meal texts (Deut 12:13–19; 14:22–29; 16:1–17) are understood as formulated "for a preexilic audience familiar with the experience of the political and ideological domination by the

Neo-Assyrian Empire in Judah" (241). Altmann concludes that "these texts highlight Yhwh's beneficence and strength through his willingness and ability to provide the community of Israelites who accept his claim to covenantal kingship with rich concrete blessings in the form of plentiful feasts, especially at the central sanctuary, but also in their local villages" (241).

There is much to be commended in Altmann's book. First, he addresses in a serious way the important topic of meals in biblical texts. Second, Altmann shows how texts and iconographic materials from the ancient Near East are helpful for understanding these meal texts. Third, he has shown how methods of the study of food in sociology, anthropology, and ritual theory can illuminate biblical texts. Fourth, Altmann makes a persuasive case for the origins of these meal texts in the Neo-Assyrian times of the eighth century. One of his stated goals is found on page 65, where he says, "In conclusion, in order to address the meaning of Deuteronomic rhetoric, I plan to heuristically reconstruct the rhetorical potential of the cultic ritual meals in late Iron Age I." He has accomplished this goal.

Altmann has provided helpful interpretations of these three Deuteronomic texts. He explains important conceptual background for understanding them. Much of his exegesis, however, relates to the compositional history of these texts and the isolation of earlier levels and later redactional changes. Since he was interested primarily in the stage of the text that arose in Neo-Assyrian times, later stages are only briefly mentioned and not explained in much depth. While it is justifiable to interpret the meaning of earlier levels of texts, one must realize that all such work is conjectural and open to question, since all we have is the final level of the text. One also wonders if earlier stages of a text can be adequately understood without giving greater attention to the growth and final shape of the text. One problem with the method of compositional history of texts is that there is a tendency by interpreters to see a text as a collection of pieces that are added sequentially. A text is a whole entity with a shape and meaning of its own that is more than an addition of its parts.

Altmann does not clarify precisely why he treats some texts in Deuteronomy and not others, but presumably it is because of his dating of texts. He does indicate that there are four meal texts in Deuteronomy (12:13–27; 14:22–29; 16:1–17; 26:1–15), but he only addresses the first three, since he thinks that 26:1–15 was a later development of the cultic meal in the Deuteronomic Code (3 n. 8). He later mentions chapters 26 and 27, which are cultic meals, but he says they are later than the three he addresses (227). It is at least arguable that Deut 15:19–23, which deals with firstlings, and 18:1–8, which deals with offerings of food for priests, could be considered as meal texts as well. One might wonder if one should disregard these texts entirely in explaining the other three meal texts of Deuteronomy.

Altmann is critical of synchronic approaches that address the whole book of Deuteronomy because they do not pay enough attention to the history of the growth of the text, but he did not present a treatment of the whole book either. Altmann's diachronic approach may help contribute to this larger concern—an understanding of food and meals in the whole book of Deuteronomy. Altmann himself says that he would like to address Deut 26:1-15 in the future (3 n. 8). There should be further work on food and meals in the final shape of the book of Deuteronomy. Besides the other meal texts previously mentioned, there are other texts related to food that should be addressed, such as Deut 8, which deals with issues of feeding in the wilderness and food in the land, and the treatment of clean and unclean food in Deut 14:1-21.

There is much useful information in Altmann's book that could be helpful in interpreting other language of food and meals in the Bible. There are sections of illustrative material such as "Diet and Archaeozoology" and "Iconography and Records of Meat and Banquets in the Ancient Near East" that will be helpful for explaining and understanding other biblical food texts. Altmann himself has been engaged in encouraging other scholars to join him in further scholarly work on meals in the Old Testament and presenting papers of their research at the SBL and ASOR meetings. In Altmann's monograph on the festive meals in ancient Israel, he provides many examples of various methods and materials that can be used to better understand meals in ancient Israel.

"When Gods Were Men": The Embodied God in Biblical and Near Eastern Literature," by Esther J. Hamori. Beihefte zur Zeitschrift für die alttestamentliche Wissenschaft 384. Berlin: de Gruyter, 2008. Pp. xvi + 185. Cloth. $97.00. ISBN 9783110203486.

Michael B. Hundley, Ludwig-Maximilians-Universität Munich, Munich, Germany

Hamori's work is part of a welcome trend in scholarship that addresses divine corporeality in the Hebrew Bible (see also, e.g., Benjamin Sommer, *The Bodies of God and the World of Ancient Israel* [Cambridge: Cambridge University Press, 2009]; Andreas Wagner, *Gottes Körper: Zur alttestamentlichen Vorstellung der Menschengestaltigkeit Gottes* [Gütersloh: Gütersloher Verlaghaus, 2010]). In particular, her study examines Gen 18:1-15 and 32:23-33, which portray God in the form of a "man" in the context of terrestrial divine-human interaction, and their relation to their closest biblical and ancient Near Eastern analogues.

In the first chapter, Hamori introduces the concept of "human theophany" (1) with these two passages from Genesis that refer to God as a "man" (*'iš* or *'anāšîm*), who "appears in the literal, physical body of a man" (3). She then offers a sketch of Gen 18:1-15 and 32:23-33 in which she argues for the compositional integrity of both passages and that the *'iš* language should be taken as literally as theophany language elsewhere. In her analysis of Gen 18, she notes that YHWH appears with such "anthropomorphic realism" that Abraham perceives the divine nature of his visitor through verbal rather than visual clues. In Gen 32, the divine nature of Jacob's combatant (here El instead of YHWH), is likewise revealed through the dialogue. In fact, she argues, God is so tied to realistic human form that he cannot win the fight. In the course of her analysis, she convincingly refutes the notion that Jacob wrestled with the numen of the River Jabbok, as argued in particular by Gunkel (13–18).

Chapter 2 begins by noting the imprecision with which scholars in general and biblical scholars in particular discuss anthropomorphism. She then proceeds to offer her own helpful taxonomy of the physical anthropomorphisms of the divine in the Hebrew Bible. Her first category, "concrete anthropomorphism," to which Gen 18 and 32 belong, refers to concrete, physical divine embodiment. "Envisioned anthropomorphism" refers to the "sight of the deity in a dream or vision" and includes such texts as Gen 28:13 and Amos 9:1 (29). Texts in the "immanent anthropomorphism" category (e.g., Exod 33:9 and 34:5–6) describe God in anthropomorphic terms and suggest divine immanence, yet do not explicitly depict God as physically embodied. To the "transcendent anthropomorphism" category (to be distinguished from Hendel's use of the same descriptor in a different way ["Aniconism and Anthropomorphism in Ancient Israel," in *The Image and the Book* (ed. van der Toorn; Leuven: Peeters, 1997), 207–8]) belong texts that describe the deity in anthropomorphic terms without being concretely embodied, explicitly envisioned, or immanent (e.g., Gen 1, 2; Ps 82:1). The final category, "figurative anthropomorphism," refers to texts that figuratively describe divine body parts, such as YHWH's strong hand or eye (e.g., Isa 41:10; 42:6). As is to be expected, "many texts reflect a mixed approach to divine anthropomorphism" (33).

Chapter 3 examines philosophical approaches to anthropomorphism. In it Hamori surveys the development of the negative evaluation of divine anthropomorphism that led to classical theism's contention that God does not and cannot have a body. In light of this prevalent perspective, scholars often understand divine anthropomorphisms to be either metaphorical or primitive. However, despite these reservations, all theism remains anthropomorphic to some degree. Thus, rather than speaking of anthropomorphism as an either/or phenomenon, Hamori suggests that scholars should identify it as a spectrum. To this end, she posits alternative approaches to anthropomorphism that take seriously the possibility that Israelite texts portray God in concretely anthropomorphic terms with some theological sophistication. First, she speaks of theophany as analogical language, which must be both affirmed and denied, such that God is "literally embodied, but without fully identifying himself as a human being" (54). In other words, theophany, like all analogical language, is multivocal, not univocal. Second, building on Wittgenstein, Hamori discusses theophany as a language-game in which the meaning of a word is determined by its use. For example, "God in embodied form does not have the same fixed meaning as a human in human form" (58). Thus, (concrete) anthropomorphisms do not limit the deity; rather they express divine freedom, which is "not limited even in regard to embodiment" (64).

Chapter 4 returns to the primary texts of inquiry, Gen 18:1–15 and 32:23–33. Hamori contends that Gen 18:1–15 and 19 form a single, early unit and that some elements of 18:17–33 were originally present to connect the two chapters. She then compares this unified text to Canaanite material in which scholars have assumed it finds its origin, arguing instead that, "as theophany, it is simply different from anything known from the region, with no reason to treat it either as evolved from any previous Canaan-like phenomenon or as evolved toward some proto-Jewish perspective" (82). In particular, she notes that, although the closest Ugaritic parallel, the Tale of Aqhat, displays many similarities (e.g., an unexpected anthropomorphic visit of a deity to a man followed by a meal), the differences are more striking. Most notably, Hamori stresses that, while YHWH and the two angels appear indistinguishable from humans, Kothar-wa-Hasis is so large that he can be seen from one thousand fields away. As a result, she contends that Gen 18:1–15 "reflects an early Israelite depiction of Yahweh in a manner that is not attested in Ugaritic literature" (95). Hamori likewise argues for an early date of Gen 32:23–33, especially since it is the source text for Hos 12:4–5. In the conflict it describes, Jacob fights with El instead of Esau as expected, who confirms to Jacob the patriarchal promise. Hamori contends that the "intense anthropomorphic intimacy" in both Genesis passages serves to establish the "unusually close bond" between God and Abraham and Jacob (102).

Chapter 5 explores the 'îš theophany in the context of biblical portrayals of the larger divine society, especially angels. Against the common identification of angels as anthropomorphic, Hamori argues instead that, "in the majority of mal'āk texts, the angels are depicted in specific non-human forms, or not on earth (in dreams or calling from heaven), or on earth in an unspecified form" (114). In the closest parallels to the 'îš theophanies, the angels either reveal their superhuman status by performing miraculous feats (Gen 19; Judg 13) or identify themselves as divine from the outset and refrain from graphically human behavior such as eating or fighting (Josh 5). Regarding the divine society in general, Hamori asserts that, while in heaven, its members are largely undifferentiated, overlapping in form and function, yet while on earth they have clearly distinguished roles, and their form is overtly related to their function. She concludes that the form of the 'îš theophanies, like these other manifestations of divine beings, is related to their function. Genesis 18 depicts YHWH's final confirmation of the blessing and promise to the first patriarch, while Gen 32 describes God's confirmation that the blessing and inheritance originally due Esau now belong to Jacob. Both texts stress the intimacy of the encounter and specialness of the divine-human relationship.

Chapter 6 offers a useful survey of anthropomorphic realism in the ancient Near East (Mesopotamia, Ugarit, Egypt, and Hittite Anatolia), with a special focus on Mesopotamia. She contends that, although similar in many respects, the ancient Near Eastern evidence never portrays "gods interacting with humans in anthropomorphically realistic form, indistinguishable from humans, for the purpose of divine-human communication" (149). Thus, Hamori argues that the 'îš theophanies are unique both in the Hebrew Bible and in the ancient Near East. Finally, in chapter 7, she offers her conclusions.

Hamori is to be lauded for a fine work that offers numerous valuable insights. Indeed, although her focus on two texts is rather specific, she brings in a wealth of helpful and impressive supporting material and theory. To name a few, her contention that anthropomorphism is unavoidable and that depictions of the divine should thus be regarded as falling along an anthropomorphic spectrum, her more precise taxonomy of physical anthropomorphism, her discussion of philosophy, her identification of theophany as a type of analogical language, and her survey of ancient Near Eastern evidence and biblical evidence for other beings in the divine world and their comparison with her 'iš theophanies all are worthy of careful consideration and significantly bolster her argument and the value of her contribution.

However, while often a strength, her breadth of analysis is also at times a weakness, leaving insufficient space to provide an in-depth analysis of her primary texts. Similarly, she occasionally seems more interested in establishing the uniqueness of her texts than in describing the texts themselves. As such, her analysis ironically at times does not do enough to establish the uniqueness of her primary texts and at other times leaves elements of these texts unexplained. For example, she only mentions in passing the role of hospitality without offering any supporting evidence (9). In other words, she does not establish that Abraham's treatment of his guests was standard practice in its ancient Near Eastern context. As such, she does not refute the alternative possibility that Abraham knew his guests were special from the outset but was not yet sure of their identity, thereby suggesting that, although they appeared as men, something about their appearance suggested that they were somehow more. In addition, although Hamori indicates that God loses the fight with Jacob (e.g., 102), she does not explore the implications. If God is no stronger than Jacob, why should Jacob trust him to carry out his promises? More broadly, why would the authors depict God in such a way? Hamori's analysis of angels also at times focuses too much on differentiating them from God in the 'iš theophanies, such that she unnecessarily minimizes the anthropomorphic depiction of angels. For example, her most prominent evidence for a nonanthropomorphic portrayal of the angel in Exod 3 is inconclusive. The text merely states that an angel appeared to Moses in the fire without saying anything more about the angel's form (cf. Ezekiel's depiction of God in 1:26–8). There must have been something about its appearance to indicate that it was an angel, especially when it is God who does the speaking from the bush (3:4). Indeed, although in the majority of texts angelic forms remain unspecified, when specified, they are predominantly anthropomorphic. Likewise, YHWH and his attendants in chapter 18 are unnecessarily distanced from his envoys in chapter 19, especially if, as she asserts, the texts are meant to be read as a unity. In both texts the divine beings appear initially as men, yet their speech (18) and actions (19) reveal them to be something more. The fact that YHWH reveals his otherness through speech instead of deed then should not be used to sharply divide the two theophanies. In addition, although very helpful, Hamori's ancient Near Eastern survey is at times unnecessarily bent on establishing the uniqueness of the 'iš theophanies. For example, Isis's encounter with the ferryman is dismissed rather cursorily, leading Hamori to conclude with regard to Egypt that "the gods do not take human form for the purpose of divine-human communication" (147). However, what other purpose could it serve in this instance when Isis takes human form for the express purpose of convincing him that she is an old woman and thus worthy of ferrying across the river? Finally, in positing a unified text in Gen 18 and 32, she does not take into account more recent German scholarship on its composition (Seebass's commentary is her most recent entry). Nonetheless, despite these shortcomings, which are inevitable in such an ambitious undertaking, Hamori's study is highly recommended and essential reading for anyone interested in divine anthropomorphism and theophany.

Methods for Exodus, edited by Thomas B. Dozeman. Methods in Biblical Interpretation. Cambridge: Cambridge University Press, 2010. Pp. xiv + 254. Paper. $24.99. ISBN 9780521710015.

Brian D. Russell, Asbury Theological Seminary, Orlando, Florida

Methods for Exodus, edited by Thomas B. Dozeman, is the fourth volume in the series Methods in Biblical Interpretation. Earlier volumes include *Methods for Luke*, edited by Joel B. Green; *Methods for Matthew*, edited by Mark Allan Powell, and *Methods for the Psalms*, edited by Esther Marie Menn. The Methods in Biblical Interpretation series from Cambridge University Press seeks to introduce students and general readers of the Bible to six distinct hermeneutical approaches to the Hebrew Scriptures and the New Testament. Methods included range from traditional historical-critical "world behind the text" approaches to new "world in front of the text" methodologies influenced by the globalization and democratization of biblical studies. Each volume includes an introductory essay followed by six essays penned by a leading practitioner of a discrete interpretive method. Each essay introduces the student to a specific hermeneutical method by reviewing its history of development. The scholars then discuss each discrete method's applicability to the given biblical book. Finally, the writers apply the methods to the same set of texts. By assigning each writer the same texts, Methods in Biblical Interpretation allows the reader to see the similarities and differences between the various approaches to the text. Moreover, the authors themselves attempt to point out connections between their approach and the exegetical lenses of others.

Dozeman's *Methods for Exodus* offers a strong addition to the series. Dozeman is a leading scholar on the book of Exodus and has gathered an impressive band of exegetes to contribute to the volume. Dennis T. Olson writes the chapter on "Literary and Rhetorical Criticism." Kenton L. Sparks covers "Genre Criticism." Suzanne Boorer discusses "Source and Redaction Criticism." Jorge Pixley describes "Liberation Criticism." Naomi Steinberg illustrates "Feminist Criticism." Gale A. Yee proffers an introduction to "Postcolonial Biblical Criticism."

Dozeman's introductory essay (1–12) sketches out the aims of the book. First, *Methods for Exodus* seeks to introduce the above six methodologies that help readers to understand the book of Exodus. Second, *Methods for Exodus* hopes to show the ways that these discrete approaches relate to one another in terms of similarities and differences. Toward this second end, Dozeman notes that the divide between the approaches turns on how one understands the authority of the book of Exodus. Traditional historical-critical approaches locate authority in the "world behind the text" of its authors and reconstructed social setting. More recent ideological methodologies locate authority in the "world in front of the text" rooted in the social location of its modern readers. Dozeman argues that these approaches find common ground in that both "behind the text" and "in front of the text" methods reflect critically on the historical setting of the literature. Moreover, certain flavors of historical-critical methods such as genre criticism recognize the role of the modern reader in creating meaning. Dozeman then moves to describe the content of the book of Exodus in broad brushstrokes. He divides the book of Exodus into two sections: 1:1–15:21 and 15:22–40:38. The first division narrates the conflict between God and Pharaoh over the service of Israel. The second describes the means and manner in which God will be present with God's people as they move toward the promised land of Canaan. Next, Dozeman introduces the two texts that will serve as the common text to explore the various methodologies used to study Exodus: Exod 1–2 and 19–20. Dozeman concludes his introduction by providing a synopsis of the remaining chapters.

Dennis Olson's "Literary and Rhetorical Criticism" (13–54) offers a brief history of the rise of "text-centered" and "reader-centered" approaches as they emerged against the more traditional "author-centered" focus of historical criticism. Olson concentrates principally on text-centered reading methods over against reader-centered methodologies that deploy literary/rhetorical techniques such as feminist. Olson, as will be true of all of the authors in this volume, offers a strong survey of the literature as represented by its best practitioners. Olson offers the clearest example of how to practice literary/rhetorical criticism by adopting Phyllis Trible's step-by-step outline from her seminal work *Rhetorical Criticism: Context, Method, and the Book of Jonah* (Minneapolis: Fortress, 1994). By describing and adopting a clear-cut methodology, Olson's chapter may be the most helpful for students because it can easily be appropriated into their own exegetical work.

Kenton Sparks's essay on "Genre Criticism" (55–94) describes the emergence of the discipline as a corrective out form criticism. The goal of genre criticism is to achieve reader competence in terms of understanding the verbal discourse of a given piece of literature. Reader competence implies that a reader recognizes how a given type of literature works and as well as the ability to understand it. The advance that genre criticism makes over traditional form criticism is the recognition that ideal types of literature do not exist. Rather, readers group types of literature together in terms of common traits rather than in relationship to an ideal type or form. Sparks demonstrates the necessity of a close reading of the text in ways similar to the other methods in the book as well as the importance of extrabiblical comparative literature in attaining reader competency. Part of this competency as it relates to the book of Exodus is recognizing the diversity of interests and concerns embedded in the final form of the text.

Suzanne Boorer writes on "Source and Redaction Criticism" (95–130). This is the most traditional approach in this collection of essays. Boorer rehearses the history of source/redaction criticism, including its interplay with form and traditio-historical methods. There is not much new ground broken in this essay, but her review of the literature is probably the broadest and most helpful in the collection. The complexity and subjectivity of identifying discrete sources as well as the vastly different conclusions reached by competent scholars applying the method will remind the reader of the reason for the rise of the newer text and reader-centered hermeneutical approaches.

Jorge Pixley's chapter on "Liberation Criticism" (131–62) is a lively and compelling read. Pixley is a leading and well-respected liberationist whose commentary on Exodus broke new ground in the field (*On Exodus: A Liberationist Perspective* [New York: Orbis, 1987]). Pixley emphasizes the importance of the social location of the reader. He notes the irony and artificial nature of introducing a "method" to Western academics when it originally developed among poor and marginalized persons of faith living in the remote villages or in the urban slums of Latin America. Liberation theology reminds the reader that the reader's *context* matters profoundly in interpretation. Pixley demonstrates that the book of Exodus is foundational for developing a theology of liberation. He argues that the prophets drew their liberationist and justice-centered themes from the book of Exodus rather than creating these themes that are so central to the Torah.

Naomi Steinberg covers "Feminist Criticism" (163–92) well. Her introduction to the discipline is brief. She traces the rise of feminism among North American Anglo women and its spread to more marginalized groups in North America and around the world. She focuses the bulk of her chapter on illustrating a feminist reading of Exod 1–2 and 19–20. Her engagement with these common texts is the most thorough in the book and helps the reader to experience the range of interpretive options and the diversity within feminist criticism in terms of class, gender, and ethnicity. Steinberg also compiles the most extensive bibliography in this volume.

In the final chapter, Gale Yee introduces "Postcolonial Biblical Criticism." Her chapter spends a significant amount of space on introducing the philosophical roots of postcolonial theory. Postcolonial method is jargon-heavy, and readers encountering it for the first time may find themselves lost in the array of new vocabulary. Yee, however, is an able guide and demonstrates the powerful lens that postcolonial theory provides for illuminating new dimensions in the text of Exodus. She notes that Exodus may be read in support of both liberation and oppression. This leads her to remind her readers to ask two questions of their own interpretations: Whom does my interpretation help? Whom does it harm? Good questions, indeed.

Each chapter concludes with a bibliography of key secondary resources for further study. *Methods for Exodus* also includes a glossary, name index, and scripture index. The glossary is particularly helpful, since the various hermeneutical approaches introduce a plethora of specialized jargon into the English language that can be bewildering to the beginning student. The glossary gathers the most common terms together and offers a brief definition.

Methods for Exodus is an excellent resource for advanced exegetical courses in colleges and seminaries. Its stated target audience is students, scholars, and interested clergy. I think that this may be overly optimistic. This is a book best suited for advanced students and scholars. It is well-written but assumes a solid grounding in the current climate of biblical hermeneutics. *Methods for Exodus* does achieve its goal of illustrating how six different methodologies read the book of Exodus.

Reading Law as Narrative: A Study in the Casuistic Laws of the Pentateuch, by Assnat Bartor. Society of Biblical Literature Ancient Israel and Its Literature 5. Atlanta: Society of Biblical Literature, 2010. Pp. ix + 219. Paper. $27.95. ISBN 9781589834804.

Thomas B. Dozeman, United Theological Seminary, Dayton, Ohio

Assnat Bartor's well-written and interesting study of the narrative dimensions of casuistic law in the Pentateuch was originally written as a doctoral dissertation at Tel Aviv University for Gershon Brin and Ed Greenstein. The interest of both mentors in the literary interpretation of biblical law looms in the background. Yet Bartor takes the reader on her own journey, intertwining her experience as a lawyer and as a biblical interpreter in an exploration of literary techniques that fashion case laws into miniature stories or "narrative laws." She anchors her study in tradition, noting the rabbinic interest in exploring the mutual connections between halakah and haggadah. She further situates her work in the contemporary study of law and narrative through a helpful review of the current state of scholarship in the fields of "literature in the law" (e.g., Martha Nussbaum) and in the literary study of biblical law (e.g., Calum Carmichael, Bernard Jackson, James W. Watts, Harry P. Nasuti).

Bartor contributes to the growing field of the literary study of biblical law by exploring the narrative elements in the laws of the Pentateuch and the techniques employed by the authors to influence the readers, both past and present. The strategy for describing the function of the narrative elements is to interpret the laws of the Pentateuch as "embedded stories" within the larger "frame story" of the narrator (ch. 1). Bartor explains that, when a character takes center stage in the Pentateuch, the episode is an "embedded story," where the speech of the character must be distinguished from the voice of the narrator, even though the discourse often relates to the larger "frame story" of the narrator. The casuistic laws in the Pentateuch function in the same way. They, too, are "embedded stories" in which internal literary devices function to relate the law to the larger "frame story." "Embedded laws" can even serve as an interpretive guide to the "frame story." The identification of the narratological techniques that relate law and narrative gives rise to a poetics of case law in the Pentateuch, according to Bartor.

She separates the investigation into four topics: "The Lawgiver as Narrator" (ch. 2); "Representation of Speech" (ch. 3); "Representation of Inner Life" (ch. 4); and "Point of View" (ch. 5).

The description of "The Lawgiver as Narrator" (ch. 2) is the most extensive chapter in the book (23–84). The central question is how to identify the ways in which the narrator as lawgiver participates in the events of law. The starting point for study is to separate the personality of the "lawgiver-narrator" from the identity of characters in the promulgation of law, such as YHWH or Moses. Bartor describes two literary techniques by which the lawgiver or the addressees enter the legal process: participation and perceptibility. Participation describes those times when the addressees or the lawgiver take part in the events of the law along with the other characters. Participation can vary from a minor role (Exod 21:22–25) to full participation, where second-person speech fully involves the addressee in relieving the distress of an animal: "if *you* meet *your* enemies" (Exod 23:4–5). The lawgiver also participates in legislation in the law of centralization where personal comment is added: "you will bring all *that I command you*" (Deut 12:11). Bartor describes this technique as the introduction of a "self-conscious narrator or lawgiver" whose function is to bolster authority. Perceptibility describes those instances when the lawgiver responds to the content of the laws, thus influencing the perceptions and process of the legislation. Examples include the interjection in the law of the female slave, "since he has dealt faithlessly with her (Exod 21:8), the rhetoric of persuasion in some laws in Deuteronomy (e.g., Deut 20:16b–17a), and the formal style ("this is the law of") or diagnostic comments ("it is a depravity") in Priestly legislation. The techniques of participation and perceptibility underscore that the case laws in the Pentateuch are communicative texts.

The "Representation of Speech" (ch. 3, 85–131) explores the power of speech to create the illusion of reality. A hallmark of narrative, according to Bartor, is "the ability to create an illusion of reality by means of imitation (e.g., *mimesis*)." When action is described and characters acquire speech, readers enter the illusion of hearing their voices and seeing the events with their own eyes. Casuistic laws are also "reality-mimicking texts" that dramatize scenes through direct speech, interior speech, and mixed discourse. Characters make direct speeches in law, such as the formal declaration of the slave: "I love my master" (Exod 21:5). Direct speech also influences laws by occurring during formal judicial procedures (e.g., Deut 21:18–21) or as oaths, as in the case of the *sotah* in Num 5:11–31, who provides the "terrified stammer": "Amen, Amen." Interior speech occurs when a omniscient narrator allows the reader to enter the thoughts of characters, such as the craving for flesh in Deut 12:20–21, which Bartor concludes highlights verisimilitude. Mixed discourse is free indirect discourse where the narrator may incorporate more than one perspective on law without quotation. An example is the law of lending to the poor, where the style of Exod 22:26–27 provides the law, while also incorporating the perspective of the poor person without quotation.

Chapters 4 and 5 explore "Representation of the Inner Life" (133–61) and "Point of View" (163–81). The representation of the inner life builds on the technique of interior speech from chapter 3 but moves in a different direction to explore motive and how it functions as plot in case laws. The law of homicide (Deut 19:2–7) and the law about the woman who grasps the genitals of a man (Deut 25:11–12) explore the motives of the characters, indicating the interest of the lawgivers in the dynamic relationship of characters. Point of view examines those instances where the lawgiver abandons a neutral stance through the use of verbs of perception (e.g., see, hear, know, understand), as in the law of war (Deut 20:1–4) or the law requiring compassion for animals (Deut 22:1–4). Multiple designations of a character can also provide point of view (e.g., brother, neighbor, wife, young woman).

Bartor states at the end of her study that "the narrative reading of casuistic laws is of very little use … for understanding their normative dimensions." She adds that the narrative reading does provide insight into the human meaning in the events that are embodied in the laws. To this end she leaves the reader with four insights that narrative interpretation reveals about casuistic laws: (1) they have a mimetic quality that exposes the world of emotions and thought; (2) they are by nature communicative and dialogic; and (3) the mimetic and communicative qualities of case laws in the Pentateuch do not readily translate to the broader corpus of ancient Near Eastern law-codes. The fourth insight summarizes my evaluation of the book: "a narrative reading [of case laws in the Pentateuch] provides a rich and emotionally stimulating reading experience."

FORMER PROPHETS

The Transjordanian Palimpsest: The Overwritten Texts of Personal Exile and Transformation in the Deuteronomistic History, by Jeremy M. Hutton. Beihefte zur Zeitschrift für die alttestamentliche Wissenschaft 396. Berlin: de Gruyter, 2009. Pp. xvii + 449. Cloth. $140.00. ISBN 9783110204100.

Walter Dietrich, Theologische Fakultät, Universität Bern, Bern, Switzerland

Dies ist ein wahrhaft gelehrtes Buch—und doch ist es ein Erstlingswerk: eine unter Leitung von Jo Ann Hackett an der Harvard University entstandene Dissertation. Der Autor hat sich eine höchst anspruchsvolle, eigentlich interdisziplinäre Aufgabe gestellt, indem er das Thema „Ostjordanland" unter drei grundverschiedenen Gesichtspunkten angeht: dem kulturanthropologischen, dem historischen und dem exegetischen. Die Exegese beansprucht den Löwenanteil des Buches; sie bietet nicht weniger als eine umfassende Redaktions- oder Kompositionskritik der Samuelbücher, und zwar auf mehreren Stufen: von der deuteronomistischen (dtr) Geschichtsschreibung zurück zu einer übergreifenden vor-dtr Redaktion und nochmals zurück zu den ältesten zugrundeliegenden Quellen. Das Motiv der Jordan-Überquerung dient dabei als heuristischer Leitfaden, führt aber nicht zu einer Blickverengung (etwa nur auf Texte, die direkt vom Jordan handeln). Der Autor hat sich ungeheuer breit informiert, und er diskutiert intensiv die unterschiedlichsten Ansätze. Auf vielen Seiten ist der Fussnotenapparat umfangreicher als der Haupttext, und die Bibliographie umfasst vierzig Seiten (wobei alte wie neueste ‚continental' Literatur verschiedenster Sprachen einbegriffen ist, die der Verfasser auch wirklich und intensiv studiert hat!).

Ausgangspunkt ist der Umstand, dass innerhalb des dtr Geschichtswerks (mit dem Hutton erfreulicherweise nach wie vor rechnet) mehrfach das Motiv der Überschreitung des Jordans in östlicher Richtung und der Rückkehr ins (israelitisch-judäische) Westjordanland begegnet. Hutton bringt dies mit der van Genep'schen Kategorie der „rites des passages" in Verbindung. Das Ostjordanland habe für Dtr ein doppeltes Gesicht: Einerseits sei es israelitisches Territorium, andererseits sei Jhwh dort nicht eigentlich zu Hause. „[I]n the literary logic of the DtrH, Transjordan serves as a place of exile, refuge, and incubative transformation for prospective personages of power" (5). Es sind drei Arten von Personen, die den Jordan überqueren: Retter (Ri 3; 8; 1Sam 11), Herrscher (2Sam 2; 15–19; 2Kön 9) und Propheten (2Kön 2; 3).

In einem interessanten historischen Durchgang (51–78) wird die Geschichte der Region nachgezeichnet: mit einem Akzent eher auf der „longue durée" als auf Einzelereignissen. Die Bewohner Ostjordaniens waren im Prinzip indigen, ihre angestammte Wirtschaftsform der „agropastoralism". Es gab ökonomische Bande sowohl zum (israelitischen) Westjordanland wie auch zu den (ostjordanischen) Ammonitern und Moabitern. Die transjordanischen „israelitischen" Stämme waren „originally autonomous ethnic units" (63); erst nach und nach entdeckten bzw. etablierten sie ihre Verbundenheit mit den ‚Brüdern' im Westjordanland. Sprache und Schrift der Texte von Deir Alla sind bezeichnenderweise „separate from both Hebrew and Aramaic" (65). Noch die—historisch vermutlich zutreffenden—Berichte vom Aufenthalt Eschbaals und Davids in Mahanajim lassen erkennen, dass „Transjordan existed as a separate political entity" (74).

Der grosse Rest des Buches gilt der Feststellung von „Sources of the Deuteronomistic History" (79): angeblich zum Zweck einer genaueren Verortung der genannten drei Typen von Jordan-Übergang; in Wahrheit aber hat die hier vorgelegte, umfassende literarhistorische Analyse ihren Zweck in sich selbst. Hutton erweist sich als ein klar *diachron* arbeitender Exeget, der nur gelegentlich und in Fussnoten auf die im anglophonen Raum verbreitete *synchrone* Exegese Bezug nimmt. Er will genau wissen, welche älteren und ältesten Textquellen es gibt, wann und wo sie entstanden und wie sie miteinander vereint worden sind, ehe sie in die dtr Geschichtsschreibung Eingang fanden.

Hutton setzt ein mit ungemein intensiven, kritischen Forschungsberichten. Am Anfang steht die Erforschung des dtr Geschichtswerks (81–101). Dieser Bericht ist nicht der erste, aber ein besonders kundiger. Er rekapituliert die grundlegenden Thesen von Noth und Jepsen, die Einwände von Wolff und von Rad, die Differenzierungen durch die „Cross (Harvard) School" und die „Smend (Göttingen) School"—wobei er nur gegen die letztere „Objections" anmeldet und damit zugleich seinen eigenen Standort zu erkennen gibt: bei der Cross'schen Hypothese eines ersten vorexilischen Geschichtswerks, das exilisch überarbeitet wurde.

Danach (102–56) geht es um die vor-dtr Textbestände. Als erstes wird die Möglichkeit einer umfassenderen vor-dtr Redaktion der Sam- (und Kön-) Bücher erkundet. Geduldig präsentiert (und kritisiert) Hutton die verschiedenen Vorschläge hierzu, die *entweder* von dem angeblich disparaten Formelgut in 1-2Kön ausgehen (Weippert, Barrick, Campbell, Lemaire, Provan, Halpern, Vanderhofft, Eynikel, Aurelius) *oder* mit einer prophetischen Edition rechnen (Nübel, Mildenberger, Macholz, Schüpphaus, Weiser, Fohrer, Birch, McCarter, Mayes, Campbell, O'Brien, White) *oder* noch andere Wege einschlagen (Vermeylen, Dietrich, Kratz, Römer). Huttons Belesenheit ist enorm, sein Urteil nie herablassend und immer sorgfältig begründet. Er selbst positioniert sich in der Nähe Campbells und dessen These eines von 1Sam 1 bis 2Kön 10 reichenden, aus der Zeit der Jehu-Dynastie (zweite Hälfte des 9. oder erste Hälfte des 8. Jh.s) stammenden „Prophetic Record".

In einem an dieser Stelle unerwarteten (und durchaus problematischen) Zwischenschritt wird die „Royal Apology" hethitischer und assyrischer Provenienz vorgestellt und behauptet, dies sei auch im königszeitlichen Israel eine mögliche Literaturform gewesen (157–75)—womit für das Folgende sehr viel präjudiziert ist. Denn angeblich sind die allermeisten der in den Sam-Büchern zu fassenden Quellen apologetischer Natur: sei es, dass sie die Herrschaft Sauls oder Davids oder Salomos oder Rehabeams oder Jehus legitimieren wollen. Dies wiederum hat eine relative Frühdatierung des Grossteils der Texte zur Folge: überwiegend ins 10., teilweise ins 9. (oder frühe 8.) Jh. So entpuppt sich das überaus gelehrte und gescheite Buch Huttons in diesem Punkt als überraschend konservativ. In anderer Hinsicht gibt es sich dezidiert modern-liberal: Immer wieder wird der Unterschied zwischen historischer Faktizität und literarischer Fiktion betont. Generell wird nach der ideologischen und politischen Funktion der Texte gefragt, wogegen Kategorien wie Narrativität, Ästhetik, Ethik oder Theologie zurücktreten.

Das Herzstück der Arbeit sind die literar- oder kompositionskritischen Analysen dreier klassischer Textkomplexe: der sog. Thronfolgegeschichte (176–227) und der sog. Aufstiegsgeschichte Davids (228–88) sowie der Erzählungen vom Aufstieg Sauls (289–363). Bei dem Versuch, ihre Entstehung aufzuhellen, scheut Hutton weder detaillierte Argumentationen noch gewagte Hypothesen.

Der Ausgangspunkt der „Succession Narrative"—hier bewegt sich Hutton in den Bahnen Kratz'—sei ein knapper Bericht von Davids Ringen mit Abschalom gewesen (2Sam 13*; 14,33*; 15,1–6.13; 18,1.2a.4b.6–9.15b–18a). Dieser Grundtext wurde schon zu Lebzeiten Davids zur „Court-History of David" 2Sam 13–20* ausgebaut, das heisst, die gesamte Thematik von Davids Übertritt ins Ostjordanland und seiner Rückkehr (2Sam 15–17*; 19–20) ist eine sekundäre und betont apologetische Ausweitung.[2] Zur Zeit Salomos sei die „Court History" um

---

2. Ich selbst vertrete ebenfalls die These eines gesonderten Berichts von Abschaloms Aufstand; doch gehörte zu ihm m.E. von Anfang an das Motiv des Rückzugs nach Mah-

die „Solomonic Apology" 2Sam 11–12* + 1Kön 1–2* zur „Solomonic Succession Narrative" erweitert worden. Ist das aber glaubhaft? Sind diese Kapitel nicht viel eher ein Entwicklungskern des Ganzen? Und bieten sie mit ihrer doch recht ungeschminkten Darstellung von Untaten Davids und Salomos wirklich „all the elements needed to fulfill the structure of ancient Near Eastern royal apologetic" (185, näher ausgeführt 192–96)? Zur Zeit Rehabeams, also Ende des 10. Jh.s, sei die „Succession Narrative" mittels der sog. ‚benjaminitischen Episoden' in 2Sam 2–4; 16,1-14 und 19,17-41 sowie der David-Meribaal-Erzählung 2Sam 9 mit einer bestimmten Version der „History of David's Rise" verbunden worden; mit diesem Werk habe man Herrschaftsansprüchen aus dem israelitischen Norden entgegentreten wollen. Etwa ein Jahrhundert später, auf der Ebene des „Prophetic Record", wurde der Auftritt des Gerichtspropheten Natan in 12,1-15 eingeschaltet und dem Ganzen eine zweite Version der Aufstiegsgeschichte vorgeschaltet (191–92); dieses grosse Literaturwerk diente der Legitimation der Herrschaft Jehus. Erst in der Folgezeit wurde aus dem Saul-Sohn Meribaal ein Sohn Jonatans (217.221—eine Anleihe bei Veijola). Am Ende dann setzte die dtr Redaktion 10,1–11,1 + 12,26-31 ein und situierte so die Geburtsgeschichte Salomos im Kontext eines Ammoniterkriegs (190–91—eine m.E. unwahrscheinliche Spätdatierung).

„The Mystery of the History of David's Rise" (228) sucht Hutton, weitgehend im Gefolge Halperns, durch Quellenscheidung aufzuklären: Er rechnet mit *zwei* Aufstiegsgeschichten, beide entstanden in der Davidszeit und beide erschaffen zur Legitimierung des Machtwechsels von Saul auf David. Beide benutzten dazu einen Nachkommen Sauls als Vehikel der Macht: die eine seine Tochter Michal, die andere seinen Sohn Jonatan. Die beiden Geschwister bildeten eine funktionale Dublette, die wie zahlreiche weitere Dubletten in diesem Textbereich nach literarkritischer Trennung riefen. Dies ist eine weitreichende und, mit Verlaub, altmodische Entscheidung. Gewiss gehen die Michal- und die Jonatan-Erzählungen auf je eigene Traditionen zurück, sicher auch bilden die verschiedenen Versionen von Davids Eintritt in die Gefolgschaft Sauls (1Sam 16,14-23; 17) oder die beiden Attacken Sauls auf David (18,10-11; 19,9-10) oder die beiden Verschonungen Sauls durch David (24; 26) oder der zweimalige Versuch Davids, zu den Philistern überzutreten (21,11-16; 27,1-4), oder die beiden Berichte von Sauls Tod (1Sam 28; 2Sam 1) Doppelungen—doch wer sagt, dass nicht *ein* Autor zwei oder mehr Varianten des gleichen Erzählstoffs nebeneinander stellen und diese Technik geradezu als literarisches Kunstmittel einsetzen konnte? Speziell problematisch ist es, wenn innerhalb der Goliat-Geschichte 1Sam 17

---

anajim; und der Text erlangte erst im späten 8. (oder frühen 7.) Jh. seinen jetzigen Umfang. Vgl. W. Dietrich, Die Fünfte Kolonne Davids beim Abschalom-Aufstand, in: W. Dietrich (Hg.), Seitenblicke. Literarische und historische Studien zu Nebenfiguren im zweiten Samuelbuch, Fribourg / Göttingen 2011 (OBO 249), 91–120. Übrigens vertritt und variiert dort auch Jeremy Hutton seine Sicht der Dinge.

zwei vollständige Erzählversionen einfach entlang den textkritischen Trennlinien postuliert werden: die eine identisch mit dem kürzeren Text von LXX^B, die andere bestehend aus den Überschüssen im masoretischen Text. Die so resultierenden parallelen Erzählreihen nennt Hutton „HDR1" und „HDR2". Die erste, auf Michal fokussierte, umfasste folgende Texte (die folgenden Angaben jeweils etwas vergröbert): 1Sam 16,14–23; 17* (in der LXX^B-Fassung); 18,6–29; 19,8–17; 21; 22,1–13; 24; 28; 31; 2Sam 5–6. Die zweite, um Jonatan zentrierte, enthielt 1Sam 13–14 (eine Vorform); 17* (die MT-Überschüsse); 18,1–5; 19,1–7; 20,1–4.18–22.24–39; 23,14–28; 26; 27; 29; 30; 2Sam 1; 2,1–4. Die Ladegeschichte 1Sam 4–6 gelangte erst auf der Ebene des „Prophetic Record" an ihren jetzigen Platz—wobei die Frage nach der Zugehörigkeit von 2Sam 6 zur „Ark Narrative" oder zu „HDR1" Hutton einiges Kopfzerbrechen bereitet (278.283).

Schliesslich die Saul-Geschichten. Gestützt auf eine wiederum stupende Literaturkenntnis nimmt Hutton eine alte Zweiteilung auf: Einer seiner Meinung nach dtr Textreihe in 1Sam 7–8; 10,17–27; 12 (so 293) stehen zwei ältere, unabhängig voneinander entstandene Traditionen gegenüber: 1Sam 11,1–11 und 9,1–10,16 (wobei der Abschluss der zweiten Erzählung in einer Vorform von 14,6–16 gelegen haben soll: eine m.E. trotz der ausführlichen Begründung 349–61 implausible These). Als „basic thrust" der beiden „Narratives of Sauls Rise" könne gelten: „Saul as *king*, rather than *deliverer*" (306). Es handele sich um „components of an authentically archaic stratum of 1 Samuel" (312) und um eine „apology for Saul's kingship" (311). Die prodavidischen Autoren von HDR1 hätten sie aufgenommen, um so die Gottgewolltheit des (inzwischen ja auf David übergegangenen) Königtums in Israel zu belegen (307).

In einem abschließenden Kapitel „Conclusion: A Composite Motif" fasst Hutton seine Ergebnisse zusammen: zuerst die zur „Composition History of 1 Samuel 9–1 Kings 2*" (364–71), dann die zu „The pre-Deuteronomistic *Bricoleur* and the Transjordanian Landscape as Palimpsest" (371–77). Ich gestehe, dass sich mir trotz dieses nochmaligen Versuchs einer Zusammenführung beider Themen deren untrennbare Zusammengehörigkeit nicht voll erschlossen hat. Im Grunde, so scheint es mir, handelt es sich um zwei Abhandlungen in einem Buch. Dieses, so sei gern hervorgehoben, ist mit ausserordentlicher Sorgfalt gefertigt. Das zeigt sich allein schon an einem fast 30-seitigen Stellenregister. Von Anfang bis Ende ist es in einer gehobenen und prägnanten, nicht immer ganz einfachen Sprache abgefasst. Es weist fast keine Form- oder Schreibfehler auf; ein besonders hübscher darf gleichwohl vermerkt werden: „Ritterbuch" statt „Retterbuch" (152).

Zweifellos wird „The Transjordanian Palimpsest" die weitere Forschung zur Entstehung der Samuelbücher, aber auch zur Geschichte des Ostjordanlandes nachhaltig beeinflussen.

The Surprising Election and Confirmation of King David, by J. Randall Short. Harvard Theological Studies 63. Cambridge: Harvard University Press, 2010. Pp. xiii + 244. Paper. $25.00. ISBN 9780674053410.

David G. Firth, St. John's College, Nottingham, United Kingdom

This well-presented study is derived from the author's doctoral thesis, which he submitted to Harvard Divinity School under the guidance of Jon D. Levenson, Gary A. Anderson, and Paul D. Hanson. In it, Short subjects the so-called History of David's Rise (HDR, roughly 1 Sam 16–2 Sam 5) to a new analysis in which he seeks to overthrow the largely political reading of these chapters that has become dominant since P. K. McCarter's ground-breaking essay that argued that these chapters represent an apology for David that sought to justify his rise to the throne as someone who lacked obvious legitimacy. McCarter's approach has been particularly influential in some recent studies of David, especially the biographies of McKenzie and Halpern, who independently develop this thesis to suggest that the historical David probably committed most of the crimes for which he seems to obtain an alibi in these chapters. Because Short restricts his analysis to 1 Sam 16–2 Sam 5, he does not therefore examine their even more provocative claim that the one murder he probably did not commit was that of Uriah the Hittite (2 Sam 11), but there is no doubt that his approach raises significant questions about the interpretation of the whole of the books of Samuel and how their content might relate to the historical David. In particular, Short seeks to move away from a political reading of these chapters where the primary concern is to justify David's usurping of the throne toward a theological one that focuses on the surprising nature of David's election and confirmation as king.

Short begins with a brief introduction that helpfully sets out his approach and outlines the direction the study will take in the five chapters that follow before a conclusion ties the argument together. Within this he includes a brief note on his understanding of the text of the books of Samuel. This is a notoriously complex issue due to the MT's own difficulties as well as the differences found in LXX and the Qumran manuscripts, especially 4QSam[a]. Short outlines his reasons for largely following MT (while acknowledging its difficulties), as it represents the common ground for most interpreters, and, of course, at many points the variants would not affect his conclusions. Although this is a valid position to take, it was disappointing that he did not engage with some of Graeme Auld's work on how the different textual traditions might point to different editions of the book. His conclusions would stand, but the case would be stronger had more attention been given to some of the textual issues.

The first chapter provides an overview of scholarship on HDR, an important element within the books of Samuel, though one that has not gained as much attention as the so-called Succession and Ark Narratives. Nevertheless, HDR is an important element in the source-critical analysis popularized by Rost, but one that has been interpreted differently. In part, this is because it was the least developed in Rost's analysis, but it is also because different scholars have meant different things by it. Thus, for some HDR needs to be examined for its own redaction history, while for others it is basically equivalent to our 1 Sam 16–2 Sam 5. Short deftly leads us through this material in order to come to his principal concern, which is McCarter's treatment of HDR (minus redactional accretions) as a political apology that justifies David's place on the throne. At the same time, he is careful to indicate that in his opinion HDR cannot be separated from the other material in the books of Samuel because it is so closely woven into the finished book. Short is therefore skeptical of the claims of those who believe they can "excavate the tell in the text" and uncover the stages that take us back to the historical David, though he does trace the various stages McCarter identifies in determining what he sees as the HDR's rhetorical posture.

An important element of McCarter's case builds on the work of Herbert Wolf and Harry Hoffner. This drew on the Hittite Apology of Ḫattušili, a thirteenth century BCE account from a usurper who justified his seizure of the throne. In truth, this was always a weak element in McCarter's case (and also of those who follow him) because it requires that HDR be an independent composition written to accomplish for David what the Apology did for Ḫattušili. In his second chapter, Short goes through the main analogies drawn to show that none of them matches the content of the HDR, quite apart from the fact that the Apology is a discrete first-person account, whereas HDR exists only as an embedded third-person narrative section of the books of Samuel.

But it is still possible that, even if the analogies with the Apology are overdrawn, at least part of the rhetorical goal of HDR is to demonstrate David's innocence. Accordingly, in his third chapter Short considers the seven underlying charges against David that McCarter finds in HDR. To do so, Short enlists speech-act theory as a methodological tool, though the introduction he offers here does not go much beyond the seminal work of J. L. Austin, though since his primary approach is to demonstrate that the illocutionary force of the text does not support McCarter's claims it is probably sufficient. Nevertheless, if one intends to use an analytical tool such as this, it would be helpful to draw on more substantial work, such as that of Searle or Grice. Taken as a rebuttal of McCarter's case, Short's arguments work well, demonstrating that there is a significant element of circular reasoning that operates in it. Thus, McCarter and those who have followed him have been overly controlled by their own externally established assumptions, and these have controlled their reading of the text and its implications. Even so, the failure to articulate more clearly how speech-act theory enables this leaves Short open to the claim that his own attempt to read HDR is also shaped by his own external assumptions, even though these are not as clearly developed as those he critiques.

Having rejected the apologetic reading of HDR as a source, Short then turns in his fourth and fifth chapters to read the text in the form we now have it. Since he has a particular focus on David's election, his primary focus is on 1 Sam 13–31. This is not HDR as it is commonly reconstructed (even allowing for differences in how its boundaries are determined) but could be considered as a discrete unit within the books of Samuel. However, it is certainly not the only point at which the material we now find in Samuel could be divided, so again Short's case could be strengthened by providing clearer argumentation in favor of this; indeed, if this were to prove to be the appropriate point for dividing the content of Samuel, then the whole argument about HDR would need reconsideration. Nevertheless, he makes a persuasive case for seeing David's election as the primary purpose of the narrative. He achieves this initially by a close reading of 1 Sam 16 but with some attention to 1 Sam 17, where the theme of Yahweh's choice of David is particularly prominent. What is stressed is the surprising nature of David's election: unlike Ḫattušili, there is no particular reason why David should be chosen, as he is the son of a nobody and the least (not merely youngest) of Jesse's sons who through the narrative becomes *the* son of Jesse, then Saul's son so that he is finally Yahweh's son and even elevated over Saul in his own eyes. These themes are not developed in order but rather are disentangled by Short for the sake of his argument, though in reality they are bundled together in the text. There are again points at which Short's argument could be strengthened—for example, in 1 Sam 16 the elders of Bethlehem are told to consecrate themselves prior to a sacrifice but Samuel separately invites and consecrates Jesse, which could suggest he was not an elder—but on the whole he makes a persuasive case for the priority of David's election and its surprising nature through the narrative.

A brief conclusion then largely summarizes the earlier chapters, though here Short acknowledges that once the apologetic purposes are removed, so that David's presentation is geared more toward understanding Israel's election, then our ability to construct the text's historical context is much less, since it could have arisen in a number of periods. However, its primary goal was to present David as the representative figure for Israel in its covenant relationship to Yahweh, and as such modern readings that focus on politics have missed the point.

Short has presented a challenge to the largely dominant reading of these chapters that is generally persuasive. A political reading does seem to import more to the text than we find in it, though it is not impossible that the text may have subsidiary purposes that include showing that David was innocent of an attempt to usurp the throne even though his surprising election is more central. As noted above, there are points where his argument needs to be supplemented. This is especially in his use of speech-act theory and also his decision to focus his own reading on 1 Sam 13–31, which is not the same textual boundaries as those he criticizes. But with these caveats noted, we can be grateful for a stimulating and close examination of the text.

The Demise of the Warlord: A New Look at the David Story, by Daniel Bodi. Hebrew Bible Monographs 26. Sheffield: Sheffield Phoenix, 2010. Pp. vii + 270. Hardcover. $85.00. ISBN 9781906055820.

Jeremy Hutton, University of Wisconsin-Madison, Madison, Wisconsin

The figure of David is an ambiguous one in the book of Samuel. His shining star rises throughout 1 Samuel, reaching its zenith in the first several chapters of 2 Samuel. After Nathan conveys a divine promise to him (2 Sam 7), however, the meteoric rise of this new king of Israel and Judah halts abruptly. Within the span of only eight subsequent chapters, David and his kingdom have become embroiled in a seemingly intractable international conflict, he has disgraced himself with the wife of one of his soldiers, murdered her husband, lost one child emotionally to an incestuous rape, lost another physically to murder, and lost the loyalty of a third, who launches a rebellion against him. The luster is tarnished, and the reader is forced to question whether and how David's reputation may be salvaged.

Bodi's book examines two of these chapters (2 Sam 11–12), asking whether the opprobrium with which the narrative treats David in the aftermath of the Bathsheba affair might be linked to a larger motif prevalent throughout the ancient Near East. This motif, he argues, comes in two thrusts. First, there exists the common ideal that warlords must lead a "warlike existence"; dallying with women and avoiding war is worthy of rebuke. The second aspect of the motif is the belief that resident aliens remain a somewhat protected class and may not be treated with impunity. Bodi argues cogently, through both a literary and historical-critical analysis of the text, that these two themes find their expression in the episode of David's "dalliance" with Bathsheba.

In a brief introduction (1–4), Bodi lays out the problem, provides a helpful overview of the book's structure, and, finally, discusses an interpretive principle adopted from the work of Moshe Held: "if one can show how insights gained from the study of newly discovered ancient Near Eastern texts have been anticipated by medieval rabbis who did not have access to these buried ancient Semitic documents, then the probability that one's interpretation is plausible may be increased" (4). Bodi relies heavily (and fruitfully) on this principle in the remaining chapters of the book.

Bodi provides a history of research on 2 Sam 11–12 in an initial chapter (5–18). This sketch is dutiful and will be familiar to anyone who has worked with this text. But the creativity in Bodi's work relies on his fluid movement between modes of analysis: the history of literary research serves as a précis for a short reflection on the *historicity* of the Davidic kingdom. In Bodi's opinion, "The use of the term 'Monarchy' is a misnomer and should be abandoned when talking of Saul, David and Solomon. … Therefore, in describing the reigns of these rulers, in the present work I have adopted the expressions 'tribal chieftain' or 'warlord', believing that they better describe their position among ancient Israelite tribes. Moreover, the domains they governed less resembled full-scale 'states' and more 'chiefdoms'" (16). Although there is a growing literature on the state/chiefdom debate that Bodi has not been able to fully engage in the space of this monograph, his recognition of the variety of governance-types is commendable; nonetheless, eschewal of "state" terminology is an interpretive move allowing him to draw connections more closely with the rhetoric of Amorite chieftains (without asking specifically about the status of their territorial holdings in Mari, for example). All in all, I believe Bodi's inclination to identify early Israel's political structure as of a similar type to that of the early Amorite "chiefdoms" of Syria (which are usually spoken of as "kingdoms") is correct. I would be less inclined to make such a hard-and-fast distinction between kingdoms and chiefdoms, however, and would point to the following comment of Bodi's as an example of the degree to which he himself permits some (nonpatrimonial) bureaucracy to have infiltrated the nascent "state": "David had adopted a new manner of exercising power that is different from traditional Bedouin warlords. He does the fighting beyond his borders through the medium of his general, officers, messengers and subordinates sent to do his bidding" (24).

Chapters 2 (19–70) and 3 (71–100) comprise a detailed literary reading of the biblical text. After providing his own translation of the text with a few annotations noting important repetitions of lexemes or other stylistic devices in the Hebrew (19–22), Bodi launches into his examination, discussing problems as diverse as the structure of the Ammonite war accounts (2 Sam 10:1–19; 11:1; 12:26–31; pp. 22–28); the timing of the New Year and, concomitantly, of campaign season (28–32); the meaning and intention of the reading Myk){lm in 11:1 (33); compositional causes and literary effects of "original" versus "secondary inclusio" (35–38); the historico-literary parallels between cities and women (38–41); the name, age, and status of Bathsheba (50–56); and many others. Throughout this analysis, Bodi demonstrates a solid and diverse knowledge of previous interpretations (both modern and rabbinic), deep familiarity with ancient Near Eastern cognate literature, and a keenly sensitive reader's eye.

After establishing his own reading of 2 Sam 11–12, Bodi includes two chapters detailing the ancient Near Eastern literary *topoi* that he finds particularly important in comprehending the biblical text: chapters 4 (101–37) and 6 (157–91). The former investigates the Akkadian-language (specifically, Amorite) instantiations of what Bodi calls "the Bedouin ideal of the warlike existence." As Bodi memorably claims, "The ideology expressed here is the exact opposite of the modern slogan 'Make Love, Not War'" (126). The latter chapter details Egyptian, Hittite, and Mesopotamian texts implying disdain for the ill treatment of the "resident alien" (Akk. *ubāru*) and argues for Uriah's identity as an Aramean (i.e., Western Semite) of some sort, rather than being of Anatolian Hittite origin. Bodi's analysis of what is meant by Akkadian *ubārum* (and its Hittite reflexes) in various literary corpora (167–81) is of particular note for its detailed argumentation and philological rigor. In each of these chapters Bodi adduces ample literary evidence for his theory, usually providing both the normalized (but sometimes merely transcribed) Akkadian version of the text and an annotated translation, as well as a thorough exposition. In short, it is not necessary for the reader to know Akkadian in order to be able to follow along, although familiarity with the language will allow the reader to track each of the arguments a bit more closely.

Intervening between these two discussions is "a brief account of the history of Mari and the importance of the Amorites for Biblical Studies" (ch. 5, pp. 138–56). Although this sequence of chapters may strike some as somewhat forced, the necessity of inserting the historical chapter between the two comparative literary chapters can be explained: it serves to show that the literature from Mari deriding those men who "eat," "drink," and "lie down" (i.e., have sexual intercourse) while their compatriots are off at battle has a clearly identifiable context in a society that is undergoing a transition from a more segmentary and nomadic organization to a more urban and bureaucratic organization—it is the former ethos from which this trope derives. Bodi's discussion of the social and economic organization of Mari's society is well-documented and nuanced, although picky readers may balk at his use of the term "Bedouin" to designate the practitioners of enclosed nomadism or transhumant pastoralism (a bit more could have been stated at the outset, I think, separating Bodi's "Bedouin" from the specifically Arabic-speaking groups designated by the same moniker today). Similarly, Bodi uses the rather vague term "nomadism" a bit too frequently without specification or elaboration. Despite this potential for confusion in the mind of modern readers, Bodi's brief analysis helpfully summarizes a great deal of data and serves as a welcome corrective to overly simplified views of ancient Near Eastern social structure.

Chapter 7 (192–211) discusses "the retribution principle in 2 Samuel 12 and its Amorite and ancient Near Eastern background." Bodi's goal in this chapter is to have us recognize that the principle of divine retribution for wrongdoing is not an invention of Hebrew literature but is rather a much older, demonstrably Amorite, *Weltanschauung*, one that may be found in later Greek and Egyptian texts as well. Although some of the examples are stronger than others (for example, the comparison of Sargon's punishment in the *Weidner Chronicle* with Saul's cultic misdeeds in 2 Sam 13 [200–202] is somewhat loose), Bodi adduces enough similarities here at least to make the suggestion a credible one worthy of further consideration. The most troublesome aspect, though, of this endeavor is that he has not gone through a full reading of the biblical text of 1-2 Samuel and analyzes it solely from a synchronic standpoint. The final section of this chapter asks, "When could the Story of the House of David have been written?" To this question, Bodi responds with a somewhat nebulous discussion of previous suggestions. He concludes, finally, that a postexilic dating of the Story of the House of David is unnecessary; all the themes central to the plot of 2 Sam 11–12 were currently in circulation well before the end of the Judahite monarchy.

A final, somewhat ancillary chapter 8 (212–24) rounds out the book's bulk. In it Bodi discusses Rashi's suggestion that Uriah had given his wife a *gēṭ*, a letter of divorce given by departing soldiers to their wives, which would become effective retroactive to the date given should the soldier die in battle. This rabbinic tradition parallels similar Assyrian legal conventions (216–20), even if we cannot establish a precise mode of transmission whereby the Assyrian legal tradition was adopted by the Israelite or Judahite legal system. (Bodi does posit, however, that such transmission may have occurred directly between these two cultures during the Neo-Assyrian or Neo-Babylonian periods [221].)

In a short conclusion (225–28) Bodi recapitulates the main points of his argument: "the *topos* seems to have been a literary reflection of the Amorite Bedouin warlord ideology dating from the eighteenth century BCE as attested in three Mari texts. ... The same ideology found further literary elaboration ... in the ninth-century BCE Babylonian *Poem of Erra*" (226). But in these final pages of the book, Bodi adds a complicating hypothesis to what has, until then, been a relatively straightforward argument: "The novelty of the Hebrew narrative is the *deconstruction of the traditional warlord ideology*. ... While David is blamed for his shameful and criminal behavior, history nevertheless continues with his descendants. ... The critique of the traditional warlord ideology, showing the uselessness of trust in military valor and bravura, might have occurred in the late pre-exilic period when Judah repeatedly faced superior military power—the Assyrians in 705 [*sic*] and the Babylonians from 605 BCE onward." This critique Bodi locates in wisdom circles (227).

This provocative and underargued closure to the book is jarring, both because of the degree of its speculative impulse following an otherwise tightly argued and cogent analysis of the biblical text and because of its implications and assumptions concerning the compositional unity and date of 2 Sam 11–12. Although the reader may not always agree with Bodi's exposition of the biblical text in chapters 2 and 3, his arguments are cleverly intriguing and worthy of further reflection. (For my own part, I find Bodi's assertion that Uriah is portrayed as having sensed little or nothing of David's exploitation of Bathsheba during the former's absence [e.g., 60–62] difficult to affirm on the face of it; nonetheless, the interpretive upshot from this assertion—namely, that Uriah's rebuke in 2 Sam 11:11 is an example of the larger, pan-Semitic trope that Bodi wants to highlight—becomes an important adjunct to his larger argument.) But this final, casually considered hypothesis seems to neglect the possibilities of redactional elaboration and of subsequent (re)interpretation: a number of recent volumes (e.g., Jacques Vermeylen's La loi du plus fort: Histoire de la rédaction des récits davidiques de 1 Samuel à 1 Rois 2 [BETL 154; Leuven: Leuven University Press, 2000]) have argued that 2 Sam 11–12 underwent a long process of redactional revision. One must wonder, then, the degree to which the Amorite trope, "Make War, Not Love," was in fact indigenous to the passage's Grundschicht (I would affirm that it was) and—contra Bodi, if I have understood him correctly—indicative of the author's(/authors') true sympathies. Is it possible that the story in its original form was in fact intended to levy this particularly Amorite accusation against a king who had essentially been caught (or who was at least plausibly accused of) "eating, drinking, and lying," only to have received interpretive revision in the ensuing decades and centuries? Or, if Bodi is correct in his assessment that the topos was wielded ironically in its earliest appearance, is it plausibly much earlier than the seventh century B.C.E.— perhaps even early enough to serve as a justification of the many bedmates of

Solomon (who is, after all, claimed to have been "a Lover, not a Fighter," in another popular formulation)?

A bibliography (229-255), citation index (256-65) and author index (266-70) round out the book.

All in all, this volume is both fascinating and thought-inducing. Its primary audience should be scholars and students interested in the history of the interpretation of Samuel, although it will also undoubtedly be of interest to anyone concerned with the literary interactions between ancient Israel and the wider ancient Near East. I am pleased to recommend it as a captivating interpretation of the David and Bathsheba affair, a complex and provocative text in its own right.

Jonathan Loved David: Manly Love in the Bible and the Hermeneutics of Sex, by Anthony Heacock. Bible in the Modern World 22. Sheffield: Sheffield Phoenix, 2011. Pp. xv + 185. Hardcover. $95.00. ISBN 9781906055509.

John Barclay Burns, George Mason University, Fairfax, Virginia

The relationship between David and Jonathan has generated considerable debate. Anthony Heacock engages in a critical reexamination of the relevant literature, including major interpretations, the influence of critical theories from the traditional to the postmodern, and insights from related fields in cultural studies. He offers his own contribution based on reader-response criticism and queer theory. Heacock believes that the fundamental question is, Did David and Jonathan engage in a prohibited sexual relationship or, as he puts it, "are David and Jonathan gay?" (2).

Chapter 1 lists the "prooftexts" from 1-2 Samuel and investigates the words that are used to support major interpretations. *Ḥesed*, conventionally translated "loyalty," expresses a friendship with overtones of God's covenant with Israel. The word *'āhēb* ("love") is customarily understood to express feudal or treaty obligations, though this need not preclude love between David and Jonathan. *Berît* ("covenant") and *šebû'â* ("oath") signal dynastic obligations ensuring both David's succession and the continuing protection of Jonathan, but a warm personal relationship may also be discerned. Saul's outburst against Jonathan's "shame" in 1 Sam 20:30 is understood either as rage at the latter's disloyalty or as indicating a homosexual dimension to the relationship. Similarly, David's characterization of Jonathan's love as "passing the love of women" (2 Sam 1:26) has been taken as an exercise in self-justification or as an expression of deep grief at a lover's personal loss.

In chapter 2 Heacock addresses the three controlling interpretations of the relationship, political-theological, homoerotic, and homosocial, and analyzes the major commentators. The political-theological reading appeals to those who envision the relationship in terms of dynastic replacement and succession, inspired by the divine will. This allows conservative commentators to dismiss any hint of sexual entanglement. Some champions of the homoerotic interpretation allow both a political and a sexual component to the relationship, though a minority focuses on the purely erotic that is expressed in homogenital contact. The homosocial stance permits an appreciation of the two positions but acknowledges the difficulty of adopting rigid positions on an ancient text and culture.

Chapter 3 traces the development of the historical study of homosexuality in the modern period. Following scholars such as Foucault, Heacock argues that our contemporary understanding of homosexuality derives from late nineteenth-century categorizations of sexuality allied with the traditional Christian viewpoint. In the ancient world the Greek concept of pederasty was socially permissible but regulated according to a strict code of conduct. Mature males' attraction to adolescent youths was natural; for a grown man to be sexually passive was not. Interpretations of sexuality in Mesopotamia to date rely mainly on Mesopotamian (Assyrian) and Hittite law collections, which, like Greece, are concerned with the male role in society, centering on status rather than morality. In ancient Israel, Heacock maintains, the only direct references to homogenital behavior, Lev 18:22; 20:13–14, "unequivocally prohibit and condemn such behavior between men" (90). The tales of Sodom (Gen 18:26–19:29) and the Levite at Gibeah (Judg 19:1–30) are both demonstrations of humiliation by homosexual rape, the rape of the Levite's concubine adding the dimension of violation of property. Leviticus 20:13 absolutely condemns both the active and the passive partners in a homogenital act. Thus, while ancient Israel shared similar notions of masculinity and femininity with its neighbors, there is the distinction that both parties were equally guilty and the transgression is set firmly in the context of religious identity rather than simple gender role or social status (91).

In chapter 4 Heacock probes scholarly interpretations of male-male friendship in ancient and contemporary societies. The Epic of Gilgamesh and the *Iliad* are the key texts. The majority of commentators acknowledge the possibility of a sexual component to the relationship of Gilgamesh and Enkidu, some more confidently than others. Classical scholars note that the mature Patroclus assumes feminine characteristics in his relationship with Achilles but are similarly divided as to whether there was a homogenital relationship: Plato certainly thought so. The openly affectionate friendships among men that flourished in the eighteenth and early nineteenth centuries became suspect once inflexible categories of heterosexuality and homosexuality came to dominate Western constructions of human sexuality. Thus, contemporary male-male friendships are inhibited and limited to "side-by-side" expressions (118).

Chapter 5 employs reader-response criticism as a way of breaking the impasse in the three major interpretations that emerge from traditional historical-critical methodologies. For Heacock, the reader-response theories of Iser and Fish allow the existence of an open text with which the reader engages in a dynamic relationship, producing the possibility of multiple interpretations, including that of queer theory.

In chapter 6 Heacock claims that the interpretations based on reader-response criticism are as valid as historical-critical ones, themselves projections of a scholarly bias onto an imagined past. For him, queer reading produces a fresh understanding of the David and Jonathan's friendship in the context of contemporary gay male friendships. He argues that their friendship was a complex one, with David adhering to a normative masculinity, while Jonathan's attitudes and actions subverted this; like Patroclus, Jonathan adopts feminine qualities: David's affection was constrained by his status, Jonathan's liberated by his love. Only after Jonathan's death was David willing to express his true feelings. Though he believes that it was a loving relationship, Heacock is unwilling to make any final claim to a sexual component, concluding, "we do not know … and, quite frankly, it is none of our business" (151).

Heacock has produced a well-documented and honest study with an outstanding bibliography. He faces the plain fact that the Hebrew Bible is opposed to any homogenital expressions of male-male love and is rightly suspicious of the school that discovers gays "under every green tree." However, his own reading, based on male-male contemporary friendships, is essentially a variation on the queer theme and, like similar readings, quite speculative. It is a pity that he does not include insights from modern male-dominated tribal cultures, which may be closer to any "real" David and Jonathan.[1] These reservations aside, this book is a fine contribution to an increasingly relevant but divisive topic that many have made "their business."

The Surprising Election and Confirmation of King David, by J. Randall Short. Harvard Theological Studies 63. Cambridge: Harvard University Press, 2010. Pp. xiii + 244, Paperback, $25.00, ISBN 9780674053410.

Steven L. McKenzie, Rhodes College, Memphis, Tennessee

This revised Harvard dissertation challenges the interpretation of the David story, especially the "History of David's Rise" in 1 Sam 16–2 Sam 5, as apology, arguing instead that it is best understood as dramatic confirmation of David's election as YHWH's "beloved son." In the introduction, Short presents a prospectus of the project and explains his reasons for adopting the MT as the basis for his study in lieu of an eclectic text drawn from critical comparison of the MT, LXX, Qumran fragments, and other witnesses. The first chapter then purports to summarize modern scholarship on the HDR. Its real focus is McCarter's reconstruction of an HDR followed by its successive integration into a "Prophetic History" and then a first edition (Dtr¹) of the Deuteronomistic History. While Short finds fault with some of the details of McCarter's reconstruction, he does not seek to offer an alternative redactional model but rather questions the entire

---

1. For example, Lawrence of Arabia praised the "voluntary and affectionate" sexual relationships among Bedouin tribesmen. See Michael Korda, *Hero: The Life and Legend of Lawrence of Arabia* (New York: HarperCollins, 2010) 364.

redaction-critical enterprise (19), arguing that it is circular to the extent that it seeks to isolate stages in a text that addressed historical realities that occasioned them. McCarter's view that the HDR is fully appreciated in the tenth-century context to which he ascribes it is a case in point. The rest of the chapter summarizes McCarter's argument for the HDR as apology based on the comparison of themes between it and the Apology of Hattušili. Short contends that important themes of the HDR are not included in McCarter's list because they do not suit his comparison—another accusation of circularity.

The second chapter reappraises the HDR in comparison with the Apology of Hattušili by following the structure of the latter identified by Hoffner: introduction; historical survey: noble antecedents; historical survey: the unworthy predecessor; the coup d'état; the merciful victor; and the edict. Short characterizes each of these sections of the Hittite work, emphasizing differences he finds between them and the HDR. Thus the introduction and section on noble antecedents work to affirm Hattušili's right to the throne, while the HDR presents David as a nobody and does not draw at all on the notables of his genealogical heritage. In the third section, the Hittite apologies present the predecessor as unfit to rule, while the HDR casts Saul as a tragic figure rather than a villain, and David is also portrayed with a good deal of ambivalence rather than as a one-dimensional "good guy." In the fourth section, the Hittite apologies admit that a coup d'état has occurred, and they seek to justify it, while the HDR neither assumes nor justifies a coup d'état, and such subtlety would be out of place in the ancient Near East anyway. In section five, Hattušili is depicted as merciful to those whom he has vanquished, while David does not defeat Saul at all but leaves that to YHWH. Finally, the HDR lacks any edict proclaiming legal reforms or the like. Short closes the chapter by noting two other differences: the Apology of Hattušili is an independent document in the first-person, while the HDR is written by an omniscient narrator as part of a larger literary work that has relevance beyond the person of the king for the entire people of YHWH.

Chapter 3 critiques the apologetic reading of the HDR by making use of speech-act theory to assess the seven allegations that McCarter found addressed in it: (1) David sought to advance himself at Saul's expense, and he was (2) a deserter, (3) an outlaw, (4) a Philistine mercenary, and implicated in the deaths of (5) Saul, (6) Abner, and (7) Ishbaal. Short's main contentions are that the apologetic reading is inevitably circular in assuming the history behind the text that it (the text) purportedly addresses and that it (the apologetic reading) is not self-evident; there are other potential illocutionary forces and perlocutionary ends that the apologetic reading fails to recognize. The text is explicitly apologetic at the locutionary level only in the case of Abner's death, and Short finds it extremely odd that this—rather than Saul's death or those of his direct heirs—represents the only explicit assertion of David's innocence. He also asks how the account continued to make sense to generations long after the death of the historical David.

The final two chapters put forward Short's reading of the HDR. In chapter 4 he explores different dimensions of the verb in the final clause of 1 Sam 16:1, *rā'îtî*

... *lî melek*, through different English translations: "I have seen/found/chosen/provided myself a king." His contention is that 1 Sam 13–15 present YHWH's decision about David's election as having been made before David is revealed as the choice. Hence, Saul's rejection and David's election are *faits accomplis* by 16:1, and "the implied or ideal reading community is not looking for exoneration of David from this point forward" (144). Then in the final chapter, Short seeks to show how the election of David in place of Saul is presented in the HDR as surprising in view of his and his family's relative insignificance and how it is confirmed first by David's replacement of Jonathan as Saul's beloved son and heir and then by the actions and words of various characters and groups of characters (the public, Saul's family, "all Israel," and even Saul himself) who approve David as YHWH's anointed in place of Saul.

This study raises some important questions relating especially to the reconstruction of an HDR as an independent source and its dating the time of David. However, such considerations do not necessarily refute an apologetic reading of the Samuel material, and the alternate approach that Short adopts is thoroughly problematic. Eschewing historical-critical postulations of levels of composition in the narrative, Short's solution is essentially to ignore the narrative tensions that give rise to such theories. Because of some verbal and thematic links between different sections of the narrative, he jumps to the conclusion that source-critical explanations are "atomistic" and "give up more than they gain" (137n, 156n). Since diachronic analysis can account for both tensions and connections in the compositional process, it is actually Short who gives up an enormous amount by examining only the surface of the text and dismissing matters relating to its depth.

As a result of this superficial approach, Short is quite vague about the audience he envisions for the David story. He alludes to a postexilic setting (116–19, 197–98) and refers to "YHWH's covenant community," "faithful readers," and "YHWH's people" as the implied audience (5, 97, 199), who nonetheless "approach the narrative naively" when it comes to David's ancestry and genealogical lists (163n). The question of audience is muddled all the more by Short's insistence on limiting his analysis to the MT, a move that is indefensible in post-Qumran biblical scholarship, especially in Samuel. Short's reasoning that the consonantal MT "closely approximates a version of the biblical text that was authoritative, and thus relatively stable, as early as the third century B.C.E." misrepresents the diversity of textual versions of biblical books available at the turn of the eras, as illustrated particularly clearly in the witnesses to Samuel. His statement also greatly oversimplifies the question of these and other writings in their various textual forms at this period. Short's acknowledgement that the MT is inevitably interpretive (8) highlights the anachronistic nature of the conclusions he draws from analyzing it alone and points to the circularity of his own approach.

Given the starting point and method that Short adopts, his conclusion is neither surprising nor novel. Members of various religious traditions have been reading the David story as a synchronic unit recounting YHWH's happy choice of David as his beloved elect for millennia. Indeed, a diachronic reading of Samuel allows for the possibility that older apologetic materials were adapted to present just such a portrait of David in final form. If Short, by contrast, intends to exclude an apologetic interpretation of this literature, he singularly fails. The main contrasts that he draws between the Apology of Hattušili and the David story fade on examination. The HDR could not emphasize David's right to the throne as the Apology does for Hattušili because it presents Saul as Israel's first king, and there was no other family with a hereditary claim to kingship. Likewise, while the interpretation of Saul a tragic figure has some validity, the narrative also clearly depicts him at points as a villain who, for instance, executed *ḥerem* against Yahweh's own priests (1 Sam 22) even though he had failed to carry it out against Yahweh's enemies (1 Sam 15). The story of David in 1 Samuel is certainly a longer and more sophisticated literary work than the Apology of Hattušili, and there are obvious differences between them (e.g., third versus first person), but the similarities noted by McCarter persist as indicators of the rhetorical posture of the David material. Short's admission that the apology is explicit in the case of Abner's death (2 Sam 3) seriously undercuts his case, as does the fact that a series of scholars (Weiser, Lemche, VanderKam) perceived the apologetic posture of this material independently of McCarter and without comparison to Hattušili. In fact, Short repeatedly acknowledges that the apologetic reading remains plausible, despite his criticisms of it (119, 127–28, 129), and his counter case in chapter 5 is full of provisional statements about how one "might" read the narrative—surprising tentativeness for an interpretation in agreement with thousands of years of Jewish and Christian tradition.

Short's book can be construed as a defense in its own right—of the traditional, precritical reading of the David story. It is useful as a reminder of the richness of the story and the variety of possible readings to which it lends itself. But the dismissal of text-critical evidence and narrative tensions that Short requires for his reading constitute a step backwards for a work of biblical scholarship.

The Fate of Justice and Righteousness during David's Reign: Narrative Ethics and Rereading the Court History according to 2 Samuel 8:15–20:26, by Richard G. Smith. Library of Hebrew Bible/Old Testament Studies 508. New York: T&T Clark, 2009. Pp. xviii + 274. Hardcover. $135.00. ISBN 9780567026842.

Walter Dietrich, Universität Bern, Bern Switzerland CH-3084

Das zu besprechende Buch hat eine längere Vorgeschichte. Laut „Preface" (xiii) lag eine Vorformim Jahr 2000 an der Universität Cambridge als Dissertation vor. Darin wurde vorwiegend unter narratologischen Gesichtspunkten die Joab-Gestalt behandelt; die Gutachten stammten von Katherine Dell und Gordon McConville. Für die Drucklegung scheinen die Reihen-Herausgeber, Andrew Mein und Claudia V. Camp, einen stärkeren Akzent „on descriptive narrative ethics" gewünscht zu haben—eine Akzentverschiebung, die das Buch zweifellos interessanter macht. (Übrigens lautet der Untertitel, für mich unverständlich, auf dem Buch-Cover anders als in der Titelei: „Narrative Ethics and Rereading the Court History according to 2 Samuel 8:15–20:26"; es ist zu hoffen, dass die Differenz nicht zu bibliographischen Konfusionen führt.)

Dem Aufbau der Arbeit ist die nachträgliche Veränderung durchaus anzusehen. In der zweiten Hälfte (Kap. 5–8, S. 107–228) bietet sie ein „close reading" von 2Sam 8–20 in verschiedenen Unterabschnitten: vermutlich der Kern der ursprünglichen Dissertation. In der ersten Hälfte (Kap. 1–4) werden die methodischen Grundlage für das „close reading" (26–40: „Narrative Criticism"), vor allem aber für „narrative ethics" gelegt (5–10: „Problems for Descriptive Narrative Ethics",10–26: „Theology and Ethics" sowie 42–64: „Justice and Righteousness as Ancient Near Eastern Ethical Ideal and Hermeneutical Construct"). Das anschliessende Kapitel: „Redefining the Court History according to 2 Samuel 8:15b–20:26 as a Literary Unit" (65–106) bietet einen ersten Durchgang durch das Textmaterial unter den gewählten Gesichtspunkten.

Eigentlich ist mit diesem 4. Kapitel alles Wesentliche bereits gesagt: Die „Court History" beginnt in 2Sam 8,15b (also nicht mit der Siegesliste 8,1–14, auch nicht mit 2Sam 7 oder der Ladegeschichte) und sie reicht bis 2Sam 20,26 (also nicht bis 2Sam 24 oder 1Kön 2). Sie ist keine Thronfolgegeschichte, auch keine Familiengeschichte Davids, sondern eben eine ‚Geschichte über das Schicksal von Recht und Gerechtigkeit während Davids Herrschaft'. Der erste Halbvers schlägt (angeblich) das Thema an, das (angeblich) bis zum Schluss durchgehalten wird.

Sogleich stellen sich Fragen: Kann 2Sam 8,15b der Einsatz einer umfangreichen Grosserzählung sein? Ist tatsächlich „Gerechtigkeit" deren leitendes Thema? Ist 2Sam 8–20 wirklich eine Einheit? Kann man 1Kön 1–2 davon abtrennen? Wie steht es mit den mannigfachen Rückbezügen auf vor 2Sam 8,15 Berichtetes? Wie vertragen sich die vielfach düsteren Einzelerzählungen mit dem positiven Leitwort 8,15b?

Um das Letzte gleich zu klären: Nach Meinung des Verfassers reichen die positiven Schilderungen von Davids Bemühen um Gerechtigkeit kaum über 2Sam 10 hinaus, und schon in 2Sam 9–10 (in seinen Massnahmen gegenüber Mefiboschet und den Ammonitern) wirken sie unangemessen und unlauter. Das 4. Kapitel und das „close reading" in Kap. 5–8 dienen im Wesentlichen dem Nachweis, dass und wie „Recht und Gerechtigkeit" während der Herrschaft Davids vollends unter die Räder kamen. 2Sam 8–20 ist demnach eine scharfe Abrechnung mit einem David, der dem altorientalischen Königsideal nicht genügte.

Nach Leonhard Rost war die „Thronfolgegeschichte" bekanntlich „trotz allem ... in majorem gloriam Salomonis" (et Davidi!) geschrieben. Ludwig Delekat interpretierte sie dagegen als generell antidavidisch. Nachfolgende literarkritische Arbeiten (Ernst Würthwein, François Langlamet, Timo Veijola, Sophia Bietenhard) wollten die davidfreundlichen und die davidkritischen Seiten auf verschiedene literarische Ebenen verteilen. Literarkritik ist die Sache des Verfassers nicht; er meint, per „close reading" eine eindeutige Aussageabsicht der Gesamterzählung erheben zu können, und diese soll antidavidisch sein. Das weckt von vornherein Zweifel. Kann man auf der Endtextebene etwas anderes feststellen als eine *ambivalente* Haltung gegenüber David, ein Sowohl-als-Auch, ein Einerseits-Andererseits in der Einschätzung seiner Herrschaft? Diese Anfrage wird später noch zu vertiefen sein.

Zunächst zur methodischen Grundlegung in Kap. 2 (7–41). Hier wird deutlich, dass im Grunde eine inter- bzw. bidisziplinäre Arbeit angestrebt ist, die Ethik und Exegese miteinander verbindet. Der Verfasser verwendet viel Mühe darauf zu klären, wie sich hinter Erzähltexten stehende ethische Maximen erfassen lassen. Dazu setzt er sehr hoch an: bei der „Philosophy of Theology" und bei „Doing Theology" (mit Gewährsleuten wie Gerhard Ebeling und Wolfhart Pannenberg) sowie bei „Aspects of Modern Moral Philosophy" (mit den Referenzgrössen James Fieser, Tom Beauchamp/James Childress und William Lillie). Abgesehen davon, dass er hier weitgehend aus zweiter Hand lebt, fragt man sich bisweilen, was diese Ausführungen für die Exegese der Samuelbücher austragen. Später werden, wie sich dem „Index of Authors" leicht entnehmen lässt, die hier aufgeworfenen Grundfragen nicht wieder aufgenommen, sondern recht pragmatisch die konkreten Texte analysiert. Anders ausgedrückt: Die systematisch-theologischen Klärungen zu Beginn wirken etwas aufgesetzt, sind in das Ganze der Arbeit nicht voll integriert.

Dies ist anders bei den Erwägungen zu „Narrative Criticism", wo Mark Allen Powell, John Barton und Gordon Wenham die Hauptreferenzen sind (Robert Alter und Shimon Bar-Efrat auffälligerweise viel weniger). In ihren Spuren wird der Verfasser die Davidererzählungen auslegen. Dabei will er zwar, im Gefolge Bartons, auch auf diachrone Textsignale achten, doch wird er faktisch zur Annahme verschiedener Textschichten kaum Veranlassung finden, weil seiner Meinung nach in 2Sam 8–20 ein einziges Thema vollkommen kohärent abgehandelt wird.

Dieses Thema soll in 2Sam 8,15b—angeblich dem Anfangssatz des Werks— mit dem aus dem Alten Testament wohlbekannten Begriffspaar „Recht und Gerechtigkeit" (*mišpāṭ ûṣedāqāh*) benannt sein. Ihm und seinem akkadischen Äquivalent (*kittum u mīšarum*) widmet der Verfasser ein eigenes Kapitel. Viel Neues vermag er zum Thema nicht beizutragen: Die Gesellschaft und insbesondere der König haben im Rahmen dieses Konzepts auf eine ausgeglichene, friedvolle Ordnung hinzuwirken. Im Innern wie nach Aussen muss das ‚Gute' durchgesetzt, das ‚Böse' ferngehalten, ‚Zuwendung' (*ḥæsæd*) soll speziell Schwachen (‚Witwen und Waisen') gewährt werden. Dazu ist ‚Weisheit' unentbehrlich, doch letztlich ist die Verwirklichung von „Recht und Gerechtigkeit" ein göttliches Geschenk.

In 2Sam 8,15b nun wird David angeblich nicht zugesprochen, er habe während seiner Herrschaft *mišpāṭ ûṣedāqāh* bewirkt; vielmehr werde dies hier als vor ihm liegende Aufgabe bezeichnet: „And David *began* to establish justice and righteousness for all his people" (S. 69). Das ist eine überraschende Übersetzung von *wajjehî dāvīd 'ōśæh mišpāṭ ûṣedāqāh lekål 'ammô*. Sie hängt wesentlich vom Verständnis des vorangehenden Satzes ab: „*And so* David *became* King over all Israel" (68). Das scheint wenig plausibel: erstens weil dem Kontext nach David die zuvor aufgezählten Kriege geführt hat nicht *bevor*, sondern *nachdem* er zum

König Israels geworden war (2Sam 5,3); zweitens weil—analog zu den sog. Jahwe-Königs-Hymnen—*wajjimlōk* kaum bedeutet „er *wurde* König", sondern „er *war* König (über ganz Israel)". Beide Sätze machen also Aussagen über die (gesamte) Regierungszeit Davids, nicht nur über deren Anfang. In diesem Sinne übersetzen und verstehen sie wohl alle einschlägigen Kommentare (z.B. Alter, Anderson, McCarter). 8,15b ist demnach zu übersetzen: „Und David übte (beständig) Recht und Gerechtigkeit an seinem ganzen Volk". Schon an diesem syntaktischen Sachverhalt droht das gesamte, in diesem Buch aufgebaute Konstrukt zu scheitern.

In einem Kurzdurchgang sucht der Verfasser „Recht und Gerechtigkeit" als Thema von 2Sam 9–20 zu erweisen (70–77). Davids Freundlichkeit gegenüber Mefiboschet (2Sam 9) sei als *mīšarum*-Akt zu Beginn einer Regierungszeit zu verstehen (was nach dem eben Gesagten in Zweifel zu ziehen ist). Der Krieg gegen Ammon (2Sam 10) „reflects the traditional relationship between a king's establishment of justice and righteousness and his responsibility as a warrior to protect his people and cities from enemies and to punish wrongdoers" (73). Ab dann gehe es mit David und der Gerechtigkeit nur noch bergab: natürlich in der Batscheba-Urija-Affäre (ob allerdings Urija der *Hetiter* als armer unterdrückter *Ausländer* hingestellt werden soll, ist fraglich) und im Amnon-Tamar-Skandal, aber auch in der Abschalom- und der Scheba-Geschichte. Die ‚Weisheit' diene hier überall nur als pervertiertes Mittel zum bösen Zweck (stimmt das aber für Huschai oder die ‚weisen Frauen' in 2Sam 14 und 20?).

Intensiv bemüht sich der Verfasser um den Nachweis, dass 2Sam 8–20 eine literarische Einheit ist (87–105). Acht Argumente für Uneinheitlichkeit listet er auf, um sie nach Kräften zu widerlegen—wobei freilich die wichtigsten fehlen: die Herauslösbarkeit von 2Sam 12,1–24a, die Fremdheit der sog. benjaminitischen Episoden im Kontext und die Verbindungen von 2Sam 8–20 zu vorangehenden und nachfolgenden Stoffen. (Besonders wenig überzeugend sind die Argumente zugunsten einer Abtrennung von 1Kön 1–2, S. 103–5.) Bedauerlicherweise wird nirgends der Versuch unternommen, das postulierte Erzählwerk literaturgeschichtlich und historisch einzuordnen. Es finden sich nur sybillinische Andeutungen, wonach es als Sonderstück für sich existiert haben könne, aber nicht müsse (229), und dass es von einem Augenzeugen, aber auch Jahrhunderte nach der erzählten Zeit geschrieben sein könne (232). Das sind gar zu vage Aussagen!

In der zweiten Hälfte des Buches folgt, wie gesagt, ein „close reading" von 2Sam 8–20. In gewisser Weise ist dies ein durchgehender Kommentar, freilich einzig auf der narratologischen Ebene und mit Blick auf die in den Texten vertretene Ethik. Dabei zeigt der Verfasser wenig Sinn für die Gespaltenheit von Personen und die Ambivalenz von Situationen. Was ihn einzig interessiert, ist die Moral, und die muss immer eindeutig sein: gut oder schlecht. David ist bzw. handelt immer schlecht—ausser vielleicht ganz am Anfang. Doch schon mit dem Gnadenakt für Mefiboschet fügt er Ziba Unrecht zu, was sich später rächen wird. Die Kondolenzdelegation nach Rabbat Ammon besetzt er womöglich mit Armeeoffizieren, was die besorgten Nachbarn nicht ohne Grund als Aggression werten.

Die Behandlung der unterworfenen Ammoniter ist ohnehin bar jeder Menschlichkeit („12:26–31 offers more parody than praise", 135; „David becomes an oppressive Ammonite king", 145). Über die Verwerflichkeit von Ehebruch und Mord in 2Sam 11 muss man gar nicht reden. David ist indes auch verantwortlich für die Vergewaltigung Tamars und für die Ermordung ihres Vergewaltigers Amnon. Dieser ist natürlich auch schlecht, und Abschalom handelt richtig, indem er an seinem Bruder „a legitimate execution" vollzieht (S. 156). Nur David will dies partout nicht begreifen, er sieht in Abschalom einzig den Brudermörder. Joab und die Frau von Tekoa können ihn davon nur mit fragwürdigen Mitteln abbringen. Doch längst hat das widerfahrene Unrecht Abschalom in einen schlechten Charakter verwandelt, der auf Rache und Rebellion sinnt. Auf der Flucht vor ihm lässt David seine Konkubinen zurück, um sie hernach zu internieren: ein Verstoss gegen die Fürsorgepflicht für Witwen! Joabs Mord an dem Aufrührer Abschalom ist vollkommen gerechtfertigt. David aber ist nicht bereit, darin eine von Gott verfügte Strafe zu sehen. So ist der General mit der Zurechtweisung des um seinen Sohn trauernden Königs völlig im Recht. David wiederum handelt unrecht, als er nicht nur Joab durch Amasa ersetzt, sondern Israels Angebot zur Versöhnung ablehnt. So trägt er die Verantwortung für Joabs Mord an Amasa und für den Aufstand Schebas sowie für dessen brutale Niederschlagung.

Man sieht: Einen Text, der übervoll ist von inneren Konflikten, von undurchsichtigen Motiven, von tragischen Verstrickungen und ambivalenten Handlungen, löst der Verfasser auf in ein Neben- und Nacheinander von Gut und Böse, Schwarz und Weiss. Die Zwischentöne verschwinden, aus Kunst wird Moral. Ein kleines Beispiel nur: Der ausserordentlich zweideutige Text in 2Sam 13,39/14,1 (hatte David sich über Amnons Tod „getröstet"—oder wollte er ihn „rächen"?) wird auf das Zweite hin vereindeutigt und als Beweis für Davids nachtragenden Charakter gewertet (157–63)[1]. Gleich im Anschluss daran findet sich allerdings ein Beispiel für ein gelungenes „close reading": eine höchst intensive Auslegung von 2Sam 14,2–22, Davids Begegnung mit der Frau von Tekoa (163–76).

Dieses Buch besitzt viele Vorzüge. Die grundlegende Kombination von Exegese und Ethik ist mutig und weitet den Horizont. Der Verfasser hat sich nicht nur eingehende methodologische Gedanken gemacht, sondern sich mit den biblischen Texten eingehend befasst und zahlreiche interessante Beobachtungen zu ihrer sprachlichen Gestalt und ihrem sachlichen Gehalt gemacht. Zu Differenzen

---

1. Leider kennt der Verfasser meinen einschlägigen Aufsatz „David, Amnon und Abschalom (2Sam 13). Literarische, textliche und historische Erwägungen zu den ambivalenten Beziehungen eines Vaters zu seinen Söhnen" (in: A. Rofé / M. Segal / S. Talmon / Z. Talshir [Hg.], Text Criticism and Beyond. In memoriam of Isac Leo Seeligmann, *Textus* 23, 2007, 115–43) nicht. Daneben vermisse ich im Literaturverzeichnis ausser meinen Büchern über *The Early Monarchy in Israel* (2007, deutsch 1997) und *David. Der Herrscher mit der Harfe* (2006) auch wichtige Arbeiten von Erhard Blum, Georg Hentschel, Ulrich Hübner und Timo Veijola.

zwischen hebräischer und griechischer Textfassung finden sich in z.T. ausführlichen Fussnoten fundierte textkritische Erwägungen (ohne dass freilich eine bestimmte Position zur Textgeschichte der Samuelbücher erkennbar wird). Die Sprache des Verfassers wirkt, jedenfalls für einen Nicht-Muttersprachler, gediegen und jederzeit klar. Regelmässig fasst er in „conclusions" das zuvor Erarbeitete übersichtlich zusammen. Eine reichhaltige „Bibliography" führt bis an die gegenwärtige Forschung heran, Indices („Biblical References" und „Authors") helfen das Buch und die Forschungslage erschliessen. So lässt sich dieses Werk durchaus mit Gewinn nutzen—auch und gerade, wenn man gegenüber seinen Grundthesen Zurückhaltung wahrt.

LATTER PROPHETS

Die nachexilische Prophetentheorie des Jeremiabuches, by Harald Knobloch. Beihefte zur Zeitschrift für Altorientalische und Biblische Rechtsgeschichte 12. Wiesbaden: Harrassowitz, 2009. Px + 334. Hardcover. €78.00. ISBN 9783447061148.

Christl M. Maier, Philipps-Universität Marburg, Marburg, Germany

The book under review is a revised PhD thesis submitted to the Protestant Department of Ludwig-Maximilian-University Munich and written under the tutelage of Eckart Otto as well as in conversation with Christoph Levin, Georg Fischer, Hermann-Josef Stipp, and Jörg Jeremias (see Vorwort). Otto's studies on the intertextual relations between Jeremiah and the Pentateuch and his model of the formation of the Pentateuch form the basis for Knobloch's thesis, with which he seeks both to critically continue Otto's hermeneutics and to offer a self-contained contribution to the research on the interrelationship between prophecy and torah (11; see further references to Otto's Pentateuch model at 13–15).

Chapter 1 introduces the topic, range, and method of the study (1–18). Knobloch uses a structuralist and descriptive approach that highlights the *intra*textual relations (i.e., citations, allusions, catenation of keywords, and specific motifs) within the book of Jeremiah as well as *inter*textual relations between Jeremiah and other texts, especially from the Pentateuch (12–13). Knobloch's leading question is how prophetic circles that conveyed Jeremiah's prophecy in postexilic times responded to priestly circles that conveyed the Pentateuch (10–11). His thesis is that Jer 26; 36 are literarily coherent and closely connected chapters that were produced by the same group of scribes in the postexilic temple community in Jerusalem, in the second half of the fifth century B.C.E. (283). They offer a theory of prophecy that subversively interprets the Deuteronomistic laws on king and prophets (Deut 17:14–20; 18:9–22) and simultaneously refutes the claim of the Pentateuch redaction (Deut 31:9–13; 34:10–12) that there is no prophet after Moses. Responding to the priestly redactors of the Pentateuch, the scribes claim that not Moses but Jeremiah was the last prophetic mediator of YHWH, whose words directly express YHWH's *torah* and that Baruch, not Moses, put this *torah* into writing (286–87). While the thesis of the book is stated from the beginning and throughout the book, its substantiation is successively built up in the chapters.

Chapter 2 (19–72) starts with a review of current scholarship on the literary character of and source-critical solutions to Jer 26. Knobloch seeks to refute all observations of literary incoherence in Jer 26 with arguments about intertextual relations within the chapter as well as between Jer 26 and 36. Where other scholars find a logical incoherence, as in the change of attitude of the people against Jeremiah (Jer 36:8, 16), Knobloch argues that the author intentionally created this tension in order to refute the idea of Deut 18:20–22 that true prophecy can be discerned in retrospect (57–58; see also 256–57).

In chapter 3 (73–122) Knobloch also reviews current interpretations of Jer 36 and aims at demonstrating that the whole chapter is coherent and artistically structured in three parts (vv. 1–8, 9–26, 27–32). In discussing the contrasting portraits of Josiah (2 Kgs 22–23) and Jehoiakim (Jer 36)—on the basis of current scholarly theses instead of a new textual analysis—Knobloch argues that both texts relate to the question of origin of the written divine word: since both Jeremiah's and Huldah's prophecy are seen as the divine word, the texts side with each other against the Pentateuch's idea that only Moses mediated the *torah* (118, with reference to Otto's dating of 2 Kgs 22:15–20 as post-Deuteronomistic, i.e., postexilic).

Chapter 4 (123–52) demonstrates "horizontal relations" between Jer 26 and 36, such as a common style, a setting in the temple precinct, similarities in composition and contents, and common rhetorical goals, which result in the assumption of common authorship.

Chapter 5 (153–227) analyzes the intertextual relations of Jer 26 and 36 to the book of Exodus (esp. Exod 32–34) in detail, resulting in the thesis that the authors of Jer 26 and 36 used Exod 32–34 as a direct *Vorlage* that was shaped by the Pentateuch redactor. Against the claim of Exod 33:11 and Deut 34:10 that Moses directly talked to YHWH and is the sole mediator of the divine word, the authors of Jer 26; 36 declare, according to Knobloch, that Jeremiah, even more than Moses, was commissioned to be the mouth of YHWH (Jer 1), a mediator of divine words, and even the location where God is present (227).

Chapter 6 (228–82) deals with intertextual relations between Jer 26 and the passages on false or true prophecy in Deuteronomy (Deut 13:2–6; 18:9–22), on the one hand, and between Jer 36 and the law of the king (Deut 17:14–20), on the other hand. Knobloch argues that the authors of Jer 26 allude to Deut 18:9–22 in a subversive way indicating that the proof of true prophecy in retrospect was not helpful and that Jeremiah absorbs the Mosaic role of mediator. Their negative portrait of King Jehoiakim, who destroys the scroll with YHWH's words (Jer 36), alludes to Deut 17:18–20 in order to show that the legitimacy of the Judean monarchy found its end already under Jehoiakim. In this perspective, the oracle of doom against this king (Jer 36:30–31) is not "unfulfilled prophecy," as many scholars argue, but an intertextual reversal of the fate of the *torah* reader in Ps 1:2 (274). According to Knobloch, the authors of Jer 36 unhinge the law of the king in Deut 17:14–20 in their intentional rejection of monarchy (275–76).

Chapter 7 (282–301) summarizes the results of the previous chapters and sketches a redaction history of the book of Jeremiah, which remains hypothetical, as Knobloch concedes, because the present study takes only two chapters in the book of Jeremiah into account.

Knobloch's study presupposes that its readers are familiar with both the texts and the current scholarship of the book of Jeremiah. The presentation of arguments spread out over several chapters is often hard to trace and requires investigative skills, as the following example may demonstrate. Against Winfried Thiel's argument that Jer 26:3 belongs to the Deuteronomistic redaction of Jeremiah with its pattern of alternative preaching ("Alternativpredigt"), Knobloch argues that the verb *nḥm* "to regret, to be sorry" in verse 3 is also used in Jer 26:13bα, 19aγ and thus builds a coherent idea of God's repentance within the whole chapter (48). He further posits that Jer 26:3 explicitly refers to the Sinai pericope in its post-Deuteronomistic shape (Exod 32:14). Instead of substantiating this claim, he refers the reader to chapter 5.1 (49 n. 108), where he, however, starts out to argue for a literary dependence of Jer 36:3b on Exod 34:9b on the basis of an almost exclusive use of the verb *slḥ* "to forgive" (154–55). On page 155, Knobloch refers his reader to 134–37, where he argues that Jer 36:3 and Jer 26:3 mainly use the same expressions and thus derive from the same author. The main theological difference between the idea of God's forgiving the iniquity and sin of the people (Jer 36:3 *slḥ*) and regretting the punishment (Jer 26:3 *nḥm*), however, is played down by Knobloch's argument that the author of these texts states such a possibility for the beginning of Jehoiakim's reign while he denies it later on (135). Only the persistent reader finds out that the allusion of Jer 26:3 to Exod 32:14 is analyzed in detail on 161–63. In sum, the reader has to suspend his assessment of Knobloch's argumentation until he or she has read the whole book, with the effect of a strong impression of circularity.

The book has merits in analyzing the intertextual links of Jer 26 and 36 in detail and with regard to the direction of literary dependence. The intertexts in Exod 32; 34; Deut 13; 17; 18, however, are not scrutinized on their own but dated and evaluated according to Otto. While most Jeremiah scholars would acknowledge the necessity to approach the question of true prophecy and the relation between *torah* and prophet in the book of Jeremiah with regard to intertexts in Deuteronomy (and even more passages in the Pentateuch), Knobloch is the first to claim that only one specific model of the formation of the Pentateuch leads to adequate results. His thesis of a "Neukonstitution jeremianischer Prophetentheorie" by "Tradentenpropheten von Jer 26 und Jer 36" (287) stands or falls with the acceptance of Otto's Pentateuch model because its dependency from Otto's ideas and interpretations is obvious throughout the book. Although Knobloch hopes to offer "einen eigenständigen Beitrag für die Forschung" (11), his apparent reliance on the work of his mentor does not allow for an innovative argument on his own.

While every interpretation necessarily ties in with or refutes other scholars' work, Knobloch's language is sometimes rather inappropriate. Otto's interpretations are either called "plausible" (11, 90) or at least positively cited and acknowledged

(14–15, 37–40, 44, 131-32, 146 n. 80, 153, 161 n. 32, 163 n. 38, 175 n. 63, 185 n. 90, 191 n. 107, 208–14, etc.), whereas interpretations of Jeremiah scholars with whom Knobloch disagrees are only granted the status of "hypotheses" (e.g., 21 Stipp; 34 Schmid; 70 n. 178 Stipp; 86 Wahl; 219 Stipp), deemed "circular reasoning" (29 Sharp; 61 n. 151 Maier), "with problematic assumptions" (251 n. 86 Köckert), "basic aporia" (188 n. 102 Finsterbusch), or even "*contradictio in adiecto*" (194 Seitz). Such depreciative dealing with dissenting interpretations may not enhance serious engagement with German exegesis among other scholars.

Admittedly, Jer 26 and 36 are both in setting and contents crucial for any theory of the formation of the book of Jeremiah. To date these texts *in toto* to the second half of the fifth century or even later, as G. Fischer and now Knobloch do, immediately stirs the question of who handed down the Jeremiah tradition during exile and the decisive time of an early postexilic reorganization of the Judean community. As long as this connection and the shape of the book of Jeremiah during these periods are not explained, any late dating remains a thesis that still requires substantiation.

You Are My People: An Introduction to Prophetic Literature, by Louis Stulman and Hyun Chul Paul Kim. Nashville: Abingdon, 2010. Pp. xvi + 323. Paper. $25.00. ISBN 9780687465651.

Steed Vernyl Davidson, Pacific Lutheran Theological Seminar and the Graduate Theological Union, Berkeley, California

You Are My People represents an artful view of prophetic literature. Situating prophetic literature in multiple locations of interpretation, the authors provide innovative readings of prophetic books. Louis Stulman and Hyun Chul Paul Kim pay less attention to the well-worn and debated histories of prophets and instead focus their gaze on communities, past and present. Employing the hermeneutic of trauma and survival, they situate this corpus as the work of ancient history's losers being read by contemporary global winners.

The book's four parts divide along standard canonical sections of the three major prophets and the Book of the Twelve. However, the individual chapter divisions demonstrate appreciation of the literary shape of each book. The introductory chapter advances the case for reading prophetic literature as disaster and survival literature. Chapter 1 follows with an exhaustive list of the characteristics of written prophecy as distinct from oral prophecy that at times risks being too definitional, given the complexities of the prophetic corpus. Without rehearsing much of the technical steps that leads from orality to textuality, Stulman and Kim insist on the importance of the written text both for the community that codifies the final form as well as for the contemporary reading community.

Chapters 2 and 3 cover Isaiah, and while chapter 2 deals largely with Isa 1–39, the authors commit to this division principally on historical grounds. Situating justice as a foundation of First Isaiah, they narrate the prophet's critique of religious activity. A brief exploration of Isaiah's work with Kings Ahaz and Hezekiah precedes a much longer section that mines the theme of hope in these early chapters. Having focused the theme of hope in Isa 1–39 instead of Isa 40–66, where traditional readings would place it, chapter 3 instead focuses on the crises of exile. The exploration here shows how the exilic crises erupt in the metaphors about God, the servant of God motif, daughter Zion imagery, and the tensions over transitions in the reconstruction community.

With three chapters dedicated to Jeremiah, the authors take advantage of the opportunity to offer a unique structuring of the book. These chapters reveal the authors' style at its most poetic and soaring. Chapter 4 vibrates with the theme of hope leading to what in the ends sounds like a symphony but in actual fact reflects acceptance of the illusive, intricate, and textured nature of hope in the book of Jeremiah. The authors examine three strategies employed by the book of Jeremiah for dealing with issue of crisis in chapter 5. While they employ this reductionist tactic, the contents of the chapter by no means simplifies how the book deals with disaster. In fact, they point out that Jeremiah stands as "a labyrinth of thick theological interpretations of sufferings" (115). Chapter 6 revisits the theme of hope in Jeremiah but presents new material. While it repeats the view of chapter 4 about the complexity of hope in Jeremiah, this chapter emerges from reflection on the narrative of Jer 26–52. Here the authors are able to ground hope in the context of suffering and marginality that at the same time grapples with imagined futures.

The reflections on the book of Ezekiel in chapters 7 and 8, though insightful, appear less gripping after the solid chapters on Jeremiah. Given that the book of Ezekiel naturally lends itself to what the authors are trying to do, it is to their credit that they are able to offer a look at the trauma of exile as it affects God. In chapter 7 they show God's exile but in chapter 8 focus on God's holiness, God's provision for the future, God's resolve to provide new leadership, and God's deep involvement in the life of Israel.

While most introductions to the prophets appear to be well spent by the time they reach the Book of the Twelve, not so *You are My People*. Chapters 9 and 10 serve up exciting fare for those convinced that the Book of the Twelve is more than just leftovers. Dividing the corpus into two along a dispersion/gathering axis, Stulman and Kim treat the books of Hosea–Micah in chapter 9 and Nahum–Malachi in chapter 10. Chapter 9 begins with some themes already seen in Hosea, Joel, and Amos. Their treatment of Amos resembles that of their work on earlier books, while they focus attention on gender abuse in Hosea and the agricultural crises in Joel. However, they present a chiasm that stretches from Obadiah to Zephaniah built around the oracles against the nations in these books. In this chiasm, Obadiah's oracle against Edom as well as Jonah's handling of anti-Assyrian issues finds their counterpart in Habakkuk's oracle against Babylon and Nahum's anti-Assyrian rant, respectively. They then connect Micah and Zephaniah as books dealing with the fate of Judah (217). Stulman and Kim suggest that, after dealing with northern Israel as a test case of sorts in Hosea–Amos, the collection turns its attention to answering "the questions of theodicy, justice, and hope" (202). They treat the last three books of the collection, Haggai–Malachi along with Nahum–Zephaniah in chapter 10. They show how these books come to terms with God's justice and set the stage for the rebuilding of Jerusalem. While the note of hope emerges again in their exploration of Haggai–Malachi, so also do issues relating to the character of God, holiness, covenant, and Torah obligations as the path to defining a place in the world.

You Are My People offers a new hermeneutic for reading prophetic literature that locates this body of literature in the domain of the disempowered rather than the powerful. As the literature of the losers, prophetic literature fully displays the issues of disaster, survival, exile, deportation, and the numerous concerns that emerge among a disempowered and dislocated people. Stulman and Kim provide a venue for reading this collection of texts from a new and more relevant social location. Their constant dialogue with the social context of the United States makes their hermeneutical endeavors more relevant to the United States rather than an invitation to disaster tourism in an exotic location. They achieve this by bracketing the usual "noise" of historical dates for text and prophet. This book helps to dispel the myth that a biography of the prophet provides an interpretative insight into reading these books. Stulman and Kim prove all too well that the later communities that shape the material as well as the contemporary reading communities hold more value in reading and appropriating this material.

Implicit in much of Stulman and Kim's work lies the notion of power. They artfully channel the notion of power into the service of hope and recovery from disaster. While such a reading strategy makes sense from the perspective of the underside, a fuller exploration of some of the issues relating to power in prophetic literature goes unexamined, especially as it relates to construction of the new world order. The destruction of human empire takes place with the tools of empire, only to be replaced by an otherworldly empire exercising power in the manner of human empire. The seduction that the alternative that emerges after the disaster will be benevolent remains all too real, especially given that the scribal elite responsible for framing these texts serve the surviving ruling elite. The authors exercise skeptical caution at times in dealing with this material. For instance, they point to where theodicy turns out to be blaming the victim (104, 167). Despite this, they appear to lose sight of the contours of trauma in rendering God as traumatized in Ezekiel. The description of God in exile, driven out by the excesses of Jerusalem, "shattered and traumatized beyond words" (158), applies the exilic condition too easily to the powerful deity described on the previous page.

The treatment of the Book of the Twelve and the integrity of its component parts stand out in this work. The novel notion of the formation of the collection around the oracles against the nations brings the book to a compelling conclusion. Not only does this offer an organizing principle; it also provides a way in to reading these books. While the diagram on page 202 serves a useful purpose to communicate their thinking, it takes reading through several pages to fully understand the relationships. Missing in the diagram are the relationships between Obadiah–Jonah and Nahum–Habakkuk, among others. A fuller narration of the notions that bind the three books on either end of the list does not appear later. Nonetheless, making a case for Micah as the center of the collection of the Masoretic version holds merit. Micah's concern for the areas and people lying outside of Jerusalem rather than the overlay of Zion theology that marks Micah's final form show the central thesis of this book. For Micah's turn to Bethlehem for the forthcoming ruler, the daring critique against central power, as well as its refusal to buy into notions of Jerusalem's invincibility, makes it much more representative of the victims of various forms of power than if its singular concern lies with the fate of Judah.

Stulman and Kim incorporate several pieces of contemporary culture into their reading of the texts. These anecdotes establish their point about the immediacy of disaster and survival in the lives of contemporary readers. Complementing these with insights of the use prophetic literature by later communities in their path to survival would have added a masterful stroke to the work. Even so, the authors make the book accessible on several levels and yet appealing to the specialist reader. The resources at the end of the book and background conversation on specialist issues make it as viable as any other technical introduction to the prophets.

You Are My People stakes out new ground in reading prophetic literature. It offers exciting, creative, subversive avenues for the use of prophetic literature in contemporary classrooms and faith communities. While this work can stand on its own as an introduction to prophetic literature, reading standard introductions without this book omits a critical voice.

Transforming Visions: Transformations of Text, Tradition, and Theology in Ezekiel, edited by William A. Tooman and Michael A. Lyons. Princeton Theological Monograph Series. Eugene, Ore.: Pickwick, 2010. Pp. 350. Paper. $42.00. ISBN 1556352859.

William R. Osborne, Midwestern Baptist Theological Seminary, Kansas City, Missouri

Were the Old Testament prophets innovators or transmitters? According to *Transforming Visions: Transformations of Text, Tradition, and Theology in Ezekiel*, the answer is both. This collection of essays, edited by Michael Lyons and William A. Tooman, seeks to mark aspects of transition and transformation in the prophetic material of Ezekiel. The study recognizes the value of the traditions (textual, ideological, and theological) that shaped the prophet and his interpretation of those traditions within the specific context of the Babylonian exile. It also offers a helpful summary of recent research in Ezekiel, while raising questions for future study.

Michael Lyons opens the work with his discussion of the Holiness Code (H) in Ezekiel. Drawing on his earlier work *From Law to Prophecy: Ezekiel's Use of the Holiness Code* (T&T Clark, 2009), Lyons presents several intertextual methods that offer needed linguistic guidance for the difficult task of determining the direction of literary dependence. Once having found evidence of literary borrowing through shared lexemes, he identifies modifications or changes and then seeks to account for these changes by contextual clues, incongruities, or conceptual dependence. Lyons builds on this method by offering five "techniques of modification" (12). According to Lyons, Ezekiel rhetorically transforms his tradition in order to: (1) bring accusation against his fellow exiles, (2) "turn the conditional covenant punishments of Lev 26 into descriptions of present or imminent judgment" (16), (3) provide authoritative instruction, (4) reveal God's concern for his own reputation, and (5) instill hope by giving a transformed picture of restoration built on divine initiative. Lyons's conclusions are sensible, well-argued, and clearly observed in the text.

Next, Tova Ganzel examines the textual and traditional relationships between Ezekiel and Deuteronomy. Acknowledging the assumed relationship between Ezekiel and the pentateuchal Priestly tradition, Ganzel turns to examine the textual and traditional relationships between Ezekiel and Deuteronomy. His study focuses specifically on the language of idolatry employed by the prophet and highlights lexical similarities between the two books, especially Deut 4 and Ezek 8 and 20. Ganzel's examples, while not overwhelming, are substantive and prove strong enough to support his modest thesis: Ezekiel drew from both Priestly and Deuteronomic sources in communicating idolatry to his fellow exiles. Perhaps the greatest contribution of the article is Ganzel's concluding proposal that Ezekiel blended the Priestly concept of impurity with the Deuteronomic concept of exile and divine abandonment to present a theology of idolatry that polluted the land and explained the exiles' current state in Babylon.

William A. Tooman's "Transformations of Israel's Hope: The Reuse of Scripture in the Gog Oracles" proposes that the Gog oracles (Ezek 38–39) reflect a compositional method, that is, thematic pastiche, commonly employed in Second Temple Judaism and therefore are to be recognized as the product of a later author. In support of his thesis, Tooman seeks to demonstrate that the vocabulary of the Gog oracles is similar to the rest of the book, but ultimately he reveals only an imperfect imitator. These imperfections are subtle (i.e., same locutions used in slightly different contexts)—so subtle that Tooman sees them where many may not. The oracles themselves are filled with innerbiblical allusions to other texts in Ezekiel, the Psalms, Isaiah, and Genesis. These texts—grounded largely in other prophetic and/or international passages—are transformed to fit within the universal scope of the Gog oracles and address the issue of Yahweh's involvement in the future of the nations. While Tooman offers many insightful intertextual connections between the Gog oracles and other biblical texts, several of his locutionary connections seem vague and authorially unintentional. In his introduction to an exhaustive appendix of intertextual cross-references he writes: "[T]his chart does not distinguish between deliberate reuse and simple sharing of language that might be common to a genre, social class, or school. It serves only to illustrate [the Gog oracles'] linguistic overlapping with other scriptural texts" (93). Unfortunately, this disclaimer seems to apply to more than just the appendix. Since the idea of a "thematic pastiche" requires the cognitive activity of a compiler, the appearance of unintentional literary borrowing makes Tooman's proposal less compelling.

Turning from antecedent texts to transformations in tradition, Jill Middlemas argues for an overlooked rhetorical feature in the book of Ezekiel: aniconism. Examining the prophet's portrayal of idols, cities, and Yahweh himself, Middlemas argues that, "[b]y distancing divinity from things occurring in the natural order, Ezekiel also accomplished an important preliminary step towards the creation of an aniconic ideal" (122). This ideal is ultimately relayed in the restoration of the temple in chapters 40–48, where there is no description of Yahweh and "[t]he image of Yahweh is transformed into the word of Yahweh" (136). Middlemas rightly recognizes the central role of idolatry in the book and offers helpful comments on the *imago dei* and personified cities in Ezekiel. However, as Middlemas acknowledges, "a paradox" (127) remains in the fact that Ezekiel—the aniconic prophet—uses more detailed imagery in his visions of Yahweh than any other biblical prophet.

Paul Joyce's contribution addresses "Ezekiel and Moral Transformation." Like his previous study *Divine Initiative and Human Response* (JSOT Press, 1989), Joyce argues in this essay that Ezekiel does not present a heightened moral view of the individual. Passages such as Ezek 18, which have led some to see Ezekiel as a transition from corporate to individual morality, need to be interpreted in light of the larger context of a community in exile. Joyce does not dismiss all notions of individualism, only that they must be tempered by their rightful place in the community. He goes on to argue that Ezekiel's moral transformation is instead exhibited in his strong theocentric position. Highlighting theocentric language such as "you shall know that I am YHWH," "in the sight of the nations," and "for the sake of my name," Joyce writes, "[I]t would seem that the primary purpose of YHWH's activity is the vindication of his reputation" (154). Ezekiel's portrayal of future restoration is contingent not upon human activity but on divine initiative and divine self-interest. Such God-centeredness combined with powerful imagery of sin, judgment, and salvation may be less than palatable to some, but Joyce presents a reasoned argument that such was the view of the prophet.

Next, Thomas Kruger offers a detailed examination of Ezekiel's perspective on Israel's history with Yahweh. Krüger begins his work with a commentary on the chapter highlighting what he believes are contradictions revealing a varied compositional strata. Krüger argues that Yahweh's "no-good laws" in verse 26 demonstrate a change in Israel's perception of how they are to react to the divine word. He writes: "[N]ot every 'statute and ordinance' of Yahweh is good and supports life, and for Israel it is not always good simply to do what Yahweh says" (181). The "tradition-critical stance of Ezekiel 20" (178) is a transformation from earlier supposed obedience- and tradition-driven postures recorded in the Hebrew Bible and Ezekiel. Throughout its history with Yahweh, Israel was to grow and develop in its "heart" and "spirit" (Ezek 11:19-20; 36:26-27) in order that Israel might determine whether or not divine directives propagated life, freedom, and justice. According to Krüger, "The god of Ezekiel 20 would not have praised Abraham for his readiness to kill his child, but blamed him for not having shrunk back from such a horrible act" (178). Such a theological perspective is truly a radical transformation, but the question could be asked as to whether or not that perspective is actually present in Ezek 20. Krüger's libertarian exegesis appears strained when dealing with such a strong deterministic text. His tripartite hermeneutical and ethical construction of human life, freedom, and justice seems like a remote interest to a text driven by Yahweh's concern for his own glory. Krüger hints at the possibility of irony in the text but settles on a rigid interpretation that all but ignores any rhetoric or irony found in Ezekiel's history lesson.

Paul Raabe's article on Ezekiel's oracles against the nations offers a summary of chapters 25–32, focusing on the content and rhetoric of these passages. Recognizing that Ezekiel's theocentric perspective produces an internationally sovereign Yahweh, Raabe posits two reasons for the judgment of these foreign nations: (1) the conduct of the nation, and (2) the pride of the nation. According to Raabe, the first reason is demonstrated in the "because … therefore" sequence observed in Ezekiel's oracles against the nations, with *lex talionis* functioning as the standard for judgment. The second reason is observed in Ezekiel's rebuke of the prince of Tyre (28:1–10, 17), Pharaoh (29:1–16), and the king of Assyria (31:1–18). Despite these two "efficient causes" (198), the "final cause" (198) for Yahweh's acting toward the nations is the recognition formula. Raabe goes on to argue that the rhetorical purpose for the prophet proclaiming these oracles against the nations are also twofold: to warn the people not to envy these foreign nations, and to hope in a future where these enemies will be dealt with by Yahweh. Perhaps the most interesting contribution of Raabe's essay is his rationale for the preservation of these oracles. He writes: "Ezekiel's oracles were probably meant to be taken in a typological way. The announced judgment against these particular nations typified divine judgment against all nations" (204). Raabe's work is clear and accurate; however, its rudimentary nature makes the chapter appear slightly out of place in the present volume.

In "Transformation of Royal Ideology in Ezekiel," Daniel Block examines the past, present, and future perspective of the prophet's portrayal of Israel's monarchy. Block recognizes that, when referring to the leaders of Israel, Ezekiel appears to prefer the Hebrew word נשיא ("prince") over מלך ("king"). He argues that in the prophet's mind "the [latter] expression carries overtones of independence and arrogance, while נשיא expresses, more appropriately, the king's status as a vassal of YHWH" (212). Block describes Ezekiel's view toward Israel's contemporary leaders by focusing on chapters 17, 18, and 19. His interpretation of these passages posits that the prophet is addressing the last four kings of Judah in their historical order. Ezekiel demonstrates his transformative tendencies when he begins to speak of Nebuchadnezzar actually delivering the people from their own wicked rulers. According to Block, Ezekiel's negative portrayal of the Davidic line served to destroy any false assurance maintained by the people when hearing of Yahweh's impending and sustained judgment. He writes: "Ezekiel declared that Jerusalem should not be viewed as a pot protecting the people from danger, but as a trap holding them for the outpouring of divine fury, and the exile should be interpreted not as a sign of divine rejection, but of election" (233). When Ezekiel's programmatic restoration comes to an end in chapters 40–48, the נשיאים are recognized as cultic and religious leaders, not political figures. Block's article offers a compelling argument for the prophet's understanding of the monarchy that fits well within the overall message of restoration communicated throughout the book and demonstrates the sometimes significant changes Ezekiel exerted on established traditions.

The third major division of the book focuses on the textual transformation of Ezekiel and begins with Timothy Mackie's essay on Ezek 7. In this work Mackie builds upon the work of text-criticism giants such as Tov and Lust by asserting that the Old Greek of the LXX preserves an earlier, shorter *Vorlage* of the Hebrew text of Ezekiel. Thus, the study seeks to understand the rationale behind the later Hebrew expansions of the MT. Mackie focuses his attention on three discrepancies between the LXX and the MT found in Ezek 7: 12c, 13b, and 13c—all of which make reference to a horde of the צפירה. He argues that "The additions about the *ṣephirah* are an attempt to identify the *agent* of judgment in Ezekiel's oracle as the 'insolent king' in Daniel's visions (Dan 8:23); he is the one who will carry out the destruction of the temple described in Ezek 7:21–24" (264). Therefore, the purpose of the expansion is to show that the oracle of judgment recorded in Ezek 7 actually spoke to a later historical phenomena portrayed in the latter chapters of Daniel. Mackie's real contribution lies in his insistence that textual insertions referencing later historical events were not merely a community's response to history but, more precisely, "a response to an emerging corpus of literature held to be sacred Scripture by its tradents" (267). The purported emendations of the MT reflect an early community interpreting its Scripture alongside its history. Mackie's study proves to be a helpful exemplar for future research seeking to examine the textual history of Ezekiel. The proposed literary relationship between Ezekiel and Daniel, if true, presents an interesting glimpse into the interplay between the fields of text criticism and canonical theology. However, much of Mackie's study hangs on his tenuous interpretation of הצפירה.

The final contribution of the collection, Beate Kowalski's examination of the intertextual relationship between Ezekiel and Revelation, seeks to contribute to the extensive research previously published on the topic by offering a more comprehensive analysis that tries to understand the hermeneutical and interpretive principles guiding John's use of Ezekiel. According to Kowalski, the book of Revelation is "rightly considered to be a mosaic built from OT texts" (284). He points to John's use of Old Testament texts (Exod 3:14; 15:1–9), institutions (e.g., twelve tribes, temple, Zion theology), characters, and geographical traditions as "deliberate signals" (291) that the apostle's Jewish-Christian audience would have recognized. Kowalski kindly provides his linguistic criteria and working definitions for what he calls a "citation," an "allusion," a "mixed allusion," and "contextual and non-contextual usage" (293–94). One can debate his rationale and definitions, but including them provides a helpful level of objectivity to the study. Kowalski claims that his study has confirmed that John's use of Ezekiel cannot be compared with the rules of rabbinic exegesis and that, on the whole, it reflects a "continual contextual usage" of the Old Testament text (294). Denying a typological approach to the New Testament's use of the Old Testament, Kowalski concludes that John's overall use of Ezekiel could best be described as "A *relecture* of the OT the light of Christ" (300). John's rereading and use of Ezekiel highlights the similarities of experience both prophets had in speaking to estranged and persecuted communities waiting on an eschatological restoration.

As illustrated above, the overall academic quality of *Transforming Visions* is apparent. While the debate on the prophets' relationship to their traditions will continue, this volume has made it clear that Ezekiel cannot properly be understood as purely an innovator of texts, ideas, or theology. Despite being a compilation of essays, the book exhibits a high level of continuity and reads easily from start to finish; as with every collection of essays, each reader will value certain articles more than others. However, provided the breadth of the present volume, any serious student of prophetic literature—and especially Ezekiel—will find *Transforming Visions* an informative and helpful contribution to current discussions and research in the study of Ezekiel.

The Book of Hosea, by J. Andrew Dearman. New International Commentary on the Old Testament. Grand Rapids: Eerdmans, 2010. Pp. xiv + 408. Hardcover. $45.00. ISBN 9780802825391.

Heinz-Dieter Neef, Eberhard-Karls-Universität Tübingen, Tübingen, Germany

Der von J. Andrew Dearman (= Vf.) verfasste umfangreiche Hoseakommentar erschien in der Reihe „The New International Commentary on the Old Testament". Diese Kommentarreihe verfolgt nach den Worten ihres Herausgebers R.L. Hubbard Jr. das Ziel, „recent methodological innovation in biblical scholarship, for example, canon criticism, the so-called 'new literary criticism', reader-response theories, and sensitivity to gender-based and ethnic readings" (x) für die Kommentierung der biblischen Bücher fruchtbar zu machen. "NICOT volumes also aim to be irenic in tone, summarizing and critiquing influential views with fairness while defending their own." (x) Die Kommentarreihe lebt von der Überzeugung "that the Bible is God's inspired Word, written by gifted human writers, through which God calls humanity to enjoy a loving personal relationship with its Creator and Savior" (x). Diese Überzeugungen sind in dem Hosea-Kommentar von J. Andrew Dearman hervorragend umgesetzt.

I.

Der Kommentar setzt mit einer umfangreichen Einleitung (3–73) ein. Im Abschnitt „Origins and Transmission" (3–8) stellt Vf. seine Grundüberzeugungen dar. Nach ihm geht das Hoseabuch auf den Propheten Hosea sowie seine Schüler zurück. Hosea selbst sieht er zugleich als „Propheten" und „Poeten" an. Die im Buch sich findenden Prophetien habe Hosea gesammelt und zu einem Buch geformt. An dieser Formung hätten auch die unbekannten Schüler Hoseas mitgewirkt. Es ist die Überzeugung des Vf.s „that little or nothing in the book itself requires a date later than the end of the 8th century B.C. As noted, elements of the book may have originated at a later, or even considerably later, date, but nothing in the vocabulary itself or allusion to historical events demands such a conclusion" (6). Vf. möchte zudem von der "final form of the text as the proper focus of attention" (6) ausgehen.

Im Abschnitt "Literary Features and Composition" (9–21) beschreibt Vf. die literarischen Besonderheiten des Hoseabuches: „the use of metaphors..., paronomasia or wordplays, and allusions to prior national history" (10). In dem Exkurs "Similes and Metaphors for Political Actions in Hosea 4–14" (11–13) stellt Vf. entsprechende Textstellen zusammen. Vf. geht in diesem Abschnitt auch auf die Verse ein, die "Juda" betreffen: 1,1; 4,15 u.ö. Verstehe ich Vf. richtig, so ist er skeptisch, diese Verse durchweg einer judäischen Redaktion zuzuordnen.

Es folgen ein informativer Überblick über den historischen Hintergrund der Prophetie Hoseas (21–29) mit einer nützlichen chronologischen Tabelle (28–29) sowie einer Darstellung der Theologie Hoseas in 10 Punkten (29–44): 1. Jahwe ist der Gott, der Israel aus Ägypten geführt hat (12,9; 13,4); 2. Jahwe hat Israel in der Wüste erkannt (13,4–5); 3. Jahwes bedingungslose Liebe (14,5); 4. Mose als Führer und Prophet (12,14); 5. Israels Bundesbruch und Übertretung der Tora (8,1); 6. Gericht für Israel (8,1); 7. Kritik am Kult (8,5); 8. Kritik an der Baalverehrung (2,10); 9. Israel und Juda als Einheit (2,2); 10. Hoseas Sprache: Metaphern, Wortspiele. Vf. sieht in dem Begriff des „Hauses" (בית) das zentrale Theologumenon des Hoseabuches: „household terminology" (49–50). Zum Umfeld dieses Theologumenons rechnet Vf. auch die Rede vom „Bund" (6,7; 8,1) sowie von der „Ehe". „The prophetic model of marriage and covenant in Hosea grows from the root metaphor of Israel as YHWH's household/family" (59). Der Einleitungsabschnitt schliesst mit einer umfangreichen Bibliographie (60–73).

II.

Der umfangreichste Abschnitt des Kommentars ist die Exegese der 14 Kapitel "Text and Commentary" (77–346). Vf. unterteilt das Buch in 5 Abschnitte: 1,1 Überschrift; 1,2–3,5 Hoseas Familie; 4,1–11,11 Gott und sein Volk I; 12,1–14,9 Gott und sein Volk II; 14,10 weisheitlicher Schluss.

1. Die Überschrift 1,1 rechnet Vf. einer Redaktion zu. Er charakterisiert sie als „Yahwists who moved southward in the aftermath of Israel's demise" (79).

2. 1,2–3,5: Die Abschnitte in 1,2–3,5 (S. 80–145; 1,2–9; 2,1–3; 2,4–25; 3,1–5) mit den Hinweisen auf Gomers "harlotry" (85) deutet Vf. metaphorisch. Das Verb זנה mit seinen Variationen sei „metaphorical and indicates primarily faithlessness in religious practice or social ethics. This is the most common use of the term in the OT, and it is too difficult to sort out from there the precise nature of Gomer's

sexual offenses. ... we must be cautious with any conclusion defining the nature of her particular sexual offense. Her representation of Israel is the primary matter in every aspect of her portrayal" (85).

3. 4,1–11,11: Vf. unterteilt diesen Block in folgende Unterabschnitte: 4,1-3; 4,4-19; 5,1-7; 5,8-7,7; 7,8-9,9; 9,10-10,15; 11,1-11 (S.145-294). Hier werde das Thema der prophetischen Familie von Hos 1-3 verlassen und durch dasjenige des "Bundes" abgelöst. Der These eines Bundesschweigens Hoseas steht Vf. ablehnend gegenüber. Eine deuteronomistische Herleitung von 8,1b hält er nicht für möglich. „There is no compelling reason to posit a Deuteronomic *origin* for the vocabulary of 8:1b as apposed to the conclusion that Hosea and the Deuteronomy (or the Deuteronomist) shared the term *bĕrît* and some of the vocabulary of 8:1b" (218). Die Rede vom"Bund" füge sich hervorragend in die Theologie Hoseas ein.

4. 12,1–14,9: Der 3. und letzte grosse Abschnitt des Hoseabuches fordert nach Ansicht des Vf.s den Leser und Hörer in besonderer Weise heraus, denn er stehe in der Spannung von Jahwes Kritik an Israel und seinem gleichzeitigen Aufruf zur Rückkehr zu ihm. Er untergliedert den Block in folgende Unterabschnitte: 12,1-15; 13,1-14,1; 14,2-9 (294-344). Sehr ausführlich geht Vf. auf Kapitel 12 mit seinem schwierigen Verständnis von V.4a ein. Er bietet nicht nur eine Synopse unterschiedlicher Übersetzungen, sondern konfrontiert zugleich den Hoseatext mit den entsprechenden Genesistexten (301-11). Er gibt zudem einige Übersetzungen von V.4a aus unterschiedlichen Kommentaren wieder (305-6). Die Jakobgestalt in Hos 12 sieht er in einer doppelten Rolle: „On the one hand, the manner in which his actions are described is drawn from traditions about him known to Hosea and presumably to his intended audience. On the other hand, in his deceit and strength, he also encountered God" (304).

5. 14,10: Den Schlussvers des Hoseabuches tituliert Vf. als „Epilog", er sei „sage counsel to readers of Hosea, formulated as proverbial instruction in both form and content" (345).

III.

Der Kommentar schliesst mit 10 kurzen und inhaltsreichen „appendices" (349-82) 1. Baal in Hosea (349-52): Vf. diskutiert die Stellen des Hoseabuches, an denen „Baal" begegnet. Er kommt dabei zu dem Schluss, dass diese „are all best interpreted as references to deities other than YHWH, even if their veneration in Hosea's day may be partially due to alliances concluded by Israel's leaders with other states" (351). 2. Das Lied des Mose (Dtn 32,1-43) und Hosea (353-55). Vf. vergleicht beide Texte und beobachtet "a common matrix of traditions *and* similar points of view" (354). 3. Flora und Fauna Metaphern. Überblick über die Rede von Gott und Israel mit Hilfe dieser Metaphern (mit Stellenangaben; 356-57). 4. Das Verständnis von „Liebe" im Hoseabuch: „The book presupposes a forceful historical judgement on Israel, but the last prophecy in it declares the way open to a more merciful nature" (360). 5. Psalm 106 und das Hoseabuch: Vf. listet die inhaltlichen Übereinstimmungen zwischen Psalm 106 und Hosea auf (361-62). 6. „Sexual Infidelity in Hosea" (363-68): Vf. untersucht hier Begriffe mit sexueller Konnotation. Er kommt dabei zu dem Schluss: „The real shock of the book … is not the negative portrayal of 8th-century Israel, but the portrayal of a God who feels justly wounded, who refused to let the failures of his people stand as the last word on human culpability" (368). 7. Erwählungsterminologie: Vf. fragt nach der Bedeutung der Verben "umwerben" פתה Pi., „nehmen, heiraten" לקח, „zurufen" קרא; „finden" מצא; „wissen" 8 .(70–369) ידע. Das Ostjordanland bei Hosea: Vf. fragt nach der Bedeutung u.a. von 5,1f; 9,10; 6,8; 10,14f.; 12,12 mit ihren Bezügen zu ostjordanischen Traditionen (371–74). 9. Kultzentren: Bethel, Sichem, Samaria, Gilgal (375–78). 10. Ex 34,6f und Hosea: „It would be fair … to say of Hosea that no other prophet draws more deeply on YHWH's dynamic self-definition in rendering him as God for his hearers" (381). Der Kommentar schliesst mit einem "Index of Subjects" (383–85), "Index of Authors" (386–89), Verzeichnis der Bibelstellen und antiker Texte (390–404) sowie einem "Index of foreign words" (405–8).

IV.

Der Hosea-Kommentar des Vf.s besticht durch eine sorgfältige und verantwortungsvolle Auslegung des Texts. Man spürt als Leser deutlich das Bemühen des Vf.s, die Verse sachgerecht auszulegen. Dazu zählen sowohl die vielen nützlichen Exkurse, die zur Verdeutlichung eingeschoben wurden (95, 100, 141–42 u.ö.) als auch die neutestamentlichen Ausblicke, die eine in Umrissen erkennbare gesamtbiblische Sichtweise erkennen lassen (102–3, 279, 329–30). Vf. bemüht sich aber auch mit Erfolg, die inneralttestamentlichen Bezüge des Hoseabuches zu zeigen (vgl. etwa 301ff.). Auch die Forschungsdiskussion wird soweit als möglich eingearbeitet (81–82).

Kritisch ist zu dem Kommentar m.E. folgendes zu bemerken: Das Hoseabuch zeichnet sich durch eine höchst komplizierte Textüberlieferung aus. Im Kommentar werden entsprechende Textprobleme bisweilen etwas knapp und ohne Diskussion behandelt (vgl. u.a. 275, 295). Hier wäre an zahlreichen Stellen eine ausführlichere Diskussion nötig gewesen. – Die Gemeinsamkeiten des Hoseabuches mit Dtn 32; Ps 106 werden zwar gut herausgearbeitet, aber die literarischen Bezüge bleiben offen. Hierzu gehört auch die die jüngste Forschung dominierende Frage nach dem Hoseabuch im Kontext des Dodekapropheton. Wie sind die Bezüge zwischen Amos und Hosea zu erklären? Welches Buch steht in literarischer Hinsicht am Anfang? Wie sind die literarischen Bezugnahmen des Amosbuches auf Hoseaworte zu erklären? Vgl. Amos 3,2 und Hos 13,5; 1,4; 2,15; 4,9.14; 8,13; 9,9; Amos 7,9 und Hos 6,5–6; Amos 2,8; 5,25; 6,8; 1,5 und Hos 4,7–8; 8,11–13; 10,1–2; 5,5; 7,10; 12,8–9; 13,6. Die Fragen nach den Anfängen der Schriftprophetie bleiben im Kommentar weitgehend ausgeklammert. Zudem bleibt zu fragen, ob wirklich alle Texte des Buches auf Hosea zurückzuführen sind und ob nicht doch Fortschreibungen und spätere Interpretationen greifbar sind (Hos 3?; Hos 14?)?

Trotz dieser Anfragen darf nicht bezweifelt werden, dass J. Andrew Dearman einen herausragenden Hoseakommentar verfasst hat, der sowohl im wissenschaftlichen als auch im gemeindlichen Bereich mit grossem Gewinn benutzt werden kann. Dem Vf. dient aufgrund seiner enormen Arbeitsleistung und gelungenen Auslegung Respekt und Dank!

The Book of Amos in Emergent Judah, by Jason Radine. Forschungen zum Alten Testament 2/45. Tübingen: Mohr Siebeck, 2010. Pp. xii + 270. Paper. €59.00. ISBN 3161501144.

Daniel C. Timmer, Reformed Theological Seminary, Jackson, Mississippi

Originating as a dissertation written under Brian Schmidt at the University of Michigan and accepted in 2007, this monograph presents an approach to the book of Amos that draws upon recent developments in historiography, archaeology, and genre theory in order to recast its nature, literary development, and function. It falls roughly midway between synchronic approaches like that of F. I. Andersen and D. N. Freedman (Anchor Bible, 1989) and redaction-critical approaches like that modeled by J. Jeremias (Alte Testament Deutsch, 1995), favoring a relatively simple redaction history for the text that is motivated more by historical and pragmatic factors than by theological interplay between various groups in Judah (and, later, Yehud).

After an introductory chapter, Radine argues in chapter 2 that the earliest form of the book ("most of Amos 2:6–9:10," 130, thus excluding the oracles against the nations and Judah in 1:3–2:5; the Amaziah narrative in 7:10–17; and 9:11–15) probably came into existence shortly after the fall of Israel. With this he cuts the Gordian knot of in/authenticity with regard to this or that pronouncement, at least for those that appear to contain anachronisms (5:26) or impossibly precise predictions of the future (5:27; 6:2). He rejects the arguments of N. Na'aman, A. Maeir, and others that the upheavals suffered by Calneh, Hamath, and Gath could be other than those caused by Tiglath-pileser III (56–60), and finds it "more likely" that the deities referred to in 5:26 were worshiped in the Levant after the fall of Samaria than before, although the latter scenario is "possible" (60–67).

Radine is less willing to attribute material to later redactions on the basis of its grammatical or syntactical awkwardness (e.g., he considers "on the dust of the earth" in 2:7 to be authentic, 21) or on the basis of theological differences associated with the sources identified by historical criticism (e.g., he rejects the argument that "in order to profane my holy name" in 2:7 has Deuteronomistic and Priestly roots on the simple ground that such phrases and logic fit well the earliest form of the book, 22). He also suggests that chiasms of moderate length are more likely original rather than otherwise (30, with respect to 5:1–17, a pericope that notably includes the doxology in 5:14–15). He judges the report of the prophet's confrontation with Amaziah to be an addition, however, because it "interrupts the series of vision reports" (40). The book as a whole "is best understood as a redaction of various materials or large blocks of text rather than a single composition of the exilic or post-exilic time period" (125).

Having defended a view on which most of the book originated in the last decade or two of the eighth century B.C.E., Radine argues in chapters 3 and 4 that the text is not prophetic in the sense of prediction but that it probably was a theodicy meant to explain the fall of the northern kingdom and to help its southern audience avoid the same fate. (Radine suggests that there was probably no united monarchy in Israel and that the northern kingdom developed first under the Omrides; on this view the various Neo-Assyrian incursions in the northern kingdom would account for his southern audience being largely of northern origin, 2.) The post-722 date that Radine assigns to the book's basic form alleviates the tension between the delays of judgment in the first two visions (7:1–6) and the apparent inevitability of destruction for Israel in the last three (7:7–9; 8:1–3; 9:1–6), although further explanation of how the same tension would be avoided if the book were addressed to those in Judah prior to the fall of Jerusalem would be helpful (37, 125).

Because Radine concludes that prophecy is best defined as the mediation of otherwise-inaccessible communication of purportedly divine origin, he suggests that the book of Amos, in part because of its retrospective nature, is not a prophetic text. Rather, the author adopted a "prophetic style" (87 and especially 110–29) while authoring a book that differs in various ways from the more common ancient Near Eastern genre of prophecy. Radine highlights "social criticism" as the most prominent difference between Amos and its analogues at Mari in the eighteenth century B.C.E. and in Neo-Assyria in the seventh (94–101), although there is limited critique of the king for both cultic and social justice offenses in the Mari texts. These considerations lead him to suggest that the genre of Amos is not prophecy (primarily because of its "length, sophistication, and … broad range of topics"), but "literary-predictive" (109).

Radine finds the closest analogue for Amos in the Akkadian Prophecies (including the Marduk, Shulgi, Uruk, and Dynastic Prophecies), which are "surveys of the past in predictive form" (110, following M. DeJong Ellis). This genre is well-suited to the "newly emergent state" of Judah, which Radine argues in chapter 5 was the book's most likely audience. With the influx of northerners shortly before 700 B.C.E., "it is likely that the Jerusalem government would have gone on the ideological offensive (or defensive), producing political rhetoric to handle this new situation" (136). Specifically, the book of Amos would have explained YHWH's wrath against the northern kingdom and presented the southern kingdom as the only legitimate nation of YHWH (140, 169). Radine might have further explained how an audience of refugees from Israel would have viewed Amos's lengthy invectives against the abuse of wealth and power, both of which they probably no longer possessed following the Assyrian onslaught. As for its postexilic audience, Radine suggests that the oracles against the nations were added after the return of Judahite exiles to Yehud in order to reactualize the book's original message in its new context (183), while the epilogue of 9:11–15 espoused the "fantastic hopes for a better future that were being simultaneously written into the books of Zechariah and Joel" (211).

Radine's work makes a valuable contribution to Hebrew Bible/Old Testament research by revisiting the composition and function of Amos, often taken to be the earliest writing Hebrew prophet. Such a reappraisal is timely in light of the present shift on the part of some from confidence in Israel's existence as a united monarchy to a scenario in which Judah comes into its own as a province only after the fall of the northern kingdom. The author is well-read in the literature on Amos as well as in the adjacent fields upon which his study draws; he merits special commendation for bringing his original dissertation thoroughly up to date (even though only three years passed between its completion and publication) by integrating significant literature published in 2008 and 2009 and even a work or two from 2010 (231). In keeping with the series in which it is published, the volume is clearly printed and well-bound and contains exhaustive indexes as well as an ample bibliography.

A methodological point or two should be raised here in order to highlight some perennial questions facing those who interpret ancient texts and other artifacts with a view toward historical understanding. Radine observes that references to the united monarchy are rare in the biblical prophetic literature and infers (not on that basis alone) that its historicity is doubtful (45). Similarly, he demurs before Na'aman's argument that Calneh was taken by Hazael prior to 738 (an argument based in part on two horse harness ornaments on which it is inscribed that Hazael took them from Unqi, Calneh's capital), in part because "the evidence of Hazael's conquest of Calneh is slim" (58). Historiographic decisions such as this are unavoidable, and rarity of reference may be a point in favor of nonhistoricity, but ancient texts are inherently selective, and the archaeological record far more so. The inevitably partial (and often very minimal) nature of the evidence for ancient events may require that frequency of attestation not be made a first-order criterion.

A related question concerns the relative historiographic values of textual and archaeological data. Because Amos is a polemical work, Radine cautions against using it as "a source of accurate information for the historical reconstruction of social conditions in ancient Israel" while cautiously endorsing the use of knowledge gained from other sources to illuminate the book of Amos (218). Since all texts are written by authors with various ideologies, questions of bias apply not only to polemical works such as Amos but to all texts, perhaps especially those with royal origins (almost certainly the most frequent type of text preserved), the ideological aspects of which are well-recognized. Additionally, the often heated debates over interpretation of archaeological data demonstrate how difficult it is to excise ideology and exercise perfect objectivity in a more scientific discipline. Further reflection on the relative priority of written and archaeological sources, and of ways to account for the biases present in text, artifact, and interpretation alike, remains a pressing need; note the recent contribution of N. Na'aman, "Does Archaeology Really Deserve the Status of a 'High Court' in Biblical Historical Research?" in *Between Evidence and Ideology: Essays on the History of Ancient Israel* (ed. B. Becking and L. Grabbe; OtSt 59; Leiden: Brill 2011), 165–83, and the reply of I. Finkelstein in *JHS* 10 (2010), article 19 (http://www.arts.ualberta.ca/JHS/Articles/article_147.pdf).

Despite the inevitable foment surrounding these questions, the overall tone and argumentation of Radine's work is measured and reflective, avoiding extremes that go beyond the evidence and showing spirited engagement with dissenting opinions while remaining self-critical and reasonable. It is also a laudable effort to read Amos's historical, literary, and religious/theological aspects together, and it is a welcome addition to the literature on Amos.

Collective and Individual Responsibility: A Description of Corporate Personality in Ezekiel 18 and 20, by Jurrien Mol. Studia Semitica Neerlandica 53. Leiden: Brill, 2009. Pp. xvi + 290, Hardcover, $154.00, ISBN 9789004170438.

Karin Schöpflin, Georg-August-Universität Göttingen, Göttingen, Deutschland

Der vorliegende Band ist die englische Übersetzung der niederländisch verfassten Dissertation Jurrien Mols aus dem Jahr 2002, die von der Universität Utrecht angenommen wurde. Einleitend (1–11) stellt Mol fest, dass nach landläufiger Auffassung in Ez 18 von individueller Verantwortlichkeit die Rede sei, während Ez 20 kollektive Verantwortung im Mittelpunkt stehe. Für diesen Gegensatz innerhalb des Buches habe es unterschiedliche Erklärungsversuche gegeben: der Prophet Ezechiel habe keine in sich stimmigen Gedanken geäußert oder habe eine gedankliche Entwicklung durchgemacht oder aber redaktionelle Bearbeitungen machten sich hier bemerkbar. Ein weiteres Erklärungsmodell bildet die Hypothese einer „corporate personality", die Henry Wheeler Robinson erstmals 1935 aufstellte. Sie ermöglichte es, einen fließenden Übergang zwischen Individuellem und Kollektivem zu sehen und so dem Gegensatz zwischen Ez 18 und 20 die Schärfe zu nehmen bzw. ihn auszuräumen. Wheeler Robinsons Hypothese wurde seinerzeit in alt- und neutestamentlicher Exegese aufgenommen, erfuhr jedoch auch—durchaus berechtigte—Kritik, die eine Neudefinition des Begriffes erforderlich mache. Außerdem bietet die Einleitung einen knapp gehaltenen forschungsgeschichtlichen Überblick über Modelle zur Genese des Ezechielbuches anhand ausgewählter Positionen beginnend mit Smend und Hölscher bis hin zu Greenberg. Schließlich präsentiert Mol einen Ansatz, der auf drei kurzen Beiträgen aus der Feder von R. E. Clements beruht und die vorliegende Untersuchung bestimmen soll. Clements betrachtet anders als Zimmerli die redaktionelle Arbeit am Ezechielbuch nicht als Fortschreibung, sondern als kommentierend-adaptierende Auslegung, die im Blick auf einen neuen historischen Kontext nach Art der Pescharim geschieht (Rekontextualisierung). Unter dieser Maßgabe wählt Mol einen hauptsächlich synchronen Zugang zu den Ezechieltexten, der im Bedarfsfall um diachrone Rückfragen ergänzt werden soll.

Die beiden ersten Kapitel der Studie wenden sich Ez 18 und 20 zu. Kapitel 1 (13–67) bietet jeweils eine Übersetzung von Ez 18 und 20 mit anschließend versweise erfolgenden Bemerkungen zu textkritischen, philologischen und grammatischen Detailfragen. Kapitel 2 (69-110) nimmt dann eine strukturelle Analyse vor, um so die innere Kohärenz und literarische Gesamtkonzeption von Ez 18 und 20 zu erweisen. Nach einem kurzen Blick auf den Gesamtaufriss des Buches—die grobe Dreiteilung 1-24; 25-32; 33-48 wird teils in einzelnen Passagen durchbrochen—stellt Mol die Struktur von Ez 1-24 dar (vgl. die Übersicht 74-76), um dann festzustellen, dass Ez 18 aufgrund des Genres, Ez 20 aus inhaltlichen Gründen an die jeweilige Position gerückt wurde. Sein Vorschlag einer Strukturanalyse—er hält ausdrücklich fest, dass es mehr als eine mögliche Analyse gebe—orientiert sich an den Kriterien der Wiederholung von Wörtern und Phrasen, ähnliche grammatische Konstruktionen und rhetorische Mittel, vor allem der Chiasmus; hinzu treten inhaltliche Parallelismen. Mit Hilfe von Synopsen (81, 85, 108-9) veranschaulicht er die engen Berührungen zwischen den Unterabschnitten in Ez 18,5-17.21-29 sowie 20,5-26. So ermittelt er eine—gewachsene—literarisch stimmige Struktur von Ez 18 und 20.

Die Kapitel 3-5 wenden sich dem Begriff der „corporate personality" zu. Kapitel 3 (111-44) schildern Wheeler Robinsons Biographie und seine erstmals 1935 vorgetragene Hypothese einer „corporate personality", die vier Punkte enthält: die Gruppe wird Generationen übergreifend definiert, so dass die Verstorbenen und Ungeborenen dazu zählen; in ihren einzelnen Gliedern aktualisiert die Gruppe sich jeweils repräsentativ; die Übergänge zwischen dem Einzelnen und der Gruppe sind in beide Richtungen fließend; das Konzept besteht auch bei zunehmender Individualisierung grundsätzlich weiter. Wheeler Robinson wandte dies Konzept in drei Bereichen des AT an: bei der Betrachtung prominenter Einzelgestalten wie Erzvätern, Königen und vor allem Propheten, dem Verständnis des „Ich" in den Psalmen und Gottesknechtsliedern sowie der hebräischen Ethik als einer Verhältnisbestimmung zwischen (nomadischer) Gruppe und dem Einzelnen. Mol stellt außerdem Hintergründe und Quellen für Wheeler Robinsons Hypothese breit dar, nämlich dessen eigene Einschätzung hebräischer Anthropologie und zeitgenössische ethnologische Studien über „primitive Völker". Das 4. Kapitel (145-86) beschreibt die Anwendung der Hypothese durch Wheeler Robinson selbst bei seiner Auslegung der Prophetengestalten, der Deuterojesajas und der Psalmen, sowie die—doch relativ schmale—Verwendung in den Arbeiten anderer zum Alten (Psalmen, Gottesknechtlieder, Ez 18) und Neuen Testament (Paulus' Adam-Christus-Typologie; christliche Kirche als Leib Christi). Das 5. Kapitel (187-207) ergänzt kritische Stellungnahmen zu Wheeler Robinsons „corporate personality", vor allem Rogersons Auseinandersetzung (in: JTS 1970) damit, die zahlreiche Mängel und Ungenauigkeiten aufzeigte. Nachdem Mol die Einwände, die sich vor allem auf die anthropologischen Voraussetzungen und deren ethnologischen Grundlagen beziehen, zusammengefasst hat (199), zieht er den Schluss, dass die Hypothese der „corporate personality" so, wie Wheeler Robinson sie auffasste, nicht haltbar mehr ist. Dennoch möchte er die Grundeinsicht „that corporate ways of thinking constitute part of the Israelite *Weltanschauung*" (204) beibehalten und die Möglichkeit einer Neudefinition ausloten.

Kapitel 6 (209–56) beleuchtet Ez 18 und 20 im Blick auf das Spannungsverhältnis zwischen kollektiver und individueller Ausrichtung. Zurückgewiesen werden die Standpunkte aus bisheriger Forschung, die von einer Widersprüchlichkeit und daher Unvereinbarkeit der beiden Kapitel ausgehen; die eine Entwicklung vom Kollektiven zum Individuellen im AT annehmen und Ez 18 als Wendepunkt begreifen; die Ezechiels Individualismus in Kap. 18 als innovativ auffassen. Auch die neuere These Lapsleys („Can These Bones Live?", BZAW 301, Berlin 2000), in Ez 18 stehe die grundsätzliche Möglichkeit menschlicher Verantwortung zur Debatte vor dem Hintergrund eines Determinismus, der in Ez 16, 20 und 23 gegeben sei, lehnt Mol ab. Denn er geht in Übereinstimmung mit Matties (Ezekiel 18 and the Rhetoric of Moral Discourse, SBLDS 126, Atlanta 1990) davon aus, dass Individuelles und Kollektives zunächst in Ez 18 miteinander verknüpft seien. Für das Thema der göttlichen Vergeltung verwendet Ez 18 die Sprache des israelitischen Strafrechts, d.h. eine singularische Ausdrucksweise. Die Abfolge der Generationen, die Ez 18 thematisiert, verweise auf die Familie, die als Metapher für das Volk diene. Ez 18 sei stärker individuell ausgerichtet als Ez 20. In Ez 18 werde der Einzelne in kollektivem Rahmen an seine Verantwortung gewiesen. In Ez 20 findet sich hingegen ein kollektiver Hauptakzent, der grammatisch an der hauptsächlichen Nutzung von Pluralformen ablesbar sei—die Singularformen in 20,11.13.21 könne man unterschiedlich, unter anderem auch kollektiv verstehen. Den individuellen Akzent in Ez 18 erklärt Mol mit der Position des Kapitels zwischen Ez 17 und 19, die sich mit dem Königshaus befassen. In seinem unmittelbaren Kontext macht Ez 18 deutlich, dass der Einzelne sich nicht hinter der Schuld der Könige verstecken und das Exil nicht nur den Vergehen der Könige anlasten kann. Das Sprichwort in Ez 18,2 zeige, dass nicht die Verantwortung für die Tat, sondern die Folge des Tuns, nämlich das Exil, entscheidend ist. Auch die Exilierten hätten innerhalb ihrer eigenen Generation Verantwortung zu tragen sowohl individuell als auch kollektiv. Im Ergebnis stellt Mol fest, dass „corporate personality" keine Option mehr darstelle; doch gilt es an einem kollektiven Anliegen des AT festzuhalten. Dieses spiegele sich im Begriff „Haus Israel" wider, d.h. in der Metapher der Familie. In diesem Sinne seien Ez 18 und 20 an der Generationenfolge interessiert, böten aber kein unterschiedliches Verständnis von Verantwortlichkeit. So plädiert Mol abschließend dafür, die Familie als „corporate personality" zu begreifen und Wheeler Robinsons Begriff in diesem Sinne zu revidieren. Eine Dichotomie zwischen Einzelnem und Familienkollektiv im Denken des AT sei nicht annehmbar. Als Gewährsmann aus neuerer anthropologischer Forschung zieht Mol für seine Auffassung G. Samuel (Mind, body and culture, Cambridge 1990) und dessen „multimodal framework" heran.

Zum Abschluss (257–63) fasst Mol seine Untersuchungsergebnisse ausführlich zusammen. Eine Bibliographie und ein Verzeichnis moderner Autoren beschließen den Band.

Lesenswert sind vor allem die Kapitel, die sich mit Ez 18 und 20 befassen, d.h. die sorgfältig gearbeiteten Untersuchungen am Text dieser beiden Einheiten. Bedenkenswert sind auch die Erwägungen im 6. Kapitel des Bandes zu einer inneren Bezogenheit und Durchdringung individueller und kollektiver Aspekte, die man in der Tat nicht immer so sauber voneinander trennen kann, wie in bisheriger Forschung häufig angenommen. Die recht detaillierten forschungsgeschichtlichen Ausführungen über Wheeler Robinson und dessen Begriff der „corporate personality" sind dagegen allzu ausführlich geraten, insbesondere wenn man bedenkt, dass Mol dies alles letztlich verwirft und lediglich den Grundgedanken eines Verflochten-Seins von Individuum und (Familien)Kollektiv daraus gewinnt.

Nahum: A New Translation with Introduction and Commentary, by Duane L. Christensen. The Anchor Yale Bible 24F. New Haven: Yale University Press, 2009. Pp. xxxiv + 423. Hardcover. $65.00. ISBN 9780300144796.

Donatella Scaiola, Pontifical University Urbaniana, Rome, Italy

Il libro di Naum è stato spesso considerato un testo minore oltre che problematico per vari motivi, ad esempio per la violenza che sembra trasudare dalle sue (poche) pagine e per l'immagine di Dio che comunica. Esso è poco presente nella liturgia, sia ebraica che cristiana, ed è citato in tutto un paio di volte dal Nuovo Testamento. Alcuni autori sono arrivati addirittura a sollevare dubbi circa il suo valore canonico, mentre, paradossalmente, questo libro sembra aver suscitato recentemente un certo interesse negli esegeti che si occupano del libro dei Dodici all'interno del quale Naum svolge un ruolo significativo.

Per i motivi suddetti, e altri se ne potrebbero aggiungere, è degno di lode il fatto che Christensen abbia dedicato a Naum un commento ampio e articolato come quello che presentiamo. Si tratta infatti di più di quattrocento pagine, corredate da una vasta bibligorafia (67–148), peraltro non esautiva, come egli dichiara fin dall'inizio, tuttavia imponente.

La metodologia seguita da Christensen per commentare lo scritto di Naum costituisce un esempio particolare di un progetto più vasto che egli definisce "logoprosodic analysis", una metodologia utilizzata per analizzare testi poetici contando le sillabe, le parole, i versetti che li compongono. L'autore mostra che questo tipo di analisi affonda le sue radici in un passato neanche tanto recente, e che dunque si tratta di una metodologia consolidata, anche se il lettore avverte un certo senso di spaesamento quando si imbatte in calcoli che appaiono vagamente imparentati con la ghematria, ai quali viene attribuito un significato simbolico.

Evidentemente la Bibbia ebraica in generale, e il libro di Naum al suo interno, sono stati scritti e pensati in un contesto diverso da quello attuale, soprattutto dal nostro, moderno e occidentale, quindi è del tutto plausibile che vengano adottati al suo interno degli espedienti di natura retorica coerenti con quel tipo di mondo che a prima vista possono sconcertarci, ma che tuttavia presentano numerosi paralleli nell'ambito delle letterature coeve del Vicino Oriente Antico. Il disagio tuttavia permane, soprattutto quando si leggono frasi come questa: «Nahum and Jonah are closely connected in the Book of the Twelve Prophets—as literary complements, as books perhaps even from the same hand, and at least in terms of their numerical composition» (2).

La relazione tra questi due scritti è molto forte, come poi l'autore mostra in maniera più analitica, ma ci pare veramente azzardato supporre che siano stati scritti dalla stessa mano, un'ipotesi convalidata dall'analisi della loro composizione numerica!

Dichiarata fin dall'inizio la perplessità che proviamo di fronte alla metodologia utilizzata, che viene ampiamente spiegata e giustificata già a partire dall'Introduzione generale, resta il dato di fatto che il commento a Naum è molto interessante, ampio, documentato.

L'Introduzione generale (1–66) affronta molte questioni preliminari, oltre a quelle di natura squisitamente metodologica. L'autore si occupa, ad esempio, del genere letterario del libro (a proposito del quale esiste una certa discussione, ma, per il momento almeno, nessun consenso tra gli esegeti), del profeta Naum, del quale anche si sa pochissimo, anzi quasi niente, al di fuori del luogo da cui proveniva, Elkos, che è peraltro sconosciuto, ricostruisce poi un'interessante storia dell'esegesi dello scritto e offre pure una esaustiva descrizione della storia della città di Ninive.

Degno di menzione è il tentativo di collegare lo scritto di Naum al libro dei Dodici, un tema oggi molto dibattuto e in particolare a Giona. I due scritti sono tra loro connessi, come hanno già fatto notare molti autori, e per vari motivi: essi sono gli unici libri della Bibbia che terminano con una domanda, si occupano entrambi di Ninive, citano Es 34,6–7, ecc. Dal confronto tra i due libri emerge un dato teologico importante: essi riflettono sulla natura di Dio, mettendone in luce rispettivamente l'aspetto misericordioso (Giona) e quello punitivo (Naum), entrambi presenti e correlati nella celebre formula di Es 34,6–7, che, aggiungiamo noi, costituisce un motivo ricorrente all'interno del libro dei Dodici.

Naum è un libro che parla della giustizia di Dio e lo descrive come forte, potente, capace di intervenire per punire chi compie il male. Si tratta di una rappresentazione di Dio che rimane valida anche per noi oggi, che preferiamo sottolineare altri aspetti del Signore, dimenticando che pure le vittime del male hanno dei diritti e che il fatto di chiedere a Dio di liberare dal male chi soffre, implica, correlativamente, che il malvagio venga neutralizzato. Tutto ciò ha a che fare con la giustizia, non con la vendetta, e rimane una componente fondamentale della rivelazione di Dio, valida anche per il Nuovo Testamento. Di conseguenza, il libro di Naum resta attuale e ci invita, provocatoriamente, a confrontarci con ciò che vorremmo rimuovere, cioè l'esistenza del male nel mondo e le domande che esso suscita.

Ninive nel libro è un esempio emblematico, una città storicamente esistita, che però assurge al valore di simbolo, al quale può essere sostituito il nome degli imperi, di ieri e di oggi, che presentano caratteristiche analoghe e che, di conseguenza, suscitano interrogativi simili.

Dopo aver chiarito la problematica teologica e aver affrontato una serie di questioni preliminari, il commento vero e proprio del testo di Naum occupa naturalmente la parte principale del volume. Il testo viene commentato in modo analitico seguendo la struttura presentata e giustificata nell'Introduzione. Non ci sono note a piè di pagina, per favorire in tal modo anche il lettore "qualunque", quello che ha un interesse per Naum, ma non è aduso allo stile accademico che prevede l'utilizzo di un certo apparato critico.

All'interno del commento si possono però trovare tutti i riferimenti agli autori citati nella vasta bibliografia iniziale, di cui abbiamo già parlato in precedenza.

Il volume è infine corredato da una serie di utili indici: degli autori, dei soggetti, delle citazioni bibliche ed extrabibliche, delle lingue, oltre a quello generale, che si trova all'inizio.

WRITINGS

Lamentations, by Robin A. Parry. The Two Horizons Old Testament Commentary. Grand Rapids: Eerdmans, 2010. Pp. vii + 260. Paper. $22.00. ISBN 9780802827142.

Timothy J. Stone, Greenport, New York,

Interest in theological exegesis or interpretation is on the rise, as is the genre of theological commentary. This can be seen in number of SBL papers given on such matters, the production of a new dictionary devoted to the subject (*Dictionary for Theological Interpretation of the Bible*), and the addition of another journal in 2007 entitled *Journal of Theological Interpretation*. In the area of commentaries, the pitfalls and promises of the Brazos Theological Commentary on the Bible series have been much discussed. To this bourgeoning enterprise one can now add the Two Horizons series (other similar series are being developed), which counts "theological exegesis and theological reflection" as its two distinguishing features (editors' introduction). With Genesis, Joshua, and the Psalms already out, Robin Parry's commentary on Lamentations is the fourth to appear in The Two Horizons Old Testament Commentary series. The series' focus is "deliberately theological" and includes examining a book as it relates to the "whole of Scripture," contributes to "biblical theology," and engages with the "constructive theology of today." The editors note that the project of theological interpretation is in its "infancy" and explain that the series is written primarily for "students, pastors, and other Christian leaders" (editors' introduction).

The commentary consists of 34 pages given to introductory matters, 122 pages to translation, structure, and verse-by-verse commentary, and 77 pages to twelve short essays that explore the theological horizons of Lamentations. I will briefly examine each of these sections and then offer a short evaluation.

The introductory materials cover the standard issues of author, date, ancient Near Eastern context, exilic context, poetry, structure, canonical location, reviews of past work, and a short outline of the author's own view of Lamentations' theology. Parry introduces his subject by observing Western culture's aversion to pain and tragedy in general and the church's slim theological engagement with the book in particular, which leaves one with little help when examining the book "theologically as a Christian" (2). Lamentations was not written to "construct a theology" nor was it "*by* Christians or *for* Christians" but was received by the early church as a book that continues to address God's people; thus Parry states, "Christians reading Israel's Scriptures cannot read those text as if Jesus had not come" (2, emphasis original). However, Parry still maintains that one should hear the book on its own terms and listen to its distinctive "pre-Christian voice" (2–3). Thus the first half of the commentary is to hear the book's distinctive voice, and the second is to listen to how "the acoustics change" when heard in the "Cathedral of Christ" (3). The focus of the commentary is not on the prehistory of the text but on the literary whole of the final form (4). After reviewing major contributions to the theology of the book, he sets out his own, which is mostly in agreement with Paul House's work (19–28). Parry's own view is that the book's theology of sin and punishment must be located in the context of the covenant (28), which means that Israel's suffering is a "direct consequence" of breaking the covenant (29). The book's focus, however, is not Israel's sins but their agony and pain (29). The vivid expression of their terrible plight is not meant to undermine YHWH's righteousness but rather to make him "feel uncomfortable" "*precisely because* he is righteous" (30, emphasis original). There is no denial of or escape from the fact that YHWH is in total control even as human freedom is affirmed. This means that, regardless of God's ultimate control, all humans are responsible for their actions and culpable for their violent behavior (30–31). In the face of God's great anger, hope remains, according to Parry, because of the covenant. God will not reject Israel forever; though he afflicts, he will show mercy. "In the end mercy will always triumph over judgment because of the nature of the God revealed in Israel's story. This vision of God underlies Lamentations" (33).

Parry's analysis of the structure and content of the book is careful, concise, and clear. In line with the series' intended audience, the commentary avoids technical jargon and succinctly summarizes scholarly debates. Even though it is not as detailed as Adele Berlin or House's commentaries, it still adequately addresses the major critical and interpretive issues. Essential to Parry's analysis of the book is the prominent role he gives Lam 3 (92). He reads this central chapter in light of the whole of Lamentations and vice versa. The man of affliction in chapter 3 is representative of Israel and embodies their sufferings (93–96; see also 97, 115). As such, he is also a model for the community to remember YHWH's covenant mercies (93). Moreover, the man's salvation experience is a foretaste of Israel's future. In short, the man, then, is a model "to emulate and a source of hope" (95). The turning point for the man occurs in Lam 3:22–24 when he recalls God's character based on Exod 34: 6–7 (101). Just as Parry's sees a progression from despair to hope in chapter 3, so he tentatively suggests, against the view of most recent scholarly works, that the book has the same movement. In line with this, Parry does not think the book ends by "giving up on God" or with "the triumph of despair" but rather "with a plea for restoration in the face of ongoing divine anger" and with the realization that "any divine response to this prayer is agonizingly still future" (154).

The last 77 pages expand into theological topics as diverse as the liturgical use of Lamentations, the place of lament in Christian spirituality, the rule of faith, and the area of political theology. This last section is by far the most fruitful and contains the heart of the volume's contribution. After some quick reflections on the liturgical use of Lamentations and other performative contexts in which the book has been read, Parry examines Lamentations in the context of Jeremiah, Isa 40–55, and the New Testament. First, according to Parry, reading Lamentations after Jeremiah is a vital "reading strategy" for expanding the intertextual resonances of Lamentation within the larger canonical context (161). Readers who approach Lamentations from Jeremiah will be inclined to see the enormity of Israel's sin and the catastrophe of Lamentations as the climax of a long story of God "patient endurance" (161–62). They may also see more clearly that God loves Judah, is reluctant to punish her, and even though judgment is the prominent theme, there is still hope because of God's covenant of love for Israel (162). Second, expanding the context to include Isa 40–55 reveals a canonical response to the book as well as a bridge that connects Lamentations more firmly to Christian theology. Parry lists several convincing connections whose overall effect is to reveal a *"radical reversal"* of Jerusalem's plight (163). For instance, there is none to comfort Lady Jerusalem in Lamentations, but this theme is directly reversed in Isa 40–55, where God speaks words of comfort to Jerusalem that her exile has ended and her iniquity has been pardoned (163–64). Parry goes on to argue that the man in Lam 3 has influenced the Servant figure in Isa 40–55. The suffering of both figures parallels that of Lady Zion (167). Since Isaiah's Servant has strong ties to the New Testament portrait of Christ, it is then possible to see the man in Lam 3 "as a partial type of Christ" (167). Third, Parry sets up is discussion of Lamentations in the New Testament by drawing connections between humanity, Israel, Christ, and the church. Following the work of N. T. Wright, Parry proposes that "Adam's story has been told in light of Israel's story, with the effect that Israel's story is presented as a retelling of Adam's" (169). The Targum on Lamentations supports such a notion when it declares that the punishment of Jerusalem is similar to that of Adam and Eve when they are expelled from the garden of Eden (170). In the New Testament, then, since Christ represents Israel, his suffering on the cross should rightly be seen as "participating in Israel's exilic sufferings" (171). This invites one to "read Lamentations in light of the cross and the cross in light of Lamentations" says Parry (172). Based on this, he concludes, "The potential for fresh insight emerging from such imaginative theological engagement with the text is immense and very open-ended" (172).

In two small sections labeled "Expanding Context" Parry explores Christian anti-Semitism and political theology (174–80). His first point is that Christian have played the role of the *"oppressive nation"* when they have persecuted Jews and should then hear the voice of their victims in the anguish and sorrow of

Lamentations. This perspective should chasten the church and expose their actions for the atrocities that they are (175–76). This certainly could help the church hear voices they have ignored or silenced, but in my view it should also be said, when such an analogy is being made, that the reverse is not true: the church's unjust persecution of the Jews is *not* part of God's judgment on them for their sins. Parry does not even hint at the reverse of this analogy, and his sensitivity to this issue in other places in the commentary reveals that he would not make such a claim. His second point discusses how Lamentations functions as a "critique of empire" as it witnesses against the horrors of political turmoil that are on display through the use of "excessive and indiscriminate military force" (178).

Parry then turns to the rule of faith as a way to focus on Christ among the diversity of the canonical books. First, he compares Christ with Lady Jerusalem. Of course, Jesus' suffering was not identical to Zion's, yet they overlap in a number of ways (181–82). Second, he compares Christ's death with the destruction of the temple. Matthew 27:39 appears to echo Lam 2:15 as it describes those who pass by Jesus on the cross. From here Parry explores the idea that Israel's temple represented the entire cosmos and thus when destroyed it symbolizes the destruction of the earth (184). Thus, "Heaven and earth symbolically end with the death of the Messiah-temple, and his resurrection is the foundation of the renewed heavens and earth" (184). Parry concludes the section on the rule of faith by discussing the relationship between the "valiant man" of Lam 3, righteous victims (cf. Lam 4:14 and Matt 23:35), and the captured Messiah in Lam 4:20 to Christ (185–90). With so many comparisons between Christ's suffering and Lamentations, Parry then asks if this neutralizes Lamentations. In other words, does the Christian hope of resurrection nullify the extreme pain of Lamentations? "It does not trivialize the suffering any more than the resurrection trivializes the cross," declares Parry (191).

The last few essays deal with God's anger, the day of YHWH and the cross, theodicy, Christian spirituality, the practice of coping with theodicy, and Lamentations and ethics. Each of these could be examined, but I want to end by looking at how Parry handles the question of theodicy because it is at the heart of his theological analysis of Lamentations. He notes that Lamentations is not concerned with the philosophical problems of theodicy, but it may partially address this question, since it claims "suffering is a just punishment for sin" (202). Yet this is inadequate even if true, since Lamentations also recognizes that the righteous can suffer (202–3). Parry shifts God's relationship to the sufferer from "God-standing-over-against-the-afflicted to God-standing-with-the-afflicted" (203). God in Christ does not stand apart from pain, but in solidarity he participates fully in suffering even to the point of death. This does "not *explain, excuse,* or *justify* God in the face of horror" according to Parry, but it does reshape the contours of the discussion (206, emphasis original).

I will conclude with a short evaluation of Parry's commentary on Lamentations. The introductory material and the verse-by-verse analysis that make up most of the commentary display well-reasoned, carefully qualified, and sound judgments throughout. It is perfectly pitched to the intended audience of students and pastors, yet there is plenty for scholars to take note of. In short, this part of the commentary is outstanding. The heart of the commentary and its greatest contribution, however, are found in the theological essays that make up the last third of the volume. This last section breaks new ground and raises a number of richly theological questions. Of course, taking roads less traveled means that one has few dialogue partners and that one may occasionally take a wrong turn. In view of the explicitly theological interests of the work, I was surprised not to see Parry dialogue with Christopher Seitz; particularly the essays in *Word without End* (Waco, Tex.: Baylor University Press, 2004) on "Isaiah and Lamentations: The Suffering and Afflicted Zion" and "The City in Christian Scripture" could have sharpened and added to the discussion. Even if one thinks that Parry has made several wrong turns—I, for instance, am not convinced by Parry's argument that Lamentations is a "critique of empire"—the work is fresh, provocative, and an invaluable resource for anyone interested in Lamentations' theology. If there is a failing of the commentary, the fault is not Parry's but the difficulty with which the particular function of Lamentations fits into the mold of commentary writing in general. Lamentations is not Romans. In this regard, more could have been said about the liturgical reception and performative function of Lamentations in the living communities that treasure it as Scripture (of course, Parry touched on these subjects), but even this would not have overcome the problem. Explanations of Lamentations in the liturgy, set to music and dramatically read, are just that, explanations. When Parry discusses the "grotesque and shocking" (85) images of Lamentations, his explanations are insightful, but something is still missing. Perhaps this is because the book's design is not so much to kindle the mind as it is to break the heart.

Finally, I want to offer a closing word on what Parry's commentary reveals about the project of writing theological commentary in general. Parry's work is of a high quality from beginning to end. When viewed as a whole, however, the commentary sets in relief a pressing issue of the genre. Even in its infancy, as the editors suggest, the genre of theological commentary appears to be constrained by its medium from growing into its full stature. These growing pains are clearly in view by the juxtaposition of the first 158 pages devoted to traditional aspects of the medium and the last 77 to theological essays. By far it is the last and smallest section that is the most theologically fruitful. Of course, to bridge the gap between biblical studies and theology one must have deep exegetical roots, but I wonder if rehearsing information that has been covered many times, even if adding nuances here and there, is worth the space. Parry's essays open lots of theological doors (a great improvement from other works on Lamentations), but seldom are these explored at any length. Perhaps a more synthetic approach would not only reveal the exegetical foundations of theology in Lamentations but also provide more space to develop that theology. The Theology of the Book of ... series with Cambridge University Press is a good example of this (I am thinking specifically of

Walter Moberly's contribution on Genesis), but even here the small size of the volumes inhibits the breadth of theological reflection. It is time for a publisher to be bold enough to break with a good-selling format and create a new genre for the theological interpretation of the Bible.

Psalms, by William P. Brown. Interpreting Biblical Texts. Nashville: Abingdon, 2010. Pp. xiv + 185. Paper. $20.00. ISBN 9780687008452.

Harry P. Nasuti, Fordham University, Bronx, New York

According to its editors, the Interpreting Biblical Texts series is pedagogical in intent, more concerned with "guiding the reader" to the present interpretation of a particular book than with "engaging in debates with other scholars." In keeping with these aims, William Brown has not attempted to present a formal introduction to the book of Psalms as much as to outline a "series of interrelated approaches in which the Psalms can be fruitfully interpreted by a new generation of students." His aim is more to open up discussion than to provide definitive answers.

As one might expect from such a noted psalms scholar, Brown succeeds admirably in what he sets out to do. This is an informed and engaging guide to the most recent trends in psalms research, one that opens up creative possibilities for both classroom and community use. As part of his presentation, Brown provides expert expositions of a number of individual psalms, as well as perceptive insights on relations between the psalms and magisterial articulations of broader themes. While this work is primarily meant for those unfamiliar with more recent psalms scholarship, more advanced students and fellow scholars will undoubtedly be interested in Brown's judicious positions on a number of issues that are being debated at the present time.

Given Brown's previous fine work on the poetry of the psalms, it is fitting that he begins his overview with a discussion of those elements that distinguish poetry from prose. The first of these is poetry's artistic or aesthetic quality, which shows itself in imagery and a "synergy between sense and sound." Second, poetry has a density of expression, a convergence of verbal compactness and semantic intensity that generates ambiguity and multiple readings. Finally, poetry has performative power, an ability to provide an experience for the reader, who is brought into an intimate relationship with the poem's speaking voice.

Much of the present book consists of Brown's demonstrations of the ways in which the psalms share these characteristics of poetry. With respect to the aesthetic quality of the psalms, Brown devotes most of the first chapter to a consideration of parallelism. He first explains the historically significant work of the eighteenth-century scholar Robert Lowth, with its influential categories of synonymous, antithetical, and synthetic parallelism. He then takes note of the way more modern scholars (such as James Kugel, Robert Alter, and Adele Berlin) have developed Lowth's categories into a more dynamic and comprehensive approach.

He concludes this chapter with an extended discussion of Ps 147 that analyzes in detail the prosody of its line by line poetic movement before addressing the psalm's overall coherence and perspective.

The focus of the second chapter is metaphor, the subject of Brown's earlier book, *Seeing the Psalms: A Theology of Metaphor* (Louisville: Westminster John Knox, 2002). As in the first chapter, Brown begins his analysis with a brief general discussion. Drawing on both classical and contemporary views, Brown argues that metaphors bring together analogous and anomalous elements to create new meaning that is naturally polyvalent with a surplus of semantic connections. He then goes on to illustrate this process with perceptive analyses of the shepherd metaphor in Ps 23 and the water imagery in Ps 42.

Brown's third chapter looks at the genres of the psalms along the form-critical lines of Hermann Gunkel. The genres he discusses here (hymns, thanksgiving songs, royal songs, complaint songs, etc.) will be fairly familiar to most biblical scholars. Less familiar, perhaps, will be the flexible approach that Brown takes to a number of genre issues, such as the way he sees many possible reasons for the sudden shift in mood that one finds in complaint psalms. In keeping with this flexibility is the way that Brown sees the boundaries between genres as "fuzzy," allowing him to locate them along a spectrum from complaint to praise, with thanksgiving in the middle. With regard to setting, Brown also argues for a more flexible approach, noting that the psalms were not functionally restricted to their "generic settings" but were able to be reused in different contexts.

This reuse of the psalms by subsequent individuals and communities forms the basis of Brown's next chapter, on the psalms as performance. Here Brown considers the way the psalmist's words become the reader's words, as that reader is "compelled" to take on the subject position of the first-person speaker of the psalms across a full range of emotions and ritual activities. Of particular importance is the way that Brown sees the psalms as shaping the reader's desire for God and the temple. Building on the work of Sigmund Mowinckel and Walter Brueggemann, Brown sees the psalms as transformative, both in their ritual and in their more "meditative" usage. Worthy of particular note here is Brown's refusal to follow those who see these two usages in opposition to each other. For Brown, both involve "performing" the psalms in an active and transformative way.

In the next two chapters Brown turns to the way that these texts now exist in the book of Psalms. He first looks at the collections and clusters that make up the "motley and complex" corpus of the Psalter. These include collections identified either by their personal superscriptions (Davidic, Korahite, Asaphite) or by other more literary distinctions (Elohistic collection, enthronement hymns, songs of ascents, hallelujah psalms). Brown looks in detail at a number of these groupings and sets forth some thoughts on the way that the psalms in these collections "become dialogically engaged as we read them sequentially in their juxtaposed positions." He concludes with a detailed discussion of Pss 15–24, which he sees as a literary cluster with a chiastic arrangement that highlights the "cosmic Torah" in Ps 19.

Of particular interest in this chapter is Brown's discussion of the Davidic psalms, which follows recent trends in retrieving David's significance for the book of Psalms. While acknowledging the obvious historical difficulties, Brown sees the Davidic connection as providing an important new layer of interpretation with a distinctly pastoral function. By reading the psalms with David in mind, an individual takes on David's own voice, identifying with him and coming to share in his intimate relationship with God. These psalms humanize and "democratize" David, even as they "Davidize" those who read them in this way.

Brown's next chapter looks at the book of Psalms as a whole. While taking note of the work of a number of other scholars who have engaged the Psalter as a book, Brown takes what he sees as a somewhat different, though not unrelated, approach. Crucial for him are Pss 1 and 2 (the Psalter's "hermeneutical spectacles"), whose themes he then traces throughout the rest of the book. In keeping with his concern for the performative nature of the psalms, Brown also is interested in the Psalter's "rhetorical dynamics," the way the reader assumes the positions of speaker and addressee throughout. After explaining his method, Brown provides an extended analysis of the way the rest of the Psalter engages its opening themes of "righteousness and refuge, *tôrâ* and Zion, judgment and protection, justice and kingship, instruction and dominion, pathway and sanctuary, individual and king, happiness and wrath."

In his last substantive chapter, Brown looks at what these texts tell us about the nature of God and humanity. In keeping with his earlier observations, Brown freely acknowledges the difficulties that the psalms' metaphorical and situational nature poses for constructing a coherent "theological anthropology" on the basis of these texts. It is, however, the fact that the psalms offer a performance-based "messy" theology "from below" that allows them to make their unique theological contribution.

Brown approaches this theological task from the perspective of the different psalm genres, moving from what he sees as the "anthropocentric" orientation of the complaint petitions to the "theocentric" orientation of the hymns (which are for him the "culmination of Israel's understanding of God and God's way in the world"). In his examination of each of these genres, Brown looks first at their picture of the human self and then at their image of God. He concludes with a view a humanity that is both dignified and dependent and a view of God that includes both "transcendent power" and "providential immanence."

Brown concludes his book with a short chapter that highlights the metaphor of the psalms as temple. For Brown, the book of Psalms is a house of prayer and instruction, rooted in the *tôrâ* of God's word and work and climaxing in the human response of praise. For a reliable tour of this temple and the way it is currently understood, both students and other readers can be most grateful for Brown's own clear and illuminating work.

Gleaning Ruth: A Biblical Heroine and Her Afterlives, by Jennifer L. Koosed. Studies on Personalities of the Old Testament. Columbia: University of South Carolina Press, 2011. Pp. xiv + 173. Hardcover. $39.95. ISBN 9781570039836.

Helen Leneman, Bethesda, Maryland

This beautifully written book breaks new ground, discussing the book of Ruth from several unfamiliar perspectives: anthropology, ancient and modern farming customs, kinship practices, even some history of food production. Koosed also includes reception history, with a discussion of film, fiction, and poetry. She treats the central theme of harvest metaphorically in order to stress the social and geographical context of the story. The author's highly eclectic approach offers many compelling insights into one of the most popular books of the Hebrew Bible.

In her preface, Koosed highlights the centrality of food in Ruth. More than the motivator of the plot, it is "intimately linked to gender, sexuality, reproduction, and ethnicity" (x). Though this has been noted before in other studies of Ruth, Koosed is the first to delve into the disciplines of anthropology and archaeology in her examination of agriculture and eating in Iron Age Judah. This additional scholarship greatly enhances her literary study of the book. She makes a convincing case for her thesis that the season and setting of the book of Ruth are not just a backdrop, as they are often viewed, but are central to the whole story.

Koosed herself obviously feels a strong personal connection to the earth and to farming. She writes with poetic lyricism: "Ruth stands in the fields of grain, each leaf transforming the inorganic to the organic, each seed a nexus of sunlight, water, and soil" (xi). She closes her preface with a nod to Ruth's afterlives in different times and cultures—through "theologians and rabbis, writers and directors" (xi). Koosed might have gone a few steps further and included later artistic representations of Ruth, which she barely touches on (discussing Exum's work in this area, 58–59) and music. Surprisingly, Koosed makes no mention of my 2007 book on Ruth as reinterpreted in music. Though most of Koosed's attention is on literary afterlives, a brief foray into musical afterlives would have further enriched this aspect of her book.

In the first chapter, "Gleaning," Koosed discusses a variety of different approaches to Ruth. Chapters about agriculture are interspersed with those on literary analysis: chapters 2, 5, and 7 are called "Agricultural Interludes" and keep the book focused on this theme. In other chapters Koosed discusses Ruth's relationships with four other characters: Orpah, Naomi, Boaz, and Obed.

Koosed's literary analysis in chapter 1 is a good summary of other scholars' work. She tries to explain the key word *hesed*, which cannot be translated by a single English word. She says it embraces "actions and attitudes of love, kindness, mercy, care," then claims that Ruth embodies all these values. This very traditional view of Ruth is almost immediately contradicted by the author herself. On the very next page Koosed admits that there are gaps between Ruth's words and actions and that she is "Janus-faced, a trickster in the fields and on the threshing-room floor" (6, 73).

Koosed gives a disproportionate amount of attention to an avant-garde documentary film about gleaners by French director Agnes Varda. As Koosed herself admits, Varda never refers to Ruth, making this film irrelevant to a greater understanding of the biblical narrative. Its importance to Koosed is in its depiction of the gleaners, but the discussion does not really add to her book. She moves back and forth between the Varda film, Millet's and Breton's nineteenth-century paintings of gleaners, and a Cynthia Ozick essay on Ruth whose jumping-off point is another painting of a gleaner (7). Though her discussion of Varda's film is too lengthy, Koosed does present a variety of scholarly views on the book of Ruth's origins, its genre, and the genealogy at the conclusion of the book.

Koosed tries to make a case for Ruth as a comedy, which has been attempted before, most notably by Nehama Aschkenasy, but Koosed does not support the assertion that most of Ruth is "told primarily through witty dialogue." She should have offered examples of this blanket statement. Her opinion of Naomi's early speech in the book as "bawdy" (15, 16) is also debatable. Later in the book, however, the picture of Ruth laden down with grain and trying to sneak home at dawn could certainly be seen as a comic or bawdy scene, as Koosed suggests (93). Koosed considers the removal of the shoe to seal the legal arrangement in the final scene to be an element of humor, but it is simply a legal convention that would not have been viewed as humorous in its time. Yet her concluding advice to the reader to shift expectations in order to allow the true character of Ruth to emerge is excellent; as she says, this will allow Ruth to "look out from between the pages, wryly grin and wink at the reader" (16).

Each "Agricultural Interlude" opens with Koosed's personal and often dreamlike memories of growing up on a farm. She then moves seamlessly back to the centrality of food in the plot of Ruth, creating a convincing parallel. As she says, "no other biblical book foregrounds actual agricultural practices" the way Ruth does (21). In chapter 2 Koosed draws on a book about life along the United States–Mexican border and applies many of its concepts to the story of Ruth. As she says, "both Ruth and Naomi are border crossers" (26), and the implications of this condition are universal. This new and fresh approach to Ruth's story greatly enriches its reading.

Themes in Ruth often highlighted by commentators—Ruth's Moabite origins, Orpah's motives, the idea of conversion, and many others—are discussed from a wide range of perspectives. Koosed includes rabbinic midrash, recent scholarship, and an excellent discussion of both colonial and postcolonial interpretations, such as the popular 1885 novel *King Solomon's Mines*, by H. Rider Haggard (41–45). In addition to stressing how postcolonial interpretation can lead to new ways of seeing Ruth, Koosed also points to the importance of letting the characters "speak with their own voices and not become just puppets mouthing contemporary woes" (49). This important caveat is too often not heeded by commentators.

In chapter 4 Koosed offers a wide-ranging discussion of Ruth and Naomi's relationship. She includes more than one queer reading, leading to discussion of the 1987 novel *Fried Green Tomatoes at the Whistle Stop Café*, by Fannie Flagg (56–57).

Koosed's conclusions are based on a close reading and understanding of the Hebrew text, in which the ambiguity is very possibly intentional. As she says, commentators who try to find a single answer to the ambiguous Ruth-Naomi relationship are closing off the possibility that the very uncertainty is itself the meaning (63).

Chapter 5, the second "Agricultural Interlude," is a fascinating examination of the history of bread-making. Bread is central to Ruth, even if it is not overtly mentioned; its centrality would have been understood by contemporary readers. Koosed draws on books of food history that have never been used in analyzing Ruth, offering a deeper and more comprehensive picture of the story than other commentaries. Very interesting factoids are sprinkled throughout the chapter: barley was considered the bread of the poor, inferior to wheat, thus immediately indicating Ruth's low economic status to contemporary readers of the book (68). The words "company" and "companion" are based on the Latin "with bread" (69 n. 27). Koosed engages in "idyll-bashing" in demolishing the common romanticized notion of the "pastoral" book of Ruth. As she points out, farming is back-breaking labor involving hours of working in the sun and wind, living on the edge of disaster (69).

Chapter 6 explores the Ruth-Boaz relationship, and Koosed offers more of her insightful analysis. Always keeping the contemporary context in the foreground, she points out that Ruth did not need Boaz's kindness or permission to glean; this was her right under the law. Koosed therefore perceives a mocking tone in Ruth's exaggerated expressions of gratitude for his "generosity" (76). Throughout the chapter Ruth's speech is misleading and mocking; Koosed asserts that she is "laughing at Boaz, at Naomi, and ultimately at God" (77), though she does not support this final assertion textually. Koosed returns to the Varda film to make a tenuous but unconvincing connection to its representation of gleaners (78). She offers a convincing portrait of an "arbitrary" God in Ruth (83) but not of Ruth's attitude to God. She discusses a novel, *The Book of Ruth*, by Jane Hamilton (1988), even though its connection to the biblical book is tenuous at best. Koosed tries to link the two through the themes of its agricultural setting, the meaning of compassion, and the absence of God (84), but it is not much more convincing or enlightening than her use of the Varda film.

Koosed mentions that the notion of a great love between Ruth and Boaz is common in popular interpretations, and she cites popular Hollywood movies and nineteenth-century poetry. This discussion would have benefited from familiarity with my article about musical interpretations ("Ruth and Boaz Love Duets as Examples of Musical Midrash," *lectiodifficilior* [2006]; see http://www.lectio.unibe.ch/06_1/leneman_love_duets.htm).

Koosed returns again and again to the centrality of the earth, harvest, and grain in the book of Ruth. In chapter 7, the third "Agricultural Interlude," she writes in a lyrical and densely metaphorical passage (94): "Grain is another character in the book of Ruth, omnipresent yet overlooked, ubiquitous yet unseen. The roots wrap around every letter in the text, its shoots sprout between the verses." In the same vein, she later states:

> In Ruth the plot, characters, and setting converge to demonstrate human interdependence. When the grains in Ruth are viewed not just as prop but as character, interdependence goes deeper and farther. … the entire universe coalesces in a seed of barley carried home in Ruth's apron to Naomi. (100–101)

This chapter offers similarly fascinating historical and biological facts about grain as a previous chapter had offered about bread. Koosed comments on the centrality of grass to life on earth. Almost everything we eat ultimately derives from grass (actually from grass species): "all flesh is indeed grass" (95). This existential phrase awakens the reader to the centrality of grain not only in the book of Ruth but in life itself. She explains the difficulties of translating the different Hebrew words for grass, plant, vegetation, and similar terms, before introducing and discussing Walt Whitman's poetry collection *Leaves of Grass* (1855–1892; 100). His poetry expresses the convergence between nature and the self, between the cosmos and humanity—ideas that inspired Koosed to read Ruth in a new light. Koosed eloquently concludes the chapter with a paean to photosynthesis: "Tonight [Ruth] will eat the sunlight and soil stored in the seeds, captured by these blades of grass" (102).

In chapter 8 Koosed tackles the thorny issues surrounding Obed's birth. The verse that has sparked commentary over the years is in chapter 4, verse 17, where the people proclaim, "A son has been born to Naomi." Koosed proposes that the story of Ruth is about "the fluidity of kinship," suggesting that family can be a matter of choice rather than blood or legal obligation (105). She discusses a broad range of interpretations of this chapter of Ruth, including the legal issues and the implications of Naomi's being called the mother of Obed. In Koosed's own radical interpretation, Ruth hands Obed over to Naomi as an act of "resistance of a final assimilation into the Israelite community," declining "to raise the son whom she has borne" because she rejects the role of good Israelite wife and mother (118). Koosed is momentarily indulging in the kind of noncontextual interpretation she so adamantly criticizes elsewhere in her book. This interpretation is not supported by the text. But her assertion that the book of Ruth leaves open questions about how we are defined in terms of culture, religion, and ethnicity is absolutely correct, and she has made that point very well throughout the book.

The final chapter offers a fine survey of Jewish and Christian liturgical uses of Ruth. Koosed discusses the Jewish festival of Shavuot, when the book of Ruth is customarily read. This holiday was transformed into the Christian Pentecost, though Ruth is not read in any official liturgical way in the Christian community. She is, however, named in a prominent place (the Gospel of Matthew, the first book of the New Testament).

The title of Koosed's last chapter is "The Story Begins Where It Ends," and this is her final point: the genealogy opens up Ruth to all her afterlives. She discusses an Israeli film in which the book of Ruth figures prominently. The director, Amos Gitai, includes many twists in his parable of exile. Koosed ends on a personal note, comparing her own recent planting and reaping of tomatoes to Ruth's gleaning. The voice of the author gives this book a unique stamp. It is thoroughly academic and well-researched, including several disciplines not usually interwoven with biblical studies. Yet because of the personal voice and the lyrical writing, this book could be enjoyed equally by the lay or scholarly reader. This cannot be said about many books in the field of biblical scholarship. Koosed deserves kudos and appreciation for her wonderfully rich contribution to the field.

Unrelated to the book's content, many passages throughout the book are hard to grasp because of a serious lack of commas. Whether due to the author's or editor's oversight, it is a serious grammatical error. To offer only two egregious examples from near the end of the book:

> As Gitai's movie demonstrates the immigrant continues to wander in and out of different lands. (132)

> When discussing Ruth early Christian commentators note her outside status. (128)

Dozens of such poorly constructed sentences are found throughout the book, marring the overall effect, especially in a book filled with such eloquent writing.

Torah as Teacher: The Exemplary Torah Student in Psalm 119, by Kent Aaron Reynolds. Supplements to Vetus Testamentum 137. Leiden: Brill, 2010. Pp. xv + 249. Hardcover. €103.00. ISBN 9789004182684.

Steven Dunn, Alverno College, Milwaukee, Wisconsin

With its repetitive use of keywords for Torah, acrostic structure, and great length, Ps 119 has long been neglected and even derided as tedious, constricted, and uninteresting. In *Torah as Teacher*, Kent Aaron Reynolds provides a comprehensive and refreshing response to these views by showing how the psalm's "striking message" portrays an "exemplary Torah student" as a means to teach readers to internalize Torah as an aspect of character formation. The author of Ps 119 creates the complex persona of the "exemplary Torah student" using "traditional religious language"—particularly elements of lament and wisdom motifs—to promote an expansive conception of Torah and its central role in righteous living. This complex development of the exemplary Torah student utilizes first- and second-person pronouns that personalize his voice, emotions, and beliefs as part of the rhetorical goal to persuade readers to internalize Torah. Reynolds notes that chapter 3, on "The Exemplary Torah Student," and chapter 4, "The Concept of Torah," form the "heart" of his study (15). This book developed from his dissertation under Michael V. Fox at the University of Wisconsin.

Chapter 1, the introduction, begins, appropriately, with examples of negative views of Ps 119 by scholars and moves quickly to present Reynolds's alternative view. The speaker of Ps 119 yearns for, delights in, and obeys Torah; depicting the speaker in this way provides an example of the "ideal Torah student" for readers to emulate. Torah, represented by eight synonymous keywords, serves as a stand-in for God. Reynolds provides a solid analysis of the poetic patterns of the psalm and its acrostic structure, key words, and themes. His analysis of the genre of Ps 119 is particularly insightful, showing how the psalm transcends classification into specific genres but rather uses "traditional religious language"—particularly from laments and wisdom literature—as part of its rhetorical strategy. These observations apply to a number of psalms that combine diverse elements that defy rigid classification. Psalm 119 is neither a lament, as some scholars claim, nor specifically a wisdom psalm, though it utilizes elements of each in its goal of presenting Torah as the key to the life of the righteous.

Chapter 2, "The Use of Traditional Religious Language," compares parallels between Ps 119 and other psalms and books of the Hebrew Bible—particularly Deuteronomy—using key words, phrases, and themes. Reynolds classifies these elements in three categories: the language of *piety, lament, and wisdom*. He effectively shows how the author of Ps 119 was influenced by the language and theology of Deuteronomy and the close parallels between the psalm and Proverbs. Elements from Deuteronomy include the motifs of "give me life" and "not forgetting"; in both cases Torah serves as a stand-in for God. In Ps 119 one gets "life" through Torah, and forgetting Torah would be equivalent to forgetting God (see 48–49). Wisdom motifs in Ps 119 and Proverbs include the "trope of the path" and way (54). Reynolds provides a clear presentation of the linguistic and thematic parallels between Ps 119 and Proverbs.

Chapter 3, "The Exemplary Torah Student," describes how the speaker of Ps 119 must "model the message." The psalmist describes him using the traditional religious language discussed in chapter 2. Reynolds rejects the classification of Ps 119 as a wisdom psalm because it lacks admonitions or exhortations (57). It is best to recognize that Ps 119 contains wisdom elements and language. Because the psalmist creates a complex and multifaceted depiction of the ideal Torah student, the psalm depicts the speaker in a variety of emotional states and contexts, which in turn explains the great length of the psalm. This is a much more plausible and positive interpretation of the psalm's length than arguments that the need to fill out the acrostic structure requires all 176 verses. Reynolds examines various "exemplary types," the first being the righteous person. Similar to the paradigm of the righteous person in Ps 1, the speaker in Ps 119 is "an *instantiation* of the exemplary type" (60, emphasis added). Psalms 15 and 112 contain similar connections with Ps 119. "David" serves as a paradigm in the Psalms for the righteous (62–63). The book of Proverbs likewise includes examples of persona worthy of imitation in the "exemplary women" and "the wise" (63–65).

Reynolds examines Ps 119:1–3 as an introduction to the psalm describing *a group* of people—whereas the body of the psalm focuses on an individual—who exemplify Torah observance; this prepares for the repeated contrasts between those who live by Torah and the wicked who disobey or ignore it (68). Reynolds provides a detailed analysis of the literary strategies used by the psalmist to emphasize the ideal Torah student: the psalmist utilizes first-person language, devotional language, the language of distress, and the "language of character formation." This last category has strong affinities with wisdom literature to show how the speaker internalizes Torah to develop "fear of God"—a primary character trait (87). "Inconsistencies in portrayal" are used to portray the speaker as "a complex and compelling Torah student in a variety of situations" (92); in addition, a variety of settings and repetition are used to fill out this depiction of the student who always remains faithful to Torah. Cumulatively, the psalmist creates this complex and multifaceted character for "suasive force"—a speaker who models the message in all aspects of life.

Chapter 4, "The Concept of Torah," examines the complex and diverse ways that Torah is presented in Ps 119 through the use of key words that are used in both abstract and specific ways. Reynolds frequently uses the term "instantiations" for the use of key words as specific commandments.[1] Reynolds convincingly shows that, rather than a "thoughtless" use of the eight key terms to fulfill the constraints of the acrostic, the psalmist uses these terms with "semantic overlap" as part of his strategy to present Torah as a "composite of ideas about God's word that can be found" throughout the Hebrew Bible to portray the divine-human communication (146). In this sense, Ps 119 serves as a precursor to later rabbinic Judaism, which more systematically describes the implications of Torah as an expression of God's will for humanity. A very important implication of this chapter is the recognition that at one level Torah dwells in the "heavens," the realm of God, but is expressed in human language on earth among humans. Though not explicitly stated, this reflects Reynolds's observation that Ps 119 is late and reflects a transition toward rabbinic Judaism, where Torah replaces the temple and sacrifice as the primary locus of the divine-human relationship.

Chapter 5, "Psalm 119 in Context," argues that, in light of the preceding analysis, Ps 119 presents Torah as a central theological concept in the Hebrew Bible for the final compilers of the Psalter and Hebrew Bible (148). Structurally, Pss 1:1, 112:1, and 119:1 begin with the term אשרי and have the verb אבד in their concluding verse; all three psalms run from א to ת and depict someone who delights (חפץ) in Torah (154–55). I note that Ps 2:12 contains both אשרי and אבד. Reynolds examines several other lexical links in Pss 19, 73, 89, 94, 111, 112, and 146–150 to reveal the theme of Torah in the structure of the Psalter. He then examines in detail proposals by Erich Zenger and Reinhard Kratz (155–66); he favors Kratz's views, who likewise views Ps 119 as part of the final editing of the Psalter (160). Reynolds provides an interesting parallel of the Priestly Blessing in Num 6:27 with Ps 119:32 as evidence of the psalmist's use of outside texts and con-

---

1. Reynolds finally gives a specific definition of what he means by this term on page 136: "the individual commandments, stipulations, and promises."

cludes that Ps 119 reflects the final editing of both the Psalter and Hebrew Bible (166). He then provides an extended analysis of the word עקב ("to the end") in Ps 119 and cross-references in the Hebrew Bible to show how the psalmist's use of the term "activates the theology of Deuteronomy" (176), that there are consequences for observing or disobeying Torah; this in turn reflects important theological emphases in developing Judaism (179).

A short conclusion (181–83) summarizes Reynolds's research and the role of Ps 119 in emphasizing the central role of Torah study. Psalm 119 was composed during the latest stages in the development of the Psalter and Hebrew Bible; its focus on Torah study prepares for rabbinic Judaism (183). The book concludes with a commentary (185–212) that would be better placed with the translation(1–11).

Critique: To Reynolds's claim that verses 3, 37, 90, and 122 lack key words for Torah (18), I would note that verses 3 and 37 have the word "way" (דרך), which serves as a euphemism for Torah (e.g., Pss 25:9, 12; 27:11). Depending on one's criteria for what constitutes a "wisdom psalm," Reynolds's rejection of this classification for Ps 119 is open to debate; one could argue that the psalm's emphasis on instruction, use of Torah and other wisdom key words, and contrast between the righteous and the wicked qualify it as a "wisdom psalm." I take issue with the claim that Psalm 119 avoids terms for wisdom, claiming that the following words are "missing": 131 (חכמה משכיל שכל נבון תבונה בנה חכם); in fact, several of these words or their roots are found throughout the psalm. For example, 119:98–99 contains the verbal forms of שכל, חכם, while verse 104 has אתבונן. Reynolds's research is impressive, and he cites several German and Modern Hebrew sources for which he provides his own translations and the original in footnotes. Reynolds seems overly dependent at times on Michael Fox's commentaries on Proverbs, which seems odd considering his claims that Ps 119 is not a "wisdom psalm." He overuses the term "instantiation" (four times each on 107, 114 and throughout the work), which he should have defined early on considering how often it appears in this study.

Reynolds provides a clearly written and extensively researched analysis that provides new insights into the rhetorical and theological function of Ps 119; this should contribute to a greater understanding and appreciation of the psalm's role in the development of Torah study as a primary focus of Judaism. This study will help fill a void in the scholarship on this often-neglected but very important psalm. This book is a must for theological libraries, Psalms scholars, and anyone researching the role of Torah in the Hebrew Bible. It would be a useful text for graduate-level courses on Psalms or Deuteronomic theology.

The Music of Psalms, Proverbs and Job in the Hebrew Bible: A Revised Theory of Musical Accents in the Hebrew Bible, edited by Jeffrey Burns, David Bers and Stephen Tree. Wiesbaden: Harrassowitz, 2011. Pp. xii + 495. Hardcover. $102.00. ISBN 9783447061919.

Rebecca A. Mitchell, Miami University of Ohio, Oxford, Ohio
Matthew W. Mitchell, Canisius College, Buffalo, New York

This curious volume, an entry in Harrossowitz's series on Jewish music and culture, sees publication as a posthumous work (Jeffrey Burns having died in 2004). As befitting a book on biblical texts composed by a musician/musicologist and edited by both a graphic designer and an author, its domains of knowledge require two reviewers (a historian of music and a biblical scholar) to do its project justice.

To begin with, the book's physical production is unusual enough to comment upon, as it is in fact a very slender volume in print form. Pages 164–495 are only on the enclosed CD in Portable Document Format (pdf), a CD that also contains embedded audio files linked to the pdf version of the book. Issues with this formatting will be discussed below, but as part of the book's reconstruction of the performance of biblical music relies on computer software, it clearly is an attempt to make use of digital sound as a relatively seamless part of the presentation of this research.

According to Burns, the examination of biblical music, in particular the use of the Masoretic טעמי המקרא, has not been the focus of those who have the expertise to make sense of this material. The טעמי המקרא, although known to be indications of music, have not traditionally been the subject of investigation by musicians or musicologists, but rather by grammarians" (3). Burns acknowledges that this is likely due to "the virtual absence of any source material on the subject" (4) but argues that, in fact, performing musicians have often relied upon forms of musical notation that require them (or the composer) to "add something extra to the score as part of the live performance" (11). He suggests that recognition of this performance tradition might well hold the key to unlocking the meaning of *t'amim* in the poetic books (Psalms, Proverbs, Job).

The basis of Burns's reconstruction of the musical meaning of *t'amim* in these books is built upon examination of three different source bases: the pedagogical tradition related to interpreting *t'amim* (33–44), living practice expressed in contemporary cantillation styles among Yemenite, Sephardic and Ashkenazic Jews (44–46) and a statistical analysis of the appearance and placement of all *t'amim* in the "twenty-one" other books of the Bible (48–49). Burns argues that the *t'amim* provide "essential" musical notation: basic information on the musical rendition of a text that singers were trained to decipher (10–12). Despite "superficial melodic differences" between cantillation traditions among different Jewish communities, Burns claims that there is a "basic similarity of motives" or "primordial melodic forms" underpinning all these traditions. (20). The absence of precise melodic pitch notation in this system demonstrates that exact melodic contour was simply not an essential component. Having established that the *t'amim* provide sufficient essential information for musical performance, Burns goes on to offer a detailed reassessment of the interpretation of *t'ame hamiqra* in the twenty-one other (nonpoetic) biblical books. He analyzes the various sequences in which the *t'amim* appear, dividing them into four hierarchical levels based upon their placement within the text. While building upon pedagogical tradition (in which three or four hierarchical levels of accents were recognized), Burns reorganizes the hierarchical placement of several of the accents advanced by other scholars to better preserve the syntactical division of the text.

In doing so, he insists on the interrelationship between the text and the accents in defining appropriate musical rendition (47–76). Finally, having established his reworking of the hierarchical division of accents, Burns offers musical examples of the rendition of accents based upon his *luakh zarqa* (a pedagogical table that provided a list of all the names of the *t'amim* that appear in Scripture together with a melodic rendition) of the East European (Ashkenazic) elaborate tradition of Torah singing (76–87).

Burns then turns his attention to deciphering the *t'amim* of the poetic books, arguing that there is a clear similarity both in accents and their combinations between the prose and poetic texts, so much so that it is possible to extrapolate the performance of the poetic texts (for which no living cantillation tradition exists) from the prose texts (for which such a tradition does exist [101]). The bulk of material included on the CD, including the computer-generated audio files, demonstrates Burns's careful reconstruction of this performance tradition (165–468). While extrapolating performance practice for the poetic texts from existing cantillation tradition requires a certain leap of faith, Burns goes even further in his analysis, suggesting (based upon his analysis of the dualist structure of the *t'amim* in the prose books) that the surviving cantillation tradition was itself based upon the older tradition of singing the poetic texts. In this way Burns resolves the puzzle that he voiced earlier in relation to the prose texts: "the *t'amim* are highly structured according to a system with its own rules [which] exist more or less independently of textual considerations" (87). The reason for this, Burns concludes, is that "the dualistic, hierarchical elements of the system of *t'amim* originate from the poetry" (150–51). The book concludes with an introduction to tutorials based on his reconstruction and a bibliography.

There are a number of things that can be said about a project of this breadth and its attempt to incorporate technology into its presentation. Given that it touches upon issues pertaining to a variety of scholarly fields, it would be uncharitable to expect anything resembling completeness or exhaustive surveys of literature. At a basic level, however, one has to ask whether the stated aims of the project and what it achieves are two quite different things. What the book achieves is a not implausible reconstruction that may persuade some readers that the poetic books may contain the more original form of notation and that the modern cantillation traditions he cites have all developed in a relatively natural manner from a common framework that the Masoretes preserved. Whether or not people are persuaded that his reconstruction of a common Tiberian tradition is completely accurate is neither here nor there, however, since the book makes much broader claims about the antiquity of the tradition preserved by the Masoretes. The book does not, however, move back from the Tiberian tradition to anything approximating the biblical time period, nor does it even provide any compelling reason to believe that the Masoretes preserve a system that has anything like that kind of antiquity to it. Optimism about this ability to reconstruct the more distant past based upon this reconstruction is simply asserted in a relatively unproblematic manner.

The book also cites very little contemporary scholarship on the Bible, musicology, or any of a variety of topics. That the bibliography on Hebrew textual traditions is limited is one concern; the broader issue is that, after claiming that grammarians or philologists and not musicians have examined a problem, the book proceeds as if there has simply been no recent Jewish musicology. Idelsohn's volume on Jewish music is cited, but it is some eighty years old at this point. While Suzanne Haik-Vantoura's 1976 *La musique de la bible révélée* is included in the bibliography (in its 1991 English translation), it receives little critical engagement in the primary text (though Burns's own work seems to draw on this earlier study). Moreover, with the partial exception of Eric Werner, no musical reconstructions attempted from other ancient traditions that may provide comparative insight are cited. There is little sense that reconstructing music from textual sources happens in a variety of settings (e.g., church music, Byzantine chant, the music of the ancient Greeks), some of which overlap in time and region with the Masoretes. That a notation system provides "primary melodic forms" rather than a specific melody is not a novel suggestion: some of these other traditions are also believed to preserve a general melodic framework or structure within which variations may occur. At first glance, then, a comparative approach would seem to hold potential insight; if the author saw his work as fundamentally different, it would have been of value to learn how he considered his approach to differ from other attempts to reconstruct ancient musical notation.

Given that this a posthumous work, some of the editing issues are likely the result of the book's author not being able to complete it (e.g., terminological inconsistency such as referring to other biblical texts as the "Twenty-One books" or the "prose" books, occasional grammatical infelicities), and one wonders what changes the author would have made before publication. In its current form, the question of to whom this book will appeal is unclear. The lack of direct engagement with much of the relevant scholarship will diminish its value for many academicians, although for those readers with a previous knowledge of and interest in Jewish cantillation traditions, it should hold a fair amount of interest. The tutorial and accompanying CD offer a potential approach for those desiring a revised performance approach to the *t'amim*. Ultimately, though, the work stands as a testament to the author's lifelong devotion to Jewish cantillation practice, a devotion that comes across to the reader, regardless of any reservations raised by the above critiques.

Ezra and Nehemiah, by Andrew E. Steinmann. Concordia Commentary. St. Louis: Concordia, 2010. Pp. liii + 675. Hardcover. $42.99. ISBN 9780758615961.

Antje Labahn, Kirchliche Hochschule Wuppertal, Wuppertal, Germany

Der umfangreiche Kommentar zu den Büchern Esra und Nehemia von Andrew E. Steinmann ist in der Serie „Concordia Commentary" erschienen. Wie die anderen bereits erschienenen Werke folgt auch dieser Band den grundlegenden Prinzipien, wie sie von den Herausgebern der Serie „Concordia Commentary: A Theological Statement of Sacred Scripture" im Vorwort festgehalten werden (xiii–xvi). Basierend auf einer lutherischen Hermeneutik soll eine christologische Auslegung präsentiert werden, die die Schrift als heiliges, inspiriertes und unfehlbares Wort Gottes versteht, das als Gesetz und Evangelium ergeht. Für diesen Ansatz verweisen die Herausgeber auf die 1580 erschienene Konkordienformel (FC) unter den lutherischen Bekenntnisschriften, mit deren Grundsätzen sich das Concordia Publishing House als Verlag eines konfessionellen Luthertums in Übereinstimmung erklärt (xiv). Auf diesem Hintergrund intendiert der Kommentar, Pfarrern und Pfarrerinnen, Predigerinnen und Predigern, Missionaren und Lehrenden eine Interpretationshilfe an die Hand zu geben (xiii). Es stellt sich aber die Frage, ob die hermeneutische Vorgabe das historische, philologische und textgeschichtliche Potential des Esra-Nehemia-Buches nicht eingrenzt.

Andrew E. Steinmann nimmt fügt seine Auslegung von Esra-Nehemia in diese Grundsätze ein. Er sieht seine Rolle als Exeget vor allem darin, theologischen Inhalten nachzugehen, wie er sie als Hauptthemen der ausgelegten Schriften in der Einleitung zusammenstellt (78ff.). Dazu zählen: *Gottesdienst* („worship", 78) mit den von ihm als Unterthemen bestimmten Aspekten Tempel, Feste, Opfer, Musik, Heiligkeit des Sabbats, Tempelpersonal und Gebet in ihrem Bezug zu dem religiösen und profanen Leben in Jerusalem; *Schrift* einschließlich der Frage nach der Tora des Mose (91ff.); Eheproblematik (94ff.); das *Gesetz* in den Büchern Esra und Nehemia (98ff.). Die Darstellung in der Einleitung fällt nicht sonderlich detailliert aus und nimmt auch keine Unterscheidung zwischen Quellen und Redaktion vor, obwohl Steinmann selbst angibt, dass Esra und Nehemia in erster Linie Editoren waren mit einem nur geringen Eigenanteil an den Worten (Esra 21 %, Nehemia 7%). Schließlich führt Steinmann hier auch die Frage nach „God's Gospel in Ezra and Nehemiah" an (103ff.). Mag dieser Gedanke ein wenig überraschen, so findet Steinmann dennoch eine ansprechende Interpretation in der Bestimmung, dass das Evangelium sich im Rettungshandeln Gottes an seinem Volk in der Geschichte erfüllt (103f.). Man könnte bei der Zusammenstellung der so genannten Hauptthemen, wie Steinmann sie präsentiert, leicht heraushören, dass ihre Auswahl und Akzentsetzung von einer konfessionellen lutherischen Hermeneutik vorgeprägt ist. Dies gilt vor allem für Sätze, in denen er z.B. von „sacramental nature of worship in the house of God" spricht (80), dessen „important principle" lautet: „Worship begins and ends with God's promises of forgiveness and life" (80); ebenso gilt für Steinmann auch, dass „sacrifices forshadowed Jesus" (81).

Steinmann geht wenig kritisch mit dem Text und seinen vermeintlich authentischen Dokumenten und berichteten geschichtlichen Ereignissen um. Den im Text des Esra-Nehemia-Buches gegebenen historischen Daten und angeführten bzw. zitierten antiken aramäischen Dokumente traut Steinmann eine hohe Verlässlichkeit und folglich Historizität zu. In der Einleitung des Kommentars geht Steinmann kurz auf die geschichtliche Epoche der achämenidischen Regentschaft ein, wobei er seiner Darstellung die erzählte Zeit zugrundelegt, die er mit dem Herrschaftsantritt von Kyros dem Großen und dem Kyrosedikt beginnen lässt. Es folgt eine Präsentation der achämenidischen Herrscher (22ff.), die (abgesehen von den Abbildungen archäologischer Grab- und Gedenkstätten) an den biblischen Zeugnissen orientiert ist, wie sie einerseits das Esra-Nehemia-Buch selbst bietet und wie sie andererseits in Prophetenschriften (z.B. Hag 1:1.14f.; 2:18; Sach 1:1.7; 3:1; 4:6) zu finden sind. Dies gilt auch für die einzeln vorgestellten Hohenpriester im perserzeitlichen Jehud sowie für die Erwähnung der Gouverneure (51-62). Die moderne Exegese würde sich hier mehr einen kritischen Dialog mit den zeitgenössischen antiken Quellen achämenidischer Provenienz und mit den hellenistischen Geschichtsschreibern sowie mit Josephus (vgl. Ant 11), mit den Papyri (vor allem aus Elephantine) sowie mit zeitgeschichtlichen Siegelabdrücken und Münzen wünschen, aufgrund derer die biblischen Quellen in einem weiteren Kontext zu stehen kommen.

In dem als historisch bestimmten, literarischen Rahmen ordnet Steinmann die beiden Protagonisten des Esra-Nehemia-Buches ein. Sowohl für Esra als auch für Nehemia, die er beide als „great leaders of God's people" bezeichnet (108), nimmt Steinmann eine Wirksamkeit während der Regentschaft Artaxerxes I. (464-424 v.Chr.) an. Steinmann rekonstruiert die Ereignisse hinter den Berichten in Esr-Neh folgendermaßen: Nach dem Kyrosedikt 538 v.Chr., der ersten Rückkehrerwelle 533 und der Tempelweihe des 2. Tempels in Jerusalem 515 gelangte Esra mit der zweiten Gruppe von Rückkehrern 458 nach Jerusalem und begann das Leben der Judäer zu regeln. Wenig später wurde 445 Nehemia beauftragt, um als Gouverneur in der Provinz Jehud die achämenidischen Interessen zu vertreten (s. die Übersicht über die Datierung und Abfolge der in Esr-Neh berichteten Ereignisse auf Seiten 66f.). Mit diesem Datierungsansatz folgt Steinmann der älteren Theorie (vgl. Esr 7:7; Neh 1:1). Trotz Anfragen an seine historische Einordnung bleibt festzuhalten, dass die Historiographie der Schriften eine Neukonstituierung des Volkes in Juda bzw. Jehud nach dem Ende des Exils mit einer Außen- und Innenansicht reflektiert, die mit der Integration der Rückwanderer aus Babylon in die im Land verbliebene Bevölkerung befasst ist (vgl. z.B. Esr 4:1f.; Neh 5:8).

Aus der Kombination von Erzählpassagen in erster Person und Berichten in dritter Person Singular werden hinter dem Esra-Nehemia-Buch herkömmlich unterschiedliche Quellenschriften wie die Esra-Memoiren (Esr 1-6 [und möglicherweise auch Neh 8-10]) und die Nehemia-Denkschrift (Neh 1-7 [und möglicherweise auch Neh 11-13]) unterschieden. Steinmann macht diese aber nicht weiter für seine Interpretation der Komposition fruchtbar.

In einem letzten Abschnitt der Einleitung fragt Steinmann nach Quellen und Traditionen. Zunächst geht er dem Verhältnis des Esra-Nehemia-Buches zum griechischen 1Esdras der Septuaginta nach, das er als spätere Nach- und Neuerzählung der hebräischen Schriften bewertet. Sodann fragt er nach dem Verhältnis des Esra-Nehemia-Buches zur Chronik, wobei er sich zur These eines Chronistischen Geschichtswerkes bestehend aus 1/2Chr und Ers/Neh so äußert, dass er eine zunächst separate Entstehung der Schriften annimmt. Ebenso setzt er eine zunächst eigenständige Entstehung auch für die beiden Schriftteile Esr und Neh voraus. Die Autoren beider Schriften des Esra-Nehemia-Buches treten nach Steinmann in erster Linie als Editoren hervor, die Material sammeln, zusammenstellen und dies mit wenigen eigenen Kommentaren herausgeben. Während Esr stärkeres Interesse am Tempel zeigt, ist Neh mehr an der Stadt Jerusalem interessiert (17). Für die Komposition der beiden Schriften Esra-Nehemia nimmt Steinmann eine Entstehung um 335 v.Chr. an (21).

Das Nachwirken in den apokryphen und pseudepigraphischen Schriften vor allem Esra betreffend (z.B. die apokryphen Schriften 2–5Esr) stellt Steinmann schließlich kurz vor (108–19). Aus dieser Übersicht hebt er die gewandelte Bedeutung Esras im Frühjudentum als „prophet and seer who learns divine mysteries" hervor und versteht in Esra der Rolle als „example, perhaps even a prototype, of faithful Judeans in the next centuries who relied on the written Word of God" (118).

Der Kommentierung geht eine detaillierte Gliederung voraus (68–77), die zugleich einen Überblick über die berichteten Ereignisse bietet und die theologischen wie historischen Deutungen, die den Kommentar prägen, aufnimmt.

Vorangestellt ist den einzelnen Abschnitten im exegetischen Teil (127ff.) erneut eine Gliederung sowie eine Einführung zu den Hauptthemen der jeweiligen Textpassage, wobei die in der Einleitung zusammengestellten theologischen Hauptthemen der Schrift wieder beggnen. Die Interpretation erfolgt in einem Dreischritt: Übersetzung, „Textual Notes", „Commentary". Die Übersetzung von Steinmann ist einerseits recht wörtlich, andererseits fällt die Verwendung theologischer Semantik für Veraltungsbegriffe auf, was eher ungewöhnlich ist. Die theologische Interpretation dieses Kommentars spiegelt sich in der Übersetzung wider.

In den „Textual Notes" zu ausgewählten Idiomen präsentiert Steinmann Beobachtungen zu Aspekten der Semantik, diskutiert Parallelen in anderen Schriften der Hebräischen Bibel und geht auf sprachliche, lexikalische und grammatikalische oder seltener textkritische Aspekte ein. Als Beispiel kann auf die „hölzerne Säule" oder das „hölzerne Podest" (*migdal-ez*) in Neh 8,4 verwiesen werden, das zumeist als eine Rednertribüne ähnlich einem *bema* interpretiert wird, von der aus Esra, flankiert von 13 Personen, die Tora Gottes dem versammelten Volk vorliest. Steinmann geht dem Bedeutungsspektrum von *migdal* nach, gibt aber keine Sacherklärung für den „watchtower" (503).

Unter den Bemerkungen der „Textual Notes" finden sich auch Hinweise auf altorientalische Parallelen, vorzugsweise in sprachlicher Hinsicht als Hilfsmittel zur Erhellung der Semantik eines Begriffs (besonders aus den Elephantine-Papyri; vgl. die Bezüge auf TAD in den Anmerkungen z.B. auf den Seiten 238.256.258). Gelegentlich werden in diesem Abschnitt auch Realien erläutert und kurze historische Erklärungen gegeben, wie etwa zum achämenidischen Herrschaftssitz in Ekbatana (mit Verweis auf Quellen der hellenistischen Geschichtsschreiber Herodot und Xenophon, 256); die Quellenbelege sind zumeist literarischer und seltener archäologischer Natur. Der Materialfülle dieser „textual notes" ist manches interessante Detail zu entnehmen, was in anderen Kommentaren in dieser Weise und Fülle so nicht zu finden ist. Hierin liegt die Stärke des Kommentars.

Unter der Überschrift „Commentary" stellt Steinmann seine theologische Interpretation der Textstelle vor. Darunter schildert er, wie die göttliche Führung die Geschichte zum Ziel kommen lässt, wie das Wort Gottes sich erfüllt und ausbreitet. Als Beispiel sei die Zusammenfassung zu Esr 1:1–4 zitiert: „God is reestablishing worship at the temple in Jerusalem. He is graciously providing for a place where his people can come into his presence, offer sacrifice pleasing him, and receive forgiveness from him." (137)

Gelegentlich finden sich in „Commentary" auch Erläuterungen wie etwa zur Mauer um Jerusalem zur Zeit Nehemias (als Exkurs, 412–16) oder zu den Toren und Personen, die in den biblischen Berichten als Bauleute ausgewiesen werden (425–33) und deren Charakteristik im Kommentar von Steinmann entsprechend vorgenommen wird (vgl. zu den Toren, ebd. 425: „The palces are approximations based on Nehemiah 3 and the toponomy of ancient Jerusalem").

Der Kommentar legt wenig Wert auf die Klärung sozialer und sozialgeschichtlicher Größen. Da die Angaben über Ämter und Funktionen, Personen und Gruppen in der wissenschaftlichen Diskussion zu Esr-Neh durchaus umstritten sind, sind entsprechende Erörterungen notwendig. Als Beispiel sei angeführt, dass der Posten des in 6:13 u.ö. genannten „Gouverneurs von Transeuphratene" (spannungsvoll vor allem im Verhältnis zum „Gouverneur von Judäa" in 6:7) nicht weiter erklärt wird, wie auch eine Ausführung über die Gruppen der Priester, Leviten und Restbevölkerung aus der Gola in 6:16, die als „Israeliten" und nicht als „Judäer" (wie anderweitig in Ers-Neh gebräuchlich, z.B. 6:14) bezeichnet werden, zu vermissen ist.

Demgegenüber fallen unkritische Bewertungen auf wie die, dass Dareios „consulted Judean religious authorities before composing this decree" (269 zu Esr 6:12). Dass die Historiographie in Esr-Neh die achämenidischen Herrscher so darstellt, dass sie auf Geheiß Jahwes hin agieren und mit den jüdäischen Autoritäten einvernehmlich umgehen und sogar die Interessen und Aktionen der Verantwortungsträger wie des Volkes in Jehud unterstützen, entspricht dem Darstellungsinteresse der Schriften. Doch können solche ideologisch-historiographischen Präsentationen und theologischen Interpretationen nicht mit historischen Urteilen in eins gesetzt werden.

Um Passagen, in denen solche theologischen Aussagen im Kommentar behandelt werden, hervorzuheben und leichter zu finden, sind am zeitlichen

Außenrand neben dem Text verschiedene, ca. 7 cm lange „icons" gesetzt. Die Erklärung der insgesamt 15 verschiedenen icons (xxiv–xxv) gibt an, ob es sich um Ausführungen z.B. zu Trinität, Taufe, Sünde und Tod, Auferstehung, Sakramente, Tempel und Gottesdienst oder Inkarnation handelt. Die Verwendung dieser Zeichen, die für die Serie Concordia Commentary charakteristisch ist, mag für manchen Leser, der mit diesem System nicht so vertraut ist, ein wenig verwirrend sein, zumal die Kategorien systematisch-theologischer Art sind und bisweilen einen Fremdköper in einem Textbereich mit einer andern historischen und sozialgeschichtlichen Herkunft darstellen.

Dem Kommentar ist eine Literaturliste vorangestellt (xxvi–liii), die sowohl klassische als auch neue Literatur umfasst und in der überwiegenden Mehrheit englisch-sprachige Titel bietet; deutsche und französische Werke bilden die Ausnahme.

Zwei ausführliche Register schließen den Kommentar ab: „Index of Subjects" (614–37) und „Index of Passages" (638–675) mit biblischen Quellen (Hebräische Bibel und Septuaginta: 638–72) sowie außer-biblischen Referenzen (672–75). Die Indizes sind eine hervorragende Hilfe, um die Details dieses voluminösen und großformatigen Kommentars zu erschließen.

Der Kommentar stellt eine eigenständige, konfessionell geprägte Auslegung vor; hierin liegt seine Besonderheit, die zwar kritische Rückfragen nach sich zieht, doch auch wertvolle Einzelbeobachtungen enthält. Die exegetischen Möglichkeiten vielfältiger gegenwärtiger Methoden werden in dem Kommentar aber leider nicht ausgeschöpft.

Yahweh's Winged Form in the Psalms: Exploring Congruent Iconography and Texts, by Joel M. LeMon. Orbis Biblicus et Orientalis 242. Fribourg: Academic Press; Göttingen: Vandenhoeck & Ruprecht, 2010. Pp. xiv + 231. Hardcover. $87.00. ISBN 9783525543641.

Jeremy M. Hutton, University of Wisconsin-Madison, Madison, Wisconsin

LeMon's publication of his 2007 Emory dissertation provides a well-written, concise meditation on the issues involved in the study of ancient Near Eastern iconographic representations corresponding to biblical tropes. The author has selected for study here the imagery of the winged form of Yhwh , as viewed in six psalms (17, 36, 57, 61, 63, 91). This trope appears elsewhere in the biblical text as well, most famously (and obviously) in Mal 3:20 (= Eng. 4:2): "But for you who revere my name the sun of righteousness shall rise, with healing in its wings" (nrsv). However, by limiting his study to the image as it appears in a single corpus, LeMon is able to provide a more homorganic and circumscribed discussion of the trope. The problems addressed in this book are just as much methodological as they are exegetical, and LeMon's volume handles both facets of the study capably.

Previous commentators on the Psalms have usually handled the imagery of Yhwh's wings in one of five ways: this trope is alternately viewed as (1) "*common aviary imagery"* of a mother bird protecting her young; (2) representing a *"winged sun disk"*; (3) a trope borrowed from *"general Egyptian symbolism"*; (4) invoking a *"protecting goddess"*; or (5) relating to the outspread wings of the cherubim in the Jerusalem temple (1–2, emphasis original). LeMon intends to determine which of these possibilities is plausible through study of the "congruent iconography"— that is, iconographic representations of divinity representing the same form as described in the text. The task is a complex one, since the domains of iconography and text tend to remain somewhat separate from one another. Contrary to the situation in ancient Egypt and Babylon, where illustrations were often accompanied by texts whose contents correspond thematically, there are very few ancient texts from Syro-Palestine in which graphic art and textual data coincide (for example, on some interpretations of the various graffiti from Kuntillet 'Ajrud). Achieving a precise and exacting methodology for elucidating one through the other, therefore, is a necessary goal of LeMon's study.

LeMon adopts what he calls an "iconographic-biblical approach," wherein "one consults ancient Near Eastern iconography for the express purpose of interpreting the Bible's literary imagery and figurative language" (14). The foremost practitioners of this approach—LeMon interacts primarily with Martin Klingbeil, Othmar Keel, Christoph Uehlinger, and his former teacher and current colleague Brent Strawn—have been methodologically adept in their interpretation of iconographic images: they examine images as elements in "constellations," not as independent units to be excised from their contexts and viewed in a sterile, uncontaminated environment ("fragmentation"). Conversely, iconographic study of the biblical text has often not proceeded with the same emphasis on holistic interpretation, suggests LeMon. It is this aspect of the book—the avoidance of "fragmentation" of the biblical text in iconographic study—that LeMon considers to be one of the primary contributions of his work.

Adopting and augmenting a theoretical framework adopted from William Brown (*Seeing the Psalms: A Theology of Metaphor* [Louisville: Westminster John Knox, 2002]), LeMon proposes a way of reading psalms that uncovers the "iconic structure" of each individual poem. This process "entails understanding the psalm as composed of a constellation of literary images in the same way that an artistic scene is comprised of numerous motifs that come together to convey its meaning" (16). For each psalm examined in its own separate chapter (chs. 3–8), this process involves an examination with attention to: (1) its basic structure; (2) its rhetorical movement; (3) its form and setting; (4) its presentation of the psalmist; (5) its presentation of the enemy/enemies (even if abstract); and (6) its image of God. Along with offering his own translation of each psalm under discussion (a task that has occasioned some solid text-critical work as well), LeMon provides a discussion of each of these elements, combining them into a briefly described "iconic structure." The constellation of literary images in each psalm is then compared to the variety of iconographic representations available in the ancient Near Eastern world in order to find congruencies. This project has required a painstaking examination of the iconographic record; for each artifact, LeMon has had to consider (24): the total iconographic context portrayed on the artifact, its historical and geographic context (i.e., archaeological provenance or likely point of origin if unprovenanced), and its material composition (LeMon handles mostly small artifacts, such as stamp seals, although larger works are sometimes addressed as well. One wonders, though, whether the possibility of forgeries should caution against the uncritical use of some of the unprovenanced materials).

The methodological centerpiece of LeMon's book is the second chapter (27–58), in which he discusses the iconographic representations of wings found throughout the ancient Near East. Wings appear on five distinct categories of birds (griffon vultures, falcons, doves, ostriches, and "other birds"), as well as on several different types of numinous beings, both *Mischwesen* and deific, the latter in both anthropomorphic and nonanthropomorphic forms. In each case, LeMon traces the individual associations of the image, as discernable from the various iconographic contexts in which it is found. He discovers that each image (or we might use the term "glyph" here to indicate a single graphic element divorced from a larger constellation of elements) connotes a slightly different meaning. For example, although the wings of the vulture connote protection (when spread, but not when folded), they do so by referring subtly to the mother goddess Mut, whom the vulture symbolized (28–31). This stands in slight contrast to the protection offered by the falcon, which symbolized Horus; the latter is frequently associated with kingship and, moreover, can often be represented simply as a pair of outspread wings over the king (31–34).

Some of the associations adduced in this chapter seem clearer than others from a cursory reading. To a large degree, this is due to LeMon's dependence on Keel and Uehlinger's preceding attempts to wrestle meaning from iconography and their collection of a much larger corpus than LeMon works with. So, although the initial argument may feel strained, the reader would do well to follow the trail of notes in order to find greater documentation of the tropes discussed. For example, in his discussion of ostrich imagery, LeMon points to a rather understated stamp seal featuring a figure with raised hands standing between two ostriches. "The iconography," he says,

> represents the idea that lordship over this animal is equivalent to lordship over the steppe region these animals inhabit. Mastery of ostriches also represents mastery of chaos itself. These animals were an apt symbol of chaos in part because of their habitat and because they were difficult to tame. Furthermore, the body of an ostrich is itself chaotic; it breaks all the "rules" of the avian world.... In short, the representation of an ostrich's nonfunctional wings highlights the bird's chaotic nature. (37)

Without recourse to Keel and Uehlinger's massive study (*Gods, Goddesses, and Images of God* [trans. Thomas H. Trapp; Minneapolis: Fortress, 1998]), this set of associations, mustered around one seal, would be rather unconvincing; in light of the data provided by Keel and Uehlinger, the full set of associations becomes more plausible. However, one wonders if Keel and Uehlinger's formulations should not still be considered tentative, insofar as the soundness of their interpretation is directly proportional to the propriety of the associations that they have drawn between iconography and biblical texts. For example, to support their connection of the "Lord of the Ostriches" motif with a deity who "just like the god Yahweh, … originally came from southeast Palestine (northwest Arabia), the region that served as home for the Shasu," Keel and Uehlinger cite Judg 5:4–5; Deut 33:2; and Hab 3:3, 7 (*Gods, Goddesses, and Images of God*, 140). This means, of course, that in order to elucidate the biblical text, LeMon has relied on a set of interpretations of iconography that is itself predicated on Keel and Uehlinger's application of the biblical text to elucidate the iconography. Thus, much of the descriptive power of LeMon's explanations rises or falls with one's assessment of Keel and Uehlinger's use of biblical and extrabiblical texts to elucidate the iconographic motifs of the ancient world, which are sometimes far from obvious. Despite running this risk of circularity, there remains much justification for examining these iconographic tropes as informing our interpretation of biblical texts. At the very least, we may recognize the continuing need for a dialogue between iconography and texts that is both mutually affirming and reciprocally correcting, and requires much close interpretation on the part of the researcher; I do not believe this point greatly conflicts with LeMon's theoretical and methodological stance.

The ninth chapter of this book (187–94) cogently summarizes LeMon's findings. In short, he argues that all six psalms examined participate to some degree in visualizing a nonanthropomorphic image of Yhwh, conceptualized as a winged sun disk offering protection to the psalmist. This imagery directly contradicts any attempts by scholars to imagine the "wings" of each psalm as those of the cherubim in the temple and concomitantly dismantles a good number of proposals for each psalm's *Sitz im Leben* as occurring in some (otherwise unattested) temple-based ritual. LeMon's proposals in this regard are especially judicious and well-argued. But LeMon pushes the point further, again, with good reasoning: he also argues that each individual psalm displays a slightly different constellation of imagery and thus participates in a total set of associations unique to each psalm. There is, he argues, "no single iconographic trope [that] provides the key to interpreting the images of Yahweh's wings" (190); "As the literary contexts change, the meaning and significance of the motif of Yahweh's wings change" (192).

LeMon's project is largely successful, thanks to his close readings of texts and the methodological sophistication he brings to bear on the problem. This book is well-structured and prudently organized, demonstrated in part by the conscientious decision to collect all the images, scattered throughout the book, in a helpful appendix ("Figures," 195–209). (This decision was especially foresightful in light of multiple scattered references to individual images; the reader needs only to turn to this appendix for an easily accessible copy of the image.) The author proves himself to be an insightful and creative reader, while at the same time rarely pushing beyond what the evidence reasonably indicates. Both Biblicists and students of iconography will find this concise volume a helpful reflection on the benefits and pitfalls of using iconography to expand our understanding of biblical texts.

APOCRYPHAL/DEUTEROCANONICAL AND OTHER JEWISH WRITINGS

Studies in the Book of Wisdom, edited by Géza G. Xeravits and József Zsengellér. Supplements to the Journal for the Study of Judaism 142. Leiden: Brill, 2010. Pp. x + 234. Cloth. $138.00. ISBN 9789004186125.

Erik Eynikel, Radboud University Nijmegen, Nijmegen, The Netherlands

The volume under review collects the papers presented at the Fourth International Conference on the Deuterocanonical Books, organized by the Shime'on Centre for the Study of Hellenistic and Roman Age Judaism and Christianity of the Reformed Theological Academy in Pápa, Hungary. The volume comes without an introduction by the editors, and the ten contributions are classified in alphabetical order of the authors' names.

In the opening contribution, Matthew Goff of Florida State University establishes that both Wisdom and 4QInstruction utilize Gen 1–3 for describing the ideal type of humankind, the "image of God." But apart from similarities that exist between Wisdom and Qumran's treatment of the creation stories, there are important differences. Nevertheless, Goff demonstrates that to understand Wisdom better the Qumran literature needs to be studied, in order to get to know the Jewish Palestinian background that may have influenced the Wisdom of Solomon.

Michael Kolarcik's essay "Sapiential Values and Apocalyptic Imagery in the Wisdom of Solomon" evaluates the claims made by some authors that Wisdom has affinities with the apocalyptic literature. He concludes that, although there are similarities in themes and motifs between the two, the worldview of Wisdom is definitely sapiential with its specific characteristics.

Luca Mazzinghi of the Pontifical Biblical Institute in Rome studies the connection between Wisdom and Greek philosophy with regard to the "law." He very clearly shows that Wisdom, unlike Philo, does not equate the law of Torah with the natural law of the philosophers but retains a much more "biblical" viewpoint stressing creation and history as important elements in the giving of the law.

Moyna McGlynn studies chapters 7–9 in the Wisdom of Solomon and its "parallels" in 1 Kgs 1–10. In these chapters the request for wisdom is central. Once the request is granted, it results in Solomon's knowledge and in his achievement of building the temple, teaching wisdom, and making right judgments. McGlynn demonstrates how these capacities attributed to Solomon in 1 Kings are developed and expanded in Wisdom to make him an idealized philosopher-king in the Platonic sense. That this knowledge is presented in Wisdom as a route to immortality through the virtues and justice is an element common in Platonic philosophy. She therefore demonstrates how the Wisdom of Solomon interpreted the traditions of Solomon's wisdom in Kings in a Platonic and Hellenistic philosophical context of the ideal kingship.

Tobias Nicklas investigates "the food of angels," as manna is called in Wis 16:20. The contemporary traditions of the book of Wisdom, like Philo, Josephus, and Testament of Abraham, have problems with the idea that angels would eat earthly food, so they offer creative solutions such as: the angels, while visiting humans, were only pretending that they were eating. But some texts, such as the Septuagint of Ps 77:24-25 and Joseph and Aseneth, speak of angels eating some kind of food, among which is manna. This food grants immortality and is comparable with the food that the Greek gods ate that gave them immortality. Nicklas demonstrates that the Wisdom of Solomon and other Jewish texts in late antiquity incorporate Hellenistic concepts in their editing of the Hebrew traditions.

Angelo Passaro of the theological faculty in Sicily studies the last verses of the book of Wisdom, more specifically the theme of renewed creation therein. He demonstrates that this theme is developed in Wisdom in the line of the prophetic traditions of the Old Testament, not the apocalyptic traditions, as often argued. He comes to conclusions close to the ones made by Kolarcik in his contribution above.

Another expert of Wisdom literature, Friedrich Reiterer of Salzburg University, treats the first verses of the book of Wisdom. In this sole German contribution to the collection, he discusses the question whether this pericope is an independent passage that could have existed prior to the incorporation in the book or whether it was created new in the light of the whole book of Wisdom. After a thorough analysis of Wis 1:1-15, he concludes in favor of the first option but points also to the many connections of this passage with the rest of the book, which explain the hesitations regarding its independence.

Greg Schmidt Goering approaches a thematic problem in Wisdom: Is the binary classification in Wisdom between righteous and unrighteous along ethnic lines (Jews- Gentiles) or not? He concludes that, since the distinction between the two categories righteous/unrighteous is not based on election by God but on human initiative to seek God and more specifically to seek divine knowledge, righteousness is within the reach of all humans and not only Jews.

Stefan Schorch investigates points of contact between Wisdom and traditions known from ancient Jewish mystical and magical texts. He specifically focuses on Wis 10:10, which retells the story of Jacob's dream and 18:21-25 concerning the high priest Aaron.

The last contribution by one of the two editors of the book, Jozsef Zsengeller, also concentrates on manna in Wisdom and on the theme of exodus as a whole. Regarding the manna, his conclusions are very much the same as Nicklas's earlier in the book. Zsengeller explains the focus on the exodus in the book of Wisdom as a result of the equation of Torah with wisdom. Further, since the Torah was given at Sinai during the exodus, the importance of the exodus is evident.

To conclude: this collection is a very valuable contribution to the study of the Wisdom of Solomon, and the editors are to be congratulated.

Apocalypse against Empire: Theologies of Resistance in Early Judaism, by Anathea E. Portier-Young. Grand Rapids: Eerdmans, 2011. Pp. xxiii + 462. Hardcover. $50.00. ISBN 9780802865984.

Benjamin E. Reynolds, Tyndale University College, Toronto, Ontario, Canada

In *Apocalypse against Empire*, Anathea Portier-Young argues that the Jewish historical apocalypses of Daniel, the Apocalypse of Weeks (1 En. 93:1–10 + 91:11–17), and the Book of Dreams (1 En. 83–90) are resistance literature. These earliest Jewish apocalypses were written as resistance to the Seleucid Empire and Antiochus IV Epiphanes. Central to her view is the understanding that apocalypses are not a retreat from reality or an escape into the supernatural and otherworldly realm, but that they are instead a call to active resistance through the revealing and inverting of visible power structures of domination and hegemony (44, also 37).

In part 1, "Theorizing Resistance," Portier-Young addresses theoretical and methodological issues related to the meaning of resistance. Part 2, "Seleucid Domination in Judea" (chs. 2–6), focuses on Seleucid rule in Judea and particularly in Jerusalem leading up to and including the persecution under Antiochus IV. The third and final part, "Apocalyptic Theologies of Resistance" (chs. 7–10), provides a close examination of Daniel, the Apocalypse of Weeks, and the Book of Dreams, while highlighting the way that each of these texts resists imperial power.

In ch. 1 (part 1) sets the theoretical stage for what follows. Rather than provide a definition of resistance, Portier-Young offers three points "that provide a conceptual framework for the understanding of resistance" (11). First, "Domination, its strategies, and the hegemony that reinforces it provide the conditions for and objects of resistance." Second, "Acts of resistance proceed from the intention to limit, oppose, reject, or transform hegemonic institutions … as well as systems, strategies, and acts of domination." Third, "Resistance is effective action. It limits power and influences outcomes, where power is understood as an agent's ability to carry out his or her will" (11). Regarding hegemony, Portier-Young highlights that it is a nonviolent means of control (11, 14). On domination, she states, "I understand domination as the social and ideological structures that create and maintain conditions of subordination as well as particular strategies and actions that aim to establish, maintain, or augment these structures" (26). Portier-Young interacts with James C. Scott on hidden transcripts and argues that imperial domination structures can be invisible but that apocalyptic literature seeks to make those structures visible. The use of pseudonymity in the Jewish apocalypses is not intended to hide the author but instead connects the authors to a tradition and highlights that "they were not the originators of this counterdiscourse" (35, also 37, 43).

Chapters 2–6 contain Portier-Young's description of Judea under Seleucid domination. In chapter 2 she highlights the way in which Hellenistic rulers portrayed themselves as conquerors and military rulers. As a result of this "royal-military ideology," Judea was caught in six wars between 274 and 168 B.C.E. (54–55). While certain provisions were granted to the leaders and people of Judea by Antiochus III (ca. 200 B.C.E.), Portier-Young argues forcefully that the people of Judea still lived under imperial control with the accompanying stresses: "lack of political autonomy, imperial exploitation, military occupation, rapid political change, the ravages of war, personal and economic hardship, internal division, and unequal distribution of privilege" (73). Portier-Young, in chapter 3, focuses on the years 188–173 B.C.E. She notes how the Heliodorus Stela indicates the Seleucid Empire's control and influence over the administration of regional temples, including the temple in Jerusalem. She also draws attention to the way in which Judaism was not necessarily pitted against Hellenism. She claims that rejection of empire was not equated with rejection of Hellenism. In chapter 4 Portier-Young interprets Antiochus's attack against Jerusalem after his forced withdrawal from Egypt as a re-creation of empire, a reconquering of the conquered. In doing so, Antiochus was able to place a new set of requirements on the people of Jerusalem and Judea. Using theories of terror and trauma in chapter 5, Portier-Young emphasizes Antiochus IV's use of state terror through massacres, abductions, home incursions, and plundering the temple. Chapter 6 centers on the edict of Antiochus and how the edict removed all previous aspects of Jewish autonomy and subjected the people of Judea and their religion to Antiochus.

With this as the background, Portier-Young explains in chapters 7–10 how "[a]pocalypse answered the empire" (217). Chapter 7 provides the reader with an extensive look at Daniel as resistance literature. Portier-Young argues that the book of Daniel was written or compiled by those who belonged to a group of "wise teachers" (229–33). In Daniel, resistance is achieved through knowledge and interpretation. Further resistance can be accomplished through prayer, penitence, and teaching in order to make people righteous. Daniel and his friends serve as examples of nonviolent resistance that takes place through waiting on the Lord (Dan 3; 6). Daniel commissions the reader to understand and to act nonviolently through knowledge, prayer, penitence, and teaching.

Chapter 8 introduces the Enochic literature. Portier-Young highlights the astronomical concerns, cosmologies, epistemologies, and the elevated role of Enoch in the Enochic literature. She argues that the dearth of references to Moses and the Mosaic law are not anti-Mosaic bias, and she suggests that it may be that the Mosaic *torah* was used the Seleucid empire for its own purposes (302–7). In chapter 9 Portier-Young argues that the Apocalypse of Weeks promotes the view that the righteous are the ones who will carry out judgment and that they are the ones who will be agents of change in the world (323). This perspective is not the passive, nonviolent approach of Daniel. Portier-Young's view is primarily grounded in 1 En. 93:10 and 91:11 (329). She contends that these actions of witnessing to righteousness, uprooting violence and the structure of deceit, and effecting justice are an overturning of power structures and a resistance to empire. Regarding the Book of Dreams (ch. 10), Portier-Young understands resistance as having open eyes and ears. The challenge to the audience is not to be blind to idolatry but to see and "cry out" like the prophets (i.e., Moses, Elijah, and Enoch). She argues that there is also a call to armed revolt in the imagery of the lambs growing horns (372–73) and that crying out, lamenting, and prayer can take place in the midst of the battle (374–75).

In the conclusion, Portier-Young provides a summary of the book, highlighting the significant points of her argument. Here she reminds her readers that apocalyptic faith can see beyond the visible structures to the reality of God's control over all creation (389). She concludes the book with an epilogue in which she suggests five areas for further study.

Apocalypse against Empire is an excellent study of Judea during the Seleucid period, especially in the way that Portier-Young makes use of various methodological theories, such as resistance, trauma, and terror. Her examination of resistance, domination, and hegemony provides helpful lenses through which to understand the plight of the Jewish people under the Seleucid Empire. Portier-Young's study will also serve to push scholarship forward regarding the purpose(s) of the Jewish apocalypses (see John Collins's foreword, xii). She is to be commended for the enormous work she has done on this project. The bibliography is valuable in its own right, and not merely for those interested in Jewish apocalypticism.

While I am persuaded that the Jewish apocalypses do present a response to empire, I wonder about the degree to which the apocalypses may be considered resistance literature. Is hope in God, God's redemption, and salvation primarily or secondarily an inversion of domination structures? There may be resistance to empire in the act of prayer, lamentation, and crying out, but if these actions are spoken to God, to what extent can they be called an act of resistance against empire? To what extent may they be theological or sociological?

A second question involves the ascent apocalypses. If the historical apocalypses can be seen as resistance literature, how do the ascent apocalypses function in relation to empire, if at all? Portier-Young discusses the Book of Watchers in chapter 1 as an example of "critical inversion strategies" (15, 16–20). But can we say this of other ascent apocalypses? How far might we take the resistance theology idea to the apocalypses not written during the Seleucid period?

Apocalypse against Empire is not just for those with an interest in apocalyptic literature. Portier-Young's in-depth look at apocalypses in relation to the Seleucid Empire and Judaism is a substantial work in the field of biblical studies.

Creation, Nature and Hope in 4 Ezra, by Jonathan A. Moo. Forschungen zur Religion und Literatur des Alten und Neuen Testaments 237. Göttingen: Vandenhoeck & Ruprecht, 2011. Pp. 206. Hardcover. $87.00. ISBN 9783525531037.

Karina Martin Hogan, Fordham University, New York, New York

This book is a lightly revised Ph.D. dissertation, completed in 2008 at the University of Cambridge under the direction of William Horbury. It consists of two brief introductory chapters situating the work in relation to that of other scholars on 4 Ezra and on apocalyptic literature in general, three substantial chapters advancing the argument, and a short "summary and conclusions" chapter. The book is a "thematic study of 4 Ezra's 'theology of creation'" (22) from three perspectives: what the author says about "creation in the beginning" (ch. 3), the status of the natural order in the author's present and what it can reveal about "the ways of the Most High" (ch. 4), and the relation of the present world to the world to come, or the role of the material world in the author's eschatology (ch. 5). Moo argues that the pessimism of 4 Ezra regarding human nature and the possibility of salvation for most people is balanced by a surprising positive view of the rest of creation and hope for its eschatological renewal.

In the first chapter, Moo aligns himself with the positions of Christopher Rowland and Crispin Fletcher-Louis against "making eschatology definitive of apocalypticism" (15) and with Klaus Koch's objection to the term "dualism" as applied to the Enochic literature (17). Nevertheless, he acknowledges that 4 Ezra presents a difficult case for those scholars who want to see Jewish apocalyptic literature as essentially world-affirming. The task Moo sets himself is to show that, despite its fixation on eschatology and its pessimism regarding human salvation, 4 Ezra takes a positive view of the (nonhuman) natural world and allows for more continuity between this world and the world to come than is generally acknowledged.

The second chapter begins with a helpful overview of the transmission history of the work, focusing on the Latin version. An attention to textual criticism is one of the strengths of this study; there are numerous footnotes that explain anomalies in the Latin text by referring to the other extant versions and reconstructing a plausible Hebrew original and primary Greek translation. In light of Moo's evident linguistic gifts and his skill in applying them in difficult passages, he seems somewhat naïve in his introduction (24–25) and in a discussion of "the vocabulary of creation" at the beginning of chapter 3 (35–37) about the pitfalls of using a lexical approach to analyze a theme such as creation in a text that exists only in secondary and later translations.

Chapter 3 analyzes three main passages in 4 Ezra that deal with the creation of humankind and of the world "in the beginning": 3:4–6; 6:1–6; and 6:38–54. These analyses are careful and thorough and yield a number of original insights. For example, regarding Ezra's unusual statement that the earth "gave [God] Adam, a lifeless body" (3:4–5; cf. 7:116), Moo tentatively suggests (42) that the author may be reading back into his description of human creation a common view of the resurrection as the earth's "giving back" the bodies (and souls) committed to it (7:32; cf. 4:41–42). An important conclusion of this section is that neither Ezra nor Uriel "suggests that it is materiality or 'earthiness' *per se* that makes creation susceptible to evil" (44). Against such a cosmological dualism, Moo argues that the elements of creation mentioned in 6:1–6 demonstrate that the boundaries between earth and heaven are porous in 4 Ezra (58).

Although the category of a "liminal creation" is an original way of describing the elements of the world singled out in 6:1–6, Moo's arguments about the relationship of creation to eschatology in general and about paradise and Zion in particular owe much to the work of Michael Stone. Perhaps in an effort to distinguish his view from Stone's, Moo is unfairly critical at times of Stone, as when he states, "Stone fails to deal with the evidence from *4 Ezra* itself that 'paradise' is, at least at present, in the heavenly realm" (51). Apart from the fact that the "evidence" for the location of paradise in the present is far from clear, Moo appears to be citing Stone's dissertation here (if so, the date given in the footnote is incorrect), instead of Stone's commentary on 4 Ezra, in which he deals with the ambiguity of the location of paradise thoroughly, in several places (*Fourth Ezra: A Commentary on the Book of Fourth Ezra* [Hermeneia; Minneapolis: Fortress, 1990], 68–69, 156, 204–6, 213–14, 221–22, 286–87).

Chapter 4 deals with how the created order in the present functions in the book, arguing for "an implicit natural theology that emerges in the dialogues between Ezra and the angel" (71). The first section examines the problem of universal judgment and how non-Israelites can be expected to know and keep God's laws. Moo concludes that "'natural law,' in the wider sense of the possibility of knowledge of God and the divine law apart from special revelation, seems required to explain the passages we have examined" (81). Here he acknowledges in a footnote that others (namely, Stefan Beyerle and I) have come to similar conclusions, but he engages in hair-splitting in order to differentiate his view from those already published (Stefan Beyerle, "'Du bist kein Richter über dem Herrn': Zur Konzeption von Gesetz und Gericht im 4. Esrabuch," in *Recht und Ethos im Alten Testament: Gestalt und Wirkung: Festschrift für Horst Seebass zum 65. Geburtstag* [ed. S. Beyerle, G. Mayer, and H. Strauss; Neukirchen-Vluyn: Neukirchener, 1999], 315–37; Karina Martin Hogan, "The Meanings of *tôrâ* in 4 Ezra," *JSJ* 38 [2007]: 530–52). Of Beyerle, Moo simply claims that he has made the case for a natural theology in 4 Ezra "via a somewhat different route" (different how?), but he seems to invent a difference with my argument: "Although I accept Hogan's suggestion that 'law' comes in *4 Ezra* to include all of the Jewish Scriptures restored in the end by Ezra (as in the later rabbinic usage), I do not think that the author so clearly distinguishes between the 'law' recorded there and that which is somehow accessible to all of humanity" (81 n. 38). The point of my article is that the author did *not* distinguish between the Torah of Moses and what we might call natural law "in the wider sense" in which Moo uses the term, but it is possible for the modern reader to see that the author is using "law" to mean several different things.

In general, Moo has a tendency to exaggerate his differences with other scholars when he takes a position that is not original to him. On the other hand, he argues very well for his own ideas. The remainder of chapter 4, in which Moo explores various explanations for the corruption of the present world, is quite persuasive. He shows that the author of 4 Ezra consistently blames human sinfulness, not material nature, for the corruption of the present age. Since "the cosmic and the anthropological are inextricably linked for the author of *4 Ezra*," Moo argues, "there is a profound need for both a transformed humanity *and* a cosmic new creation that restores, replaces or transforms the present corrupted world" (103).

The fifth chapter analyzes all of the important passages relating to the eschatology of 4 Ezra, focusing on the role of the created order in the age to come. Moo wisely avoids making a sharp distinction between the messianic age and the new creation when looking for evidence of continuity between the present and future world-ages, because of "the fluidity in the book's portrayal of the end" (127). For example, the eschatological Zion and paradise are not consistently associated with the temporary messianic age, and the earth itself survives to "give back" the dead (7:32) at the beginning of the new world-age (131). The first three episodes (the dialogues) are treated in considerably more detail than the last four (the visions and epilogue).

Nevertheless, Moo's most interesting and original arguments in this chapter pertain to the visions. First, noting the link between "mother Zion" and "mother Earth" in Ezra's address to the mourning woman (10:6–17), Moo suggests that it "could imply in light of the wider context of the book that just as Zion and the earth share a common plight and a present sorrow, their hopes for a future restoration are also inextricably linked" (144). Second, regarding the "field of flowers where no house has been built" (9:24), where the mourning woman is transformed into the New Jerusalem, Moo ventures that by eating the flowers of this field, Ezra "participates proleptically in the paradise that is to come," or perhaps he has found a bit of creation that has not been corrupted by human evil (146–48). The latter interpretation is supported by the mention in the sixth episode of the success of the lost tribes in keeping the commandments in "a more distant region, where humankind had never lived" (13:41). Perhaps there are places in the present world, Moo suggests, where the original goodness of creation has not been lost (152–53). If so, the existence of such places and the "liminal creations" mentioned in 6:1–6 call into question the sharp dualisms often ascribed to 4 Ezra.

This is a well-conceived and well-executed study of the "theology of creation" of 4 Ezra, a theme that has been largely neglected by scholars of apocalyptic literature. Apart from the tendency noted above to exaggerate at times the originality of his interpretations, Moo shows himself to be both a careful and an imaginative scholar. His work provides a valuable corrective to the common assumption that apocalyptic literature is necessarily world-denying and antithetical to a responsible environmental ethic.

Judaism Defined: Mattathias and the Destiny of His People, by Benjamin Edidin Scolnic. Studies in Judaism. Lanham, Md.: University Press of America, 2010. Pp. v + 246. Paper. $35.00. ISBN 9780761851172.

Daniel R. Schwartz, The Hebrew University of Jerusalem, Jerusalem, Israel

This is a very Jewish book, one written from a point of view that is implicitly contemporary and explicitly partisan. The introduction opens with a reference to the annual Jewish celebration of Hanukkah, "the holiday commemorating the valiant deeds of the Maccabees" (1), and the chapter on forced circumcision (1 Macc 2:46) opens with the explanation that the issue was assimilation and that Mattathias well understood "that for an ethnic group, continuity is maintained through difference from the rest of society" (99)—a formulation that fits the Jews of the United States today much better than those of Judea in the second century B.C.E. Similarly, the chapter on Mattathias's decision to allow defensive warfare on the Sabbath (1 Macc 2:39–41) closes by underlining that the decision did not bespeak any lack of respect for Jewish law. Rather, "the innovation was really a modification made out of necessity in order to save Jewish lives from slaughter. The Maccabees were religious keepers of the Sabbath who believed that while Jewish law sometimes needs to be bent, it should never be broken" (215). This sounds more prescriptive than historical and contributes to the goal of restoring faith in the heroes of Hanukkah. As Scolnic frankly puts it, "my purpose is to counter the work of those scholars who would make the Maccabees into merely self-serving, ambitious, non-idealistic, non-pious Hellenistic leaders who used Judaism as a tool for their own advancement" (2)—and thus restore our confidence that it is right to celebrate a holiday commemorating their victory.

Accordingly, the book is built as a series of arguments against views that would undercut the traditional story as told by 1 Maccabees, Josephus, and the ancient (and modern) rabbis. After the introduction, chapter 2 argues (in the face of denials based, inter alia, on the silence of 2 Maccabees) that Mattathias really existed; chapter 3 builds on the premise that ambition was not "the primary ambition for the initial act of rebellion" (19); chapter 4 defends (against suggestions that the Hasmoneans fiddled around with biblical lists) the ancient claim that Mattathias was indeed of priestly stock; chapter 5 argues both that the Hasmoneans were not motivated merely by self-serving ambition and that ambition is not necessarily a vice; the eighty pages of chapter 6 are dedicated to showing that forcible circumcision of uncircumcised Jewish babies (1 Macc 2:46) testified to Mattathias's zeal and idealism (thus again undermining the charge of self-serving ambition); chapter 7 is dedicated to showing that Mattathias's decision to fight in self-defense on the Sabbath (1 Macc 2:39–41) should not be viewed as evidence for his scorn for religious values; and chapter 8 argues (against arguments that it is composite, late, and/or inaccurate) that 1 Maccabees, which provides virtually all of the evidence for this study, is a unitary work written not long after the events it describes and, therefore, worthy of trust. Indeed: "I have studied the different aspects of the Mattathias narrative in 1 Maccabees.... In each case, I have found reason to accept the validity of the text's claims about this important figure" (229).

In the nature of things, some of Scolnic's arguments are better than others. To claim that 2 Maccabees' silence about Mattathias indicates how important he was, for "were he a trivial figure his name would have appeared, even if it were just as Judas' father," so "ironically, the omission of Matthathias in 2Maccabees speaks to his historical importance" (11), seems to be a wonderful example of *petitio principii*. To claim that the fact that there is figural evidence for otherwise nude Greek athletes wearing a *petasos* means that when 2 Macc 4:12 says

Jewish athletes in Jerusalem wore a *petasos* readers should assume they were naked (118)—a point necessary for the case that 1 Macc 1:15 is to be believed when it reports (if it reports; see below) that numerous Jews underwent epispasm—is akin to proving that Socrates was a cat because cats are mortal and so was Socrates. In general, moreover, there is something problematic about a book that amounts to a detailed commentary on 1 Macc 2 but only rarely deals with its Greek text or the underlying Hebrew original. Thus, for an egregious example, there is something problematic about a long discussion (104–17) defending the notion that Jews of the period practiced epispasm that builds solely on Goldstein's Anchor Bible translation of 1 Macc 1:15, "and underwent operations to disguise their circumcision" (Scolnic, 106), without asking if that really corresponds to the much simpler Greek (καὶ ἐποίησαν ἑαυτοῖς ἀκροβυστίας, literally, "and they made themselves foreskins") and without looking for other contemporary evidence for epispasm. That quest would have uncovered the bothersome fact that there seems to be virtually no evidence for epispasm before the first century C.E. Similarly, it is surprising to see Scolnic rejecting B. Bar-Kochva's conclusions (*Judas Maccabaeus* [Cambridge: Cambridge University Press, 1989]) about the relative sizes of the Jewish and Seleucid armies as arbitrary ("He picks and chooses what to accept in 1 Macc; if the numbers of soldiers given do not fit his scheme, they are considered unreliable," 214) without any discussion at all of the data. This leaves the reader suspecting that Scolnic's criticism might derive mainly from the fact that the traditional Jewish prayer for Hanukkah ('Al HaNissim) praises God for giving the wicked "many" (Seleucids) into the hands of the righteous "few."

On the other hand, there is much that is valuable in this book. Perhaps, primarily, its value is to be sought precisely in the point of view underlined above: it shows us what a knowledgeable advocate of Judaism in general, or of the Hasmoneans in particular, might think about the events narrated in 1 Macc 2. Particularly important here is Scolnic's attempt, at various points, to minimize the differences between 1 Maccabees and 2 Maccabees, differences that have usually been noted as part of a characterization of the former as nonreligious (or, as Abraham Geiger put it, Sadducean). How could a book that, as especially the contrast with 2 Maccabees underlines, has no reference to miracles, resurrection, and angels, that advocates warfare on the Sabbath, that makes no reference to sin and atonement, that has no interest in theodicy and little use for martyrs, and, especially as it goes on, makes little reference to God or to prayer be a religious book? Scolnic's response is to argue, at each turn, that the differences are not so polar. Thus, for example, if scholars have often asserted that 2 Maccabees forbade war on the Sabbath and viewed that as a sign of its religious orientation as opposed to the worldliness of 1 Maccabees, Scolnic, in his comparison of 2 Macc 8:25–29 to 1 Macc 4:15–16 (202–3), admits that 2 Maccabees strives to emphasize the importance of Sabbath observance but urges us to remember that "1Macc 3–4 is a passage remarkable for its piety: it is full of prayer, Torah-reading and references to the saving acts of God in the people's history."

Frequently, moreover, Scolnic's approach leads him to detailed observations that are off the beaten path. Thus, for example, most scholars who discuss the importance of circumcision in antiquity view those who insisted upon it, despite the dangers and other costs, either as demonstratively establishing a (more or less) indelible boundary marker or as simply persevering in fulfilling the law. Such scholars might well take notice of Scolnic's detailed and sensitive discussion (127–52) of the relationship of circumcision to immortality and of just what the threat of "excision" (*karet*), imposed upon the uncircumcised by Gen 17:14, can mean to Jews. Similarly, Scolnic's campaign to show that the Hasmoneans did not lightly abandon doubts about the permissibility of defensive warfare on the Sabbath leads him first to interpret 1 Macc 9:44, in the days of Jonathan, as a proclamation by Jonathan that it is permissible to fight in self-defense on the Sabbath, then to argue that Josephus must have been bothered by the question why Mattathias's innovation of the same permission (2:39–41) did not suffice. According to Scolnic, Josephus may well have inferred that Mattathias's decision was not taken to be a legal precedent. Rather, as Scolnic puts it, Josephus may have "understood something very important," that "fighting on the Sabbath was always an ad hoc measure, not so much halakhah or policy as something that was done only when there was no choice. While Mattathias may have stated that it was acceptable, he never created a policy as such" (211). It is clear that both the interpretation of the meaning of Jonathan's words and the inference concerning Josephus's understanding of the legal status of Mattathias's decision derive from a rabbinic interest in issues of Jewish law that does not always characterize commentators of 1 Maccabees. From this point of view, Scolnic's contribution is quite salutary.

SEPTUAGINT

"Translation Is Required": The Septuagint in Retrospect and Prospect, edited by Robert J. V. Hiebert. Society of Biblical Literature Septuagint and Cognate Studies 56. Atlanta: Society of Biblical Literature, 2010. Pp. xvii + 248. Paper. $31.95. ISBN 9781589835238.

Karen H. Jobes, Wheaton College and Graduate School, Wheaton, Illinois

This collection of thirteen papers resulted primarily from an international conference in September 2008 at the Septuagint Institute at Trinity Western University of many of the leading lights in Septuagint studies, as well as scholars in other disciplines from France, Germany, England, and North America. Both the conference and this collection of essays address not only the Septuagint as a translation but also issues arising from recent translations of the Septuagint into English (*New English Translation of the Septuagint*), French (*La Bible d'Alexandrie*), and German (*Septuaginta Deutsch*). It will, therefore, be of interest not only to those in Septuagint studies but also to those involved in translation studies more generally.

The collection leads off with an important paper by Albert Pietersma, "Beyond Literalism: Interlinearity Revisited," which discusses and clarifies his theory first introduced in the 1990s. He stresses that interlinearity as he defines it does not address the *Sitz im Leben* of the Septuagint but rather a linguistic relationship between the Greek and its parent text that has certain inherent and constitutive characteristics. Pietersma's theory rests on Gideon Toury's descriptive translation studies (DTS), which does stress the sociocultural position or function of a translation—a small distinction from its *Sitz im Leben*. Furthermore, referring to the theory as the "interlinear paradigm" suggests the modern interlinear Bible, which has its own function in our society, and would, in accordance with linguistic relevance theory, understandably tilt one's mind toward such construals as Pietersma wishes to distance himself from. So Pietersma's clarification is necessary reading for anyone conversant with this aspect of Septuagint studies.

This interlinear paradigm is one aspect of the *New English Translation of the Septuagint* and the forthcoming Society of Biblical Literature Commentary on the Septuagint, so Pietersma's essay is an apt introduction for the three essays that reflect either on issues of translation or the exegesis of a translated text. Benjamin Wright's "Moving beyond Translating a Translation: Reflections on *A New English Translation of the Septuagint* (NETS)" discusses Toury's DTS as a methodological framework of the NETS project, then considers the alleged function of the Septuagint as described by the Letter of Aristeas in view of Toury's principles. He observes that the sociohistorical function of the Greek translation as reported by Aristeas does not match at all the linguistic character of the translated text. He surveys three recent works that start with the character of the translated text and apply translation theory to reflect on possible sociocultural contexts and specific historical circumstances of its origin. According to Wright, Cameron Boyd-Taylor's 2005 doctoral dissertation, "Reading between the Lines" "offers the most detailed articulation of, and arguments for, the interlinear paradigm" (37). Theo A. W. van der Louw's published dissertation *Transformations in the Septuagint* discusses how the Septuagint translation corroborates certain translation universals. Naomi Seidman's book *Faithful Renderings*, while not limited to biblical translation, ancient or modern, explores "translation narratives" as "religious and political" texts, again calling attention to the function and value of translated work.

Cameron Boyd-Taylor makes an important contribution in "*The Semantics of Biblical Language* Redux" by applying James Barr's work of a similar title to exploring the semiotics of a translated text. His chapter discusses the semantics of "hope" (*elpizo*) in the Greek Psalter and how that contributes to a rhetoric of hope, which in turns points toward a theology of hope.

Two papers reflect on methodological concerns in reference to specific biblical books of the NETS project. In "Ruminations on Translating the Septuagint of Genesis in the Light of the NETS Project," Robert J. V. Hiebert demonstrates the importance for developing and consistently implementing sound translation methodology of the distinction between a translation as produced by someone who had access to the *Vorlage* and the translation as subsequently received by those who did not and, consequently, for whom translation was required. Through five examples he critiques Susan Brayford's translation and commentary on Septuagint Genesis in the Brill series, highlighting the theoretical differences between the Brill series and the forthcoming IOSCS commentary series.

In "Translating a Translation: Some Final Reflections on the Production of the New English Translation of Deuteronomy," Melvin K. H. Peters reviews observations about the Greek translation of Deuteronomy, especially where it disagrees with the Masoretic Text (MT), and uses those data to defend "secular Septuagintalists" (133) against those scholars who, in his opinion, allow their faith commitments to unduly privilege the MT and who resist the idea of the pluriformity of Hebrew Scripture and multiple textual traditions. He argues passionately that the viability and relevance of Septuagint studies depend on ridding the field of the hegemony of the MT.

In "Some Reflections on Writing a Commentary on the Septuagint of Leviticus," Dirk Büchner remarks primarily on its Greek grammar and syntax, the lexicology of pentateuchal technical vocabulary, the Septuagint Pentateuch, and Greek religion. He highlights two aspects of the translator's approach: the intent to provide equivalence even at the expense of good Greek and the need to contextualize by making sense of the Hebrew through Greek cultural conventions.

In more narrowly focused studies, Larry Perkins investigates "'Glory' in Greek Exodus: Lexical Choice in Translation and Its Reflection in Secondary Translations," concluding that the Greek translator was emphasizing the theological concept of Yahweh's *doxa*. Jan Joosten examines the translation of various Hebrew idioms in "Translating the Untranslatable: Septuagint Renderings of Hebrew Idioms," finding that, though different techniques were employed to translate idiomatic expressions, the form of the source text was often preserved. August Konkel looks at "The Elihu Speeches in the Greek Translation of Job," arguing that the shorter length of the Greek Job in comparison to the MT is the creative work of the translator in forming an alternate literary version, not because of a shorter *Vorlage*, and should not be taken as a translation equivalent to the Hebrew version.

In "At the Beginning: The Septuagint as a Jewish Bible Translation," Leonard Greenspoon presents an interesting historical contrast between the approaches of Max Margolis and his student Harry Orlinsky toward the relationship between the Septuagint and the Masoretic Text, perhaps providing an example of the point Melvin Peters makes about the hegemony of the MT.

Alison Salvesen's "A Well-Watered Garden (Isaiah 58:11): Investigating the Influence of the Septuagint" is an excellent survey of daughter versions of the Greek Septuagint in Syriac, Old Latin, Armenian, Coptic, Ethiopic, Christian Palestinian Aramaic, Christian Arabic, Georgian, and church Slavonic. Her contribution gathers much essential information about these daughter versions.

Wolfgang Kraus presents "The Role of the Septuagint in the New Testament: Amos 9:11–12 as a Test Case," taking the reader step by step through the issues involved in understanding the contribution of the Amos quotation in an important New Testament text and questioning the search for the "original focus" of the biblical text in light of textual pluriformity.

Finally, Brian Anastasi Butcher explores the question of the reception and use of NETS by English-speaking Christians of the Eastern Orthodox and Byzantine-Rite Catholic Churches. In "A New English Translation of the Septuagint *and the Orthodox Study Bible: A Case Study in Prospective Reception*," he argues that the "criteriology" of Orthodox biblical translation, the challenges of confessionalism, and the use of Scripture in the Orthodox liturgy will weigh against the use of NETS by this potential audience.

The volume concludes with the panelists' introductory statements made at the conference by Pietersma, Wright, Joosten, and Kraus.

A common thread connecting the many issues addressed throughout this volume is arguably the importance, often overlooked, of distinguishing between the translated text as produced and the translation as received by subsequent interpreters in various religious communities, geographical regions, and of different theological persuasions. This volume is a must read for those involved or interested in modern Septuagint studies or the issues of translation more broadly.

On Conditionals in the Greek Pentateuch: A Study of Translation Syntax, by Anwar Tjen. Library of Hebrew Bible/Old Testament Studies 515. New York: T&T Clark, 2010. Pp. xvi + 267. Hardcover. $120.00. ISBN 9780567575463.

Randall X. Gauthier, Houston Graduate School of Theology, Houston, Texas

Tjen's objective in this work, as the title suggests, is to examine conditional (protasis-apodosis > if/then) clauses in the "oldest recoverable Greek translation" (2) of the Pentateuch. Methodologically, Tjen begins from the standpoint of "translation technique," as popularized by Soisalon-Soininen and further developed largely by the so-called Helsinki school. As such, Greek "conditionals" are examined from the standpoint of their origin as translations from a Hebrew text, and thus his seven-chapter study begins with the Hebrew text (7). More specifically, Tjen sets out to make sense of the "translation syntax" that arises when rendering such clauses from source to target. Central to this objective is the task of determining which conditional constructions in the Greek Pentateuch result from the translation process itself (via linguistic interference from the Hebrew) and which are attributable to regular vernacular Greek expression (2-3). This two-pronged approach necessarily scours original classical and Hellenistic Greek compositions as a point of comparison for what may or may not be deemed "natural." As is typically the custom in LXX studies, the Masoretic Text (MT), in this case Cod L (B19^A), serves as the working representative of the presumed *Vorlage*. Nevertheless, Tjen is cognizant of textual criticism, so other texts (e.g., Samaritan Pentateuch, Dead Sea Scrolls) are considered when necessary. The Greek text is based on the critical Göttingen edition (ed. Wevers), although the Cambridge (Brooke-McLean) edition as well as Alfred Rahlfs's *Handausgabe* (1935) are also utilized in the process. Tjen also helpfully offers English translations of his examples throughout his first two chapters.

Chapter 1 (10–32) begins with a survey of Hebrew "conditionals," and concludes, in concert with Joseph Greenberg's postulate on word order with respect to universal grammar, that in the Pentateuch the protasis normally precedes the apodosis, except in certain formulaic expressions such as those found especially in Deuteronomy (11). Beginning with a survey of *real* conditions (or particles of "lower hypotheticality" such as אם ,כי) and *unreal* conditions (לו) negated by לולי ,לולא, and אלו (לוא)?, 14), as well as doubtful markers (e.g., ה־, הנה, הן, אשר, אבי אולי, 14), Tjen then traces overt markers of the apodosis (resumptive *waw*, כי עתה, כי אז, כי) as well as unmarked conditionals and specialized instances such as elliptical constructions (protasis and apodosis) and wish-oath clauses. He then considers three taxonomies as applied to verb forms and conditionals (*yiqtol* and *weqatal*), those of S. R. Driver (i.e., with respect to temporal reference/realization), C. van Leeuwen (certainty), and Hatav and Hendel (modality). In the end he concedes that the traditional bipartite distinction many grammars make between fulfillment and realization are likely accurate (12, 32), and, without morpho-syntactic criteria (the lack of which are indicative of Driver's and van Leeuwen's taxonomies), there is no need to further subcategorize them.

Chapter 2 (33–67) begins with a survey of Greek "conditionals," focusing primarily on the system in the Koine and secondarily on "diachronic changes from the Classical system from which it is derived" (33). Although Greenberg's universal word order (see above) has been challenged (so Wakker) despite strong support, Tjen contends that the issue requires a more comprehensive investigation. Concrete markers of the protasis include εἰ + indicative or optative, and ἐάν + subjunctive, whereas concrete markers for the apodosis such as ἀλλά, δέ, τότε, τότε δή, and οὕτως are more flexible and optional. Tjen provides a list of four "major" collocations of conditional markers and verb forms (38–39) and surveys additional instances of rare collocations and elliptical expressions (41–48).

Turning next to conditionals with the optative in the LXX, Tjen interacts with Turner's count of twenty-six. From there he reduces the number first to thirteen (thirteen are in 4 Maccabees alone because of "Atticizing"), and then to nine, since the remainder of instances are contested text-critically. Of these, Tjen discounts the "only" example in the Psalms (138[139]:9) as secondary but overlooks the complex conditional string in Ps 7:4–6, where אם + *qatal* (protasis)/jussive string (apodosis) is rendered by εἰ + indicative (protasis), followed by ἄρα + optative string (apodosis). This example is noted as a conditional on page 26 of the previous chapter with respect to the Hebrew text. Further, he does not explain the presence or meaning of the optative in the witnesses that do support it. If anything, *later* inclusions of the optative should be explained, since the optative is seen to be "phasing out" by the time of the Koine. If they are indeed secondary, what motivated them?

Tjen provides a substantive overview of ways in which scholars have classified Greek conditionals. These are presented primarily in time-oriented systems (e.g., Goodwin) and mood-oriented systems (Gildersleeve, 56). More recent variations include those of Boyer's "class" system (1st, 2nd, 3rd, 4th; 58–59); Porter's attitudinal semantics (assertion, projection, 59–60); Ruijgh, Rijksbaron, and Wakker's traditional mood classification; and Young's speech act classification (61). Tjen, however, prefers a modified form of Godwin and Porter's position in terms of degrees of "hypotheticality."

Chapter 3 (68–107) examines different constructions that have been rendered as conditionals in the LXX. Tjen recognizes the difficulty in his task, since many particles that mark conditional sentences (אם, כי, לו) are multifunctional and often designate other functions altogether. Nevertheless, אם and כי (= εἰ or ἐάν) are the most prevalent markers of conditionals in the Pentateuch. With explicit markers such as כי, clauses are both temporal and conditional, and the distinction between the two is often subtle. Indeed, the LXX sometimes opts for ἐάν instead of ὅταν, even where כי is more clearly temporal (78–79). Tjen contends that conditionality is more evident in situations where the promised land is in view, and this betrays the speaker's (the translator's?) doubt over its realization. However, he does consider that the predominance of ἐάν may in fact be evidence of Hebrew interference. His survey considers many other constructions, such as כי אם ... אם, ב/כ, פן, בלתי, ה־, מן, אולי, הנה, הן, אשר, אי, לו(לא), אם + the infinitive construct, various paratactic constructions, attributive particles, and, finally, conditionals involving text-critical issues (e.g., לא read as לו). Tjen shows that the translator adjusts certain unmarked instances to make better conditional sense in the Greek.

Whereas chapter 3 examined the question of how the Greek construes conditionality from various Hebrew constructions, generally, chapter 4 (108–37) specifically examines the "choice of verbal and non-verbal equivalents as well as their collocations with conditional markers" (108). Of particular importance for the author is "the use of different tense-forms and moods in Greek conditional constructions," and especially so in the protasis unless the apodosis requires attention. He concludes that the change in tense forms/moods largely indicates the sense division between protases and apodoses. He examines *yiqtol-weqatal* conditions, since these are the most common in protases (109). Since conditions are typically found in the nonpast domain, *yiqtol* forms are naturally abundant. Likewise, where there is a verbal sequence within a complex conditional, *weqatal* normally takes over. These are generally matched by the Greek subjunctive, which according to Tjen is "genre driven," given the precedent in legal formulations throughout Hellenistic and classical Greek. This likewise explains the predominance of ἐάν over against εἰ in the Pentateuch. In most cases (excepting two; see 117–19) ἐάν + subjunctive is future referring or pertains to some level of hypotheticality or possibility.

Conditionals in the Pentateuch prefer the aorist subjunctive as the unmarked alternative (120), but the choice of tense, in accordance with representative aspectual theory, is still a matter of the translator's "subjective preference for voicing the verbal occurrence as either a single whole, or with regard to its internal constituency" (122). Although εἰ + indicative is an uncommon construction, seventeen occur as *yiqtol-weqatal* renderings. The author also considers that אוּלי + *yiqtol* underlies εἰ + future indicative or ἐάν + present subjunctive, although his title alludes to a match with the aorist (125). Other constructions considered include εἰ + present indicative, εἰ + aorist indicative, אם + *yiqtol* (in oath formulas), participles, infinitives (i.e., nonfinite verbal constructions), pluses and minuses in the LXX, *weqatals* in paratactic constructions, and instances in which verbs clarify ambiguous and lengthy sense division. Tjen offers a helpful summary at the end of this chapter.

Chapter 5 (138–80) continues the theme of chapter 4, but shifts from *yiqtol-weqatal* renderings, the most common in the Pentateuch, to *qatal*, *wayyiqtol*, *qotel*, and other forms. *Qatal* forms are evenly distributed among Genesis, Leviticus, and Numbers, with a relatively even split between indicative and subjunctive verbal forms in the Greek. Tjen spends some time on the εἰ + aorist indicative renderings of *qatal*, since these confirm the tendency for the aorist to convey background material in past-time narrative. Εἰ + perfect indicative reflects stativity, which both the stative aspect (Greek) and *qatal* can do. Following on the discussions of aorist and perfect indicative conditionals is a consideration of the idiom אם מצאתי חן בעיניך ("if I have found favor in your eyes"), since it is rendered equally with aorist and perfect tense verbs (εἰ εὗρον/εἰ εὕρηκα). Furthermore, εἰ + present indicative appears to favor stative *qatals*, as one would expect. The remainder of the chapter is a detailed survey of the other minor collocations and idioms (150–58).

Wayyiqtol forms in conditionals are typically rendered with the aorist subjunctive (ἐάν + subjunctive), as may be expected, but there are also examples noted where the aorist indicative, perfect indicative, present indicative, and aorist participle take that role. Tjen moves next to what he calls "nominal conditionals," opting to place predicative *qotel* forms here. The LXX renders these in various ways, including εἰ + present and future indicative and ἐάν + subjunctive. Instances where non-*qotel* forms occur in nominal situations with particles of existence or nonexistence tend to evoke an explicit verb (εἰμί) in the Greek (169). There are also several interesting instances where ἐάν is followed by nominal clauses (170–72), as well as verbal clauses and other infrequent collocations. Chapter 5 concludes with a helpful summary of the many details discussed.

Whereas most of the prior study concentrated on the protasis of conditional statements, the clause that is distinctly conditional, chapter 6 (181–21) looks at translation technique in the apodosis. Tjen's survey begins with the Greek rendering of *yiqtol* and *weqatal* forms as future indicative and imperative. He demonstrates from contemporaneous Greek literature that the "imperatival" future, often considered to be a Semitism, especially by New Testament scholars, is in fact a natural phenomenon; its *frequency*, however, is because of Hebrew interference. He also examines imperatives (for *yiqtol* and *weqatal*), subjunctives (for *yiqtol*), optatives (for *yiqtol* and *weqatal*), secondary verbal forms (imperfect, aorist), the *participium coniunctum* (adverbial participle), and nonverbal equivalents. The following major sections in this chapter examine the translation technique of *qatal* forms in the apodosis, as well as *wayyiqtol*, nominal sentences, elliptical apodoses, and instances involving text-critical decisions. This chapter closes with a survey of apodotic markers, including apodotic ו, כי, and עתה כי.

Chapter 7 (222–29) provides a brief summary and conclusions. Tjen's concludes that the translators had mixed motivations. The LXX Pentateuch is often riddled with unidiomatic and awkward Greek structure and wording, due to interference and narrow segmentation, but also betrays many instances in which conditionals succeed quite well in their linguistic contexts. This is also evident in the choice of tense vis-à-vis the genre at hand (e.g., interactive and legal-instructional material). The use and freedom of apodotic markers also, for Tjen, betrays mixed motivations. Finally, Tjen concludes that Hebrew interference is prevalent throughout the Greek conditionals of the Pentateuch. Otherwise, the Greek conditionals of this corpus conform to contemporaneous Koine usage.

Tjen has clearly made a novel contribution with this work. Not only are his surveys of conditionals in Hebrew and Greek helpful resources on their own merit (chs. 2–3), but his thorough and systematic approach toward translational syntax in the area of conditionals will be a welcomed contribution for those engaged in the inherently complex field of Septuagint studies. Owing to the complexity of this work, which makes for dense reading, it will undoubtedly serve as a reference for those pursuing this angle or others pertinent to this topic of research.

HEBREW BIBLE/OLD TESTAMENT THEOLOGY

Ethical and Unethical in the Old Testament: God and Humans in Dialogue, edited by Katharine Dell. Library of Hebrew Bible/Old Testament Studies 528. New York: T&T Clark, 2010. Pp. xv + 287. Hardcover. $150.00. ISBN 9780567217097.

Walter Brueggemann, Columbia Theological Seminary, Decatur, Georgia

This volume consists of fourteen essays that have been presented over time in the Cambridge Old Testament Seminar, Cambridge University. The essays feature exactly what one might expect from such an erudite company, namely, closely reasoned, critically informed, discerning, and reliable exegesis, with a reticence about any contemporary connection with the ancient material. The rubric of "ethical" is to be only loosely construed, even though the term "ethics" recurs in the titles of many of the essays. The general topic, even loosely construed, suggests the way in which this distinguished seminar has focused somewhat away from the usual "historical" questions to more venturesome interpretive issues.

Many of the essays include sound critical attention to specific texts. These include Robert Gordon on truth-telling in Gen 2–3, Diana Lipton on desire in Gen 39, Adam Mein on Ps 101 and royal ethics, Janet Tollington on "holy war" in the traditions of Judges, Hilary Marlow on restorative justice that pertains to the land, Graham Davies on friendship in the wisdom traditions, Daniel Estes on the "strange woman" in Prov 1–9, and Philip Jenson on the stratification and hierarchy of commandments in biblical law. In these several essays the writers probe fresh questions in responsible and suggestive ways, while some essays, predictably, are more generative than others.

Among those, of special interest is the essay by Lipton on Joseph and Potiphar's wife in Gen 39. Lipton shrewdly notes the tension between the law and the values and ideals that the law intends to promote, thus allowing for a flexibility of interpretation that keeps the law viable. She probes the way in which Potiphar may be regarded, in the narrative, not only as a courtier but also as a eunuch. In the latter case, the agenda that his wife may pursue through Joseph is the production of an heir in the face of a barren husband. Lipton considers the way in which gender power is at work in the narrative and so offers an important departure from our usual reading.

The volume includes three essays on "postbiblical perspectives" that will be of special interest to readers who know less about this material. Charlotte Hempel considers "family values" in the Second Temple period through a comparative study of Ezra-Nehemiah and the Damascus Document. Both textual traditions are in the wake of the exile and reflect the power of the ideology of the exile. She shows that the Damascus Document is much more severe and coercive in its management of family life, which was taken to be a bearer of holiness, so that priestly supervision was of immense importance. The Damascus Document focuses on an "Examiner" who is to supervise children's nurture, education, and discipline to the enhancement of the priesthood at the expense of fatherly authority.

Carol Dray considers strategies for translation that are evident in the Targums in which the translators exercised immense freedom and imagination in adjusting the texts to fit later circumstance and perspective. She contrasts that evident freedom with the standards of modern translators who, for the most part, attempt (or claim to attempt) to be faithful to the text itself, not only in its verbal rendering but also in its more general intent. She judges that the matter of "translational ethics" is reflected in the work of these ancient translators and that they made deliberate decisions to accent or "whitewash" elements of the texts that they rendered. Her study has important implications for the current "battle for the Bible," concerning the nature of the text as a fixed script under the rubric of "original intent" or as a score to be freshly rendered in each "performance." Clearly, freedom and fidelity are characteristically in deep tension.

Ed Noort offers a study of the way "death is on the move" in the postbiblical tradition in the interest of postmortem existence as the tradition develops. In the end, the extension of life in this way served, he opines, to satisfy and resolve the issue of divine justice in a "deeds-consequences" scheme. It is curious that in his study Noort does not appeal to the important work of Jon Levenson, who would link that development to the restoration of Israel.

Finally, three essays converge concerning what must be the deepest theological issue of the Hebrew Bible/Old Testament, namely, the "dark side" of God. First Ronald Clements, senior among these contributors, a founder of the seminary, and an honoree of the volume, probes the force of "divine anger" in the text. Clements pays attention to the way in which the tradition allows for divine anger and the way in which modern interpreters attempt to soften or explain the force of divine vengeance and jealousy. He offers a strong dose of realism about the subject:

> In any case, we do not need the biblical prophets to tell us about divine anger, since life confronts us with sufficient painful experiences to raise questions about the kindness and justice of the Creator. Experience of the injustices and undeserved pain that pervade the entire created world compels us to question notions of the beneficence of its Author. (95)

The felt awkwardness of divine anger in critical scholarship creates a "stretch" for interpretation:

> It is arguable that modern historiography has frequently left biblical scholarship uncomfortably stretched between defending the essential historicity of the Bible and an inability to explain how divine and human actions interact. (99)

Clements makes an unflinching connection between the raw witness of the text and the actual world we inhabit and, in his gentle way, chides interpreters who try to cover over that telling connection.

Second, John Barton explores the hiddenness and arbitrariness of God and considers attempts to underplay that textual reality by focus on the deep emotional attachment of love that belongs to the person of God in this testimony:

> We cannot have it both ways: if we want to believe in a God who is emotionally engaged, then we have to accept that this will mean a God who knows anger and vengeance as well as forgiveness and love. (126)

Against every attempt to soften the claim of the text, Barton judges that we must, soon or late, "recognize an irreducible core of inexplicable darkness in the Old Testament God" (131). In response to every vigorous scholarly attempt at an "explanation," he finishes with the hardest question:

> Is monotheism really coherent as an account of the world we see around us? I hope the answer is yes, but the Old Testament does not make it an easy question to answer; and it gives us plenty of ammunition if we want to fight on the other side. (134)

Third, Katharine Dell, editor of the volume, considers the conduct of God in the book of Job. She concludes that God in the divine speeches is about power and not justice and is beyond human comprehension and beyond human ethical thought:

But in a sense, that is precisely what God is saying in his vision of the created world—that there is a seeming arbitrariness to wild animals and to gratuitous rain. … However one-sided it may be, all human beings can do it live with the paradox of hoping for ethical treatment by God but without expectation of it. The speeches of God show that there are no guarantees and indeed that to expect such guarantees is to seek control and belittle God in his infinite greatness and wisdom. (182)

She ends by warning against every human effort to reduce this awesome holiness to what is "acceptable" to human ethical reasoning.

These three essays, taken together, are a vigorous recognition that the God witnessed in this text is wholly other and does not conform to our best expectations or govern according to our most serious ethical requirement. The sum of these articles is what I have termed Israel's "countertestimony" that does not fit well with Enlightenment rationality or with the usual confession of the church. These articles are a serious recognition that the God of the text is well beyond our control, beyond our usual scholarly tradition, and beyond the confidence we have long had in the crucial project. They serve to attest, against both the critical tradition and the confessional tradition in which many of us stand, that the God of this text is now a compelling counterpoint to the world we now inhabit. Such rendition is a bold and welcome offer from this most impressive of academic venues.

This volume, rich in its diversity, attests to the lively energy that is now present in critical exegetical work that refuses all of the old "assured results." The volume is, predictably and lamentably, overpriced, so that many who would benefit greatly from its fine work will be denied access.

Oral Tradition in Ancient Israel, by Robert D. Miller II. Biblical Performance Criticism. Eugene, Ore.: Cascade, 2011. Pp. xv + 154. Paper. $20.00. ISBN 9781610972710.

Raymond F. Person Jr., Ohio Northern University, Ada, Ohio

In this short study Miller sets out to produce "a comprehensive study of 'oral tradition' in the narrative books of the Old Testament" (xiii). In chapter 1 he briefly surveys the secondary literature on oral tradition in Old Testament studies from Gunkel to the present, including the "Oral Formulaic Theory" that he associates with the Parry-Lord school (in which he includes not only Milman Parry and Albert Lord but also Walter Ong and Jack Goody) and its impact on Old Testament scholarship. In chapter 2 he rejects the approach of the Oral Formulaic School and argues instead for "the simultaneity of orality and literacy" (20–27). In chapter 3 he presents "the best ethnographic analogies to the biblical material"—Homer, Icelandic sagas, and Arabic epic poetry—and concludes with his notion of "gobbets," which he defines as "intentionally crafted *aides-mémoires* that are constitutive for narration and function as generic markers" (37). Consistent with his rejection of the Oral Formulaic School, he explicitly states that his notion of gobbets is superior to "Lord's formulas and themes" because they are "far more flexible in expression than formulas" (37). Chapter 4 reviews the arguments of William Schniedewind, Susan Niditch, and John Van Seters (among some others) concerning orality and literacy in preexilic Israel and concludes that they "minimize the extent to which Israel was always a society of oral literature full of literate individuals" (54). In chapter 5 Miller returns to his discussion of Icelandic sagas and Arabic epic poetry as "orally derived" literature that is "probably the nearest approximations to the oral literature of ancient Israel" (60). In chapter 6 Miller draws from his comparative evidence in order to extend his notion of gobbets to a methodology by which he hopes to identify "orally derived texts" in the Old Testament. When he applies his own methodology, he concludes that Gen 49 and Judg 5 are two examples of orally derived texts. In his brief conclusion, he summarizes his argument as follows:

> We have seen that any continued reliance on the oral-formulaic school of Parry and Lord, and Goody and Ong by biblical scholars would be highly misguided. There is no formulaic test for orality in a written text, oral poets do not always compose on the spot, societies are seldom entirely oral or entirely literate, and there is no philosophical difference between those that are. (121)

Miller's approach suffers from two significant flaws, both of which are due to his apparent misreading of the secondary literature in the study of oral traditions, especially in the Parry-Lord school. He misrepresents the Parry-Lord school as it exists in its contemporary forms; therefore, his own approach is, on the one hand, simply a restatement of some generally accepted understandings in the Parry-Lord school and, on the other hand, a resurrection of an early approach to the study of oral traditions that has been abandoned by the Parry-Lord school because of its naïve simplicity.

Miller's misrepresentation of the Parry-Lord school begins with his continuing label for the school as "Oral Formulaic." Although it may be the case that in the early work of Parry and Lord the definition of "formula" was too narrow and the compositional role of formulas was overemphasized, this does not remain the case today. For example, over twenty years ago John Miles Foley, who is widely recognized as the foremost contemporary scholar in the Parry-Lord school, concluded as follows concerning the limitations of focusing exclusively upon formulas in order to understand the traditions represented by Homer, *Beowulf*, and Serbo-Croatian epic:

> the best, most faithful characterization of the diction had to be as a heterogeneous collection of both formulaic and not demonstrably formulaic language—all overseen by traditional rules. (*Traditional Oral Epic: The Odyssey, Beowulf, and the Serbo-Croatian Return Song* [Berkeley: University of California Press, 1990], 390)

That is, Miller's critique of the Parry-Lord school is based on (mis)understandings of the early work of Parry and Lord that have already undergone significant self-critique within the school itself, so that the caricature that Miller produces does not fairly reflect the positions of the current adherents of the Parry-Lord school. Thus, his conclusion—"There is no formulaic test for orality in a written text, oral poets do not always compose on the spot, societies are seldom entirely oral or entirely literate, and there is no philosophical difference between those that are" (121)—does not require a rejection of the Parry-Lord school, since prominent scholars in this school (such as Foley) have already rejected such simplistic notions.

We have just seen one example of how Miller's misreading of the Parry-Lord school leads him simply to restate a current understanding within this school, even though he thinks that he is rejecting the school's position. Another case in which he is simply restating a basic conclusion of the contemporary Parry-Lord school is his notion of what he calls "gobbets." On the one hand, his rhetoric suggests that his notion of gobbets is superior to "Lord's formulas and themes" (37) and, therefore, the Oral Formulaic School should be rejected. On the other hand, his own footnotes to others work in his discussion of gobbets includes references to those who are within the Parry-Lord school or at least draw substantially from its observations (e.g., Foley, Lauri Honko, and Ruth Finnegan on 37 nn. 68–70, 73, 75). In fact, his notion of gobbets is simply a restatement of Foley's notion of "traditional phraseology" and "register," which is widely accepted within the Parry-Lord school (see Miller's own footnotes, 37 nn. 70, 73).

Miller justifiably rejects what is often referred to as the "Great Divide thesis," the notion that orality and literacy are so incompatible that one can develop a simplistic oral-formulaic test that will determine if an ancient or medieval literary work is orally derived or not. His argument of the "simultaneity of orality and literacy" is completely consistent with the notions of the interplay of the oral and the written especially in primarily oral societies such as ancient Greece, Anglo-Saxon England, and ancient Israel found in discussion of the Parry-Lord school of today. Although this critique erroneously leads him to reject the Parry-Lord school, he nevertheless falls into the same type of dichotomous thinking of the "Great Divide thesis" itself when he develops his own methodology for identifying "orally derived texts." In his discussion of biblical texts in chapter 6, the following dichotomies are clearly in play in his analysis:

oral versus written
poetry versus prose
early (preexilic) versus late
northern (=Israelite) versus southern (=Judean)

Such simplistic dichotomies have been rejected by the Parry-Lord school with ethnographic evidence clearly demonstrating the falsity of such claims. It is for these reasons that scholars such as Foley have abandoned the whole enterprise of trying to identify which ancient texts are orally derived and which are not, even though they continue to insist that all literary texts with roots in oral tradition, no matter what the exact mode of composition may have been, must nevertheless be understood within a cultural context in which the oral and written engage in significant interplay so that even written texts often betray an oral aesthetics (e.g., Foley, *Traditional Oral Epic*, 3–5). Thus, for example, Miller's analysis of Judg 5 would have profited significantly from the more cautious approach of Susan Niditch (*Judges: A Commentary* [Louisville: Westminster John Knox, 2008]), who similarly concluded that we must read Judges with an oral register in mind but, in contrast to Miller, without necessarily concluding that Judges is orally derived literature. Ironically, Miller rejects the Parry-Lord school based on an outdated assessment of its approach and then turns right around and falls into the same trap that he uses to (falsely) condemn the school.

Lest I give the impression that I learned nothing from this study, let me state that his summary of the Icelandic sagas and Arabic epic poetry in chapter 5 is suggestive, so that I am interested in learning more about these traditions as possible analogues to the Old Testament. Therefore, those who are familiar with the Parry-Lord approach to oral traditions may find a few helpful insights in this short work. However, because of its serious flaws, I cannot recommend it as an introduction to the study of oral tradition in the Old Testament. Susan Niditch's *Oral World and Written Word: Ancient Israelite Literature* (Louisville: Westminster John Knox, 1996) remains the best introduction, even though it is now somewhat dated.

JUDAISM: GENERAL

The Ancient Synagogue from Its Origins to 200 C.E.: A Source Book, by Anders Runesson, Birger Olsson, and Donald D. Binder. Leiden: Brill, 2010. Pp. x + 327. Paper. $69.00. ISBN 9789004161160.

Adele Reinhartz, University of Ottawa, Ottowa, Ontario, Canada

The study of the synagogue is important for Jewish history and Jewish life in antiquity in general, but also more specifically because the synagogue provided the sociopolitical and religious setting for the formation of Judaism and Christianity (the "parting of the ways"). *The Ancient Synagogue from Its Origins to 200 C.E.* is the first comprehensive sourcebook to cover the full range of textual, archaeological, and epigraphical material pertinent to the origins and nature of this central Jewish institution. The limit of 200 was chosen in order to provide some post-70 sources up to and including the Mishnah.

Chapter 1, "Introduction," provides a brief history of synagogue studies, with particular focus on the challenges that face a researcher in this area today. One such challenge pertains to the varied and often loaded ways in which the term "synagogue" has been used in both the ancient and modern literature on the topic. The study of the synagogue has often been based on two widespread but false assumptions: (1) that the term "synagogue" has always referred to an institution separate from the church; (2) that church and synagogue have always been binary opposites in constant conflict. These assumptions arise from the retrojection of often anti-Jewish attitudes from the second century and later back into the first century. The current intellectual climate encourages a reevaluation of such long-held assumptions. Another factor in synagogue research has been the tendency to confuse the different types of usages of the term both in the primary sources and in the secondary literature. The introduction notes that synagogue research tends to fall into four broad topics that are separate but interrelated: spatial, liturgical, nonliturgical, and institutional. Recent scholarship has also highlighted the role of women in synagogue leadership and the presence of Gentiles, including those who may have adhered to the worship of the God of Israel as well as those who did not.

The introduction provides a brief but useful history of the term. In the Second Temple period "synagogue" and its synonyms were used by Diaspora Jews to seek understanding and evoke friendly attitudes from Greco-Roman neighbors and rulers interested in maintaining law and order. In the first century, the earliest Jesus community used it to describe intra-Jewish interactions, whether friendly or hostile. With the growth of Gentile Christianity arose a negative, monolithic, and stereotyped portrayal of the synagogue as representing any and all opposition to Christianity and the polarized portrayal of church and synagogue as rivals. After the Christianization of the Roman Empire, these views became mainstream and contributed to the marginalization of Jews and to antisynagogue legislation. By the rise of Islam in the seventh century, the social separation of synagogue and church was a fait accompli. One might add that the current push toward rethinking the early relationships between Jews and the Jesus community, of which the synagogue is merely one element, stems at least in part from a desire to undo the binary opposition between Judaism and Christianity ("synagogue" and "church") that has been so firmly entrenched over the course of the past two millennia.

Chapters 2 and 3 provide the sources pertaining to synagogues in the Land of Israel (ch. 2) and the Diaspora (ch. 3). Each of these chapters has two main divisions—"Identified Locations" and "General References and Unidentified Locations"—and is further divided into subsections for each separate site. Each subsection presents any literary references in the original language and then in English translation, followed by a short list of references in secondary literature and some brief comments. These references are followed by a listing and discussion of archaeological data and, where available, drawings. Chapter 2 covers twenty sites from the Land of Israel—from Caesarea to Tiberias—as well as general references to synagogues in the Galilee and Judea and from the land of Israel more generally. Chapter 3 covers sites from Achaia, Asia, the Bosporan Kingdom, Cyprus, Cyrenaica, Egypt, Galatia, Hungary, Italy, Macedonia, Mesopotamia and Syria—fifty-two in total—and three general references to Diaspora synagogues found in literary sources (two in Philo's treatises and one in Jas 2:6).

Chapter 4 presents and discusses seven major literary sources, from the New Testament (2 Corinthians and Acts), Philo, as well as Artemidorus, Cleomedes, Tacitus, and Justin Martyr. Chapter 5 does the same for Jewish temples outside

Jerusalem, specifically in Babylonia (Casiphia), Egypt (Elephantine, Leontopolis), Idumea (Lachish and Beesheva), Syria (Antioch), and Transjordan ('Araq el-Emir), as well as some unspecified locations in Egypt and Transjordan.

The catalogue of sources is followed by a bibliography; lists of illustration credits, abbreviations, and sigla; indices of primary sources, subjects, and names; synagogue terms; and a map of the synagogue sites referenced in the sourcebook.

The sourcebook includes explicit references to synagogues as well as passages or inscriptions that may plausibly be read as references to synagogues. For example, Paul's 2 Cor 3:14–15 is cited as a "general reference" (item no. 197, p. 254). Relevant here is the reference to hearing the reading of the "old covenant," which the editors explain as a "probable reference to the reading of Torah in the synagogues." More tenuous perhaps is the use of John 2:6 as a source for the synagogue at Cana. This verse refers to the six large stone jars used for the ritual of purification. The editors argue that the sheer size and number of these jars would indicate that they were not portable jars but rather were permanent and that the most reasonable location for these would be the synagogue. This is quite plausible, but it should be noted that ritual handwashing was required as part of Sabbath, holiday, and festive meals associated with life-cycle events that were not often or necessarily conducted in a synagogue building. Thus, in the Land of Israel stone jars may well have been located in a public square, village gate, or other public indoor or outdoor space.

This volume will be extremely helpful for scholars and general readers interested primarily in synagogue buildings prior to the third century C.E. As the editors point out, however, studies of the synagogue inevitably must tackle the ambiguity both in the literary sources and in the scholarship between the synagogue as a social institution and the synagogue as a building. The editors provide a good if necessarily brief discussion of this and other ambiguities, pointing to the anachronistic application of contemporary criteria and realities to the ancient synagogue. But the collection itself seems to lean toward a primarily architectural understanding of the term, which may itself be anachronistic. Today, of course, we think of synagogues as buildings in the first instance, but whether and to what extent this was the case in the first century still remains to be determined.

Nevertheless, this sourcebook serves its purpose admirably. The book is user-friendly due to the numbering system, the detailed and well-organized table of contents, and the various indexes. To my knowledge, the sourcebook is complete, within its stated geographical and chronological parameters, except, of course, for sites uncovered since its publication, such as the first-century synagogue structure uncovered in 2009 at Magdala (the identification of this new site as a synagogue is much more certain than the 1976 find by Loffreda and Corbo, discussed on p. 55, item no. 27). The inclusion of literary references in both the original languages and in translation is valuable. A desideratum for a future edition would be an index of modern authors that would steer readers who might want quick and easy access to who has written about which site. These references are included under each item, but a full listing would be welcome.

The book is a most welcome addition to the reference shelf of scholars working in the areas of Second Temple Judaism, early Christianity, archaeology, ritual, and many others, particularly now that it is available in paperback and therefore more affordable edition. One hopes that it will be updated periodically in order to reflect new discoveries and that it will be joined by a similar sourcebook for the period from the third century c.e. and beyond.

Ancient Judaism: New Visions and Views, by Michael E. Stone. Grand Rapids: Eerdmans, 2011. Pp. xiv + 242. Paper. $30.00. ISBN 9780802866363.

Joseph L. Angel, Yeshiva University, New York, New York

This book is a collection of seven essays dealing with a variety of central topics in the study of Second Temple Judaism. In the preface, the author expresses his principal compositional motivation: "to engage some assumptions and axiomatic beliefs that have helped determine the directions of scholarship in the field during the last half-century." Stone, a virtuoso who has produced significant research in the field for nearly fifty years, could not be better suited for the task. The attractive volume includes a substantial bibliography and indexes of subjects and names and ancient sources.

Chapter 1 ("Our Perception of Origins: New Perspectives on the Context of Christian Origins") exposes one of the gravest ills plaguing the study of Second Temple Judaism. The problem arises from the fact that the written sources from this era (barring the Dead Sea Scrolls and other epigraphic evidence) have been transmitted and filtered through Jewish and Christian orthodoxies that developed only after the age in question. In general, Second Temple period traditions reinforcing these later religious configurations were retained while incompatible ones were discarded. Since modern scholars operate in a world formed by the same orthodoxies that have selected the available data, a vicious circle emerges whereby scholarship tends to perceive in the preserved material "evidence that accords with and buttresses those orthodoxies" and "to privilege the elements that are in focus through those particular 'spectacles,' even if other phenomena are present in the same data." The way out of such distortion, avers Stone, is through the integration of all the available evidence into a balanced picture fostered by scholarly introspection and avoidance of the "spectacles of orthodoxy." One of Stone's key contributions here is his agenda for future scholarship. He argues convincingly for the need to increase the available pool of data through the search for still-unknown sources in existing Jewish and Christian manuscript traditions and for the incorporation of evidence preserved in such "obscure" languages as Armenian, Georgian, and Slavonic. In chapter 2 ("Adam and Enoch and the State of the World"), Stone compares two significant explanations for the origins of evil bequeathed by Second Temple Judaism: the "Enoch-Noah axis," which attributes the evils of the present world to demonic forces born out of the primordial rebellion of the watchers, and the "Adam and Eve axis," which views the evils of the world as stemming from human disobedience. Since the library of Qumran contains almost no interest in the latter, but an intensive interest in the former (represented by numerous copies of a variety of pre-sectarian compositions), Stone justly concludes that the former worldview was favored by and fundamental to the Qumran sect. Significantly, he locates an "allied focus" in the pseudepigraphic traditions preserved at Qumran concerned with the priestly line of the patriarch Levi. These traditions unexpectedly incorporate Noah into the primordial priestly genealogy as the originator of sacrifice. This Noahic focus is linked to the Enochic axis, according to which Noah represents a sort of second Adam who nurtures postdiluvian humanity by transmitting his knowledge of sacrifice and antidemonic techniques. The author concludes that the emphasis on Noah as progenitor of priestly lore may be understood as the product of the alienation of a stream of Judaism from the Jerusalem temple in the third century B.C.E. Here Stone's warnings from the previous chapter come back into focus. Since we have no way of determining how prevalent the ideas in these pseudepigrapha were, we cannot assess the pervasiveness of either axis in Second Temple society in general. Moreover, it should be recalled that the Adamic and Enochic axes were not the only explanations for the present world order available at Qumran. Danielic material, for instance, survives in numerous manuscripts, and it is not clear that such complexes of ideas developed in complete isolation from one another.

Chapter 3 ("Apocalyptic Historiography") presents a nuanced discussion of the shift from prophetic to apocalyptic conceptions of history that characterized the Second Temple period. Stone charts two vital and intertwined developments: the introduction of the notion of an eschaton, which made possible the conceptualization of history as a coherent and meaningful whole, and the yearning to bridge the chasm between the Deuteronomic ideal of retribution and actual historical events, which resulted in the projection of the resolution into transcendent temporal and spatial realms. Numerous typical elements of apocalyptic historiography, such as the schematization of all of history into grand patterns and the lack of concern with individual historical events, are to be understood as flowing from these conceptual shifts. The clarity and conciseness with which Stone sets forth these rather complex issues ensure that this chapter will remain of enduring value for students of apocalyptic historiography.

Chapter 4 ("Visions and Pseudepigraphy") contains a plea for the integration of the understanding of religious experience as a fundamental factor behind the composition of ancient Jewish religious writings, particularly the apocalyptic pseudepigrapha. To those scholars who view these writings as fictional manifestations of a stereotypical literary convention (and thus not reflective of true experience), Stone devotes a sustained response. First (rehashing in some detail the well-known thesis from his Hermeneia commentary), he argues that the uniqueness of the portrayal of the experience of the visionary in 4 Ezra precludes dependence on stereotypical literary influences and most likely illustrates reliance on "direct or mediated knowledge of religious experience." Second, the dependence on stock traditions characterizing other pseudepigrapha does not exclude the possibility of an underlying authentic religious experience, since we should expect authors to express such experiences in the traditional terms and cultural language available to them. Although he concedes that criteria to determine whether a particular author is relating personal experience or drawing on transmitted stores of knowledge do not and may never exist, Stone maintains that "religious experience always stood in the background, whether at first, second, or third remove." A second section of the chapter explores the emergence and function of the phenomenon of pseudepigraphy, and the implications of the fact that real visionary activity is expressed in pseudepigraphic form.

In chapter 5 ("Bible and Apocrypha") Stone weighs in on the intense discussion surrounding the formation of the canon of the Hebrew Bible. While agreeing that the terms "canon" and "Bible" are not applicable to the Second Temple period, he warns that underplaying the existence of collections of authoritative writings is equally unacceptable. The codicological data from Qumran as well as other evidence indicates the crystallization of the Pentateuch by the third century at the latest (and Stone prefers a much earlier date going back to Ezra). This detail should serve as a warning to those who would deny the special status of the Torah in relation to such rewritten biblical works as Jubilees. The Prophets collection likely included all of the books of the present corpus, but it was not fixed and probably contained a broader selection of works. The situation was fluid and complex, with different groups maintaining different views of the authoritative written tradition. Moreover, revelation was multiform in this period, and certain writings could be venerated as inspired (e.g., the pesharim) without being considered "biblical."

Chapter 6 ("Multiform Transmission and Authorship") treats the phenomenon of "clusters," or groups of texts representing multiple configurations of the same apocryphal material. Specifically, Stone examines examples associated with Adam, Ezra, and Elijah. (Although this evidence stems from the first millennium C.E., he justifies the inclusion of this discussion in the book because it "affects the transmission of texts relating closely to the Second Temple period.") Rejecting attempts to explain the variety of text forms by means of traditional stemmatic analysis, he suggests origins in oral and fluid monastic settings. By his own admission, this is far from a complete solution, but Stone succeeds in his chief goal of illuminating an important direction for future research. One can only hope that scholars will take measures to overcome the imposing language barriers impeding such important textual work.

Chapter 7 ("The Transmission of Apocrypha and Pseudepigrapha") charts the process by which the nonbiblical Jewish writings of the Second Temple period were transmitted by the oriental Christian churches and subsequently "rediscovered" by European scholars in the eighteenth century. Stone suggests that the choice of living Jewish tradition to reject these works relates to a change in the understanding of authority and a shift in literary genres (from individually authored pseudepigrapha to collections of legal and homiletical material). Fittingly, the chapter (and hence the book) concludes with two suggestions for the direction of future scholarship. First, Stone expresses pleasure with the recent shift toward broadened chronological range in pseudepigrapha studies, as it moves the field away from the dominating orthodoxy-conditioned question of what these works can teach about Christian origins. But as long as this concern continues to be valued above others, distortion remains inevitable. Second, he once again calls for the mining of known and very diverse Jewish and Christian manuscript traditions for remnants of ancient traditions that will ultimately contribute to a more complex picture of Second Temple Judaism.

In a concise presentation, this book manages to illuminate several of the fundamental issues in the study of Second Temple Judaism with a methodological distance and clarity not often encountered in the field. In an academic environment of narrow and all too often atomized specializations, Stone's broad grasp of the contours of the preserved data (with due attention to both what is present and what is absent) as well as his ability to assess their overall significance have produced a stirring reminder of the "bigger picture" to which even the narrowest scholarly endeavors are to be related. Perhaps more importantly, his contribution has spotlighted the need to reexamine and move beyond the artificial boundaries imposed by the field that have been perpetuated, largely unconsciously, for generations. The introspective approach championed by Stone is a step forward on the path toward a more accurate and highly complex view of Second Temple Judaism. Further progress will demand dedication to a balanced consideration of the ever-expanding corpus of data unfettered by the "baggage" of inherited orthodoxies.

Issues of Impurity in Early Judaism, by Thomas Kazen. Coniectanea Biblica New Testament Series 45. Winona Lake, Ind.: Eisenbrauns, 2010. Pp. viii + 201. Paper. $34.95. ISBN 9781575068114.

John W. Fadden, University of Denver/Iliff School of Theology, Denver, Colorado

In *Issues of Impurity in Early Judaism*, Thomas Kazen offers a collection of eight articles on various issues relating to impurity and purification in early Judaism. Chapters 1, 2, 5, 6, and 8 are new, while chapters 3, 4, and 7 are previously published. The chapters work well together, exploring diverse yet related issues. The collection is a welcome contribution to the ongoing discussion of impurity in early Judaism.

The first chapter (1–12) introduces the book. Kazen frames the purpose of the book as a discussion of some of the issues of impurity in early Judaism, as opposed to a general overview or a systematic discussion of Second Temple period purity (1–2). The issues he plans to touch on in the following chapters include the relationship between impurity and sin, discrepancies that are evident within and between various purity laws, notions of purity "systems" and graded impurity and graded purification, the isolation and expulsion of impurity bearers, and the practice of eating ordinary food (*chullin*) in purity (10ç12). Kazen also provides a basic historical context for his discussion of impurity. He locates the development of purity concepts within the Second Temple period temple-state under Persian sovereignty (9). Additionally, Kazen suggests that concepts of purity developed in both "home" and "cult" realms (10).

The second chapter (13–40) provides an interesting and potentially fruitful attempt to use the tools of the cognitive sciences to suggest that three emotions—disgust, fear, and sense of justice—are important for ideas of impurity and the rituals handling impurity (13). In so doing, Kazen endeavors to provide an explanation of the relationship between impurity and sin. Unlike other theories of impurity that have struggled to explain the blending of moral and ritual impurity in early Judaism, Kazen argues that a common denominator in both categories is in underlying cognitive-emotional experiences (16). He suggests that emotions are intimately involved in human reasoning, judgment, and behavior. Negative emotional responses underlie the idea of impurity. Disgust involves moral evaluation and is a socially conditioned emotion. Dietary laws, contact contagions, and impure behavior, Kazen proposes, are based on the emotion of disgust (20–23). Furthermore, the divine threat associated with impure behavior and unclean states suggests that the emotion of fear is also involved in the ideas of impurity and purification (23). Kazen puts forth that some purification rites contain vestiges of more ancient beliefs connecting impurities to demonic powers in need of exorcism (25). Finally, taking sense of justice as a distinct emotional complex, Kazen proposes that a fundamental sense of justice requires the removal of impurities and a restoration of equilibrium that is accomplished through *kipper* rites (39).

Chapter 3 (41v61) highlights the discrepancies that remain after the systematic shaping of the purity laws. There is no one explanation of these discrepancies (60). Kazen suggests that some of the discrepancies within Lev 15 are better explained from early conceptions of impurity that make distinctions between the bearer of impurity and the impurity of the discharge (54). As for discrepancies between Lev 15 and Num 5, Kazen proposes that impurity associated with demonic threat may help to explain some of these differences (60).

In chapter 4 (63–89), Kazen argues that 4Q274 deals with the behavior of impurity bearers at an intermediate stage of lesser impurity compared to more permanent impurity bearers and, as such, the text witnesses an early origin for the ideas of graded impurity and graded purification (63). Kazen gives special attention to the case of the menstruant, suggesting that her initial impurity is mitigated by a first-day purification water rite that is analogous to other first-day water rites (e.g., the biblical rule for "lepers" and the ablution for those with corpse impurity). Kazen argues that first-day ablutions for corpse impurity developed and became a widespread practice in the Second Temple period, which is extended to the menstruant as a systemic necessity. This is not just a practice of sectarians but a developing expansionist practice that served the purpose for social integration and eating in purity (89).

Kazen takes up the question of isolation and expulsion of impurity bearers in chapter 5 (91–111). A key thrust of the chapter looks at the status of the *zavah* at the end of the Second Temple period with an eye toward the woman with a blood flow in Mark 5. While there is a basic systemic shaping of the discharge laws of Lev 15 at the end of the Second Temple period, Kazen points out that there was not complete harmonization of every detail. Kazen shows how the various impurities in Lev 15 appeared to be treated at the end of the Second Temple period. While the case of the "lepers" was relatively clear, the case of dischargers was more difficult. Of all the dischargers, the *zavah* was the most vulnerable. As long as irregular bleeding continued, the *zavah* was unable to lessen contamination potency by a first-day rite. Kazen suggests that the *zavah* was worse off than any impurity bearer besides the "leper" at the end of the Second Temple period, subject to restrictions and likely isolation in stricter locations (111). Kazen suggests the story of the woman with a blood flow in Mark 5 is a Greek, pre-Markan tradition incorporated by Mark. He notes that Mark alludes to Lev 15 but makes no explicit point about it. In other instances where purity is a concern, Mark includes necessary details for his uninformed, Gentile audience as needed. His failure to do so here suggests that Mark is not interested in considering the purity issues. Rather, Mark is concerned with the miraculous aspect of touch. Nonetheless, the narrative does conform to the general picture of the *zavah* at the end of the Second Temple period (109).

In chapter 6 (113–35), Kazen takes up the issue of hand washing before ordinary meals to eat the meal in purity, and he relates the issue to Mark 7. Kazen takes issue with those who would describe eating ordinary food in purity as "priestly." Rather, it is a practice that results from the desire to achieve as high a degree of purity as possible (115). With a general view of graded impurity and graded purification, the washing of hands is one of many practices intended to increase one's purity. This is a practice that, among certain portions of the population, was widely practiced at the end of the Second Temple period and advocated by the expansionist groups. Kazen suggests that Mark 7 is concerned with inner (moral) impurity and outer (ritual) impurity, which is not identical with hand washing and food impurity (128). It is an earlier Jesus tradition that was concerned with the question of hand washing and food impurity. Mark has shaped the earlier tradition for his later Gentile audience, thus Kazen rejects an early dating of Mark.

Chapter 7 (137–49) looks at the Lukan parable of the Good Samaritan. Kazen offers an argument for giving it a prehistory within the Palestinian-Jewish context addressing first-century C.E. Jewish purity concerns (137). The implicit view sees the relative value of humanitarian concerns to purity concerns. Kazen's discussion of the topic also highlights that the story's view is by no means unique in the Palestinian-Jewish context, but it would be in conflict with some other Jewish opinions. This would, then, be evidence of an early voice criticizing the priorities in applying corpse impurity rules, a criticism with similarities found in later rabbinic discussions (148–49).

In the final chapter (151–67), Kazen provides a review of Meier's fourth volume of *A Marginal Jew*. This review also serves as a summary of some of Kazen's views expressed in earlier chapters and, as such, is a fitting conclusion to Kazen's collection. While Kazen has points of agreement with Meier's interpretation of purity halakah, he also finds disagreement with Meier. Kazen criticizes Meier for failing to allow the general picture of diversity toward impurity to play a substantial role in Meier's view of Jesus and purity (156). Kazen shows how his reading of Mark 7:15 leads is preferred to Meier's conclusions. Meier's method leads to the conclusion that purity was not an issue for Jesus (166). For Kazen, Jesus may have had a relative priority of concern in which the kingdom vision was a crucial factor for his attitude toward halakic issues (167).

This collection does well in positioning Kazen within the ongoing conversation of impurity and purification in early Judaism and the relationship of Jesus and purity. The topic of impurity has been a source of vibrant scholarship in recent years, and Kazen's articles are a fine contribution to this conversation. This book is not for someone looking for a general introduction to impurity in early Judaism, but, for those with a general knowledge, it will be a welcome addition to current scholarship on diverse issues of impurity in early Judaism and on the relationship of Jesus to purity issues.

JUDAISM: DEAD SEA SCROLLS

Qumran and Jerusalem: Studies in the Dead Sea Scrolls and the History of Judaism, by Lawrence H. Schiffman. Grand Rapids: Eerdmans, 2010. Pp. xx + 483. Paper. $35.00. ISBN 9780802849762.

Matthew A. Collins, University of Bristol, Bristol, United Kingdom

This latest installment in the Eerdmans Studies in the Dead Sea Scrolls and Related Literature series constitutes a collection of articles by Lawrence H. Schiffman on the broad topic of "Qumran and Jerusalem," representing "a cross between a book of collected studies and an independently written volume" (x). Most of the essays have been previously published (1987–2007), though, while written separately, "are essentially part of an ongoing research project that is brought together here, properly organized and able to express the overall thesis that serves as the basis of these various studies" (x). Thus the volume is not merely a collection of disparate essays but is intended to form a coherent whole, with the finished product serving as a "companion" or "follow-up" volume to Schiffman's earlier work, *Reclaiming the Dead Sea Scrolls* (Philadelphia: Jewish Publication Society, 1994).

In terms of content, the unifying factor tying these essays together is their focus upon "the Qumran sectarians within the wider context of Second Temple Judaism" (xi), examining the "close relationship" and "basic commonalities" between the Judaism of the scrolls (the identification of a Qumran sect behind the collection is assumed) and that centered in Jerusalem. Indeed, the author pointedly suggests that "one cannot study Qumran without Jerusalem nor Jerusalem without Qumran" (xi). Despite having originally been written and published over a twenty-year period, the articles have been "substantially revised" and updated (e.g., to reflect more recent publications and discussion, as well as for the sake of stylistic coherence), while "readers will often find that the chapters here have been reorganized, and in some cases that material has been omitted to prevent duplication or to remove excessively specialized discussions," in the interest of making the volume "understandable to a wider audience" (x). This latter aim has also resulted in the deliberate omission of "overly specific or philologically-based studies" (xi), while essays focusing specifically on the Temple Scroll have likewise been excluded since they are intended to appear in a separate volume.

Following the preface (x–xiii), the acknowledgments (xiv–xvi) helpfully list the original publication details for each of the articles reprinted here. This is in turn followed by a list of abbreviations employed (xvii–xx). The main bulk of the volume constitutes an introduction plus twenty-five further chapters (divided between six separate sections: "The Scholarly Controversy"; "History, Politics, and the Formation of the Sect"; "Jewish Law at Qumran"; "Religious Outlook of the Qumran Sectarians"; "Qumran Sectarians and Others"; "Language and Literature"), together reflecting twenty-four previously published articles (one split into two for chs. 8 and 9) and one previously unpublished (ch. 21). Space prohibits a thorough discussion of all twenty-six essays, but, in order to provide something of an overview, a brief description of each contribution will be offered, along with some consideration of the collection as a whole.

The introduction, "The Qumran Scrolls and Rabbinic Judaism" (1–11 [orig. 1999]), forms a backdrop to the entire volume, arguing that halakic issues and disputes are the key to understanding Jewish sectarianism in the Second Temple period, noting further that these legal rulings "also function as sociological boundary markers" (6). A brief look at sectarian halakah (e.g., regulations for entry into the group, punishment, charity) is followed by a concise but astute discussion of "common halakah" (e.g., the practice of wearing phylacteries), in which the reader is reminded that "the vast majority of legal rulings ... were common to Second Temple period Jews" (8), stressing the important point that "our sources tend to emphasize disagreements over commonalities" (9). The introduction ends by drawing some preliminary conclusions about the role of the scrolls in understanding pre- and post-70 C.E. continuity, highlighting the fact that they "negate the assumption of a monolithic Judaism" and yet play a part in helping us understand how "this period of great variegation gave way to that of standardization and consensus, and the emergence of rabbinic Judaism" (11).

The first of six main sections, "The Scholarly Controversy" (13–78), contains three chapters. Chapter 1, "The Many 'Battles of the Scrolls'" (15–43 [orig. 2001]), constitutes a general introduction to the topic, revisiting the history of discovery and publication and providing a brief overview of the various theories of origin, the nature of the collection, the relationship to early Christianity, and the significance of the biblical material. Chapter 2, "Literary Genres and Languages of the Judean Scrolls" (44–62 [orig. 2007]), examines the different literary genres and compositions reflected in the Qumran, Masada, and Bar Kokhba texts, then goes on to discuss the evidence contained therein for the linguistic situation in late antiquity, in particular as it relates to the use and diversity of Hebrew and Aramaic language/dialects. Chapter 3, "Halakhah and History: The Contribution of the Dead Sea Scrolls to Recent Scholarship" (63–78 [orig. 1999]), notes that "it is virtually impossible to separate Jewish law and Jewish history from one another" (63) and looks at the role played by the scrolls in modern studies of Jewish halakah, highlighting in particular the impact of the Temple Scroll and MMT.

The second section, "History, Politics, and the Formation of the Sect" (79–139), contains four chapters. Chapter 4, "Community without Temple: The Qumran Community's Withdrawal from the Jerusalem Temple" (81–97 [orig. 1999]), addresses the community's attitude to (and withdrawal from) the temple, identifying an eight-stage development documented within the texts, from disagreements with temple authorities through to eschatological expectations of a new, divinely built temple. Chapter 5, "Political Leadership and Organization in the Dead Sea Scrolls Community" (98–111 [orig. 2003]), examines the evidence for leadership structures, organization, and "the separation of powers" (98), focusing on the following areas: kings and priests; priests and laymen; courts and the rights of the accused; sectarian leadership; royal and priestly Messiahs; and the messianic assembly. Chapter 6, "The New Halakhic Letter (4QMMT) and the Origins of the Dead Sea Sect" (112–22 [orig. 1990]), turns to 4QMMT and its potential historical significance for shedding light on the halakic disputes lying behind the origins of the Qumran community. Chapter 7, "The Place of 4QMMT in the Corpus of Qumran Manuscripts" (123–39 [orig. 1996]), continues the theme of the previous chapter by discussing the various constituent parts of 4QMMT (the calendar, the legal section, the homiletical section) in the wider context of other Qumran texts, noting the many similarities with other documents believed to date from the formative period of the sect.

The third section, "Jewish Law at Qumran" (141–215), contains five chapters. Chapter 8, "Legal Texts in the Dead Sea Scrolls" (143–69 [orig. 2007]), surveys the major (CD, 4QMMT, 1QS, 1QSa, 11QT, 4Q265) and minor (4Q251, 4Q274, 4Q276–277, 4Q284a, 4Q477) legal texts, commenting upon their structure and contents. This is followed up in chapter 9, "Codification of Jewish Law in the Dead Sea Scrolls" (170–83 [orig. 2007]), by a discussion of these texts in the context of legal codes and codification, especially in terms of redactional activity and the "interpretation, reconciliation, and homogenization" (172) of underlying scriptural passages. Chapter 10, "Pre-Maccabean Halakhah in the Dead Sea Scrolls and the Biblical Tradition" (184–96 [orig. 2006]), attempts to identify pre-Maccabean (ca. 450–168 B.C.E.) Jewish law in the scrolls, extrapolating from what sources we have (including late biblical sources, such as Ezra and Nehemiah) in order to comment upon wider historical issues and promoting an early (pre-Maccabean) date for both the origins of the Pharisee/Sadducee halakic dispute and the development of midrashic and mishnaic approaches to legal texts. Chapter 11, "Contemporizing Halakhic Exegesis in the Dead Sea Scrolls" (197–203 [orig. 2005]), briefly examines the phenomenon of contemporizing exegesis (e.g., as known from the pesharim) within halakic texts (in particular, CD and 11QT), noting, for instance, the attempt by the author of the Temple Scroll to create, via differentiation and contemporization, "an up-to-date way of realizing the halakhic requirements of the Bible in his own age" (198). Chapter 12, "Halakhic Elements in 4QInstruction" (204–15 [orig. 2004]), looks at what little halakic material can be found in 4Q415–418a, 4Q418c, and 4Q423 (specifically, regarding the vows of a married woman, the law of mixed species, and laws of the firstborn), concluding that 4QInstruction is not sectarian in character.

The fourth section, "Religious Outlook of the Qumran Sectarians" (217–318), contains six chapters. Chapter 13, "The Early History of Jewish Liturgy and the Dead Sea Scrolls" (219–34 [orig. 1987]), evaluates liturgical patterns in the scrolls and compares them with early rabbinic traditions. Chapter 14, "The Concept of Covenant in the Qumran Scrolls and Rabbinic Literature" (235–55 [orig. 2004]), compares presentations of the covenants of Noah, Abraham, Jacob, Sinai, and Levi and Aaron in Qumran and rabbinic texts, as well as looking at the concept of covenant within Qumran sectarian ideology. Chapter 15, "Holiness and Sanctity in the Dead Sea Scrolls" (256–69 [orig. 2006]), examines issues of holiness and sacred space in the texts, highlighting two fundamental schemes present in the texts: spatial/geographical and individual/group holiness. Chapter 16, "Messianic Figures and Ideas in the Qumran Scrolls" (270–85 [orig. 1992]), turns to the question of messianic expectation in the scrolls, addressing the "diversity and pluralism" (271) attested across the corpus. Chapter 17, "The Concept of Restoration in the Dead Sea Scrolls" (286–302 [orig. 2001]), focuses on sectarian concepts of restoration, across various "spatial, temporal, and spiritual" (287) planes, identifying three main themes: present versus eschaton, Israel versus the sectarians, and restoration versus utopia. Chapter 18, "Jerusalem in the Dead Sea Scrolls" (303–18 [orig. 1996]), surveys both explicit and implicit references to Jerusalem in the scrolls, dividing these into three separate yet complementary categories: the Jerusalem of history, of religious law, and of eschatology.

The fifth section, "Qumran Sectarians and Others" (319–80), contains four chapters. Chapter 19, "The Pharisees and Their Legal Traditions according to the Dead Sea Scrolls" (321–36 [orig. 2001]), assesses the Qumran evidence for the Pharisees (making several assumptions about which sobriquets refer to this group), concluding that, "contrary to widespread scholarly opinion, tannaitic literature preserves reliable information about the pre-70 C.E. Pharisees" (335). Chapter 20, "Pharisees and Sadducees in Pesher Nahum" (337–52 [orig. 1993]), continues the theme of the previous chapter by attempting to extract historical information about the Pharisees and Sadducees from 4QpNah, again concluding that the Qumran material essentially confirms the picture provided by the later sources. Chapter 21, "Inter- or Intra-Jewish Conflict? The Judaism of the Dead Sea Scrolls Community and Its Opponents" (353–64 [previously unpublished]), addresses the question of Judaism versus Judaisms in the context of the scrolls and the Second Temple period, examining points of consensus and disagreement and suggesting that, in the view of the sect, "there was only one Judaism, which some followed and most violated" (363). Chapter 22, "Non-Jews in the Dead

Sea Scrolls" (365–80 [orig. 1997]), focuses on attitudes to non-Jewish groups and Jewish/non-Jewish relations, particularly in terms of legal rulings governing interaction between the two.

The sixth and final section, "Language and Literature" (381–423), contains three chapters. Chapter 23, "Pseudepigrapha in the Pseudepigrapha: Mythical Books in Second Temple Literature" (383–92 [orig. 2004]), investigates the phenomenon of "fictitious pseudepigrapha" (383), references in Second Temple literature, not to lost books, but to texts that may never have existed. Chapter 24, "Second Temple Literature and the Cairo Genizah" (393–410 [orig. 1997–2001]), evaluates the impact of the genizah texts (specifically Ben Sira, CD, and the Aramaic Levi Document) and their relation to the Qumran corpus. Finally, chapter 25, "Inverting Reality: The Dead Sea Scrolls in the Popular Media" (411–23 [orig. 2005]), examines presentations of the scrolls in the media (newspapers, documentaries), highlighting the curious manner in which reality is often inverted in favor of fringe or sensationalist theories, itself "a double-edged sword" (412), increasing public interest in the scrolls but generating a potentially skewed image of the field.

The volume concludes with a bibliography (424–56) and indices of modern authors (457–63), subjects (464–70), and ancient sources (471–83).

For a collection of essays produced over a twenty-year period (and in an order different from that presented here), the train of thought flows remarkably well from one chapter to the next, testimony to both the "overall thesis" (x) in the mind of the author and the careful editing work that has taken place. The finished product is a single study with a single thematic thread (the scrolls in their Jewish context), which nevertheless covers an astonishing array of topics, debates, and approaches. There remains, however, a slight degree of ambiguity about the status of the final piece, since its composite nature is betrayed by some repetition between chapters (e.g., the frequently stated equivalence of the terms *Zadokite Fragments* and *Damascus Document* [noted in the introduction and chs. 1, 3, 4, 5, 8, 9, 10, 11, 12, 16, 17, 19, 22, 24] or the suggested pun on הלכות in דורשי חלקות [noted in chs. 1, 3, 19, 20]), unlike what one might expect from a normal monograph (where it would suffice to note such things on the first occurrence), which may suggest that the book is, after all, still primarily intended to function as a collected volume (where such repetition might be justifiable or indeed necessary) rather than read as a unified whole.

The footnotes have been substantially updated throughout (easily recognizable by the references to items published after the original publication date of the article), with the essays adjusted accordingly to reflect more recent discussion where appropriate (e.g., replacing old nomenclature with new, such as Testament of Levi with Aramaic Levi Document [41]). In chapter 18, even the author's translation of the "Apostrophe to Zion" (317–18) has been revised in the light of Hanan Eshel and John Strugnell's subsequent "Alphabetical Acrostics in Pre-Tannaitic Hebrew" (*CBQ* 62 [2000]: 441–58). Aside from one or two very minor issues (e.g., a seemingly incorrect heading level on 136), this is an extremely clean work with an admirable level of coherence and consistency achieved between its component parts. The result is a volume that can be fairly described as simultaneously both an archive of Schiffman's work in this area over the past twenty years and a new up-to-date contribution to the field—in both senses an invaluable addition to the study of the scrolls in their wider Jewish context.

New Idioms within Old: Poetry and Parallelism in the Non-Masoretic Poems of 11Q5 (=11QPsa), by Eric D. Reymond. Society of Biblical Literature Early Judaism and Its Literature 31. Atlanta: Society of Biblical Literature, 2011. Pp. xiv + 228. Paper. $29.95. ISBN 9781589835375.

John Engle, Columbus, Ohio

Eric Reymond examines here seven out of the eight of the non-Masoretic poems/psalms from 11QPsalmsa/11Q5. He omits Ps 115B because of its "fragmentary nature" (115). Reymond devotes a chapter to each of the poems in which he provides an introduction, presents the Hebrew text in strophic form with a grammatical and semantic analysis, and then makes notes on the translation. These are then followed by occasional poem-specific discussions, a section devoted to "reading and structure," "line length, parallelism, and allusion to Scripture," and a conclusion. In his parallelism discussions he deals with four types: repetitive, grammatical, semantic, and phonetic. Reymond's scholarly findings will be of interest to biblicists and Dead Sea scroll scholars alike. Less-advanced students may find the book a bit heavy going, however, since there is a general presumption of familiarity with 11QPsalmsa, and the Hebrew text is rather small and compact.

Reymond opens with Sir 51:13–30 (11Q5, XXI, 11–XXII, 1) because it permits "a review of the features that distinguish Sirach poetry from biblical poems" and provides "a backdrop against which to compare the other compositions in 11Q5" (21). But because the latter half of the poem is nearly entirely missing from the scroll, he offers a reconstructed reading. The reconstruction is largely unobjectionable except for a missing א in משה in verse 26 and his reading of סורו אלי נבלים in verse 23. Most other scholars reconstruct סכלים or פתיים instead of נבלים, and this does accord better with the hardened nature of the נבל in the Bible. Reymond's defense of the reading based on the LXX's translation of נבל as ἀπαίδευτος in Prov 17:21 does not rest on the safest methodology, since ἀπαίδευτος translates several Hebrew words, and נבל is translated into more than one Greek word in the LXX. Reymond's lexical methodology overall is sound, but at places it is uncertain and narrowly supported. He, for instance, seems to rely entirely on Jastrow and Cline's *The Dictionary of Classical Hebrew*. The reader is left to wonder why Even-Shoshan and Canaani were not employed. The reader is also left to wonder how תר (< תאר) of verse 14 translates into "beauty" when elsewhere he translates it with the more standard "appearance" (48, 54), how גרע of verse 15a translates into "wither" when the notes discuss "to form globules, drop" and "to drip" as options, and how טרד נפש and שלה of verse 19a–b translate into "weary oneself" and "be lazy," respectively. As far as his overall findings are concerned, he maintains that the "common ways that parallelism is deployed in this poem are all the more significant since they are, by and large, not shared with the Masoretic or non-Masoretic material from 11Q5. Together with the consistencies between the approximate length of the lines in 51:13–19c–d (as attested in the 11Q5 scroll) and the length of lines in the later chapters of Sirach, these common traits suggest that Ben Sira was, in fact, the author of this poem, more specifically, the author of the Hebrew version of this poem as it appears in 11Q5" (50).

Reymond turns next to Ps 151A (11Q5 XXVIII, 3–12). He observes, "A definitive interpretation of the poem seems difficult, if not impossible, because of the numerous linguistic variables, including ambiguous readings of the pronominal suffixes" (52). Still, he leads the reader well through all of these difficulties and provides a solid reading of the poem. His findings again are for the more advanced student, as he does not address the spelling of צון (< צואן) in verse 1 (contrast his treatment of תר in Sir 51:14). Further, he leaves unaddressed the possibility of reading ואשימה of verse 2c as a plain volitive instead of a "pseudo-cohortative" (56). Lastly, his entire system of grammatical and syntactic analysis will be a challenge for anyone to use facilely. Verse 4c–e's אדון הכול ראה / אלוה הכול הוא שמע / והוא האזין illustrates this well. The reader's guide to the grammar at this point is the cumbersome "S2V// S2SV//SV" and to the semantics is the recondite "a+bc//a'+bdc'//dc'"" (54). Not only do these systems fail to address the *casus pendens* of verse 4d; they also do not indicate the continuative nature of verse 4e in relation to 4d as evidenced by the *waw* of והוא. Reymond does provide a key for understanding these notes in the introduction, but vocalizing the text at critical spots and devoting more space to arrangement of the Hebrew text would have done more to facilitate understanding—especially in those places where the Hebrew must be divided contrary to his own verse paragraphs in order to accommodate all these letters.

Reymond examines Ps 154 (11Q5 XVII, ? –XVIII,16) next and finds that "if the text has been expanded from a sorter unit consisting of only vv. 1, 3, 16, 17, 18b–c, and 20, then the secondary material seems to bear the closest resemblance in thought to Sirach and, therefore, suggests either a common time of authorship, a similar theology, or an actual dependence." His notes here are a little more friendly to the less-advanced reader. He explains "על אוכלמה" of verse 13 with, "I translate 'while' and assume that this temporal nuance has grown out of the sense of accompaniment that the preposition sometimes expresses or its sense of 'in addition'" (86). At the same time, he does not mention the *mem sofit* in word internal position or that in both of his elucidating references of 1QM IX, 11 and 11Q19 LI, 11 [*sic*, = 12] the syntagm can be read as על + infinitive construct. This would seem to be especially relevant, since the 11Q19 passage has changed Deut 25:4's בדישו into על דישו. The reader is informed, however, that the preposition is translated "'on' for 1 Sam 25:8" (86)! He likewise helpfully explains the lack of subject/verb agreement of verse 16's עיני יהוה תחמל "as a result of haplography, the *wāw* at the end of the word having fallen off due to the immediately following *wāw* conjunction," something he neglects for the רחקה / אמר disparity of verse 15. But he then remarks that "such nonagreement is not without many parallels, even when the noun comes directly before the verb (e.g., עיני קמה in 1 Sam. 4:15)" (88). This particular example, however, is not felicitous, since קמה can be explained as the old perfect third feminine plural ending (see Brockelmann, *Hebräische Syntax*, 50a; Sivan, *Ugaritic Grammar* [Hebrew], 73). The reader may also want to note that in the discussion of repetitive parallels אבוא should be juxtaposed with פתח and not מפתח (97 n. 86) and that an alternate understanding of חבר (v. 12 in the light of בית חבר as "מקום הומה ורועש"; see Sivan, *Ugaritic Grammar*, 4) may add a valuable nuance to the parallelism of the line. We would than have "eating to satiety" אוכלסה בשבע paralleled with "drinking with a ruckus" שתותמה בחבר.

Reymond next addresses Ps 155 (11Q5 XXIV, 3–17), which he finds an alphabetic acrostic and divides into two-verse paragraphs. He observes, "The purpose of this two fold structure is to demonstrate the effectiveness of appealing directly to God and, more generally, to illustrate God's mercy" (115). With regard to the alphabetic pattern he observes that it "is more than a mere ornament or memory device; it helps bridge the different parts of the poem and, thereby, highlights the fulfillment of the poet's plea for salvation and assistance" (115–16). He also finds that "the poem can be read as a coherent whole" and was heavily influenced by Pss 3 and 143 (124). Although he puts up a valiant effort to demonstrate an alphabetic structure, the poem itself does not seem to want to cooperate. For instance, Reymond has to assume that יהוה was being read as אדוני to start the א cola, that the א cola are overloaded, and that the ז line ends a tricolon and demarcates a fresh line of alphabet but that the same is not true of the ב beginning the tricolon of the next verse of the l of verse 17. He does, however, partly justify these procedures by noting that the "inconsistent deployment of cola for each given letter of the alphabet is not something unique to this text" (105).

Reymond also finds that the next poem he treats, the Apostrophe to Zion (11Q5 XXII, 1–10), is an irregular alphabetic acrostic. He further observes that, "[a]lthought the poem is , without question, interacting with these biblical texts, affirming some ideas while qualifying or undermining others, I believe that the most interesting aspect of the poem ... is the way that Zion is evoked as a concept, as something that exists in the mind of the pious (126–27). In those cases where the poem has altered negative biblical contexts into positive ones, we see "attempts to reconceptualize Zion and provide hope to the reader concerning Jerusalem's future" (151). His treatment of the poem is fairly thorough but at times seems forced. For instance, he notes on verse 13 that "the perfect נכרתו and the *wāw*-consecutive ... indicate the future deliverance of Zion, not its past deliverance; this is assumed based on the poem's initial lines" (137). Yet the same structure is rendered as past tense in verse 9. His translation of verse 4 is largely unobjectionable, but then he defends it by saying, "[T]he first colon is essentially a *casus pendens* clause and the *wāw* conjunction at the head of the second colon is an epexegetical *wāw* (i.e., *wāw* of apodosis)" (134). To buttress the claim further, he cites Jer 33:24. The reader, however, is left to wonder how a *wāw* can serve epexegesis and apodosis functions at the same time and how the Jeremiah reference, which is continued by *wāw* consecutive, can lend support to his reading.

Reymond turns next to Plea for Deliverance (11Q5 XVIII, ? –XIX, 18). Here he finds that the "text uses language and imagery common in the Bible to emphasize the dejected state of humanity in general (characterized as inherently sinful and wormlike), and to underline that humanity is saved only through the mercy of God" (168). He further finds, "Overall, the poem argues that praising God and offering thanks are linked intimately with the expectation of divine assistance" (165). The fact that language from the Plea appears elsewhere in Qumran literature leads Reymond to suggest "the possibility that later poetry alluded to and/or echoed the non-Masoretic poems of 11Q5" (167). The explanatory notes for the poem are sometimes uneven. For example, בעויה of verse 16 receives no mention of being an Aramaicism (see Dan. 4:24), but then ירשו of verse 18 elicits due notices of Aramaic influence along with a detailed account of the scholarship behind seeing the *shoresh* of the word as רשה.

Reymond concludes the book with Hymn to the Creator (11Q5 XXVI, 9–15) and a summarizing chapter. He finds that the Hymn, too, was alluded to in other Qumran literature, and from this the surmise arises "that, although the poem recycles many expressions and images from biblical text, it still was understood to be a significant work in its own right" (169–70). He goes on to note that "the poem's language, as well as its allusion to other biblical text (especially those in Jeremiah and Pss 97 and 135), suggests that it is concerned to comment on and to offer qualification to the humanlike representation of Yahweh found in biblical texts such as Isa 6. The poem implies that Yahweh is beyond human description" (183). As far as the concluding chapter is concerned, he observes, "The poems, in all likelihood, derive from different milieus and from different periods of time within the late Persian and Hellenistic eras" (185). He also observes that "the poems are not overwhelmingly consistent in their structures or ideas" (185). This inconsistency does not, however, extend to line length, since he remarks that "consistency of verse length was not a major concern of the poets (Ben Sira excluded), something that is interesting, given the fact that the poems often exhibit strong parallelistic patterns between verses" (186). The poems also, of course, rely heavily on biblical language, and this leads Reymond to the conclusion that "in repeating almost formulaic expressions, the poet (and/or the congregation reciting these texts) suggests that the words are not his or her own, that they derive from God, for the general purpose of his praise" (189).

The "Mysteries" of Qumran: Mystery, Secrecy, and Esotericism in the Dead Sea Scrolls, by Samuel I. Thomas. Society of Biblical Literature Early Judaism and Its Literature 25. Atlanta: Society of Biblical Literature, 2009. Pp. xvii + 311. Paper. $39.95. ISBN 9781589834132.

Carol A. Newsom, Emory University, Atlanta, Georgia

The emergence and function of the category of "mystery" in Jewish literature of the Second Temple period and in early Christian writings is a topic that has been repeatedly addressed in the scholarly literature. Most recently, two complementary monographs have returned to this topic, Benjamin L. Gladd's *Revealing the Mysterion: The Use of Mystery in Daniel and Second Temple Judaism with Its Bearing on First Corinthians* (Berlin: de Gruyter, 2008) and the book under review here. While Gladd's survey is more comprehensive, Thomas provides an in-depth analysis of the concept in the Qumran literature.

In the first chapter Thomas identifies the focus of his study as the lexeme *rāz* and the concept to which it refers, noting the incomplete match between the concept of mystery in English and the concept indexed by *rāz*, hence the scare quotes in his title. While other words from the semantic field (e.g., *sôd, nistārôt*) are also examined in the course of the work, the distinctiveness and importance of *rāz* is clearly established. It is not just the meaning of "mystery" that concerns Thomas, however, but also its function, a topic that he explores further in subsequent chapters.

Chapter 2, "Esotericism, Sectarianism, and Religious Discourses" establishes the conceptual framework for the book, discussing the ways in which the phenomena of secrecy and secret knowledge have been studied across religious traditions. Drawing in particular on the work of sociologist Edward Tiryakian and historian of religion Kocku von Stuckrad, Thomas situates the Qumran discourse on mysteries within the phenomenon of religious esotericism more generally but also locates it in relation to the role of esoteric knowledge within ancient Near Eastern scribalism. The five key features of Qumran esotericism he identifies as (1) "The rhetoric of a previously hidden truth delivered by mediation by a specific authority"; (2) "The notion of a chain of 'initiates' and sages who determine the course of revelation"; (3) "The claim that knowledge is combined with individual religious experience"; (4) "Comprehensive cognitive mappings of nature and the cosmos, and of the ontological reflections of ultimate reality"; (5) Ritual initiation of new members by those already holding esoteric knowledge" (52).

Chapter 3, "Secrets, Mysteries, and the Development of Apocalyptic Thought," investigates the historical background and context for the concept of mystery, exploring notions of the divine council in prophetic and sapiential texts and speculations about the primal human and antediluvian sages, as well as the occurrences of the word *rāz* in pre-Qumranic texts. The most important findings are that the key developments occur in Aramaic speaking priestly-scribal guilds who appear to have been responsible for the introduction of the term *rāz* and its association with apocalyptic themes, paving the way for the development of a new range of uses and meaning for the concept of mystery.

In chapter 4, "A Lexicogology of Mystery in the Qumran Scrolls, Thomas provides a semantic map of *rāz*, as well as other words from the same semantic field. Although very thorough and carefully executed, the analysis of the texts presents few surprises, though it is striking that Qumran texts, especially those of sectarian composition, exhibit such a distinct preference for using *rāz* in construct phrases (e.g., "mysteries of wonder," "mysteries of knowledge," "mysteries of evil"). Thomas helpfully provides a chart of the various verbs employed with *rāz*, noting that they fall mostly into the categories of verbs of revealing, concealing, perceiving, or knowing. The domains of knowledge to which the category of mystery is applied are cosmological, eschatological, and theological.

In the final chapter, "Prophetic, Sapiential, and Priestly 'Mysteries,'" Thomas attempts to sort the uses of the term according to the type of discourse in which they figure, acknowledging that the categories overlap in significant ways. While there is some use of mystery terminology associated with the calendrical and cultic concerns of priestly discourse, the more important findings have to do with its role in sapiential and particularly in prophetic contexts. Thomas demonstrates that *rāz* is closely associated with the notion of continuing revelation as it occurs both in experiential and exegetical modes. Even where the revelatory medium is textual, the mode of contemplation of the mystery is often described in visual terms, particularly through the verb "to gaze" (*nābaṭ*), suggesting not only the possible influence of traditions related to Moses (cf. Num 12:8; 21:4–9) but also a somewhat mystical turn in the understanding of the revelatory process. The book concludes with an appendix on the Persian etymology of the word *rāz*.

The virtues of this volume are significant. Thomas is methodologically rigorous, careful in his analysis, and prodigious in his research. The bibliographic notes are astonishing in their comprehensiveness. But does the book deliver on its intention to analyze the functions of mystery language in the Qumran scrolls? To a significant extent it does, though one is left with the sense that the threads of the research never quite come together as significantly as they might. One of the reasons for this is that arguments about the functions of mystery language are taken up in different parts of the book and not fully integrated into a comprehensive picture. Early on Thomas makes the commonsensical argument that mystery language is as much about issues of authority and symbolic power and the strategies for asserting such power (2). Later, he takes up the boundary-marking function of claims to esoteric knowledge and rightly notes the role of this discourse in the self-fashioning of a community that attempted to construct a new identity for its members (67–68). These are both important claims, though they are the "low-hanging fruit" of the argument and remain at a level of generality. Thomas does begin to get at some of the more fine-grained analysis of the self-fashioning in the arguments he makes in the final chapter about the role of the discourse of mystery in the phenomenon of continuing revelation and the transformation of religious practices and religious experiences as a result. One senses, however, that there is yet more to be said on the ways in which the language of mysteries functions both within particular texts and within the Qumran community. Thomas's excellent work accomplishes much and provides a superb foundation for further work on this issue.

JUDAISM: RABBINIC AND MEDIEVAL

Brothers Estranged: Heresy, Christianity, and Jewish Identity in Late Antiquity, by Adiel Schremer. Oxford: Oxford University Press, 2010. Pp. xx + 272. Hardcover. $74.00. ISBN 9780195383775.

Peter J. Tomson, Faculteit voor Protestantse Godgeleerdheid, Brussels, Belgium

The study under review may be seen as part of a new interest from Jewish scholars in early relations between Jews and Christians. This involves a critical though empathizing approach on ancient Judaism, neither swallowing rabbinic traditions as gospel truth nor rejecting them as sacred fiction, and a readiness to envisage different varieties of Judaism, including unsympathetic features such as banning infidels. It is likely that the Qumran scrolls have helped produce a more sober look on such varieties, with earliest Christianity as another interesting one. What specialists of the New Testament and of early Christianity have still so much difficulty in doing is more within reach for a new generation of Jewish scholars: carefully utilizing rabbinic literature in order to flesh out these varieties.

Adiel Schremer's book is about the early rabbis and their attitude to *minut*, "heresy," as this regards Christianity. It involves an ambitious and important endeavor at a new explanation of the split between Jews and Christians that occurred in the second century. It offers no easy reading; often brilliant analyses of rabbinic midrashim are couched in convoluted reasoning whose successive steps are not always made explicit. Meanwhile, a well-reasoned methodology in utilizing early rabbinic literature is presented, with clear thinking about how Jews and Christians before the rupture can be viewed as belonging to one larger religious community. In Schremer's analysis, the rupture was produced when at a given point in time the rabbis started to include Christians in the category of *minim*, "heretics" or "infidels." This happened in the climate of crisis and disorientation following the defeat of the Jews by the Romans in 70 and 135 C.E.

The introduction sets parameters in different directions. A "new outlook" on early relations of Jews and Christians is gaining ground in which these are no longer seen as mother and daughter religions but rather, following Alan Segal and others, as rival siblings born from Second Temple Judaism. Some even explain the very rise of rabbinic Judaism from polemics with Christianity. Schremer reminds us, however, that second-century Christianity was at most a tiny minority. Also, since midrash is extremely difficult to contextualize, anti-Christian polemics is hard to establish without external corroboration. Actually, how significant was Christianity for the rabbis? More fundamentally, we must query the axiomatic "otherness" of early Christianity and Judaism as though they were different entities from the start. Daniel Boyarin has pointed the way here in his *Border Lines*, but in speaking of competing Christian and rabbinic "discourses of heresy," even he assumes two independent communities. When speaking of "heresy," we must begin from zero, carefully reconstructing the rabbinic concept of *minut*. Its contents was not damnable theology but social separatism; here Schremer follows David Flusser. A society in crisis needs to create boundaries in which "minor issues become important identity markers." Not the issues themselves are the critical point, but the historical circumstances that cause society to be nervous about identity and frantic about borders. As to method, this concerns a historical essay that consciously intends to utilize midrash as a source. This is possible because midrash is "responsive in nature": direct or indirect reflections of contemporaneous circumstances can be detected. Furthermore, we must be careful and primarily use the Tannaitic texts redacted in the third century. Nor should we be hyper-critical and reject Tannaitic attributions wholesale, as Jacob Neusner has proposed, but cautiously operate with cumulative and converging data.

Chapter 1, "'Where Is Their God?' Destruction, Defeat, and Identity Crisis," explores "the traumatic impact of the destruction of the Second Temple and the failure of the Bar Kokhba revolt on Palestinian Jewry of the second and third centuries C.E., as it is reflected in earliest rabbinic literature" (26). For the Jews, the Jerusalem temple was the place of God's presence where his power was palpable; its destruction manifested his defeat. This is traceable in Tannaitic literature. While explicit discussions of the destruction are late, "voices of doubt about (God's) power and providence" are echoed in second-century traditions. A shared discourse of power surrounded the temple, both on the Roman and the Jewish side. Thus a series of early Tannaitic midrashim are analyzed involving the themes of God's power and its publicly being challenged by Titus or other non-Jews. The sense of defeat and despair peeping through is inescapable.

Chapter 2 is not about the people targeted by the term *minut* but about its basic contours: "Conceptualizing *Minut*: The Denial of God and the Renunciation of His People." Theology is not the point. In early rabbinic literature, "doubts concerning God's power and providence and separation from the community" are felt to be "two sides of the same coin, which is the heart of *minut*" (49). Minim deny God's existence or confess "two powers in heaven"; in other words, they deny God's power in the political reality of the early second century. With the Jews defeated and the temple destroyed, bowing to the cult of the victorious emperor meant denying God. Both Seth Schwartz and Gedalyah Alon have pointed out the post-70 phenomenon of defection to the enemy camp. A Roman analogy is found in Cassius Dio's report of Romans "drifting into Jewish ways," which is seen as "atheism." "It appears that the rabbinic discourse of *minut* is, in a sense, an internalization of the hegemonic Roman discourse and its application in a reverse direction. ... For the rabbis, *minut* was constructed in terms of becoming Roman and was conceived as a theological denial of God" (67–68).

Chapter 3 reflects on "Laws of *Minim*," the concrete rules drawing the line vis-à-vis the infidels listed in large part in t. Hullin 2:19–20. On the level of theory, drawing boundaries and defining deviance can be seen as a matter of social power. Typically, the dominant group sets down what is right and what is wrong. The comparison with Qumran instructively reveals the opposite: a minority group setting the standards. Theirs were laws of *seclusion* or, in their own words, of "separating themselves" from the rest of society. The rabbinic laws of *minim* are those of a majority: they are laws of *exclusion*. The attributions point to a date no later than the early second century, that is, the period of revolt and defeat by the Romans. Who were targeted by the terms *minim* and *minut*? Regarding some thirty mentions found in Tannaitic literature, "a thorough examination ... reveals that *minim* and *minut* are broad terms that may refer to Jewish sectarians and deviants of various types"—Samaritans, gnostics, Sadducees, Boethusians, and other sects. Only in one passage does it unequivocally refer to Christians.

Chapter 4 focuses on that passage, t. Hullin 2:21-24: "Producing *Minut*: Labeling the Early Christians as *Minim*." It is not, as is often thought, another passage about Christians as *minim*. It is unique in addressing "the question of whether the followers of Jesus should be considered, too, as *minim*." Indeed, in the passage Rabbi Eliezer does identify one of the followers of Jesus as a *min*. The same story also warns against associating with *minim*. One implication is that the teachings of the *minim* were distractingly similar to Jewish tradition. Another would be that this in fact was the moment of rupture. This is confirmed by the attribution of many statements about *minim* to Tannaim of the early second century. Confirmation is also found in the fact that during the same period Christianity began to be seen as an independent religion in Roman discourse.

Chapter 5, "Christian Belief and Rabbinic Faith," cautions against narrow "Christianizing readings" of rabbinic sources: polemics against Christianity everywhere being read into rabbinic texts. Objections against the language of "son of God" might well refer to the imperial cult and power, and "sons of God" are also mentioned in Qumran texts. The rabbis resisted the deification of Pharaoh, Sennacherib, and "the Prince of Tyre," possibly a sobriquet for the emperor. Similarly, rabbinic praises of the commandments need not imply a condemnation of Pauline theology. In this connection, Schremer elaborates on the rabbinic homily "Great is *amana*." Its intention is not to condemn Paulinism but to uphold *amana*, "faithfulness," in the face of Roman power. Christianity was combated for other reasons. "Having seen that *minut*, for Palestinian rabbis of that era, was a matter of social and communal sense of loyalty and belonging, it is possible to suggest that the followers of Jesus were introduced into the category of *minim* because they were known to have established their own congregations, separated from the rest of Jewish society, much more than a result of their specific beliefs" (117).

Chapter 6, "Significant Brothers," addresses the later empire. Does the rabbinic saying "The Kingdom shall turn into *minut*" really refer to Christianity? The Christianizing of the empire was a much slower process than is often thought. "Augustine did not live in a Christian world" (MacMullen). This also holds true for Palestine. Liturgical poems of the Byzantine period contain few explicit anti-

Christian references and rather address Roman idolatry and power. The "wicked kingdom" is disliked because of its violence and confiscation of property. Christianity made no great change. "The widespread hermeneutical procedure that takes references to Rome in post-324 rabbinic dicta as references to Christianity is, ultimately, nothing but *petitio principii*" (126). Conversely, there is an identifiable rabbinic tradition presenting Jews and Romans as brothers.

The "Conclusion: A Different Perspective" reiterates the insight that *minim* are not one single category but include Boethusians, Samaritans, gnostics—and also Christians. It is not "heterodoxy" but the "sense of communal solidarity that matters."

Of course, questions must be asked and adjustments made. We should not exaggerate the post-70 crisis and extrapolate despair. On a pedestrian level, life went on as it always had. Yet the point made in chapters 1 and 2 deserves consistent consideration. Furthermore, if it is true that the rabbinic concept of "heresy" is not preoccupied with theology, similar things can be said of second-century Christian discourse. The language of Alexandrian theology was often teasingly similar to that of Gnosticism, and the latter's error was seen more in the sphere of authority and loyalty. Also, if rabbinic *amana* means "faithfulness" rather than "belief," the same can be shown to be the case for New Testament *pistis*.

More fundamentally, if *minut* is not about wrong theology but lack of loyalty, why would Christians have been included in that category from the early second century onwards and not earlier? Schremer gives no more specifics than the feeble remark that Christians had their own congregations. We probably should go on and ask whether things were different for Gentile Christians and Judeo-Christians, what was the attitude of the Roman administration in this respect, and how the rabbinic movement would relate to the latter. Such questions become more pressing if it is true that the term *minim* was used to designate pre-70 sects such as Boethusians, Sadducees, and Essenes. Then can the language of *minim* and *minut* impossibly predate the second century, as Schremer seems to maintain, adducing the post-70 introduction of the prayer of Eighteen Benedictions, correct in itself, as proof (58–59)? Asking these questions is one thing, answering them another.

Yet one more thing. Not only because they view relations of Jews and Christians from the other side, but because of their more verifiable dating, early Christian sources could help Schremer's argument immensely. The triple reference to the "excommunication" of Christians in the Gospel of John may have been used incorrectly to corroborate the introduction of the *birkat ha-minim* during the early second century. It does give, however, strong confirmation to Schremer's lucidly argued theory that from precisely that time onward the rabbis started targeting Christians with the laws of *minim*.

Feasts and Sabbaths: Passover and Atonement, by David Instone-Brewer. Traditions of the Rabbis from the Era of the New Testament 2A. Grand Rapids: Eerdmans, 2011. Pp. xviii + 382. Hardcover. $60.00. ISBN 9780802847638.

Joshua Schwartz, Bar-Ilan University, Ramat-Gan, Israel

This is the second volume to appear in TRENT (Traditions of the Rabbis from the Era of the New Testament). The aim of this project is to present texts of the earliest layers of rabbinic literature in a way that is accessible to the non-specialist (in rabbinic literature) and particularly for students and scholars of the New Testament. The first volume in the series was *Prayer and Agriculture* (TRENT 1; Grand Rapids: Eerdmans, 2004). Future volumes of the series are planned on *Fasts and Festivals: Tabernacles and Purim*, *Women and Marriage*, *Crime and Punishment*, *Offerings and Temple*, and *Pure and Impure*.

The methodology of the series is presented in detail in the first volume.[1] While for the most part I shall make reference to the brief recapitulation presented in the present volume under review, since the methodology of the author here is consistent with the principles stated in this first volume,[2] I should like to cite the opening sentence to the project from the first volume: "The aim of this series is, for the first time, to provide ready access for New Testament scholars to the invaluable collection of those rabbinic traditions which can be shown to originate before 70 CE." In this volume, perhaps as a result of some of the sharp criticism of the reviewers of the first volume, Instone-Brewer states that his work represents the first attempt to identify the earliest layers of rabbinic literature and analyze the dating of these texts. He apparently means the same thing as stated in volume 1. In any case, immediately, and somewhat perplexingly, he then plays down the innovative nature of his project and adds that he is actually *not the first* to do this and that many scholars "from (Anthony) Saldarini onwards have clearly carried out this kind of task for themselves, but they have not published their notes." Indeed, the present work often reads like "notes."

At first Instone-Brewer was skeptical about finding any actual words of the rabbis that survived unedited from before 70 C.E. In the first volume he realized that editors were often reluctant to edit pre-70 C.E. rabbinic traditions they had received, even if this resulted in a clumsy or untidy text. During his work on the present volume, however, he came to the conclusion that some texts from the early first century C.E. or even earlier (!) may have survived in the Mishnah. Thus, Mishnah Yoma, for example, appears to be an expansion of an early foundation

---

1. The author makes large parts of volume 1 available at http://www.tyndalearchive.com/TRENT/Vol1/.

2. And even earlier; see his *Techniques and Assumptions in Jewish Exegesis before 70 CE* (TSAJ 30; Tübingen: Mohr Siebeck; 1992), based on his Cambridge University dissertation. See also idem, "Review Article: The Use of Rabbinic Sources in Gospel Studies," *Tyndale Bulletin* 50 (1999): 281–98.

text, perhaps priestly, that survived in the final version. In order to make it quite clear to the reader what is early or pre-70 C.E., those Mishnah (and Tosefta) texts are printed in bold font. Later texts or texts that cannot be dated are printed in regular font. There is quite a lot of bold text in this volume. The year 70 C.E., the date of the destruction of the Jerusalem temple, is an important cut-off date not only for the Jews but also because it marked the completion "of most or all of the New Testament," at least according to Instone-Brewer, allowing for the relevance of early rabbinic traditions for early Christian traditions.

The first volume was not received with enthusiasm in all quarters, and there were some sharp reviews. I find little to disagree with regarding the major criticisms and shall briefly recapitulate some major points of criticism, as they are for the most part still relevant. Thus, Catherine Hezser in her review of volume 1 (*JJS* 56 [2005]: 347–49) accused the author of not being up to date regarding relevant scholarship on rabbinic literature. Since Instone-Brewer on principle refrains from citing secondary literature, at least so far in the project, it is not easy to determine what he knows or does not know, and lacunae are evident only when there are blatant mistakes; Hezser pointed out a number of such mistakes. Hezser also attacked Instone-Brewer on his dating methods, particularly his claim regarding "early" material that had been preserved and particularly regarding the temple. I shall come back to this point below. Following up on Hezser some years later, for example, Günter Stemberger devoted a study to the question of whether there is "a legitimate way to date rabbinic traditions to the period of the New Testament and to use them directly for its interpretation."[3] Stemberger devotes an entire section of his study to this issue and, like Hezser, points out the dangers of postulating a continuity between pre-70 C.E. and post-70 C.E. traditions and/or Judaism and adding with respect to the New Testament that Instone-Brewer tends to interpret the New Testament on the assumption that already in Jesus' time, the people, including Jesus and his followers, observed rabbinic halakah in the smallest detail.[4] As mentioned above, I agree with the above criticism and find it relevant also for the present volume. I shall expand now on issues pertinent to the volume under review.

I start with a number of comments regarding Instone-Brewer's choice of texts and editions of Mishnah-Tosefta. While the texts of Mishnah-Tosefta provided by Mechon (*sic*!) Mamre (http://www.mechon-mamre.org/b/b0.htm), Instone-Brewer's choice for the Hebrew text of Mishnah and Tosefta, might be readily and conveniently available for free on the Internet, they are hardly the ideal choice for such a project.[5] There are many other, and more scientific, versions of rel-

---

3. Günter Stemberger, "Dating Rabbinic Traditions," in *The New Testament and Rabbinic Literature* (ed. Reimund Bieringer et al.; JSJSup 136; Leiden: Brill, 2010), 92. For the entire study, see 79–96.

4. Ibid., 92–96 (= "Rabbinic Traditions from the Era of the New Testament?").

5. The site, for instance, states that they use the Vilna edition of Tosefta!

evant texts and manuscripts available today, such as the Bar-Ilan Response Project (http://www.responsa.co.il/home.en-US.aspx), admittedly not free; the "Primary Textual Witnesses to Tannaitic Literature" project of Shamma Friedman and Leib Moskovitz (http://www.biu.ac.il/JS/tannaim/); and the wealth of texts and manuscripts found in the relevant sites of the Hebrew University of Jerusalem and the Jewish National Library (e.g., http://jnul.huji.ac.il/dl/talmud/tosefta/selectti. asp, http:// jnul.huji.ac.il/dl/talmud/mishna/selectmi.asp). As it is clear from his own Internet site (http://www.tyndale.cam.ac.uk/index.php?page=david-instone-brewer), Instone-Brewer is quite computer savvy, and he is undoubtedly aware of all this. Why deprive the reader, even those with little background, of all this? Instone-Brewer's answer that the Mechon Mamre version is more in keeping with English translations is hardly appropriate or convincing. Rather than provide any of this information, the author sends the readers to the Giessen Mishna project begun in 1912 and not yet complete.

The "Major Modern Editions and Reference Works" are so lacking that it is difficult to know even where to begin in commenting on this. True, the author might respond that he does not intend to cite secondary material, but if, for example, he includes the first two volumes of the CRINT (= Compendia Rerum Iudaicarum ad Novum Testamentum) project from 1974–1976, why not cite the CRINT volume actually relevant to Mishnah and Tosefta that appeared in 1987?[6] It is also difficult, for example, to understand how a volume on Mishnah Shabbat does not mention the excellent text and commentary of Avraham Goldberg on this tractate.[7] The relevant volumes of the Safrai *Mishnat Eretz Israel* commentary apparently appeared too late to be used by the author. This is somewhat of a shame, since this is one of the few works on Mishnah today that is willing to postulate the possibility of early material, or at least the active recollection of such; it might have helped the author.[8]

While pre-70 C.E. material need not refer to only temple or cultic events, a good deal of the material in the tractates under discussion here seemingly does, at least according to the methodology of the author; therefore, I shall devote my specific comments to this type of tradition. The very claim for such early temple or cultic strata, however, has come under attack recently, and during the last few years a number of studies have appeared that abrogate any possibility whatso-

---

6. Shmuel Safrai, ed., *Oral Tora, Halakha, Mishna, Tosefta, Talmud, External Tractates* (Assen: Van Gorcum, 1987). This may not be the latest on Mishnah and Tosefta, but it is certainly better than something from 1974–1976. The second part of this volume, which appeared in 2006, after a long hiatus, is not relevant for Mishnah-Tosefta.

7. Avraham Goldberg, *Perush la-Mishnah, Masekhet Shabat* (Jerusalem: Jewish Theological Seminary of America, 1976).

8. Shmuel Safrai and Ze'ev Safrai, in cooperation with Chana Safrai, *Mishnat Eretz Israel: Tractate Shabbat, Parts A–B, Tractate Pesahim, Tractate Shekalim, Tractate Yoma* (Jerusalem: E. M. Liphshitz College Publishing House, 2008–2010).

ever of learning about the goings on on the Temple Mount or in the temple from rabbinic literature, even those strands considered in the past to be early, or still apparently considered early by the author.[9]

Our first example comes from m. Yoma 7:3, which the author deals with at great length (304–11). I shall discuss just one point of his discussion. Thus, the author marks off the requirement that the high priest offer two rams on the Day of Atonement as an early stratum. The number of rams to be offered on the Day of Atonement was not clear (cf. Lev 16:5; Num 29:8–11). Mishnah Yoma 7:3 mentions two rams offered by the high priest. The author in his comments correctly refers to the Temple Scroll (25:14–16), which states that *three* rams, not two, were offered. With a very little bit of maneuvering Instone-Brewer claims that there is no conflict between the seemingly two early sources, and he moves on to analyze in detail other aspects of the mishnah. What he does not mention, though, is that both Josephus (*Ant.* 3.240–242) and Philo (*Spec. leg.* 1.188) state that three rams were sacrificed, just as stated in the Temple Scroll. Thus, all the proven and agreed-upon early sources have three rams, while the rabbis have two. If the rabbinic tradition were also early, just what is going on? Two rams or three? If three, as the (real) early traditions state, how can the rabbis have been ignorant of the number of rams slaughtered on the holiest day of the year? It is more likely, of course, that the rabbinic tradition is late and the difference of opinion becomes a less acute issue.

The Day of Atonement rite is replete with such cases. To cite another example regarding the blood of the bullock, according to m. Yoma 5:3, it was tossed *once* upwards and seven times downwards. This, according to Instone-Brewer, was probably pre-70 C.E. (284–85). However, Josephus (*Ant.* 3.242–243) simply states that the blood was sprinkled seven times. Can both traditions relate to the period before the destruction? Once again, it is likely that Josephus (not mentioned here by Instone-Brewer) is early and the rabbis late.

The same problem exists regarding the Passover traditions in the Mishnah. Thus, according to Exod 12:3–4, 7 the Passover meal was considered a family sacrifice, eaten at home, while Deut 16:2 states that the Passover was sacrificed and eaten "at the place the Lord will choose as a dwelling for His name," that is, at the temple, as we find in the Passover of Josiah (2 Chr 35). In these sources it is understood that one sacrifices and eats at the same place. According to rabbinic sources, the sacrifice was offered in the temple but could be eaten throughout Jerusalem (m. Pesaḥ. 5:10; cf. m. Zeb. 5:8). This is included in the bold early sections of Mishnah, according to Instone-Brewer (147). The Book of Jubilees, clearly early, devotes a long passage (49:16–21) to stress that this sacrifice must be eaten within

---

9. See, e.g., Ishay Rosen-Zvi, *The Rite That Was Not: Temple, Midrash and Gender in Tractate Sotah* [Hebrew] (Jerusalem: Magnes, 2008); and Naftali S. Cohn, "The Ritual Narrative Genre in the Mishnah: The Invention of the Rabbinic Past in the Representation of Temple Ritual" (Ph.D. diss., University of Pennsylvania, 2008).

the precincts of the sanctuary, as opposed to the "early" tradition in the Mishnah. Instone-Brewer, while referring in general to this passage in Jubilees (138), does not seem to be aware of the difficulty in terms of the Passover meal, or at least does not comment on it. Is the Mishnah early? What, then, of the tradition in Jubilees? Where was the sacrifice eaten?

It is also not clear how it was offered. Thus m. Pesaḥ. 5:5 states that the Passover sacrifices were offered in three groups. The Mishnah then goes on to discusses details relating to the comings and goings of the three groups. Instone-Brewer correctly point out that the introductory section of the Mishnah mentioning the three groups is not early (143–44). However, he includes the details of the three groups in bold as reflecting early traditions. Not mentioned, though, is the fact that Philo (*Spec. leg.* 1.145) knows nothing of these three groups. The same is true for Josephus (*B.J.* 6.423). Josephus, however, does mention smaller groups that gather around the sacrifice, reflecting perhaps the custom of "registration" described in m. Pesaḥ. 8. Ironically, this is considered by Instone-Brewer to be post-70 (154), in spite of the corroborative evidence of Josephus here.

I could go on and on with other such examples, as well examples of a noncultic nature from tractate Shabbat. Admittedly, what I have cited is a drop in the bucket regarding a work that dates hundreds, if not thousands, of traditions of rabbinic literature. However, as I and others have stressed the problematical nature of the methodology, there seems no purpose in going further. I have also refrained from discussing dating issues with respect to the New Testament traditions cited by the author and the subsequent relationship between the two types of traditions. Instone-Brewer is certainly correct that rabbinic literature should be known and used by New Testament scholars, and there is indeed a surge of interest in rabbinic literature by such scholars during the last few decades. Rabbinic literature is no longer *terra incognita* for them. This being the case, it would be best to present a somewhat more normative view of the importance of rabbinic literature for the study of the New Testament. David Instone-Brewer offers much of interest to his readers, but to get to it they must also wade through much material of a problematic nature.

Stories of the Babylonian Talmud, by Jeffrey L. Rubenstein. Baltimore: Johns Hopkins University Press, 2010. Pp. xv + 366, Cloth, $55.00, ISBN 9780801894497.

Joshua Schwartz, Bar-Ilan University, Ramat-Gan, Israel

Stories of the Babylonian Talmud is the continuation of the author's two previous books, *Talmudic Stories: Narrative Art, Composition, and Culture* (Baltimore: Johns Hopkins University Press, 1999) and *The Culture of the Babylonian Talmud* (Baltimore: Johns Hopkins University Press, 2003). In those works Rubenstein argued that the redactors of the Babylonian Talmud (Bavli), the Stammaim, made important contributions not only to talmudic law but also to talmudic narrative, creatively reworking the versions they had received from their predecessors. As the present work is not only a continuation of these two works but dependent upon them, it is important to summarize the methodological and theoretical arguments of these two works, as indeed the author does himself in his introduction.

Talmudic Stories developed an approach to the study of stories in the Babylonian Talmud that combined literary analysis with methods of talmudic scholarship such as source criticism and form criticism. Rubenstein argued for a "close reading" in keeping with contemporary literary methods, and each of the six chapters of that work analyzed a Bavli story. However, since the stories of the Bavli are an integral part of the Babylonian Talmud, which is essentially a work of legal traditions, and the Talmud does not distinguish narratives from legal discussions, it was necessary also to use critical methodologies associated with the literary study of legal passages such as source-criticism, form-criticism and redaction criticism.

The same redactors who composed the legal passages composed the stories and haggadic passages of the Talmud. These were a group of anonymous sages known as the Stammaim, named for the Hebrew term for anonymous, *stam*. Just as they reworked legal passages, they composed talmudic stories by reworking earlier narrative sources they received from either Palestine or from earlier Babylonian sages, in particular the Amoraim, the (very often) named sages usually identified with talmudic tradition. The "fingerprints," as it were, of the Stammaim were revealed in the methods and techniques of composition of the haggadic narratives, and these were basically the same as those found in the legal material. These Stammaim functioned somewhere between 500 and 700 c.e. Clearly it makes a difference if a story should be situated in the second and third century c.e., as was often thought before, as opposed to the sixth or seventh century. I shall briefly comment on this issue below.

Rubenstein's second work, *The Culture of the Babylonian Talmud*, sought to place the stories of the Bavli in their correct cultural context as opposed to earlier Palestinian or (Palestinian and Babylonian) Amoraic material. Late Stammaitic culture, according to Rubenstein, was scholastic and academic. Many of the stories took place in the academy and dealt with academic concerns such as leadership, protocols, etiquette, and conflicts. In this milieu, dialectical ability was especially important. Argumentation became a value, not just a means to an end. The academy became competitive and agonistic. Heated debates were often personal, not just academic. The Stammaim were elitist and looked down on nonrabbis or on all those who were not part of their Torah study enterprise, whether these were the unlettered and nonlearned *'am ha'arets* or even their own wives. All of this was different than the cultural-academic milieu of the earlier Amoraim, who studied in disciple circles and small schools that stressed rabbinic masters.

As mentioned above, the present volume is a direct continuation of the previous two works. *Stories of the Babylonian Talmud*, seeks, first, "to expand the corpus of *Bavli* stories analyzed with critical methods." A second focus of the book is to highlight the processes of reworking and composition of the stories, carefully documenting how the Bavli Stammaim storytellers changed earlier versions to produce new stories of their own creation. A good deal of effort is also devoted to fine-tuning the methodologies for determining the signs of Stammaitc reworking, since, as we remember, they were anonymous, and as I shall point out, not all scholars agree as to the scope of their presence and/or activity, especially in haggadic literature. Rubenstein also seeks to continue other avenues of investigation found in his previous works, such as study of the poetics of Bavli narratives, the specific culture of the Stammaitic academy, the redactional context and function of stories, the relationship between law and narrative, and the overall cultural context of the stories.

The work contains ten chapters. The first is an introduction that lays the theoretical framework described above. Chapters 2–5 feature stories dealing with aspects of academic life, such as insults in the academy, the need to leave it on account of poverty, and the famous story of Honi, his seventy-year nap and his return to the academy. Chapters 6 and 7 treat stories of masters and disciples, with one chapter dealing with a rebuke of a master to his student and the other with the heresy of Jesus within the framework of the breakdown of relationships between masters and disciples. Chapters 8 and 9 focus on stories that feature important aspects of the Stammaitic worldview. Chapter 8 assesses stories of dire predictions of astrologers and examines how the Stammaim engaged certain theological issues, and chapter 9 analyzes the story of Moses' visit to the academy of Rabbi Akiba, which deals with the difficult theological issues of the expansion of Torah throughout the generations and the suffering of the righteous. The final chapter, the conclusion, organizes the findings of the individual chapters according to topic and provides a taxonomy of the primary techniques of Stammaitic composition.

While the thrust of this work is literary-redactional, with an emphasis on understanding the compositional techniques of the Stammaitic storytellers, Rubenstein builds his technical discussions on sterling analyses of the haggadic Bavli traditions he examines. He has read all the relevant literature and is aware of all the methodological issues that must be dealt with prior to any discussion of Stammaim. Also, his "text" work and knowledge of relevant manuscript traditions and variants are impeccable, although this is very much in the background. However, the bulk of his discussion revolves around uncovering the Stammaim; thus, a good deal of effort is put into the analysis of the stories in terms of such seemingly technical matters as wordplay, symbolic character names, irony, keywords and repetitions, dialogue, interior monologue, order, and structure. All of this helps illustrate the culture of the Stammaitic academy as well as the mechanics of Stammaitic composition, particularly the borrowing from earlier Babylonian or Palestinian sources. These borrowings are of special concern, and they often involved "patterning" in which lengthy sections or passages are borrowed. There were also different types of "patterning" in these stories of the Bavli, such as "summary patterning," "weak patterning," and the related process of duplication. While all of this might be considered highly technical and of interest only to specialists, Rubenstein's lucid prose makes for extremely interesting reading, even for the nonspecialist in haggadah. The structure of the book also allows student, scholar, or interested lay reader to make use of parts of the literary analysis without always being compelled to accept the redactional analysis. This, as we shall now see, is of great importance.

The analysis of haggadah, whether in Bavli or in any other branch of rabbinic literature, has to relate to the substance of haggadic tradition. The rabbis of these traditions are expressing theological and social concerns, at times even economic or political concerns. Within the text are reflected numerous extratextual matters. While there is nary a scholar today who will claim that one might learn "straight" history from these sources, there is a strong consensus, although not universal, that rabbinic texts do yield cultural and historical information. The issue at hand based on the works on Rubenstein is not so much how to mine this information but rather whose cultural world is reflected. As we have pointed out above numerous times, in Rubenstein's view, this is the cultural world of the late Babylonian redactors, the Stammaim, not that of the Palestinian rabbis, even if there are borrowings from them, and not that of the earlier named and famous sages, the Amoraim.

The basic methodological problem of this work, as well as of the other two volumes mentioned, is that there is really no proof for the existence of the elusive, anonymous Stammaim. The very phrase is a modern invention of scholarship. The tenth century C.E. Rav Sherira Gaon, head of the Babylonian academy in Pumbeditha, does mention a group coming after the Amoraim and before the Geonim, and they were called Savoraim. This group was not anonymous, and we know a few sages of their group by name. The Savoraim, unlike what has been postulated for the Stammaim, engaged not in creative literary activities but rather in editorial matters of the utmost technical nature, filling in the occasional lacunae of the earlier Amoraim, and their work usually has clear and distinctive editorial features. In the present volume, Rubenstein makes no mention of this group, and they do not even merit an entry in the index. In the *Culture of the Babylonian Talmud*, he seems to imply that they are the same as the Stammaim, but this is somewhat difficult in view of the fact that the activities of the two groups seem to have been markedly different. Thus, there is always the gnawing possibility that the Stammaim are not mentioned because they did not exist. If this is the case, then a good deal of what Rubenstein claims to be late Babylonian rabbinic culture would revert to the earlier Amoraim. Some of the conclusions might be the same, but the social context would be very different, and for the historian this would certainly be of great importance. This would also make the Palestinian material more relevant, since it would allow for better comparison with nearly contemporary Babylonian material. Thus, the stakes here are much higher than one might imagine regarding a book devoted to seemingly very technical literary and redactional issues.

Obviously, I cannot discuss all the texts analyzed by Rubenstein, so I cite one example from chapter 3, "Ilfa's Desperate Challenge (Taanit 21a)," which deals with events basically outside the academy but very much connected to it. The literary chronological framework is, of course, of great importance for understanding the cultural-religious implications of the tradition.

Babylonian Talmud 21a describes two third-century C.E. Palestinian sages, Rabbi Yohanan and Ilfa, who being very hard pressed by poverty left the academy to seek their fortune in commerce. They sat down under an unsound wall to eat. Two angels, seeing the sages, said to one another that they should kill these "former" sages for having abandoned eternal life for temporal life. Rabbi Yohanan heard the conversation, Ilfa did not; the former returned to the academy, the latter went out and apparently made his fortune in commerce. Years later Ilfa returned to the academy to find that Rabbi Yohanan was head of the academy. A number of students said to him that had he remained in the academy, he, Ilfa, would have been the head, not Rabbi Yohanan. Ilfa went up to a sailyard of a ship (a play on his name, which means boat, or representing his success in commerce?) and challenged those present to question him on *baraitot*, or external teachings, and if he did not answer based on the teaching of a Mishnah (and not on an external teaching), he would plunge from the sailyard to his death.

We cannot, of course, go into details regarding Rubenstein's fascinating analysis. Apart from literary issues, the tradition deals with the broad cultural context of subsistence versus Torah studies. Leaving the academy was seemingly a crime punishable by death, yet Ilfa seems to have managed to study Torah outside of the academy even when he was engaged in commerce. The story in the Palestinian Talmud (Palestinian Talmud Qiddushin 1:1, 58d), however, simply relates to an "academic" challenge of Hilfai (= Ilfa) to be thrown into a river if he cannot answer questions. There does not seem to be any issue of mortal challenge, and the "broader" cultural context of the Bavli seem to be nonexistent here. For the historian, or for anyone seeking to understand the cultural context of the Bavli tradition, it is of course important to know whether the tensions between subsistence and poverty were the reality of the late Stammaim or whether these problems existed earlier during the period of the Amoraim and contemporary to what was described in the Palestinian Talmud. Were they there during a good part of the talmudic period or just at its tail end?

Ultimately, however, it is impossible to prove anything, although obviously all camps have those who are convinced. Whether one accepts the Stammaim or not in the world of Babylonian haggadah, the brilliant analyses of Jeffrey Rubenstein enrich our understanding of talmudic literature, and I cannot imagine the study of haggadah without recourse to this book and the other works of Rubenstein cited above. We await his future volumes on additional haggadic traditions in Bavli.

The Arabic Translation and Commentary of Yefet ben ʿEli the Karaite on the Book of Esther: Edition, Translation, and Introduction, edited byMichael G. Wechsler. Études sur le Judaïsme médiéval 36; Karaite Texts and Studies 1. Leiden: Brill, 2008. Pp. xx + 444 + xii. Hardcover. $202.00. ISBN 9789004163881.

John Kaltner, Rhodes College, Memphis, Tennessee

Yefet ben ʿEli ha-Levi, whose Arabic name was Abū ʿAlī Ḥasan ibn ʿAlī al-Lāwī al-Baṣrī, was a prominent Jerusalem Karaite from Basra who was active in the second half of the tenth century and the early part of the eleventh century. He was the author of a number of grammatical works that are no longer extant, as well as a few religious poems, some books of prayer and liturgy, and commentaries. His commentaries cover all books of the Hebrew Bible, and they include Arabic translations of the original text. In this volume Michael G. Wechsler presents an edition, translated into English, of Yefet's Arabic translation of and commentary on the book of Esther. Wechsler's translation takes up the second half of the book, with the first half given over to a discussion of Yefet's exegetical approach, his work's relationship to other Karaite commentaries on Esther, and an overview of the manuscripts Wechsler consulted. His basic text is the earliest dated witness to Yefet's Esther commentary, MS JTSA ENA 1651, which is dated 1466.

Yefet's work on Esther has been influential because it is early and richly detailed. He addresses many interpretive issues that even modern-day scholars continue to wrestle with, and Wechsler notes that Yefet's successors rarely treat new or unexplored aspects of the text because Yefet was extremely thorough in his analysis. His work on Esther is one of the earliest attempts to translate the book into Arabic, and he adopts a pericope-by-pericope approach, like that of his Rabbanite predecessor Saadia Gaon, rather than the verse-by-verse format that was more common at the time.

The first part of the volume, in which Wechsler contextualizes Yefet and his work, is a very thorough and illuminating treatment that broadens the coverage beyond a discussion of Yefet's Jewish environment to situate him within the framework of his Islamic and Arab contemporaries. Given the many interactions among Muslims and Jews during this time period and the influence going in both directions between them, this is a vital issue to explore, but it is sometimes the case that it is ignored or downplayed in scholarly discussions. One area in which we see this attention to the wider context is in Wechsler's explanation of Yefet's rationalistic mode of exegesis, which he discusses in relation to Muslim Muʿtazilite thought. A rationalist tendency is typical of Karaite exegetes, and it stemmed in part from their rejection of rabbinic authority and nonbiblical sources. Wechsler neatly lays out the connections between Yefet's rationalism and that of the Muʿtazilites, a rationalist sect within Islam that was founded in the eighth century. The close relationship between the two was acknowledged during Yefet's time. Certain Islamic sources of the tenth century considered the Karaites to be the Jewish equivalent of the Muʿtazilites, and Jewish scholars like Maimonides sometimes noted the Muʿtazilite influence on Karaite thought. Wechsler argues that Yefet clearly knew of the Muʿtazilites, but the degree to which he was influenced by them remains uncertain. He describes the question as a "tangled state of affairs" and believes each case needs to be judged on its own merit and assigned to one of three somewhat fluid categories: (1) direct borrowing/ influence; (2) indirect borrowing/influence; (3) independent development.

Wechsler demonstrates the parallels with this Islamic school of thought by showing how in Yefet's introduction to his Esther commentary he refers to all five of the main foundations of Muʿtazilite doctrine. Those foundations are the following: God's unity; God's justice; God's fulfillment of promise and threat; the existence of an intermediate state; and the obligation for believers to enjoin good and refrain from evil. But Wechsler is quick to point out that in some cases these ideas are presented in modified form to better reflect Yefet's Karaite perspective. In this way, he shows that Yefet was not simply parroting Muʿtazilite ideas but presenting them in a manner that fit his aims and purposes.

Another way that Wechsler makes use of Islamic concepts to discuss Yefet's work is in his response to the claim sometimes made that Yefet's approach is overly literalistic. He refutes that charge by citing the practice of *ijtihād*, or independent reasoning, in Muslim jurisprudence, which often takes the form of arguing by analogy. Wechsler sees examples of such analogical reasoning in Yefet's Esther commentary through his use of figurative, nonliteral language that should not be taken at face value. It is also present, he argues, in those instances where Yefet adopts a more psychological approach toward reading a passage and infers certain motives or feelings on the part of a character that are not explicitly stated in the text. For example, Wechsler points out that in a number of places Yefet's Esther is more active and engaged in bringing about the outcome of certain events in the story than most prior rabbinic commentators tend to view her. By appealing to *ijtihād*, Wechsler brings into his analysis a key Islamic idea that continues today to be a source of discussion and debate regarding how the Qur'an should be read and interpreted. At the same time, he provides a novel idea regarding how Islamic thought might possibly have informed Yefet's approach to the biblical material.

An interesting aspect of Wechsler's translation is the way he effectively calls attention to how Yefet often acknowledges the role of an agent he identifies as the *mudawwin* in the communication of the text. It is a somewhat elusive term that can have a number of different meanings, including "composer," "recorder," "redactor," and "narrator." According to Wechsler, the latter two senses are how the word *mudawwin* is most commonly understood in Yefet's Esther commentary. A few of Yefet's predecessors refer to the *mudawwin* in their own exegesis, but Wechsler points out that Yefet is the first to develop the concept in a coherent and detailed fashion, and in this way he anticipates later developments in biblical studies. When the term *mudawwin* is used in reference to the redactor, this indicates that Yefet is acknowledging the difference between the person who wrote the text and the one who gave it its final form. Similarly, when he uses it in reference to the narrator, Yefet is able to distinguish between the voice of the character(s) and the voice of the narrator. Using the term in the latter way also allows Yefet to analyze the text in ways that are very much in line with the conventions of modern narratological analysis. For example, Wechsler points out how Yefet's identification of the *mudawwin* as narrator enables him to highlight the literary technique known as "gapping," whereby certain information is left unreported in the telling of a narrative.

Wechsler notes that Yefet does not engage in complicated grammatical discussions in his commentary, so the solutions he proposes to the textual problems he encounters are often found in the translation choices he makes. Consequently, Wechsler warns that we must be particularly attentive to the nuances of the translation from Hebrew to Arabic. This is a very important point, and we are well advised to follow Wechsler's advice on the matter. But the same thing applies to his own work and the translation from Arabic to English. He, like Yefet, does not always provide an explanation for the choices he makes, so we must examine those choices with care. Doing so raises some questions about the Arabic resources Wechsler consults in his translation work. The most obvious concern is that he sometimes relies on dictionaries that are less trustworthy, either because they do not provide a full treatment of the lexicographic data or because they are limited chronologically or geographically. Three in particular are worth mentioning: J. G. Hava's *Al-Farā'id: Arabic-English Dictionary*; M. Piamenta's *Dictionary of Post-classical Yemeni Arabic*; and H. Wehr's *A Dictionary of Modern Written Arabic*. Each of these, in one way or another, is deficient for Wechsler's purposes. The works of Piamenta and Wehr, as their titles suggest, are primarily concerned with modern forms and meanings of Arabic words. Hava's dictionary, along with the other two, simply lists meanings without providing a thorough treatment of how those meanings have evolved over time. Undoubtedly, these resources often contain ancient material that is relevant for Yefet's work on Esther, but it is impossible to know when this is the case unless one consults other works. Wechsler would be on firmer footing if he were to avoid reliance on dictionaries of this sort and base his translations on more reliable resources that help to contextualize a given meaning.

This book is the first in a series co-edited by W. and Meira Polliack titled Karaite Texts and Studies, and he is to be congratulated on this very fine inaugural volume. Its careful attention to textual and contextual matters serves as an excellent model for future contributions to this series, which will help make Judeo-Arabic and Arabic sources more readily available for scholars.

Targum and Testament Revisited: Aramaic Paraphrases of the Hebrew Bible: A Light on the New Testament, by Martin McNamara. 2nd edition. Grand Rapids: Eerdmans, 2010. Pp. viii + 359. Paper. $32.00. ISBN 9780802862754.

Joshua Ezra Burns, Marquette University, Milwaukee, Wisconsin

Targum and Testament Revisited is a revised edition of McNamara's 1972 study *Targum and Testament,* also published by Eerdmans. The original publication was based largely on the author's doctoral thesis, published in 1966 as *The New Testament and the Palestinian Targum to the Pentateuch* (Rome: Pontifical Biblical Institute; repr. 1978). In each of these earlier volumes, the McNamara proposed to read the Targumim, the classical Jewish Aramaic translations of the Hebrew Scriptures, as keys to the sometimes opaque language of New Testament. This principal objective is maintained in the present revision. The decades, however, since McNamara developed his approach have seen major changes in the critical study of the Targumim potentially deleterious to his basic analytical premise. These changes were facilitated in part by McNamara's own *Aramaic Bible* project (Wilmington, Del.: Glazier; Collegeville, Minn.: Liturgical Press, 1987–2007), a celebrated series of English-language translations and commentaries on all of the extant Targumim. The present volume represents McNamara's effort to update his earlier work in light of certain vital lessons learned from that project. The result is impressive.

As noted, the basic premise of *Targum and Testament Revisited* is identical to that of the book's first edition. McNamara begins by acknowledging that Jesus and his disciples spoke and thought primarily in an Aramaic idiom rather than in the Greek idiom of the New Testament. This observation naturally entails the now commonplace assumption that Jesus and his earliest followers partook of their native Galilean Jewish culture to an extent typically underrepresented in the Christian Scriptures. Aiming, therefore, to recover evidence of the New Testament's Aramaic background, McNamara proposes the Targumim as viable witnesses to the patterns of language and thought present occasionally underlying its Greek text. In view, however, of the acknowledged distances between the dates and locations of the extant Targumim relative to the New Testament, McNamara appeals chiefly not to these treatises themselves but to a theoretical precursor commonly known as the Palestinian Targum. Although no longer extant itself, this targumic prototype would have represented the version of the biblical text in common Jewish use during the first century C.E. This document, in turn, would go on to serve as the textual basis for the later surviving targumic texts still in our possession. As a result, McNamara submits, these the extant Targumim might well preserve authentic witnesses to the Palestinian Targum original and, by extension, to the Aramaic substratum of the New Testament.

McNamara's conception of a seminal Palestinian Targum is not of his own design. In fact, the idea of a lost proto-Targum was current to the time of the author's original research on the subject and remains popular in some circles to this day. In that original publication, as in the present revision, McNamara carefully documents the evolution of this theoretical treatise as an object of critical discussion in modern scholarship. Nevertheless, McNamara now acknowledges that recent scholarly advances have eroded critical confidence in the integrity of so-called Palestinian Targum as a fixed textual corpus. To this end, he prefaces his revision with an instructive discussion of current research to this effect conducted principally by contributors to the *Aramaic Bible* project (1–16). As McNamara duly concedes, the conclusions of these scholars have complicated the possibility of tracing the numerous and diverse Targumim in our possession to a common base text analogous to that once unequivocally construed as *the* Palestinian Targum. As a result, while McNamara remains confident in the basic viability of his project, he now qualifies his hypothesis with a cautious proviso: "It may be that the time has come to re-evaluate the possible contribution that the Targums may have for the study of Judaism of the New Testament period and of the New Testament itself (15)."

McNamara's sustains his tempered optimism throughout the present revision. The book is organized into three major units. The first eight chapters present an extensive and thoroughly documented overview of modern research nominally pertaining to the origins of the Targumim and their significance toward the reception of the Hebrew Scriptures in early Jewish culture. Unfortunately, the impact of McNamara's recent methodological reevaluation is scarcely evident in these chapters, which largely reproduce the corresponding contents of the book's first edition. The major revisions here appear in updated footnotes rather than in meaningful modifications to the body of the text. That notwithstanding, McNamara makes a cogent case. Assembling witnesses from such diverse sources as the Dead Sea Scrolls, the New Testament, and the Mishnah, he provides ample documentary evidence for production and use of Aramaic treatises analogous to the Targumim throughout the Second Temple period and well into the rabbinic age. In the process, he paints a rich and nuanced portrait of ancient Jewish thought and practice reaching well beyond the scope of his present inquiry.

On the whole, these chapters serve to establish ample grounds upon which McNamara proceeds to base his comments on the Aramaic background of the New Testament. Yet discerning scholars of the classical Jewish tradition will find much to object to in these pages. McNamara's major points of reference on the history of the Jews in antiquity are sorely out of date. Citations of Schürer, Moore, and Dalman abound. While perhaps excusable in 1972, McNamara's reliance on these and other nineteenth- and early twentieth-century scholars does not inspire confidence in the currency of his analytical assumptions about the modes and forms of exegesis he claims to have influenced the Targumim. Some readers will wince at his casual use of the term "midrash" as a catch-all category of Jewish reflection on the Hebrew Scriptures. Others will undoubtedly take issue with his regular association of the Targumim with such dubious ancient religious movements as late Judaism, Old Testament Judaism, official Judaism, and orthodox Judaism. The mere presence of these retrograde denominatives does not severely undermine McNamara's basic argument. To his credit, he seems much better attuned to the interpretive dilemmas inherent to these terms than his lexicon suggests. The effect, however, of his antiquated language upon readers sensitized to the complexities of describing Judaism in antiquity might be disconcerting.

The second part of the book is arguably its centerpiece. Chapters 9–16 present a series of case studies focusing on select theological terms and concepts featured prominently in the New Testament and reflected, according to McNamara, in the language of the Targumim. These chapters are likewise adapted from the book's first edition, although here McNamara undertakes a number of significant revisions to his base text in view of his revised methodological sensibilities. Topics of common Jewish and Christian identification covered in these chapters include the origins of select devotional terms for God, the ontological relationship between sin and virtue, and the language of eschatological speculation. One chapter is devoted exclusively to Aramaic resonances in the peculiar Greek of the Gospel of John. None of these discussions will be especially revelatory to readers already knowledgeable of the Jewish background of the New Testament. Indeed, many of McNamara's observations on these topics might be taken for granted by scholars already attuned to his widely accepted analytical premise. Yet by highlighting the linguistic features of that background, McNamara assembles an impressive array of evidence. To the mind of this reviewer, the sheer weight of evidence connecting the language of the New Testament to the language of the Targumim adds up to a substantial argument in support of his thesis.

However, many of the specific arguments raised in these chapters are subject to question. As noted, McNamara proposed in the book's first edition to connect the New Testament to the extant Targumim using the conjectural Palestinian Targum as his preferred intermediary. His certainty about the precise features of this text now diminished, McNamara now finds himself drawing ever more tenuous connections between the Christian Scriptures and sundry Jewish biblical translations still amenable to comparison. Inevitably, these indirect textual affinities appear more convoluted than the direct affinities drawn in his previous work. I do not mean to suggest that McNamara's efforts to salvage his old arguments are misguided. In fact, I am quite taken by the degree of critical sophistication McNamara has applied to his correction of the relatively simple logic of his previous treatment. To the minds, however, of some readers, his newly revised technique might demand more concrete evidence for many of his theoretical claims than McNamara is able to provide.

A brief example will suffice to illustrate my point. In chapter 11 McNamara adduces a series of targumic witnesses to the Jewish doctrine of the holy spirit, or the *ruaḥ haqqodeš*. Acknowledging its traditional association with the voice of prophecy, he cites several examples in which the Targumim seem to assign Moses access to God through *ruaḥ haqqodeš* or some analogous mechanism (e.g., Targums Neofiti and Pseudo-Jonathan on Exod 33:16 and Num 7:89). McNamara proceeds to trace echoes of this concept in Paul's homily in 2 Cor 3:7–4:6, where the apostle speaks of Moses—and, by extension, the Mosaic law—as an unnecessary intermediary between God and the Spirit for those who are in Christ. Paul's rhetorical figure, McNamara argues, assumes his familiarity with the targumic notion that Moses spoke for God through the "spirit" of *ruaḥ haqqodeš*. Paul, of course, argues to the opposite effect. But McNamara's point is clear. "Apparently," he concludes, "Paul is merely christianizing a midrash already formed within Judaism (173)."

McNamara presents his chapter on the Holy Spirit in *Targum and Testament Revisited* exactly as in the first edition. Then, in an addendum (174–76), he responds to critics of his earlier work who have questioned the likelihood that Paul was familiar Jewish exegetical traditions unattested in his era. While it is possible that Paul was familiar with the formative Jewish doctrine of the spirit, the association with Moses articulated in the extant Targumim appears to have been an exegetical embellishment of the targumists themselves. These translators were active hundreds of years after Paul's time. Their work, McNamara now concedes, might be entirely inadmissible as witnesses to Paul's formative Trinitarian theology. Nevertheless, he continues, "I still believe that the evidence in question merits consideration." Paul, argues McNamara, may well have taken it upon himself to adapt elements of the pentateuchal narrative to his novel distinction between the old and new covenants. "Such a combination of related biblical texts is a feature of Jewish midrash.... Paul may have 'christianized' some traditional Jewish understandings of the Hebrew Scriptures already at the beginning of his career, during his sojourn in Arabia." It was, after all, in this vicinity that "Jewish tradition located many of the events of the original revelation and the giving of the Law to Israel" (176).

Say what? In light of McNamara's previous comments, it is clear that we can trace no channel of direct influence between Paul and the Targumim. But while McNamara acknowledges that his original argument has been weakened, he likewise recognizes that it has not been definitively disproven. His logic, however, in defending his old position is puzzling. I do not disagree in principle with the possibility that Paul detected in the biblical text traces of the same exegetical impulses later applied to the targumic portraits of Moses. I furthermore sympathize with McNamara's impetus to describe Paul's homily as a prototypical variation of rabbinic midrash. This observation, in fact, might account for a great deal of the apostle's innovative readings of the Hebrew Scriptures. But I am at a loss to understand how Paul's physical proximity to the supposed site of Mount Sinai might have informed his knowledge of Jewish exegetical traditions pertaining to Moses' revelation. This contrived argument actually serves to diminish the credibility of McNamara's otherwise valid defense of his original position. It seems to me as though McNamara does not wish to let his argument of plausibility stand on its own merit, yet here, as elsewhere in the present revision, he simply cannot adduce evidence strong enough to make the plausible absolutely certain.

The book's third major unit, incongruously listed in the table of contents as an appendix, constitutes a comprehensive introduction to the Targumim. The four chapters of this section cover all of the extant full and fragmentary Jewish Aramaic translations of the Pentateuch, the Prophets, and the Hagiographa. A special chapter is devoted to the sometimes vexing but always fascinating geographical referents of the Palestinian Targumim to the Pentateuch. McNamara here focuses primarily not on the contents of these texts but on their origins, their publication histories, and their respective places in modern targumic research. These chapters have been expanded and extensively modified since the book's original publication to reflect the results of McNamara's *Aramaic Bible* project and other recent and ongoing research initiatives. These chapters are truly remarkable. McNamara has produced what is easily the most accessible English-language handbook for the critical study of the Targumim currently on the market. Students of both the Hebrew Scriptures and the New Testament relatively new to the field of targumic studies will find much of value in these chapters. I wonder whether the author might have served his argument placing these vital pages in the front of the book rather than relegating them to the back.

While the final chapters of McNamara's study might be its strongest, they are not without fault. In view of the author's aforementioned relative lack of attention to current scholarship in the field of rabbinic literature, his overview of the field of targumic studies suffers a significant gap. Missing from his methodological survey are any significant references to the work of scholars presently conducting research into the cultural contexts of the Targumim in late ancient Jewish society. Recent years have seen tremendous efforts on the parts of such scholars as Alexander, Fraade, Shinan, and Smelik to demonstrate the use of the Targumim and other Aramaic biblical translations in Jewish scriptural pedagogy, Hebrew language instruction, and liturgical composition both within and without the ancient rabbinic academies. The contributions of these and other scholars bear directly on the old theories of the origins of the Targumim cited by McNamara (see, e.g., ch. 3) and assumed throughout his study. But their absence is especially patent in the book's closing chapters. Granted, these studies do not have much to do with the New Testament. It is nonetheless regrettable that what might otherwise have been a comprehensive guide to modern targumic research seems to fall flat where the objectives of that inquiry diverge too far from McNamara's own.

Like many commendable studies, *Targum and Testament Revisited* has its flaws. To my mind, however, the positive aspects of McNamara's work far outweigh the negative. This is an excellent resource for critical readers of the New Testament wishing to gain entry into the complex and sometime daunting world of the classical Targumim. As in the original edition, McNamara's writing style is straightforward, easily accessible, and conducive to novices and experts alike. The editing, moreover, is nearly impeccable. With the present revision, McNamara has turned an obscure and unjustly neglected work into a necessary companion and key to the *Aramaic Bible* series. Despite, therefore, my stated reservations, I would not hesitate to recommend this book to my students and colleagues. While McNamara's book might not be to everyone's taste, I doubt that many would not stand to benefit from its instructive and thought-provoking lessons.

JUDAISM AND CHRISTIANITY

Studies in Rabbinic Judaism and Early Christianity: Text and Context, edited by Dan Jaffé. Ancient Judaism and Early Christianity/Arbeiten zur Geschichte des antiken Judentums und des Urchristentums 74. Leiden: Brill, 2010. Pp. xvi + 248. Hardcover. $146.00. ISBN 9789004184107.

Peter J. Tomson, Faculteit voor Protestantse Godgeleerdheid, Brussels, Belgium

This volume results from a symposium organized in Paris in 2007 by Shmuel Trigano and Dan Jaffé; it contains papers both in French and in English.

Daniel Marguerat opens with "La quête du Jésus de l'histoire et la judaïcité de Jésus." The Third Quest of the historical Jesus correctly brought the teacher from Nazareth back home in Judaism. However, the pendulum has swung too far and has resulted in what Marguerat calls a "complete re-Judaization" of Jesus. In reaction, a remake of liberal Protestant doctrine is presented: in Jesus, a singular moral consciousness overruled legal exigencies. His incompatible singularity is exemplified in three features: the radicality of his command to love even one's neighbor; a positive, "offensive" attitude toward ritual purity that "relativizes dietary ritual" for the sake of moral purity; and an overriding sense of eschatological urgency expressing itself, for example, in the command to delay one's offering when reconciliation with a brother is still outstanding. Though similar, the latter command is thought to differ from the rabbinic idea that Yom Kippur only atones in combination with repentance (m. Yoma 8:9), where the rabbis' attention is attuned only to the "correctness of the ritual." Thus Marguerat arrives at the traditional view that it was the singularity of Jesus that eventually was to make Christianity a religion independent from Judaism (9).

A distinctly different emphasis in heard in François Blanchetière, "Jésus le Nazaréen 'fondateur' ou 'rénovateur'?" Jesus was not a "founder," certainly not of a new "religion." He was a "reformer," conscious of being sent, like his predecessors the prophets, "to the lost sheep of the house of Israel," come "not to abolish the law but to fulfill" it. Blanchetière's paper exudes what in retrospect one misses in Marguerat's: a sympathetic affinity with Judaism that carries the historical analysis of early Christianity. The big question, then, is how the rupture with Judaism and Jewish culture came about. Here Blanchetière also reverts to a traditional explanation: the growing dominance of pagano-Hellenistic Christians. The ancient term "Christianity," in fact, would cover only that segment and not the Semiticizing branch of Jesus' followers of Jewish culture originally called Nazarenes. The underlying theory classically underestimates the importance of Greek-speaking Judaism and the openness of ancient Jews, rabbis included, to Greek as a language of expression. The break between Judaism and Christianity is neither really explained from doctrinal dissent (Marguerat) nor from cultural or linguistic divergence (Blanchetière). Other causes must be sought.

Next is the study by Barak S. Cohen, "'In Nehardea Where There Are No Heretics': The Purported Jewish Response to Christianity in Nehardea (A Reexamination of the Talmudic Evidence)." The essay seems a bit off focus in the framework of the volume, but it is a piece of decent scholarship. Contrary to the opinion of a number of earlier scholars, including Isaac Halevy and E. E. Urbach, Cohen demonstrates that talmudic Nehardea, a town on the Euphrates River at the center of present-day Iraq, at most had an insignificant Christian presence and that passages from the Babylonian Talmud thought to prove the opposite are often quoting traditions from Palestine, where the sages were of course confronted with a sizeable Christian presence. The author adds that Babylonia should not be considered uniform in this respect. One would agree and wish to add that Arbela, present-day Arbil, counted a significant Christian church from the late first century onward.

A study by editor Dan Jaffé follows bearing the title, "Représentations et attraits du christianisme dans les sources talmudiques: Proposition d'un nouveau paradigme." It confronts the reader with the unfortunate combination of keen insights and methodological gaffes. It is announced that a central rabbinic passage, the story of Rabbi Eliezer arrested for "heresy," will be analyzed and that in so doing the three themes mentioned in the title will be addressed: the representation of Christianity in rabbinic sources; its possible attraction for ancient Jews; and the proposition of "a new method of reading oriented toward a paradigm shift." Other than the remark that this last feature relates to "the diachronic historical-critical approach," the essay explains neither this new method nor the nature of the new paradigm. Then, a different set of three questions for investigation are proposed: Does the passage document a rapprochement between rabbinic Jews and Judeo-Christians? How does it represent Christianity? Why was it inserted in the talmudic corpus? The story intended is found in t. Hullin 2:24 and b. Avodah Zarah 16b–17a. The instructive differences between both versions are explored only in part; at times the author speaks indiscriminately about the intentions of "the talmudic redactor" in incorporating the story. The phrase "it is written in your Torah" from b. Avodah Zarah 16b is taken to reflect the view of the later talmudic editor, but it is also thought that the early Tanna R. Eliezer was actually attracted to Christianity; criteria for such diverse judgments are not made clear. An illuminating insight is that the story's portrayal of Jesus as a proficient midrashic teacher distinctly differs from his representation as a fraud and a deceiver elsewhere in the Talmud. Then again the supposed "Tannaitic background" of a quotation from 'Abot de Rabbi Nathan is underpinned with a simple reference to Menahem Kister's pertinent *Studies*, although on the intended pages Kister only points out the extremely complex entanglement of "old" and "new" in that work. In final analysis, the Rabbi Eliezer story is thought not to be meant "to exclude the dissident" but rather to instruct Jews associated with the sages to steer free from Christianity.

Next is Avinoam Cohen with "'The Lord Shall Lift Up His Countenance upon You' (Numbers 6:26)—An Anti-Christian Polemical Midrash by the Sages?" Some forty times in rabbinic literature, the verse from the Aaronite blessing quoted in the title is confronted with Deut 10:17, "The Lord who does not lift up any countenance," meaning that he is impartial. In true midrashic manner, a contradiction is read here, which is then resolved by explaining either that the Numbers verse does not signify God's partiality but his just retribution, or by saying that the verses refer to different situations, or again by conceding that the conflict is justified because sometimes God is partial. All this is talmudic rhetoric and well-known. The problem is that both medieval commentators and early Tannaim were also aware that, from a linguistic point of view, there is no contradiction at all, since the difference is between God "lifting his own countenance," that is, his being favorable, and his "lifting someone's countenance," his being partial. Why all the fuss about a fictional contradiction? The answer is derived from the information that the contradiction is first reported of the second generation of Tannaim, the period after the first revolt against Rome. Unfortunately, the inference that it concerns a rhetorical ploy reflecting "the fierce theological debate" of the sages "with their Christian neighbors" (67) does not convince. None of the supportive quotes explicitly involves Christians, and for confirmation Cohen refers only to historical accounts in which it is said that around this time the rabbis took anti-Christian measures.

Daniel Schwartz follows with "On the Jewish Background of Christianity"; a footnote informs us that it concerns the updated form of a 1992 publication. Extremely clear in structure, it is also somewhat schematic and to that extent not among the best of this eminent scholar. In last analysis, it is about "what distinguishes us (Jews) from Christians," that is, the readiness to live with unresolved tensions surrounding three main vectors of Jewish identity: place, pedigree, and law. As to these tensions, three main figures of early Christianity brought about a one-sided "resolution": John the Baptist, Paul, and Jesus. The Baptist undercut "pedigree" as a pillar of Jewish existence, and Paul relativized "place" and "law." In this, actually, they only did more radically what other Jews also did, namely, the Qumranites and Hellenistic Diaspora Jews. Schwartz even associates the Qumranites with Diaspora Jews, because they avoided the Jerusalem temple and used the language of "exile." To be sure, Jesus' preaching of the Davidic kingdom of God was in line with what his Palestinian fellow-Jews believed. However, after his death, via the belief in his resurrection, he did become a factor of "universalization and spiritualization" of "the value of Land and People." If simple conclusions were intended, Christianity would be understood as Judaism gone wrong, and Hellenistic and Qumranic Judaism as Judaism gone a little less wrong.

The next paper, "The Jewish-Christians' Move from Jerusalem as a Pragmatic Choice," by Jonathan Bourgel, is largely identical with a chapter from the author's 2009 Tel-Aviv dissertation, "Jewish Christians and Other Religious Groups in Judaea from the Great Revolt to the Bar-Kokhba War." It is a solid reassessment of the patristic story about the flight of the Christians from Jerusalem, dealing especially with S. G. F. Brandon's arguments and avoiding, as the author says, "the twofold pitfall" of either accepting the story wholesale because it confirms traditional ecclesiology (as does P. H. R. van Houwelingen) or rejecting it just as squarely for the same reason (with Jos Verheyden). Bourgel's cautious estimate is that a large part of Jerusalem Christians surrendered to the Romans when the besieging legions began closing in during the spring of the year 68 and were then settled under Roman supervision at Pella. This maneuver fit in the larger movement of submission and defection encouraged by the Romans and exemplified by the priest-commander Josephus and the Pharisaic leader Yohanan ben Zakkai; here Bourgel judiciously selects from the arguments of Gedalyahu Alon and Jacob Neusner. His proposal also explains why the Christians returned, so that Eusebius could report of a succession of Jerusalem bishops "from the circumcision" after 70 and before the banning of Jews from the city in 135.

Continuing his prolific studies on the sects, priesthood, and ritual of the later Second Temple period, Eyal Regev follows with "The Temple in Mark: A Case Study about the Early Christian Attitude toward the Temple." Regev correctly rejects the interpretation widely shared among New Testament commentators that Mark and his main character, Jesus, had a negative attitude to the Herodian Temple. On the contrary, in a refreshingly original analysis of major Markan passages where Jesus interferes with or refers to the temple, Regev finds a basically positive attitude, especially in Jesus' comments on the poor widow's donation and on the bread and wine at the Last Supper (Mark 12:41–44; 14:22–24). A distinction is made between traditional Jesus sayings and Markan redaction, although this is not strictly carried through. A final section puts these results in perspective. It finds radical criticism of the temple and its ritual only in Hebrews and Revelation. The Gospel of John would definitely need to be added here, while the inclusion of Hebrews could suffer some discussion.

Emmanuel Friedheim, author of a brilliant study on the ample knowledge of the ancient rabbis about pagan cults, offers "Quelques réflexions historiques sur les origines païennes présumées du christianisme primitif." The well-documented essay makes a pendular movement between two great specialists of ancient religion, Franz Cumont and David Flusser, and between two key dates: the destruction of the Jerusalem temple in 70, before which hardly any openness toward paganism can be seen in Judaism, and the end of the Bar Kokhba revolt in 135, after which Christianity became a predominantly Gentile movement and began to show a growing influence of Greek culture. The latter observation was made by Flusser, with whom Friedheim basically agrees on this matter. Cumont was more optimistic about pagan influences on early Christianity, especially where angels and *mystêria* are concerned. However, Friedheim shows that this word (possibly of Semitic origin) was widely used in Judaism. The critical essay by Walter Burkert on ancient mystery cults could also be mentioned in this connection. Friedheim's conclusion is that neither in the Gospels nor in Paul nor in the other parts of the New Testament can exclusively pagan influences be found.

Finally, Stéphanie E. Binder presents a sample of her 2009 Bar-Ilan dissertation under the title "Jewish-Christian Contacts in the Second and Third Centuries C.E.? The Case of Carthage; Tertullian and the Mishnah's Views on Idolatry." The Mishnah tractate Avodah Zarah and Tertullian's treatise *De idololatria* are roughly contemporary and have much in common as concerns the attitude to pagan cults, which incites obvious questions about common contexts and shared sources. The study begins with a survey of scholarly opinions on the nature of the Christian and Jewish communities in Carthage, concluding that Carthaginian Jews probably were familiar with traditions about idolatry related to tractate Avodah Zarah. A comparison between both texts follows on a number of items. The many similarities in outlook lead to the conclusion that Tertullian must have used Jewish traditions. Because both Christians and Jews maintained clear boundaries toward each other, the two treatises are further proof that the ways had not yet really parted by the end of the second century.

The volume, which undeniably contains some excellent studies, is completed with an index of ancient sources and of modern authors. The book has four sections whose titles are of only limited relevance to the contents of the papers. The main purpose of the symposium announced in the introduction, "to outline the origins of Christianity," is not really carried through. The English sections of the book and especially the introduction abound with solecisms and misprints.

GRECO-ROMAN WORLD AND HELLENISM

The Ituraeans and the Roman Near East: Reassessing the Sources, by E. A. Myers. Society for New Testament Studies Monograph Series 147. Cambridge: Cambridge University Press, 2010. Pp. xv + 216. Hardcover. $95.00. ISBN 9780521518871.

Mark A. Chancey, Southern Methodist University, Dallas, Texas

Itureans figure only tangentially in most discussions of the Roman Near East. Drawing upon a few vague references by Josephus, Strabo, Luke (3:1), and other ancient authors, modern scholars have typically described them as an Arab tribe prone to banditry that dwelled in the southeastern Lebanon, the Golan Heights, the Hermon Massif, and perhaps Galilee. In her review of the literary and archaeological data, however, E. A. Myers argues persuasively that such depictions are not only problematic but also troubling. She also calls into serious question the practice of delineating the outlines of Iturean settlement by tracing the extent of usage of a particular type of pottery, suggesting that the association of certain ceramic forms and fabrics with the Itureans is unjustified or at least premature. Her own reassessment of the sources sheds new light on the Itureans by contextualizing the little we know of them within the larger world of the Roman Near East, while simultaneously demonstrating that the gaps in our knowledge are significant. The book is a fine review of the methodological challenges facing those who seek to recover the history of local peoples who were ultimately subsumed into the Roman Empire.

A revision of a 2007 University of Toronto dissertation written under the direction of Peter Richardson, the book is structured around eight chapters that include a review of previous scholarship, discussions of different categories of evidence (ancient literary references, putative archaeological remains, coins, and inscriptions), exploration of the question of Iturean ethnicity, a limited sketch of Iturean history, and concluding comments. The book includes two appendices, one on small archaeological finds that may be associated with the Itureans and another that helpfully compiles epigraphic data regarding Roman auxiliary units that had names referring to the Itureans. Ten photographs illustrate the Itureans' geographical setting and key artifacts discussed in the text.

Myers's investigation of what recent scholarship and ancient texts have said about the Itureans is illuminating. Despite the frequency with which scholars characterize Itureans as Arabs, no ancient writer makes the association until the Roman historian Dio Cassius in the third century C.E. (*Roman History* 59.12.2). Earlier writers are vague about their ethnic identity, sometimes even distinguishing them from "Arabians" (Strabo, *Geography* 16.2.18). Myers notes that what writers in antiquity meant by the terms "Arabs" and "Arabians" is unclear, and modern usage is often no more precise, and she raises the possibility that the Itureans could have been Arameans or members of another ethnic group. Uncritical modern linkage of Itureans to Arabs becomes particularly problematic, she emphasizes, when scholars take generalizing references by Strabo and Josephus to the Itureans as "bandits" at face value, thereby fostering negative stereotypes of Arab cultures, even if unintentionally so. Such characterizations, she argues, must be interpreted in light of the biases, literary and political agendas, and limits of knowledge of the writers who made them, not as objective descriptions of entire populations. Myers also notes that scholars are imprecise in their geographical situating of the Itureans, neglecting the importance of the Bekaa Valley as the heart of their territory and misplacing them in Galilee on the basis of careless readings of Josephus's reports of the conquests of Aristobulus I (*A.J.* 13.319).

The most concrete information about Itureans provided in ancient texts concerns their first-century B.C.E. rulers (Ptolemy, Lysanias, and Zenodorus), although, unsurprisingly, the depictions of those kings clearly reflect the agendas of the writers. When Josephus describes Iturean interaction with Jewish rulers, for example, he is far more interested in the latter than with the former. The issuing of bronze coins by Iturean rulers that identified themselves as tetrarchs and chief priests attests to a level of political stability and accomplishment. The fact that the coins bore Greek inscriptions, depicted Greek deities, and followed the basic Seleucid style reflects Hellenistic influence, while the appearance of Roman emperors on later issues shows the changing cultural climate. Because virtually the entire corpus of Iturean coins is unprovenanced, lying in private collections and museums, it is difficult to draw broader conclusions from it.

Myers's discussion of the epigraphic evidence is particularly strong. She considers several inscriptions that have been described as Iturean on the basis of their find spots (cultic inscriptions at Har Senai'm, for example), but she notes that none of them includes any actual reference to Itureans. In contrast, numerous funerary inscriptions, military diplomas, and other inscriptions by or about soldiers refer to Roman auxiliary units (at least six of them) with names associating them with

Itureans, such as the *Cohors I Augusta Ituraeorum*. Known for their archery skills and stationed in Egypt, Mauretania, and various places in Europe, such units were initially recruited from Itureans. Their ethnic identity would have faded over time, however, as the units shifted from one deployment to the next, until eventually only the name provided any indication of their original composition.

Perhaps the most controversial suggestion of Myers is her rejection of a particular ceramic type as Iturean. After the Israelis gained access to much of Mount Hermon and its vicinity after the 1967 war, excavations soon uncovered regional pottery made of gritty pinkish and light brown fabric that began appearing in the Late Hellenistic period. Although the pottery was initially identified as Golan Ware, some archaeologists (particularly Shemariah Gutman, Moshe Hartal, Shimon Dar) quickly began regarding it as Iturean Ware. Myers observes, "The suggestion appears to rest mainly on taking as fact the historical textual sources, and assuming Ituraeans controlled the Golan, the Hermon, the Huleh and regions to the east." In her opinion, these assumptions are largely unproven, as the extent of Iturean settlement and control (two related but different issues, she argues) is unknown. No epigraphic evidence confirms the Iturean nature of the sites that have yielded this pottery, and even if a significant number of Iturean coins turned up at them (which has not happened thus far), those coins would not constitute an unqualified indicator of Iturean habitation. Furthermore, because our knowledge of sites in adjacent Lebanon and Syria is so limited, it is entirely possible that the usage of this pottery extends much farther north and east and thus well beyond the territories ancient writers associated with the Itureans. Given the difficulty of determining the ethnicity of the makers and users of the pottery, Myers suggests returning to the nomenclature of Golan Ware.

Myers largely succeeds in demonstrating that conventional wisdom about the Itureans does not do justice to them. Whoever they were, they could hardly have all been bandits, an observation so obvious it is surprising so many scholars have been willing to repeat so blithely ancient writers' characterization of them as brigands. Myers also convincingly shows that there is little reason to suppose the Itureans ever made significant inroads into Galilee, despite traditional (mis)readings of Josephus to the contrary. Her challenges to the identification of Golan Ware as Iturean Ware are worthy of serious consideration. Scholars have not found it necessary to name a specific ethnic group for the users of Galilean Coarse Ware, settling instead on the conclusion that they were from an unidentifiable group of Gentiles. Why the rush to associate this pottery with Itureans, especially when our knowledge of it is itself still so fragmentary? There are aspects of the book that could be stronger, to be sure. While its primary goal is to explain the context of the Itureans, sometimes so much attention is given to context that the focus on Itureans themselves is lost; the book as a whole would have flowed better had more background information been relegated to the footnotes. Excessive geographical, geological, and climatological details sometimes weigh down the discussion; this information also could have been pruned considerably. Especially given the importance of topography in Myers's discussion, a map or two would have been enormously helpful. Still, this is an important book for its topic, and it easily replaces the handful of earlier article-length discussions of the Itureans as the definitive study. Scholars interested in the Hellenistic- and Roman-period archaeology of Palestine, Hasmonean and Herodian history, and the fate of local peoples in an age of empire will appreciate the fine care with which Myers approaches her task.

Greco-Roman Associations: Texts, Translations, and Commentary, Volume 1: Attica, Central Greece, Macedonia, Thrace, edited by John S. Kloppenborg, and Richard S. Ascough. Beihefte zur Zeitschrift für die neutestamentliche Wissenschaft und die Kunde der älteren Kirche 181. Berlin: de Gruyter, 2011. Pp. xxxvi + 488. Hardcover. $180.00. ISBN 9783110253450.

Alicia J. Batten, University of Sudbury, Sudbury, Ontario, Canada

Scholars of classical literature, papyrologists, archaeologists, and anthropologists, among others, have long been engaged in attempts to describe the social world of Greco-Roman antiquity. This volume is an important addition to these efforts, combining insights, as it does, from all of the above fields in its rich presentation of a wide range of inscriptions for ancient associations. Such groups were plentiful in Mediterranean antiquity, and their study provides significant contextual information for situating the nature and practices of ancient Christ-groups. As Kloppenborg and Ascough point out in the book's foreword, once one has studied these inscriptions in detail, one observes that "Christ-groups could fit rather comfortably within the spectrum of ancient associations" (vi). However, scholarship in the field of early Christianity has traditionally only engaged a small number of ancient associations in comparison to Christian communities and often appealed to the same examples, such as a well-known inscription from Philadelphia (*Syll*[3] 985), which notably refers to "internal" attributes such as good intention (εὔνοια), instead of a broad range of this sort of material evidence. In contrast, this collection provides translation and analysis of a selection of ninety-one inscriptions. It is of note, as the authors point out, that it would be impossible to be exhaustive, so they seek to be representative in the collection offered.

The book is the first of a projected three-volume set that will include translation and analysis of inscriptions of associations not only from Attica, Central Greece, Macedonia, and Thrace but Asia, the Aegean Islands, the Bosphoros region, and Syria-Palestine (vol. 2) and, subsequently, Egypt, North Africa, Germany, Pannonia, Dacia, and Moesia (vol. 3). The present publication is structured in a straightforward and usable manner. After the foreword, sigla, abbreviation lists, calendars (Athenian and Macedonian), short glossary of terms, some maps, and a general introduction about ancient associations, the book organizes the inscriptions in sections according to provenance. Within the Attica section the texts, translations and notes are arranged chronologically, while those of the other regions appear alphabetically. The dates of the chosen examples range from 400

B.C.E. to the third century C.E. The inscriptions are also numbered, which facilitates quick and efficient discovery of the desired text and easy correlation of the inscriptions with various items organized in the indices at the back.

The introduction furnishes an overview of associations in the Greco-Roman world, taking into account the most recent research. As Kloppenborg and Ascough explain, life in ancient Greek and Roman cities revolved around two main poles: the *polis* and the family. Participation in the *polis* was limited to male citizens, and the family reflected a strong hierarchical structure, while at the same time providing a sense of identity for many. Between these two poles lay the association: groups of people who shared the worship of a particular deity, a profession, neighborhood, or possibly a common ancestor, if they were somehow related to one another. These associations were private, often permanent, and obviously tremendously diverse. Some allowed slaves, women, and freed people to belong, while others did not and were limited to people of high social levels. But given that many slaves, former slaves, and freeborn people were displaced from their own families and region of origin, the possibility of joining an association would be tremendously attractive, as this could supply a context for sociability, often including cultic acts, both of which could engender a sense of belonging and identity. In addition, some associations made available important "social services," such as support for funerals, loans for various members' needs, or simply contacts and benefits that would serve the mutual interests of the participants.

The honoring of specific individuals, often those who had contributed financially to the association, is reflected regularly by the inscriptional evidence. Kloppenborg and Ascough indicate that in many ways the associations replicated the honorific practices of the *polis* and "internalized the hierarchical structures of the ancient city," whether the members were citizens or not (6–7). Honors were bequeathed not only by identifying and lauding a specific individual for his or her contributions to the association, financial and otherwise, but by assisting with funerals, as already mentioned, and thereby, through a more costly funeral, increasing the honor of the deceased (8). Moreover, these groups were not generally subversive to the state (although this should not be ruled out in all cases) but regularly honored their wealthy patrons and/benefactors as signs of gratitude and loyalty or appointed such powerful people to important roles within the life of the association.

The authors indicate that such clubs were central in the establishment of foreign cults throughout Greece and Rome. Merchants, traders, metics, and possibly slaves were able to set up cults to foreign deities, such as Isis, the Phrygian Mother of the Gods, Adonis, and Men, among others. Political alliances and cooperative efforts among different associations also contributed to the creation and management of new cults. But clearly the geographic migrations of peoples because of war or other disasters, or from trade and commercial ventures, led to the displacement of persons, which, in turn, led to the establishment of new cults. The founding of these institutions and their preservation would have been easier to achieve, given the widespread incidence of such clubs that could, in turn, serve as social models with which many would be familiar.

Finally, based upon their extensive work with these materials, the authors state that, although these associations were highly diverse, one can observe general patterns within their internal organization. The Attic inscriptions regularly refer to a supervisor, treasurer, and secretary, which no doubt imitated the Athenian administrative practices, and there are additional forms of "civic mimicry" found in Thracian and other inscriptions (11). However, despite the presence of wealthy patrons and benefactors in some associations, and the imitation, to some extent, of civic structures, these groups often afforded opportunities for noncitizens, including slaves and women, to participate and hold office, even if only for one year, within the association. As Kloppenborg and Ascough maintain, "associations provided a venue where those excluded from civic office might achieve an honoured place within these cities 'writ small'" (11).

Throughout the book each inscription includes identification of where it is from, approximate date, where it has been published, the publication used, current location, and a physical description of the stela, followed by the Greek text, then the English translation. Line-by-line notes follow, then a series of comments and often references to any secondary literature that has been produced. The erudition of the book's authors is especially apparent in the notes, wherein appear cross-references to other inscriptions, as well as to a range of other ancient literature. The inscriptions are highly variable. Some, especially grave inscriptions, are short and simple (e.g., *IG* VII 685–688), while others are quite extensive, such as the rule of a Bacchic association from Athens that was known as the *Iobakchoi* (*IG* II^2 1368). This inscription contains a long list of functionaries, describes the different sorts of meetings and banquets that the group would have, and details the processes for disciplining the members. Reading through the inscriptions, one meets various individuals and groups, perhaps most striking being the women (e.g., *IG* II^2 1334) and slaves who were recognized for their work in the association or even simply named on the stela, which was an honor in itself. The latter phenomenon is illustrated by an association of the cult of Sabazios at Pireaus that honors Athenian citizens, metics from other areas, and, judging from their names, freedmen and slaves (see *IG* II^2 1335). Such a mixture of peoples reminds us of the authors' introductory point that these groups provided some sense of belonging for a range of people throughout the ancient world and underscores the fact that the mingling of different social levels was quite possible within the same organization.

The authors imply that a rationale for the book is its value for the study of ancient Christ-groups. Although such a reason may not be necessary, as these associations are interesting in and of themselves, some might be surprised that more comparisons to early Christianity were not made throughout the text (there are notable exceptions to this, such as the discussion of the Cult of Men [*IG* II^2 1365 + 1366], for example). However, I understand the intent of the volume to be the provision of a tool that others who study early Christianity can use to enrich their own work. Both authors, moreover, have made extensive use of inscriptional evidence in other publications that focus on ancient Christ-groups.

Greco-Roman Associations is the result of a great deal of painstaking work, and Kloppenborg and Ascough deserve recognition for such an achievement. The book will be an essential addition to the libraries of those working on the creation and development of Christ-groups within the ancient world and of considerable interest to classicists and historians of religion interested in social history more generally. I look forward to the publication of the subsequent two volumes. All three will be important reference tools in university collections because they will provide up-to-date background to numerous inscriptions to which some scholars will not otherwise have easy access.

The Gospel 'According to Homer and Virgil': Cento and Canon, by Karl Olav Sandnes. Supplements to Novum Testamentum 138. Leiden: Brill, 2011. Pp. xii + 280. Hardcover. $146.00. ISBN 9789004187184.

Dennis R. MacDonald, Claremont School of Theology, Claremont, California

Karl Olav Sandnes and I have been crossing swords over Homer and Christian origins for six years; *The Gospel 'According to Homer and Virgil'* is his latest thrust and parry, and this review could have been mine, but my task here is to introduce readers to this welcome contribution to the topic. Sandnes first took issue with *The Homeric Epics and the Gospel of Mark* (2000) in his "*Imitatio Homeri*? An Appraisal of Dennis R. MacDonald's 'Mimesis Criticism,'" *JBL* 124 (2005): 715–32. I responded to him (and to an article by Margaret M. Mitchell) in *My Turn: A Critique of Critics of "Mimesis Criticism"* (IACOP 53; Claremont: The Institute for Antiquity and Christianity, 2008). He then published *The Challenge of Homer: School, Pagan Poets, and Early Christianity* (LNTS 400; London: T&T Clark, 2009).

In his newer book he claims that largely because of an exchange between us at the 2006 meeting of the SNTS in Aberdeen, Scotland, he took on the challenge of the *Homeric Centos*. Although the study makes many contributions, its place in this ongoing discussion pertains to assessing what light, if any, the Greek centos of Homer and the Latin centos of Virgil might shed on the composition of the Gospels.

In chapter 1, "Introduction: The Context of the Study," Sandnes fairly and concisely locates his book within this dispute over mimesis criticism, introduces the centos (poetic paraphrases of the Gospels that adopt, adapt, or imitate classical poetry to retell Gospel stories), presents evidence for the ubiquity of the *Iliad*, the *Odyssey*, and the *Aeneid* in the world of the first Christians, offers criticisms of my mimetic readings of the Gospel of Mark and the Acts of the Apostles, and sets out his strategy for comparing the uses of classical epic in the Latin and Greek centos and proposals about such uses in the Gospels. "Are there contemporary analogies to the procedure adopted by advocates of Mimesis Criticism, and if so, what can be gleaned from them with regard to the question of *mimesis*?" (22). Sandnes argues throughout the volume that, whereas the centos exemplify a maximalist form of mimesis insofar as the Christian poets announce in nearly every line their dependence on Homer or Virgil, mimesis in the Gospels is so minimalist that their readers would have been unaware of such influence. The chapter ends with a splendid overview of growing scholarly interest in the centos for their own sake.

Chapter 2, "The Rhetorical Context of Biblical Epics," asks several important questions regarding the application of mimesis to texts (29): (1) Do similarities between two texts issue from authorial intent or the reader's imagination? (2) Do the similarities demonstrate "borrowing, imitating, or allusion"? (3) Are the similarities "conscious or accidental"? (4) Does the author imitate "a text or a story" that the author could have known independent of the text? In each case, Sandnes favors the latter options, whereas I generally prefer the earlier ones, that Mark's mimesis usually is authorial, imitating, conscious, and textual. Sandnes provides a handy introduction to *paraphrasis* in ancient education, including *mimesis* and *emulation*, or literary rivalry. He rightly shows that ancient imitators often disguised their imitations, but when they rivaled them, they advertised the mimetic targets: "The more significance and transvaluation one attributes the intertextual links, the more difficult it becomes if these are subtle, and even hardly noticeable" (41). "A fundamental step in reading literary contests involving transvaluation is to recognize the body of texts involved. … If, however, no sign of advertisement is found on the macro level, alleged intertextual links on the micro level should be approached with corresponding caution" (49–50). Sandnes may be surprised to learn that on this important point I agree with him, but I would insist that Mark and Luke fully expected their more perceptive readers, if not all of them, to see the mimetic markers strewn throughout their works.

"Why Imitate Classical Texts?" is the title of chapter 3, and Sandnes answers this question with two helpful responses. First, the earliest examples of "biblical epic" were "caused partly by what was considered the crude style of the biblical Gospels: they did not meet the standard of the classical legacy" (65). This chapter then ably illustrates this observation and uses it to object to mimesis criticism: "If there is some truth in claiming that the epic Gospels written in classical style were attempts at improving upon the reputation of the canonical Gospels, it is hard to understand how precisely these compositions may serve as models for how the canonical Gospels come into being" (83–84). My response is simple: whereas Juvencus (the Latin epicist and Sandnes's prime example) wished to elevate "the crude style of the biblical Gospels," Mark and Luke wished to transvalue what they perceived to be the crude religion of epic poetry, even if in many cases that "did not meet the standard of the classical legacy."

Sandnes's second answer to "Why imitate classical texts?" pertains to Julian's decree against Christians teaching classical Greek literature (361–363 C.E.). Indeed, most poetic imitations of the Gospel appear after this decree, and chapter 3 gives a fair assessment of them. Strangely, Sandnes sees in this reaction to Julian reason to suspect mimesis criticism on the Gospels, not because they were written much earlier but because "it is difficult to understand why the Emperor then directed the Christians to read the Gospels instead of Homer, thus trying to keep them away from Homeric and classical influences" (96). But the Gospel of Mark and the Acts of the Apostles surely are not simply Homer for Christians.

Not until chapter 4 does Sandnes answer the question "What Is a Cento?" This is one of the most original and significant contributions of the book, one long overdue. With respect to mimesis criticism, I would simply note that he surely is right in observing that the uses of Homeric epic in the *Homerocentones* and the Gospels are not strictly analogous. The later poets did not create their narratives; they adorned biblical narratives with verse. Although the centos display a *Kulturkampf* of sorts, generally they are friendlier to the epics than were Mark and Luke, who more consistently attempted to rival them. Clearly, the centoists advertised their links with Homer more blatantly. I will return to these differences at the end.

Chapter 5, "Faltonia Betitia Proba: The Gospel 'According to Virgil,'" begins not with the *Homerocentones* but a Latin centoist who wrote in the midst of Julian's ban on Christians teaching the classics (362). Sandnes discusses the Greek centos in some depth in the following chapter, "Eudocia Athenais: The Gospel 'According to Homer.'" This amazing woman composed her work during the first half of the fifth century, probably in exile in Jerusalem. Both chapters are helpful contributions to understanding the uses of Homeric and Virgilian epics in this period.

Chapter 6, however, has a major deficiency. One gets the impression that the Eudocia and subsequent Greek centoists imitated the epics somewhat atomistically, ripping out a line or two from one scroll and pasting them alongside others to retell an episode in the life of Jesus. Entirely absent are examples of several lines in the same sequence that surely suggest that the poets recognized profound similarities between the biblical accounts and tales in the epic. For example, in recension 2, the poet retells the story of Jesus' triumphal entry by borrowing no fewer than twenty-four lines from *Od.* 7, Odysseus's picaresque entry into the city of the Phaeacians (*Hom. Cent.* 2.1228–1261). In the same recension, the first thirteen lines for telling the story of the Gerasene demoniac come from *Od.* 9, Homer's introduction of Polyphemus (*Hom. Cent.* 2. 782–793).

The same phenomenon appears in recension 1. For example, the poets astutely retell the story of the hemorrhaging woman (Mark 5:25–34 and par.) by borrowing eight apt lines from the staunching of Glaucus's wound in *Il.* 16.

Hom. Cent. 1.1015–1016, 1028, 1034–1037, and 1044–1045
(≅ *Il.* 16.517a and 518b) "For I have this awful wound, and my blood
(≅ *Il.* 16.519) is not drying up.
      *   *   *   *   *

= *Il.* 16.523) "But you, lord, heal this terrible wound."
      *   *   *   *   *

(= *Il.* 16.528) Immediately he stopped the pain, from the painful wound
(= *Il.* 16.529) dried the black blood and put strength in her will.
(≅ *Il.* 16.530) Then he knew in his mind and called out,

(= Il. 6.441) "These things concern me as well, woman."

* * * * *

(≅ Il. 16.530) Then she knew in her mind and was glad,
(≅ Il. 16.531) because a great god had quickly heard her prayer.

Such examples could be multiplied, but these should suffice to demonstrate that the Byzantine poets recognized affinities between the biblical stories and the Homeric stories that seem to have informed the Evangelist in the first place.

It is in chapter 7, "Summary," where Sandnes's observations about mimesis criticism are most pointed and important. I heartily concur with the following:

> The Christian centoists relate to their hypotexts, be they Homer or Virgil, in various ways. They sometimes approach the hypotext as a quarry from where more or less isolated units are found appropriate; it is then simply a matter of coincidence in language. At other times, they engage with the wider context in more conscious ways, often in a contrasting or transcending way. This has been labelled "Kontrastimitation," "transformation," "transvaluation," "transposition" or "Verfremdung." Through contrasts, unexpected bendings, astonishments and curiosity, a heightened understanding of the hypotext is achieved. Dennis R. MacDonald has rightly called this a *Kulturkampf*, and I have argued that this corresponds to a hermeneutical *synkrisis* at home in rhetorical criticism. (233)

Sandnes makes several distinctions that will be important for further research. First, he surely is right in making a distinction, as the centoists did themselves, between the *res*, *sensus*, or subject of their poems, which invariably is biblical, and the *verba*, or language and style, which are Homeric or Virgilian (234–36). This distinction does not apply to Gospel narratives. Second, one must be careful, as I apparently have not been, about using the centos as analogies to the use of Greek poetry in the New Testament (238–40). Whereas the Gospel authors used epics as models for the creation of their stories (*res*), the centoists inherited their *res* from the Bible and ornamented them with dactylic hexameters (*verba*).

Sandnes restates his most biting criticism of mimesis criticism in the last five pages: here is the heart of our disagreement.

> [MacDonald] may well be right that readers well-versed in Homer may find allusions to his epics, perhaps most densely in the passion story as a Jesus-Hector comparison. But ... the absence of advertised intertextuality is indeed problematic. Cultural struggle between texts requires identification far beyond general accessibility in the culture. ... In my opinion, the fact that these two great poets [Homer and Virgil] were generally accessible cannot make up for the lack of advertising, especially if the purpose is to embark upon a *Kulturkampf*. (239–40)

I agree that textual transvaluation requires "advertised intertextuality," but I would disagree that such advertising is absent in the Gospel of Mark or the Acts of the Apostles, both of which contain enough mimetic glue to their narratives to stick to their epic models. We have not noticed this glue because we generally are ignorant of the Homeric epics. The authors of the *Homerocentones* were not and thus found a way to link the texts in new ways. One great virtue of Sandnes's books are their contributions to bringing the epic tradition into conversation with New Testament scholarship.

The end matter of the book contains a valuable bibliography and indexes.

NEW TESTAMENT: GENERAL

Torah in the New Testament: Papers Delivered at the Manchester-Lausanne Seminar of June 2008, edited by Michael Tait and Peter Oakes. Library of New Testament Studies 401. New York: T&T Clark, 2010. Pp. xvii + 278. Hardcover. $130.00. ISBN 9780567006738.

William Loader, Murdoch University, Perth, Australia

This volume brings together papers read at the 2008 joint colloquium held at Manchester of Bible scholars teaching in Lausanne, Geneva, Sheffield, and Manchester. It is a rich and diverse collection touching on a wide range of issues related to understanding attitudes toward Torah in the New Testament.

James Crossley's piece on "all foods clean" (Mark 7:19) leads off the collection with a provocative attempt to challenge consensus views, setting his own contribution within the context of the struggle against the ideology of such majorities. Accordingly, he seeks to make it plausible (and with caution claims no more than this) that Mark's comment on the controversy over handwashing declares that no clean food is rendered unclean by impure hands, so that rather than declaring all foods, including unclean foods, clean, Jesus is here doing the opposite, upholding biblical laws about clean and unclean food and addressing only the former. Such a reading runs against the grain of the immediate context, which by implication argues the irrelevance of the clean-unclean distinction by employing a rationalistic argument about human digestion, which would surely apply to all foods, clean and unclean.

Next, Arseny Ermakov highlights the life-giving nature of Torah as underlying Mark's discussion of the commandments, which focus on the Decalogue, Lev 19, and Deut 6. There follows a well-researched and convincing discussion by Andreas Dettwiler on Torah in Q that shows Torah's normative value, with "no trace of overt criticism" (63), though facing the challenge of relating Torah to the new element introduced by the kingdom. Thomas Römer and Jan Rückl then endeavor to make a case that one can find traces of Jewish hope for a Messiah son of Joseph in the Gospels, though acknowledging that the references are at best allusive, not direct. In his discussion of Torah in John, Sean Winter argues that the author's comments about Torah should be seen as part of the construction of his Christology rather than as reflections of conflict expressed in redactional layers of the Gospel. But conflict need not be tied to theories of redaction. Christological construction and contextual conflict need not be seen as alternatives—especially when one goes beyond 1:14–18, Winter's focus in this short piece, and considers the Gospel as a whole. Thus ends part 1 on the Gospels, where one might have expected treatment of Matthew and Luke, but it is the nature of such a collection not to be comprehensive.

Part 2, on Acts, does engage us with Lukan material, beginning with a superb article by Daniel Marguerat, who addresses the depiction of Paul's attitude toward Torah according to Acts. In it he identifies the tension between the way Luke's Paul rejects Torah as a way of salvation yet at the same time has Paul and Jewish Christians being Torah-observant. The resolution of the conflict lies in Luke's concern to portray Christian Jews as showing respect for the customs of their ancestors in conformity with values affirmed by the Romans. "To abandon the law of the forefathers is a disgraceful act" (116). Accordingly, the apostolic decree "confirms the co-existence of the two regimes, one applying to Judaeo-Christians who remain constrained by the Law, the other applying to the pagano-Christians, free with regard to the Law save for the four prohibitions laid down by the decree" (113). While one might argue with his reading of Luke 16:16–17 and the conclusion that Luke's focus is primarily ethical, Marguerat has produced a challenging and insightful analysis that goes to the heart of the issues in Luke-Acts. The paper by Simon Butticaz is a strong companion piece, focusing on the apostolic decree and arguing that its provisions are concerned with establishing a *modus vivendi* to ensure that Jewish Christians can remain true to the their ancestral law. Emmanuelle Steffeck also turns to the apostolic decree, arguing, less convincingly to my mind, that its concern is with countering the influence of pagan cults, including cult prostitution, but the existence of the latter is much debated.

Part 3 turns to the letters. In relation to Paul, the focus falls on Galatians. Peter Oakes examines statements about the law in relation to four aspects of Paul's theology in Galatians: ideas about God; Christ and the Spirit; the universe and its inhabitants; salvation and time. As a result, he challenges Dunn's distinction between "works of the law" and "the law" and also Räisänen's view that Paul is torn in two directions. Instead, he argues for a paradoxical coherence in Paul's view that denies the law's continuing validity while using Torah texts to urge this is so. Barry Matlock offers a detailed critique of the approaches of Stendahl, Sanders, Dunn, Wright, Donaldson, and Stanley, on Gal 3:10–14, focusing in particular on the notion of the law's unfulfillability. He argues that the way forward may not be to explain Paul's statement away as making no sense in the context of Jewish understandings of his day (or ours), but to see it as employed over against fellow Christians where such assumptions no longer play such a role. In the third paper George Brooke turns to Jude and to its apparently broad understanding of what constitutes Torah, which includes so-called rewritten scripture such as the Testament of Moses and, most notably, the Enochic tradition.

Part 4 begins with a refutation by Michael Tait of the notion of messianic Torah as an alleged aspect of Jewish expectation. Neither so-called canonical, pseudepigraphic Jewish literature, nor New Testament texts support such an idea, which, he argues, would surely have been exploited by Paul in his disputes with fellow Jews and Jewish Christians had it been known. Roger Tomes then compares statements in Philo and Josephus that attempt to explain Torah to Gentiles with the New Testament. He argues that the perspectives of New Testament writers would have included that the law was "given by God," has been "embodied in a particular culture," that "some laws are more important than others," and that "new circumstances call for new laws and new approaches to law" (208). The paper would have been stronger had it taken into account the differences among the various approaches among the New Testament writers when making such comparisons. Gerald Downing's contribution notes how Aristotle sees legislation as a means of also promoting virtuous living, practice thus facilitating inward change. Such an understanding of law, whether directly or indirectly from Aristotle, appears, he argues, to have informed New Testament writers. This is an important article in that it broadens the perspective in discussion of law beyond the limits of Jewish-Christian discourse and counters the assumption that this discourse had a monopoly on the notion of ethical transformation in relation to internalizing law. The final chapter takes us way beyond the New Testament to Gregory of Nyssa, but does so in order to employ his reflections as a way of highlighting the importance within the New Testament of temple and cultic imagery, also an integral part of Torah, and their associated assumptions.

This is not a comprehensive coverage of the theme, but it offers a rich collection of contributions to many of the important aspects of attitudes toward Torah in the New Testament. Despite some unevenness, the reader is well-rewarded.

What's in the Word: Rethinking the Socio-rhetorical Character of the New Testament, by Ben Witherington III. Waco, Tex.: Baylor University Press, 2009. Pp. viii + 195. Paper. $29.95. ISBN 9781602581968.

Richard L. Rohrbaugh, Lewis & Clark College, Portland, Oregon

In yet another book on what he calls the "socio-rhetorical" method of New Testament interpretation, Witherington seeks to demonstrate that socio-rhetorical criticism *"changes various readings and paradigms of NT studies in significant ways, and if we allow these readings to have their due weight, it will change the way we view early Christianity, including the way we view its theology and ethics"* (5, emphasis original).

In a very fundamental way, Witherington is making the case that a *historical* understanding of what the New Testament authors said, in their own time and place, together with an analysis of the methods by which they sought to persuade their largely nonliterate audiences, is the *sine qua non* of New Testament study. He emphatically rejects the notion of an "autonomous text," as if language is ever devoid of context, along with the idea that somehow historical analysis is of purely antiquarian interest or a means of avoiding personal engagement with

Scripture. Making good use of Philip Esler's devastating critique of those who cry "intentional fallacy" whenever they hear talk of authorial intent (*New Testament Theology: Communion and Community* [Minneapolis: Augsburg Fortress, 2005]), he easily demonstrates that history and theology simply cannot be separated.

The chapters in Witherington's book cover a variety of texts and topics. He begins by emphasizing the growing recognition that New Testament texts are not "texts" in the modern sense of that word but rather surrogates for oral communication. They were meant to be orally performed for largely nonliterate audiences. A second chapter claims that there was no ancient epistolary convention that made pseudepigraphical writing acceptable, and its presence in the canon is unlikely. However, not all will be convinced by the evidence he adduces that this is not a prime example of the anachronism he deplores. A third chapter explores the way the scribal culture that produced the Hebrew Bible shares much in common with the setting that produced the New Testament. A chapter on sermons and homilies in the New Testament nicely fleshes out the discussion of texts as surrogates for oral communication.

An intriguing chapter on Paul's seemingly personal struggle in Rom 7 suggests that rhetorical analysis changes everything. Instead of Paul describing his own life prior to becoming a Christ-follower, verses 7–13 offer a Pauline impersonation of Adam, and verses 14–25 describe the experience of those in Adam. Other chapters assert that Lazarus was the author of the Fourth Gospel, that eyewitness oral history rather than informal oral tradition produced the Gospels, that *eidolothyton* in 1 Corinthians warns against idolatry in pagan temples, that the divorce exception clauses in Matt 5 and 19 do not refer to marital infidelity but to incestuous relations like that of Herod Antipas, that Gal 3:28 refers to the creation of a spiritual equality in the body of Christ, and that apostolic and eyewitness testimony was the basis of a canonizing process that had already begun in the writings of Luke.

What is it that ties together such a varied and seemingly eclectic collection of studies? In Witherington's own words, it is the "historical socio-rhetorical way of reading NT texts" (5). So far so good; exactly that is demonstrated, often convincingly, throughout book. What is unacknowledged, however, and what is a clear part of the unstated agenda in the book, is an attempt to use this type of historical method to make the case for a very conservative view of historical reliability. To that end, speculation and leaps from the plausible to the certain abound. Phrases such as "we may assume..." or "it is likely that..." or the probability is..." are uncomfortably common. There is no doubt all of us spin the evidence in the interests of an agenda; here the unspoken character of this particular agenda will be significantly disconcerting to some readers.

One final comment regarding method. The spin notwithstanding, the case Witherington makes for the necessity of sociorhetorical analysis is often as convincing here as it is in many of his other writings. He demonstrates the earthbound character of the texts with great skill. One might suggest, however, that for all of the rightful emphasis he places on social history, he pays no attention whatsoever to the fact that language encodes a *cultural* world as deeply as it does a sociohistorical moment or the conventions of rhetorical practice. The first is every bit as historical as the other two and is especially critical when examining writings that function as surrogates for oral communication. If New Testament language does not float free of the sociohistorical moment that produced it, neither does it escape the ancient culture that it encodes.

Jesus and Paul: Global Perspectives in Honor of James D. G. Dunn for His Seventieth Birthday, edited by B. J. Oropeza, C. K. Robertson, and Douglas C. Mohrmann. Library of New Testament Studies 414. New York: T&T Clark, 2010. Pp. xxvii + 240. Hardcover. $140.00. ISBN 9780567629531.

Bernard Ukwuegbu, Seat of Wisdom Major Seminary, Owerri, Nigeria

This Festschrift, dedicated to James D. G. Dunn on the occasion of his seventieth birthday, contains essays by seventeen former students and two forewords by eminent scholars best described as Dunn's interlocutors in the ongoing dialogue in New Testament scholarship in the last few decades. The essays are grouped into two principal parts along the line of topics on Jesus and Paul, "two persons whom Jimmy's own studies have frequented."

In the opening essay, James F. McGrath ("Written Islands in an Oral Stream: Gospel and Oral Traditions") explores the roles of oral traditions in the composition of the Gospels, with a focus on Matthew and Luke. For McGrath, the truth that later New Testament authors had access to written sources does not rule out the fact that "they do not bear witness to independent oral tradition." In the quest for recovering these sources and determining which sources pre- or antedate the other, contemporary scholarship stands to benefit from insights of scholarly investigation of orality.

Stephen Wright ("Debtors, Labourers and Virgins: The Voice of Jesus and the Voice of Matthew in Three Parables") focuses on three Matthean parables (Unforgiving Servant [18:23–35]; the Laborers in the Vineyard [20:1–16], and the Ten Virgins [25:1–13]) in the light of recent research by Luise Schottroff and Klyne Snodgrass. Relativizing the tendency in certain strands of scholarship to dismiss the Gospels as "sources for Jesus," Wright argues that in these parables we can hear "the voice of Jesus" and the impact of that voice on his followers.

Jey Kanagaraj ("Jesus' Message of the Kingdom of God: Present and Future Tensions Revisited") revisits, through a study of selected sayings of Jesus from the Synoptic tradition (Mark 1:15; Matt 12:28; and Luke 11:20; Matt 6:10 and Luke 11:2; and Mark 9:1), the *now* and *not-yet* tensions in the eschatology of Jesus' message of the kingdom of God. Kanagaraj argues that the kingdom, although expected to come at the end time, is accessible to human beings in the person of Jesus and in his challenge to his audience to experience life in the kingdom by repentance and faith. In this way, the author illustrates how, in the imminence of God's kingdom, both present and future aspects converge.

Drawing on the story of Luke 7:36–50 in which a woman considered a "public" sinner anoints Jesus' feet, Ellen Christiansen ("Sinner according to the Words of the Law...") explains, through the identification of the status of the characters in the story, how the Lukan Jesus challenged existing boundaries. For Christiansen, the woman's identification as a sinner is designed to contrast her status to that of the respected Pharisee. By forgiving the woman, Jesus presented himself as the prophet of the kingdom who challenges boundaries and declares a new status and a changed identity.

Graham H. Twelftree ("Jesus and Magic in Luke-Acts") examines, through a consideration of the stories of Simon Magus, Elymas or Bar-Jesus, the slave girl with a spirit, and the seven sons of Sceva, Luke's definition of magic and his defense of Jesus against any charge of magic. Equating magic with false prophecy, Luke, so Twelftree, defended Jesus against the charge of magic by his portrayal of Jesus as a true prophet (against his understanding of magicians as false prophets), as a humble servant (against magicians' tendency to self-aggrandizement), and as one detached from wealth and possession (in contrast to magicians' avariciousness). Helen K. Bond ("Barabbas Remembered") argues that the significance of Barabbas depends not so much on who he really is as on how he was remembered in the Gospels. A cursory presentation of the different images of Barabbas in the four Gospels (an insurrectionist in Mark, a famous prisoner in Matthew, a murderer and rabble-rouser in Luke, and a violent criminal in John) enables Bond to conclude that the different pictures derive from lively oral traditions seeking to make sense of the Messiah and his death and in the attempt to draw on and transform a historical character connected with Jesus' last hours.

The next two essays address an issue central to the new perspective on Jesus (championed by Dunn): the possibility of preaching the Gospels without anti-Semitism. After a consideration of the development of the Judas figure in the history of interpretation, Arie W. Zwiep ("Judas and the Jews: Anti-Semitic Interpretation of Judas Iscariot, Past and Present") concludes that, not only is the study of *Wirkungsgeschichte* essential to the exegete's historical task, but fidelity to that task requires an ethic of interpretation to avoid disastrous effects of misguided readings. J. Martin C. Scott ("Jews or Christians? The Opponents of Jesus in the Fourth Gospel") focuses on the "typification" of the 'Jews' in the Fourth Gospel. Drawing a parallel with the history of the birth of Methodism, Scott demonstrates, through a consideration of texts where the typification is played out, that at stake is a case of inter- and inner-group struggle that must not necessarily have been heard by the ideal reader as "incipient anti-Semitism." Read within the wider context of the Johannine community, the "Jews" concept reflects the desire of the ideal author to communicate to readers the ongoing demand to continue to believe in their conception of the Messiah, despite other views to the contrary.

Simon Gathercole ("New Testament Christology in Recent British Scholarship: A Sketch of Distinctives and Debates") outlines some features of British research on Christology, highlighting areas that have been neglected (wisdom Christology and atonement) and areas that have received sufficient attention

(Adam Christology and Jesus' inclusion within divine identity). He ends by pointing out areas where British scholarship could benefit from developments in other regions. Kenneth I. Schenck, in the last essay in the Jesus part of the collection ("The Worship of Jesus among Early Christians: The Evidence of Hebrews"), studies the worship of Jesus in the Letter to the Hebrews. While not denying the fact that Hebrews uses "highly exalted language of Jesus" that smacks of worship, Schenck concludes that such language should not be understood as violating conventional Jewish monotheism.

C. K. Robertson ("Inheriting the Agitator's Mantle: Paul and the Nature of Apostleship in Luke-Acts") introduces the Paul section of the collection by exploring the remark in Acts 7:58 that the witnesses laid their coats "at the feet of a young man named Saul." Robertson sees in the remark a Lukan ploy of linking Paul's ministry through Stephen to Jesus and ultimately to Elijah and Elisha. Saul seemingly agrees with the actions of the mob because he sees what the apostles seem to miss: that in Jesus the distinctions between insiders and outsiders have disappeared. Since this was championed first by Stephen, the laying of the cloak at Saul's feet could be seen as the transfer of Stephen's spirit and vision to Saul following the Elijah/Elisha succession motif. B. J. Oropeza ("Running in Vain, but Not as an Athlete (Galatians 2:2): The Impact of Habakkuk 2:2–4 on Paul's Apostolic Commission") notes that, while the athletic metaphor is behind most of Paul's usage of the running imagery, the same is not the case with Gal 2:2. Rather, Paul here identifies himself with the tradition of prophetic heralds and interprets his traveling to different towns on his missionary journey proclaiming God's message of righteousness by faith in a way similar to "the herald in the Habakkuk's vision." Paul's apprehension that the running might be in vain, so Oropeza, rather than indicating doubts that the Jerusalem apostles could nullify his calling, reflects his concern for the future effectiveness of his gospel.

Douglas C. Mohrmann ("Of 'Doing' and 'Living': The Intertextual Semantics of Leviticus 18:5 in Galatians and Romans") reviews allusions to Lev 18:5 in Hebrew Bible and extrabiblical Hebrew literature, showing how the usage of the text exhibited patterns and innovations expedient to the needs of the times of the various users. Since the intertext is open to transformations, Mohrmann defends the legitimacy of Paul's innovative use of the intertext in Gal 3:12 and Rom 10:15 in the light of the novel situations he faced in the two letters. Against the backdrop of selected passages in the Hebrew Bible, Don Garlington ("Israel's Triumphant King: Romans 1:5 and the Scriptures of Israel") explores the reference in Rom 1:5 to "the obedience of faith" owed to the chief hero of Paul's gospel. For him, Paul brings together a number of texts concerning the Davidic king (Gen 49:10; Num 23:21–24; 24:17–19; Deut 33:5 LXX; 2 Sam 7:1; 1 Chr 17; Pss 2; 68; 72; 110; Isa 9:1–7; 11; 19:19–24; Zech 9:9-10) "who would claim the nations as his own" to justify his eschatological and christological reading of Israel's Scriptures.

Lung-kwong Lo ("Paul and Ethnicity: The Paradigm of Glocalisation") shifts the focus to contemporary implications of Paul's message. For Lo, when read in the light of the tensions between Jews and Gentiles in the early first century c.e.,

Paul's vision of "neither Jew nor Greek (Gentiles) (3:28) is better appreciated in terms of "glocalisation," a coinage that joins the characteristics of both "globalization" and "localisation." Unlike the tendency in some versions of globalization, Paul does not seek to *erase* cultural specificities but to *relativize* them. Similarly, Lo sees the Pauline injunction: "Jews first and then the Gentile" (Rom 1:16) as Paul's strategy to keep the distinction between Jews and Gentiles in their living context while at the same time championing the cause of their unity in Christ. He cautions against the temptation (inherent in missionary history) to require conformity, under the assumption that "there is only one form of Christianity."

Allan R. Bevere ("*Cheirograph* in Colossians 2:14 and the Ephesian Connection") argues for reading the χειρόγραφον in Col 2:14 as a reference to the Mosaic law in the light of the common connection between Colossians and Ephesians (where the phrase explicitly refers to the Mosaic law). Bevere, however, admits that his reading of χειρόγραφον does not rule out understanding the concept in terms of the two other alternative proposals of "a certificate of indebtedness" and "a heavenly book of deeds." The last essay in the collection (John Byron, "The Epistle to Philemon: Paul's Strategy for Forging the Ties of Kinship") presents Philemon as a "window into Paul's practice of pastoral ministry." Through an examination of the identity of Philemon and Onesimus and an assessment of the legal and social aspects of Onesimus's status as a slave, Bryon sees Paul's reinterpretation of Onesimus's status from a "slave" to his "child" and a "beloved brother" as signaling that the new bonds of kinship erected by Paul undermines the artificial structures of slavery.

Biblical scholarship continues to diversify, and as this process of diversification continues into the future, the need for dialogue between different approaches to the Bible and their practitioners will become more acute. Especially with regard to the academic study of the New Testament, the variety of essays in this collection testifies to Dunn's ground-breaking contribution to this ongoing process. No doubt the collection will aid readers to become more conversant with the many approaches used in understanding the New Testament texts that Dunn champions.

NEW TESTAMENT AND CHRISTIAN ORIGINS

In the Beginning Was the Meal: Social Experimentation and Early Christian Identity, by Hal Taussig. Minneapolis: Fortress, 2009. Pp. x + 262. Hardcover. $39.00. ISBN 9780800663438.

Pieter J. J. Botha, University of South Africa, Pretoria, South Africa

The title of Taussig's book proposes an underlying hypothesis "for the beginnings of Christianity" (ix), even though his study undermines the idea of Christian origins itself. With this focus on meals, Taussig wants readers to gain a different perspective on many aspects of the first hundred years of the various movements related to and in memory of Jesus. Those movements were primarily formed as associations that kept meals, argues Taussig, so he "looks to what can be learned about early Christianity through examining one of its major social practices" (5). "The emergence of early Christianity is impossible to contemplate without the meal and the organizational form of Hellenistic associations" (100). In the meal activities of the early Christians we find the particular forms of "social experimentation" that created Christian identity. "The festive meals of early Christianity were a social stage on which early Christian identity was elaborated. Thus, studying them participates in the methodological shifts from heroic figure to social formation, from belief to social practice, from origins to identities, and from essence to performance" (19).

In the first four chapters Taussig establishes the basic shape and dynamics of early Christian meals by investigating the character of Hellenistic festive meals and the early Christian participation in such meals. Chapter 2 is a critique of the conventional "imagination" of Christian origins. Building on the work of Karen King, Burton Mack, Judith Lieu, and Jonathan Z. Smith, Taussig endeavors to portray the dynamics of early Christian social practice as manifested in their shared meals.

By "meal," Taussig refers to the "Hellenistic" meal with its homogeneous form and shared meanings practiced widely throughout Greco-Roman antiquity. Anchoring his work to studies by Matthias Klinghardt and Dennis Smith, Taussig identifies five shared features of the Hellenistic meal: (1) a multihour event in which eating and drinking were central to the evening's activities, (2) a three-part event in which the community shared in both a meal (*deipnon*) and a period of conversation and drink (*symposium*), separated by (3) a ceremonial libation, (4) the leadership of a president, and (5) the presence of several marginal persons, such as servants and uninvited guests. Taussig is clear that the shared Christian meal event was distinguished from other Greco-Roman meal events only by the libation to Christ and by the content of the conversation. He emphasizes that the Christian Mass or Eucharist was a later Christian phenomenon that grew out of this shared meal. According to Taussig, this shared meal, as a pervasive institution within the Greco-Roman world, provided a "safe space" for early Christian communities to challenge the domination of the Roman Empire.

The Hellenistic meal had fairly standard social dynamics, expressing (or consolidating) community, friendship, boundaries, obligations, stratification, and equality. Taussig notes the utopian dynamic, the idealized significance attached to some ancient discussions of the Hellenistic meal. These dynamics provided early Christians with a social institution that was both "closed" and "open," hence opportunities for social "innovation" in a "safe" environment.

In the last four chapters Taussig elaborates the ways early Christians' meals became a primary social practice. He discusses the involvement of early Christianity with larger society, how meals related to, and provided opportunities for resistance to, the Roman Empire. In his investigation, Taussig attempts to show how actions within these meals reproduce, negotiate, perfect, and contemplate difficult social issues of the Hellenistic era. In an epilogue he raises questions for current Christian worship from what has been seen in his account of this ancient social practice.

Taussig combines his understanding of Greek and Roman festive meals with insights of ritual theorists to argue that early Christians regularly reclined for meals; they offered libations, some with hymns to Christ; and they celebrated the forerunner of the Eucharist with the partaking of more wine after the libation, but in a setting of teaching, discussion, and fellowship. It is in these meal contexts that the early christological hymns were possibly composed (ch. 5, reflecting on early Christianity's concern with "larger society"). It is in these meal situations that the stories that would eventually form the Gospels were retold, adapted, or invented. Finally, it is here that believers experimented with new configurations of social order, creating less hierarchy than was typical and elevating the role of women and the poor. By means of these meals early Christians used food both to unify and to differentiate with regard to ethnic tensions. Here, as in certain other voluntary associations in the Roman Empire, resistance to imperial hegemony was implied by drinking to a deity above the emperor himself.

Though these early Christian meal rituals entailed social experimentation, Taussig is careful to point out that nothing in society at large may have changed as a result. Meal participants were vividly confronted with new *possibilities* for status identification and interaction. The meal ritual helped the early Christians to deploy new resources to social issues, but "in a curiously implicit, semiconscious manner" (66). These festive meals allowed actions to became opportunities for thinking about the way the world could be different: "even though ritual engages social dynamics so strongly, it almost never does so in direct address. It provides a somewhat removed and safe environment and usually in coded gesture and language reproduces a social conflict or problem. This indirect, veiled engagement of important social dynamics commonly provides a more effective address of intractable and frightening social issues" (145).

In chapters 7 and 8 Taussig uses a more detailed exegetical approach to reveal how early Christian meals may have been "performing" a new identity amid the massive displacements and struggles of the Hellenistic world. He brings together various insights to explore what meals "did" in shaping social relationships internally and toward "the outside world" in early imperial society in general and within early Christian communities in particular. The possible forms of "social experimentation" that were taking place in those meals as they were becoming what might later be called "Christian" were linked both to resistance to Rome (or, more precisely, to Roman imperial ideology) and to the emerging interpretations of Jesus. The character of early Christian resistance to the Roman Empire was, essentially, an insinuated resistance, in disguised form (see, e.g., 140–43).

In sum, according to Taussig, early Christian meals allow us to bring Christian beginnings, Christian theologizing (early Christian rhetoric), and the development of identity together. In the "performances" associated with the meal we find the early Christians negotiating life issues as believers.

When engaging Taussig in dialogue we should be appreciative of his interpretive stance. He is not just paraphrasing New Testament texts (as is wont among many scholars), and he does not simply accept early Christian literature as direct access to historical reality. For instance, "it appears that Paul missed both the important performative reflection that the meal was working on and the difficulty of the larger issue of Jews and gentiles in the broader environment. ... the meals in the community to which Paul was writing were in the process of working creatively on complicated and intractable issues" (73). Another example, about the Jesus stories dealing with eating: "Whether they were real or imagined meals, the point still holds that the social symbolism of meals, the prevalence of meals, and the important functions meals played in ordinary people's imagination of society made some meals an occasion for serious social experimentation. Telling an imaginary story about a meal in relationship to hungry and shamed people participated in the socially experimental vocabulary of the larger meal practice" (156).

This is an important study (even though parts are repetitive and components of the argument are derivative). Taussig formulates carefully and goes to great lengths to avoid simplistic and naïve claims. He avoids stark contrasts (such as between Christian and "pagan" meals), and attention to historical, contextual issues is not wanting. Significantly, his arguments do not suffer from academic insularity.

It is with reason that Taussig presents his case with confidence, but one should point to (at least) the following topics for further discussion and analysis. In order to understand how the deployment and manipulation of rituals constructed meanings for the audiences (participants) who shared the sponsors' (benefactors') ritual knowledge—*and of those telling us about these events*—it is obviously necessary to reconstruct as much as possible of that knowledge. It seems to me that just too many aspects involved with ancient meals as ritualized processes are left out of the picture or not covered adequately, such as the development of authority structures in early Christianity (the growth and extension of control and supervision by early Christian leaders).

There hangs an air of anachronism around Taussig's presentation. Surely those early Christians had some sense of a grand narrative (a mythology) and a physical model of being (without which, Mary Douglas is adamant, no ritual can be understood). It is correct to say early Christian practices cover a range of expressive vocabularies exploring alternative social visions (e.g., 20), but what were ancient (Greco-Roman) social visions, and hence what could those alternative expectations be? How would we know about these alternative social visions? Friendship, status, equality, even gender are not just phenomena to be linked to; they are constructs, historically and culturally unique. In a way, in Taussig's study historical embeddedness remains at a level of generality.

In addition, Taussig presents very little of the actual primary sources for our knowledge of festive meal practices. His presentations of (especially Christian) meals are highly selective conflations of very diverse sources. Reading the ancients' actual discussions of their festive meals, one is struck by how those festivities after the libation differ from Taussig's narrative images.

The issue of theory also require some reflection. Taussig uses selected elements of (essentially) five recent ritual theorists. Quoting Catherine Bell, he emphasizes that rituals help participants sort through basic cultural and social schemes (by reproducing functions); from Jonathan Z. Smith, he notes that rituals create a provisional perfection of that which is symbolized. Pierre Bourdieu contributes the insight that rituals as processes help to construct human identities ("Rituals are ways people negotiate social and cultural power by the way their performance brings tensive dynamics together," 62). Victor Turner is included to allow the use of the concept of liminality and to accentuate the blurring of social boundaries and the *communitas* that can result. Mary Douglas is involved to legitimize the claim that the details of a meal signify the social relations among the participants. It is a question whether these theorists are actually discussing quite the same thing, even though they share the use of the word *ritual*. Taussig creates a very neat picture of ritual as processual behavior, but basically it is an eclectic collection of statements dovetailed to allow a very attractive construction of early Christian meals. How does his theory enable self-reflexivity and critique, and how does it provide an interpretive platform that is different from predictable exegetical outcomes? In other words, does his theory allow conclusions about "meaning" *not* readily or self-evidently relevant to our needs and situation?

Above I noted that Taussig believes that early Christian meals provided "a more effective address of … social issues" (see 145)—how would we know that? What theory underpins the claims about effectiveness? When Taussig claims that as "good rituals do, these meals were reproducing for reflection and eventual deployment complex tensions in the larger situation" (73), how would we know they were "good" rituals?

However, Taussig has provided us with a very useful platform to constructively add to our understanding of early Christianity.

Maranatha: Women's Funerary Rituals and Christian Origins, by Kathleen E. Corley. Minneapolis: Fortress, 2010. Pp. xvi + 262. Hardcover. $35.00. ISBN 9780800662363.

Nicola Hayward, McGill University, Montreal Quebec, Canada

In her most recent book, *Maranatha: Women's Funerary Rituals and Christian Origins*, Kathleen Corley continues her work on women in early Christianity by focusing on the liturgical context of women's funerary meals and laments. According to Corley, focusing on women's ritual laments provides one of the best setting for solving many of the problems of Christian origins, as it "give us the oral core of what became the passion narrative" (1) as well as the resurrection and appearance accounts.

Chapter 1 discusses the shift in meal practices from 200 B.C.E. to 300 C.E., whereby respectable women began to experience more freedom, which enabled them to attend formal banquets "with or without their husbands," as well as being depicted reclining at the banquet in funerary images (6). Corley argues that, while much of the literary evidence suggests that this newfound freedom was not widely accepted, the Gospels, Matthew in particular, do exhibit signs of acceptance, or at least a willingness to engage in the debate. It is Matthew's Gospel, according to Corley, that is the most open to women's participation in the meal, as he narrates their role in the miraculous feeding accounts in which women and children recline alongside men, an aspect the other Gospels leave out. Furthermore, Matt 21:31–32 is the only Gospel that aligns Jesus directly with both "tax collectors and prostitutes" and places women noted for their bad reputation in his genealogy. According to Corley, Greco-Roman voluntary associations share many similarities with early Christian communities and as such offer the best comparison for understanding early Christian group formation. In Greco-Roman associations, men and women gathered to share in the communal meal, as well as being provided with financial assistance toward funerary costs. Early Christians also met for gender-inclusive meals and provided the necessary requirements to honor the dead. Much of the meal celebration in honor of the dead took place either at the house of the deceased or later at the site of the tomb. Corley notes how the "bawdiness of these repasts" (19) eventually became a problem for the church, which, by the time of Augustine, imposed restrictions on funerary celebrations at the tomb.

Chapter 2 focuses on the participation of women in ancient funerary rites and funerary meals, an aspect of women's activity that has been neglected by scholars. Often referred to as the "cult of the dead," women played a central role in the care for the deceased. They often washed and anointed the body for burial, prepared the meal, and led the community and family in bereavement. The mourning women would perform lamentations at the site and offered food to the dead, specifically fish and bread. Corley rightly points out that these occasions were public, not private, affairs, as the whole community would attend. Legislation enacted in the seventh to third centuries B.C.E. curbed women's participation in funerals. This legislation restricted women's display of grief and excessive wealth, and at Delphi the funeral procession was carried out in silence. Similar funerary restrictions were also written into Roman law, limiting the expression of women's grief. According to Corley, however, despite legislative efforts to curb the role of women's liturgical activity, many continued to visit the tombs and to sing laments to their loved ones.

Corley notes that, as a result of their association with the cult of the dead, women participated in the ritual lamentation of heroes and gods, such as the Egyptian Isis. Women were also depicted in the noble death scenes of Socrates, Hercules, and Moses. The disapproving nature of women's lament is expressed when Socrates dismisses the women on account of their weeping. A similar incident is repeated in Seneca's *Hercules Oestaeus*, when Hercules tells his mother to stop weeping. Hellenistic Jewish literature also reflects similar attitudes to women's lamentations, as in the case of Josephus's account of the death of Moses. The cult of the dead, however, continued to flourish in early Christian communities. Early Christians often gathered at the tombs of family and friends to honor the dead and partake of the Eucharist. During these occasions women "led the funerary meal, and raised a cup at funerary meals to toast the dead and lead the group in liturgical recitations" (57). Her analysis of women's leadership roles in ritual laments, particularly the festive meals, raises the question of women's participation, if not leadership, in the celebration of the formal eucharistic meal.

Chapter 3 addresses the New Testament and Jesus' inclusive meal practices. Corley argues that the early Christian meal was not hinged on issues of gender, nor was it concerned with the presence of Jesus at the meal, but it was rather concerned with inclusivity and class equality. Evidence that Jesus encouraged an egalitarian meal setting can be demonstrated by examining the parable of the feast (Matt 22:1–14; Luke 14:16–24; Gos. Thom. 64:1–12) and the tradition that Jesus dined with tax collectors and sinners (Q 7:34; Mark 2:15). Accusations that Jesus dined in mixed company indicate the Jesus movement as one of the groups that was affected by the changing practices to Greco-Roman meal customs. Conversely, the Didache contains what is possibly the earliest text of early Christian meals that did celebrate the presence of Jesus. The earliest is an agape meal and proclaims "Maranatha" in the last verse. The second is a eucharistic meal but without the words of institution.

The fourth chapter focuses on Jesus' meals with women. Drawing from the feeding narratives in Matthew, the Syro-Phoenician woman, and the anointing woman, Corley argues that women played an active role in the formation of tradition. As a collection, these stories emphasize several perceptions regarding the role of women. She identifies the story of the Syro-Phoenician woman as predating Mark and coming from a collection of miracles concerning Elijah in 1 Kgs 17:7–16, 17–24. The story portrays a stereotypical Christian funerary feast in which a woman uses her wit to secure not only her daughter's well-being but also the inclusion of a Gentile mission. The anointing woman "boldly anoints" (109) Jesus at a meal for burial, causing his disciples to react negatively. Although pure speculation, Corley suggests these accounts may have derived from the creative role of women in the community and in the formation of tradition. The Last Supper accounts, however, shift the focus from women and ground the eucharistic meal in the person of Jesus himself.

In her fifth chapter, Corley argues against the idea that the passion narrative and the empty tomb were produced by elite men. Concerns are also raised when the tradition that links Mary Magdalene as the first witness to Jesus' resurrection is placed secondary to Paul's earlier description of an appearance to Peter (1 Cor 15:3–11), a passage that omits women as the first witnesses to Jesus' resurrection. The development of these traditions, however, comes under question when viewed against the background of women's and ordinary people's roles in ancient funerary rites and the function of gender in the narratives of dying heroes. The presence of these women at the tomb of Jesus may be compared to the noble death scenes of heroic individuals such as Socrates and Hercules. Corley proposes that the Hellenistic custom of women's laments on the third day influenced the Gospel tradition of the women going to the tomb of Jesus on the third day. She argues that the overall effect of the empty tomb, however, silenced and marginalized the women followers of Jesus. The origin of the passion narrative has its oral roots in the women and ordinary people who visited the tomb over and over again to lament and sing over the death of Jesus.

Corley makes a significant contribution to the problem of uncovering early Christian origins. Not only has she brought our attention to the pervasiveness of women's funerary laments in Hellenistic customs, but she has also successfully matched these customs with the passion narrative in the Gospels. Given the political nature surrounding the death of Jesus, further research into the political form of female laments would prove fruitful in uncovering the history of early Christian women. Corley's book is a valuable source for those interested in uncovering Christian origins, but more specifically for those interested in women's participation in the creation of the passion narrative and the empty tomb stories.

JESUS

Jesus, Gnosis and Dogma, by Riemer Roukema. New York: T&T Clark, 2010. Pp. xi + 231. Paper. $24.95. ISBN 9780567466426.

James F. McGrath, Butler University, Indianapolis, Indiana

Riemer Roukema's *Jesus, Gnosis and Dogma* is an ambitious volume that seeks to disentangle the intertwined threads mentioned in the book's title and investigate what history can and cannot answer regarding traditional Christian doctrinal views of Jesus and the variations on and alternatives to them found not only within Gnosticism but also other groups such as Jewish Christians.

The first chapter sets forth Roukema's goals. He aims not only to trace the development of orthodox Christology (as well as of other views) but also to distinguish as clearly as possible what can be said *historically* about Jesus from that which can only be asserted *theologically* (3). Roukema immediately acknowledges the challenging character of such an undertaking, since impartiality and objectivity are elusive, with bias and subjectivity being factors not only for the historians of today but also for the ancient Christian authors from the first several centuries whose writings will be the focus of the book (4). History and theology may be distinguishable and need to be distinguished, but they are intertwined as far back as we go. Roukema outlines key criteria of authenticity used in the quest for the historical Jesus, and traces chronological developments across time through a variety of sources, interacting in the process with the treatment of them by major scholars such as Dunn, Meier, and Pagels. The latter's preference for the Gospel of Thomas is pointed to as an example of a *theological* preference that should not be allowed to color the historical evidence, which suggests that much in the Gospel of Thomas is *historically* secondary (13).

The next three chapters form a series, focusing on Jesus' origin and identity, his teaching, and his death and resurrection, respectively. Chapter 2 begins with a brief mention of some basic information in Luke and the other Synoptics, then turns quickly to Paul and proceeds chronologically from there. Paul is considered to have viewed Jesus as preexistent. The evidence in the Gospel of Mark is understood to "identify" Jesus with "God the Lord" (28), although whether this identification means a close connection, a shared nature, or something else is not specified. The authenticity of every act and saying is not considered, since here Roukema is tracing the development of theological views of Jesus, not assessing their historicity (32). The Christology of the remaining Synoptic Gospels is surveyed, and of them Roukema writes, "In a more or less concealed manner, they refer to his heavenly origin and therefore his pre-existence with God" (39). Turning attention to the Gospel of John, Roukema argues that its expression of this view of Jesus is found to be much more emphatic. Roukema then returns to the relationship of history and theology and writes, "On a theological level, we can determine that Paul and the authors of the gospels thought of Jesus in this way, but that does not imply that they were right in their theological views. ... [E]ven if one believes that the testimonies of the New Testament about Jesus as the Lord and as the pre-existent Son of God go back to his own life, it remains impossible to determine by historical means that he was truly so" (45). The chapter continues with a survey of the Gospel of Thomas and of later works reflecting a gnostic viewpoint and concludes that, while historical tools cannot determine whether the viewpoint found in the New Testament or in later gnostic works is *correct*, it *can* be shown that the formulation of a gnostic interpretation of Jesus is a *secondary development* beyond, based on, and at times running counter to the depiction of him in earlier sources.

Chapter 3 focuses on the teaching attributed to Jesus in the same range of sources as the previous chapters, drawing a similar conclusion to the previous one. While the theological development of Gnosticism is described as understandable in the context of its time, the earlier evidence for Jesus taking a positive view of the Jewish Scriptures excludes the possibility of his having held or taught the views found in later gnostic sources (87). Chapter 4 focuses on interpretations of the death and resurrection of Jesus. Roukema notes our historical uncertainty about what interpretation, if any, Jesus may have offered for his own future death. In surveying the sources, there is sometimes a tendency to flatten the evidence, so that, for instance, even after noting the lack of atonement theology in Luke-Acts, Roukema nevertheless sums up his treatment of that source by writing, "All in all it is clear that, according to Luke, Jesus' death and resurrection have a redemptive effect" (97). But in other instances, the chapter offers very interesting insights into the distinctive outlook of ancient sources. The best example is the treatment of the view that Simon of Cyrene rather than Jesus was crucified as resulting from a close reading of ambiguity in Mark 15:20–24 (109–10). The possibility that

Thomas' atonement-free outlook could have early roots is acknowledged, as is the inability of historical inquiry to evaluate Jesus' resurrection and ascension as historical facts.

Chapter 5 is a brief one, recapping what proceeded and presenting what will be the focal points in the remaining chapters. Chapter 6 examines the phenomenon of Jewish Christianity and discusses whether the sorts of views found in later Jewish Christian literature such as the Pseudo-Clementines might go back to the earliest period in the history of the Christian movement. Chapter 7 considers whether Jesus had a secret teaching. While several New Testament and extracanonical works make reference to such private instruction, these texts also *record that teaching*, making it unlikely that any of them refer to an esoteric teaching not recorded in the piece of literature that referred to it (137). Thus Roukema concludes that the popular notion that the church suppressed the true teaching of Jesus, which was passed on by "heretics," "is fiction and has no historical foundation" (144). Chapter 8 examines whether exalted christological statements found in early Christian texts could fit within the framework of early Judaism. Considering Philo, Targums, and other Jewish literature such as Ezekiel the Tragedian and the Prayer of Joseph, and interacting with scholars such as Larry Hurtado and Daniel Boyarin, Roukema draws the conclusion that early Christology would not have seemed out of place in early Judaism. Chapter 9 builds on the preceding chapter, beginning with the claim that "Judaism knew a plurality in the one God and left room to other heavenly figures besides God, so that the exalted conceptions which were made of Jesus were not completely unfamiliar to contemporaneous Judaism" (164). The chapter then proceeds to consider a number of developments in the way Christians related Christology and monotheism, including adoptionism (spelled "Adoptianism" in the book), modalism, Origenism, Arianism, and the Nicene formulation. The chapter concludes by recognizing that the "orthodox" view of Jesus cannot persuade all Christians (188) and asks instead whether the Nicene Creed offers "a proper interpretation" of what is said about Jesus in the New Testament (189). Roukema believes that it does, although he acknowledges that historical study cannot answer the question of how this view of Jesus compares to Jesus' own self-understanding. The final chapter offers an overview and seeks to bring together the threads running through the book, concluding with a doxology.

Although the attempt to distinguish between what can be said historically and theologically is of crucial importance, at times I felt that matters were significantly more complex that Roukema indicated. The evidence is surveyed with questions raised by later Christian doctrine, or at least other Christian texts, already in mind, and this often colors the interpretation of evidence in precisely the way that Roukema warns of the potential for theological preference to influence historical judgments. If one reads the Gospel of Luke, for instance, asking whether there are any hints at Jesus having a preexistent heavenly origin, then one may indeed find some. If, however, one asks what a reader would have understood if the reader did not have those questions in mind, then the matter of preexistence will simply never come up for the reader of Luke, and the same may be said likewise for the other Synoptics. Since Roukema's express aim was to distinguish the historical and the theological, even if they could not always be separated, then it must be noted that a survey that brings topics from systematic theology or later confessions into the picture and allows them to set the agenda is a *theological* survey, not only in the sense of a survey of New Testament authors' theologies, but also in the sense that it is a survey of them through a particular theological lens.

Of course, the entanglement of theology and history is the very reason Roukema wrote, and it was perhaps inevitable that such a volume should not only present the problem but at times illustrate it. Roukema regularly does an admirable job of not merely acknowledging but highlighting the fact that doctrinal statements to which he subscribes are matters of theological choice and not something susceptible to historical demonstration.

There were other aspects of the book that were problematic, and if they are somewhat minor, they nevertheless detract from the volume's overall effectiveness. The reference to Jesus having "swept clean" the temple's outer court shows a lack of awareness of the size of the structure (62), and the discussion of the Secret Gospel of Mark features several inaccuracies, including the claim that no one other than Smith ever saw it and that it has recently been "irrefutably demonstrated" to be a falsification, when in fact it is not the case that everyone finds Stephen Carlson's treatment persuasive, much less the final word on the subject (137–38). The statement that Jesus' use of "son of man" necessarily implies a consciousness of having preexisted in heaven (194) shows a lack of awareness of the range of meaning of the underlying Aramaic phrase.

This book may be useful for students in a conservative theological setting coming to the historical study of Christology for the first time, since it will begin to introduce a number of key concepts and issues, without overwhelming them with challenging material and perspectives at their first encounter. Those working with students from a different background or from diverse prior experiences will probably find the book less suited to their needs. While Roukema's attempt to tackle an important and difficult topic is to be appreciated, many will feel that the several gems of insight found within the book do not counterbalance the problems with it. Nevertheless, where there are shortcomings, to at least some extent these reflect the difficulty of bringing together topics, methods and areas of expertise as diverse as historical criticism, New Testament studies, patristics, Gnosticism, and systematic theology and seeking to distinguish them clearly while at the same time allowing them to interact constructively. Roukema's effort to do precisely that is to be appreciated.

Key Events in the Life of the Historical Jesus: A Collaborative Exploration of Context and Coherence, edited by Darrell L. Bock and Robert L. Webb. Grand Rapids: Eerdmans, 2009. Pp. xvii + 931. Paper. $70.00. ISBN 9780802866134.

Richard Horsley, University of Massachusetts, Boston, Massachusetts

In the field of biblical studies, which includes scholars of widely differing theological views, there is often a tacit agreement to disagree. This is nowhere more important than in investigation and interpretation of the historical Jesus, so "loaded" with implications for faith. Fortunately, the agreement to disagree is rooted not simply in professional toleration and civility but in an appreciation that those with different theological or secular perspectives can learn from each other. This volume by eleven evangelical or "biblically orthodox" Christian scholars, who met together in a "seminar" for thorough-going discussion of their respective essays over a period of ten years, presents much that those of different viewpoints can learn from.

This weighty volume includes twelve essays on key events and activities of Jesus, plus an introduction, a summary, and a substantial essay on historical method. Many of the "key events" or activities chosen are generally viewed as historical and integral to Jesus' mission: Jesus' baptism by John (Robert Webb), exorcisms (Craig Evans), the temple "incident" (Klyne Snodgrass), the Last Supper (I. Howard Marshall), and Jesus' crucifixion by the Romans (Robert Webb). The historicity of other events chosen for treatment is doubted to some degree by more skeptical scholars: Jesus and the Twelve (Scot McKnight), Jesus' table fellowship with sinners (Craig Blomberg), Peter's declaration in Caesarea Philippi (Michael Wilkins), Jesus' royal entry (Brent Kinman), and the Jewish trial of Jesus (Darrell Bock). A couple of the events have been neglected or regarded as not susceptible of historical investigation: the Sabbath controversies (Donald Hagner) and Jesus' empty tomb/ appearances (Grant Osborne).

By focusing on events and activities, this collection of essays presents a more relational, historically interactive Jesus than do books that focus mainly on text-fragments of his teaching. The portrayal of a Jesus who communicates with his followers and is engaged in conflict with opponents persists even when the authors assert his transcendent authority (as the Messiah), especially at the end of their respective essays. Among other attractive features, the essays, some of great length, are also reviews of previous scholarship, although not always complete.

Each essay aims to do three things: (1) establish the case for the probable historicity of the event on standard criteria for "authenticity"; (2) explore the sociocultural context; and (3) state the significance for understanding Jesus.

The contributors are concerned to find Gospel accounts historically credible. The analyses are generally critical, using the standard criteria of "authenticity," although sometimes, after critical assessment of the key passages, the ensuing discussion takes Gospel texts at face value as virtual transcripts of what happened. Also, at points some authors portray Jesus as the sole actor and "the onlookers" as reacting, in contrast to the interaction portrayed in the Gospel accounts (e.g., "the royal entry").

Context, for most of these essays, means a cultural context of concepts and ideas. In pointed contrast with the Jesus Seminar, which tended to focus more on Hellenistic context, these essays focus on Second Temple Jewish culture. While including late Judean texts, this often means mainly Scripture, which is sometimes treated almost as a closed system of thought. But this more general cultural context as the key to interpretation is broader than the Jewish eschatological scenario within which the neo-Schweitzerians (Allison, Ehrman) locate the apocalyptic Jesus or the Cynic philosophers that provides the key to the liberals' sapiential Jesus (Crossan). Only a few of these essays pay much attention to the concrete historical (political-economic) context, such as the effects of Roman rule on the Judean temple-state. Only a couple of the contributors give some attention to the fundamental division between village life in Judea and Galilee and the Herodian, high-priestly, and Roman rulers based in Jerusalem and the newly built cities of Galilee. As with much study of "the historical Jesus," the concrete aspects of historical religious-political-economic life remain obscured by continuing use of the broad essentialist constructs of "Judaism" and "(early) Christianity." Most of the essays assume that the framework of Jesus' actions was Jewish "restoration eschatology," although not in the more grandiose biblical-theological synthesis of some recent interpreters of Jesus.

While it is impossible to comment on all the essays, let me deal briefly with some salient points in a few. In contrast to the frequent practice of treating fragments of "data" piecemeal, Scot McKnight points out that Jesus' choosing "the Twelve" is present in various strata and forms of Jesus traditions (Mark, Q, Paul; narrative, sayings, lists, a creed). Of special importance as we begin to recognize the importance of tradition in the formation of a movement, he lays out the much greater depth of the twelve tribes and twelve pillars, stones, bulls, lambs, goats, staffs, and pieces of a robe in Israelite tradition than previously discussed. "Twelve" symbolizes the people Israel (not "nation," which is a modern concept) as a whole, but not necessarily the particular twelve tribes (e.g., Elijah's altar of twelve stones). Twelve representative leaders of Israel-in-restoration then appear prominently in Qumran texts and other late Second Temple texts. In the cultural context of this deep Israelite tradition, McKnight suggests, on the basis of accounts of Jesus and the Twelve, that Jesus chose the Twelve as representative of the people Israel, but not to represent each tribe. Jesus commissioned them to extend his own mission of healing/exorcism and proclaiming the kingdom and limited their mission to Israel. They thus symbolize that his mission was the restoration or renewal of Israel. Looking for links and broader patterns (unfortunately unusual for Jesus-interpreters), he suggests that the renewal was also a covenant renewal, which was also linked with John's baptism (as in Webb's essay). He even suggests that constitution of the Twelve representative leaders of Israel undergoing restoration was part of a political mission to replace the Jerusalem rulers.

Robert Webb's contribution to the volume is by far the most extensive (250 pages out of 850), the most distinctive (essays on Jesus' baptism by John, on Jesus' crucifixion by Pilate, and a fine essay on "doing" history), and the most important. In his three lengthy essays, Webb is unusual, not only among contributors to this volume, but among Jesus scholars in general, in several respects. More than the other contributors he attends to sources beyond the canonical Gospels. Further, the most important contribution to historical Jesus studies in the volume may be Webb's twenty-seven-page discussion of historiography and historical method in chapter 2, rarely discussed by historical Jesus scholars. Particularly suggestive is his summary on history/historiography as representation. But taking this seriously would, of course, require the authors of these essays, like other historical Jesus scholars, to recognize that the Gospel sources are also representations, only "evangelical" representations, without the critical historical awareness of current critical historiography. Of special importance for historical Jesus scholars is critical self-awareness (self-criticism). One would think that this would mean that Jesus scholars would recognize how the questions they bring to the "data" and the context in which they understand the "data" are derived from the New Testament branch of theology, not from critical (postmodern) historiography, hence are limiting and distorting, reducing and obscuring particular historical relations in synthetic essentialist constructs such as "Judaism" and "Christianity" or "eschatological" and "the Messiah." Further, Webb's courageous discussion of "historical explanation" and the "supernatural" raises the question of whether there should be a special historiography for Jesus with different explanation as distinctive among historical figures. "Natural" and "supernatural" are modern concepts, not features of ancient worldviews. Should critical historiography of Jesus or of any ancient figure couch its representation in distinctively modern concepts? Or should historians attempt to discern and understand and represent in terms of the appropriate ancient worldview of historical figures and their culture?

Unusual among Jesus scholars, Webb himself moves beyond the standard issues rooted in traditional Christian faith/doctrine and the theologically based agenda of New Testament studies. To deal with Jesus' crucifixion as a rebel leader by order of a Roman governor, Webb seriously investigates the Roman rule of Judea and Galilee, perhaps the major factor that determined life and events there. He discerns the fundamental division in Roman Palestine between the Herodian and high-priestly rulers, who were appointed by the Romans, and the ordinary people. He recognizes that there was (thus) political conflict between John the Baptist and Antipas in Galilee-Perea and between Jesus and the high priests and Pilate in Jerusalem. In contrast with most interpreters, Webb sees that Jesus was not merely an individual teacher and healer but was generating a popular movement. Also unusual for Jesus scholars, who discuss Jesus in terms of christological titles and/or scholarly constructs, Webb recognizes that historical figures act in particular roles that are given in their particular cultures. Appropriately, Webb attends to how John the Baptist and Jesus were acting in a role attested by evidence for first-century Judean and Galilean society (thus a "leadership" popular prophet or a popular king/messiah, but not "the eschatological prophet" or a Jewish "Cynic sage," which are both modern scholarly constructs).

Attending to the social roles in which our sources portray Jesus as acting, as only appropriate to an investigation into a historical figure, however, leads to some tension in the volume's interpretation of Jesus. As many would probably agree, both the accounts of the theophany (perhaps) at his baptism and the accounts of his association with John, indicate that Jesus assumed the role of a prophet (like Moses and/or Elijah). But to what extent do the Gospel sources suggest that Jesus himself claimed to be (acted as) "the king of the Jews," on which charge Pilate ordered him crucified? There is considerable tension in the Gospels and Jesus traditions themselves about whether Jesus was acting as a (popular leadership) prophet like Moses and Elijah and/or as a (popular) king/messiah.

In addressing the significance of their essays for understanding Jesus several of the contributors make elaborate claims, particularly regarding the transcendent authority of Jesus, clearly a major issue for evangelical scholars. Yet the tension within the Jesus tradition and other New Testament texts about how, when, and in what role Jesus had or gained what authority goes largely unaddressed in these essays. Authority is not only an issue for faith and theology. It is also a historical issue. Rulers cannot control populations for long by propaganda and the threat of violence alone. They must have some sort of legitimacy, that is, legitimate power. By the time of Jesus, the high-priestly aristocracy had lost much authority. In "Roman" Palestine the Romans and their Herodian clients had virtually none. Authority is/was relational. Jesus did not already have authority to heal, but in the historical circumstances he generated authority by healing (in the recognized role of a new Elijah) and thus gained authority/power to heal. In Q Jesus has authority as a (martyred) prophet. Mark presents Jesus acting mainly as a prophet (like Moses and Elijah) and is uneasy about how or whether he was a messiah. The speeches in the early chapters of Acts present Jesus has having become the Messiah at his exaltation only after his crucifixion. Paul proclaims Jesus Christ as transcendent Lord. It seems clear that there were some disagreements among Jesus' followers about how and when he exercised authority.

In sum, this volume features an important shift in focus from Jesus' teaching to events and activities in which Jesus was involved, the stuff of which history is made. What remains is to deal with events and activities as relational and in historical political as well as cultural context, as represented in some (but not most) of these essays and in the Gospel sources for the historical Jesus.

A Hitchhiker's Guide to Jesus: Reading the Gospels on the Ground, by Bruce N. Fisk. Grand Rapids: Baker, 2011. Pp. 320. Paper. $22.99. ISBN 9780801036064.

Timothy D. Howell, Montreat College, Charlotte, North Carolina

After teaching introductory classes on the Gospels for sixteen years, I can think of no better approach than what Bruce Fisk has given to students with his

Hitchhiker's Guide. He has considered both the student with a strong religious foundation and the student with a skeptical inquiry to travel down the same path without compromising either one's academic convictions. Fisk considers the life of Jesus with honest, intellectual integrity. He does not set aside religious tradition but, instead, advances historical appraisals of valid features within biblical studies. By applying a narrative style to New Testament concepts, postmodern students feel at ease to explore new ideas. Fisk makes scholarship a fun journey through the eyes of Norm. Norm is a recent college graduate in religious studies who travels to the Middle East seeking to bridge gaps created in his academic pursuit. Ultimately, the question of how faith exists despite the rigors of a historical approach to Jesus that frames the *Hitchhiker's Guide*.

The foundational truth that Jesus did exist in history demands the attention of the first chapter. Fisk introduces various critical scholars in Jesus studies (Bultmann, Bornkamm, Reimarus, Strauss, Wrede, Schweitzer, and Wright). By weaving quotes and summaries from their writings, Fisk introduces students to critical ideas and questions that must be addressed in a historical approach to the life of Jesus. He also employs ancient writers such as Pliny, Tacitus, and Josephus to convey a wider spectrum of first-century Mediterranean thought to the life of Jesus. Fisk relies on Josephus as the greatest evidence for Jesus' existence outside the New Testament.

Chapter 2 concentrates on the person of John the Baptist. It is unusual for a whole chapter to be devoted to the influence of John the Baptist within introductory studies. The rationale for doing so can be explained in how Fisk uses various means to study the historical record of John the Baptist and his influence on the Gospel writers. Fisk introduces the historical quests for Jesus by utilizing the criteria of authenticity as applied to the Gospels. It can be determined how the writers had an agenda in their compositions by comparing the Gospel presentations of John the Baptist. The descriptions of his décor allow Fisk to discuss the Qumran community and the Dead Sea Scrolls, emphasizing the diversity within first-century Judaism. Finally, the use of Old Testament allusion by the writers is exhibited in a chart formation. The strength of this section is the attention brought to the literary nature of the Gospels.

The use of intertextuality by the Gospel writers is the focus of chapter 3. Fisk discusses the virgin birth by first examining what higher critics have concluded was a comparable rendition similar to ancient pagan myths. He allows the critics to speak through his former professor, Dr. Randall Guilder, as the reader is privy to email correspondence between the two. I found this to be an attractive medium for making higher-critical ideas more reader-friendly in introductory studies. By reading the questions Norm has in response to Dr. Guilder (84), the reader has a good example of applied critical thinking within biblical studies. Norm displays openness to ideas without the dogmatism of either position controlling the discussion. Through Norm, Fisk compares the infancy narratives to the Old Testament narratives of Joseph and Moses. He introduces the concepts of *scripturized history* and *historicized prophecy* (98) as legitimate means employed in the Gospel compositions. This chapter demonstrates how the Gospel writers did not write merely to record facts about Jesus' birth. Instead, they wrote in an oral climate immersed in both Hellenistic and Old Testament narratives. Stories were told to convey theological meaning, and former paradigms could be employed to tell the story of Jesus' significance.

With chapter 4, discussions center on the miracles of Jesus. The purpose of this chapter is to ascertain whether historical criteria can be useful in evaluating Jesus' miracles (105). Fisk is quick to point out that historical inquiry is about possibilities, not certainties (106). This is a good principle for students to learn early in their studies. Throughout this section Norm describes the scenes for the reader. By describing the pool of Siloam, the shore around Capernaum, and the house of Peter, Norm exposes the reader to the impact of tradition. Fisk seeks to separate centuries of tradition with appropriate historical inquiry. The miracles involving exorcisms, walking on water, and the feeding of thousands are discussed from both a literary and historical context. Norm experiences an Arab wedding and compares it to the wedding at Cana, asking questions of the text in light of Mediterranean customs. One conclusion Fisk offers is the blending of "historical facts with embellishment" as a possibility in understanding the miracle stories (130). However, Fisk emphasizes that the symbolic nature of miracles was a foreshadowing of Jesus' significance that forms the basis for our understanding. Even so, Fisk warns that miracles were not parables in disguise (147). The literary medium was written to convey theological truth as witnessed in historical settings.

Chapter 5 focuses on the perceptions of Jesus' kingdom message and self-identity. Fisk allows Norm to experience Pan's Cave on rocky Mount Hermon. The messianic affirmation by Peter is discussed in light of the geographical features of Pan's Cave (deep chasm). Norm also meets a young man living on a kibbutz who expresses his hope of the rebuilt temple on the Temple Mount. A theological formula is deduced that is remarkably similar to Norm's experience and the Matthean composition: "a Messiah, a stone, a holy building, and certitude" (162). The next discussion is over the kingdom Jesus announced. Cleverly, Fisk utilizes discussions among scholars in Norm's dream to demonstrate various theories of Jesus' kingdom message. Comparable to *Alice in Wonderland*, there are three doors from which to choose (171–76). The theories of Meier, Crossan, Dodd, McKnight, Wright, Schweitzer, Allison, Ehrman, Dunn, and Meyer are found among the three doors. Norm struggles to comprehend a Jesus with limitations with a Jesus who could predict the future as a psychic. What Norm realizes is the difference in time orientation between our Western society (future orientation) contrasted to a peasant one (present orientation). The suggestion offered is that prophetic imagery compares to abstract art.

The focus of six major events leading to the time of Jesus' death is covered in chapter 6. First, the understanding Jesus had about his impending death is seen in light of the resurrection of Lazarus. Second, the lamentation of Jesus over Jerusalem points to its failure to recognize his divine role. Third, Jesus' riding into Jerusalem on a donkey is discussed more than I have seen in other introductory studies (193–201). However, I was impressed with Fisk using Norm's tour to make allusions to Israel's history and present situation in clarifying Jesus' entrance. Fisk illustrates how the populace would have understood the entrance of Jesus as confirmation of being the successor to David (199). Fourth, an event given more notice than usual is Jesus overturning the tables in the temple. Fisk understands this event analogously to the prophets' announcement of judgment due to Israel "presuming on grace" (211). Fifth, Judas's betrayal is discussed in light of its differences between the Gospel accounts. The benefit of this section is how the Matthean composition parallels Zechariah and Jeremiah through intertextuality and allusion (218). The sixth event Fisk discusses is the Last Supper. Fisk discusses the various meanings one could have of Jesus' death in light of the bread and wine offered to the disciples. As Norm is thinking about the differences between the Gospels concerning the Last Supper, an editorial reminder is provided for the student who may feel lost in the discussion. For Norm, his study provided him with more confidence, not over the reliability of the Gospels, but with an ability to think of them differently (221).

The death and resurrection of Jesus is the heart of chapter 7. Norm realizes that the Gospels do not give gory details, as heard in many sermons. Instead, the writers' emphasis is that Jesus died by crucifixion. Norm finishes his tour by going to the traditional burial site of Jesus. A popular theory that Jesus' body was moved by his family is discussed and dismissed by Norm. He leaves his discussion of the resurrection by noting that, at the very least, the tomb had to be empty. I would have liked more discussion over the theological ramifications of the resurrection and not just the historical evidence for or against it. There was no mention of his postresurrection appearances and conversations as narrated in the Gospels.

Fisk has an extensive note and bibliography section that completes the worth of this book. I enthusiastically endorse *Hitchhiker's Guide* as a valuable read for any student wanting a grasp of the Gospel compositions and the interpretive history behind them. Through the example of "one student's adventure," we can hope others will be challenged to do the same.

Jesus and the Powers: Conflict, Covenant, and the Hope of the Poor, by Richard A. Horsley. Minneapolis: Fortress, 2010. Pp. viii + 248. Paper. $29.00. ISBN 9780800697082.

Kevin B. McCruden, Gonzaga University, Spokane, Washington

In this most recent of his many historical studies that treat both the social and imperial background of the Gospels, Richard Horsley offers a compelling reconstruction of the public ministry of Jesus that focuses on Jesus' role as a prophetic figure who advocates for the renewal of Israel. Horsley's study comprises eight chapters framed by an introduction and brief conclusion. The first three chapters mainly serve to sketch the political and economic contours of the advanced agrarian society in which Jesus conducted his ministry, while the final five chapters focus on the nature of Jesus' ministry as one informed by popular Israelite traditions of liberation and social justice.

In the introduction Horsley summarizes specific Western assumptions that, in his judgment, continue to hamper historical Jesus research. His first observation is broadly literary in scope. Much as proponents of the narrative-critical approach shift attention away from isolated episodes in the Gospels in order to discern larger narrative patterns, Horsley likewise stresses the necessity of reading the Gospels as sustained narratives. Unlike narrative critics, however, who tend to focus on the synchronic dimension of the Gospels, Horsley's interest is decidedly diachronic or historical. According to him, it is precisely the narrative frame of the Gospels that imparts historical coherence to the individual sayings and episodes contained in the Gospels. While it would be a mistake to view these narratives as historically reliable in every detail, Horsley contends that they do provide historical verisimilitude, particularly in terms of reflecting Jesus' overall program of covenant renewal and bold confrontation with the powerful elites of his day. Horsley goes on to affirm that modern historical reconstruction goes amiss when it neglects to attend to the political and economic conflict endemic to Jesus' ministry and focuses instead on Jesus as a religious figure addressing individual persons. The latter Western proclivity becomes especially problematic when interpreters construe religion as a matter of individual faith or belief divorced from the concrete economic and political realities faced collectively by peasants in the advanced agrarian setting of Jesus' day.

Foundational for Horsley's assessment of Jesus' public ministry is the analysis he devotes to the numerous powers experienced by persons in antiquity. In chapter 1 he explores the power of empire, especially the way in which the elite representatives of the Babylonian, Egyptian, and Roman Empires exploited the labor and produce both of their own population as well as of subject populations. The bulk of this chapter, however, focuses on the socially disintegrating effects of Roman military expansion on both the peasant soldiers of Italy as well as of the inhabitants of Palestine after the invasion by Pompey. Horsley demonstrates how the increasing Roman expansion into the Mediterranean effectively displaced much of the Italian peasantry, who through debt foreclosure found themselves alienated from their ancestral and. In terms of Roman military expansion, Horsley notes that the ideology of empire rationalized violent conquest on the pretext of bestowing civilization, peace, and stability to subject peoples.

In chapter 2 Horsley provides an insightful account of the main contours of the ancient Israelite tradition of liberation as seen in the books of Torah. He views much of the narrative plot of Torah as depicting the struggle of the ancient Israelites to resist the political, economic, and natural powers of ancient Middle Eastern empires. Beginning with the Book of Genesis, Horsley observes how Yahweh appears as a power substantially different from the natural, political, and economic powers of Middle Eastern empires. Specifically, Yahweh is a force of political, economic, and social liberation who, in initiating a covenant with the Hebrews, summons the recently redeemed slaves to embody an alternative society that will live by a code of mutuality and nonpredatory economic relationships. Although the emergence of the monarchy effectively altered this vision, both the memory of liberation and the vision of a contrast society abided.

An important feature of Horsley's study is the attention he gives to the various forms of Jewish resistance that emerged in response to the experience of overwhelming exploitive power. In addition to popular messianic and prophetic movements, a distinctively intellectual mode of resistance appears in the scribal circles responsible for such texts as the book of Daniel and 1 Enoch. Horsley makes the point in chapter 3 that highly literate intellectuals sometimes struggled with the tension of serving as retainers for powerful elite leaders who frequently ignored the scriptural traditions of liberation and social justice that the scribes were expected to preserve and cultivate. In response to this situation of mixed loyalties, these scribal circles employed the coded language of apocalyptic to criticize the very leadership who frequently functioned as their patrons.

The remainder of Horsley's study beginning with chapter 4 focuses on the reconstruction of Jesus' public ministry. Horsley contends that the indispensable starting point for understanding Jesus' ministry is the recognition of the disintegration of the traditional life of Galilean peasants due in large measure to the exploitive layers of tribute they were forced to endure. Horsley contends that, in response to such a social crisis, Jesus engaged the peasantry through acts of healings and teachings that served to energize the peasantry. Jesus saw his mission as one of cultivating community renewal in accordance with ancient Israelite traditions of liberation and social justice. While in some ways Jesus resembled the charismatic prophetic movements of his day, Jesus was distinctive, according to Horsley, in that he focused his missions on reform from within the village setting. Rather than retreating into the wilderness to await a dramatic sign of liberation, Jesus chose instead to empower the people to live alternative lives offstage that challenged the exploitive powers arrayed against them.

Chapter 5 treats the healing activity of Jesus, in particular his many acts of exorcism, as concrete expression of Jesus' program of community renewal. Here Horsley makes the important observation that the experience of demon possession is likely misunderstood whenever Western bio-medical and psychological categories are brought to bear on a phenomenon so strikingly alien to our modern Western assumptions about what counts as reality. Employing the by now familiar sociological distinction between disease and illness, in addition to the more recent insights of medical anthropology, Horsley probes in this chapter the social, emotional, and political dimensions of the phenomenon of possession. With the account of the healing of the Gerasene demon-possessed man as his conversation guide (Mark 5:1–20), Horsley argues that spirit possession functions as a defensive and concealed response to exploitive forms of overwhelming power.

Whereas the focus of chapter 5 was on Jesus' exorcisms, chapter 6 dwells on the teaching ministry of Jesus. The essential thesis that frames this chapter is the claim that Jesus addressed his teachings concerning covenant renewal to entire village communities, not to individuals. Hence the mission discourses contained in both Mark and Q depict the disciples as engaged in a program of community outreach and not conversion, while the Sermon on the Mount/Plain represents a kind of covenant-renewal charter. Addressed to peasants, Jesus' teachings functioned to provide guidelines for an internal community ethic where mutuality and solidarity were the prime values. Influenced especially by the debt codes contained in Torah as well as prophetic witnesses such as Jeremiah, Jesus' program of covenant renewal especially targeted the predatory wealthy.

Chapters 7 and 8 deal largely with the final stages of Jesus' prophetic ministry. While there is little evidence to suggest that Jesus advocated violent revolt, he nonetheless displayed resistance to exploitive power in two principal ways. First, by empowering peasants to live out an alternative lifestyle of solidarity and mutuality in their own community enclaves, Jesus challenged the exploitive ethic of both the Roman Empire and its aristocratic collaborators. Second, and more provocatively, Jesus engaged in coded behavior that directly challenged both Roman and high-priestly rule. Horsley sees Jesus as making a highly intentional trip to Jerusalem in order to confront the ruling aristocracy. Once in Jerusalem, Jesus directly confronts exploitive power through actions that signaled God's condemnation of the temple and conveyed God's judgment over the illegitimacy of the Roman tribute. Chapter 8 is perhaps the most provocative section of the study. In this chapter Horsley argues that the event of Jesus' crucifixion, not the experience of his resurrection, provided the main impetus for the emergence and expansion of the primitive Christian movement. According to Horsley, a method of execution designed to humiliate subject peoples became instead, paradoxically, a symbol of solidarity with one who challenged exploitive power, even to the point of death.

To the degree that Horsley views covenant renewal as the focal point of Jesus' message of the dawning kingdom of God, this study complements well other recent historical reconstructions that take seriously the Jewish backdrop of Jesus' public ministry. Horsley's insistence, moreover, that the Gospel narratives reveal irreducible political and economic conflicts at the heart of Jesus' ministry is especially well taken. His study provides an important reminder that much can seriously be lost in historical reconstruction when the religious dimension of Jesus' ministry is viewed as somehow separate from the predatory political and economic dynamics of his day. Horsley's reflections become more speculative, however, when he claims that it was primarily the event of the crucifixion of Jesus that provided the real breakthrough event for the communities that identified with him. Horsley himself attests to the thousands of crucifixion victims executed for their defiance to Rome. Why did a movement not form around these figures? Put another way, what was especially empowering or distinctive about Jesus' program of covenant renewal such that communities of persons would identity with this particular crucifixion victim? Moreover, even if Horsley is correct that the teachings contained in such passages as Mark 8:34–10:52 depend largely upon a memory of Jesus' own agenda of covenant renewal, it is also likely that from the earliest stages communities treasured the words of Jesus because they heard in them the voice of someone whom they felt was alive in a new and transformed way.

SYNOPTIC GOSPELS

Honor among Christians: The Cultural Key to the Messianic Secret, by David F. Watson. Minneapolis: Fortress, 2010. Pp. x + 229. Paper. $29.00. ISBN 9780800697099.

Jonathan A. Draper, University of KwaZulu-Natal, Pietermaritzburg, South Africa

Wilhelm Wrede's famous discovery of the "messianic secret" in Mark's Gospel has in many respects set the agenda for all subsequent scholarly work on the Gospel. As each new critical methodology has been applied to the Gospel, it has had to attempt to answer the riddle of the passages where Jesus prohibits demons and those he heals from telling anyone about what has happened and yet achieving the opposite effect. The application of models from cultural anthropology to the New Testament texts is no exception, and the challenge has already been probed by members of the Context Group, such as Bruce Malina and John J. Pilch, who have mainly been concerned to explain Jesus' secrecy in Mark. This book by David Watson provides a plausible attempt to read the whole Gospel consistently from the perspective of the model of honor-shame and patron-broker-client relationships.

After setting out in brief the *status questionis*, Watson proceeds to address the question of secrecy. His patient analysis of the texts shows that secrecy is, in fact, peripheral to the main concerns of the Gospel. Jesus does not consistently conceal his miraculous healings; indeed, he heals many people in public without any word of caution. Rather, Jesus in Mark rejects the patron-broker-client values and practices of the ancient world, by which honor is ascribed and acquired. His prohibition of spreading praise in response to a benefaction (healing or exorcism) is an attempt to turn the traditional understanding of what is honorable and what is shameful on its head. Illustrating his thesis with contemporary texts from the Greco-Roman world, Watson argues that members of Jesus' community reflected by Mark's Gospel are expected to reject the "grab for honor" (and power) and value instead self-denial, the no-honor role of a child, to identify the most extreme form of shaming in the ancient world with what is most honorable. Joining the community resulted in being shamed by the world, something now seen as providing honor within the new community that will finally be recognized at the return of Jesus.

Watson turns next to the so-called "contradictions" to or "gaps" in the secrecy theme (e.g., the exorcism of the Gerasene demoniac), where Jesus heals openly and makes unambiguous statements and acknowledgements of who he is. Watson points out that such openness is by no means anomalous and denies that the messianic secret is the rule that is contradicted. Instead, such open public behavior is "conventional" in the Gospel. The secrecy injunctions are connected directly to the theme of Jesus' rejection and subversion of traditional understandings of honor-shame, while the public demonstrations are related to other themes in the Gospel. In an oral-aural context of performance of Mark, which would be the overwhelming norm for the reception of the text in the ancient world, no contradiction would have been noticed or experienced between the "secrecy" theme and the "conventional" passages. Taking up the terminology of Walter J. Ong, Watson finds oral characteristics of *additive*, *aggregative*, and *redundant* expression designed to imprint the narrative on the minds of the hearers. Likewise, the "narrative gaps" (Wolfgang Iser) play the role of drawing the hearer into the world of the narratives as they filled in the missing pieces in a way that "made sense" in their cultural milieu. The role of these features in the narrative of Mark's Gospel is compared with the (roughly) contemporary narrative of the *Life of Aesop*, where the contradictions do not hinder the major themes of honor-shame in the narrative but support it. In fact, the Aesop narrative is designed to puncture and deconstruct normal understandings of honor and shame in a satirical fashion in a way not dissimilar to Mark's narrative. Both narratives "make sense" in their own cultural context and would not have been perceived as showing internal contradictions in the same way they might do in our modern context.

Watson concludes that the problem of the "Messianic Secret" in Mark is a modern Western construct that disappears once read against the background of the deconstruction of conventional notions of honor and shame and the construction of an alternative social universe that reverses them. Watson ends with a brief consideration of the kind of ostracized community that might embody these countercultural values in a new fictive kinship group.

This is a slender, readable volume that paints with broad brushstrokes but puts ample material in the footnotes for interested readers to follow up. It presents a helpful picture of a text that "means" against a quite different cultural matrix to that of modern readers (in the West). It will certainly provide newcomers to the debate with an excellent introduction to the study of Mark's Gospel from a cultural-anthropological standpoint and has many original insights beyond that. My reservation with the methodology would first be its assumption of a uniform "ancient Mediterranean" culture, despite the common perspective of a thoroughly hellenized Palestine in the first century C.E. that has prevailed since Martin Hengel. Living, as I do, in South Africa, which has been colonized and exposed to global Western cultural influence for over four hundred years, I can observe all around me the persistence of cultural particularity and indigenous knowledge systems despite the massive impact of modern media and educational systems that were not available in the ancient world. Mark, like the Christian community, stands at the interface of cultural difference and cultural conflict. The significance of this needs to be argued in more depth. Second, while any acknowledgement of the impact of orality/aurality in New Testament studies is welcome, scholars working in the field of orality studies have for many years problematized the model of Walter Ong that is used here, even while acknowledging a debt to his work. These caveats aside, I would recommend this book for its freshness and for demonstrating the fruitfulness of a new methodology for approaching an old question such as the venerable messianic secret.

Feeding the Five Thousand: Studies in the Judaic Background of Mark 6:30–44 par. and John 6:1–15, by Roger David Aus. Studies in Judaism. Lanham, Md.: University Press of America, 2010. Pp. xvii+187. Paper. $31.50. ISBN 9780761851523.

James Crossley, University of Sheffield, Sheffield, United Kingdom

Roger Aus has long been publishing detailed studies on haggadic influences on New Testament passages, particularly passages from the Gospels. This latest edition, on the feeding of the five thousand, again shows Aus's profound knowledge of a wide range of Jewish sources, from the Hebrew Bible/Old Testament to rabbinic literature, and their usefulness for historical-critical examination of Gospel texts. In *Feeding the Five Thousand*, Aus strengthens the view that the Elisha story and its retellings are the most significant Judaic tradition in the illumination of Mark 6:30–44 and parallels and John 6:1–15.

Chapter 1 covers the importance of feeding in the context of famines. Using various sources, notably 2 Kgs 4:38–44 and those concerning the 'omer offering (Lev 23:9–14), Aus illustrates how a Palestinian audience would have been only too aware of the physical dangers of famine. He also looks at use of the relevant language, including language of bread, in relation to "spiritual" matters, especially Torah teaching (cf. Mark 6:34). Part of the 'omer offering concerns the "common" or "inferior" barley bread (cf. 2 Kgs 4:42) and the second day of Passover (involving the 'omer offering of barley sheaves and flour), which is picked up in the Johannine version (John 6:9).

Chapters 2 and 3 look at the parallels between Elisha and Jesus, including their respective functions as successors to Elijah and John the Baptist, with particular focus on their roles as miracle workers, itinerant prophets, holy and single men, righteous ones, and teachers with disciples. These similarities are again developed in chapter 6, which compares Jesus praying (Mark 6:41) with Elisha praying, including some discussion on standard praying gestures in early Judaism, a counter to those scholars who have claimed that Jesus' prayer actions were somehow unique.

As is common in the work of Aus, several chapters analyze precise words and phrases, typically with the Elisha background in mind. Chapter 4 briefly covers the term "denarii" (Mark 6:37) and how it may have involved a reading of a Targumic rendering of the Elisha story. Chapter 5 looks at further Semitic word association concerning John 6, this time involving 1 Sam 9:1–10:27 (including, as ever, subsequent readings of the passage), such as: Baal-Shalishah and Shalisha (cf. 2 Kgs 4:42); the "boy," a "sign"; withdrawal and being made king; reclining at a banquet; blessing and/or thanks for food; and first fruits, Passover, barley loaves, much grass, and gathering fragments. Chapter 7 continues with reference to the background of Mark 6:39 and phrases involving doubling, garden beds and rows, hundreds and fifties, and reclining in groups, including a Passover timing. Chapter 8 covers eating satisfaction and the assumption of saying grace after meals (Mark 6:42), while chapter 9 looks at the baskets and leftover pieces. Chapter 10 assesses the gender-specific significance of "five thousand *men*" in Mark 6:44 and the second Elisha feeding narrative (cf. 2 Kgs 4:38, 43), with comments on the Matthean addition of women and children, which presumably makes the miracle more dramatic in number (ca. twenty thousand!).

A number of chapters are also concerned with contextualizing the Markan and Johannine passages. Chapter 11 looks at Bethsaida as a possible location and its (re)building with the name Julias, after the renaming of Livia Drusilla as Iulia. Iulia was also honored as divine in the eastern Empire, had her own cult, and was venerated as a mother goddess. In feeding five thousand, Jesus is constructed as a superior alternative with local resonances. The following chapters concentrate on more "literary" contextualization. Chapter 12 looks at Markan and Johannine redaction, while chapter 13 looks at the function of the passages in Markan (especially Mark 6 as a whole) and Johannine contexts. Chapter 14 further emphasizes the Semitic background but also briefly locates the miraculous feeding motif in the history of religions. Major narrative motifs are discussed in chapter 15, such as the role of Jesus as greater than (/more than) other Israelite heroes (including, or especially, Elisha) and Roman/pagan heroes. Minor motifs are also noted, such as Jesus as Lord of hunger, redemption through the Messiah at Passover, foretaste of the messianic banquet, and Jesus as the eschatological Davidic shepherd-Messiah. Genre issues are raised in chapter 16, and, in line with what is identified as the main thrust of the narrative, Aus classifies the passage as a "miracle of surpassing." Historicity is discussed in chapter 17, and, unsurprisingly, Aus is able to show with ease that the story does not have a historical core, not least because this would be to misunderstand the nature of haggadah and an original writer and audience who would not necessarily have been thinking in terms of "historical" versus "nonhistorical." Chapter 18 ends the book by looking at the two Markan feeding narratives and the role of the feeding of the five thousand as part of a miracle collection.

As often with Aus, specific details may be questioned, but the argument of collective weight is persuasive, particularly in stories (such as this one) with such clear haggadic features. Many of the general benefits of this book typically apply to other works by Aus. For instance, he shows emphatically that familiarity with rabbinic sources (and their original languages) is crucial, and, while careful reconstructions are obviously required, such sources should not be lazily dismissed as "late" without serious engagement first. The most specific benefit of *Feeding the Five Thousand* is that the argument in favor of the Elisha context now has its most forceful advocate. Any historical-critical study of this story, in whichever Gospel, will now have to grapple with Aus's arguments and the sources he presents.

There are areas that might be developed further. On the contextualization of Mark 6:30–44 in Mark 6 and in Mark's Gospel, for instance, it may be helpful to expand the immediate literary context right up to and including Mark 8:21, which seems to be the end of a distinct section in Mark's Gospel. Not only do we have a second feeding miracle but also plenty of further links with bread and eating (as Aus notes with reference to Mark 6). In addition to the unsurprising mention of bread in the two feeding miracles (6:38, 41, 43, 44; 8:4–6, 8), there are also notable occurrences in-between: Mark 7:2 has the disciples eating bread when criticized for eating with unclean hands; Mark 7:27 talks of the bread of the children; and in 7:28 the Syro-Phoenician woman speaks of the crumbs under the table. Furthermore, after the second feeding miracle the disciples forget to bring bread and have only one loaf of bread in the boat (Mark 8:14). Verses that follow make mention of the yeast of Pharisees and of Herod and wondering and questioning about the significance of bread (Mark 8:16–21).

What might this obsession with bread mean? One possible option could be the link between Torah teaching and bread mentioned by Aus (5–6) or a related Torah-Wisdom-bread connection, all generally established links in rabbinic times (e.g., Philo, *Change of Names* 259–260; Gen. Rab. 43:6; 54:1; 70:5). In the context of Mark 6–8, Mark 7:1–23 gives us plenty of Torah teaching, such as the contrasting of the commandments of God with "tradition," *qorban*, and the details of hand-washing and purity. It may well be that the connections between bread and Torah teaching picked up by Aus are important here, particularly in light of recent scholarly moves that have pushed for a more law-observant Mark than has traditionally been suggested and on the basis of Mark 7:1–23 (including a rereading of Mark 7:19).

Further links between the two feeding miracles, and more generally across Mark 6–8, could have also been developed with reference to an inclusion (to some extent) of Gentiles, which starts to become an issue after, not insignificantly, the vice list of Mark 7:21–23. There is the trip to the notorious region of Tyre (Mark 7:24), deemed a bitter enemy of Jews (*Apion* 1.70; cf. *War* 2.478; 4.105; Acts 21:3–4; and with Sidon, cf., e.g., Isa 23; Jer 25:17–22; 47:4; Ezek 26–28; Joel 3:4–8; Amos 1:9–10; Zech 9:2–4). In "Gentile" territory we meet the Syro-Phoenician woman (Mark 7:24–30) whose ethnicity leads to the label of (Gentile) "dog" and the affirmation that they are still very much secondary to the (Jewish) children (Mark 7:27–28). The theological geography culminates in more "Jewish" territory after the second feeding miracle and followed by the reappearance of Pharisees in Mark's narrative (8:10–11). Presumably, then, there is good reason to follow the view that the lesser second feeding miracle is also aimed at a narrative inclusion of Gentiles in the eschatological banquet, even if they are inferior, mere dogs feeding on the crumbs of the children and being represented by "just" four thousand.

Clearly, these points do not contradict Aus's main arguments; on the contrary, they are suggestive of some of the ways in which his detailed work can be developed. Such narrative connections certainly give us further insight into what Mark was doing with these traditions. Indeed, these suggestions may well boost Aus's argument for the author of Mark being a Jewish Christian (167–68). Similarly, in light of the above, we might add that we should perhaps be emphasizing, and further investigating, even more the haggadic influence at the level of Gospel redaction.

Aus has again produced excellent research in an area that most New Testament scholars cannot. Even if, or perhaps especially if, those New Testament scholars do not have Aus's familiarity with haggadic texts, his work provides an extremely helpful resource that ought to be used in addition to the commentaries.

Methods for Matthew, edited by Mark Allan Powell. Methods in Biblical Interpretation. Cambridge: Cambridge University Press, 2009. Pp. xvi + 261. Hardcover. $85.00. ISBN 9780521888080.

Daniel A. Smith, Huron University College, London, Ontario, Canada

This volume is one of the first in the Cambridge University Press series "Methods in Biblical Interpretation," whose purpose is to "introduce students and general readers to both older and emerging methodologies for understanding the Hebrew Scriptures and the New Testament" (iii). Essays are contributed by well-known scholars with expertise in specific methodologies pertinent to the biblical writing under investigation in the volume. At present, volumes have appeared that cover the book of Exodus (ed. Thomas B. Dozeman, 2010), the Gospel of Luke (ed. Joel B. Green, 2010), and the Gospel of Matthew. The present volume contains six essays: Donald A. Hagner and Stephen E. Young, "The Historical-Critical Method and the Gospel of Matthew" (11–43); Mark Allen Powell, "Literary Approaches and the Gospel of Matthew" (44–82); Elaine M. Wainwright, "Feminist Criticism and the Gospel of Matthew" (83–117); Craig A. Evans, "Historical Jesus Studies and the Gospel of Matthew" (118–53); Bruce J. Malina, "Social-Scientific Approaches and the Gospel of Matthew" (154–93); Fernando F. Segovia, "Postcolonial Criticism and the Gospel of Matthew" (194–237). Each chapter introduces the method under discussion, where possible with a special focus on its general application to Matthew, then illustrates how the method works in an analysis of Matt 27:57–28:15 (the first three chapters) or 8:5–13 (the last three). Powell also contributes an introduction (1–10) in which he gives a very basic introduction to the six methods and how they compare to one another. In general, the essays presume little or no knowledge of the methodology under discussion, typically use little jargon (or define it carefully, with some exceptions), and provide clear and accessible insight into both the theoretical foundations of the method and its application to Matthew. As such, this volume would be an excellent addition to the reading list for a course on the Gospel of Matthew or an introductory course on the Gospels. The book also includes a glossary (239–43), an annotated bibliography (245–49) that covers important works on the methodologies used in the book (but not commentary literature or monographs on Matthew!), and subject and scripture indices (251–61).

Hagner and Young, in their essay on the historical-critical method, attempt first to situate this method in the context of current scholarship. The discussion ranges from contemporary reactions to the historical-critical method and brief descriptions of how "text" and "interpreter" tend to be understood within the historical-critical method (11–18), to descriptions of specific approaches typically understood as operating within the historical-critical method, specifically, source criticism, genre and form criticism, redaction criticism, and historical/cultural background studies (19–31). The section on source criticism acknowledges that the "most widely held solution to the Synoptic Problem" is the Two-Source Hypothesis, mentioning only the Two-Gospel (or Griesbach) Hypothesis as a competing theory, but gives no indication of the data that these theories attempt to explain. Instead, the student is advised to "[wrestle] personally with the evidence in the gospels themselves" (21). A beginning student might wonder how these theories arose and how they compare as explanations of the data. In the section on genre criticism, Hagner and Young note the general trend to view the Gospels as ancient Greco-Roman biographies but interpret the tendency of biographies to focus on a single individual as a reason for adopting a primarily christological hermeneutic in reading the Gospels (23). This statement could have been nuanced considerably. While of course the Gospel of Matthew is "about" Jesus, it also tells us about Matthew and his community, and this should not be understood as a "distraction" (their word) from the primary interpretive goal of understanding "what [Matthew says] about Jesus," for sometimes that is the most it can tell us. The section on historical and cultural background rightly emphasizes that the historical-critical method can often profit from insights gained through the application of other methods sometimes considered as separate approaches, for example, social-scientific approaches (30). The chapter concludes with a brief historical-critical treatment of Matt 25:57–28:15 (31–43) that tends to focus on issues of language (e.g., *taphos* for tomb instead of *mnēmeion*, 27:61) and historicity (e.g., the Matthean material about the guard at the tomb, 27:62–66; 28:11–15).

Powell's chapter on contemporary literary approaches is concise and useful, covering basic topics of analysis such as, in relation to the text, plot, events, character, and setting, and, in relation to the reader, social location, reading strategy, empathy choice, and conception of meaning (45–54). Different approaches such as reader-response criticism, *Wirkungsgeschichte*, ideological criticism, postmodern criticism, and narrative criticism are also briefly explained (55–60). Powell's overview of literary criticism as applied to Matthew covers the implied reader (what the text expects of that reader in terms of knowledge, beliefs, and values), major characters (Jesus and the religious leaders), and basic plot lines (65–70). Powell's observation here that the expected reactions of the implied reader applies to the "story world" of the text is important because it allows readers to disengage from drawing historical conclusions from the world the text of Matthew creates (68). As in the previous chapter, there is a short application of literary approaches to Matt 25:57–28:15. Powell describes the function of Joseph of Arimathea as a foil to the disciples who have deserted Jesus (71–72), the deep irony of the religious leaders' labeling of Jesus as a "deceiver" (72–73), the challenge that the commissioning of the women at the tomb levels against received values about gender (73–77), and the ambivalence of the conclusion of the plot line involving the opposition of the religious leaders (77–80).

Wainwright's section on feminist criticism begins with a twenty-five-year retrospective of feminist approaches to Matthew (85–100), discussing the contributions of authors such as Janice Capel Anderson and Elisabeth Schüssler Fiorenza (2003) and her own work on Matthew (1991), noting how more recent approaches merge feminist analysis with, for example, postcolonialism, with the result being a more "multidimensional" hermeneutic (99). In her application of feminist criticism to Matt 25:57–28:15, Wainwright makes use of Vernon Robbins's sociorhetorical approach, examining the passage's "inner texture, intertexture, social and cultural texture, and ideological texture," each of which is briefly defined (100). She notes that reading with a gendered lens allows one to see Matthean interconnections beyond the limits of the passage assigned for study, connections that, for example, allow for a critical reading of androcentric approaches to isolated passages such as Matt 28:16–20 (101–3). The analysis then turns (103–11) to human reactions to the death of Jesus (those of the centurion and others, the women disciples at the cross, Joseph of Arimathea, and the women who attend the tomb) and finds that each reaction contributes to a reversal of the shame of Jesus' death and burial (111). Finally, Wainwright discusses the appearance of the risen Jesus to the women (Matt 28:9–10) and suggests that the narrative may have served a legitimating function in relation to the authority of such figures as Mary Magdalene (116).

In his chapter on historical Jesus studies, Evans discusses basic issues about the goals and methods of this approach in general (118–42), including questions of appropriate sources, historical context, and methods and criteria. Concerning sources, Evans discusses a few noncanonical texts (Thomas, Egerton Papyrus 2, the Gospel of Peter, and "Secret Mark") and concludes that these "are not as old and are not as well connected to the first generation of Jesus's movement as are the New Testament Gospels" (130). His discussion of historical context focuses mainly on refuting the Cynic hypothesis (something of a minority position), but this section remains useful for readers new to historical Jesus research because of the information Evans presents concerning Jewish life and practices in the Galilee (136–38). The discussion of methodology covers the standard criteria of authenticity (138–42). Evans then applies a historical Jesus approach to Matt 8:5–13, first of all comparing the Matthean version with Luke 7:1–10 and John 4:46–54, finding that "[t]he appearance of this story in three forms and in what are probably two distinct literary traditions (Synoptic and Johannine) … tells against the late wholesale fabrication of the story" (151). Evans also finds that the story coheres well with what may be known of the historical and religious-cultural context of Jesus (152). (I note a small "autocorrect" typo: on. p. 152 it should read, "[t]he Q source … may even date as early as the 40s or 50s," not "the 1940s or 1950s"!) He concludes that the event is authentic but was "preserved in three creative, interpretive presentations, suggesting new meaning and significance for the emerging Church" (153).

Malina's chapter on social-scientific approaches and Matthew begins with some basic definitions and a short history of social-scientific approaches to New Testament interpretation (154–64). In his description of the "presuppositions of social-scientific approaches" (164–70), Malina notes that language, and its use and interpretation, is culturally embedded to the extent that contemporary readers of Matthew, for instance, must attempt to become "considerate readers," that is, "to bring to [their] reading a set of scenarios proper to the time, place, and culture of the biblical writer" (167). Or, put differently, the Gospel of Matthew originated in a "high-context society," one in which little is spelled out explicitly (168). Malina also offers a very useful set of historical observations that aid in reading Matthew; these include observations about the social institutions, understandings of economy and history, and so forth (170–75). In a substantial discussion preceding his social-scientific analysis of Matt 8:11–14 (185–92), Malina analyzes Jesus as a first-century holy man (175–80) in light of anthropological insights into the cross-cultural phenomenon of "holy person," discusses the centurion and the military (180–82), and offers observations about the first-century Mediterranean healing system (182–85).

Segovia's essay has two parts: a survey of postcolonial biblical criticism as to its history, theoretical foundations, and methodology (195–216); and its application to Matthew, first in general terms, then in relation to Matt 8:5-13 (216–37). The discussion of the history of postcolonial approaches to biblical studies is insightful and covers the main developments in what Segovia calls the "period of formation and definition" (1996–1999), as well as important contributions since. Segovia acknowledges the variegated and tensive nature of postcolonial biblical interpretation but says that "a monolithic understanding of both the problematic and the approach" should be resisted (212). In the section on postcolonial approaches to Matthew (216–28), Segovia discusses contributions by Musa Dube (Matthew as "imperializing") and Warren Carter (Matthew as "counterimperial" and as "conflicted"). As to Matt 8:5–13, Segovia notes that "the exchange between Jesus and the centurion provides a key insight into imperial-colonial relations from a Matthean perspective" (228). This insight, which involves status pronouncements from both the centurion (he is not worthy to receive Jesus in his house, vv. 8–9) and Jesus (he says the centurion's faith surpasses what he has found in Israel, vv. 10–12), is evaluated in light of Matthew as imperializing, counterimperial, and conflicted (234–36).

This book is very well conceived, and the individual essays provide excellent and highly readable introductions, by noted experts, to both traditional and emerging methodologies that are relevant to the study of Matthew. The end result is something that will very easily be adapted to a university or seminary course on the Gospel of Matthew but that could also serve as a useful introduction to these methods in an introductory course on the Gospels (with Matthew as a sample text). Highly recommended.

Mark and the Elijah-Elisha Narrative: Considering the Practice of Greco-Roman Imitation in the Search for Markan Source Material, by Adam Winn. Eugene, Ore.: Pickwick, 2010. Pp. 148. Paper. $18.00. ISBN 9781608992010.

Dean Deppe, Calvin Theological Seminary, Grand Rapids, Michigan

According to Winn, scholars have placed too much emphasis on the putative oral sources of the Gospel of Mark, thus lamentably failing to employ literary source materials in their investigations of the Gospel. He further argues that the standard methodologies have failed interpreters of the Gospel in several ways: (1) source criticism made the search for Mark's literary sources irrelevant by establishing Markan priority; (2) form criticism removed the need for the search altogether by promoting oral traditions as Gospel source material over literary ones; and (3) redaction criticism's standards for demonstrating literary dependence (e.g., agreement in details and order; strong verbal agreement) proved so strict that a search for Mark's literary sources became next to impossible (7). In light of this failure of the standard methodologies, Winn emphasizes the role of memesis, or imitation, in developing criteria for determining literary dependence.

In chapter 1 Winn reviews the classic case of imitation, Virgil's rewriting of Homer's *Iliad* and *Odyssey* in his *Aeneid*. He develops six episodes that exhibit imitation and demonstrates how Virgil creatively imitates a former literary work. Virgil reverses the order in the narrative, conflates two episodes into one, diffuses a single episode into multiple stories, intensifies the action, changes the particular artistic mode from song to visual art, creates role reversals, and enhances the central character to demonstrate Aeneas's superiority to Odysseus. From this study Winn develops various criteria for determining literary dependence: (1) plausibility demonstrated by the date of composition and availability; (2) similarity in structure and order of events; (3) shared narrative details and actions; (4) verbal agreement; and (5) the weight of these combined criteria.

In chapter 2 Winn investigates Dennis MacDonald's thesis that the first thirteen chapters of the Gospel of Mark imitate Homer's *Odyssey* and the last three chapters re-present the *Iliad*. Winn applauds MacDonald for bringing the practice of imitation into the light and for providing interpreters with a storehouse of Homeric themes, characters, and episodes that contain intriguing parallels to the Gospel of Mark. However, Winn disputes MacDonald's contention that Homer's works are the primary literary model for Mark's Gospel, since not a single Homeric quotation or a single Homeric character can be diagnosed in Mark. Winn unearths the weaknesses of MacDonald's comparisons between Jesus' stilling of the storm (Mark 4:35–41) and Odysseus's crew releasing the winds (*Od.* 10.1–69) as well as Jesus' entry into the city of Jerusalem and the entry of Odysseus into the city of the Phaeacians. Jewish parallels in the book of Jonah and the Maccabean rulers' entries into Jerusalem contain more parallel material.

In chapter 3 Winn analyzes Wolfgang Roth's *Hebrew Gospel: Cracking the Code of Mark* to demonstrate the use by Mark of the Elijah–Elisha narratives. Although Winn places more significance than I would upon many of Roth's parallels outside the miracle stories, he questions Roth's identification of John and Jesus with Elijah and Elisha. Mark does not restrict Elijah imagery to John the Baptizer alone. Roth's overabundance of subtle parallels draws attention away from the significant parallels that are clearly found in the narratives. Winn also challenges Roth's presupposition that the Elijah–Elisha narrative provides an interpretative key for Mark. However, Winn's failure to propose an alternative interpretative explanation removes some of the sting of his criticism.

Chapter 4 marks the beginning of Winn's own conclusions. First he develops the general similarities of genre, narrative length, episodic style, and geographical structure in chapter 4. Winn's most profound insight is that no other Old Testament narrative contains such a quantity and frequency of miraculous events and fulfilled prophecies as the Elijah–Elisha narrative.

Chapter 5 begins a survey of Mark that investigates the connections with the Elijah and Elisha traditions. Mark begins his Gospel with a quote alluding to Elijah in Malachi and presents John the Baptizer as an imitation of Elijah. Winn argues that Mark 1:12–20 reproduces the flow of material in 1 Kgs 19:4–21 with parallel wilderness accounts, parallel proclamations about the kingdom of God, and parallel call narratives.

Chapter 6 concentrates on Jesus' Galilean ministry and demonstrates important connections between (1) Jesus' healing of the leper (1:40–45) and Elisha's healing of Naaman, the leprous Syrian official (2 Kgs 5:1–19); (2) Jesus' multiplication of five and seven loaves for five thousand and four thousand and Elisha's multiplication of twenty loaves for a hundred people (2 Kgs 4:42–44); and (3) a healing ministry to Gentiles in Tyre and Sidon in Mark 7:24–30 and 1 Kgs 17:7–16. One doubtful allusion concerns the connections between Jesus' healing of the paralytic (2:1–12) and King Ahaziah's fall from the roof in 2 Kgs 1, since no healing is involved in the Old Testament account and the thesis of a deliberate plot reversal seems unnecessary.

Chapters 7 and 8 move away from the genre of miracle story and consider references to Elijah connected with Jesus' passion predictions and the parable of the Wicked Tenants. Winn attempts to trace Jesus' threefold passion prediction in Mark to the three successive predictions made to Elisha regarding Elijah's ascension, but the use of triplicates was a common storytelling device in Semitic oral and written traditions. Winn contends that the third misunderstanding by James and John in Mark's Gospel is structurally different from the first two misunderstandings, just as the third conversation about Elijah's ascension is different from the first two, but his arguments are not convincing and question a scholarly consensus. Regarding the parable of the Wicked Tenants, Winn argues that, because Isa 5 leaves many features of Mark's parable unaccounted for, the story of Jehu in 2 Kgs 9 fills this gap. However, although there are many allusions in the Gospels to the works of Elijah and Elisha, the acts of the Israelite kings in these chapters bear little resemblance to the events in the gospel.

Chapter 9 turns to Mark's passion and resurrection narratives. Again Winn contends that Peter's triple denial is modeled upon Elisha's triple affirmation of

Elijah in 2 Kgs 2, but both narratives demonstrate a common storytelling device. Behind Winn's conclusion could be the presupposition of his mentor, Thomas Brodie, that all references to oral tradition are unfounded, unworkable, and unnecessary (see ch. 6 in *The Birthing of the New Testament*). Surprisingly, Winn does not discuss the misunderstanding of Jesus' lament from the cross as a call for Elijah. It is tied closely to the offering of wine, which could relate back to Jesus' statement in the upper room that he will not drink of the fruit of the vine until the coming of the kingdom. Then the arrival of the kingdom occurs on the cross and assumes the arrival of Elijah. It is interesting that both Mark's Gospel and the Elijah–Elisha cycle conclude with a resurrection (2 Kgs 13:20–21), but the Old Testament event certainly does not explain the abruptness of Mark's ending as Winn surmises. Neither does Winn claim that the order of the events throughout the Elijah–Elisha cycle supplies the narrative sequence for Mark's Gospel.

Winn's book is a fine review of the interconnections between the Gospels and the Elijah–Elisha narrative, including clarifying charts to envision literary allusions. Importantly, Winn concludes that Mark's primary literary dependence centers upon Jewish texts rather than Greco-Roman literature (50). Winn demonstrates convincingly that Mark alludes to material found in the Elijah–Elisha narrative, but to say that he is imitating this material could imply that the order and details of the Old Testament events are controlling Mark's presentation. I am not so sure why Winn finds it so important to define the connection as literary imitation rather than just literary allusion. The differences between literary allusions and literary imitation (if there is any difference) are not really spelled out in the book. Finally, what is the purpose of the imitation? Winn does not say. Through this omission, the work proves ultimately unsatisfying, since the author refuses to deal with the issue of the significance of Mark's literary dependence upon the Elijah–Elisha cycle (60). However, the reader surely benefits from a review of the important interconnections between these two sections of scripture as well as through his critique of other works that consider Markan imitation.

He of Whom It Is Written: John the Baptist and Elijah in Luke, by Jaroslav Rindos. Österreichische Biblische Studien 38. Frankfurt am Main: Lang, 2010. Pp. 291. Hardcover. $76.95. ISBN 9783631605509.

Clare K. Rothschild, Lewis University, Chicago, Illinois

This book is the author's doctoral dissertation under Klemens Stock, S.J., at the Pontifical Gregorian University in Rome, defended February 2009. Its aim is to show, against a veritable torrent of studies to the contrary, that Luke portrays John the Baptist as Elijah, just as Mark did. The book has five chapters, not including the introduction and conclusion. The introduction covers *status quaestionis* and methodology. In terms of the former, Rindos argues that scholarship focuses on Luke's depiction of Jesus', over John the Baptist's, depiction as Elijah—at the expense of the truth. The present monograph, therefore, focuses on Luke's depiction *of John* as Elijah. In eleven pages (16–27), Rindos helpfully lists the views of all of the major monographs and commentaries on the topic of Elijah in Luke. He subsequently groups the approaches by whether they endorse or reject the depiction of John as Elijah (28–30). Those who advocate an association between John and Elijah (Rindos included) also support an association between Jesus and Elijah (30). He contends that the studies rejecting depiction of John as Elijah overemphasize Lukan omission of two Markan associations of John with Elijah. "I do not believe," writes Rindos, "that we can learn much from the gaps. Certainly, the comparison of Luke with Mark is indicative, and Luke's omissions are instructive and should be taken into consideration, but rather in the light of his positive exposition of the John-Elijah association" (33). We will return below to this important methodological point—without argument, eschewing redaction criticism.

Setting out to establish the Baptist-Elijah association, Rindos analyzes four passages in Luke: (1) 1:5–25; (2) 1:68–79; (3) 3:1–20; and (4) 7:18–35. His approach to the analysis is "synchronic" (defined as interpreting a pericope in its current narrative setting, 34) and narratological. These emphases occur within a wider scope of historical-critical methods (24–28). Rindos concludes the section on method by noting that he will extend to the text the benefit of the doubt in instances of apparent disagreement between Luke and Acts (34). Notably, he will offer no attempt to square his conclusions based on narratology with divergent findings of scholars using other methods, including redaction criticism.

Chapter 1, "The Origins of John the Baptist" examines Luke 1:5–25 in the detailed style of a commentary, frequently including, for example, text-critical issues. Most of the material is tangential to the book's thesis. The chapter never argues for the author's central thesis about John the Baptist in Luke; it is purely descriptive. The "recapitulation" (73–76) concludes with the following narrative summary: "This unit introduces the name of Elijah for the first time in Luke's work, [where the] angel of the Lord links the future of John the Baptist to 'the spirit and power of Elijah' in his announcement of the birth of John to his father Zechariah (Luke 1:13–17). This announcement, from the author's perspective, presents a 'narrative program' providing the essentials for the future of John and his role" (73).

In much the same manner, chapter 2 descriptively analyzes Zechariah's canticle in Luke 1:68–79. Chapter 3, on John's "public mission," likewise follows the same pattern. A great majority of the textual examination in individual chapters is sound, if repeating information of standard commentaries, especially J. Fitzmyer and D. Bock. In chapter 3, Rindos asserts that Luke 3:1–20[22] ("public mission of John") constitutes "a 'performance' of the narrative program" established by Luke 1:5–25 and 1:68–79" (101). Toward this goal, the author argues that Luke 3:1–2a reflects the political situation of Ahab and Jezebel (104–5). Even though the "word of God" formula associated with John in Luke 3:2 is, as Rindos shows, widespread in the LXX, it indicates to Rindos a reference to Elijah (108). Rindos argues this point on the basis of the Elijianic program that Rindos claims began in Luke 1–2 and his interpretation of subsequent passages in 3:19–20. That Luke omits Elijah's clothing in Mark 1:6, Rindos explains as Luke's assertion that John comes in ἐν πνεύματι καὶ δυνάμει Ἠλίου (Luke 1:17)—not in Elijah's clothes. John's preaching at the Jordan is likewise explained as correlating with the beginning (1 Kgs 17:3, 5, 8) and ending (2 Kgs 2:6–14) of Elijah's ministry (112–13). That the common word ἐγείρω occurs in Luke 3:8 with respect to John ("raise up children to Abraham") also occurs in a story about *Jesus* modeled on 1 Kgs 17:17–24 suggests to Rindos that *John* not Jesus is Elijah, never mind Luke 7:22, where the verb applies to Jesus (119–22 and 160). John's reference to fire in 3:16 is the Holy Spirit *and* Elijah on Mount Carmel (1 Kgs 18:38, pp. 141, 162). In chapter 4 Rindos argues that Jesus as Lord qualifies John as the Elijah-like messenger in Malachi (Luke 7:27, pp. 177–84, 191). Chapter 5 concludes that: (1) John is explicitly designated as Elijah in Luke; (2) the fact that Jesus is also described as Elijah is explained by Luke's love of parallels and Elijah's message as universal (i.e., both John and Jesus can share it); (3) Luke's omission of Mark's references to Elijah's clothing (1:6) and John's designation as Elijah (9:11) are both explained by Luke's specification that John comes, not literally as Elijah, but ἐν πνεύματι καὶ δυνάμει Ἠλίου (Luke 1:17). If, Rindos speculates, John *had* come in Elijah's clothing, those flocking to him in the desert might have misconstrued him as *actually* the old prophet Elijah, rather than as the new Elijah of Malachi, preparing the way of the Lord (Mal 3:1, p. 198). Presumably, new Elijah is different from old Elijah, on Rindos's argument, only in that the new Elijah is the figure returned to earth after being taken up. It is difficult, therefore, to understand how anyone who knew enough to recognize Elijah on his return could mistake him for his old self. Methodologically, it is very significant that the author simply ignores the significance of the redaction-critical observation that at two key points Luke passes over Mark in silence. Rindos's method is emblematic of much work in the last twenty years: simply asserting (without argument!) that one can instead (!) use literary methods. If one simply ignores contrary findings from another method, there is arguably a lack of scholarly control in the *use* (note: *not* in the method itself) of narrative criticism.

Careful exegetical commentary and philological work are the best features of this book. (Understandably, Rindos relies on commentaries that do not close the door on John's depiction as Elijah in Luke; see his list on the bottom of 29). The monograph's topic is worthwhile, attested by its rich history of interpretation. On the weaker side, the study admits no tension between the Markan and Lukan portraits of John, despite a solid review of scholarship demonstrating the contrary. Thanks to methodological peculiarities, Rindos's study leaves the impression of making a fundamentally canonical argument: because John is clearly depicted as Elijah in Mark, John may *also* be seen as Elijah in Luke. For a scholar to find the results of one method (in this case, narratology) more compelling than another (here, redaction criticism) is perfectly acceptable. But simply to ignore Luke's authorial freedom to change Mark leaves the impression that Rindos has not yet grasped the work of Conzelmann (*Die Mitte der Zeit*, 1953; [2]1957; ET: *The Theology of St. Luke*, 1960), bequeathed to us nearly six decades ago. The primary prooftext of Rindos's argument is Luke 1:17, that John will come "in the spirit and power of Elijah." But the author never considers the possibility that attributing *only* Elijah's spirit and power to John *denies* him Elijah's identity, as does Luke's omission of (1) John's clothing, (2) John's diet, (3) Jesus' statement that John was the Elijah who was to come (Mark 9:11–13||Matt 17:10–13). John is not Elijah, but possesses his spirit and power much as Elisha did (2 Kgs 2:15). Zechariah's prophecy in Luke 1:76 alludes to Isa 40:3 but does not designate John as Elijah. Finally, Luke 7:24–27 cites Isa 40:3 but never mentions Elijah.

Instead of the study under review, I strongly recommend to readers the elegant and concise treatment of these very problems in James A. Kelhoffer, *The Diet of John the Baptist* (WUNT 1/176; Tübingen: Mohr Siebeck, 2005), 129–32; cf. 7–12, mentioned once in Rindos's book (51 n. 117). Referring to passages about John's diet in the Synoptics, Kelhoffer writes: "The flawed tendency in scholarship toward harmonization of two or more of these Synoptic passages … cannot be overemphasized" (10). The situation is exponentially worse when John's other Elijianic qualities are considered.

The Case for Mark Composed in Performance, by Antoinette Clark Wire. Biblical Performance Criticism 3. Eugene, Ore.: Cascade, 2011. Pp. 238. Paper. $26.00. ISBN 9781608998586.

Larry W. Hurtado, University of Edinburgh, Edinburgh, Scotland, United Kingdom

A senior scholar well known for her contributions to the study of the New Testament, Wire writes out of the conviction that the Gospels "were composed, not by individual authors with pens in hand, but orally in performance" (2). In this very readable book she lays out her argument that Mark in particular was composed in this manner, building upon similar observations and arguments offered, for example, by Joanna Dewey, Pieter J. J. Botha, and David Rhoads (curiously, Whitney Shiner, *Proclaiming the Gospel: First-Century Performance of Mark*, is not mentioned by Wire). Indeed, Wire's book appears in a series devoted to promoting Biblical Performance Criticism, an approach based on the view that the biblical writings derive from "oral composition" and "performance," the written forms that we know simply textual artifacts (residue?) of these processes. The foreword to the series states as the aim "to shift academic work on the Bible from the mentality of a modern print culture to that of an oral/scribal culture" and hails Wire's book as presenting "an alternative paradigm for the emergence of Mark." Given its ambitious aim, it is appropriate to devote some sustained consideration to Wire's book.

Early in the introduction she notes that the Gospels are "not signed by their composers" (1) and urges that this should signal that these texts are not really to be seen as literary productions of individual authors but much more as bodies of material heavily "shaped in the telling" (2). She goes on to portray a distinction between composition by an author and composition in "oral tradition": "Authors may draw on given traditions in the process of a story or an argument, but they do so in order to make their own particular statement. Performers of tradition are understood to be transmitting a given tradition of the community" (3). Wire urges that to treat Mark as a story "told by several favored oral performers rather than as the product of a single writer" leads to understanding the text differently in several ways. Instead of thinking of "an urban male shaped in the Greek language and Hellenistic culture," we can allow for "composition over decades" and by various people, such as individuals who knew Jesus, hosts of Christian circles, and/or others who simply were good at storytelling or whose physical attributes advantaged them in public speaking. This also means that, instead of seeing Mark as responding to "a single historical and social setting," we take it as reflecting "multiple contexts of composition" (5). Moreover, she grants "the heavy weight of tradition" (exercising a conserving effect) over against "the near freedom of a modern novelist." Finally, not only in content but also in its textual character, she proposes, Mark "will reflect the oral traditions and embody the oral performances that lie behind it" (6).

Wire then briefly reviews "Twentieth-Century Rediscovery of Oral Tradition," summarizing work from Parry and Lord (on Serbo-Croatian epic singers) on through studies of Homeric epics (Nagy), folklore of various peoples, recent studies of early Jewish and Islamic oral tradition, and "Gospel oral tradition" (from early form criticism through to recent study of "orality" (e.g., Dewey, Botha, Horsley, Draper, Foley, Dunn). But, judging that "the default setting has not changed" in most of this recent work, she urges that "it is time to make the case for Mark as an orally composed tradition" (17). She concludes her introduction by listing anticipated objections to her thesis, framing her arguments in succeeding chapters to answer them.

In Part 1, Wire lays out "external evidence" of Mark's composition in performance. But chapter 1 really addresses anticipated objections to her thesis from those for whom the biblical texts are canonical and authoritative and from advocates of "postmodern theory." In chapter 2 she turns to how Mark appears in ancient manuscripts, underscoring the frequency of variants, the paucity of early manuscripts (only P45 before 300 C.E.), and what she describes as the comparatively "free text" of Mark. Along with some valid observations, however, I think her description of the early textual transmission of Mark and the other Gospels is flawed, reflecting a lack of "hands-on" acquaintance with manuscripts and their data (regrettably, an all-too-common shortcoming among contemporary New Testament scholars).

Wire proposes that P45 reflects an earlier, less-controlled copying practice and that a subsequent, more "strict" copying is exhibited in P66 and P75 (36–37). But, although the early Gospels papyri reflect varying copyist abilities and tendencies, this is hardly a basis for the large claim that she makes. Given that we have only one copy of Mark among these manuscripts, it is not possible to distinguish a supposedly earlier and later approach to copying this text. Actually, the most substantial variant in Mark, the "long" ending, first appears in manuscripts of the fifth century and later. Moreover, all the papyri that she cites are roughly from a similar period (indeed, P66 and P75 are typically dated a bit earlier than P45), suggesting that whatever textual tendencies they individually reflect were roughly contemporary.

In chapter 3 ("Mark Found in Writing: The Setting"), she first discusses "writing and reading in the Greco-Roman world" and again makes what I regard as sweeping and debatable claims. For example, how does one square the statement "In general, reading and writing were not a part of life except in small scribal and ruling circles" with the abundant evidence of popular-level use of writing/reading reflected in the thousands of Greek personal letters, which are undeniably from people of various walks of life? Likewise, there are the many other "documentary" texts (e.g., marriage certificates, land transfers, bills of lading, invoices) that suggest at least a "utilitarian" use of writing/reading among various social levels well below "small scribal and ruling circles." For a fascinating demonstration of how much we can learn about everyday life from this material, see Peter Parsons, *City of the Sharp-Nosed Fish: Greek Lives in Egypt* (London: Weidenfeld & Nicolson, 2007). Wire rightly emphasizes the prominence of speaking and hearing in the Roman world, but I think she errs in appearing to play off "orality" against "textuality." I submit that the full range of evidence suggests a rich interplay of both, "authors" as well as "performers."

Chapter 4 explores further "the event" of Mark being written. Wire reviews briefly various putative scenarios for why someone wrote it, judging that most scholars "seem to exaggerate the significance of writing as the turning point in the Markan tradition" (56). Having made a somewhat similar point years ago ("The Gospel of Mark: Evolutionary or Revolutionary Document?" *JSNT* 40 [1990]: 15–32), I am inclined to agree, basically, that in content and even in stylistic matters, there is likely considerable congruity between Mark and the "pre-Markan" transmission of Jesus-tradition. But I remain less confident than Wire that this pre-Markan tradition involved the oral recitation of accounts that map so directly onto Mark. Wire does not engage adequately the arguments of scholars such as Richard Burridge that the Gospels comprise a noteworthy event in the literary history of earliest Christianity, reflecting the Christian adaptation of and participation in "bios" writing.

Judging a "lack of any authorial presence in Mark," Wire doubts a "literary writer" at work and prefers a view of the text as "a scribe's re-performance of the tradition" (57). This, however, summarily goes against the judgments of a goodly number of scholars that Mark reflects the work of an author. To be sure, the anonymity of the Gospels indicates that their authors were not concerned to promote their own status but likely saw themselves as serving the message and movement for which they wrote. Wire's approach rightly cautions us against too much of a "cult of the individual" in our approach to the Gospels. But I doubt that she will convince many that the Gospels do not reflect real authors exercising their individual efforts to give inspiring "renditions" of Jesus.

Wire goes on the claim that "the written Mark would have been unwieldy and very difficult to read" and so "was likely reserved in a case for symbolic value or used for pedagogical purposes in its early decades while oral performers continued their composing task" (58). These comments, I fear, further reflect an unfortunate lack of acquaintance with the material evidence. For example, consider P66, which was originally a 78-page copy of John in a codex with pages circa 16.2 x 14.2 cm. John is a considerably larger text than Mark, but this manuscript would hardly have made an "unwieldy" item. Even as a bookroll, any of the Gospels would have made an entirely portable text.

Moreover, to judge from the earliest extant remnants of New Testament manuscripts, they were prepared to be used, read from, typically in Christian group-occasions, and certainly not placed in a "case for symbolic value." In format, these manuscripts make an interesting contrast with the high-quality copies of pagan literary texts, which William Johnson cogently showed were designed to reflect the elitist circles in which they were used: *Readers and Reading Culture in the High Roman Empire: A Study of Elite Communities* (Oxford: Oxford University Press, 2010). By contrast, New Testament manuscripts typically have elementary punctuation and use spaces to mark sense-units. They also often have breathing marks, somewhat larger writing, and wide line-spacing (with fewer lines per column-inch), all of which seem to be reader's aids intended to facilitate the public reading of these copies. I have discussed these and other features of early Christian manuscripts in *The Earliest Christian Artifacts: Manuscripts and Christian Origins* (Grand Rapids: Eerdmans, 2006), urging their importance for wider historical issues about early Christianity.

In chapter 5 Wire reviews questions about the languages used in the Roman East. Somewhat curiously, she also highlights here what she regards as "a remarkable aspect of the Markan narrative … that Jesus' ministry takes place strictly in small towns and the countryside" (67) and takes this as perhaps reflecting "a cultural alienation from the values represented by the cities" (68). Hmm. Maybe. Maybe not. In any case, it is not clear how this pertains to her larger case.

In part 2 Wire offers "internal evidence of composition in performance." In chapters 6–8, she points to Mark's use of parataxis, the repeated καὶ, simple vocabulary, and quoted speech. In chapters 9–11, she discusses several kinds of "repeated scenes" in Mark: exorcisms, controversies, healings, the vision of a heavenly voice, and "the vision of one coming on the clouds." Chapter 12 focuses on showing that the Markan narrative "as a whole has been shaped in the telling" (110), that is, that it exhibits features that could derive from oral "performance" of Jesus-tradition.

Chapters 13–14 treat "the story pattern" of Mark, focusing on motifs of conflict a "report of a prophet's sign." This focus on themes and motifs continues into part 3, "Soundings in Mark." These include Mark's emphasis on Jesus' identity (ch. 15), in which (curiously, to my mind) she alleges a "minimal Christology" in Mark, by no means a consensus view. Chapter 16 is given to Mark's treatment of God's kingdom as announced and arriving. Chapter 17 deals with Mark's ending (at 16:8), Wire briefly exploring the possibility that women's testimonies may be reflected in the Markan tomb scene, yet also accepting the view that the women are presented as not speaking to anyone at all about the empty tomb (even though a growing number of scholars have inclined to David Catchpole's proposal that 16:8 should be read as the women not speaking to anyone else than those to who they were sent).

In part 4, Wire engages in interesting speculations about whether the link of the text to "Mark" (a figure connected in Acts 12 with "the house of Mary") may reflect a derivation from "the telling of Jesus' story that might have been taking place in Mary's house" in the decades prior to the writing of the Gospel, or whether Mark derives from Jesus-tradition "among women in Galilee." In chapter 19 she reviews her arguments, then concludes by addressing "our own context" (192–94).

Wire's handling of themes and motifs in Mark is clear and often persuasive, but her specific claim that Mark is essentially a recording of a particular "performance" of its narrative leaves me unconvinced. On the one hand, there certainly are factors that suggest a strong connection of Mark with the prior and larger transmission of Jesus-tradition, including particularly oral transmission. On the other hand, for the sort of reasons mentioned briefly here, I regret to say that I find some of Wire's claims somewhat simplistic (as if we have to choose between oral tradition and authors) and weakened by an insufficient grasp of the material evidence of the transmission and reading of texts in early Christianity. To be sure, early Christianity was, and throve in, a Roman environment in which "orality" was important. But, as Harry Gamble showed, early Christianity was also remarkably invested in the composition, copying, distribution, and reading of texts (*Books and Readers in the Early Church: A History of Early Christian Texts* ([New Haven: Yale University Press, 1995]).

New Perspectives on the Nativity, edited by Jeremy Corley. New York: T&T Clark, 2009. Pp. xi + 215. Paper. $34.95. ISBN 9780567629043.

Mark R. C. Grundeken, Katholieke Universiteit Leuven, Leuven, Belgium

Jeremy Corley's introduction (1–3) puts the claim that the volume offers "new perspectives on the nativity" into perspective: "While nothing is entirely new, these essays develop earlier approaches in novel ways, offering a wide variety of perspectives—literary, political, feminist, theological, poetic, Islamic, and liturgical—on the familiar Christmas story" (1).

Henry Wansbrough (4–22) surveys the issues that developed in scholarly discussions on the infancy narratives since the second edition of Raymond E. Brown's *The Birth of the Messiah* (1993). He observes that, in line with Brown's conviction as to the priority of theological and christological over merely historical analyses, in recent studies on the first two chapters of Matthew and Luke, various new approaches have been elaborated (especially literary and feminist ones), while use of the stories to establish historicity has declined.

Next, four chapters focus on Luke's infancy story. Ian Boxall (23–36) draws parallels between the readings of recent narrative-critical (and other literary)

approaches and artistic interpretations of Luke's birth narrative. He argues against Brown that there is a link between Jesus' manger and his tomb (Luke 2:7; 23:53). Brown dismissed this link on the basis of the different vocabulary in the two passages (*Birth*, 399). Boxall notes that already Domenico Ghirlandaio's altarpiece "The Nativity and Adoration of the Shepherds" (1483–1485) depicts Jesus' birth in a way that foreshadows his death.

Barbara E. Reid (37–46) notes that the three women (Elizabeth, Mary, and Anna) in Luke 1–2 embody the prophetic mission and prefigure the ways in which Jesus is presented as a (rejected) prophet in the remainder of Luke's Gospel. Similar to Jesus, the women persist in their mission despite all the disbelief, opposition, and silencing they encounter. Reid suggests that they can model for women in today's church how to express their experience of God in their own voice.

Leonard J. Maluf (47–66) contends that the first part of Zechariah's utterance (Luke 1:68–75) does not refer to Jesus—Messiah and descendant of David—but to the Davidic house itself. It is not intended to evoke the messianic era but the Old Testament story and the notion of salvation as deliverance from Israel's enemies. This salvation does not coincide with the one announced by John the Baptist (Luke 1:76–79), the forerunner of Jesus Christ, namely, salvation (consisting) in the forgiveness of sins in the messianic age to come.

Nicholas King (67–76) defends the traditional view that *katalyma* in Luke 2:7 means "inn" and argues that this is one of the themes in the first two chapters of Luke-Acts that anticipates the unfolding plot. Luke expresses the idea that Jesus encounters many difficulties in his life ("there was no room for them in the inn") but that God will make sure that every obstacle in the divine project will eventually be removed.

Thereafter, four essays deal with Matthew's infancy story. Warren Carter (77–90) states that Roman imperial power plays a central role in the first two chapters of Matthew's Gospel. Jesus' birth foreshadows his future life and his death on a Roman cross. The narrative guides Jesus' followers by showing that at times imperial power may serve or enact the divine purposes but that it is ultimately at odds with God's plan. It will eventually turn out that no power is stronger than God.

Benedict T. Viviano (91–109) argues that Matthew's three-part genealogy is an extract from a larger seven-part scheme. He writes that Matt 1:2–17 is perhaps a fusion of a scheme of a world-week of seven thousand-year periods of history and a scheme of generations grouped by major figures or events. He concludes that Matthew presents his genealogy as a theology of history, with Jesus' birth as the beginning of a new stage of salvation history.

Bernard P. Robinson (110–31) designates Matthew's Gospel as "creative historiography" (113) that is partly fictional and may partly follow some historical substratum. He observes that Matthew's infancy narrative is characterized by its androcentricity and its (relatively) frequent use of formula citations from the Old Testament. He explains these elements as indications of the Evangelist's likely past as a Jewish scribe.

Christopher Fuller (132–47) uses Mikhail M. Bakhtin's theory on the carnivalesque to show how Pier Paolo Pasolini's film *The Gospel according to Saint Matthew* (1964) gives a carnivalesque reading of the magi in the First Gospel. Following Mark Allan Powell's *Chasing the Eastern Star* (2001), Fuller goes on to say that Matthew presents the magi as "pagan fools" in search of a king who are ignorant within the biblical view, "yet to them God reveals the truth about Jesus" (136). As such, "Matthew's narrator fashions a conflict between the high and powerful (who should be wise) and the low and ignorant (who, in fact, have access to the kingdom)" (136).

The last three essays focus on presentations of the nativity in poetry, Islamic sources, and liturgy. Ann Loades (148–64) shows how twentieth-century British poetry raised new poetic perspectives on the infancy stories. She observes that in these poetic interpretations there is generally little realism about Jesus' birth. She concludes that "it seems that we still have not reached the point where we can take such realism for granted" (155).

John Kaltner (165–79) describes Mary's (Maryam's) prominent place in Islam, referring to the Qur'an, the hadith, and extracanonical texts. He points at Mary as an example of the Qur'an's tendency to Islamize biblical characters. Since Christians and Muslims can agree on much when it comes to Mary—"she is recipient of God's message, model of faith and submission, sinless virgin mother, and a sign for all people" (179)—it is suggested that Mary may serve as a central figure around whom adherents of the two religions can unite.

Thomas O'Loughlin (180–99) expresses the idea that, "in our desire to historicize all the details, we fail to appreciate a whole approach to the mystery of Jesus" (187). According to O'Loughlin, it is the liturgy that fills this gap. Recalling the nativity liturgically means that one is not concerned with the historical details but celebrates the nativity as a sacramental event today. In the context of the Christian assembly, it is not so much the historical event as the liturgical meaning of Jesus' birth that counts and teaches what Christmas is about.

The volume ends with Patricia M. McDonald's appendix "Resemblances between Matthew 1–2 and Luke 1–2" (200–201), followed by a "Dictionary of Technical Terms, Significant Persons, and Ancient Texts" (202–4) and a "Bibliography of Studies on the Nativity, 1990–2009" (205–11).

The volume offers a welcome 'bouquet' of a wide variety of fruitful approaches to the nativity stories. Its strength is, however, also one of its weaknesses. It is quite diffuse, and the editor's attempts to put things together are rather limited. A conclusion is lacking. It is therefore somewhat surprising that the editor uses more than one third (11 of 27 lines) of the part of the introduction that evaluates some common themes in the essays to argue that he, unlike some of the contributors, considers Bethlehem as the likely historical birthplace of Jesus. He thereby ignores the argument that John consistently says that Jesus was from Nazareth and that he shows no awareness of a direct link between Jesus and Bethlehem—although John 7:41–42 mentions the Messiah-Bethlehem link (see Wansbrough, 5 with n. 10; O'Loughlin, 187 n. 19).

Another weakness is that the volume incorporates several perspectives that are, to say the least, rather contestable. It is remarkable that Wansbrough considers Jesus' resurrection without any reservations as a historical fact ("what actually happened") rather than as a theological truth (5). Maluf states that, "if perhaps Luke knew and used Matthew's Gospel, we can regard the Benedictus as containing Luke's profound meditation on Matt 1:21" and goes on to say that "in Luke 1:68–75, Luke spells out what is only implicit in the Matthean text that establishes the meaning of the name Jesus: 'He will save his people (*not from their enemies—as in Old Testament times—but) from their sins*' (Matt 1:21)" (52). An exegesis that explains Luke from Matthew and then reads Luke back into Matthew is highly problematic. Viviano is not very cautious about positing a high level of historicity when he states that the saying underlying Matt 23:35 and Luke 11:51 "very likely goes back to the historical Jesus" (101). Finally, it is one thing to say that the Evangelists interpreted the meaning of Jesus' birth in terms of familiar biblical poetry (especially Isaiah), but it goes too far to say with Loades that "it may even be the case that the poetry of Isaiah formed both Mary's own understanding of her role in bringing the divine presence among humanity … and then formed Jesus' own struggle to understand his relationship to God" (150). Here a daring leap is made from the level of the Gospel narrative(s) to the (alleged) self-understanding of (the historical) Mary and Jesus. Despite all this critique, it is fair enough to conclude with John Barclay (on the cover of the book) that the volume is "a great resource for many Christmases to come."

Mark, edited by Nicole Wilkinson Duran, Teresa Okure, and Daniel Patte. Texts @ Contexts. Minneapolis: Fortress, 2011. Pp. xvii + 237. Hardcover. $40.00. ISBN 9780800659981.

Steve Smith, University of Chichester, Chichester, United Kingdom

This collection of essays on Mark's Gospel is the second volume to be published in the Texts @ Contexts series (after the volume on Genesis). Accepting that all textual interpretation is necessarily contextual, this series celebrates a diversity of interpretive contexts whether they are related to ethnicity, gender, politics, personal biography, or personal and national ideology (among others). As such, it represents a welcome move away from the dominant Western, male, and predominantly Protestant nature of biblical scholarship by seeking to include voices less often heard in scholarship.

There are three sections to the book. Part 1 examines "Jesus as Exorcist and Healer" with three essays. Israel Kamudzandu, whose mother was a shaman in Zimbabwe, examines "The Nature and Identity of Jesus in Mark 7:24–37: A Zimbabwean Interpretation." His reading foregrounds the "mystical powers of the universe" (12), which are obvious in an African context, and notes the resemblances between Jesus' healings and those of a shaman because Jesus engages in a similar world of magic and healing. Similarly, Sejong Chun's "Exorcism or

Healing? A Korean Preacher's Rereading of Mark 5:1–20" uses a contemporary account of a shaman ritual performed in a South Korean village to throw into relief aspects of the account of the Gerasene demoniac. The conversation between the shaman and the dislocated spirit highlights the conversation between Jesus and the demon, and the observation that the spirit in the Korean account had died without honor helps one interpret why the demons appeal to go into the pigs. In both essays the context is used to interpret the text, but there is less attention to how the text differs to its contextual parallel. Nicole Wilkinson Duran examines "Other People's Demons: Reading Mark's Demons in the Disbelieving West." Her self-aware wrestling with Mark 5:1–20 from a Western perspective is enlightening because of the tensions that she notes in the process. Her Western perspective wants to deny demonic activity, but she finds herself drawn to seeing the spirits as they are shown in the text; similarly, her Western perspective wants to cross boundaries between groups, but she notes that the story presents group boundaries as a positive thing. As such, the text speaks back, and she is attracted to things that are "the converse of my own culture's values" (51).

Part 2, "Teachers, Disciples and Communities," opens with another Korean view from Jin Young Choi ('The Misunderstanding of Jesus' Disciples in Mark: An Interpretation from a Community-Centered Perspective"). She notes that discipleship with Jesus can be seen as a horizontal and communal relationship, an "egalitarian kinship model" (58) where being with Jesus is the mark of a disciple; this contrasts with Western ideas about discipleship as an individual relationship proceeding out of rational understanding of who Jesus is. Her approach is noteworthy in that it makes explicit use of Western scholarship and methods (including references to social-scientific criticism and literary methods) but concludes with ideas consistent with Korean shaman practice. In "The Markan Construction of Jesus as Disciple of the Kingdom," Osvaldo D. Vena examines the text through his own personal journey (from Argentina to the United States as a New Testament scholar), a journey from an apocalyptic interpretation to one with greater concern for issues of justice. He finds that the pressures on the Markan community arising from the Jewish uprising before 70 C.E. caused a similar refusal of apocalyptic traditions in the Gospel; instead, Mark emphasizes discipleship as a theological concern defined by the needs of his community and offers Jesus as the model for discipleship. Elsa Tamez writes from the perspective of violence and oppression. Her engaging essay, "The Conflict in Mark: A Reading from the Armed Conflict in Colombia," also focuses on the Jewish War. The similarities between her context and the Jewish War in Mark's context enables her to note two aspects of discipleship that are not detailed in conventional approaches: the references to war and violence in Mark 13, and themes of fear and silence elsewhere. This reading allows the text to speak into the Colombian situation by addressing how to live under such circumstances. Teresa Okure looks at "Children in Mark: A Lens for Reading Mark's Gospel" and notes that commentators do not often discuss children in relation to texts, even though the plight of children is an important global topic. She notes the macro-level exploitation of children as well as Jesus' identification of children as models of the kingdom.

The essays in final section, "Putting Other Readings in Context," do something different. Instead of reading the text through their context, they note how certain contexts obscure aspects of the text. Hisako Kinukawa's "Sexuality and Household: When 'Cultural Reading' Supersedes and Skews the Meaning of Texts" is concerned to demonstrate how a strongly patriarchal Japanese reading of texts about family and household has obscured Mark's meaning. She demonstrates how this context has subordinated women in divorce and also suggests that such readings in church history have distorted the Markan Jesus' teaching on sexuality. In undoing a long-standing patriarchal contextual interpretation of sexuality in the Gospel of Mark, she replaces it with an interpretation informed by her own personal context. Menghun Goh, in "The Relationship between John the Baptist and Jesus in the Gospel of Mark: A Postcolonial Interpretation from a Chinese Malaysian Context," writes from a context that, because of British imperialism, gives a sensitivity to disruption, conflict, and power plays among groups of people. He notes that Mark portrays John in an ambivalent manner (e.g., he does not recognize Jesus' mission). One would therefore expect Malaysian Chinese Christians to view John negatively; instead, they take a traditional positive view. His analysis of this is carefully nuanced and eventually embraces both perspectives. Finally, Daniel Patte's "Contextual Reading of Mark and North Atlantic Scholarship" clearly shows how conventional biblical scholarship is both blind to the role of contextual interpretation and resistant to it. He goes on to propose a series of suggestions for how Western biblical scholarship can embrace such contextual interpretations.

Overall this volume offers a reasonable sample of different interpretive contexts, and the essays from a Western perspective are helpful in emphasizing the place of contextual awareness in Western study. Three aspects of the volume prevented it from being a fragmentary reading experience. First, within each section of the book the essays all address a similar Markan theme, facilitating the comparison of different contexts and what they have to contribute to Markan studies. Second, each author introduces his or her chapter with an explanation of the author's own particular context, often with some informative personal biography. These serve as vital orientation to unfamiliar contexts (without laboring the point for a reader familiar with them) and prepare for the exegesis that follows. Third, even though the majority of the chapters approach the text by foregrounding the interpretive context, there is usually sufficient reference back to more conventional scholarship to emphasize the dialogue. All of this enables a reader situated within a conventional context (as this reviewer is) to appreciate the contextual interpretations and how they relate to conventional scholarship. As a Western male, I certainly did not agree with the exegetical results of every essay, but that is part of the point of the volume.

In a collection of essays some are always stronger than others. In places the contextual interpretation of the biblical text can be a little predictable or rely on a superficial parallelism, but most essays offer a refreshing approach to the text that yields new insights. A couple of essays did not give sufficient attention to how the text dialogues with the context and do not note where the text differs to the contextual parallel that has been noted. In contrast to this, the essay by Nicole Wilkinson Duran is a highlight. Her transparent wrestling with a Western contextual interpretation is refreshing and illustrative of the difficulties that can face other Western scholars attempting the same task. In particular, her observation that a contextual reading from a Western scholarly context is actually a denial of that very context is enlightening: Western scholarly contexts are characterized by their denial that they are contexts at all; they usually see themselves as objective and a-contextual. Daniel Patte's essay is then useful in suggesting how Western scholarship may deal with contextual interpretation. But despite this, while accepting that interpretation is affected by the interpreter's context, this reviewer would add that this is not necessarily the dominant interpretive context for a reader. The text itself has an important role in presenting interpretive contexts that have been provided by the author to enable effective communication.

Having said that, this volume clearly makes the point that interpretation is contextual, it demonstrates the great value and importance of embracing interpretations that come from outside the conventional scholarly context, and it offers some suggestions for taking things further. And it does so with some lively essays. For all of these reasons it can be recommended. One does wonder, though, whether the whole volume is a contextual reading from within a postmodern Western biblical scholarship that welcomes diversity in interpretation, printed as it is in a traditional format of a series of essays, complete with footnotes and bibliography.

Mark's Memory Resources and the Controversy Stories (Mark 2:1–3:6): An Application of the Frame Theory of Cognitive Science to the Markan Oral-Aural Narrative, by Yoon-Man Park. Linguistic Biblical Studies 2. Leiden: Brill, 2010. Pp. xx + 344. Hardcover. $169.00. ISBN 9789004179622.

James D. G. Dunn, Durham University, Durham, United Kingdom

The Linguistic Biblical Studies series is dedicated to the development and promotion of linguistically informed study of the Bible in its original languages. The subtitle of this, the second volume in the series, indicates clearly its scope: *An Application of the Frame Theory of Cognitive Science to the Markan Oral-Aural Narrative*. The starting point is the recognition of Mark's Gospel as the product of an oral-aural communication culture. That is, it "was constructed in such a way as to facilitate the memory process of a listening audience," "to facilitate the audience's memory processes such as comprehension, storing and remembering" (2, 4). In this process, "frames are the devices whereby the initial comprehension takes place and as such they determine what is remembered" (10).

Park defines a "frame" several times: for example, "Frames provide background knowledge by which one understands incoming information" and "guide the listener/reader in remembering a story" (25). Or, in more technical terms: "a frame ... consists of stereotyped knowledge which is stored through cultural and social experience" (27); "a frame is a hierarchical set of concepts which are interconnected by human experience. The hierarchical structure of a frame makes memory easier by allowing for an economical storage of a story on the part of the audience. Since parts belong in a whole, the access to the actions at the whole (higher) level readily leads to the parts" (232). A frequently cited present-day example is the "restaurant frame": the simple reference to a restaurant meal triggers an audience's familiar experience of such a meal, so that little more than the simple reference is sufficient to evoke the various elements which make up such an experience, for example, waiter, menu, order, bill; these can be alluded to, without explicit reference, on the confident assumption that the audience's "restaurant frame" will provide the taken-for-granted information that will make the allusion effective.

So the affirmation can be confidently made that "the communication between Mark and his historical audience was based on a shared body of knowledge" (32); "when the Gospels were orally performed for the first time, the audience did not hear anything completely new, but rather something which was already part of their knowledge" (74); "the early Christians were already familiar with the Jesus traditions in 'communal oral memory'" (76). Or, again in more technical language: "given that Mark's Christian audiences were well versed in the stereotyped sequences of an event frame through their social experience and linguistic knowledge in Greek, it is quite natural to assume that the audiences were readily capable of organizing the cognitive structure of the event sequences as they heard a specific episode" (114).

Most of this will be familiar to anyone conversant with the theory and practice of hermeneutics, for example, that particular usage requires knowledge of general usage to make sense, that context is vital if individual word and specific text is to be properly understood, that parts inform the whole and the whole informs the parts. Form criticism has from the first familiarized us with the idea of typical forms such as miracle or controversy stories. J. M. Foley introduced the idea of "metonymic" reference in oral communication, where a particular reference would trigger a whole sequence and complex of related cultural memories from the audience's historical and social experience.

Chapter 3 provides a useful analysis of the oral features of Mark's Gospel: for example, "homeostatic organization" (information irrelevant to present experience passes out of sight, and new elements are modified to fit in with the cultural identity); paratactic narrative; and redundancy. A lengthy chapter 4 goes into detail on different kinds of frames and how they process information. This is helpful on such features as "inferential processing" and the role of the frame in evoking an audience's expectation and increasing the impact of the unexpected. But it also becomes somewhat pedantic and an overelaboration of the basic mechanics of frame theory.

In part 2 Park turns to the text that will exemplify the benefits of frame theory in reference to Mark's Gospel: 2:1–3:6. It is clear that a "legal controversy" frame provides the best explanatory model, with its easily recognizable and repeated form: provocative events, charge, defense, and verdict. The demonstration of the explanatory force of frame theory for each of the five episodes is overall effective but soon becomes rather labored and mechanical.

Several of the suggested frames make good sense: "table-fellowship," "ritual purity," "fasting," "wedding," and, of course, "Sabbath." These were all themes that would evoke familiar experiences and knowledge and set the particular episode within the frame of a more extensive experience of such traditions and praxis. Of course, any commentator worth his or her salt for the past century or so has seen it as a fundamental part of the commentator's responsibility to fill out the background, or context, or metonymic sequence of reference and allusion that are implicit in these terms and that any teller of these stories would have been able to take for granted in the audiences addressed. Somewhat surprisingly, Park does not fill out frames such as "table-fellowship" and "Sabbath," providing examples of how the frames would have informed the audience's appreciation of and reaction to the stories. Presumably he was himself content to assume his readers' frame of awareness of the commentary tradition that had already filled out such background contexts.

However, the choice of subframes is surprising on several occasions: a "paralytic frame" in 2:1–12 (187–89), when a "serious illness and sin" frame would appear to be more appropriate and to provide more of the trigger that would set in motion the metonymic reverberations that the story provoked; a "forgiveness of sin" frame would have better indicated the theology and cultic practice that explains the surprise and indignation that Jesus' pronouncement of sins forgiven would have sparked off (Park notes the cultic dimension only later, 263). It is disappointing that the third episode is set within a "tax collector" frame and not a "sinner" frame, since it is the "sinner" element within the episode on which Jesus majored (Mark 2:17). Finally, why a "grainfield" frame in the fourth episode rather than a "hunger" frame (196) or a "withered hand" frame in the fifth episode (198), rather than a "severe disability" frame?

Nor am I persuaded by his analysis of the "frame organization of sentences," which again comes across as too mechanical. If it was indeed the case that the sequence of main verbs provided the episode's gist and best memory aids (252–53), I would have expected closer parallel between Matthew's and Luke's retelling of the same stories. The frame and the form almost certainly provided the setting for the sequence of controversy stories, but the memorable feature that embedded the episodes in the oral-aural tradition of the early Christian communities was presumably the sayings of Jesus that lifted the episodes from their familiar frames and gave them the impact that made them so memorable. Again, Park may have assumed that the commentary tradition had focused sufficient attention on Mark 2:10, 17, 21–22, 27–28, and so on, so that little more need be said. But if these sayings were crucial to the memorability of the stories, then more attention should have been given to them.

Regrettably, I have to add that the volume contains a surprising number of misprints and typesetting errors that proofreaders should have noted and eliminated.

In sum, then, Park provides a theoretical basis for understanding how the reading or performance of Mark's Gospel worked in the decades after it was written. It helps to bring home the reality of what it meant for the Gospel to function in an oral-aural culture. For that we can be very grateful. It is always good to have a theoretical basis for a practice (an explicative commentary) that has probably been more firmly rooted in common sense, although the real value will be in making for better exegesis, more sensitive to historical actuality, and only time will tell if that value is realized.

Honor among Christians: The Cultural Key to the Messianic Secret, by David F. Watson. Minneapolis: Fortress, 2010. Pp. x + 229, Paperback, $29.00, ISBN 9780800697099.

Adam Winn, University of Mary Hardin-Baylor, Waco, Texas

In *Honor among Christians*, David F. Watson (Assistant Professor at United Theological Seminary) examines the Markan secrecy motif against the backdrop of the ancient Mediterranean honor/shame value system. This review will proceed by summarizing each chapter and will conclude with a brief critique.

The book's introduction offers a brief survey of the Markan secrecy motif in New Testament scholarship, a survey that begins with William Wrede and traces subsequent research trends. Following this survey, Watson discusses his own approach to the Markan secrecy motif, an approach that relies heavily on social-scientific criticism but also incorporates narrative and reader-response criticism. More specifically, Watson states that his primary goal is to consider the Markan secrecy passages in light of the ancient Mediterranean values of honor and shame.

In chapter 1 Watson explores the meaning and significance of secrecy in the ancient Mediterranean world. After examining both the language and function of secrecy in the ancient world, Watson demonstrates that neither play a prominent role in the Markan secrecy passages. As a result, Watson formulates two conclusions: that it is unlikely Mark's audience would understand so-called "secrecy" passages to in fact be such, and therefore to use secrecy language to describe these passages is both misleading and confusing. As a result, Watson prefers to use the language of concealment rather than secrecy.

Watson turns in chapter 2 to what he calls Markan concealment passages and analyzes them through the lens of the honor and shame value system. He first considers passages in which Jesus resists "achieved honor," that is honor that Jesus has merited through his acts of healing or exorcism (Mark 1:40–45; 5:21–24, 35–43; 7:31–37; 8:22–26). For example, Watson notes that in the healing of the leper (1:40–45) Jesus acts as a beneficent patron (or perhaps a divine broker), while the leper acts as his client. He argues that Jesus' command for the leper to be silent is not an attempt to keep either Jesus' identity or his ability to heal a secret but is rather an attempt to resist the honor due him from the leper. The recipient of benefaction (the leper) would be expected to repay the benefactor (Jesus) by praising him and by spreading this praise to others—actions that Jesus' command for silence subverts.

Next Watson considers passages in which Jesus resists "ascribed honor" (Mark 1:23–28, 34; 3:12), that is, honor Jesus received through the bestowing of honorific titles. For example, Watson argues that the demon's use "the Holy One of God" (Mark 1:23–28) to identify Jesus is a way of ascribing honor to him—honor that would require reciprocation on the part of Jesus. In silencing the demon, Jesus is not seeking to keep his identity a secret but rather is resisting honor. In regard to Jesus' commands for silence, Watson concludes that Mark's first-century audience would not have asked why Jesus sought to hide his identity but would instead have asked why Jesus resisted the honor that he was due.

In chapter 3 Watson argues that Jesus' resistance to honor is only half of the story. Jesus is not rejecting the honor/shame system *in toto*—a system too deeply ingrained in ancient Mediterranean culture—but rather is offering a new vision of what is honorable and shameful. While Jesus resists the common-place markers of honor and shame (e.g., acts of power, benefaction, honorific titles), he also establishes new markers (e.g., service, self-sacrifice, suffering, and crucifixion). Jesus establishes these new markers through his passion predictions (Mark 8:31; 9:31; 10:33) and teaching on discipleship (8:34–38; 9:33–36; 10:13–16, 29–31, 35–45). For Watson, the Markan Jesus ultimately inverts standard conventions by claiming that the least, the suffering, and the servants should be honored, while the great and the powerful should be ashamed. According to Watson, the Markan motif of failing disciples serves to reinforce this inversion for Mark's readers.

In chapter 4 Watson addresses passages in which Jesus' honor is on public display but in which Jesus does not attempt to conceal or resist such honor—passages that are apparently in conflict with the concealment passages. In his analysis of many of these passages, Watson rejects interpretive efforts either to minimize Jesus' honor or to maximize elements of concealment—efforts that ultimately seek to harmonize concealment passages with publicity passages. Watson argues that these passages must be accepted for what they are, passages that publicize Jesus' highly honorable words and actions. Yet, he argues that concealment passages and publicity passages should not be understood as competing with one another. According to Watson, the publicity passages advance a number of different themes, not simply "publicity," and both these various themes and the theme of concealment are equally important to the Markan Evangelist.

Watson addresses in chapter 5 the perplexing relationship between the concealment passages and the publicity passages. His explanation of this relationship is rooted in the oral nature of ancient literary stories. Watson gives particular attention to the role of repetition and inconsistency in ancient stories. Because stories in the ancient world were often written to be heard rather than read, their thematic development was heavily dependent on repetition. Watson concludes that the Markan Jesus' repetitious rejection of honor in the concealment passages develops a clear theme that would not be missed by Mark's readers. This theme, however, would neither be the only nor the most important Markan theme, and other passages would forge additional themes, perhaps even themes that were inconsistent with the theme of rejected honor. However, Watson argues that such inconsistency is not nearly as problematic in ancient literature as it might be in modern literature. He argues that the thematic inconsistency was quite common in ancient literature and that we should not be surprised to see inconsistent themes interwoven throughout Mark's Gospel.

In the conclusion, Watson considers how the Markan inversion of the Mediterranean honor/shame system would encourage the persecuted Christians in the Markan community. He argues that such Christians would have been cut off from the honor of the wider culture. Mark's Gospel not only claims that such honor is unimportant but also provides Mark's community with a new divine standard for evaluating honor: service, self-sacrifice, and suffering. Though a Christian might be shamed by the wider culture, this shame actually brings honor in the eyes of God and in the eyes of one's new Christian family. Ultimately, Mark is telling his community how they can and should gain "honor among Christians."

Watson is to be commended for his efforts to locate the meaning of the Markan "secrecy" motif in the social world of the ancient Mediterranean people. Far too few Markan interpreters have asked the crucial question that Watson asks, "How would Mark's original readers understand Jesus' commands for silence." Watson's work on the meaning and significance of "secrecy" in the ancient Mediterranean world fills a surprising void in the copious amount of work that has been produced on the "messianic secret." He is able to make a strong case that what have often been described by modern scholars as "secrecy" passages were unlikely to have been understood in such terms by ancient readers. If Watson is right (and I believe he is), he significantly undermines previous attempts to explain the Markan "secrecy" motif (e.g., Wrede, Marxen, Burkill, Räisänen) and sets a new trajectory for future research.

Watson is also to be commended for bringing the ancient Mediterranean values of honor and shame to bear on the Markan text. Though he is not the first to consider honor and shame in Mark's Gospel, Watson's work brings fresh and rewarding insights to many Markan pericopes. Not least of these is Watson's insight that the Markan Jesus' commands for silence would be best understood by first-century readers as a surprising resistance to honor.

That being said, Watson's work is open to some critique. While Watson does well in identifying both concealment passages and publicity passages in Mark's Gospel, I find his explanation of their relationship unsatisfactory. As we have seen, Watson argues that the concealment passages work to invert (and thus subvert) the ancient Mediterranean honor/shame value system. However, he also acknowledges that the publicity passages seem to embrace (or at least presuppose) this value system and lack in them any sort of critique of it. Watson's explanation is that both types of passages are seeking to convey different themes and that such "inconsistent" material is quite common in ancient literature. But to use the word "inconsistent" to describe the relationship between Mark's concealment and publicity passages seems to be misleading. As the passage types are understood by Watson, "contradictory" seems to describe their relationship better than "inconsistent." Passages that seem to promote/presuppose the conventional honor/shame system (publicity passages) would seem to undermine passages in which the conventional system is subverted (concealment passages). Perhaps ancient readers could handle inconsistent themes (as Watson demonstrates), but would not such *contradictory* themes prove confusing to them?

This first critique raises questions about Watson's understanding of the concealment passages, namely, that through them Jesus is attempting to subvert the existing honor/shame value system and replace it with his own. If in the publicity passages Jesus is operating under the existing honor system and thus affirming it (e.g., 2:1–12; 3:1–6; 6:30–44; 11:1–11), it seems unlikely that Mark's readers would understand Jesus to be subverting that system in the concealment passages. Such mixed messages seem to undermine aspects of Watson's reading of the Markan concealment motif. As a result, I find persuasive Watson's argument that Jesus' commands for silence should be understood terms of resisting honor rather than in terms of secrecy. However, I find unpersuasive Watson's understanding of Jesus' resistance to honor, namely, that it ultimately functions to invert/subvert the ancient Mediterranean honor/shame value system—a system Mark regular presents Jesus participating in.

In this well-written and erudite book, Watson has taken a decisive step forward in our understanding of the so-called "messianic secret," and he has set a significant trajectory for any future research. All further work on Markan "concealment" passages should consider the arguments and conclusions of this book, and *Honor among Christians* should be on the bookshelf of every serious reader of Mark's Gospel.

Textos fuente y contextuales de la narrativa evangélica: Metodología aplicada a una selección del evangelio de Marcos, by Miguel Pérez Fernández. Biblioteca Midrásica 30. Estella, Spain: Editorial Verbo Divino, 2008. Pp. 549. Paper. €23.00. ISBN 9788481698008.

David E. C. Ford, Fundación Universitaria Seminario Bíblico de Colombia, Medellín, Colombia

Esta publicación es el producto de un proyecto presentado hace años atrás a la Asociación Bíblica Española, con la esperanza de formar un equipo de especialistas que produjera un comentario a los Evangelios con base en fuentes de la tradición judía bíblica y extrabíblica (rabínicas, qumránicas, apócrifas y pseudoepigráficas). Lastimosamente la idea original se redujo al estudio de unos textos del evangelio de Marcos, felizmente éste ha sido realizado por el experto Miguel

Pérez, catedrático de Lengua y Literatura Hebreas de la Universidad de Granada y fundador de la Biblioteca Midrásica.

El libro trata de 9 perícopas en el Evangelio de Marcos (1:1, 2-8, 9-11, 12-13, 14-15, 16-20, 21-28, 29-31, 40-45, 6:30-46, 11:12-14) y la metodología hermenéutica de Pérez utilizada está desarrollada en cinco pasos: (1) Mostrar los escenarios, actores, palabras y acciones de la perícopa. (2) Identificar los denominados textos-fuente bíblicos del relato del evangelio. (3) Hacer una relectura del macrotexto de cada escena como una exégesis canónica. (4) Realizar la aprobación de los textos contextuales, es decir, la literatura helenística-romana. (5) Producir una relectura final a la luz de las nuevas aportaciones.

En su estudio de Marcos 1:1, al autor trata del significado de ἀρχὴ, εὐαγγελλιον, Χριστός, e Hijo de Dios. Con cada expresión hay comparaciones con el Antiguo Testamento, la literatura apócrifa, qumránica, rabínica y helenístico-romana. Un punto interesante es que Pérez observa que en el período tannaítico son muy escasas las menciones acerca del Mesías, mientras que abundan en la literatura posterior.

En la segunda perícopa, Marcos 1:2-8, el autor incluye el análisis literario junto con el escenario, actores, dichos y acciones, y observa el paralelo entre Juan el Bautista y Elías concluyendo que la vida de Juan fue una profecía sobre Jesús. Hay dos Excursos: ¿Bautizó Jesús? y El bautismo de fuego.

La sección sobre el Bautismo de Jesús (Marcos 1:9-11) incluye observaciones sobre los calificativos que allí se le dan como el ἀγαπητός ὁ ἐκλεκτός de Dios y la conexión de este título con la 'aqedah de Isaac: "La tradición targúmica y midrásica había visto en Isaac no sólo el siervo de Dios que sufre voluntariamente sino también el que experimenta la muerte para resucitar. ... Precisamente este sacrificado, mediante su 'aqedah, se convierte el liberador" (175).

En la siguiente perícopa, El Espíritu impulsa a Jesús al desierto (Marcos 1:12-13), se muestra un gran número de alusiones al Antiguo Testamento.

La sección con el título, El Programa de Jesús, Marcos 1:14-15 indica la conexión del mensaje de Jesús con Isaías, y explora la expresión "Reino de Dios". Pérez comenta que la expresión exacta "Reino de Dios" no se encuentra en la Biblia Hebrea, aunque se pueden desarrolla temas del rey y su señorío en el Antiguo Testamento. En la cuestión de la diferencia de conversión entre judíos y cristianos, la conclusión es, "La gran diferencia está una vez más en la conversión a la Ley o la conversión a Jesús. Es cierto que, con espíritu irénico, puede decirse que ambos (Torah y Jesús) son mediadores a Dios. Pero la comprensión divina de Jesús, en definitiva la fe trinitaria, impiden cualquier reduccionismo fácil" (242).

En el tema, Llamada y Seguimiento (Marcos 1:16-20), Pérez ofrece una amplia discusión sobre el modelo Elías-Eliseo como maestro-discípulo en la tradición neotestamentaria y rabínica. "El servicio y el seguimiento son dos rasgos del discipulado rabínico especialmente enfatizados en la literatura tannaítica y amoraítica, creando unas fórmulas estereotipadas. Los mismos acentos y formulación se hallan en el Evangelio" (276). Hay dos excursos sobre El acceso a la comunidad de Qumrán, y Discipulado y seguimiento en el mundo helenístico.

Sobre la sinagoga de Capernaúm, Marcos 1:21-28, la ἐξουσία de Jesús incluye una exposición sobre los escribas y otra sobre exorcismos en el mundo helenístico-romano. Acerca de Jesús, el autor observa, "las múltiples coincidencias de su enseñanza con la de los rabinos, incluso con algunas doctrinas qumránicas. Las diferencias de contenido son, no obstante, abismales, singularmente la pretensión de Jesús de que su palabra, su acción y su misma persona se erijan sobre la Torah como una nueva Torah. Éste fue el gran escándalo para escribas y la gran novedad para sus seguidores" (316).

La sección sobre Recuperación de una mujer para la *diakonía* (Marcos 1:29-31) otra vez trata de Elías y Eliseo. Se observan temas sobre las resurrecciones realizadas, la práctica medicinal en la tradición judía extrabíblica y también sobre Rabinos curadores sin mediación medicinal. Hay excursos sobre La mujer en el mundo judío y Curaciones en el mundo helenístico (El *theios aner*).

Marcos 1:40-45, Jesús frente al "Primogénito de la Muerte", incluye información sobre los leprosos en el Antiguo Testamento y el desarrollo del tema de Mesías entre ellos en la relectura del texto. Pérez observa " la progresiva autoestigmatización del Mesías que hace la literatura rabínica, o una parte de ella, recurriendo a los mismo textos bíblicos que la tradición cristiana aplica a su Mesías. Si es correcto el cuadro que hemos contemplado en Betania, 'Jesús entre los leprosos', hemos de concluir que siglos más tarde sólo Dios sabe bajo que influencia o inspiración, vieron unos rabinos a las puertas de Roma 'al Mesías entre los leprosos'" (394-95).

La multiplicación de los panes y los peces, Marcos 6:30-46, hace una comparación con el decadente banquete en el palacio de Herodes y el banquete mesiánico-escatológico. El autor desarrolla la idea que muchas de las enseñanzas de Jesús iniciaron como conversaciones de sobremesa. Hay comentarios sobre la importancia de la comida común en Qumrán.

En la perícopa de Marcos 11:12-14, La higuera que no dio fruto, el autor discuta la pregunta sí la maldición de la higuera es milagro didáctico o signo profético. Los textos fuente de la vid y la higuera son símbolos de Israel, muestran expresiones de abundancia y paz, anuncian la visita de Dios y de Mesías. La ausencia de viñas e higueras son simbolismos del desierto, el castigo divino, aunque el pueblo sigue confiando en Yahvé.

Al final de la publicación, los índices son: Analítico; Antiguo Testamento; Nuevo Testamento; Qumrán; Mishná, Tosefta y Talmud; Midrashim y textos litúrgicos; Tárgum; Apócrifos del AT; Filón y Josefo; Autores greco-romanos y de la antigüedad cristiana; y Autores. Además hay dos bibliografías: una de 30 publicaciones citadas abreviadamente y la otra con 237 referencias relevantes.

Pero una publicación importante que falta entre las fuentes bibliográficas es el comentario de Joel Marcus *Mark 1-8* (Anchor, 2000) que también emplea ampliamente la literatura judía bíblica y extrabíblica para comentar sobre el texto del evangelio.

La fortaleza del libro es su atención al detalle de la literatura judaica: Antiguo Testamento y sus Apócrifos, Qumrán y la literatura rabínica. Es una mina de textos paralelos y la publicación es completamente diferente de libros sobre las costumbres de los judíos en la época del Nuevo Testamento. Muestra la conexión intima entre el texto cristiano y el desarrollo de judaísmo. Las fuentes extrabíblicas son llamativas porque otros comentarios nuevotestamentarios no incluyen tantas.

La obra de Pérez ayuda a los académicos y a los predicadores a apreciar más el trasfondo de 9 perícopas de Marcos. La calidad del contenido da la esperanza que el objetivo original de escribir un comentario a los Evangelios desde el punto de vista de la literatura judía, se realizará.

JOHN

The Gospel and Letters of John, by Urban C. von Wahlde. Eerdmans Critical Commentary. Grand Rapids: Eerdmans, 2010. Pp. lii + 705; xvii + 929; xii + 441 (3 vols.). Paper. $180.00. ISBN 9780802809919.

George L. Parsenios, Princeton Theological Seminary, Princeton, New Jersey

Urban von Wahlde has investigated the source and redaction history of the Johannine literature for decades. This three-volume commentary on the Gospel and Letters of John is the fully considered fruit of his labors and an important contribution to the field. At a time when interpreters focus their attention largely on the final form of the Gospels, this commentary does a great service by reminding us of the justifications and value of source and redaction criticism in Johannine interpretation. In what follows, I will question some of the first principles that motivate the study, but, when taken on its own terms and in light of its own presuppositions, von Wahlde's work is a model of rigorous and disciplined scholarship.

The starting point for the entire project is the bewildering array of *aporias* that fill every page of John and "prevent a smooth and consistent reading of the material" (1:10). Von Wahlde's introductory example of such *aporias* comes from John 10:7–13, the pericope on the Good Shepherd. This problematic passage presents Jesus as both the Shepherd who enters through the gate as well as the gate itself. That is the first concern for von Wahlde. Even more significant, the image of the Shepherd does not appear until verse 11. Prior to that point, the identity and work of Jesus is explained under the image of the gate (10:7). Thus, the thieves and robbers who come before the Good Shepherd are not false shepherds but false gates. Von Wahlde calls this "nonsense" (1:11). When shepherd terminology finally does appear, the Good Shepherd does not call out to his sheep, as a shepherd might be expected to do, but rather lays down his life for the sheep. The image of the hireling who runs away is also introduced at this point, even further complicating the basic image of the shepherd. Such a complex collection of traditions indicates to von Wahlde that "the image of the sheep and the Shepherd was so meaningful to the Johannine community that it was developed in several ways"

(1:11). As the original image was reconsidered from new perspectives, the various interpretations were gradually jumbled together into the current form of John 10. Numerous other passages reflect similar circumstances in John, causing von Wahlde to conclude, "It is unrealistic to attempt to treat the text of the Gospel as a simple, unified, and coherent composition emerging from the work of a single hand" (1:12). This commentary seeks to delineate the various hands that brought the text to its current form.

Von Wahlde discerns three distinct layers of tradition in the canonical version of John, and the entire first volume of his work (totaling 705 pages with indices) explains both his method and the characteristics of each of the three layers. It is impossible here to summarize such elaborate argument in detail, but his basic method begins with a few key issues. In addition to the *aporias* noted above, von Wahlde also focuses on John's many *Wiederaufnahme*, "repetitive resumptive" clauses (1:24). Such clauses repeat previously used material, then add a new dimension. They begin with a phrase such as "When therefore…" before they introduce this new material, as at 4:30–40. But such devices only indicate the presence of different material, not whether or not the material is earlier or later. Whether something is earlier or later can only be shown by looking at other factors. This commentary focuses on three such factors (1:26-27). The first is the use of different terms for the same object or concept. In the first edition of the Gospel, for example, the religious authorities are called Pharisees, chief priests, and rulers, but in the second edition they are called the Jews (*Ioudaioi*). Second, each edition of the Gospel has a distinct narrative orientation. "For example, in the first edition, the common people feel free to debate and disagree with the religious authorities, while in the second edition the people fear 'the Jews' and avoid them" (1:26). Third are theological criteria, where the goal is to track changes from one edition to another in issues of Christology, pneumatology, eschatology, and so forth. In the second two volumes, each section of the Gospel or Letters is treated individually. Volume 2 (the commentary on the Gospel) treats each section of John by initially addressing the composition history of a given passage. The verses attributed to each edition are then treated separately, in order to clarify the message and meaning of each edition. Volume 3 comments on the Letters and places their production between the second and third editions of the Gospel.

In tracing the lines that separate the various editions, Von Wahlde attempts to avoid the pitfalls that mar the value of previous source studies of John, especially by bringing greater nuance to the task. For example, it was said above that the terms for religious leaders change between the first and second editions, from Pharisees and chief priests in edition 1 to *Ioudaioi* in edition 2. A parallel change in vocabulary occurs with the two words for miracles: signs (*sêmeia*) and works (*erga*). As von Wahlde reads the evidence, the passages that call the leaders of Israel Pharisees (i.e., the first edition) also call the miracles of Jesus "signs," while the passages that call the leaders of Israel the *Ioudaioi* (i.e., the second edition) call the miracles of Jesus "works." Yet, von Wahlde does not trace merely the appearance of a new word but focuses his attention on a word's usage. Thus, even though the term "sign" is used for miracles in the first edition, that same term is applied to Jesus' miracles in two passages that von Wahlde assigns to the second edition (2:18 and 6:30), because the term "sign" is not used in a way typical of the first edition (1:154). In these two cases, signs are requested as christological proof, which corresponds more to the theology of the second edition. A term from the first edition (sign) functions in a manner more appropriate to the second edition and so belongs to the second edition. Von Wahlde, thus, does not trace in a superficial sense the mere appearance of a new word, but he is even more attentive to the theological value of a word in a given context. Because he argues in a similarly disciplined and careful fashion at every stage, his work will need to be carefully considered from many angles in the coming years.

Nevertheless, once we take the *aporias* seriously and do not simply ignore or explain them away, do source and redaction criticism provide the best explanation for them? I still have reservations about this claim. Take the image of the shepherd discussed above. This is not the only complicated image in the Gospel. The image of "the Way" in John 14 resembles the Good Shepherd passage in at least one important respect. In John 14, Jesus initially has a conversation about "the way" on which he goes (14:4–5), but in the very next verse Jesus announces, contrary to expectations, that he actually *is* the way (14:6). Saying both that he is the way as well as that he travels on the way sounds very much like saying both that he is the gate and that he enters through the gate. The appearance of such an unusual phenomenon in two places suggests the intentional product of a single mind, not merely the haphazard splicing of various traditions. In his treatment of chapter 14 (2:620–37), von Wahlde assigns John 14:4–5 to the second edition and 14:6 to the third edition, but he does not address the play on the term "way," a play that is obscured by his source-critical approach.

The same is true of John's use of language. As noted above, von Wahlde defines the content of his several editions by tracing changes in vocabulary and subtle changes in the meaning of words. But such an argument assumes that John's use of language should be simple and consistent and that any variety or inconsistency should send us looking for editorial activity. The opposite seems to be the case, a fact that von Wahlde even recognizes in some prominent places. When Jesus questions Peter, for instance, at 21:15–17, Jesus uses not only two different words for love (*agapan*; *filein*) but also two terms for caring for a flock (*boskein*; *poimainein*); two words for the flock (sheep, *probata*; lambs, *arnia*), as well as two interchangeable verbs for the expression "to know" (*ginōskein*; *eidenai*). When von Wahlde comments on this pericope, he relies on the scholarly consensus that the change in verbs is stylistic and not substantive (2:892–94). He takes the same approach in the alternation from *esthiein* (*phagein*) to *trōgein* in John 6:50–58, where he says, "The importance of the distinction should not be exaggerated" (2:317). The same mechanism operates with other important words throughout the Gospel. Especially interesting are the various terms for seeing: *blepein*, *theasthai*, *theōrein*, *idein*, *horan*, as well as the alternation between *niptein* and *louein* in John 13:5–10. The sending of Jesus from the Father is referred to with both *apostellein* as well as *pempein*, and even the important "hour" of Jesus can be referred to both as *hôra* (2:4; 7:30; 8:20; 12:23, 27; 13:1; 17:1) and *kairos* (7:6, 8). Such a use of language is difficult to explain, but it at least reflects the rhetorical device of *variatio* (using a new word instead of repeating the same word twice), which was common in antiquity. As in the case of John's complex use of imagery, the fact that such a shift in terminology is so common throughout the Gospel suggests that it is the result of a single mind or a single group of minds and not of the poorly edited thoughts of different generations of editors. Should this assumption have any impact on theories about the relationship between the terms "signs" and "works"? Von Wahlde distinguishes the first and second editions on the basis of these terms, but he also recognizes, as we saw above, that the distinction is not perfect. The term "sign," which identifies material from the first edition, continues to appear in passages from the second edition, but it is used differently. But, given John's tendency to use alternating terms for the same referent, is it not just as likely that a single edition employed two terms differently to describe one complicated reality?

The same questions arise in regard to the theological complexity of the Gospel. When von Wahlde discusses theological *aporias* (1:12–22), he allows for two possibilities on the part of interpreters: (1) ignoring and explaining them away or (2) addressing them through source and redaction criticism. But there is a third way: addressing with them without source criticism. While Johannine theology might reflect, as von Wahlde argues, a complicated conversation spanning a long period of time and including a great many speakers, it might also reflect the complex internal dialogue of a single mind. This way of reading was championed in previous decades by scholars such as C. K. Barrett and more recently by Paul Anderson, whose work is mentioned only briefly (1:397 n. 3, 1:423 n. 68). For these interpreters, the paradox, inversion, and negation that characterize the Fourth Gospel are designed to reflect the great mystery at the heart of the incarnation, where concealment and revelation go hand in hand. The fact that every major theological theme in the Gospel involves opposing statements (both high and low Christology, both future and realized eschatology, both a positive and a negative evaluation of signs, and many others) might well be intended to force our thinking to a higher level of reflection on the incarnation and its consequences. In this way of reading, the opposing statements are not the work of various authors and editors but of a single dialectical mind.

In the end, it seems that the interpreter is confronted with two possibilities. The final form of the Gospel of John is either the result of several layers of editing or of a single but complicated reflection on the life and significance of Jesus Christ. If we are to take the Johannine *aporias* seriously, and we do not merely erase their puzzling complexity, we must rest in one of these two camps. This is not the place to decide between these approaches in any final way, of course, and the great advantage of von Wahlde's work is precisely that he keeps the debate alive by presenting his complex and careful arguments in an eminently readable and carefully constructed fashion. Skeptics may still not be convinced, but neither will they be able to ignore this serious work. It should have a key place in Johannine conversations for years to come.

The Riddles of the Fourth Gospel: An Introduction to John, by Paul N. Anderson. Minneapolis: Fortress, 2011. Pp. xiii + 296. Paper. $22.00. ISBN 9780800604271.

Cornelis Bennema, South Asia Institute of Advanced Christian Studies, Bangalore, India

Building upon his earlier work, well-known Johannine scholar Paul Anderson has produced an introductory textbook on the Fourth Gospel. Anderson writes in a clear, lucid style, making the book accessible to a broad range of readers. That alone, however, is not sufficient reason to recommend a book. There are many excellent introductions to the Fourth Gospel available, such as A. Köstenberger (*Encountering John*, 2002), R. Edwards (*Discovering John*, 2003), W. Carter (*John: Storyteller, Interpreter, Evangelist*, 2006), R. Kysar (*John the Maverick Gospel*, 2007), and J. van der Watt (*An Introduction to the Johannine Gospel and Letters*, 2008). So, one may ask whether there was a need to produce yet another one. I had two questions in mind before evaluating the book: How is this textbook distinct from others? What contribution does it make? The answers to these questions will determine the significance of the book.

After a short introduction, the book unfolds in three parts. Part 1 introduces the reader to the numerous riddles (i.e., perplexing issues) in the Fourth Gospel: theological riddles in chapter 2, historical riddles in chapter 3, and literary riddles in chapter 4. Although these chapters contain no surprises, Anderson neatly sets out for the reader the various categories of riddles. In part 2 Anderson reveals his strategy for addressing the Johannine riddles. He starts, in chapter 5, by outlining the strengths and weaknesses of various scholarly approaches to the Fourth Gospel. Anderson positions himself along the perspectives of Alan Culpepper and Raymond Brown: "the Gospel of John is best interpreted as a literary narrative with its own claims to memory and interpretation of Jesus' ministry, *whoever its author might have been*" (123). Chapter 6 is arguably the most important part of the book, for it is here that Anderson clarifies his approach to addressing the riddles of the Fourth Gospel. Anderson's theory of so-called "dialogical autonomy of the Fourth Gospel" includes the following aspects. First, Anderson considers Mark and John the "Bi-Optic Gospels," suggesting that, while John probably knew Mark, his Gospel also shows a radical independence from Mark's account. Second, Anderson contends that the theological tensions in the Fourth Gospel are not the result of multiple sources and authors but of John's dialectical approach to holding truths in tension, working in both-and ways instead of either-or ways. Third, Anderson explains his reconstruction of the Johannine community in three phases, including no less than seven crises over seven decades. Fourth, Anderson suggests a two-edition theory of composition for the Fourth Gospel—a basic first edition, by whoever the original author, as an intentional alternative to

Mark around 80–85 C.E., and the final edition by John the Elder (who also wrote the Epistles) around 100 C.E. Fifth, Anderson considers aspects of interfluentiality (i.e., mutual influence) between John and the other traditions—Mark, Luke, Q, and Matthew—resulting in a complex diagram of interrelated oral and written traditions among the Gospels (151). Chapter 7 concludes part 2 by briefly exploring the origin and character of John's theological, historical, and literary perplexities. After having outlined his theory, Anderson returns in part 3 to the Johannine riddles and shows how to interpret them by looking at the Christ of faith and Johannine theology (ch. 8), the Jesus of history in the Fourth Gospel (ch. 9), and aspects of the church (ch. 10). A brief conclusion ends the book.

I offer a few critical remarks, focusing mainly on chapter 6, the book's fulcrum. In order to reconstruct the history of the Johannine situation, Anderson engages in a two-level reading of the Fourth Gospel where "what happened" during Jesus' time correlates to "what was happening" during the various stages in the Johannine situation. Although this approach in its various shapes has been widely accepted since its introduction by Louis Martyn more than forty years ago, it has also been challenged recently by scholars such as Richard Bauckham (*The Gospels for All Christians* [Eerdmans, 1998]), Tobias Hägerland (*JSNT* 25 [2003]: 309–22), and Edward Klink (*The Sheep of the Fold* [Cambridge University Press, 2007]). Like many others, Anderson assumes (rather than argues) that such an approach is legitimate. Although Anderson briefly mentions Bauckham in chapter 5 and even concedes his proposal "a notable challenge," there is no interaction (118). There is also no reference to Richard Bauckham, *Jesus and the Eyewitnesses* (Eerdmans, 2006), where a strong argument is made for the Beloved Disciple as the real author of the Fourth Gospel. Instead, Anderson favors composition theories that sidestep the question of authorship. For example, Anderson contends that John the Elder finalized the first edition of the Fourth Gospel, adding chunks such as the Prologue, chapters 6, 15–17, and 21, and signing it off as the witness of the Beloved Disciple (21:24) (143). However, 21:24 also tells us that this "disciple [the Beloved Disciple] … has *written* these things." Are "these things" simply everything minus the Prologue, chapters 6, 15–17, and 21? Besides, although Anderson points out the aporia in 14:31, must we immediately claim that John 15–17 is thus a later edition? While I have no problem with a later editor being at work (e.g., in 7:53–8:11 and 21:24–25), it seems rather clumsy of the editor to leave in these three Greek words that translate "Get up, let's go from here" in 14:31. Is it not equally plausible that Jesus and his disciples did get up and leave and that Jesus taught the material in John 15–17 en route to the garden in 18:1? Perhaps some of the riddles have easier solutions than Anderson assumes.

I return to the questions I first posed in order to deliver the final verdict on the book. I contend that this book is distinct from other textbooks in two ways. First, it has a unique approach in that it explores the riddles or tensions in the Fourth Gospel at the theological, historical, and literary levels. Second, Anderson is able to suggest a unique way forward, a particular perspective on the Fourth

Gospel in order to resolves its riddles. The added value of the book is found in Anderson's proposal to recognize the dialogical autonomy of the Fourth Gospel as a key to unlock its riddles. Whether or not one agrees with his reconstruction of the Johannine situation and some other issues, I think it is fair to say that Anderson has successfully produced a textbook on the Fourth Gospel that is both distinct and has added value. For this we can only applaud him.

Echoes of Friendship in the Gospel of John, by Martin M. Culy. New Testament Monographs 30. Sheffield: Sheffield Phoenix, 2010. Pp. xii + 226. Hardcover. $95.00. ISBN 9781907534102.

Anne M. O'Leary, St. Mary's University, San Antonio, Texas

This monograph marks an important contribution to the study of New Testament documents, in particular, the Fourth Gospel, in the context of Greco-Roman antiquity. As a revised doctoral thesis, "Jesus—Friend of God, Friend of His Followers: Echoes of Friendship in the Fourth Gospel" (Baylor University, 2002), completed under the supervision of Mike Parsons, it is not surprising that Culy's substantial contribution has as much to do with his methodology as it does the matter under study.

Chapter 1 is entitled "Friendship, Literary Motifs and the Authorial Audience." At the outset Culy presents the thesis of the book, that, "although key terms typically associated with the notion of friendship, such as φίλος ('friend'), rarely appear, when read against the conceptual world associated with Greco-Roman notions of friendship it becomes apparent that friendship language is consistently used throughout the Fourth Gospel and, in particular, … in the farewell scene" (2), as a tool of characterizing the relationship between Jesus and his Father and Jesus and his followers (27).

Culy begins with a survey of the most recent studies on friendship in the Greco-Roman world, the New Testament, and the Fourth Gospel. His work differs methodologically from other Johannine studies to date in that "none adequately addresses the questions of how the authorial audience, or original audience, would have understood such [friendship] language" (11). His objective is to demonstrate how the motif of *ideal personal friendship* shaped the reading of the Fourth Gospel by the authorial audience, understood as "the convergence of the implied reader and the actual historical readers" (17).

Chapter 2, "Friendship in the Ancient Mediterranean World," begins by offering some methodological considerations, the most important being Culy's aim to construct "a conceptual field" rather than a "semantic field" in relation to the topic of friendship, "since the former explicitly affirms the importance of looking beyond lexical entries when studying a conventional socio-cultural phenomenon like friendship" (34). Building on the work of R. Alan Culpepper (1983), Culy finds that, as the (implied) readers were Greek-speakers, they would "have extensive knowledge of the culture in which they lived" (38).

From an in-depth examination of Greco-Roman texts (ca. 100 B.C.E.–200 C.E.), Culy isolates three *topoi* that characterize the conceptual field of ideal friendship: *unity, mutuality, and equality* (49–58). Ideal friendships were rare and occurred mostly in the private domain; further, while reciprocity was also found to be a crucial component, it ought to be the result of friendship, not the motivation (59). He also finds that, while there is a dearth of references to friendship in Jewish canonical texts, apocryphal author Ben Sira and historian Josephus both strongly reflect Greco-Roman notions of friendship in their works (76). Finally, Culy finds that the conceptual field associated with ideal friendship is reflected in some of the New Testament books and in the writings of the early fathers. His research finds that the *topoi* listed above formed "part of the sociolinguistic world that the author of the Gospel of John would have both assumed and utilized" (86).

Chapters 3 and 4 examine the topic of friendship in the Fourth Gospel. In the former, the focus in on the relationship between "Jesus and the Father"; in the latter, between "Jesus and His followers." Culy sets the scene in chapter 3 by demonstrating how the familial metaphor of "Father-Son" is greatly amplified if put in concert with the language of ideal friendship (90). He outlines how the *topoi* listed above are introduced in the overture-like Prologue (1:1–18) and developed in the portrayal of Jesus' uniquely intimate relationship with God/the Father in John 1:19–12. He observes that, while some degree of unity and mutuality characterized Greco-Roman father-son relationships, they were not characterized by equality. By contrast, Jesus' relationship with the Father reflects absolute unity ("the Father and I are one," 10:30), mutuality ("all that the Father has is mine," 16:15), and equality of nature ("the Word was God," 1:1).

Chapter 4 begins with a study of four specific individuals who are recipients of Jesus' love: Mary, Martha, Lazarus, and the Beloved Disciple. Culy demonstrates how the nature of Jesus' friendship with his followers, introduced in John 1–12, becomes greatly amplified in the footwashing pericope and the Farewell Discourse (13–17). This relationship reflects unity ("the vine and the branches," 15:1–8; the language of in-dwelling, 14:10, 11, etc.), mutuality ("the words that you gave to me I have given to them," 17:8, etc.), and the greatest degree of equality possible between the Jesus/Logos and "the children of God" (13:1; cf. 1:12, etc.). Thus Jesus' followers no longer relate to him as a slave to a master. Rather, they share a genuine friendship with him. Their acting in obedience to Jesus is out of the love of friendship rather than out of a patron-client relationship. In this way the Jesus-follower relationship mirrors the Jesus-Father relationship. Culy ends with two further insights: that the Greco-Roman *topos* that "true friendships find their ultimate expression in the willingness of one friend to die for another" (15:13; 166) is demonstrated by the death of Jesus/the "I AM" out of love for his followers (John 18–19); and that "the disciples are to relate to one another in the way that Jesus relates to them" (13:34; 174).

In chapter 5, entitled "Reading the Gospel of John as Authorial Audience," Culy makes the case that his proposed reading would *likely* match that of the authorial audience based on current research on the pervasiveness of the notion and value of ideal friendship "at all levels of society" (183). He notes the ubiquity of the language of ideal friendship in the Gospel of John relative to the Synoptic Gospels. That it occurs "often in places where such language was not necessary or at least could have been avoided" (182) provides a clue to understanding a critical dimension of the Gospel author's agenda, which Culy describes as "theologically revolutionary" (187), that "Where Greco-Roman writers tended to expound on personal friendship as an idealistic, utopian concept ... the Gospel of John makes the startling claim that such a relationship not only exists between Jesus and the Father, but is also available to Jesus' followers" (186).

Culy's work is coherent, well-argued, and richly furnished with references and footnotes. It is a timely example of the fruitfulness of reading the New Testament, in this case, the Gospel of John, with a historical consciousness of the world of Greco-Roman antiquity of which Israel was a part. His work augments current literary-critical approaches in several ways, although I will name just two: in his development and use of audience criticism; and in his development of a methodology that takes account of the characteristics of the "conceptual field" of the authorial audience of the Fourth Gospel. The friendship motif and select *topoi* provide a hermeneutical lens for the study of the relationship of Jesus and the Father. By reconfiguring material familiar to Johannine scholars in this way, Culy greatly amplifies the thesis that "something beyond the average father-son relationship was in view" (128).

Few works are typographically free or perfectly formatted, and this one is no exception (e.g., 43, 45, 47; cf. 52 and 60 for use of the same quotation). Regarding critical remarks, I have just three. First, readers may well grapple with Culy's use of headings. For example, some major sections of chapters are followed by helpful summaries, and others are not. Moreover, some major sections are as brief as a paragraph (97–98, 108–9), while one minor summary runs several pages (143–46). The omission from the table of contents of some headings in chapter 2 that are of equal status to those included is puzzling (e.g., 43–58), as are the summaries themselves, some of which include new material and significant quotations (61–62, 145).

Second, Culy's application of the *equality topos* to the study of the relationship between Jesus and his followers (ch. 4) is perhaps the weakest link of an otherwise excellent work. Culy appears to struggle with the application of this *topos* because of the reality of the ontological inequality between Jesus and his followers, which he rightly notes. He does not address clearly the nature of equality that Jesus did share with many of his first followers, for example, his humanity and socioeconomic status. Moreover, at this point of the book, it would seem opportune to develop further how the inequality between these friendship partners (Jesus and his followers) contributes to the Fourth Gospel's high Christology. It could also be an opportunity to highlight how the Christian ideal friendship surpasses that of the Greco-Romans not only because of the degree of occurrence (186) but because of the reality that Jesus' followers can share an ideal friendship with the source of all friendships (103), the Logos, while retaining their respective differences in nature. Finally, given the prevalence of the diction and notion of "the soul" in Greco-Roman, Jewish apocryphal, and Josephus's writings on friendship, Culy's work would have been enhanced had he addressed the issue of its omission in the Gospel of John (151).

Given the above, this work is a must-read for any serious scholar of Johannine literature and/or literary criticism in relation to the works of Greco-Roman antiquity.

The Son of Man in the Gospel of John, by J. Harold Ellens. New Testament Monographs 28. Sheffield: Sheffield Phoenix, 2010. Pp. xvii + 200. Hardcover. $85.00. ISBN 9781906055998.

Cornelis Bennema, South Asia Institute of Advanced Christian Studies, Bangalore, India

This monograph is J. Harold Ellens's doctoral dissertation, supervised by Professors Jarl Fossum and Gabriele Boccaccini at the University of Michigan. Ellens sets out to examine the Son of Man logia in the Gospel of John against the backdrop of other Son of Man traditions in Second Temple Judaism. His thesis is that the Johannine Son of Man is a divine savior (resembling Daniel's heavenly Son of Man), in contrast to a human being who is exalted to heaven as the eschatological judge (as we find in 1 Enoch and the Synoptics). After having defined his topic, Ellens presents a succinct history of research in three phases: the ancient precritical phase (from the church fathers to the nineteenth century), the modern critical phase (1800–1950), and the contemporary critical phase (1950–present). Regarding the third phase, Ellens observes that there have been two main trajectories in the Johannine Son of Man debate: the nonapocalyptic Son of Man who essentially resembles the one in the Synoptics (the majority position), and the apocalyptic Son of Man (the minority position). According to Ellens, the latter trajectory "breaks significant new ground by relocating the Johannine Son of Man in its original Jewish apocalyptic context" (5). From his history of research Ellens extracts three issues that will guide his research: the identity of the Johannine Son of Man, the relationship between the Johannine Son of Man and other Second Temple Son of Man traditions, and the nature of the Son of Man as judge. Ellens concludes chapter 1 with some methodological comments. He states that Second Temple Judaism was "a varied fabric of multiple and competing Judaisms" (28), from which he chooses the Gospel of John in its final form as an expression of late-first-century Judaism. Ellens stresses that his work is "a history-of-ideas assessment of the Son of Man sayings in the Gospel of John" rather than a study of Johannine Christology (31).

In chapter 2 (the longest chapter), Ellens examines all thirteen Son of Man logia in the Gospel of John. In each logion he deals with possible text-critical issues, the context of the logion, its meaning, and its theological import. In summarizing the results of his analysis, Ellens contends that the three dominant designations of the Son of Man in John's Gospel are: (1) heavenly figure; (2) revealer of God; (3) savior. Ellens sees the following correlation between these categories: the Johannine Son of Man is a heavenly figure, the descended divine Logos, and as such he is the revealer of the heavenly mysteries of God and hence the savior of the world. Ellens stresses that the Son of Man is primarily the incarnated Logos and not the man Jesus of Nazareth; that is, the divine Logos descended to earth as the Son of Man and infested a human being, Jesus of Nazareth, with the divinity and divine agency of the divine Logos (84–85). Ellens then explains that, even though the Johannine Son of Man is the judge, he does not exercise his *exousia* as judge or prosecutor. Instead, people judge themselves by their response to the Son of Man. Hence, John's Gospel does not envisage an eschatological parousia or final judgment—the day of judgment and salvation is every day that one encounters the Son of Man (85–89).

In chapter 3 Ellens looks at the Son of Man logia in the Synoptics, using Bultmann's three categories: (1) the Son of Man as human proclaimer of God's reign and the forgiver of sins on the earth; (2) the Son of Man as the messianic suffering servant; (3) the Son of Man being exalted to heaven as the eschatological judge. Ellens argues that the Son of Man in the Synoptics is an Ezekiel-like human being, Jesus of Nazareth, whom God commissions to proclaim his imminent reign and to forgive sins on earth. In colliding with the Jewish religious authorities, the Synoptic Son of Man chooses to suffer and so identifies himself with the Suffering Servant of Isa 53. God rescues this Son of Man in resurrection and exaltation to heaven as the eschatological judge who will carry out the final judgment in the parousia at the eschaton.

In chapter 4 Ellens turns to the Son of Man notions in Ezekiel, Daniel, the Parables of Enoch (1 En. 37–71), and 4 Ezra in order to explore the extent to which they might have influenced the Gospels, especially the Gospel of John. In Ezekiel, the Son of Man is merely a man who is commissioned to proclaim the imminent advent of God's kingdom. While this view seems to resonate in the Synoptics, the Ezekiel Son of Man tradition is absent from John's Gospel. The Son of Man in Daniel is a heavenly figure (a human being with heavenly status) with *exousia* to destroy evil and establish God's reign on earth. Ellens contends that both John's Gospel and the Synoptics were influenced (in different ways) by the Danielic Son of Man tradition. In 1 En. 37–71, the Son of Man is a human being, identified as Enoch, who is exalted to heaven as the eschatological judge. Again, Ellens believes that both John's Gospel and the Synoptics drew (differently) on the Son of Man tradition in 1 Enoch. For example, Ellens concludes that the Synoptic Son of Man does not simply resemble the figure in 1 Enoch but also competes with 1 Enoch in that Jesus, not Enoch, is the Son of Man. Regarding John's Gospel, Ellens argues that the author was well-acquainted with the Enochic Son of Man tradition and set himself aggressively against it. In 4 Ezra (contemporaneous with John's Gospel), the Son of Man arises from the sea to destroy evil and institute God's reign. Ellens ends by highlighting the major differences between the Son of Man concepts in the Synoptics and John. Whereas the Synoptic Son of Man is a human being who becomes a heavenly (not divine) figure as the eschatological judge who will return in the parousia, the Johannine Son of Man is the divine Logos who descends from heaven to save rather than judge the world and who returns to his heavenly home, never to return to earth.

The final chapter contains Ellens's summary and conclusion. He contends that the contribution of his study is the result of viewing the Son of Man concepts in the Synoptics and the Gospel of John in the wider context of Judaism rather than the narrow context of the development of early Christology. Ellens stresses that the Son of Man in the Gospel of John differs significantly from the one in the Synoptics. The Synoptic Son of Man is the man Jesus from Nazareth, who is eventually exalted to heavenly status as the eschatological judge and who will return in the parousia to judge the world. In contrast, the Johannine Son of Man is the divine Logos who as the Son of Man descends from heaven and becomes incarnated in Jesus and who will return permanently to his heavenly home. In John there is no eschaton, no parousia, no final judgment, because the Son of Man as the eschatological judge chooses not to judge the world but to save it. Regarding the various Son of Man traditions in Second Temple Judaism, Ellens concludes that the presentation of the Johannine Son of Man shows (1) no influence from Ezekiel, 4 Ezra, or the Synoptics; (2) clear influence from Daniel; (3) and a reverse influence from 1 Enoch (in that John's Gospel is polemical of Enoch being the true Son of Man). The unique contribution of the Gospel of John therefore is that the Johannine Son of Man will not exercise his function as eschatological judge but will operate in the world as the divine savior.

I had most difficulties with Ellens's foundational chapter 2 on the Johannine Son of Man logia. First, although Ellens competently presents a broad spectrum of views on the meaning of the logia, he often fails to evaluate them or follow the discussion through to its logical conclusion. As a result, I was left wondering what Ellens himself had concluded, and I could not detect a consistent argument throughout. For example, after providing various scholarly views regarding the meaning of the Son of Man logion in 1:51, Ellens stops abruptly, leaving me unsure what he himself thought of 1:51 (36–38; cf. 42–46, 60–64, 66–68, 69–73). Second, in some concluding sections of the logia there was a logical jump. For example, regarding 1:51, Ellens readily concludes that the Son of Man is a heavenly figure (39), but this does not seem to follow from his discussion. Or, with regard to the logion in 3:14–15, Ellens's assertion that it depicts the Son of Man as the suffering servant is abrupt rather than from argument (53). Third, in his summary that eight of the thirteen logia present the Son of Man as a heavenly figure (85), Ellens seems to conclude more than he has made a case for. In my view, he has only succeeded with the logia in 3:13; 5:27ff.; 6:51–53; and 6:62. Fourth, the degree of realized eschatology that Ellens perceives in John's Gospel rules out any future eschatology for him. However, while I agree with his argument that people judge themselves in their response to Jesus, I wonder whether this necessarily excludes a consummation of judgment in some kind of end-time event. For example, while 5:25 depicts a present reality ("the hour is coming and is already here"), 5:28–29 seems to indicate a future reality ("the hour is coming [but is *not yet* here]"). Also, Jesus' problematic sayings of his going away and coming back and the disciples' inability to see him shortly and then seeing him again in John 14 and 16 might well include a reference to a parousia at the eschaton. Fifth, in chapter 3 on the Son of Man in the Synoptics, there could have been critical interaction with, for example, Simon Gathercole, who argues for preexistence in those Son of Man logia in the Synoptics that are coupled with the "I have come" sayings of Jesus (*The Pre-existent Son: Recovering the Christologies of Matthew, Mark, and Luke* [Grand Rapids: Eerdmans, 2006]).

All things considered, I contend that his argument on the Johannine Son of Man logia needs tidying up and that the distinction between the Son of Man in the Gospel of John and that in the Synoptics is not as stark as Ellens presents it. Nevertheless, I still think Ellens has made a valuable contribution to the Son of Man debate in general.

ACTS

Restoring the Kingdom: The Role of God as the "Ordainer of Times and Seasons" in the Acts of the Apostles, by Michael A. Salmeier. Princeton Theological Monograph Series. Eugene, Ore.: Pickwick, 2011. Pp. 224. Paper. $25.00. ISBN 9781610970983.

Richard I. Pervo, St. Paul, Minnesota

This monograph is presented as the result of "a few more years of revising and reshaping" of an Oxford thesis directed by Robert Morgan (vii). As has become increasingly common, Salmeier does not state when his dissertation was accepted. The bibliography contains a few items from 2002. During those subsequent few years some substantial commentaries have appeared (e.g., D. Bock, D. Marguerat [first half], R. Pervo, D. Peterson), as well as other publications. Salmeier does cite a number of French and German authors. The vast majority of his Greek citations are unnecessary (and he utilizes the 1979 edition of Danker's translation of Bauer's *Lexicon*). The volume is quite well written and finely produced, with notes at the bottom of the page. No indices are provided.

The driving force of the work comes from Jesus' reply to his followers' inquiry whether he is about to restore the kingdom to Israel (Acts 1:6–8): "It is not for you to know the times or periods that the Father has set by his own authority. But you will receive power when the Holy Spirit has come upon you; and you will be my witnesses in Jerusalem, in all Judea and Samaria, and to the ends of the earth." Salmeier concludes and determines that God has promised the restoration. This is no more than an implicit promise. The explicit promises in verses 4 and 8 relate to the gift and arrival of the Spirit. Salmeier devotes roughly 180 pages to arguing that the promise of restoration was fulfilled, albeit not in a literal way. Prior to that he stipulates "Ten Characteristics for a Proper Portrait of God in Acts"

(2–9). Each of these seems reasonable; they are analyzed from the perspective of a history of research. Salmeier then turns to characterization, for his ostensible method is to analyze, by literary means, God as a character in Acts (12–16). He does not take up the postmodern attack on the concept of literary character. Buttressing his argument is "a pragmatic reader-response approach" (17). It is "highly likely that the implied reader is significantly sympathetic to Jewish tradition" (18). This is the fundamental problem: those urged to read Acts as sympathetic toward the religion of Israel and its contemporary practitioners will tend to agree that it views Jews and Judaism positively, despite some difficulties. Those who attempt a neutral stance are likely to be struck by the book's hostility to Jews, who are made the villains of a melodrama.

Pages 21–48 set out the implied reader's presuppositions. For comparative works Salmeier elects 2 Maccabees and Josephus, *Ant.* 15–17, fine choices. He then launches into a study of the actions that characterize God. These include what Jesus and the Spirit do. Chapter titles are: "Who Acts for God?" (49–78), "The King Who Establishes and Restores Israel's King" (79–108), "The King Who Establishes His People" (109–63), and "The God Who Directs Everything" (164–91). God is a central character in Acts and in charge of everything. But there is more. Salmeier uses his literary analysis, thin as it becomes, in support of his contention that Acts promotes a restorationist theology. Since this theology is thoroughly transformed, it can be difficult to discover what this contribution means, in short, what new or fresh this book has to offer.

Although Salmeier devotes some pages to describing his method, he does not offer a profile of the background, contexts, and proponents of restorationist theology. His implied reader is evidently expected to be quite familiar with the subject. A subject with which Salmeier does not appear to be familiar is history of religions backgrounds, especially the Greco-Roman world. Regarding the possessed slave of Acts 16:16–18, for example, he says: "Luke describes the girl in allusion to the Delphic oracle. … the reader would recognize that her announcement points the crowd away from the God preached by Paul and toward Zeus or any other god the locals considered as the principal god" (170). These judgments depend upon a misreading of secondary comments ("Delphic Oracle"), apparent ignorance of the term "most high god" and related discussion, and inattention to the constitution of Roman colonies, as well as to the cults of Philippi.

One advantage of Salmeier's method is that it can attribute his views to the implied reader. Thus knowledge of 2 Maccabees and Josephus orients readers to the view that God exercises providential beneficence (40, 44). Pages 111–12 assure that Stephen was not opposed to the temple and its cult, given earlier positive statements and because the witnesses against him were unreliable. Cornelius was not saved until he repented, as demonstrated by 11:18. The first claim is unnecessary; the second upholds his pro-Jewish thesis; the third fits a stereotyped, individualistic view of salvation. In fact, Acts 10:44–48 does not require repentance of Cornelius and his household.

With most, Salmeier views the eschatology of Acts as both present and future (although he does not take up the relation of kingdom to church). He does not delve into the theological principle that beginning and end are correlated (*Endzeit wird Urzeit*). Intertwined with this structure is the widespread notion of a primitive golden age. Both Acts and 1 Clement view the church's story from the perspective of a decline from an ideal state. Salmeier rejects this understanding (125). He has no interest in myth as source and inspiration for theology. For this reason his reflections on the restoration of the kingdom remain close to the surface. Irony emerges in his view of that restoration as taking place in a highly nonconcrete, far from literal manner. He affirms the accomplishments of early Christian theologians while locking some of their tools in a box.

The value of this work is in the number of comments and insights, many culled from a judicious reading of a range of commentaries. The major weakness is the absence of a demonstration of what the determination that Luke was a restorationist theologian would mean. Others include evident lack of adequate mastery of background and theological matters. Those who generally agree with Salmeier's views will appreciate this contribution; scholars who hold other views are unlikely to change them.

Geography and the Ascension Narrative in Acts, by Matthew Sleeman. Society for New Testament Studies Monograph Series 146. Cambridge: Cambridge University Press, 2009. Pp. xi + 300. Hardcover. $99.00. ISBN 9780521509626.

Steve Walton, London School of Theology, Northwood,
Middlesex, United Kingdom

Matthew Sleeman here presents a fresh, stimulating, and innovative study of Acts, based on his PhD thesis presented to King's College London under the supervision of Professor Richard Burridge. Sleeman is Lecturer in New Testament and Greek at Oak Hill College, London—on the basis of this monograph, one can conclude that his students have a teacher with a lively and creative mind.

Sleeman argues that geography, that is, how space is understood, portrayed, and constructed, has been neglected in New Testament studies; history, rather, has been the main focus of such study. He comes to this study with a PhD in geography behind him (yes, this *is* his second PhD thesis), and these previous studies provide the analytical tools that enable him to read Acts freshly for its portrayal and understanding of space.

The book falls into two parts. The first (chs. 1–2) lays out theoretical perspectives, assessing the state of play in scholarship of the ascension of Jesus and outlining the key theoretical tools that Sleeman will use to study Acts. The second part (chs. 3–8) works through Acts 1:1–11:18, identifying how a spatial approach provides exegetical insights into the text and arguing that the ascension of Jesus is a key feature of the story of Acts that continues to be important and influential in the development of the storyline of Acts. There is much careful consideration of detail in these chapters, and the discussion below will only be able to provide a sampling of the good work that they contain. A brief conclusion (ch. 8) summarizes key gains of the spatial approach taken and sketches possible implications for Christian understanding of space today and for further New Testament study.

In more detail, "Ascension Scholarship at the Turn of the Century" (ch. 1) identifies three key gaps in recent Acts scholarship as significant for Sleeman's project. First, his work follows in the train of, and builds upon, earlier narrative-critical work on Acts, notably that of Mikeal Parsons, whose synchronic approach to the ascension is a key jumping-off point for Sleeman. However, Parsons's project is limited by its failure to read on from the ascension narrative into the rest of Acts to see how the ascension of Jesus impacts the plot of the book. Sleeman also finds Matthew Skinner's work on narrative settings in Acts 21–28 helpful and seeks to extend Skinner's insights by arguing that *heaven* is a key setting in Acts that shapes how earthly spaces are understood. Second, Sleeman engages with the debate over whether Jesus is present or absent in the book of Acts following his ascension and, if present, in what sense. He notes that the discussion to date has focused on whether Jesus is active on earth following his ascension and that such activity has been identified as "presence" (17), then suggests that an active/passive dualism is oversimple. In the light of recent systematic-theological work on the ascension, Sleeman proposes to reconsider how far Jesus in heaven now exercises a different kind of presence on earth that is not simply presence by the Spirit as his "alter ego." Third, therefore, Sleeman sees the need for fresh consideration of the spatiality of the ascension itself and the ascension's influence on the whole storyline of Acts and the understanding of space within Acts.

The key theoretical perspective that informs Sleeman's approach is the human geography of Ed Soja, who attacks the "historicism" that has led to considerations of space and geography being neglected or actively suppressed. Thus the modern world—and, in the context of biblical studies, the ancient world—is understood through historical spectacles using analytical tools suitable for that task. Sleeman demonstrates how such a "historicist" perspective has dominated academic biblical studies, illustrating his point from the few articles covering geographical themes in the *Anchor Bible Dictionary*—startlingly, the first major Bible dictionary to engage in any depth at all with such themes. Study of Luke-Acts, where it has considered geography, has placed Jerusalem or Rome at the center of the narrative and has focused on the historical development of the narrative, whether Hans Conzelmann's threefold schematization of history or James Scott's reading of Acts that identifies geography with tradition. Both approaches neglect the heavenly dimension of reality as constructed by Luke and the early Christians.

What Sleeman gains from Soja is the analysis of three ways of viewing space. "Firstspace" denotes external, material spatiality, the "geography" of Acts familiar from maps of Paul's journeys—here, objectivity is privileged as focus. "Secondspace" denotes how material space is conceptualized and understood, whether ideologically or architecturally; in the context of Acts, we may think of the "vibes" carried by particular locations or groups of locations, such as the

Jerusalem temple or Herod's palace at Caesarea—here, rationality and imagination are privileged. "Thirdspace" goes beyond the dualisms inherent in both firstspace and secondspace ways of seeing spaces as "simultaneously real [firstspace], imagined [secondspace] and more (both and also…)" (thus Soja, quoted on 44–45). Soja's Marxist orientation means that thirdspace is emancipatory, that is, aimed at improving the state of the world. Sleeman illustrates helpfully using the Christmas truces on the Western Front in 1914 (47).

What does this look like when Sleeman reads Acts? His seminal and key discussion is of Acts 1:6–11 (ch. 3, esp. 68–81). He notes the fourfold mention of heaven in 1:10–11 and argues cogently that the present location of Jesus in heaven is a key perspective for reading Acts' understanding of space, rejecting the dualisms offered in 1:6 (now or then? Israel or not? etc.). He regards this insight as more important than the standard reading that 1:8 provides a "table of contents" for the book of Acts that focuses on firstspace (geographical) expansion and secondspace conceptualization ("the end of the earth"—a marker signaling the whole of the created order). Rather, the ascension of Jesus and Jesus' departing words in 1:8 reconceptualize earthly space as *witnessing*-space that will create "distinctive earthly believer-spaces" (78) that draw their meaning from the presence of Jesus in heaven. The narrative, in other words, is orientated around heaven, and Christ's location in heaven rather than, for example, Jerusalem or Rome—or, for that matter, seeing Acts as the journey of the gospel message from Jerusalem to Rome (as is frequently asserted).

Reading on into 1:12–26, Sleeman notices that Judas's apostasy is spatial, for he chose his own *way* and became a guide (ὁδηγοῦ) to the Jewish authorities to invade Jesus-space in the garden. Peter thus "brokers space according to its production arising from Christ's ascension" (88) and seeks another to fill Judas's *place* (τόπος, 1:25, twice).

In chapter 4, Sleeman reads 2:1–6:7 spatially and shows the continuing role of the ascended Christ in the narrative. Acts 2:2 specifies that the noise came "from *heaven*," which is Jesus' present location, identified clearly in 1:10–11. Similarly, 2:5 notes that there are Jewish people present from "every nation *under heaven*"—while this is a secondspatial description, conceptualizing universality, it also points to a christological reading of the Pentecostal gift of the Spirit, identifying all nations as included in the gospel's reach. This perspective, Sleeman argues, critiques interpretations that prioritize Jerusalem's place in the geography of Acts, for Christ is present in heaven and events are driven from there, not from Jerusalem.

This heavenly perspective allows Sleeman to engage freshly with the role of the Jerusalem temple in Acts, long a matter of dispute among scholars. He first notes parallels between the healings of paralytics in Luke 5:17–26 and Acts 3 and observes acutely that both have a christological focus: the former is about Jesus' authority "on earth" to forgive sins (Luke 5:24), and the hearing before the Sanhedrin consequent on the latter highlights that Jesus' name alone "under heaven" saves (Acts 4:12). This leads him to argue that "Christocentric repentance" (110) is now the means and marker of membership in Israel: the temple's claims to have thirdspatial status as enabling access to God is being undermined.

When the believers pray (Acts 4:23–31), their prayer engages with this heaven-centered geography, noting that Jerusalem Jews ("in this city," 4:27) opposed the *heavenly* Jesus and his witnesses. God is the one who controls geography (4:28—as well as history, we might add) and will continue to "bridge heaven and earth" (118) with signs and wonders (4:30, 31).

Sleeman's consideration of Acts 6:8–8:3 (ch. 5) develops some of these themes and goes further. A key exegetical insight here is that 7:55–56 should be seen as part of Stephen's speech—indeed, as the speech's climax—rather than a detached comment. Sleeman cogently argues that a number of cotextual features indicate this (see 141 for details). The point, of course, is that this part of the speech locates Jesus in heaven, at God's right hand, climaxing Stephen's portrayal of sacred geography as it pertains to Abraham, Joseph, Moses, and the divine dwelling-place—it is because of his assertions about heavenly Christ that Stephen is killed. Following on the heels of Stephen's death, the scattering of the believers (8:1) carries through the geographical implications of Stephen's speech and prepares for the impact of ascension geography on the wider Roman world.

Acts 8:4–9:31 then tells stories focused in three different locations—Samaria, the Gaza road and the Damascus road—and Sleeman argues that each contains elements of ascension geography (ch. 6). The Samaritan section depends on heavenly initiative and power, both in the signs and wonders that Philip does (8:6–7) and in the descent of the Spirit (8:17). In discussing Philip's encounter with the Ethiopian eunuch, Sleeman questions the "historicist" concern for identifying the "first" Gentile convert and argues instead that there a number of "firsts" better expresses the heavenly ascension-geographical perspective of 1:6–11: Acts is more interested, in other words, in the way different Gentiles in different places come to faith in Jesus through different means and different "ministers of the word." In considering Saul's Damascus road experience, Sleeman rightly highlights the christological encounter that involves Jesus appearing *from heaven* (9:3). The absent Jesus is not inactive (201) but intervenes in Saul's travels and then in Ananias's life ("the Lord" in 9:10 is Jesus). Sleeman helpfully notes that Judas (9:11) is unlikely to be a believer, and thus the exalted Jesus is asking Ananias to enter potentially hostile space in going there. Saul's baptism leads to him moving from private space into public space (9:20) and being an agent in reordering that space in relation to the exalted Jesus (9:22).

Finally, Sleeman turns to Acts 9:32–11:18 (ch. 7). The centerpiece of this discussion is his consideration of the Cornelius story (10:1–11:18), where he notes yet again the heavenly provenance of both Cornelius's and Peter's visions (10:3, 11, 16, 22). Peter's speech expounds ascension geography as including anyone anywhere who fears God, which now means to respond in faith to Jesus, who is "Lord of all" (10:36)—Lord of all *places* and people. Heaven then intervenes in the descent of the Spirit on the auditors (10:44), which leads Peter to reorder earthly believer-space according to ascension-geographical priorities in ordering that they should be baptized (10:47-48a) and in accepting hospitality in a Gentile space (10:48b). Peter's response to the criticisms he receives on his return to Jerusalem for this last action (11:3) is to reiterate the heavenly nature of what has happened—in his vision (11:5, 9, 10: "from/to heaven"), the actions of the Spirit (11:12, 15–17), and the angel's visit to Cornelius (11:13). This is what persuades the critics to reorder their understanding of Israel-space as believer-space that can include Gentiles (11:18).

Sleeman argues that by 11:18 the ascension geography set out in 1:6–11 has been played out sufficiently so that at a firstspace level, physical location is no barrier to encountering God; at a secondspace level the nature of Israel is being renewed and reordered by the thirdspatial interventions of God, the exalted Jesus and the Spirit. Thus believer-space is now to be ordered by understanding heaven as the center of affairs.

Sleeman's "Concluding Reflections" (ch. 8) provides a helpful summary and identifies a number of benefits that flow from the spatially focused approach that he takes. He is undoubtedly right that there are insights that his approach identifies and highlights that are generally missed in other historically focused approaches. In particular, his central theme, that the ascension of Jesus has a continuing effect in the narrative so that space (first, second, and third!) is being reordered around the exalted Jesus and his priorities and concerns is persuasive and has profound implications for the reading of Acts and, we may add, other New Testament documents (particularly those that highlight the exalted status of Jesus). His discussion also begins to make sense of the interplay of Jesus' absent-yet-active role, not least in expanding the understanding of geography to include the heavenly dimension. Luther is said to have chided Erasmus, "Your ways of thinking of God are too human"; Sleeman rightly chides New Testament scholarship with thinking in too earthly a way.

In places Sleeman may overplay his hand a little, I think, in that some of what he says stems from a geographical perspective has previously been noticed—for example, his discussion of the Ethiopian eunuch identifies a number of points that his spatial approach certainly illuminates, but many of these are points recognized in other ways without the use of "space" language. That makes me wonder, in places, whether the geographical heavy artillery of Soja (who, it must be said, is not always easy to understand) is entirely necessary to the key insights that Sleeman has identified.

That said, Sleeman has utilized Soja's theoretical framework well to harvest insights into Acts that are helpful, relevant, and (in the case of his understanding of the ascension) game-changing. This is a book that deserves a very wide audience in New Testament studies, and not just in studying Acts, for its insights and approach open new vistas (even new spaces). Space may not be the *final* frontier in biblical studies, but Sleeman has shown that it is one that requires further exploratory voyaging.

Perfect Martyr: The Stoning of Stephen and the Construction of Christian Identity, by Shelly Matthews. Oxford: Oxford University Press, 2010. Pp. viii + 226. Hardcover. $65.00. ISBN 9780195393323.

Robert Brawley, McCormick Theological Seminary, Durham, North Carolina

The burden of *Perfect Martyr* is to determine the rhetorical effect of the stoning of Stephen. Shelly Matthews, formally Professor of Religion at Furman University but newly appointed at Brite Divinity School, argues with strong conviction that the account in Acts is a fictive narrative (appropriate nods to Hayden White), the rhetorical force of which is to portray Stephen in such a way as to arrogate Israel's heritage while creating Christian identity separate from Judaism. This rhetoric of identity is also a rhetoric of violence against *Ioudaioi*. To her task Matthews devotes an introduction, four chapters, and an epilogue, all packed with her own skillful rhetoric and an impressive array of information.

The introduction establishes that the *Ioudaioi* of Jerusalem (Diaspora included) are agents of Stephen's execution and participants in a discourse that creates a martyr. Reading Acts in a trajectory toward martyrologies, Matthews, along with a small but impressive cluster of Lukan scholars, locates it in the second century, conceptually close to Justin Martyr and aligned with anti-Marcionism. She construes identity as binary opposition that creates a sharp break: Christ-believers are set off against unbelieving *Ioudaioi* perniciously. Simultaneously, Acts represses imperial violence, which in the following chapter is attributed to colonial mimicry. Her arguments against the possibilities of finding a historical kernel of Stephen's death are effective. This implies Luke's increased responsibility for anti-Judaism and also dictates a methodology that focuses on rhetoric and the ethics thereof.

Chapter 1 argues that the rhetoric of Acts denigrates non-believing *Ioudaioi*, associates the identity of Christ-believers with imperial values, and responds to Marcionism. Matthews finds the narrative kyriarchal, as indicated by the lack of women who prophesy (in spite of Peter's quotation of Joel in Acts 2) and by women's silence in general. Moreover, Acts smoothes over conflict with the empire. Because cadres of scholars argue for more positive views toward *Ioudaioi* and more critical views of the empire in Luke-Acts, Matthews seeks to counter such views. Her basic criterion for determining Luke's attitude toward *Ioudaioi* is whether their status depends on belief in Jesus or not. Especially arguments for a universal perspective in Acts are countered by the notion that universalizing rhetoric advances Christian superiority. Indeed, Acts allegedly evaluates nonbelieving *Ioudaioi* as inferior subjects of empire. (Does Gamaliel not appear as a highly regarded nonbeliever?) The views toward both *Ioudaioi* and empire are located under the umbrella of second-century opposition to Marcionite ideas. So against Marcion's break between a violent God of Israel's scriptures and the merciful Father of Jesus, Luke-Acts advocates continuity between the divine warrior and the God of peace. From this second-century perspective, the desires of the characters in Luke 1–2 for peace and

Israel's consolation are ironically inverted by the actual destruction of Jerusalem into culpability of the *Ioudaioi*.

The next chapter develops a complex nexus within which to explicate the story of Stephen. Reiterations of the guilt of *Ioudaioi* and the innocence of Romans in both the death of Jesus and the persecution of Christ-believers form a matrix that is intensified by the failure of Acts to reflect the tradition of Paul's martyrdom at the hands of Romans. Further, Gamaliel's counsel passes over Roman responsibility for the demise of Theudas and Judas but lays the foundation for perceiving the actions of nonbelieving *Ioudaioi* as fighting against God. Because Stephen encounters conflict in a synagogue context but is tried before temple leadership, he comes into this matrix as a bridge between early apostolic activity in the temple and Paul's eventual activity in synagogues. The observations that after Stephen's death *ho laos* ceases to designate Jews sympathetically and occurrences of *hoi Ioudaioi* increase with the emergence of the name "Christians" are taken as indicators of separate identities. (Curiously, a positive use of *ho laos* occurs in 26:23.) Stephen's speech is taken as opposition to the temple rather than as a theological understanding of it. When the tradition of the persecution of prophets surfaces in Stephen's speech, it explicitly applies to Jesus and implicitly to Stephen and Paul. Further, Matthews notes that, according to imperial values, stoning was barbarous/un-Roman, and she attributes such imperial values to Acts.

Given a second-century setting of Acts, chapter 3 is an innovative reading of Stephen's death in comparison with the martyrdom of James the brother of Jesus. This adds confirmation to Matthew's challenge of the historical reliability of Stephen as a martyr and of the violence attributed to *Ioudaioi*. When Hegesippus's presentation of James's death is read in comparison with Stephen's story, the rhetorical strategy of providing an etiology of separate identities of Christians and *Ioudaioi* comes to the fore. In spite of Stephen's summary of a long course of Israel's history, Matthews again focuses on the temple and Stephen's Christology as the flashpoint of what she calls "lynch justice." A comparison of the Pseudo-Clementine *Recognitions* with Acts indicates that Acts is more polemical toward *Ioudaioi*. Further, in contrast to Acts, when Josephus reports the deaths of James and John the Baptist, he also reports Jewish opposition to their deaths. Matthews notes that Josephus depicts the imperial system, including the Jewish client king and Roman governor, and alleges that this is absent from Acts.

The final chapter evaluates the rhetorical function of Stephen's prayer for forgiveness. Distinguishing transitive (the meaning for those for whom the prayer is made) from intransitive readings (the meaning for the one praying), Matthews determines that the prayer is ineffectual for those who execute him but characterizes Stephen/Christianity as ethically superior to Judaism. She buttresses this argument with early Christian interpretations of such things as the final prayer of James (Hegesippus), dominical sayings regarding prayer for enemies, Jesus' prayer for his executioners, and the *lex talionis*. Matthews also aligns these prayers for forgiveness with imperial rhetoric for clemency, which makes claims for peace but by means of violence. Luke-Acts thus heaps "rhetorical violence ... upon rhetorical violence" (130).

Seldom have I learned so much from a book and simultaneously dissented so much. The book is a pearl of research, thoroughly and astutely annotated. Matthews makes the best case I have read for a second-century anti-Marcionite setting for Acts. With one exception, virtually every time questions came to my mind, the author dealt with them. The exception is the absence of God as an actant in the story. To be sure, God is characterized in terms of an anti-Marcionite continuity with Israel's story. But the way Luke-Acts portrays God's fidelity to Abrahamic covenant traditions is viewed primarily in terms of martial violence. I also consider that clemency redounding to the honor of an emperor who grants it and prayer to God, the outcome of which is unspecified, are distinct enough to put into question the rhetorical equivalence that Matthews gives them.

In a discussion about the ethics of reading, Matthews acknowledges that interpreters are responsible for their interpretations but takes my own references to the ethics of reading to mean that I claim ethical high ground for my own reading. What I had hoped to do was to make a methodological appeal for differentiating among *Ioudaioi* to the extent that Luke-Acts does and for refusing to vilify them beyond what the text does. Whereas Matthews clearly acknowledges ambivalence in Luke-Acts toward *Ioudaioi* and Rome, she opts for a monolithic characterization of both in binary rather than nuanced terms. To make a case for a nuanced reading of the Stephen incident, "some" from a specific synagogue are differentiated from its other members. They are also differentiated from the high priest and the council who interrogate Stephen, and when Stephen is stoned the last antecedent for the indefinite "they" who carry it out are those seated in the council (e.g., Acts 6:15; 7:54). What is more, does the absence of the term *Ioudaioi* in the account urge caution against calling them a "mob of Jews"? To be sure, whoever they are, they are characterized with high levels of rage. Nevertheless, as negative as their rage is, should this characterize all unbelieving *Ioudaioi* in Luke-Acts? What warrants taking the death of one Christ-believer at the hands of specific characters as implicating all nonbelieving *Ioudaioi* as "originary murderers of Christians" (78)? Is Stephen a cipher for Christianity? Do the actions of the council and some members of a synagogue who incite others tar all *Ioudaioi*? Further, should Lukan characterization of *Ioudaioi* be intensified beyond what the text says with terms such as "barbarous," "vile," "villainous," "savage," and "rabid"? One final suggestion is that, when attention is given to imperial systems of governors, client kings, indigenous ruling elites, and vanquished subjects, distinctions between *Ioudaioi* and imperial systems are not easily drawn (see Luke 3:1–6; Acts 4:25–26 [deemphasized by Matthews as pre-Lukan tradition]). These questions notwithstanding, the book is a weighty contribution to the study of Luke-Acts.

PAUL AND THE PAULINE EPISTLES

Reading Romans in Pompeii: Paul's Letter at Ground Level, by Peter Oakes. Minneapolis: Fortress, 2009. Pp. xiii + 194. Paper. $39.00. ISBN 9780800663599.

Richard A. Wright, Oklahoma Christian University, Oklahoma City, Oklahoma

Peter Oakes sets out to accomplish two tasks in this volume: (1) to show that in the first century there was diversity involving social stratification among the nonelite and to illustrate its shape from evidence at Pompeii; and (2) to imagine what it might have sounded like to hear Paul's letter to the Romans in relation to such social diversity (xi).

In chapter 1 Oakes takes the reader on a guided tour through the remains of four houses in the Insula of the Menander (region I, block 10). He describes the physical structure of each house, provides a description of the loose objects recovered from the excavations, and, finally, reconstructs the occupants suggested by the physical remains of these houses. Oakes imagines four individuals representing very different nonelite positions along the socioeconomic spectrum: two slaves and two craft-workers.

The first house explored (house 6, which is only 40 m^2) appears to have been the dwelling of someone who worked with stone; the residents lived among their work. Oakes suggests that two persons could have lived in a house this size and that they were likely freed persons who struggled to survive from day to day (10). The second house in Oakes's tour was also likely inhabited by a craft-worker. This house (house 7, which is 310 m^2) is much larger than the first. Oakes suggests that the owner of this house was a cabinetmaker (32). The occupants were not elite but were far from poverty. The third house appears to have been a local tavern (house 2–3). Graffiti on the walls indicate that a barmaid worked there. Oakes suggests that, from what we know about slaves in this type of environment, she would likely have been compelled to offer sexual favors to clients (36). Finally, Oakes takes the reader into house 4, where the painting of Menander was discovered and for whom the house (and insula) gets its name. The owner was likely a member of the elite. One feature of this house was a bath that would have required a slave to keep its furnace going. This kind of slave would not have held much hope of manumission (42).

In chapter 2 Oakes expands his data set to see the degree to which the social stratification suggested by the houses in the Insula of Menander is representative of Pompeii and Herculaneum more generally. Oakes compares the space distribution seen within the Insula of Menander to the distribution of space seen in an additional 230 houses located in Pompeii and Herculaneum. The distribution appears similar.

Oakes acknowledges that his space-distribution model is limited in that it provides data for only about an eighth of the population, that is, householders. The model says nothing about the income of half of the population: slaves or dependents of other kinds living in someone else's house or the homeless. But this kind of limitation is not unique to Oakes's model. Oakes provides a brief comparison of his model with other models, arguing that his model is no less deficient than others and that it offers the advantage of revealing "vertical scale" within a part of the socioeconomic spectrum previously less well-defined (67–68).

In chapter 3 Oakes constructs a model of a house church consisting of approximately forty people: the host (the cabinetmaker) and his wife, children, slaves, and dependent relatives; several other householders with smaller houses, some spouses, children, slaves, and other dependents; members of households whose head is not Christian; slaves whose masters are not Christian; a couple of free or free dependents on people who do not belong to the church; and a couple of homeless people. To account for the higher living expenses in a major city such as Rome, Oakes modifies his model, suggesting that a craft-worker such as the cabinetmaker could not have afforded a house of the same size in Rome. Therefore, Oakes reduces the number of members to thirty people. Oakes maintains a similar socioeconomic composition for this smaller church.

With chapter 4, Oakes begins the section of the book where he considers how members of his model house church would have heard Paul's words. Oakes divides Rom 12 into sense-units and provides a translation of the verses plus translation notes before commenting on how he thinks the words would have sounded to the characters in his hypothetical church. Not surprisingly, most of Oakes's observations focus on status and economic considerations. For example, Oakes suggests that Paul's exhortation not to think too highly of oneself and that the Roman Christians should consider themselves members of one body (v. 3) would have challenged the system of honor (101). He asserts that the body metaphor in 12:4–5 would have been a "radical assault on the hierarchical assumptions that flowed from the status system" (102). He points out that the possibility of offering hospitality (12:13) required economic resources that many of the members of the model church would not have had (116). This observation in particular follows from the physical evidence from the houses in the Insula of Menander.

In chapter 5 Oakes takes each of the constructed characters from his model church and suggests ideas or themes from Paul's letter that might have particularly resonated with that person. He argues that Paul's promise of an improved status and God's justice would have appealed to a slave on the bottom rung of the socioeconomic spectrum, such as the one who kept the bath furnace stoked (132–37). The themes of endurance and eternal life would have appealed to a destitute craft-worker like the stoneworker because of the challenges of surviving day to day (138–40). He also suggests that, even though Paul does not explicitly deal with sexual ethics in Romans, the body metaphor would have caught the attention of a barmaid who would not have had control over her body (144).

Chapter 6 focuses on the cabinetmaker. Oakes wonders how the Jewish aspects of Paul's letter would have sounded to a person who likely would have held a cultural disdain toward Jews (150–51). Oakes also wonders how the language of holiness would have sounded to a person in this social location (164). Oakes brings the study to conclusion in chapter 7, where he discusses five ways that the results of his project surprised him.

The strength of Oakes's book is in the execution of his first task: the illustration of stratification among the nonelite. For example, the data from the Insula of Menander highlights in striking ways the distance between two households (the stoneworker and cabinetmaker) that previously would have been identified as sharing the same social location. To be able to see the layout of the houses in a floor plan and see photographs of the spaces, and to have access to a list of the items discovered in the rooms, brings the living spaces of the ancient world to life in a very tangible manner.

The execution of Oakes's second task (imagining what it might have sounded like for certain social types to hear the letter) is in some ways less satisfying. This is the case in two ways. First, with respect to Oakes's reading of Rom 12, his discussion of any one topic is so brief that his observations cannot be anything more than suggestive. Oakes admits that, given the primary agenda of his project, his observations on Romans will be less substantial. He states that "it seemed important to put all these points together, even though my handling of them could undoubtedly be improved upon" (175).

A second limitation concerns his reconstruction of the "agendas" that these social types might bring to the letter. What is missing from this discussion is precisely the kind of comparative data that makes his description of the socioeconomic strata so compelling. The archaeological data provide controls for the kinds of physical spaces that might be imagined for an early Christian house church, given certain kinds of occupations. If the cabinetmaker who lived in house 7 of region I, block 10, had converted to Christianity and hosted a church in his house, we know the amount of space available and have some idea of what it would have looked like. We do not have similar controls for the subjective experiences of people in those socioeconomic layers. We do not have textual evidence that provide access to the perspectives of persons engaged in the occupations practiced in those spaces in Pompeii. So when Oakes suggests a topic in Paul's letter that might have caught the attention of one of these social types, we do not have the necessary data to distinguish what would be reasonable for a first-century person from what seems reasonable to a twenty-first-century person. Again, Oakes is sensitive to the issue. He writes, "[to] move from social types to specific agendas is clearly a radical simplification that could in fact lose the first-century concreteness of the social types we drew from the archaeological evidence at Pompeii" (129).

As a whole, Oakes's volume is a valuable contribution to our understanding of the social location of Pauline churches. He sharpens our understanding of the social circumstances in which Paul's missionary activity took place. He also provides an imaginative reading of portions of Paul's letter to the Romans in that social context. The volume includes black and white photos, floor plans for the Insula of Mender, a bibliography, and indexes of biblical references, modern authors, and subjects.

The Spirit and the Restoration of Israel: New Exodus and New Creation Motifs in Galatians, by Rodrigo J. Morales. Wissenschaftliche Untersuchungen zum Neuen Testament 2/282. Tübingen: Mohr Siebeck, 2010. Pp. xii + 200. Paper. €49.00. ISBN 9783161504358.

Sigurd Grindheim, Fjellhaug International University College, Oslo, Norway

Inspired by N. T. Wright, yet refreshingly independent, Rodrigo Morales sets out to show how Paul's gospel concerns the restoration of Israel. In this book he studies the role of the Spirit in Paul's argument in his letter to the Galatians. His thesis is that the eschatological outpouring of the Spirit accomplishes what the law was powerless to do: bring about the eschatological blessing of life. The book is a lightly revised doctoral dissertation from Duke University, supervised by Richard Hays.

Morales situates Galatians in a Jewish context and mines the Old Testament and the literature of Second Temple Judaism for expectations regarding the eschatological outpouring of the Spirit. In the Old Testament he turns to Isa 11:1–16; 32:15–20; 42:1–9; 43:14–44:8; 48:16; 57:14–21 LXX; 59:15b–21; 61:1–11; 63:7–64:12; Ezek 11:14–21; 18:30–32; 36:16–38; 37:1–14; 39:21–29; Joel 3:1–5. In these texts the outpouring of the Spirit is related to the idea of a new creation as well as to the regathering and restoration of Israel in a new exodus.

Proceeding to the literature from Second Temple Judaism, Morales finds Jub. 1; 1QS 3:13–4:26; 4Q504; 4Q521; Pss. Sol. 17; 1 En. 49; 61; 62; T. Jud. 23–25; and T. Levi 18 to be particularly relevant. Several of these texts attest to the idea that God's Spirit will address the problem of Israel's disobedience, a problem that may be located in their hearts.

The heart of the book is the chapter on the role of the Spirit in Gal 3 and 4. Morales finds the question of the Spirit to be central to this section of the letter, as Paul begins his argument with a question regarding the Galatians' receiving of the Spirit (3:2). In his discussion of these chapters, Morales finds that Paul may be inspired by a number of themes from the Old Testament prophets, particularly regarding their expectations of the outpouring of the Spirit. In general, Morales argues not for specific allusions but rather thematic connections. In the case of Gal 3:2, however, he makes an exception, suggesting that the phrase ἐξ ἀκοῆς πίστεως (NRSV: "believing what you heard") alludes to Isa 53:1 LXX: τίς ἐπίστευσεν τῇ ἀκοῇ ἡμῶν ("who believed our message"). He also thinks that Isaiah's fourth Servant Song underlies Paul's argument in Galatians.

The most detailed discussion in the book is devoted to the notorious crux in Gal 3:10–14. Morales argues that Paul did not speak in hypotheticals when he quoted the curse from Deut 27:26. Rather, this curse was already a fact that affected all Israel due to their disobedient heart. Relying on an article by Joel Willitts, Morales shows that Ezekiel and Nehemiah also understood this curse to be in effect. In contrast to James Scott and N. T. Wright, Morales observes that Paul understood the curse not as exile but as death. Israel's predicament, as it is reflected in Galatians, is not that they continue to be in a state of exile but that they cannot be free from death.

Turning to Gal 4:1–7, Morales maintains that Paul saw Israel's history as a time of immaturity and slavery under idols. Arguing that this passage refers to Jewish Christians, Morales sees the outpouring of the Spirit as the remedy for Israel's predicament, a predicament that could not be remedied by the law. In the fifth and final chapter, Morales argues that Gal 5 and 6 are closely related to Gal 3 and 4. They continue to unpack the significance of the eschatological outpouring of the Spirit.

There is much to commend in this work. It shows that there are numerous connections between Paul's argument in Galatians and Jewish eschatological expectations. Along the way, Morales points out a number of plausible connections between Galatians and various Old Testament passages. He wisely emphasizes that the connections are thematic and does not identify specific allusions. His argument is therefore difficult to falsify, which of course also makes it difficult to decide what level of certainty to attribute to the many proposed connections.

Morales's appeal to the Old Testament prophets provides solid arguments for his interpretation of Gal 3:10, that all of Israel de facto was under the curse. For his observations, Morales refers to Joel Willitts. Other scholars have presented very similar arguments, including Preston Sprinkle and myself, but Morales has reached his conclusions independently of these studies.

As much as I applaud Morales's understanding of Israel's plight, however, I cannot help but feel that he has overstated his case with respect to the solution. He concludes that "the Spirit gives the eternal life that the Law failed to produce throughout Israel's history" (162). To be sure, the gift of the Spirit is essential to Paul's understanding of the solution, but the chief contrast in Galatians is between faith and works of the law, not between the Spirit and the law.

The exaggerated emphasis on the outpouring of the Spirit can be seen in Morales's discussion of the Old Testament in chapter 1, where he concludes that "each of these texts connects the outpouring of the Spirit on all of God's people with the restoration of Israel" (40). Most of the texts in question attribute the Spirit to an individual—the messianic king, the prophet, or the Servant of the Lord—rather than to all of God's people.

In chapter 5 Morales refers to "the righteousness that one receives from the Spirit on the basis of faith" (137). This statement is presented as a paraphrase of Gal 5:5–6, but as such it is quite tendentious. Neither in Gal 5:5–6 nor anywhere else does Paul say that one receives righteousness from the Spirit.

It also seems to me that Morales tries to force Paul into a predetermined pattern when he focuses on the connection between the giving of the Spirit and the restoration of Israel and when he insists that the outpouring of the Spirit "opens up the blessing of Abraham to the Gentiles" (131). Morales argues that all the first-person plural verbs in Gal 3:10–4:7 refer to Jewish Christians. By reading the text in this way, he is able to maintain the focus on Israel's restoration. In any case, however, the starting point for the whole argument in Gal 3 and 4 is the observation that the Spirit was given to the uncircumcised Gentile Galatians (3:2), as Morales also emphasizes. Paul's question in Gal 3:2 concerns how they received the Spirit in the first place, not what the Spirit accomplished. When Morales discusses the results of the spiritual outpouring, he seems to confuse cause and effect. The Spirit does not open up for the Gentiles to receive the blessing; the presence of the Spirit proves that the blessing has already been given to them.

Morales's work demonstrates that the discussion about Paul's theology has moved well beyond the old categories of "new perspective" and "traditional." Morales fits neither label and is able to present stimulating challenges to us all.

1 Corinthians 1–4: Reconstructing Its Social and Rhetorical Situation and Rereading It Cross-Culturally for Korean-Confucian Christians Today, by Oh-Young Kwon. Eugene, Ore.: Wipf & Stock, 2010. Pp. 316. Paper. $35.00. ISBN 9781608994328.

Yongbom Lee, Dominican Biblical Institute, Limerick, Ireland

This book is a revised version of Oh-Young Kwon's doctoral dissertation submitted to the Melbourne College of Divinity under the supervision of Keith Dyer, Professor of New Testament at Whitley College in Melbourne, Australia. This study is a good example of an interdisciplinary and cross-cultural reading of Paul. Kwon utilizes a sociorhetorical approach in reconstructing the background of 1 Cor 1–4 and discerning the core of Paul's message, and he relates his findings to Korean Christianity today. Kwon considers Cicero (a first-century B.C. Roman philosopher) as the cultural representative of the first-century A.D. Roman Corinth. Similarly, Kwon considers T'oegye (a sixteenth-century A.D. Korean Confucian philosopher) as the cultural representative of the twenty-first-century A.D. Korean Confucian culture. This study involves four parties in dialogue: Paul, the Corinthian believers, the author himself, and twenty-first-century Korean Christians.

In chapter 1 Kwon provides a critical review of recent scholarship on the problems Paul addresses in 1 Cor 1–4. In chapters 2 and 3 Kwon investigates the sociorhetorical background of the first-century A.D. Roman Corinth. In chapters 4 and 5 Kwon offers his sociorhetorical analysis of 1 Cor 1–4. In chapter 6 Kwon summarizes his sociorhetorical analysis of 1 Cor 1–4 and concludes that 1 Cor 1–4 "critically engages the consequences of an uncritical use of Greco-Roman rhetorical conventions and social and patronal networks that was evident in the improper mentality and behavior of some in the Christian community" (189). In chapter 7 Kwon discusses the cross-cultural hermeneutics of 1 Cor 1–4 for Korean Christians today. In the appendix, Kwon briefly surveys the life and works of Cicero and T'oegye. Chapter 7 is particularly interesting, as Kwon compares the sociorhetorical situation of the Corinthian church with that of twenty-first-century Korean Christians. Based on his reflections, Kwon calls for the theological reevaluation of some controversial issues in Korean Christianity today, such as "Shinto shrine worship," "ancestor veneration," and "monoethnic community."

First, "Shinto shrine worship" refers to Korean Christians' response to the imposed worship practice of the Japanese imperial cult during the Japanese occupation of Korea (1935–1945). Kwon argues that, since Paul "does not speak of whether it is a sin against Christ for some of the Corinthian Christians implicitly to worship the Roman emperor and to eat food sacrificed to idols (1 Cor 8:4–6)," Korean Christians "should consider the important Pauline message of unity and love in Christian communities before they judge whether the Shinto shrine worship that their forefathers performed was idolatry" (214). Second, "ancestor veneration" refers to Korean Christians' response to the Korean traditional ceremony of ancestor worship or veneration, rooted in Confucianism: bowing down to a dead ancestor's photo and offering a food sacrifice. Korean Christians traditionally refused to participate in this familiar activity, identifying it as a cultic (or demonic) act. Even today many conservative Korean Protestant Christians refuse to participate in this ceremony. Kwon argues that, since Exod 20:4–5 and its wider context (20:1–23) forbids idol worship rather than ancestor worship, "it can be concluded, therefore, that their [i.e., those who oppose ancestor worship] understanding is taken out of its biblical context," and "they should not consider it as idolatry but as an integral part of Korean-Confucian traditional customs and thereby build up Korean cultural customs within our Christian faith" (244–46). Third, "monoethnic community" refers to the ethnocentrism deeply rooted in Korean national and cultural identity. Kwon criticizes a Korean tendency "to have an exclusive attitude towards people of different races, different skin colors, and mixed blood. This tendency further penetrates the life of Korean Christians in Korea and diaspora Korean Christians overseas, especially those of the first generation migrants" (246).

While Kwon's overall thesis is persuasive and extremely relevant to the sociorhetorical and cross-cultural reading of 1 Cor 1–4 for Korean Christians today, there are a number of difficulties to be noted. First of all, there exists an innate methodological challenge for anyone's attempt to reconstruct what happened in Corinth almost two thousand years ago. Considering the fact that we know almost nothing about the Corinthian church apart from Paul's letters, it is difficult to reconstruct the Corinthian situation with precision. Kwon generally proceeds with the following steps. He initially finds broad sociorhetorical parallels between 1 Cor 1–4 and Cicero (and the first-century A.D. Greco-Roman culture). Kwon then reconstructs the sociorhetorical reality of the Corinthian church, often heavily relying on other scholars' speculative ideas rather than his independent assessment of primary sources. Kwon finally rereads 1 Cor 1–4, forcing his reconstruction upon the Pauline text. This hermeneutical process works when the reconstruction of the Corinthian reality is accurate. If not, however, it slips into a sort of circular argument. Kwon's reconstruction of the sociorhetorical reality of the Corinthian church is convincing in many but not all cases. I will mention two particular examples.

Kwon uncritically accepts Stephen M. Pogoloff's speculation that Paul's rhetoric appealed to the educated and sophisticated people in the Corinthian church, while Apollos's rhetoric appealed to the less educated and cultured (*Logos and Sophia* [Atlanta: Scholars Press, 1992], 180–89). Following Pogoloff's speculation,

Kwon claims, "Furthermore, the majority preferred Apollos' rhetorical ability, rather than Paul's, because of his Alexandrian origin. That is why in the Corinthian congregation there were tense relations between the people of Paul and those of Apollos" (54–55). The limited data that we have in 1 Cor 1–4 does not warrant this level of precision in reconstructing the sociorhetorical reality of the Corinth church. Another example is Kwon's argument concerning *collegia tenuiorum*. Kwon claims, "Some of the Corinthian Christians may also have understood the Christian *ekklesia* to be more of a kind of *collegia tenuiorum*, formed for the purpose of arranging funerals and the appropriate burial of the dead" (161). Kwon does not support his claim with any primary source except for the phrase "baptism into Moses" in 1 Cor 10:2 (165). Kwon surprisingly misses Paul's rhetoric behind his creation of the phrase "baptized into Moses." Paul's statement in 1 Cor 10:2 ("all were baptized into Moses in the cloud and in the sea") has no parallel in the Old Testament. Besides the rhetorical expressions in 1 Cor 1:13, 15, Paul always uses the verb βαπτίζω with the preposition εἰς in order to signify Christian believers' union with Christ through baptism (Rom 6:3; 1 Cor 12:13; Gal 3:27). A more immediate clue for the background of the phrase "baptized into Moses" is found in 1 Cor 10:1 ("Our ancestors were all under the cloud, and all passed through the sea"). Paul refers to the exodus story (Exod 13:21; 14:2–27) in order to draw a parallel between that and the situation of the Corinthians concerning food sacrificed to idols, in which the Israelites' experience of crossing over the Red Sea corresponds to the Corinthian believers' baptism. Paul's goal of creating the phrase "baptized into Moses" is neither to develop a theology of "union with Moses" nor to criticize the Corinthian believers' association with Roman social *collegia tenuiorum* but to make a vivid parallel between the experience of the Israelites in the exodus story and the situation of the Corinthian believers.

While providing thoughtful alternative readings of 1 Corinthians with implications for "Shinto shrine worship" and "ancestor veneration," Kwon does not adequately represent the biblical basis of the views of those whom he identifies as "conservative Korean Christians." Space does not allow me to discuss these issues in detail but to make only a few preliminary comments. If the apostle Paul were alive today, would he push for the unity of the church or the purity of the church? This is a difficult question, and no simple straightforward answer is warranted. Going beyond Paul, for instance, the whole book of Revelation concerns Christian discipleship, that is, to refuse to worship the Roman imperial cult and to persevere in worship of God and Christ only. Refusal to participate in "ancestor veneration" based on such conviction (cf. Exod 20) seems to be no more "out of context" than Kwon's interdisciplinary and cross-cultural interpretation of 1 Cor 1–4, reading together Paul, Cicero, and T'oegye out of their contexts. Lastly, Kwon's term "Korean-Confucian Christians" is problematic. I would identify myself as a Korean Christian with Confucian cultural background, but I would never call myself "a Korean-Confucian Christian"; I do not know anyone who would. While Confucianism is a traditional way of life in Korea rather than a coherent system of religious beliefs (cf. Buddhism, Taoism, and Shintoism), calling someone "a Confucian Christian" sounds as awkward as calling someone "a Buddhist Christian."

Despite these difficulties, this study provides a critical and insightful interdisciplinary and cross-cultural reading of 1 Cor 1–4 for Korean Christians today. This is a must read not only for all Korean Christian theologians and whoever is interested in Korean Christianity but also for those who are interested in the sociorhetorical or cross-cultural reading of the Scripture.

Whom God Has Called: The Relationship of Church and Israel in Pauline Interpretation, 1920 to the Present, by Christopher Zoccali. Eugene, Ore.: Pickwick, 2010. Pp. 236. Paper. $26.00. ISBN 9781608995172.

James D. G. Dunn, Durham University, Durham, United Kingdom

This volume began as a 2009 PhD thesis at the University of Wales, Lampeter, U.K., under the supervision of William S. Campbell and Kathy Ehrensperger. As the subtitle indicates, it is primarily a review of the vigorous contemporary debate on the relationship of the church and Israel as envisaged by Paul, particularly the continuity/discontinuity issue.

The first main chapter (ch. 2) reviews the "developing debate." The review begins with the traditional view, as represented by C. H. Dodd and Ernst Käsemann, summarized in terms of "supersessionism" or "replacement theology" and now challenged by "the new perspective." The new perspective, emphasizing the continuity between Israel and church, however, poses fresh questions: Is a critique of Israel's "ethnocentrism" any less anti-Jewish in character than the old perspective's critique of "works righteousness"? If circumcision is now dispensable, does not that remove one of the defining identity marks of Israel? If "Israel" has now been absorbed into Christ, where does that leave ethnic Israel? Alternatively, if Paul does not redefine Israel in terms of Christ, and Torah-observant Jews alone constitute Israel, then how can one reckon adequately with Paul's argument that Gentile believers are as much Abraham's seed as Jews and that Gentile believers have been grafted into the one olive tree that grows from the roots of the patriarchs? Or if, to avoid all traces of anti-Judaism, one argues that Paul envisaged a "Sonderweg" for Israel, Israel's salvation as a consequence of Israel's covenant, independently of Christ, then what does this say about Paul's gospel and his insistence on justification by faith (alone)? The alternative views in the "developing debate" are clearly represented, and the points of critique, and the consequent puzzles as to Paul's logic, well enough expressed.

Chapters 3 and 4 focus on the key texts: Rom 2:29; Gal 6:16 (ch. 3); and Rom 11:26 (ch. 4). On the first, Zoccali recognizes an implicit criticism by Paul of presumed privilege on the part of ethnic Israel but finds the critique of "ethnocentrism" overstated, since the criticism is in line with earlier prophetic rebuke, as in Isa 52:5. On Gal 6:16 Zoccali argues that the "Israel of God" is a reference to the church of Jews and Gentiles, though the question whether Paul's reference to "Israel" in Galatians does not foreshadow his treatment of "Israel" in Romans needs fuller discussion.

On Rom 11:26 Zoccali finds five views in contemporary scholarship: (1) "eschatological miracle": all Israel's salvation effected by a final coming of "the Deliverer out of Zion"; (2) ecclesiological: "all Israel" as the multiethnic Christ community; (3) Roman mission: "all Israel" represents Jewish believers in Rome; (4) two covenant: the Sonderweg thesis that Israel will be saved without reference to Christ; (5) "total national elect": "all Israel" refers to the complete number of elect from ethnic Israel. Zoccali's critique of (3) and (4) is very effective, and he himself argues for (5); his case for reading the reference to "all Israel" as a reference to ethnic Israel is hard to dispute, though it does need to be stressed that Rom 9–11 is about Israel, not about the church and Israel! However, his argument against (1) is very strained, since it is so difficult to read Rom 10:14–11:32 as other than a chronological sequence: Israel's hardening in part, salvation to Gentiles, full number of Gentiles, Israel's jealousy, deliverer from Zion, all Israel saved. As becomes clear in chapter 5, Zoccali wants to read Rom 11:26 "as describing the eschatological process initiated by the resurrection of Christ" (121), but he largely ignores the rhetorical effect of Rom 9–11: of Paul's grief for the bulk of his fellow Jews' failure to respond to the gospel, answered little by little, until finally resolved in the mystery of what is happening (Israel's hardening) and what is about to happen (not least through his own apostleship to Gentiles).

The main argument of chapter 5 is that Paul was "a Jewish reformer who remained personally connected with the synagogue and presumed an open relationship, at least in potential, between the Christ movement and greater Jewish community"; Paul did not seek separation from Judaism (126–27). I agree with him that there was probably a more positive relation between synagogues and house churches in Rome than is usually thought to be the case, but it is much harder to argue a similar case in relation to the churches in Galatia, since the imagery and language of Gal 4:17–5:12 seems to imply more a closing of the door than an open relationship. In this chapter the use of "proselyte" is too casual, and "Judaism" is used in a confusing way, unrelated to Paul's own and only use of the term in Gal 1:13–14.

Chapter 6 stirs the pot a little more, arguing against the false dichotomy between apocalyptic and salvation history and that Israel's election, for Paul, was "representational and vocational." A concluding chapter reflects for one last time on the paradox of Paul's in effect double assertion that the church *is* Israel and that the church is *not* Israel—"Israel" being used by Paul in a multifaceted way, indicating "multiple identities—the continuity of church with Israel through Christ being decidedly *not* "replacement theology" but "inclusion theology." A nineteen-page bibliography and indices of texts and modern authors complete the volume.

The discussion is rather repetitive, with the same issues coming up two or three times, and the critique of the various authors reviewed in chapter 2 is scattered over the following chapters. Going round the mulberry bush several times tends to blur the case being made rather than clarifying it. Further, the layout of the book is not helpful, in that the relation of text to footnotes leaves much to be desired: the text is often cluttered with several lines of source references, which would have been better in the footnotes, and the footnotes are regularly used to carry forward the discussion, which would be more appropriate in the text. Some editorial counsel would have been helpful.

In short, it is good that the subject of the relation between church and Israel in Paul has been given such close attention, but this treatment of the issues is only moderately satisfactory.

Redescribing Paul and the Corinthians, edited by Ron Cameron and Merrill P. Miller. Society of Biblical Literature Early Christianity and Its Literature 5. Atlanta: Society of Biblical Literature, 2011. Pp. xiii + 323. Paper. $40.95. ISBN 9781589835283.

Antoinette Clark Wire, San Francisco Theological Seminary and the Graduate Theological Union, Berkeley, California

This collection of essays, largely presented from 2000 to 2004 in the SBL Seminar on Ancient Myths and Modern Theories of Christian Origin, shows how independently this group operates from other Pauline text scholars. They practice a comparative religions approach to the texts in intense and interactive sessions, dismissing what one calls "academic Christian theological modernism" (106). But they touch only in an occasional footnote or not at all on other work, such as rhetorical, feminist, postcolonial, psychoanalytical, social-science, art and archeological, and social-memory analysis. They seem to assume that one can adapt Wilhelm Bousset's Christ cult with Wayne Meeks's social history and make Paul's letters understood in twenty-first-century debate. Yet in the sustained work of this seminar, insights have surfaced that are being missed elsewhere. The best way to break through the insulation between groups of scholars that came with our field's late twentieth-century expansion may be for us to listen to what others are doing. The seven essays here, introduced and concluded by the editors, take as their task to relate mythology and social structures when redescribing two disjunctions, that between Paul and pre-Pauline tradition and that between Paul and the people he addresses.

Beginning from the seminar's earlier conclusions published in *Redescribing Christian Origins*, also edited by Ron Cameron and Merrill P. Miller (SBL and Brill, 2004), Burton Mack asks how references in Gospel sources to the martyr Jesus with the byname *christos* are related to Paul's citations of tradition in 1 Cor 11:23–25 and 15:3–5. Mack proposes that Paul has reshaped tradition so that "Christ died for the kingdom" has become "Christ died for our sins," that "raised" in the sense of exalted by God has become "raised" to life and cosmic rule, and that "appeared" in memorial meals has become "appeared" to apostolic witnesses. Similarly, the tradition of a memorial meal of bread and wine has become for Paul a "site of instruction" signifying Jesus' body and blood that make the participants one living body. These proposals of the pre-Pauline tradition changed by Paul are not so much demonstrated as suggested as plausible in light of the gap between the Jesus *christos* of Gospel sources and Paul's Christ myth in Phil 2:5–11 summarized in 1 Cor 2:2, "I determined to know nothing among you but Jesus Christ and him crucified." Mack's focus here is on Paul's message as a whole rather than on the rhetorical situation of 1 Corinthians. This means Paul's "Abraham myth" of Gentile inheritance in Israel through faith that is outlined in Galatians and Romans (as seen in Caroline Johnson Hodges, *If Sons, Then Heirs,* Oxford, 2007) is given more weight than Paul's "Spirit myth" of access to divine Spirit through himself and Christ that is stressed in 1 Corinthians. Paul is identified as the creator of Hellenistic Christianity built on the three legs of the Christ myth, the Abraham myth, and the Spirit myth, but this is not called a Christ cult because we lack evidence of "a system of rituals practiced regularly by a venerating group." Apparently Mack sees the creative religious thinker coming first, then the myths that arise from his reflection, and only then through long-term teaching a ritual practice that can be called a cult.

The other lead article, by Jonathan Z. Smith, becomes the stimulant for most of the papers when it compares the Corinthian groups addressed by Paul with a small Papua New Guinea society. The Atbalmin converted to Christianity due to native pastors' preaching in the 1970s while they were venerating dead ancestors who gave wisdom for daily life. In a short time immigrants arrived from coastal cities, a Christian revival featured spirit possession by Atbalmin women, and a nativist movement announced that the ancestors were returning. The Corinthian addressees might be redescribed comparatively as people displaced from the western Mediterranean coastlands and their ancestors' burial places now celebrating memorial meals honoring the martyr Jesus. Here they experience spirit possession, including possible mediation of spirits at the baptism of their special dead who were left behind or buried recently in strange ground. They could claim a mobile ancestor in Christ while yet contesting Paul's resurrection gospel that threatens the guidance only the dead can give. This comparison assumes that Paul's letter is not written to churches in any sense we would recognize but to households of mixed-origin people who already associate for other purposes and are alternately responsive and repelled by what Paul promotes. Smith does not mention groups of women prophesying as an obvious point of comparison, though he notes "a prime candidate for rectification would be the broad, somewhat diffuse category of enthusiasm" (34 n. 50).

William Arnal responds that these presentations have overdrawn the disjunction between Paul and his long-term interlocutors in Corinth, since Paul's own situation, coming from an ethnically uprooted people, is parallel to theirs. Therefore when Paul joins a trade or other association and persuades a faction to replace their patron with his Christ, baptizing some and getting contributions for Jerusalem from others, he offers them what they crave: integration into a lineage—Abraham's lineage through Christ—and into the spiritual and material blessings God promised to the nations. Though we might contest that Diaspora

Jews before 70 C.E. felt uprooted and might argue that the ethnic issue is not central to the Corinthian correspondence, Arnal makes sense that whatever success Paul has depends on his own social location in the Hellenistic city. If Arnal had featured what he identifies as the "inexcusable lacuna" in these discussions, namely, gender issues, and the large slave and freed population in Corinth that he discusses only in notes (89 n. 33, 101 n. 58), social interests in Corinth to which Paul responds might have allowed for the more specific explanatory reframing that Arnal sought.

Stanley Stowers contributes two essays on Paul's relation to the Corinthians. He distinguishes three kinds of meals in the culture—the home, the sacrifice, and the memorial—and sees Paul in Corinth rejecting the practice in which a man divides sacrificed meat hierarchically to symbolize levels of power from the gods down to the least participant. Paul reshapes the memorial of Jesus to be a bread-based meal in homes served by women and slaves that symbolizes a common participation in one loaf, yet he incorporates from sacrificial meals the testing of purity he took to be required for sharing with the divine. Some Corinthians object and develop their own myths and practices. Stowers then argues that Paul was cultivating something more like certain Hellenistic philosophies than like home or city piety. He sought conversion by a free and exclusive choice to a life of self-mastery modeled on the founder's noble death. This gave priority to intellectual gifts of reflection, interpretation and writing, which slighted spiritual expressions of wisdom.

John Kloppenborg sees the Corinthians whom Paul addresses less comparable to Hellenistic philosophies than to urban collegia or thiasoi. The people Paul writes are like households, since they seem to be located in larger homes where there are people of mixed status, and they are like synagogues in their use of Jewish scriptures and weekly gatherings. But Kloppenborg sees them to be most like voluntary associations or collegia that cultivate a particular trade, ethnic group, or neighborhood. They choose a patron, share meals across slave and gender status, provoke and manage conflict, and provide basic identity, mutual support, and a decent burial.

A final article, by Richard Ascough, returns to this issue of honoring the dead where Thessalonica provides him forty-four Greek inscriptions showing how Thracian, Greco-Roman, and Egyptian divinities were appealed to, dues exacted, donations given, festivals celebrated, and the dead otherwise honored. In writing Thessalonians, Paul has forbidden their ancestor cults and even forbids grief when family members die by assuring them that the "sleeping" will be first to meet Christ at his coming. For the Corinthians, who prefer baptizing their dead to believing them resurrected, Paul establishes a meal where the living memorialize Jesus for his heroic task on the cross. Jesus' rising leaves no need to care for a tomb and guarantees that all who are incorporated into him will rise again at his coming. That these are no small issues can be seen in catacomb frescoes of memorial meals at the graveside of Christian dead still in the third and fourth centuries.

Those of us who are mortal might have wished the editors had pressed some writers to focus their work more sharply rather than sought to clarify it through their own full introduction and over fifty-page conclusion (including several two-page footnotes). Yet it may be possible with their help to ferret out what the seminar found in this Pauline dig. In addition to Mack's claim that it is Paul who constructs the Christ myth from a martyr story about Jesus supplemented by other myths drawn from Israelite and Hellenistic traditions, at least three groups are identified among Paul's Corinthian addressees. A few are patrons and co-workers attracted to his foreign *paideia* who claim solidarity through interdependent hierarchy. Many nonelite people seek ties to lost or fictive homelands with hopes of spiritual communication with their dead ancestors while avoiding offense in an alien society. A large faction resist Paul's demand for sole commitment, develop other discourses about Moses and Christ, and claim a place in both the wider society and this assembly. The picture is anything but simple, yet I find it revealing.

This collection of essays is best suited for advanced university seminars or for retired professionals like myself rethinking Christian origins.

Jesus, Paul, and the Gospels, by James D. G. Dunn. Grand Rapids: Eerdmans, 2011. Pp. xx + 201. Paper. $21.00. ISBN 9780802866455.

Raymond F. Collins, Brown University, Providence, Rhode Island

Jesus, Paul, and the Gospels has its origin in an initiative of Pope Benedict XVI, who declared that 28 June 2008–28 June 2009 was to be a year in which to honor Paul, commemorating the assumed bimillennial observance of the apostle's birth. The occasion led to invitations to hosts of Pauline scholars to deliver lectures or participate in symposia on Paul. Not a few of these invitations were addressed to Jimmy Dunn, world-renowned for his study of Paul. The nine essays gathered together in this book represent some of the fruits of those invitations.

In a six-page "personal introduction" of himself, Dunn describes his own pilgrimage with Paul. A feature of this particular collection of essays is that the lectures on which they are based were delivered to audiences that presumably did not share Dunn's familiarity with and love for Paul. In the opening paragraph of the book, Dunn avows his Protestantism. Nevertheless, he delivered five of the lectures in Catholic Spain and Italy and four of them in Jewish Israel. Gathered together in this collection, these lectures form a remarkably cohesive whole. In their simplicity, they are profound.

The four Beer Sheva lectures were on the Gospels—the topic was suggested by Dunn's hosts—providing material for the volume's part 1, "What Are the Gospels." The essays focus on Jesus, the time between Jesus and the Gospels, Mark and the Synoptics, and the Fourth Gospel. Thus they provide a good introduction to the New Testament's first four books. They belong to the volume insofar as they deal with "the gospel," a decidedly important Pauline theme.

The first chapter, centering on the "characteristic Jesus" rather than on the "distinctive Jesus" so dear to the heart of many searchers for the Jesus of history, begins with four givens. These givens serve as a useful reminder even for those of us who have been around the track a few times. The four are that Jesus existed, that he was a Jew, that he made an impact on people, and that he lived in an oral culture. These facts are so true and yet are so easily overlooked by text-based researchers.

The orality of the culture in which Jesus and first-century believers alike lived is a key feature of the second and fourth chapters, another useful reminder for all of us, especially those who seek textual links between the Fourth Gospel and the Synoptics, that is, a link between the written Synoptic Gospels rather than the oral tradition on which these written Gospels were based. For Dunn, it is the ongoing oral culture that explains the similarity between the Fourth Gospel and the earlier texts. All too frequently scholars apparently assume that the oral tradition ceased once elements of the tradition were written down. That, of course, is not the case, and they would admit it, despite not factoring into the interpretation of the New Testament texts. Dunn deserves commendation for the emphasis that he places on the importance of the oral tradition in all four canonical Gospels.

The one thing that I missed in this quartet of lectures on Jesus is that when Dunn writes about Mark as "the birth of a new genre"—which indeed it was—he neglects to mention, at least in a footnote, that the Pauline letters were the first written form of the gospel, the good news whose core is the death and resurrection of Jesus.

An essay entitled "From Jesus' Proclamation to Paul's Gospel," based on Dunn's Barcelona lecture, is the only essay found in part 2, "From Jesus to Paul." The essay examines three similarities between the preaching of Jesus and the theology of Paul, namely, the openness of God's grace, eschatological tension and the gift of the Spirit, and the love command. Obviously the language and point of view of Jesus are different from the language and thoughts of Paul, but, at bottom, there are similarities that must not be overlooked.

It is appropriate that the third part of the book has as its title "The Bimillennial Paul." Its first chapter has the provocative title, "Who Did Paul Think He Was?" Dunn's response: a Jew no longer in Judaism, an Israelite in Christ. The second essay asks another question: Was Paul an "Apostle or Apostate?" Paul's own answer is clear. He did not consider himself an apostate from Judaism, and he certainly considered himself an apostle of Jesus Christ, as he declares himself to be in the greetings of several of the extant letters. Paul's own answer to the question is clear, but the question remains to this day. It is a question that needs to be answered by Jews and Christians alike, each with their respective biases.

"The Gospel for All Who Believe" is the subject of the eighth essay. Paul's conversion, the importance of God's Spirit and grace, and the double dimension of justification serve as the foci of this essay. Dunn rightly underscores the social aspect of justification and the importance of the topic for Jewish-Christian dialogue, to which the recently completed ecumenical document *The Biblical*

Foundations of the Doctrine of Justification: An Ecumenical Follow-Up to the Joint Declaration on the Doctrine of Justification is expected to make a contribution.

Speaking about Paul's Damascus experience, I count myself as one of those who prefer to speak of the apostle's commission rather than of his conversion. Moreover, I found this particular and insightful essay to be also somewhat frustrating. My little frustration came from what I would consider to be an overemphasis on Romans and the lack of distinction between the authentic and the disputed Paulines. These features of Dunn's assessment of Paul are most apparent in this essay, but in some ways they are found throughout the latter part of the book.

The church of God, house churches, the body of Christ, and the fellowship of the Spirit are the four topics of the volume's final essay, "The Church—Paul's Trinitarian Ecclesiology." I particularly appreciate the way that Dunn treats the charismatic nature of the church and its members. The chapter is to be recommended as a valuable primer on Pauline ecclesiology.

The whole collection is vintage Dunn, clearly written and forcefully expressed. Dunn occasionally tosses a zinger at those who underestimate Paul or do not preach the Pauline gospel. I assume that the zinger is directed principally at Roman Catholics such as myself. The zinger should have been tossed long ago. Hardly anyone is more qualified to toss it than is Jimmy Dunn. Fortunately, Benedict XVI's Year of Paul gave him an opportunity to do so.

"Denn wenn ich schwach bin dann bin ich stark": Die paulinischen Peristasenkataloge und ihre Apostolatstheologie, by Young Sook Choi. Neutestamentliche Entwürfe zur Theologie 16. Tübingen: Francke, 2010. Pp. x + 329. Paper. €58.00. ISBN 9783772083389.

Lars Kierspel, Trinity College of the Bible and Theological Seminary, Newburgh, Indiana

This book is a slightly revised version of Choi's dissertation, written at the Evangelisch-Theologischen Fakultät of the Johannes Guttenberg University in Mainz, Germany (Doktorvater: Friedrich W. Horn). With this study, Choi analyzes Paul's five catalogs of his own suffering in 1 Cor 4:6–13; 2 Cor 4:7–15; 6:3–10; 11:21b–30; and 12:9b–10. The catalog in Rom 8:31–39 is excluded because the sufferings mentioned there are not specifically those of the apostle.

The first part (11–42) briefly walks the reader through roughly a dozen previous studies of the last one hundred years about these lists. They are united by a tradition-historical concern for comparing Paul's lists of sufferings with those of (1) Stoics and Cynics (e.g., Bultmann 1910), (2) Isaiah's "suffering servant" and of Jeremiah (e.g., Wichmann 1930), and (3) Jewish apocalyptic texts (e.g., Schrage 1974). Choi reports the strongest points of contacts between Paul and these traditions, yet not without also highlighting significant contrasts. While Paul shows stylistic parallels to Stoic texts, he grasps the overcoming of pain not simply as a human achievement but as the result of divine assistance (28). Paul resembles

Isaiah's suffering servant, but the apostle understands his distress not only as that of a chosen vessel but also as an example for the church (32). Finally, Paul does not share the Jewish apocalyptic determinism and dualism according to which suffering is the result of an eschatological struggle between two eons (40–41).

Part 2 (45–97) examines the list of hardships in 1 Cor 4:6-13. Choi first analyzes the context of 1 Cor 1–4 and observes that Paul is interested here neither in a theology of the cross as such nor in a theology of wisdom or a defense of his apostleship. All statements in this regard serve a larger purpose: to unite the church. The exegesis of the text first tackles two interpretive problems in 1 Cor 4:6 (μετεσχημάτισα and ἃ γέγραπται, 55–70). Choi then analyzes 4:7–13 (71–87) and connects the catalog to the sacraments of baptism (see βαπτίζω in 1:13 and 12:13) and the Lord's Supper (see σχίσματα in 1:10 and 11:18) as related efforts for the unity of the church (87–95). Choi's examination is particularly helpful in demonstrating ties between 4:6–13 (e.g., μωροί, ἀσθενεῖς, ἄτιμοι in 4:10) and 1:17–31 (e.g., μωρά, ἀσθενῆ, ἀγενῆ, 1:26–28), which establish the list of hardships as the climax of Paul's argument in 1 Cor 1–4: Just as baptism and the Lord's Supper, so the apostle's suffering brings to mind ("vergegenwärtigen") the suffering of Christ in the service of unifying the church (55).

Part 4 (101–246) analyzes the four lists of hardships in 2 Corinthians. (1) The first list in 2 Cor 4:7–15 shows many terminological links to the preface in 1:3–11 (105–7) and unfolds, therefore, the key subjects of affliction (θλῖψις) and comfort (παράκλησις). The apostles have the gospel ("treasure") in "earthen vessels" (4:7), meaning in weak and fragile bodies, as the following list of hardships demonstrates. Choi emphasizes that the parallels to Stoic philosophy are only formal in nature: Epictetus seeks to minimize pain and suffering by creating a mental distance from the experience, while Paul acknowledges their reality, which needs to be "endured" (119–20). Paul's language of carrying around the "death of Jesus" (νέκρωσις τοῦ Ἰησοῦ 4:10; similarly Gal 6:17) is not a reference to a mystical experience (122) but a christological interpretation of apostolic suffering: Paul's body is a "constant" (4:11) and daily (4:15) revelation of Jesus' death and life. (2) The second list in 2 Cor 6:3–10 (138–74) serves as an apostolic self-commendation (6:4), necessary because of similar boasting of the opponents (10:12–13). That purpose also explains a peculiarity in this list of hardships: the reference to eight virtues of the apostle (6:6–7a). Also noteworthy is the antithesis in 6:10: "sorrowful yet always rejoicing" (ἀεὶ δὲ χαίροντες). Choi highlights that Paul is referring neither to a future joy (so Jewish apocalypticism) nor to a change from sorrow to joy but to a "paradox simultaneous existence of joy and sorrow" (170). (3) The third list in 2 Cor 11:21b–30 (175–223), which has the most biographical details among the lists (177), is part of Paul's so-called "fool's speech" (2 Cor 11:1–12:13, see ἀφροσύνη in 11:1, 17, 21; ἄφρων in 11:16, 19; 12:6, 11; παραφρονέω in 11:23), which stands at the center of the chiastic composition in 2 Cor 10–13 (178, so with Zmijewski). Here Paul imitates the self-boasting of his opponents, which he qualifies as foolish (181–82, 184). While the false apostles (11:13) brag about their Jewish origin (11:22), Paul "boasts" about his "weakness" (11:30; "key statement,"

175, 220) and argues that he is "more so" a servant of Christ *because* of his many sufferings (11:23)! Beside details about the individual sufferings in this list, Choi adds an excursus each about the identity of the opponents (191–95) and about the question of Paul's Roman citizenship (204–10). (4) The fourth list in 2 Cor 12:9b– 10 (225–46) is the shortest of all and finishes the "fool's speech" as a parallel to the previous list (see 11:30; 12:9b). Forced by his opponents (10:10; 12:1; p. 229), Paul mentions specific experiences of revelation and many miracles (12:1–4, 11–12). But he balances these immediately with a report about the denial of a miracle of healing, finishing with the Lord's words, "My grace is sufficient for you, for power is perfected in weakness" (12:7–9a). Paul then applies these words personally to himself and, thereby, summarizes the whole "fool's speech": he boasts about "my weaknesses that the power of Christ may dwell in me" (12:9b). Paul's weakness is here, *pace* Krug, not understood as a *condition* for the display of Christ's power (see 12:12), but it makes Christ's resurrection-power (239) better visible (240).

In part 4 (249–84) Choi analyzes Paul's understanding of his apostleship in light of the lists of hardships. She specifically investigates references in which Paul's interprets his sufferings as τὰ παθήματα τοῦ Χριστοῦ (2 Cor 1:5), νέκρωσιν τοῦ Ἰησοῦ (2 Cor 4:10), τὰ στίγματα τοῦ Ἰησοῦ (Gal 6:17), συμπάσχομεν (Rom 8:17), τῶν θλίψεων τοῦ Χριστοῦ (Col 1:24). The apostle also employs prepositional phrases according to which he suffers διὰ Χριστόν (1 Cor 4:10; 2 Cor 4:11; also Phil 3:8), ὑπὲρ Χριστοῦ (2 Cor 12:10; also 12:15; 1:6), and ἕνεκεν σοῦ (Rom 8:36). Choi quickly rejects views that regard Paul's language as mystical (J. Schneider, A. Schweitzer) or as a reference to an epiphany (E. Käsemann, E. Güttgemanns, 253–55). Rather, using Lips's basic theory of communication, Choi understands Paul's view of his sufferings as a consequence of his call to be an apostle and preacher (channel) according to which the sender (the Lord) speaks his message, the gospel, to the recipients (the churches) (255–56). A final chapter summarizes the results of this book (273–82), and an epilogue (283–84) relates Paul's notion of strength in weakness to the Korean concepts of *han* (suffering) and *hung* (joy).

Choi's detailed exegesis of the five lists of Paul's hardships rewards the reader with many exegetical insights (parts 2 and 3). The relative preference for an analysis of the Greek text over historical speculations regarding partitions of the Corinthian letters, the specific identify of opponents, and precise traditionhistorical analogies highlights not only Choi's contribution to existing studies on the subject but also enables her to use the hardship lists for a significant theological synthesis.

However, it is here (part 4) where she proceeds too fast. After the analysis of the lists of hardships in the Corinthian correspondence, Choi attempts a theology of suffering in Paul's letters. The scope of this synthesis, while focused on 1 and 2 Corinthians, extends beyond these two letters and broadens to a more topical review of Pauline literature. What I would have expected is an effort to integrate the exegetical results into a historical framework that answers the question: Why do these lists occur only in letters addressed to *Corinthian* believers? What is it in the Corinthian culture that challenged Paul's apostolic authority? Why does Paul not mention the details of his hardships in other letters? Is there a specific apostolic profile that emerges from these lists when compared to Paul's self-portrait in other letters?

Another important question that remains unanswered is: The meaning of "weaknesses" is clearly defined through the many hardships, but what is the meaning of "power of Christ" that dwells in Paul especially when he is weak (2 Cor 12:9b)? Choi explains it at one point as "resurrection power" ("Auferstehungskraft," 239) that is *not* limited to the future physical resurrection. But how does Paul experience resurrection here and now, in the middle of his daily experience of persecution and disease? The question is particularly urgent because Choi frequently insists on the "iterative simultaneous existence" ("iterative Gleichzeitigkeit") of weakness and power. While she quickly rejects a mystical understanding, that is exactly what her illustration in her epilogue to the reader reminds of: the Korean concept of "hung" as a "specifically religious" experience of joy with a "transcendental dimension" in the midst of suffering (283). Rhetorically, Paul is using this language in 2 Cor 12:9b to refute the charge of weakness (10:10), but what does this rhetoric refer to in reality? Choi explains later that the believer is "strengthened" in his or her suffering through the power of Christ's resurrection (263). Does this imply an *emotional* strength that enables courage in the midst of frightening circumstances? The antithetical experiences listed in 2 Cor 6:8–10, which Choi refers to as the "co-existence of opposites" in her exegetical discussion (173), deserve closer attention in this regard.

These areas of concern highlight open ends in this dissertation but do not minimize the strengths of Choi's diligent research and readable book.

Theodore of Mopsuestia: Commentary on the Minor Pauline Epistles, by Rowan A. Greer. Society of Biblical Literature Writings from the Greco-Roman World 26. Atlanta: Society of Biblical Literature, 2010. Pp. xliv + 839. Paper. $89.95. ISBN 9781589832794.

Frederick G. McLeod, Saint Louis University, Saint Louis, Missouri

This translation of Theodore of Mopsuestia's *Commentary on the Minor Pauline Epistles* marks the completion of a recent progressive effort to provide English translations for all of Theodore's five major works that have survived more or less intact. These translations fulfill a glaring lacuna in knowing what Theodore taught as an outstanding exegete and theologian of the late fourth and early fifth centuries. Greer is an exceptional choice to accomplish the present work. Though the blurb on its back cover does not make mention of this, Greer has previously published two well-received studies on both Theodore's theological and exegetical thought. These show that he is a specially qualified scholar to undertake the present task.

As regards the text, Greer has taken the Latin text, plus some additional extant Greek excerpts, that H. B. Swete published in his two-volume work on

Theodore's *Commentary on the Minor Pauline Epistles* (the last seven letters in the Pauline corpus from Galatians through to Philemon). Greer has updated and improved this text by examining and incorporating many of the emendations that Swete has proposed and two by U. Wickert, while rejecting many others. In my opinion, Greer offers solid, well-reasoned arguments for why he accepts some and excludes other changes. I found, however, his ten pages of reasons for rejecting the majority of Wickert's emendations as heavy reading. I think that it would have been better to place this discussion in his appendix at the end of his work and not in his introduction. But overall I believe that Greer has established and used the best and most reliable text available for his translation.

Greer presents in his book the Latin and Greek texts on the left-side page and an English translation of both on the right side. Having tried to translate Theodore's Latin and Greek texts of the present work, I appreciate how very difficult it is to render a text that is often succinct, obscure, and difficult in free-flowing, understandable English. Greer has lived up to his promise to remain as faithful as possible to what the text literally states and to do so in a clear, exact, and readable way. I have only two suggestions for improvement, all personal. I think it would have been helpful to indicate by way of a footnote that when the Latin text translates "persona" as "person" in reference to Christ, the original Greek is πρoσώπον (*prosōpon*). This is confirmed by cross-checking the Greek and Latin texts on page 182. This is especially significant for understanding Theodore's christological commentary on Phil 2:1–11 (313–27). The only jarring translation that I encountered is Greer's rendering of "magnitudo" as "greatness" in such phrases as "the greatness of his dispensations" (363). If I may judge from Theodore's use of the term in his *Commentary on John's Gospel*, it signifies that Jesus' extraordinary deeds reveal not only his exercise of divine power but his intimate sharing in the Word's and the Father's divine nature, as on page 373. There is, in addition, one line needing to be changed. On page xii, the last line of the first paragraph ought to read "many in North Africa suffered persecution for their opposition [not defense] of the Three Chapters."

As regards Greer's introduction, he first summarizes the manuscript history of the text, noting that, although the Latin translation is not always faithful to the Greek text, it can be said to be substantially reliable. He also states in passing that these commentaries on Paul were written in the latter years of Theodore's career. I think that this may be made more precise, as Theodore cites in his commentary of Galatians (43) the title of his own earlier work on John's Gospel. So if one can trust as authentic his dedication of this work to a bishop Porphyry, this would indicate that he published his commentary on John sometime around the beginning of the fifth century. If this is indeed true, then the present Pauline commentaries would likely belong to its first two decades. Greer then offers some general reflections and observations about Theodore's exegesis. One small correction needs mentioning. On page xiii, Greer states that Theodore's treatise on allegory has been lost. Lengthy passages, however, can be found in van Rompay's *Fragments syriaque du Commentaire des Psalms*. Greer does spend some time elaborating on how his understanding of *historia* as "narrative" helps to explain Theodore's strong antipathy in Gal 4:21–31 toward allegory, for it does not fully respect the narrative as a whole. While in general agreement with this view, I prefer to say that Theodore rejects the allegorists because they substitute their own imaginary projections of what a text means for what a scriptural text is actually affirming. For Theodore, the only way one can prove the spiritual meaning of a text is that this is in some way approved by a New Testament text. If it is, it is a type; if it is not, it is an allegory.

In his theological comments, Greer summarizes some prominent topics of interest in the letters. He speaks, in general, of how "Theodore's theology is fundamentally a story" (xxi). He describes Theodore's views on the two "ages" as being centered upon both the Adam and Christ stories and "represent a transition from mortality to immortality." Greer draws from this how grace and love must be balanced with human freedom and lived out in the spiritual lives of all. Admittedly Greer is limited in what he can highlight in his introduction about the specific roles that Christ's humanity plays in the present letters, as he does on page xxiv, yet it would have been helpful to expand at least a little more on (1) what Paul saw to be the fundamental weakness of the Jewish law for achieving salvation, (2) how Christ as man serves as the head of his body, the church, especially by bestowing, with the Spirit, the graces needed to be in a spiritual union with him and through him to God, and 3) what Theodore means by a type (113–23), especially as it is opposed to allegory and as it applies to the sacraments of baptism and the Eucharist.

As regards the appendix, I found the index to be highly detailed and helpful for those interested in specific topics and themes. I think that Greer's "Commentary Index by Verse" and his "Index of Scriptural Citations" will be valuable for those seeking Theodore's thought about particular verses. However, I do not know what real advantage the "Swete-Greer Concordance" offers, as Greer now provides an updated version of Swete's text and his important footnotes. Why go to Swete, when Greer is now providing an improved Latin and Greek text, with an excellent English translation!

In summary, despite discussing a number of what are my own personal interests and observations, I believe that Greer's present work will become the standard "go-to" text for those interested in Theodore's insights into the minor Pauline epistles. Because of Theodore's stress on commenting only on what he has encountered in Paul's letters, Theodore's elaborations enjoy a timeless value for those seeking to live out the Christian life as spelled out by Paul. Considering the vast amount of linguistic and theological knowledge required, the clear, graceful writing and organizing skills manifested in this work, and doubtless the countless hours of labor this whole effort has clearly demonstrated, Greer has succeeded in producing a first-rate volume that will last in its own right and be used as a valuable source and tool in future studies of Theodore.

Paul's Way of Knowing: Story, Experience, and the Spirit, by Ian W. Scott. Grand Rapids: Baker, 2009. Pp. xvii + 341. Paper. $44.99. ISBN 9780801036095.

David M. Allen, Queen's Foundation, Birmingham, United Kingdom

How did Paul expect his epistolary readers to "know" or use their powers of reason? How did he expect his audiences to make decisions, or what epistemological processes does Paul anticipate them to deploy? Such questions form the backdrop of Scott's latest work, an in-depth analysis of Paul's epistemology, and particularly the apostolic use of narrative to reason with, and exhort, the audiences so addressed. Scott ventures that Paul is operating with a coherent narrative framework and is placing his readers' experience within such a framework, albeit one that is necessarily reconfigured by the unexpected narrative developments of a crucified Messiah and the gift of the Spirit.

The book is a republication of Scott's earlier work: *Implicit Epistemology in the Letters of Paul* (Mohr Siebeck, 2006). There is no suggestion of any change in content or presentation, but perhaps the title is a more representative (or less daunting?) appellation for Scott's analysis and may give it exposure to a wider audience as a result. After a relatively short introduction, the book breaks up into three constituent sections. The first discusses the portrayal of human reason within the Pauline corpus, while the second one deals with the bigger questions of narrative and story within Paul's thinking. In the third section, Scott then turns to consider Galatians as a case study of the way in which Paul's narrative theology might be seen to function, before closing with some concluding reflections on the theological implications of Paul's epistemology. Although related in terms of content, each individual section is reasonably discrete, and one could profitably read them in isolation from each other.

Part 1 of the study engages with Paul's attitudes toward reason and rationality. Scott gives particular consideration to Rom 1:18–32 and 1 Cor 1:17–2:16, concluding that Paul actually holds rationality in high regard—it is *worldly* wisdom, rather than wisdom per se, of which he is critical. For Paul, the problem is human sin and its negative impact upon reason. He suggests that it is the Spirit who leads into truth and that humans need Spirit-empowered wisdom in order to think appropriately. Reasoning can only function properly when enabled by the Spirit, "when it is freed from the corrupting influence of the human tendency to reject God" (73).

The middle section is perhaps the heart or nub of Scott's thesis. Within four chapters he considers several different types of "knowledge" that function within Paul: "mundane," "theological," "ethical," and what one might call divine-knowledge or "knowledge of God." The discussion of "mundane" knowledge is reasonably straightforward; Scott suggests that Paul is aware of such "ordinary" ways of knowing and is happy to speak of knowledge in a way that is earthy and realistic, distinct from, for example, the idealist conceptions of the Platonic academy. The sections on theological and ethical knowledge, however, yield a more substantial analysis. Scott proposes that Paul's theological knowledge comprises an overarching story, the theological narrative that both permeates and sustains his epistolary texts; in other words, Paul has a narrative structure that underpins (or "overpins"?) his theological understanding. He ventures that "Paul's theological knowledge is … a grand unified story, an epic narrative of the relationship between humanity and its creator which stretches from creation to the final eschatological fulfilment" (108). Unsurprisingly, perhaps, Scott's analysis builds on the work of Frei and McIntyre, but not slavishly so, and it offers a well-rounded discussion of developments in narrative theology and their impact upon biblical studies.

By contrast, Paul's "ethical" knowledge is more realistic, or rather comprises the way in which the apostle suggests decisions are reasoned out within the nitty-gritty life of the churches he addresses. Rather than espousing particular ethical maxims or concepts, rather than being essentially foundationalist, Paul locates and outworks ethical decisions in the light of theological knowledge—what Scott terms "the skill of setting the mundane events of one's life properly into the context of the theological story" (155). In effect, Paul is seen to be embracing narrative ethics; it is this theological story that informs and dictates the practical reality of ethical decision-making. It is thus possible to know God and Christ in an intimate way and to share in the life of Christ and his passion.

Scott's final section is effectively a case-study approach considering Paul's narrative reasoning in the Epistle to the Galatians. One finds some attention to the familiar *topoi* such as "works of the law" and *pistis Christou*, but these are not really the primary focus of Scott's analysis. Instead, stepping through the text in extensive fashion, he teases out how the categories of theological, ethical, and divine knowledge function within the letter and how Paul seeks to bring his audience into such "knowledge." Key concepts for Scott become the notions of reconfiguration and coherency; appealing to narrative theory, he proposes that events earlier on in the story need to be reunderstood, or reconfigured, in the light of new narrative developments, but in such a way that the story remains a coherent and comprehensible one. Consequently, he considers the way in which Paul reconfigures the Abraham narrative in the light of the Christ-event or how the Pauline view on law (in Galatians, at least) is reworked in the aftermath of both the Galatians' reception of the Spirit and the crucified Messiah. Paul differentiates, Scott suggests, a way of faith and a way of law, and the law needs to be necessarily reunderstood or reconfigured as a "dead-end" (215). Likewise, the audience find themselves "re-plotted" within the story, their (new) life in the Spirit reconfiguring the story in fresh fashion. To some degree, therefore, Scott seems to endorse a version of Sanders's famous "solution to plight" dictum, something he himself seems to concede, though arriving there by a different methodology than Sanders.

In sum, Scott's argument is well-formed. There are helpful summaries at the end of each chapter, and the overall structure of the work makes for a well-presented piece of research. At one level, it offers a very useful analysis just of Galatians—there are plenty of footnotes to signpost the interested reader, and it presents a consistent reading of the letter as whole. One would not need to agree with every exegetical move that Scott makes to find his analysis of the epistle a helpful and informative piece of work.

More significantly, though, the book is a well-argued consideration of Paul's narrative theology, its focus on the way in which ideas of "knowing" operate within the Pauline discourse being particularly well-developed. This is probably the book's greatest strength; indeed, the central section on the way in which narrative theology functions is a very useful piece of work in its own right and forms a helpful introduction to the topic that one might profitably use with students in a classroom setting. It is important to note, though, that Scott is less interested in Paul's *own* understanding of the theological story or rather how Paul himself thinks theologically; instead, Scott's focus is on the way in which Paul expects his audience to locate themselves within the theological story and how they should go about the process of thought and reflection. However, it is sometimes hard to distinguish the two, especially when considering Paul's recollection of Damascus road in Galatians, and Scott, perhaps inevitably, still has some commentary on Paul's own understanding of the theological story. One cannot always separate author and text in quite so neat a fashion.

If one were being picky, one might have hoped for a more developed discussion of the way in which the Spirit is operative in Pauline epistemology. In terms of the book's subtitle, for example, one finds plenty here on "story" and plenty on its interface with "experience," but some more developed discussion of Pauline pneumatology would be beneficial, especially in the central portion of the book. But this is only a small gripe, bearing in mind the detailed and very readable presentation Scott's work otherwise provides.

Paul's Gospel in Romans: A Discourse Analysis of Rom 1:16–8:39, by Jae Hyun Lee. Linguistic Biblical Studies 3. Leiden: Brill, 2010. Pp. xviii + 582. Hardcover. $216.00. ISBN 9789004179639.

Eve-Marie Becker, University of Aarhus, Aarhus, Denmark

Der Wunsch, Texte und deren Inhalte möglichst nicht nur nach inter-subjektiv nachvollziehbaren methodischen Regeln zu analysieren, sondern mit einem ‚objektivierbaren' methodischen Verfahren dem ‚richtigen' Verstehen zuzuführen, ist häufig ein leitendes Motiv bei der exegetischen Arbeit. Gerade die Erfahrung, dass die exegetische Beschäftigung mit vielen neutestamentlichen Texten und Themenstellungen *nicht*, zumindest nicht immer zu übereinstimmenden Beurteilungen kommt, sondern zum überwiegenden Teil im Blick auf Methoden wie auf Resultate gravierende Abweichungen aufweist, verstärkt offenbar den Wunsch nach einer ‚objektivierbaren' Text- und Inhaltsanalyse, und zwar besonders dann, wenn es sich um einen zentralen theologischen Text wie den Röm handelt. Linguistische Methoden scheinen dafür hilfreich zu sein. Die vorliegende Dissertation, verfasst am *Divinity College* der *McMaster University* in Hamilton/Ont., ist von dem Wunsch nach Objektivierbarkeit spürbar, wenn auch nicht explizit getrieben. Denn der Verf. versucht hier, die theologischen Kerngedanken („*central point[s] or peak[s]*", z.B. 23) des Paulus in Röm 1–8 mittels einer linguistischen Analyse objektiv zu erheben. Dabei sollen die „linguistic features of a text itself" als ein "methodological framework" (24) dienen. Die drei für die Untersuchung leitenden Fragen sind dabei die folgenden: „*how* one can determine the author's intention, including the main and subsidiary emphases.... how can we discern *where* Paul's central point(s) is and *what* the content of that point(s) is?" (3; 23 u.ö.). Bei der Bearbeitung dieser Fragen gelangt Verf. letztlich zu der Einsicht, dass „Paul's arguments in Rom 1:16–8:39 is delivered by two descriptive frameworks. According to these frameworks, his gospel about God's salvation has one peak point (Romans 5), which shows the central role of Jesus and its result in God's salvation, and two sub-peaks (Rom 3:21–26 and Romans 8), which elucidate salvation with the stress on the role of God and the Holy Spirit" (443).

Die Untersuchung umfasst zehn Kapitel, wovon die beiden ersten und das letzte einer forschungsgeschichtlichen Einführung und Darstellung der Methode sowie einer Ertragssicherung dienen. Im ersten Kapitel (1–24) stellt Verf. insgesamt die fünf leitenden *readings* vor, die gegenwärtig bei der Interpretation des Röm Anwendung finden: Es handelt sich dabei um *social-scientific criticism, intertextual reading, narrative reading, rhetorical reading* und *linguistic discourse reading*. Die kritische Darstellung besonders der ersten vier *readings* ist klar geschrieben und überwiegend gut informiert. Sie weist auf eine dort tendenziell zu beobachtende Textferne hin, die nach dem Verf. darauf beruht, dass diese *readings* ihre methodischen Fragen auf die Texte applizieren, statt die relevanten Fragen aus der Auslegung der Texte selbst zu entwickeln. Daher kommt Verf. zu der Feststellung: „each reading has its own merits.... they share a common weakness that they do not seem to regard the text as the starting point of their analysis" (23). Unter Verweis auf *Stanley E. Porter* plädiert Verf. für *studies of the New Testament*, die „textually based" seien (23). Wiewohl diese Kritik berechtigte Fragen zum Verhältnis von Text und Methoden aufwirft, sollte sie nicht dahingehend überdehnt oder missverstanden werden, dass hier vermeintliche Alternativen postuliert werden: Texte und Methoden bzw. *readings* sind untrennbar und wechselseitig auf einander bezogen. Wie Methoden angemessen auf Texte zu beziehen seien, muss jeweils methodologisch, d.h. hermeneutisch diskutiert werden. Die Suche nach ‚angemessenem Verstehen' ist nicht gleichbedeutend mit dem Anspruch auf ‚richtiges Verstehen'. Die Pluralität von Methoden, *readings* und Interpretationen deutet vielmehr gerade darauf hin, dass die Suche nach ‚angemessenem Verstehen' fortschreitet und unabgeschlossen bleibt, wohl: bleiben *muss*. Hierin liegt nicht die Schwäche, sondern vielmehr die Stärke der exegetischen Arbeit.

Im zweiten Kapitel (25–86) konzipiert Verf. über mehr als sechzig Seiten seinen eigenen Zugang zur Textanalyse, die er im Anschluss vor allem an den englischen Sprachwissenschaftler *Michael A. K. Halliday* als *discourse analysis* begreift. Die Diskursanalyse bezieht sich dabei auf die Analyse von Sprache bzw. die Beschreibung linguistischer Strukturen und Formen—ein übergreifender ‚Diskurs'-Begriff ist hier nicht im Blick. Ebenso wenig werden die Spezifika diskutiert, die durch eine *briefliche* Kommunikation bedingt sind—eine Frage, die ja bei der Analyse des Röm durchaus relevant ist. Nach einer Charakterisierung der Diskursanalyse (26–33), bei der der Diskurs als eine umfassende Kommunikation zwischen Absender und Adressat verstanden wird, in der einerseits verschiedene kontextuelle Elemente und Ebenen, andererseits die „sequentiality and hierarchy of a text" (33) zu berücksichtigen sind, weist der Verf. den schon eingangs skizzierten drei Fragen drei analytische Methoden oder Perspektivierungen zu: Im Blick auf die Bearbeitung der ersten Frage nach den „central point(s) or peak(s)" schlägt Verf. eine Unterteilung des Diskurses in verschiedene Teile („discourse units") vor und bezeichnet dieses Vorgehen als „grouping" (33–50): Externe Kriterien („boundary markers") wie interne Kriterien („cohesion and coherence") sollen dieser Bestimmung von *discourse units* dienen. Bei den *cohesive elements* differenziert Verf. sinnvollerweise zwischen „conjunctions…, grammatical cohesion…, lexical cohesion". Im Ergebnis soll eine auf der Beobachtung von *topic changes* basierende, ihrerseits schon hierarchisierende Unterscheidung zwischen einem übergreifenden *topic* sowie untergeordneten *topics* und *sub-topics* erreicht werden (Schema: 50). Bei der Bearbeitung der zweiten Frage („what is the author's main thought?") steht die *topicality* im Vordergrund (51–61). Grundlegend ist hier die schon auf *T. A. van Dijk* zurückgehende Beobachtung, dass Absender und Adressat sich einer thematischen Entfaltung jeweils umgekehrt nähern: Während der Absender „from the top to the bottom" geht (51), erschließt der Adressat das Thema eines Diskurses zunächst von den kleinsten Einheiten, den Worten her, über Sätze zu größeren textuellen Strukturen hin. Die *topicality* der Diskurseinheiten in ihrem Verhältnis zu einander konstituiert sich dann in einer „information structure" (51), die dem Thema-Rhema-Modell ähnlich gedacht wird und die sich dann vorwiegend über semantische Komponenten analysieren lässt: „interpersonal, ideational, and textual meanings" (54). Die dritte Frage schließlich—„how can we discern the central point(s) or peak(s)?"—zielt auf die Beschreibung der *focality* (61–84), d.h. darauf, zu untersuchen, wie die *message* im Diskurs ‚verpackt' ist und präsentiert wird. Dabei sind bestimmte „linguistic devices" (67) zu untersuchen, die sich—wie „verbal aspect…, mood…, voice…, case…, conditional clause…, word order…, empathic or attention markers…" etc. (68–79)—teils auf Satzebene, teils aber auch über die Satzebene hinaus (u.a. „rhetorical structure", 80–84) bestimmen lassen. In einer kurzen Zusammenfassung (84–86) werden die zuvor beschriebenen analytischen Schritte nun auf ihre Anwendung für die Textuntersuchung hin vorbereitet.

Im dritten bis neunten Kapitel, dem Kernstück des Buches (87–430), wird die diskurskritische Analyse auf den gewählten Textabschnitt Röm 1,16–8,39 appliziert. Dabei schlägt der Verfasser folgende Untergliederung des Briefabschnitts vor: Röm 1,16–17; 1,18–2,11; 2,12–3,20; 3,21–4,25; Kap. 5; 6,1–7,25; 8,1–39. In den einzelnen Kapiteln werden die entsprechenden Textabschnitte unter den o.g. Aspekten von *grouping, focality* und *topicality* untersucht. Dabei zielt Verf. darauf, einerseits den Diskurs innerhalb eines Textabschnittes sprachlich und inhaltlich zu beschreiben, andererseits aber auch dessen Beitrag zum übergeordneten Diskurs der Kapitel 1–8 darzustellen. Röm 1,16–17 z.B. ist dementsprechend beides—zum einen eine „transition" oder „introduction of the body of the letter" (98), zum anderen aber auch eine eigenständige Vorausschau auf wichtige theologische Themen, die Paulus im späteren Verlauf des Briefes bearbeitet. Die Beschränkung der Untersuchung auf Kap. 1–8 wird zwar begründet, stellt aber eine nicht unwichtige Weichenstellung dar: Denn wenn Röm 1–8, nicht aber der Gesamtbrief als übergeordneter Diskurs begriffen werden, so wird sich die Gestalt und der Inhalt dieses Diskurses auch (nur) an den dort verhandelten Fragen und Themen bemessen lassen können. Hier ist zweifellos die eigene—keineswegs illegitime—Deutungsarbeit des Verf. mit im Spiel. Auch nimmt die vorgeschlagene Unterteilung in die genannten Textabschnitte in gewissem Sinne einige Ergebnisse der Untersuchung bereits vorweg. Die Deutung des Verf. bei der Analyse von Röm 1–8 übt zudem dadurch in nicht unerheblichem Maße Einfluss auf die Textinterpretation aus, als auf eine historische Kontextualisierung des Röm, d.h. auf eine Berücksichtigung der situativen Sprechersituation des Briefeschreibers, weitgehend verzichtet wird. So behält letztlich auch der als Linguist tätige Exeget die Deutungshoheit über den Text inne. Ein mehr als hundertseitiger Appendix (445–546!) bietet eine Übersicht über die vorausgegangene Textanalyse im Blick auf den „frame of topicality" und die „semantic domains". Es folgen die Bibliographie (547–61) sowie ein Autoren- und Stellenregister (563–78).

Die Untersuchung ist—gerade im Blick auf die eingangs skizzierte exegetische Motivation—zweifelsohne ambitioniert. Das gilt insbesondere für die wichtige Mahnung, nicht einfach *various readings* gut zu heißen, also kulturwissenschaftlich bedingte Fragen auf die neutestamentlichen Texte zu übertragen, sondern die Texte selbst in ihrer textuellen Gestalt zum Ausgangspunkt methodischer Fragen zu machen. Und doch bilden Text und Methode keinen Kontrast (s.o.). Das gilt im übrigen auch oder sogar gerade für eine linguistisch basierte Diskursanalyse, die so wie andere Methoden oder *readings* letztlich aus kulturwissenschaftlichen Fragen und Paradigmen hervorgegangen ist und daher bis zu einem gewissen Grade ihrerseits durchaus immer aus einem sachfremden Zusammenhang an einen Text wie den Röm herangetragen werden wird. Da die ‚Diskurskritik' in der vorliegenden Untersuchung jedoch nicht in ihrer übergreifenden geistes- und kulturgeschichtlichen Bedeutung entfaltet (s. z.B. *Foucault*) und auf dieser Basis der linguistische Ansatz einer Diskursanalyse bewertet und definiert wird, bleiben diese und ähnliche Fragen weitgehend unbesprochen. Man kann am Ende der Lektüre dieses Buches freilich fragen, wieweit die Diskursanalyse wirklich neue und/oder differenzierende Einsichten in die textuelle Gestalt und in den propositionalen Gehalt von Röm 1–8 erlaubt. Ferner legt eine kritische Lektüre des Buches durchaus offen, dass die Anwendung linguistischer Methoden keineswegs zur ‚Objektivierbarkeit' des Textverstehens führt, wie mancher wünschen würde. Sie führt aber—und ist darin der Philologie verwandt—zu einer hohen Sensibilität im methodischen Umgang mit der Beschreibung von sprachlichen und textuellen Strukturen. Eine exegetisch-philologische Disziplin hat daher einen großen Bedarf an linguistischer Analytik. Und genau dazu leistet die vorliegende Untersuchung einen wichtigen Beitrag.

The Great Sermon Tradition as a Fiscal Framework in 1 Corinthians: Towards a Pauline Theology of Material Possessions, by Christopher L. Carter. Library of New Testament Studies 403. New York: T&T Clark, 2010. Pp. xi + 272. Hardcover. $130.00. ISBN 9780567473042.

Philip F. Esler, St. Mary's University College, Twickenham, London

The thesis of this volume (a revised version of a doctoral dissertation submitted to the University of Aberdeen and supervised by Andrew Clarke) is that in 1 Corinthians Paul expresses a particular view on material possessions because he has learned to do so from the Jesus tradition, in particular the oral tradition that lies behind the great sermons of Matthew and Luke. In so arguing, Carter sides with those who provide a positive answer to the long-running question of whether Paul knew about the dominical tradition. This debate was inaugurated in 1808 by Hermann Cludius, who had expressed skepticism of Paul's knowledge of Jesus. Carter offers numerous epithets for "relating to material possessions," of which the most common is "fiscal" (as in the book's title). While one sympathizes with the problem, "fiscal" relates more to the finances and taxation of the state and sounds odd in this context. In addition, the locus for what the historical Jesus said about possessions was a peasant economy where barter was more common than monetary transactions.

It would have been to Carter's advantage in handling this subject if he had drawn on the literature from that area of social psychology known as social identity theory, part of which concerns how groups embed distinctive behavioral norms among their members so that group identity is maintained, especially in new and ambiguous situations. Why would this help? Let us grant (as I believe) that Paul did not invent the morality of the Christ-movement and that the words of Jesus provided the stimulus for a new and very distinctive new moral vision in the first century C.E. (with the precious fragment of Paul's oral proclamation on the subject of the love that characterizes the Christ-movement in Rom 12:9–21 providing a good example of that vision). The issue that remains is whether the new ethical norms became so embedded in group identity that Christ-followers would have acted on them whether in any particular case they could link them to a particular *logion* of Jesus or not. The more one thinks about this the more it tends to erode the significance of the question Carter and the scholars before him have set for themselves. Did Paul speak as he did in Rom 12:9–21 because he "knew" similar *logia* directly attributed to Jesus of Nazareth or because these were just the norms/identity-descriptors of the new movement he had joined and that he probably just accepted in some general way went back to Jesus? Or does it really matter which is closer to the truth? Is the whole debate about whether Paul "knew" the words of Jesus that began with Cludius in 1808 simply a survival of ways of thinking about the data that look far less interesting when more sophisticated ways of understanding group formation, maintenance, and identity drawn from the social sciences are introduced?

Furthermore, along with the vast majority of New Testament scholars at present (hopefully the position will soon change), Carter also commits a fundamental category error in understanding key first-century data. This is to assume that we are dealing with two "religions," "Judaism" and "Christianity," two entities of the same broad type, whose adherents were "Jews" and "Christians," respectively. This view is expressed regularly in New Testament studies in the misleading metaphor of the "parting of the ways," with its picture of the sorrowful divergence of two similar entities. It is in the interests of historical truth to recognize that first-century *Ioudaioi* were an ethnic group, like the fifty or so other such groups existing around the Mediterranean mentioned by Josephus in the *Contra Apionem*. Although geography is just one part of ethnicity, all of them were known by the territory from which they sprang (whether they lived there or in diaspora), so we should call them "Judeans" to avoid exceptionalism, and all of them had an ethnic identity that included a religious dimension but was far larger than it. The Christ-movement had a completely different type of identity. There is no one epithet that captures it: it was certainly not ethnic, and its locus in strongly God-oriented house gatherings where members of Judean and other ethnic groups ate from the one loaf and drank from the one cup in memory of the Lord made it highly distinctive and, to some Judeans at least, threatening¾not because such practices were "heresy" (51) but because they were more akin to treason. This was the *ekklesia tou Theou* that Paul tried to destroy (Gal 1:13).

Carter's first chapter (1–16) summarizes the debate about Paul's knowledge of Jesus traditions (1–7), before moving on to a good coverage of writings on the attitude of the Bible (Paul in particular) to material possessions (7–14). Here Carter has some appropriately sharp comments to make on capitalist and prosperity approaches for the crudity of their exegesis, but he is unjustifiably harsh on liberation theology. Given that a driving force for liberation theology was the desire to discourage the Catholic poor of Latin America from fatalistically ignoring the injustices of this life on the basis they would receive their reward in heaven, it is rather surprising to see him taxing liberation theologians for "de-emphasizing the major biblical themes of eternal salvation and eschatology." Even more remarkable is his claim that liberation theologies "sometimes catalysed bloody revolutions" (10), an assertion for which he provides no evidence whatever. Does he think everyone just shares that view? On the other hand, blood was certainly shed *in the cause of* liberation theology, as when El Salvadorean Archbishop Oscar Romero was shot dead while saying Mass in a hospital chapel on 24 March 1980.

One issue not addressed in chapter 1 is just what aspects of the great sermons Carter has in mind as covering "material possessions." We have a clue when he favorably acknowledges a recent remark of Bruce Longenecker that a comparison of the attitudes of Jesus and Paul toward the poor is long overdue (14). Yet although one's view on material possessions and attitude to the poor are related, they are not the same, and it would have been helpful for Carter to explain more clearly the precise subject of his interest and what aspects of the great sermon tradition related to it. At times we find him arguing for links between Paul and the great sermon tradition in areas that are not necessarily related to material possessions or the treatment of the poor (e.g., his use of Michael Thompson's work on Rom 12–15 at pp. 69–70). His case really requires some modeling of "material possessions" that he does not provide.

In chapter 2 Carter argues for the dominical origins of the great sermon tradition (17–41). This gives him an opportunity for a detailed coverage of the vibrant recent debate, which updates or rejects form criticism, on how Jesus traditions could have survived in the first century in a culture that was largely oral and mnemonic, but with some literacy. He ranges across important contributions by Roli de la Cruz, David Parker, Birger Gerhardsson, Werner Kelber, Samual Byrskog, Richard Bauckham, and Alan Kirk, to mention only a few. His conclusion is that the theology of Jesus has been preserved in this tradition and transmitted, even if his words have not. While this is perfectly reasonable, some eyebrows may be raised at his failure to offer any detailed discussion of the texts of the Matthean or Lukan sermons in this chapter. In addition, as noted above, it would have been desirable for Carter to assess how ethical norms become embedded in groups and members socialized to accept them as an expression of group identity. On reflection, the question of how norms functioned in the early Christ-movement in relation to its identity is just as important as that of the mechanisms by which they were transmitted, although at present the latter dominates scholarly attention.

Carter argues in chapter 3 (42–72) that Paul probably knew the great sermon tradition. First he seeks to answer the case against his position by covering topics such as the apparent indifference of Paul to the Jesus traditions (42–47) and the express statements by Paul (2 Cor 5:16; Gal 1:12; 1 Cor 15:3) that seem to point to his ignorance of the historical Jesus (47–50). Then Carter moves on to positive arguments for his position: the knowledge Paul may have derived concerning Jesus while persecuting the church (47–51) or that was expressed in preaching initially to unconverted people that can be deduced largely from Acts (51–58). Yet his confidence in Acts does not always acknowledge negative data, such as the impossibility of reconciling Paul's statement of his inaugural preaching in Thessalonica¾how he preached to ex-idolaters (1 Thess 1:9)¾with the Lukan version in Acts 17:1–4. The next area Carter covers is the body of Pauline texts suggesting knowledge of the dominical tradition (58–67).

While Paul was aware of Jesus-material (especially in 1 Cor 7:10–11; 9:14 and probably also in various places in Rom 12–15, especially 12:14, which reflects what we now have in Matt 5:44 and Luke 6:27), it is a long stretch to say that he was aware of the "great sermon" tradition as such, to the extent that he can be presumed to know other aspects of it now found in Matt 5 and Luke 6. If one looks at what Paul says about love in Rom 12:9–21, the issue of material possessions appears only once, in the injunction at verse 13 to contribute to the needs of the holy ones and to practice hospitality, or twice if we include the direction at verse

20 to give food and drink to one's enemy. But none of these precise injunctions is found in Matt 5 or Luke 6. In other words, Paul was able to urge Christ-followers to bless those who persecuted them without mentioning other aspects of the great sermon tradition. It could well be the case, as already noted, that what we find in Rom 12:9–21 may represent an original idea or outlook of Jesus that has been elaborately developed in a whole range of situations by Paul or, far more likely, the Christ-movement before him to generate norms for members that would reflect its distinctive identity.

With chapter 4 (73–105), we finally arrive at Carter's analysis of the material on poverty and possessions in Matt 5–7 and Luke 6. In my view, the organization of the book would have been improved if this had been the first substantive chapter. Carter begins with an account of "eschatology" as the hermeneutical framework for the material (scare quotes for "eschatology" here because this word has now probably passed its sell-by date in New Testament studies, as a word that substitutes for fresh thinking about the phenomena in view). Having competently run through consistent and realized eschatology, he opts for "inaugurated eschatology" as the best approach, since it alone does justice to the "now" and the "not yet" dimensions, while giving the teaching real ethical bite without turning it into legalistic entrance-requirements (73–79). He argues for an "otherwordly" dimension to the material, where there is a heavenly zone in frame with its own privileges and obligations (79–97). Finally, he shows how this ethical material requires one to esteem people over things and warns of impending judgment (97–104). It would have been interesting if Carter had undertaken more to contextualize this material (or at least what he considers its dominical core) in early first-century Galilee, as Sean Freyne, for example, has so interestingly done. This would have brought out more sharply its radical edge (for example, in the way that Jesus subverted the local honor code) and allowed it to be more fully understood. We would then have a richer sense of what it means to tell a peasant subsisting from day to day to lend (that day's bread? his only cloak?) without hope of reward (Luke 6:34–35).

Chapter 5 (106–203) is a long and closely argued chapter where Carter seeks to relate 1 Corinthians to the great sermon tradition. He organizes the material along the themes he has previously employed in relation to the great sermon: eschatology as a hermeneutical framework (117–28), arguing for an "already but not yet" dimension to 1 Corinthians (e.g., in 1 Cor 3:11–15; 5:7; 6:9–10; 15:24); an otherworldly perspective (129–69), especially covering 1 Cor 1:26–28; 5:9–11; the ethical dimensions of an otherworldly perspective (169–83); the relational perspective of an otherworldly perspective (184–90); and impending judgment (190–202). The argument in this chapter is clearly written and critically engages with a wealth of scholarship (much of it very recent) on 1 Corinthians. Nevertheless, although he argues that, "despite the absence of quotation [in Corinthians], sermonic influence is plausible" (109), in my view he only proves such influence as a possibility. This is the case, for example, when he argues that the essence of 1 Cor 1:26–28 is "blessed are the poor, for theirs is the kingdom of God" (134).

While 1 Cor 1:26–28 could indicate that Paul is writing within a community that has taken on board views of Jesus, this falls a long way short of proving that he is aware of the great sermon material. Even more problematic is the argument that the injunctions to avoid rapacious people in 1 Cor 5:10–11 state "negatively what the sermons declare positively" in relation to commanding extravagant generosity with regard to possessions (182–83). This seems to miss the huge difference between not doing something evil and doing something extravagantly good that is embedded in the Matthean version of the great sermon: "Again you have heard that it was said…., but I say to you" (Matt 5).

In chapter 6 (204–25) Carter ably works through important aspects of the first-century context (biblical Judaism, Second Temple Judaism, and the Greco-Roman world) and reaches the view that none of them provides the common view on attitudes to material possessions to be found in the Sermon on the Mount tradition and in 1 Corinthians. He finds the major point of difference to be in "inaugurated eschatology."

His main conclusion (226–29) is that "a common oral source lies behind the great sermon tradition and 1 Corinthians" (226) and that "the pervasively eschatological and otherworldly perspective" (228) of Jesus and Paul lies at the heart of what they both have to say about material possessions.

This is an important book that offers interesting new insights into the much-disputed question of how Paul related to Jesus. While I doubt that Carter has proved knowledge by Paul of anything as specific as the great sermon, he has certainly in my view done a valuable job of proving that Paul did not invent the ethical dimension of Christianity nor do violence to Jesus' teaching (as many still claim). Although unfortunately not noticed by Carter, the likely explanation for the similarities he has demonstrated between the thought of Jesus and Paul is found in that branch of social psychology known as social identity theory. This explanation is that Jesus' distinctive moral thinking in these areas (and others) was embedded in the identity of the earliest Jesus-groups as norms for behavior (or identity-descriptors) that told the members who they were in relation to how they should behave¾as a matter of course and also in new and ambiguous situations. These norms were then faithfully maintained and transmitted throughout the Christ-movement so that they crop up in the writings of later Christ-followers as diverse as Paul, Matthew and Mark, James, and so on. What makes this even more remarkable is the way that these norms emerged in the life of Jesus, a member of the Judean ethnic group in Galilee, then moved into the entirely different (nonethnic) identity of the Christ-movement. In the result, then, Carter has performed the valuable service of forcing us to confront and acknowledge phenomena (even if I have interpreted their transmission by a different mechanism) that speak of the magnificent new moral vision that Jesus released into the world, which, when you encounter it in the great sermon or in Rom 12:9–21, sounds fresh as ever. We should all be grateful to him.

Gossip and Gender: Othering of Speech in the Pastoral Epistles, by Marianne Bjelland Kartzow. Beihefte zur Zeitschrift für die neutestamentliche Wissenschaft und die Kunde der älteren Kirche 164. Berlin: de Gruyter, 2009. Pp. xvi + 241. Hardcover. $139.00. ISBN 9783110215632.

Korinna Zamfir, Babeş-Bolyai University, Cluj, Romania

This volume is based on Kartzow's doctoral dissertation, written under the supervision of Turid Karlsen Seim. She explores the discourse of the Pastoral Epistles from a less-examined perspective, more specifically in the context of ancient texts dealing with gossip. Several passages in the Pastorals are involved in gossip discourse in different ways, construct gossip scenes to blame opponents through othering, and use charges of gossip to exercise control, in particular over women.

The introductory chapters explain the premises and methods of the research. The author applies insights from sociorhetorical criticism (mainly Vernon K. Robbins) and from gossip and gender studies. Sociorhetorical criticism is briefly summarized. These perspectives allow a focus on the inner texture of the text (and thereby on semantic fields suggestive for gossip), as well as an intertextual approach, disclosing parallels with ancient texts, *topoi*, and cultural echoes. Social-scientific criticism and the investigation of the ideological texture (via feminist criticism, discourse analysis, and postcolonial criticism) permit the dismantling of gossip discourses used to construct opponents and allow the interpreter to disrupt stereotypes (gossip as typically female speech) used to sustain misogyny. Gossip studies show that, although it is most often described as a vice of second-class humans, gossip may also have a positive psychological function and, from another viewpoint, may be seen as a form of alternative discourse or a counterdiscourse. Gossip may be a "hidden transcript" (cf. James Scott), a critique of power used by the unprivileged.

Chapter 2 investigates ancient gossip discourse. Kartzow defines the criteria used to identify gossip texts (44–50). In terms of content, gossip implies evaluative talk about a known but absent third party, true or false information about a third party, disclosure of intimate details, a touch of secrecy, reports about news and scandals, and anonymous rumors. From the viewpoint of function and effect, gossip may be a light mode of communication related to pleasure and/or an efficient form of communication with potentially damaging and dangerous effects. The description of the talker involves caricature, stereotypes, and tendentious descriptions. The exploration of the semantic field shows the variety of terms that may be subsumed to gossip. Kartzow analyzes the φλύαρ-root as a test-case and explores its various meanings in ancient sources, as background for the gossip terminology of the Pastoral Epistles, based on word searches in the Perseus Digital Library and in the TLG. The research focuses on Plutarch and other authors such as Epictetus, Philo, Josephus, Dorotheus (apparently never discussed so far), Dio Chrysostom, Theophilus, Dionysius of Halicarnassus, up to John of Damascus and Hesychius's Lexicon (in this order; one may wonder whether such late sources such as Damascenus are relevant). The semantic field includes a variety of meanings, such as telling foolish or nonsensical stories, frivolous chatter, superficial speech contrasted to the talk of educated men and to philosophical discourse, talkativeness and spreading of rumours that may endanger the city, gossip associated with inquisitiveness (φλυαρία and περιεργία), foolish talk of male opponents, speech of men lacking rhetorical training or comparable to that of women and emasculated men (51–60). The investigation shows that the common translation of φλύαρος with gossiper (1 Tim 5:13) is not universally supported and is far from being a typically female trait. The rhetorical use of the term is suggestive, as it frequently aims at discrediting the speech of male opponents. Referring to men it is used to question their manliness, thus their authority and reliability.

Chapter 3 deals with ancient representations of gossip in classical Greek, Greco-Roman, and Jewish texts from the seventh century B.C.E. to the third century C.E.: Semonides, Andocides, Lysias, Plutarch (*De garrulitate, Comp. Lyc. Num., Coniug. praec.*), Juvenal, Apuleius, Philo, Joseph and Aseneth, and the Mishnah (Sotah and Ketubbot). The texts are discussed in much detail (possibly envisaging readers unacquainted with these authors). The investigation shows that gossip is frequently associated with women (as well as slaves and children). Most texts view gossip negatively and emphasize its harmful effects. Female gossipers blur the border between private and public space, as they cause leakage from the *oikos* or inadequate communication from *polis* to *oikos* that threatens social order and the stability of the *oikos*. The content of this communication sometimes goes beyond the common content of gossip (see above) and involves political matters. Gendered gossip is used as stereotype-backing misogyny. However, some texts show that information gained from gossip is useful for male citizens, gossip functioning as a sort of information management and even as instrument of control over women. Furthermore, it seems that female gossip provides an insight into women's networks and may be regarded as a form of counterdiscourse lending ways of expression to women, excluded from public speech.

Chapters 4 and 5 discuss scholarly approaches to the gossip and gender discourse of the Pastoral Epistles and the representation of female gossipers in these writings. Kartzow places texts dealing with female gossip in the context of ancient gossip discourse and shows how the negative characterization of women's speech is part of the process of othering the opponents. She discusses a number of texts that (seem to) use gossip terminology: 1 Tim 3:11 and Tit 2:3 (διάβολος); 1 Tim 4:7 (γραώδεις μύθους), and, obviously, 1 Tim 5:13. Understandably, the passage on widows (seen to refer to a widows' order) in 1 Tim 5 is discussed in more detail, given a number of terms that may be subsumed to gossip (φλύαροι, περίεργοι, λαλοῦσαι τὰ μὴ δέοντα); 1 Tim 5:13 may envisage gossip not only because φλύαρος can denote gossip but because the author constructs a typical gossip scene: women gad about, leaving the domestic space, talk nonsense, and are meddlesome. However, the broad semantic field of the φλύαρ-root shows that it is difficult to decide what exactly young widows are accused of, all the more as nothing concrete is said about the content of their speech. The association between φλύαρος and περίεργος may refer, in Kartzow's view, to three possibilities: (1) gossip and witchcraft, (2) speaking nonsense or voicing opposing views and even alternative teachings, intruding in the male field, reprehensible either because it involves theological discussions or because teaching is performed by women, or (3) a scenario constructed by the author in order to discredit widows, by the use of the *topos* of women as gossipers and busybodies (152–55). By way of conclusion, Kartzow shows that "[t]he intention of 1 Tim 5:3–16 seems to be to limit the involvement of widows with the church and of the church with the widows, and a stereotype of gossip discourse is exploited as one of the rhetorical devices" (155). Even when widows are not accused of spreading heresy but the gossip terminology is used rhetorically, together with the also stereotyped allegation of female idleness, the effects are no less damaging. As Kartzow remarks, "a stereotype is a modelling device with enormous potential for harm. It is characterized by its ability to generate certainty in support of prejudice by appearing to be unambiguous and stable. In order to promote misogyny, stereotypes are used to construct and define what is typically and essentially feminine, repeatable, and unchangeable" (115). As Kartzow puts it, "only women bound to the *oikos* life will speak, teach, and learn properly, that is to be silent towards men, not be gossipy in all-female groups, but rather follow domesticated standards" (149). The last section of chapter 5 deals with further reflection on women and gossip, dealing with the sensitive issue of widows' reputation, based on some ancient texts and passages from the Gospels.

Chapter 6 discusses the connection between gossip and masculinity in ancient texts and in the Pastoral Epistles. Kartzow shows how men's association with gossip and with other feminine traits or attitudes is used by ancient authors to deconstruct the masculinity and credibility of men. In a similar manner, the strategy of the Pastoral Epistles includes the feminization of the opponents to undermine their authority. Their speech is described in terms recalling gossip, and they are associated with subversive and silly women. Chapter 7 summarizes the findings of the research.

Kartzow's investigation addresses an important topic, is generally careful, and leads to pertinent conclusions. The study of this volume will probably be mandatory to any scholar dealing with the Pastoral Epistles especially from the perspective of gender and gendered speech. Nonetheless, a few remarks are required. It may be true that gossip actually functioned as a counterdiscourse in the case of women who were barred from public speech. The problem is that the argument is very difficult to substantiate from the ancient texts quoted in chapters 2 and 3, and the required "imaginative scenes" (116) may only lead to speculations about the real influence of female speech (whether truly gossip or merely labeled so). Whereas some texts show how female gossip could be useful to men, I could not discover in these passages cases where women communicated important contents merely branded as gossip. This is not to say, of course, that such cases did not exist.

Concerning the Pastoral Epistles, one wonders in how far the use of διάβολος in 1 Tim 3:11 and Tit 2:3 means that the author labels the speech of the women actually addressed as gossip (136–37). The first is part of a standardized qualification list and has its counterpart in 3:8 with respect to male speech (μὴ διλόγους). The second is an exhortation that does not actually accuse women of being slanderers. These texts at most incorporate a stereotype about women but do not describe the way in which the addressed women speak. Further, in the discussion of 1 Tim 5:13, a central passage from the viewpoint of the topic, Kartzow does not deal with the textual problems of this verse, namely, with the various possibilities of supplying the elliptic ἀργαὶ μανθάνοθσιν. The passage, including this matter, was discussed very thoroughly by Ulrike Wagener (*Die Ordnung des "Hauses Gottes"*), but her discussion is omitted by Kartzow. One may agree or not with Wagener's suggestion about the predicative use of ἀργαί, φλύαροι, and περίεργοι in relation to μανθάνω, yet it should at least be noted that, based on 2 Tim 3:7; Tit 3:14, and Tit 2:1, 15, Wagener understands the verse to refer to widows learning from the opponents and teaching alternative doctrines.

Some important commentaries (Oberlinner, Marshall, Fiore, to mention only a few) are not used, and one has the impression that the author relies mostly on a few English sources. The important work of Annette Merz (*Die fiktive Selbstauslegung des Paulus*) goes unmentioned.

In the end, it is not very clear what the position of the author is. Should women in the Pastorals really be seen as gossipers, or do they articulate important contents merely labeled by the author as gossip, or is gossip mentioned only as a stereotype to blame women for other transgressions? It may be true that the author engages in various gossip discourses, but the positions mentioned above are mutually exclusive. If women did indeed engage in gossip as a form of counterdiscourse of the powerless, the author may not be accused of using misogynous stereotypes. If, on the contrary, women did not entertain gossip but were communicating significant matters (e.g., they were teaching), then the author undermined their speech by qualifying it as gossip and nonsense, but women were not using gossip as a form of counterdiscourse. (The latter option seems more likely to me and probably to the author as well). It is certainly difficult to elucidate the historical context of the texts addressed to women, yet one should eventually make a decision about the meaning of the gossip discourse.

At any rate, Kartzow has made a valuable contribution to the scholarship on the Pastoral Epistles.

Colossians: Encouragement to Walk in All Wisdom as Holy Ones in Christ, by John Paul Heil. Society of Biblical Literature Early Christianity and Its Literature 4. Atlanta: Society of Biblical Literature, 2010. Pp. xi + 227. Paper. $28.95. ISBN 9781589834842.

Rodrigo J. Morales, Marquette University, Milwaukee, Wisconsin

Does the Letter to the Colossians have a clear overarching structure that drives the main argument of the text? In this new monograph, John Paul Heil argues that, indeed, the letter does betray a deliberate structure. Heil offers a new analysis of the epistle, arguing that both in its grand scheme and in the details the text follows a chiastic pattern. In other words, each of the letter's ten main units form a chiasm (A-B-C-D-E-E'-D'-C'-B'-A'), and each of the individual units similarly have an internal chiastic structure. These chiasms, Heil suggests, serve to drive the basic purpose of the letter, which he expresses in the subtitle of the book: "Encouragement to Walk in All Wisdom as Holy Ones in Christ." The letter is thus primarily an exhortation that addresses the specific problems facing the Colossian (as well as the Laodicean; see Col 4:16) church, namely, the dangerous attraction of "false wisdom."

In the opening chapter Heil addresses some of the standard questions of New Testament scholarship: authorship, audience, and methodological approach. Siding with a minority of New Testament scholars, Heil argues that the letter is a genuine Pauline epistle, though he does not insist on the point, and the question has little effect on his argument. With regard to audience, Heil suggests a Gentile Christian group being tempted by the "philosophy" mentioned in Col 2:8. Though directed primarily to the Colossians, the letter may have been a circular one to be read in the churches of Laodicea and Hieropolis as well. In terms of methodology, Heil follows a literary-rhetorical, "audience-oriented" model, using "rhetoric" in a broad sense. His method thus amounts to a close reading of the text, looking for the literary structure of the letter and its rhetorical effect on the audience.

Following the introduction, the first chapter outlines nine criteria for determining chiastic structure and then applies these criteria to Colossians. Heil rightly notes, "It must be clear that the chiasm has not been subjectively imposed upon the text but actually subsists and operates objectively within the text" (13). Among the criteria he proposes, some of the more important include: the need for clear parallelism between the two "halves" of the chiastic structures; verbal parallelism should involve important language and imagery; the outline should correspond to natural divisions within the text; and "The central or pivotal as well as the final or climactic elements normally play key roles in the rhetorical strategy of the chiasm" (13). What distinguishes Heil's analysis of the structure of Colossians is that it is based primarily on specific verbal parallels rather than conceptual or thematic ones that tend to rely on subjective criteria. Heil further argues that the original audience(s) of the letter would have been more attuned to chiastic structures, even when the different members of a chiasm seem uneven in terms of length. Before turning to the analysis of the letter, Heil makes an important point regarding the significance of chiasms. Though a clear characteristic of these structures is balance, chiasms are not simply repetitive. On the contrary, in addition to the parallels between the two halves of the structure, each chiasm exhibits "an ongoing, dynamic progression" (15). Discovering the chiastic structure of a text is thus not simply a matter of aesthetics or artistry. Rather, it can help the reader determine the key words and pivotal ideas in the argument.

The chapter then unfolds in two parts. The first analyzes the ten units within the letter, arguing that each one exhibits an internal chiastic structure. The second half of the chapter argues that these ten units are also arranged according to a chiasm at the macro level. The rest of the book goes on to develop this analysis at greater length and detail, expounding the significance of these chiastic structures for the letter's argument.

Heil is to be commended for offering sensible and precise criteria for the detection of chiasms, and his analysis of the text often leads to interesting readings and insights. There is no question that the ancients used chiasm more than we moderns do, and Colossians certainly contains a number of chiastic structures, whether or not Paul (or the "implied Paul") intended them. With regard to the macro level of the letter, the most persuasive aspect of his case is the parallels between the four inner units (D-E-E'-D'). Particularly intriguing is the way the exhortation of Col 3:16 reflects 1:28, involving the same exact verbal forms in precisely inverse order. Another fascinating insight is the connection Heil makes between the fullness of deity dwelling bodily in Christ and in the body of Christ, that is, the church. But it is the discussion of the "mini-chiasm" in Col 1:16 that really shows the usefulness of this kind of analysis, demonstrating the intricate logic of this small section of the Colossians hymn.

While Heil presents a number of interesting and persuasive analyses of chiasms on the micro level, the argument that the entire letter is a chiasm on a macro level is less compelling. This is hardly surprising; Heil is not the first to attempt to show that an entire biblical book is arranged chiastically. Most of these previous attempts were less than a ringing success, so I approached the book with more than my fair share of skepticism. Unfortunately, despite some intriguing suggestions, Heil's argument did not manage to overcome my initial skepticism.

The main problem is that at points Heil's argument fails to meet his own criteria, such that several of the chiastic structures seem stretched. A few examples will suffice. In Col 3:1–7, the E' unit of the letter, Heil argues that the language of "living" (ἐζῆτε) in 3:7 parallels the language of "seeking" (ζητεῖτε) in 3:1. While the two words no doubt sound alike, the parallel seems a bit forced. Alliterative similarity is not nearly as persuasive as thematic and lexical similarity. More problematic is his discussion of the next unit (D') on at least two counts. First, while the A unit of this section lists five vices ("anger, rage, malice, slander, obscene talk), the corresponding virtues ("heartfelt compassion, kindness, humility, gentleness, patience") appear not in the A' unit but in the B' unit. Moreover, the verbal connections between the A and A' units are the pronouns "one another" (ἀλλήλους/ἀλλήλων) and "you" (καὶ ὑμεῖς). These hardly seem to fit Heil's fourth criterion: "The verbal parallelism should involve central or dominant imagery or terminology important to the rhetorical strategy of the text" (13). On a macro level, while it is true that both C and C' units refer to "heaven," the thematic parallels seem strained, with the first unit describing Paul's preaching of the gospel to every creature under heaven and the latter unit describing the lordship of Christ in the heavens. Again, though the verbal parallels are certainly present, there is not enough thematic coherence to go along with the verbal similarities.

Despite these weaknesses, Heil's monograph offers some genuinely insightful readings of Colossians, as well as useful criteria for determining genuine chiasms.

Any future study on chiastic structures in the New Testament would do well to consult this fine monograph.

Paul, Jerusalem and the Judaisers: The Galatian Crisis in Its Broadest Historical Context, by Ian J. Elmer. Wissenschaftliche Untersuchungen zum Neuen Testament 2/258. Tübingen: Mohr Siebeck, 2009. Pp. x + 249. Paper. €59.00. ISBN 9783161498077.

Davina C. Lopez, Eckerd College, St. Petersburg, Florida

Paul, Jerusalem and the Judaisers: The Galatian Crisis in Its Broadest Historical Context is a revision of the author's doctoral dissertation submitted to Australian Catholic University under David C. Sim. This book is a reconsideration of persistent scholarly debates surrounding such weighty issues in Pauline studies as the identity of Paul's "opponents," the nature of the conflict with the so-called opponents, and to what end(s) such conflict could possibly have shaped the apostle, his gospel, and his mission. There exists a deep history and wide variety of interpretive options and opinions on these matters. No clear consensus has emerged concerning the contours of Paul's interactions with his opponents, not to mention what such interactions could have signified in and among Pauline communities. Ian J. Elmer, however, is undeterred by the possibility of contemporary exegetical impasses. Like the ancient author of Luke-Acts, he seeks here to "'set the record straight' concerning the crisis in Galatia.... my aim is not simply to recover and reconstruct the events surrounding this significant event, but to draw lessons from the exercise that have significant bearing on how we deal with the vicissitudes of Christian life today" (v). The "vicissitudes of Christian life today" with which Elmer appears to be concerned include Jewish-Christian relations as well as what Paul's conflict with the "Judaisers" practically implies: a tension between "the temptation to merely conform, live according to the Laws and regulations and the radical call to live beyond all the boundary markers and distinctions based on legalities" (221). Through linking the "Galatian crisis" to possible backgrounds, causes, and aftermaths as reported in the context of the New Testament, the author presents a case for a more thoroughgoing understanding of Paul's difficulties and disagreements with others.

Chapter 1, "Understanding the Crisis: Paul and Jerusalem," comprises a brief survey of scholarly literature where the signal exegetical studies of Paul's opponents since F. C. Baur of the Tübingen school are evaluated. The goal of the chapter is to situate the study of Paul's opponents, who are treated here as the initiators of a missionary crisis in Galatia that led Paul to write his letter to that particular assembly in that particular place. Of note here is explicit attention to methodological concerns, such as the use of Acts to reconstruct and/or corroborate issues attended to in the Pauline correspondence as well as the lack of direct evidence from the figures scholars have come to call "Paul's opponents" themselves. On the utility of Acts, Elmer maintains that, while difficult, Acts is indeed most helpful as a historically informed document for efforts toward reconstructing and understanding the events surrounding the Galatian crisis (38). On the lack of data from opponents and others besides Paul, the author develops, using the work of J. Barclay and R. Longenecker, a "reverse reading" or "mirror-reading" approach wherein Paul's relationships with his opponents, and perhaps the identity of the opponents themselves, might be detected through a careful and critical engagement with Paul's rhetoric about such matters. A detailed plan of the study outlines the steps needed to propose a reconstruction of the Galatian crisis, its "Judaising" instigators, and Paul's response.

The following chapters delineate an attempt to follow and to develop the methodological approach outlined in chapter 1. Chapter 2, "The Roots of the Crisis: Hebrews and Hellenists," locates the controversy that led to the conflict in Galatia. Elmer provides an extended discussion of the prominence of Jerusalem as the location for the origins of the so-called Galatian crisis. Privileging the Acts of the Apostles as a, if not the, major source (even if "suspect") for a Pauline and early Christian timeline, it is here supposed that the dichotomic opposition between "law-observant Judaism" and "law-free Christianity" can be traced to pre-Pauline conflicts between the "Hebrews" and "Hellenists" as narrated by the author of Acts. Indeed, in conversation with the Pauline corpus, Elmer affirms that it is this dispute that "led to the advent of two distinct liturgical groupings within the Jerusalem church, each with its own language, its own Scriptures, its own worship services, its own leadership group, and even its own missionary fields" (79–80). Chapter 3, "The Background to the Crisis: Antioch and Jerusalem," deploys this conclusion as a lens through which to interpret the Antioch incident as narrated in Gal 2. Herein the so-called "final conflict" at Antioch signifies the divergences and oppositions between the Hebrews (Jerusalem adherents to Jewish custom) and Hellenists (originally Diaspora Jews but primarily Gentiles). For Elmer, the Antioch incident is evidence of the two distinctly different forms of faith in Christ, as well as of attempts by the "mother church" in Jerusalem to curb the activity of a completely law-free Gentile mission.

It is into the space opened by the "crisis" of attempts to force law observance upon Gentiles that Paul steps. After the Antioch incident, Paul's Gentile mission, according to Elmer, is partially predicated upon a desire to elude James's influence regarding matters of circumcision for non-Jews who want to claim Jewishness. *Paul, Jerusalem, and the Judaisers* positions this conflict, and Paul's response to it, as thoroughgoing and as that which serves as the context for the letter to the Galatians. It is this epistle to which Elmer turns exegetical attention in chapter 4, "The Crisis in Galatia: Paul and the Judaisers," where he rehearses the chronology of Galatians within the Pauline corpus as well as the possible location of the Galatian assemblies. Herein Paul's articulation of his gospel in Galatians is read as an antagonistic relationship with the law, indeed, as an attempt to negotiate the law as that which no longer holds validity in the communities Paul wishes to evangelize. The Galatian crisis, then, is positioned as a continuation of the original conflict between the Hebrews and Hellenists as narrated in Acts 6, as well as a turning point in the career of Paul as an apostle to the Gentiles. Galatians, then, is a document wherein Paul attempts to outline a perspective that avoids a theological link with either Jerusalem or Antioch, which leaves him "alone" in his attempts to resist the "circumcision putsch" (163).

The last two chapters provide readers with exegetical resources for understanding Paul's letters as interconnected, and perhaps interdependent, as a coherent collection. Chapter 5, "The Aftermath of the Crisis: Paul and Jerusalem," extends the argument that the various conflicts between Paul and his opponents remain a core issue throughout the Pauline corpus. Elmer discusses the oppositional rhetoric in the Corinthian correspondence as that which develops following the Galatian crisis. Likewise, similar issues threaten the Philippian community and Paul's supposed final visit to Jerusalem on account of the collection. Herein is proposed a consistency of conflict across Paul's letters that presupposes a consistency of the various opponents' identity as Judaizers. In fact, operating in alignment with the principle of Occam's razor (212), Elmer accepts as "the simplest explanation" the possibility that the opponents to which Paul alludes in the Corinthian correspondence and Philippians are those who may have played a role in the initial conflict between Paul and James at Jerusalem, which implies that the opposition between the Hebrews and Hellenists is that which influenced the whole of Paul's mission after his initial visit to Jerusalem and the fall-out from the Antioch incident. Chapter 6, "Revisiting the Crisis: Paul, Jerusalem, and the Judaisers," concludes Elmer's study by reiterating that its purpose is to place the Galatian crisis in a broad historical context, positing that there is a "cumulative" story to be told across Paul's letters, one that coheres with the Acts of the Apostles. In his final analysis, the author raises the incarnational nature of Christian living, restating the fundamental tension between living according to law and living into a higher, "radical" moral calling to live beyond boundaries.

Paul, Jerusalem and the Judaisers includes fairly adequate footnotes, a bibliography appropriate to the study, and three indices: ancient sources, modern authors, and subjects and key terms. Of these, the last is the least thoroughly presented. Of greater importance than the technical aspects of this monograph, however, is a series of methodological questions that might be raised by this work for the study of Galatians and Pauline literature as a whole. Chief among such questions is whether the structural proposition that the "broadest historical context" for Paul's letter to the Galatians should, in fact, be limited to a canonical New Testament context, and if so, what difference that should make for interpretation. Even as the author admits that there are some limits to doing so, the reassertion of Acts as a historical source for Paul's life and mission without significant attention, at the very least, to contemporaneous sources (not to mention historiographical issues) is a cause for serious exegetical concern. Similarly, a sustained conflation of Paul's historical context with his theological one runs throughout this work. That Christianity is a distinct theological and moral configuration in the first century of the common era is a presupposition that is not without complications, and yet it is presented here without substantial justification. Furthermore, attempts to synthesize Paul's letters as a consistent body of literature exhibiting similar, chronologically arranged, increasingly developed theological responses to Judaizing opponents have been repeatedly challenged by trajectories in Pauline studies that position the letters as occasional documents evidencing little of what we might now call a systematic theological orientation. It could be said that Elmer's study suffers from a lack of contextualization within the wider Pauline studies landscape, not to mention the field of New Testament studies as a whole.

Finally, it must be noted that emphasizing the conflict between Paul and the so-called Judaizers as the occasion for the mission to the Gentiles may, in the end, not do as much to further interreligious dialogue and negotiation in the contemporary world as the author might suppose. Given the trenchant controversies surrounding Paul's life and work, the propensity of modern readers to reconstruct an apostle most useful to our own purposes, and the persistence of interpretive strategies that (dis)place responsibility for modern problems onto ancient Pauline shoulders, raises a basic unaddressed question for exegetical studies like this one (and other recent releases in the WUNT 2 series): Who benefits from this kind of analysis, and who does not? Interpreters like Elmer who deploy the discourse of constructive morality, who use Paul to make claims about theological orientations and legitimations of religious affiliation in oppositional (perhaps even implicitly supersessionist) terms, and who want to present the breaking of all (Jewish, legal) boundaries as central to Christian identity, may do well to address the centrality of power and privilege as a matter of ethical responsibility. Following Elmer's framework, it would stand to reason that such ethical reflection is a matter of banal legalism. However, such boundary-asserting propositions represent an exegetical tradition with which this reviewer, in fine Pauline fashion, (respectfully) seeks to break.

Paul, the Corinthians and the Birth of Christian Hermeneutics, by Margaret M. Mitchell. Cambridge: Cambridge University Press, 2010. Pp. xiv + 178. Hardcover. $85.00. ISBN 9780521197953.

Thomas Schmeller, Goethe-Universität, Frankfurt am Main, Germany

Wer schon Texte von Margaret Mitchell gelesen hat (und wer hat das nicht?), weiß, dass sich die Lektüre immer lohnt. Die hohen Erwartungen, mit denen man dieses neue Buch aufschlägt, werden aber nicht nur erfüllt—sie werden weit übertroffen. Es gelingt Mitchell, exegetische Analysen zu den Korintherbriefen, rezeptionsgeschichtliche Entdeckungen zu den frühen Vätern und hermeneutische Ideen, die auf Paulus selbst zurückgehen, auf vorbildliche Weise miteinander zu verbinden.

Der Band enthält sechs Vorträge, die Mitchell 2008 als „Speaker's Lectures in Biblical Studies" an der Universität Oxford gehalten hat. Was die Texte verbindet, formuliert sie so:

The story of Paul's attempt to clarify the meaning of his letters to the Corinthians becomes, as we shall see, an inner-biblical process that fashioned a storehouse of hermeneutical principles from which his devoted followers in years to come would justify their own interpretive feats. The man who called himself 'all things to all people' (1 Cor 9:22), that quintessential claim of strategic adaptability, was to become the patron and exemplar of an early Christian exegesis (extending throughout the Mediterranean landscape of late antiquity) that would emulate his interpretive variability. (x)

Wie Paulus seine früheren Briefe nach Korinth in späteren Schreiben selbst deutete und für neue Situationen fruchtbar machte, gab eine Hermeneutik vor, die von den kirchlichen Auslegern übernommen wurde. Diese kommentierten oft weniger den Paulustext selbst als ihre jeweilige Situation und rechtfertigten dabei mit rhetorischen Mitteln je nach Bedarf eine wörtliche oder allegorische Deutung.

Der erste Vortrag ist überschrieben: „The Corinthian *diolkos*: passageway to early Christian biblical interpretation" (1–17). Mit einem Abschnitt aus dem Kommentar zum Hohenlied von Gregor von Nyssa zeigt Mitchell, wie dieser Autor die prinzipielle Unterscheidung zwischen wörtlicher und allegorischer Interpretation aufhebt und als das einzige Ziel der Auslegung den Nutzen für den Hörer benennt. Gregor beruft sich dabei auf Paulus (Röm 7,14; Gal 4,20.24; 1Kor 2,10.16; 9,9–10; 10,11; 2Kor 3,6.15–16 u.a.) und dessen rhetorische, d.h. am Nutzen orientierte Schriftauslegung. Die große Bedeutung, die Gregor in dieser Argumentation gerade den Korintherbriefen zuschreibt, ist nach Mitchell nicht zufällig. Erst in der Auseinandersetzung mit dieser Gemeinde wurde Paulus zum Begründer der christlichen Rhetorik und Schriftauslegung. In einem schönen Bild ausgedrückt:

The Corinthian correspondence is the *diolokos* carrying the cargo of hermeneutical tools from one end of the empire to another, from the first through the fourth centuries, and well beyond. (9)

Diese Sichtweise ist, wie Mitchell betont, nicht davon abhängig, ob man ihre Briefteilungshypothese zu 2Kor akzeptiert. Sie sieht 1Kor als einheitlichen Brief, während 2Kor aus folgenden (hier chronologisch geordneten) Teilen bestehen soll: (1) 8; (2) 2,14–7,4; (3) 10–13; (4) 1,1–2,13; 7,5–16; 13,11–13; (5) 9. In der Abfolge dieser Briefe bemühte sich Paulus darum, seine vorangegangenen Schreiben immer wieder neu auszulegen. Er verwendete dazu verschiedene Methoden (nicht nur die allegorische), wobei er Anleihen bei den rhetorischen Mitteln machte, die man beim Grammatiker lernen konnte. Wie diese früheren Briefen zu Argumenten wurden, die im Konflikt mit den Korinthern für die Sache des Paulus sprachen, so versuchten auch die späteren Ausleger nicht nur, diese Briefe zu verstehen, sondern sie in einem bestimmten Verständnis für die eigene Sache zu verwenden. Mitchell nennt das „the ‚agonistic paradigm of interpretation'" (16).

Im zweiten Vortrag („The *agôn* of Pauline interpretation", 18–37) wird der in 1Kor 5,9–11 bezeugte Konflikt um das richtige Verständnis eines früheren Briefs besprochen. Paulus zitiert in V. 9 aus diesem Brief, weist in V. 10 ein bestimmtes Verständnis zurück und erläutert in V. 11 das richtige Verständnis. Diese Argumentation mit dem genauen Wortlaut und den Folgen einer bestimmten Auffassung gehörte zu den Techniken, die in der rhetorischen Ausbildung der Zeit vermittelt wurden. Sowohl für wörtliche wie für allegorische Textdeutungen standen hier Topoi zur Verfügung (Mitchell verweist besonders auf Ciceros *De inventione*), deren Wahl nicht von einer Vorentscheidung für die eine oder andere Richtung (Literalisten vs. Allegoristen), sondern von der konkreten Situation abhing.

Der nächste Teil („Anthropological hermeneutics: between rhetoric and philosophy", 38–57) befasst sich vor allem mit der schwierigen Deutung von 1Kor 1f. Die Antithesen Weisheit vs. Torheit, Stärke vs. Schwäche setzt Paulus als Argument für eine allegorische Hermeneutik ein: „You say foolish but you mean wise; you see weakness but you really see power" (40). Diese Hermeneutik sollen die Korinther weiterführen, und das bedeutet: Sie dürfen sich nicht in ihren Parteistreitigkeiten mit der Weisheit der Welt, die in Wirklichkeit Torheit ist, einlassen. Aber es gibt nicht nur den Dualismus zwischen Juden und Griechen einerseits und den Berufenen andererseits. Paulus unterscheidet daneben zwischen pneumatischen (= vollkommenen), psychischen und sarkischen Menschen (2,6-3,4), wobei die Korinther auf der untersten Ebene angesiedelt werden. Überraschend ist die Überlagerung eines zweiteiligen (rhetorischen) durch ein dreiteiliges (anthropologisches) Schema, die von Paulus nicht erklärt wird. Mitchell zeigt, in welche Schwierigkeiten dieses ungelöste Problem spätere Ausleger (Ignatius, Irenäus, Origenes) brachte.

In den beiden Korintherbriefen begegnen zwei Bilder für die Schwierigkeiten der Hermeneutik: der Spiegel und die Hülle. Mit diesen Texten befasst sich Mitchell in ihrem vierten Vortrag („The mirror and the veil: hermeneutics of occlusion", 58–78). Beide Bilder können zum Ausdruck von Offenheit und Verborgenheit, vollständiger und teilweiser Wahrnehmung verwendet werden. Paulus verbindet hier das agonistisch-rhetorische mit dem apokalyptisch-poetischen Paradigma: Zu ersterem gehört die Klarheit, zu letzterem das Geheimnis. In 2Kor 3 vergleicht Paulus seinen eigenen unverhüllten Dienst mit dem Dienst des Mose, auf dessen Gesicht eine Hülle lag. Damit versucht er Vorwürfe aus Korinth zu entkräften, die an seinen Briefen Mehrdeutigkeit oder Unverständlichkeit kritisierten. Im Hintergrund steht die rhetorische Variabilität des Paulus, der als Gemeindeorganisator Klarheit und Ordnung liebte, als Prophet und Dichter aber Andeutungen und geheimnisvolle Bilder. Der Konflikt mit den Korinthern könnte hier eine Wurzel haben: „some read Paul as mysterious or opaque when they sought clarity (on finances for instance), and prizing clarity precisely when they championed the mysterious aura of ecstatic speech" (67). Mit diesem Vorwurf setzt sich Paulus in 2,14–7,4 auseinander (in der Sicht Mitchells ein eigener Brief). 2Kor 3,6 war also ursprünglich keine allgemeingültige allegorische Maxime, sondern ein sehr eng auf die Situation bezogener Versuch des Paulus, seine Glaubwürdigkeit zu verteidigen, indem er den *Text* seiner Briefe als Mittel der eigenen Authentifizierung ablehnt. Während er in 1Kor 5,9–11 auf einem wörtlichen Verständnis besteht, wird hier der Text gerade abgewertet. Mit dieser hermeneutischen Strategie („he named and modelled what is […] a spectrum or 'veil scale' of carefully and strategically calibrated movement along a spectrum of the seen and unseen, the dark and the illumined", 77) fand er unzählige Nachfolger.

In einem nach Mitchells Auffassung anderen Brief, 2Kor 10–13, versucht Paulus die Korinther davon zu überzeugen, dass er auch für sie ein Apostel ist, weil er dafür drei Zeugen anführen kann (2Kor 13,1). Um diesen Text, den Mitchell für „one of the most extraordinary and inventive passages in early Christian literature" (82) hält, geht es im fünften Vortrag („Visible signs, multiple witnesses: interpretive criteria in the agonistic paradigm", 79–94). Der erste Zeuge, den Paulus für sich anführt, ist ein Narr, der Dinge über ihn sagen kann, die Paulus selbst nie für sich anführen könnte (11,1–12,13). Der zweite Zeuge ist „ein Mensch, den ich kenne" (12,2), der ins Paradies entrückt wurde. Die unpersönliche Formulierung soll den Eindruck einer Selbstempfehlung verhindern (vgl. 10,18). Der dritte Zeuge schließlich ist der Herr selbst, der zu Paulus gesagt hat: „Es genügt dir meine Gnade, denn die Kraft wird in Schwachheit vollendet" (12,9). Damit verwandelt er einen Einwand der Gegner, seine körperliche Schwäche, seine Leidensexistenz, in einen Beweis für seine Apostolizität. Paulus definiert hier Hermeneutik so, dass die Wahrheit eines Texts wie im Gerichtssaal mit Hilfe von Zeugen erkannt wird. Seine christlichen Rezipienten (Mitchell zitiert Beispiele aus Johannes Chrysostomus und Origenes) haben später diese Praxis einer skrupulös genauen Textprüfung zur Grundlage ihrer Interpretationen gemacht.

Der letzte Vortrag („Hermeneutical exhaustion and the end[s] of interpretation", 95–115) geht von 2Kor 1,13 aus: „Wir schreiben euch nichts anderes, als was ihr lest und versteht". Dieser Satz ist—wie die Geschichte der korinthischen Korrespondenz zeigt—offensichtlich falsch. Es war eben gerade nicht so, als seien die Paulusbriefe eindeutige und erfolgreiche Kommunikationsmittel gewesen. Paulus sieht sich an dieser Stelle immer noch dem Vorwurf ausgesetzt, seine Briefe hätten verborgene Botschaften und geheime Absichten. Er behauptet zunächst die Möglichkeit einfachen Verstehens, um genau ein solches Verstehen herbeizuführen. Aber er gibt in den Abschnitten 1,1–2,13; 7,5–16; 13,11–13, die Mitchell für einen eigenen Brief hält, auch Hilfen für das Verständnis der früheren Briefe. In 7,8–13 bietet er eine Lektüreanweisung zum Tränenbrief (für Mitchell 2Kor 10–13). In 2,4 verweist er auf sein wahres Anliegen mit diesem Brief, dessen Ziel nicht die Trauer war, die er faktisch verursachte. Er unterscheidet also das Geschriebene von der Absicht—ein weiterer rhetorischer Topos.

Nach einer hilfreichen Zusammenfassung (106–7) formuliert Mitchell, was heutige Exeget/innen von dem agonistischen Paradigma, das Paulus entwickelt hat und das seine frühen Interpreten übernommen haben, lernen können. Bei der Auslegung sind drei Tugenden mit einander zu verknüpfen: eine genaue Prü-

fung der Textaussagen (ἀκρίβεια), eine Ausrichtung auf den Nutzen der Leser/
innen (ὠφέλεια) und die Milde (ἐπιείκεια), die zwischen den beiden genannten
Tugenden vermittelt. Es gilt, den vermeintlich kontradiktorischen Gegensatz zwischen einem wörtlichen und einem bildlichen Textverständnis als rhetorischen
Gemeinplatz zu durchschauen. Die Auslegung muss gerade das Spektrum zwischen diesen beiden Polen, die Position auf Mitchells „veil scale" (113; vgl. o.), in
den Blick nehmen:

> texts which matter, biblical texts in this case, are of interest *because of the tension
> they embody between the plain and the unplain*, the clear and the unclear. Biblical
> scholars are not just in charge of the 'plain', but they themselves are continually
> recalibrating a kind of veil scale of disclosure of meanings hidden by authors, by
> linguistic distance, by historical recontextualization, by readerly deficiency, by
> authorial obscurity. (113)

Was Mitchell hier als die Tugenden der Auslegung formuliert, hat sie selbst
vorgeführt. Sie verbindet ἀκρίβεια, ὠφέλεια und ἐπιείκεια auf mustergültige
Weise. An der Texttreue ihrer Deutungen von Paulus- und Vätertexten gibt es
keinen Zweifel. Der Nutzen der Lektüre liegt nicht nur in neuen Einsichten in
die Geschichte und die Grundlagen der christlichen Hermeneutik, sondern
auch in der Freude beim Lesen über einen geschliffenen, ebenso niveauvol-
len wie unterhaltsamen Vortragsstil. Die Milde im Ausgleich zwischen diesen
beiden Qualitäten ist schon an Mitchells Humor, aber auch an ihrer Erfindung
eines „veil scale" erkennbar. Mitchells Buch ist—wie soll man es sonst sagen?—
ein Meisterwerk.

GENERAL EPISTLES AND HEBREWS

1 Peter: A Handbook on the Greek Text, by Mark Dubis. Baylor Handbook on the
Greek New Testament. Waco, Tex.: Baylor University Press, 2010. Pp. xxi + 202.
Paper. $24.95. ISBN 9781932792621.

John H. Elliott, University of San Francisco, San Francisco, California

This volume on 1 Peter is the most recent in the Baylor Handbook on the
Greek New Testament, with studies on Luke, Acts, Ephesians, and 1–3 John
already in print. The series in general focuses on "the mechanics of the Greek
text" (ix), with particular attention to grammar and syntax. Its aim is "to help
move linguistic insights into the mainstream of New Testament reference works"
and to reduce misunderstandings of the Greek language (ix, x), such as confusion
concerning deponency and middle-voice Greek verbs. Its volumes are intended
for readers with some facility in the Koine Greek.

Each volume treats sections of the biblical text *seriatim* from opening to
close. An initial fresh translation is followed by a verse-by-verse analysis of the

section, with comments on grammatical, lexical, syntactical, semantic, and text-critical matters. Disputed issues are identified, along with selective mention of commentators and translations favoring different options. This volume on 1 Peter, as all in the series, has a glossary of technical terms (179–83), a limited bibliography including up-to-date grammatical tools (185–92), an author index (199–202), and an especially useful "grammar index" (193–98). The Greek text used apparently is that of Nestle-Aland, *Novum Testamentum Graece*, 27th ed., although this is not explicitly stated—something to consider for future volumes in the series. This volume's author is professor of biblical studies in the School of Theology and Missions at Union University, Jackson, Tennessee, and author of *Messianic Woes in First Peter: Suffering and Eschatology in 1 Peter 4:12–19* (New York: Lang, 2002).

The Greek text of 1 Peter poses more than a few complex questions concerning grammar, syntax, semantics, and translation so that a study intent on identifying and clarifying these issues is highly welcome. Dubis's sectioning of 1 Peter (treated as an integral letter) follows, more or less, the current consensus regarding its units: 1:1–2; 1:3–12; 1:13–21; 1:22–2:10; 2:11–17; 2:18–25; 3:1–7; 3:8–12; 3:13–22; 4:1–6; 4:7–11; 4:12–19; 5:1–11; 5:12–14. His own rather wooden translation stays close to the Greek text and seeks to embody and display the results of his textual analysis. (A full intact translation, in addition to or in place of sections scattered throughout, would have been useful, especially for indicating consistencies or variations in rendition.) Analysis focuses on grammar, syntax, and word order but includes regular attention to textual variants as related to grammatical and syntactical points and occasional comment on word meanings.

Here are a few textual probes. Dubis prefers "exiles" for *parepidêmoi* (1:2; 2:11) and "sojourners" for *paroikoi* (:11), with both taken metaphorically, but with no supporting discussion and only reference to other scholarly studies. The adept and attractive alliterative Greek sequence *timiô haimati hôs amnou amômou kai aspilou Christou* (1:18) unfortunately disappears in his rendition, "with the precious blood—like that of a totally perfect lamb—of Christ" (22), with the further result that readers do not see these terms as part of 1 Peter's stress on holiness in this and other sections of the letter. Dubis notes the collective aspect of the *nomen actionis hierateuma* in 2:5 ("body, community of persons acting as priests") but translates with the limp abstract "priesthood." Despite the Petrine author's intentional stress on the distinctive *collective identity* of the believing community with this and associated terms of 2:9 (*genos* [inaccurately translated "race"], *basileion* [taken as an adjective, with no mention of its relation to *oikos* in 2:5], *ethnos, laos*) , Dubis curiously opines that "the priestly status of individual Christians would seem to logically follow" (49)—a notion neither derived from nor developed in 1 Peter but indebted to subsequent theological doctrine. He renders *hypotassô* verbs (2:13, 18; 3:1, 5, 22; 5:5) as "submit" rather than "subordinate," ignoring and obscuring the fact that the issue of social "order" (*taxis*, a paronym) underlies 2:13–3:7 and 5:1–5. The syntax of 3:3–4, Dubis recognizes, is "difficult" (86), but his attempt to sort things out is not fully successful and his translation rather awkward (83). What he refers to as a "vague phrase" (114, 177) is in fact 1 Peter's particular designation for followers of Jesus Christ (3:15; 5:10, 14) and equivalent in function to *Christianos* (4:16), though the latter term originated not with Jesus' followers (as did *en Christô*) but unbelieving outsiders. Sometimes decisions are insensitive to the culture—another crucial factor bearing on grammatical choices. Since females were socially embedded in males, the masculine term *neoteroi* (5:5) need not denote solely males (*pace* Dubis, 158, 163–64) but more likely includes males and females together as do *philadelphia* (1:22), *philadelphos* (3:8), and *adelphotês* (2:17, 5:9). *Adelphotês* (unique to 1 Peter in the New Testament) is also the likely noun implied by the *syneklektê* of 5:13 ("co-elect brother [and sister] hood "at Babylon/Rome (*pace* Dubis, 176). Commenting on Silvanus (correctly identified as courier and not amanuensis of the letter, 173–74) and the clause, "as I esteem him," Dubis apparently inadvertently speaks of "Paul" when he means Peter: "According to the standard by which *Paul* reckons faithfulness, Silvanus has indeed been faithful" (174). The reference, "see also Kittel," in regard to the meaning of *logikon* in 2:2 (44) is inadequate information for the presumed reader; "see Kittel, *TDNT* 4:142–43" would have been preferable. The translation of conditional *ei* (2:3) with "if" (36) rather than "since" is ill-advised and inconsistent with Dubis's own observation concerning the assumed reality of the addressees' cognitive and emotional experience of Christ (45). Dubis's treatment of the difficult *en hô* occurrences (1:6; 2:12; 3:16, 19; 4:4) fails, especially at 3:19, to expose the theological as well as syntactical problems at stake, with his own preferences less than convincing.

Nevertheless, the volume abounds with helpful information. I especially welcome Dubis's rendering of *psychê* as "life" rather than "soul" (1:9, 22; 2:11, 25; 3:20; 4:19), his conclusion (25–26) that numerous participles in 1 Peter function as imperatives (1:13, 14; 2:1, 12, 18; 3:1, 7, 8, 16; 4:8, 10; 5:7), and many of his choices concerning the difficult verses of 3:18–22, though he neglects to alert students to the interesting step construction appearing in 3:19–22 and miscasts the passage as a "digression" (129) when it is in reality essential to the argument of 3:18–4:6. Translators and interpreters need to pay particular attention to Dubis's instructive comments on the sense of middle-voice verbs (xi–xiii, xxi) the multiple functions of *hôs* (24–25), and those of the particle *de* (13–14). Equally valuable are the numerous comments on textual variants, which show how ancient scribes were aware of and dealt with many of these issues.

The text's grammar and syntax are the chief focus of this volume. Issues such as the structure of 1 Peter, how its major and minor units are determined, matters of vocabulary, style, the meaning of most words, and all isagogical questions (authorship, addressees and destination, social situation and rhetorical strategy, date and place of composition) are left undiscussed or are mentioned minimally in passing. The intricate literary structures of certain passages, such as 2:4–10 or 3:18–22 are not discussed; Old Testament quotations from both the Septuagint and Masoretic Text are noted, but other traditions receive no tradition-critical or form-critical analysis; passing attention is given to the nature of the letter's vocabulary and literary style.

This restricted focus is both the strength and the limit of the volume. The significant contribution of the volume (and the series) is the scrutiny and space given to important matters that usually receive only limited attention in the commentaries. The readers, presumably beginning Greek students, are shown, at the hand of Greek biblical writings, the essential importance of grammar and syntax to the meaning of texts and how translations reflect decisions in this regard. This is no small accomplishment in an age when classrooms leave students uninformed of the grammar and syntax of their *own native language*, let alone ancient Greek. The question about deponents, the communicative capacity of the Greek middle voice, and significance of doublet constructions, among many mechanical mysteries more, are in full view here.

At the same time, the book also demonstrates how frequently judgments are made based not simply on linguistic theory but also on *Sprachgefühl* and *Sachgefühl*, sense of the language and of the writing as a whole (verbs as either middles or passives; *de* as marker of new development or in some cases specifically adversative; the referents and functions of the problematic *en hô* occurrences [1:6; 2:12; 3:16, 19; 4:4]; prepositions indicating either purpose or result; taking terms as either literal or metaphorical; rhetorical aims and strategies; etc.). Appeals to logic and theological considerations also pepper the volume throughout and shape decisions on syntax and semantics. Readers and users need to keep in mind that knowing the linguistic mechanics of a writing is essential, yet by no means the whole exegetical picture.

The volume is not—nor does it represent itself to be—a complete exegetical guide to the substance, structure, and meaning of the Greek text. It is, at best, a companion volume, one important tool among others in the bulging exegetical toolbox. Scholars as well as students should hail, and avail themselves of, this series. Baylor University Press deserves our thanks for making it a reality.

Solidarity Perfected: Beneficent Christology in the Epistle to the Hebrews, by Kevin B. McCruden. Beihefte zur Zeitschrift für die neutestamentliche Wissenschaft und die Kunde der älteren Kirche 159. Berlin: de Gruyter, 2008. Pp. viii+159. Cloth. $105.00. ISBN 9783110205541.

Craig R. Koester, Luther Seminary, St. Paul, Minnesota

A hallmark of the Christology of Hebrews is the idea that Jesus was made "perfect" through what he suffered (Heb 2:10; 5:9; 7:28). The notion of perfection is evocative but difficult to define. In this helpful contribution, McCruden proposes that the terminology of perfection is applied to Jesus in order "to attest the depth of the Son's beneficent commitment to, and solidarity with, the socially marginalized members of this early Christian community" (3). More specifically, perfection points to the way the beneficent character of the divine presence is revealed through Jesus' suffering, death, and exaltation.

The first chapter clearly summarizes the range of proposals that have been made concerning the meaning of perfection (τελειόω) in Hebrews. One approach is to take the term as a summary of the way Jesus was brought through suffering to heavenly glory, which marks the completion or fulfillment of God's will for him and for those who follow. Since the exalted Jesus now serves as the heavenly high priest for the Christian community, some have also noted that the verb τελειοῦν is used in the Greek translation of the biblical expression for priestly consecration, which is "to fill the hands" (τελειοῦν τὰς χεῖρας). Some interpreters have emphasized the element of suffering in the process of perfection, construing it in terms of Jesus' own moral development that led to his present situation in glory. A more common approach, however, is to say that Jesus' suffering made him perfectly suited to carry out his vocation on behalf of others, since suffering allows him fully to identify with those he redeems.

To refine the notion, McCruden turns to the nonliterary papyri, which use the term τελειοῦν for contracts that are being put into effect. Although he recognizes that transferring meaning from the attestation of documents to the person of Jesus might seem implausible, he argues that the connotations of something being public and definitive are applicable. He points out instances where Hebrews uses language in a manner similar to the papyri in order to show that something is confirmed or sure (e.g., βεβαιόω and cognates in 2:2–3; 3:14; 6:16, 19; 9:17; 13:9).

The next question concerns what has been attested in Christ. In chapter 3 McCruden notes how Hebrews cites Ps 8, which speaks of God's purposes for humanity, and applies it specifically to Jesus (Heb 2:5–8). The idea is that Jesus can serve as humanity's representative. McCruden then notes how Jesus entered the realm of death in order to liberate people, much as Heracles had done according to Greco-Roman tradition. Jesus is similar to Heracles in that he shows beneficence and commitment. The difference is that sacrifice plays a much larger role in the example of Jesus. Putting the concepts together, he proposes that what is perfected or "attested" is Jesus' character and solidarity with his people.

Chapter 4 turns to the role of *philanthropia* for Hebrews' Christology. Since that word is not used in Hebrews, McCruden takes it as a summary of a concept that is conveyed in other ways. He notes that *philanthropia* (benevolence, goodwill) was a recognized virtue for human rulers and deities in the Greco-Roman world. The notion was then taken over into Hellenistic Judaism, where it was a theme in Philo's understanding of God. McCruden sees a bridge between the Hellenistic-Jewish notion of *philanthropia* and the theology of Hebrews in the mention of Jesus' piety or reverence (εὐλάβεια, 5:7), a context where Jesus' perfection is also mentioned (5:9)

The heart of the book is found in chapter 5, which brings together Hebrews' high-priestly Christology with the idea of divine beneficence. McCruden notes that in the context in which Hebrews was composed the audience would have been a minority group on the margin of the dominant culture. Since Christians lacked the priests and temples that were common in Greco-Roman cities, it makes sense for the author to present Christ as the highest and most noble of all high priests. At the same time, the author gives distinctive emphasis to Christ's sympathy for people, which brings his *philanthropia* to expression.

The key move in the argument is that perfection is not primarily Christ's movement from suffering into glory but the reverse: "Perfection comments on the extent of Christ's participation in the human sphere" (114). Rather than underscoring Christ's current elevated status, the idea gives central place to his commitment to humankind, which is expressed through the offering of his own flesh and blood (120). The final chapter notes that this message would have been appropriate for a community under stress in the city of Rome.

A strength of this monograph is that it takes seriously the way Hebrews emphasizes the depth of Jesus' identification with the suffering of other people. Although Hebrews begins on a high note with the portrayal of Christ in glory (Heb 1:1–14), the writer quickly shifts the frame of reference to include Jesus' suffering and death, which occurs with and for other people (2:9–10). Giving Jesus' suffering an integral place in the process of "perfection" is very important. The most distinctive aspect of McCruden's proposal is that Jesus' solidarity with human beings—extending through his life and death—is revelatory. By his suffering Jesus reveals the character of God. Given the opening lines of Hebrews, which tell of God communicating or speaking through the Son (1:1–4), it is helpful to include Jesus' suffering in that act of divine revelation.

One question that arises for me is whether the revelatory interpretation of "perfection" can encompass the full range of usage in Hebrews. At a number of points the writer speaks about Jesus being made perfect (2:10; 5:9; 7:28), but he also speaks about the faithful being made perfect (10:14; 11:40; 12:23). If perfection is revelatory when it refers to Jesus' beneficent identification with human beings, then what would that expression mean when applied to other people? Since they are already enmeshed in the realities of human existence, their perfection would presumably mean something different. Would exploring the analogy between the perfecting of Jesus and the perfecting of others alter the proposal that McCruden makes here? For me it is important to couple the shared experience of suffering more strongly with the shared promise of moving through suffering into glory, which is also a dimension of the perfection theme (2:10).

I appreciate McCruden's willingness to include the papyri in his research. Scholars have often mined Hellenistic Jewish texts and philosophical writings for help in understanding the language of Hebrews, so broadening the range of source material is helpful. Hebrews does use language that resonates with Hellenistic practices of accounts, inheritance, wills, and oaths (1:4; 2:4; 4:13; 6:16). What is less clear is that language used for the attestation or execution of a document can be transferred to Jesus. Although McCruden makes every effort to address that problem, the case would be stronger if closer precedents could be found for perfection as the attestation of a person's character. It would also be helpful to see more clearly why *philanthropia* was selected as key to Hebrews' Christology, since the term itself is not used in Hebrews and the concept was used in various ways in Greco-Roman sources.

McCruden's work encourages interpreters to explore the significance of Hebrews for readers living in an interreligious context. Hebrews clearly links themes such as priesthood to biblical antecedents, yet the implications of the book's Christology give encouragement to readers living in a Greco-Roman context, where there were competing understandings of priesthood and sacrifice. The portrayal of Jesus as a priest who fully identifies with those who struggle underscores the importance of the imagery for a beleaguered group of first-century readers. This monograph helps us see that in new ways.

La première épître de Pierre, by Jacques Schlosser. Commentaire biblique: Nouveau Testament 21. Paris: Cerf, 2011. Pp. 331. Cloth. €38.00. ISBN 9782204092579.

Jean-Paul Michaud, Université Saint-Paul, Ottawa, Ontario, Canada

Jacques Schlosser, professeur émérite de Nouveau Testament à la faculté de théologie catholique de l'université de Strasbourg nous donne ici un substantiel commentaire de *La première épître de Pierre* (1 P). Il avait déjà présenté les deux épîtres de Pierre et celle de Jude dans D. Marguerat (éd.), *Introduction au Nouveau Testament. Son histoire, son écriture, sa théologie*, Genève, Labor et Fides, 2008, 4ᵉ éd. revue et augmentée, ainsi que « Le corpus des épîtres catholiques », dans J. Schlosser (ed.), *The Catholic Epistles and the Tradition* (BETL, CLXXVI), Leuven, University Press/Uitgeverij Peeters, 2004, 3–41. C'est dire qu'il était tout à fait préparé pour ce commentaire dans la nouvelle collection de commentaires bibliques scientifiques (dont c'est le 6ᵉ volume paru à date) publiés par les Éditions du Cerf.

Il s'agit en effet d'un commentaire scientifique. Conformément aux usages de la collection, le volume commence par une bibliographie d'ensemble, suivie d'une introduction générale traitant des questions classiques : genre littéraire, destinataires, date, auteur, lieu de composition, agencement, plan et but. Le commentaire proprement dit comporte d'abord une traduction de travail la plus littérale possible, la bibliographie propre du passage étudié, suivie de deux parties, intitulées *Interprétation* et *Notes*. La partie *Interprétation* se veut accessible à un large public (enseignants et étudiants en théologie, prêtres, pasteurs, laïcs ayant une formation théologique, spécialistes des littératures de l'Antiquité). Large public, si l'on veut, mais on ne vise évidemment pas un milieu populaire ou peu scolarisé. Dans cette partie les mots grecs sont systématiquement translittérés. Le fait que pour chaque mot ou chaque expression, on évoque toutes les interprétations proposées, en donnant entre parenthèses, de manière abrégée il est vrai, les références aux auteurs concernés, au lieu de les reléguer en bas de page, ne rend pas facile la lecture de ce commentaire. Mais cela rassure sur le sérieux des opinions de l'auteur et permet aux spécialistes une vérification rapide des diverses positions. La partie *Notes*, qui garde le même modèle pour les références, est plus technique. Elle s'occupe de philologie, d'histoire et présente des états de la question sur les thèmes (de l'AT et du NT) effleurés dans l'*Interprétation*. Dans cette partie, où le grec revient au naturel (!), les spécialistes trouveront la justification des prises de position du commentaire. Le tout se termine par une série d'index (de la Bible et de la littérature ancienne, des thèmes, des auteurs modernes et des excursus) très utiles aux chercheurs.

À l'encontre de ceux qui voyaient dans le texte de Pierre un document liturgique ou une homélie baptismale, l'introduction le range fermement dans le genre épistolaire. Il s'agit d'une lettre, mais, étant donné son caractère peu concret, d'une lettre encyclique (30). Malgré la densité exceptionnelle des références à l'AT et, plus encore, l'application aux destinataires de termes et d'images issus du judaïsme, Jacques Schlosser (JS) estime que la lettre s'adresse à des communautés constituées en majorité de pagano-chrétiens (1,14.18 ; 2,10.25 ; 4,3-4), prenant ainsi position, entre autres, contre J.D.G. Dunn, *Beginning from Jerusalem*, qui croit que la lettre s'adresse plutôt aux congrégations « principally made up of Jewish believers in the Western diaspora » (1166). Une série d'observations convergentes (parmi lesquelles il faut souligner la parenté entre 1 P 2,12 et Mt 5,16 ; 1 P 3,14 et Mt 5,10 : la première trace véritable de l'évangile de Matthieu [voir la thèse de R. Metzner, *Die Reception des Matthäusevangeliums in 1. Petrusbrief*, Tübingen, 1995]) poussent à ne pas placer 1 P à une date antérieure aux années 70 et à descendre peut-être jusqu'à 90. Il s'ensuit que l'apôtre Pierre, dont la tradition place le martyre en 64 ou 65, ne peut pas être l'auteur de ce texte. Néanmoins cette lettre, écrite probablement de Rome (Babylone, en 5,13), sous un pseudonyme, « recueille peut-être en partie l'héritage de Pierre » (36). À ce propos, Schlosser renvoie à Dunn (*Beginning from Jerusalem*, 1156), lequel, cependant, sans parler explicitement d'*école* pétrinienne, met en plus grand relief « the legacy of Peter » (1157) et l'impact que Pierre aurait produit sur des communautés principalement judéo-chrétiennes, alors que les lettres de Paul nous introduisent surtout dans les communautés « of earliest Gentile Christianity » (Dunn, 1166). En fin d'introduction, le thème de la souffrance est fortement marqué : les chrétiens qui souffrent en tant que chrétiens (1 P 4,16) participent ainsi aux souffrances du Christ (4,13). Ce thème central est plusieurs fois relié à « la volonté de Dieu » (3,17 ; 4,19 ; voir aussi 2,13.19), non pas comme une invitation à se résigner à l'inévitable, mais comme un appel à la foi et à l'espérance en un Dieu protecteur des siens, défini bellement comme « le Dieu de toute grâce » (5,10).

Au moment où les études critiques s'intéressent de plus en plus à l'histoire des chrétiens du premier siècle et aux différents groupes et courants théologiques que reflètent spécialement les écrits chrétiens du deuxième siècle non retenus dans le canon, un texte comme celui de la première épître de Pierre prend, historiquement et théologiquement, une grande importance. Il témoigne, en effet, autour de la fin du premier siècle, d'une très ferme maîtrise doctrinale que certains seraient portés à dater beaucoup plus tardivement. Je note quelques-unes de ces lignes de force que le commentaire de JS met très bien en évidence, touchant aussi bien la théologie proprement dite (le discours sur Dieu) que la christologie et l'ecclésiologie.

JS souligne fortement le théocentrisme remarquable de cet écrit (62, 248, 282, 287-88). Le mot Dieu (*theos*) y est employé 39 fois (55). Ce Dieu est Saint, Père, juge, maître de l'histoire (103). Initiateur du salut « réalisé » en Jésus mort et ressuscité, c'est lui qui est au premier plan (87, 101–2). Si le Père est le plus souvent mentionné, 1 P témoigne néanmoins véritablement de la foi trinitaire (1 P 1,2 ; 1,3–12 et 2,4-5, où les sacrifices « spirituels » renvoient indirectement à l'Esprit) (124). Il faut encore noter en 1 P 4,17 la mention de l'« Évangile de Dieu », expression plutôt rare (Mc 1,14 ; Rm 1,1 ; 15,16 ; 2 Co 11,7 ; 1 Th 2,2.8–9), qui désigne bien le message chrétien, mais « en tant qu'il a Dieu pour origine » (273). Sans oublier, en toute fin (5,12), « le Dieu de toute grâce » (5,10) et cette « grâce de Dieu » (5,12), qui désigne le message chrétien véhiculé dans l'épître et dont le mot « grâce » constitue le coeur (298).

Mais c'est la christologie qui domine tout de même en ce texte. Dans une lettre consacrée à donner un sens à la souffrance des destinataires (65), c'est la souffrance ou la mort du Christ (219) qui reste le thème le plus marqué. Mais mort et résurrection ne sont pas dissociées (219). Cette dernière est rappelée sans cesse (1,3 ; les gloires de 1,11 ; 1,21 ; parole *vivante* de 1,23 ; pierre *vivante* de 2,4 ; 3,18.21…). Cette résurrection « n'est pas seulement pour le Christ une entrée dans la vie de Dieu, elle lui assure un nouveau statut, l'exaltation » (102). Ce kérygme pétrinien, à la fin du premier siècle, rejoint tout à fait celui de Paul (79). JS précise même que c'est dans 1 P qu'on trouve énoncées de la façon la plus claire toutes les étapes du kérygme : souffrance et mort (2,21 ; 3,18), résurrection/exaltation (3,21), ascension, exaltation et domination sur les puissances (3,22) (232). Un autre point que 1 P est seul à mentionner et qui est fortement rappelé tout au long du commentaire, c'est celui de la présence de l'Esprit du Christ dans les prophètes d'autrefois (1,11). Pierre est le seul à attribuer explicitement au Christ et à son Esprit une présence active dans les prophètes (79). C'est une manière de souligner la continuité de la révélation et l'unité de fond entre l'AT et le NT, une reconnaissance qui est l'une des lignes de force de ce commentaire. En révélant ainsi « la voix anticipée de l'Évangile » (82) ou cet évangile « qui était caché au creux des prophéties » (Prigent, 80), Pierre fournit une clé importante pour comprendre et apprécier les nombreuses citations de l'AT et allusions qui parsèment l'épître, en particulier celles du prophète Isaïe, cité explicitement en deux passages (1 P 1,24 et 2,6), mais à qui l'auteur fait allusion un très grand nombre de fois, utilisant même des expressions d'Isaïe (en 2,22–25) pour « exposer directement le kérygme chrétien » (83). À tel point que JS parle du quatrième chant du Serviteur comme « arrière-plan garanti de 1 P » (225) et qu'il ose affirmer, à propos de 2,24, que Pierre non seulement suit de près le texte d'Isaïe, mais « qu'il l'a sans doute sous les yeux » (177). À ceci il faut ajouter le thème de l'exode—un thème particulièrement cher à JS (voir son article « Le thème exodial dans la Prima Petri », dans *À la recherche de la parole*, Paris, 2006, 387–403)—valorisé d'ailleurs en Is 40–66, où est annoncé le renouvellement par Dieu de la merveille de l'exode. C'est une ligne de fond que JS fait ressortir tout au long du commentaire (98, 100, 104–5, 128–30, 141, 157, 294). À ce propos, on peut penser que cette extraordinaire connaissance des Écritures par ce « lecteur de l'AT » (294) qu'est Pierre aurait été un bon argument à développer en faveur de la pseudépigraphie. En raison de cette activité du Christ au temps des prophètes (1,10–12), et plus encore de la mention de ce Christ

« prédestiné avant la fondation du monde » (1,20), « il paraît indiquer, selon JS, d'attribuer à l'auteur la conviction théologique de la préexistence ontologique ou absolue du Christ auprès de Dieu » (102). On serait ainsi, avec quelques années d'anticipation, tout près de la haute christologie johannique.

Il reste que la christologie de cette lettre est liée à deux textes mystérieux que l'exégèse n'a pas encore réussi à déchiffrer parfaitement : la proclamation du Christ aux esprits en prison en 3,19 et l'évangélisation des morts en 4,6, deux références qu'on a rattachées traditionnellement à la doctrine de la descente du Christ aux enfers énoncée dans le Credo. JS analyse minutieusement ces textes. Dans l'ensemble, il se rallie à la position magnifiquement exposée par W.J. Dalton, dans *Christ's Proclamation to the Spirits. A Study of 1 Peter 3: 18–4:6* (1989). Selon cette lecture, les deux passages de 3,18–22 et 4,6 se réfèrent à des événements différents et doivent être interprétés indépendamment. Celui de 3,18–22 est alors lu à la lumière des traditions juives qui rattachent l'origine du mal à la chute des anges telle que racontée en Gn 6,1–4, traditions qu'on retrouve dans le livre d'Hénoch (1, Hén 6–10 ; 15–16 ; 19 ; 21,10 et 106,13–18) et dans celui des Jubilés (5; 7,21). Ces traditions juives, étant étonnamment reprises dans 2 P 2,4–5 (une épître qui se réfère formellement à 1 P en 2 P 3,1) et en Jude 6, fourniraient, peut-être, selon JS, le sens à donner aux « esprits en prison » de 3,19. Le *kèrussein* de 3,19 ne viserait plus alors, pour une très rare fois dans tout le NT, l'annonce de l'Évangile comprenant une offre de conversion (217), mais, selon Dalton que JS semble suivre ici, l'annonce de la victoire du Christ et la soumission des forces angéliques : « Christ does not preach to the spirits : his appearance before them as risen Lord is a proclamation, a proclamation that Jesus is Lord, that the rule of the powers of evil is ended » (*Christ's Proclamation...*, 158). Par contre, l'évangélisation des morts en 4,6 viserait, selon Dalton, les chrétiens évangélisés à un moment de leur vie et décédés depuis. Le contexte serait alors celui que reflète la première aux Thessaloniciens, où les croyants s'inquiétaient de ceux qui étaient morts avant la venue glorieuse du Christ, la parousie. Sensible peut-être aux bons argument de David G. Horrell (« Who are "The Dead" and When was the Gospel Preached to Them ? : The Interpretation of 1 Peter 4.6 », in *NTS* 48 (2003), 70–89), qui a disqualifié cette lecture, JS n'insiste pas sur ce contexte. On n'a, en effet, aucune indication que le problème qui inquiétait les Thessaloniciens soit à l'horizon de 1 P. En se ralliant, pour 3,19, au modèle explicatif de Dalton qu'il estimait « le moins mauvais » (214), JS laissait bien entendre que ce modèle n'était pas sans problème. Pour 4,6, en tout cas, il semble encore moins assuré. Il termine son commentaire sur ce passage mystérieux en rappelant la position de Horrell qui « tente de réhabiliter l'interprétation plus classique : dans un acte unique le Christ adresse, à l'ensemble des défunts qui attendent dans le Shéol, un message ouvert leur permettant d'adhérer à l'Évangile et d'être sauvés » (244). JS n'endosse pas explicitement cette position, bien sûr, mais on se demande si, en terminant sur cette perspective, il ne trahirait pas tout de même une certaine envie d'y croire ! Il laisse, en tout cas, la question ouverte : « Le dernier mot sur cette question n'est donc certainement pas dit » (244).

Découlant de cette christologie—la situation des croyants est liée intrinsèquement à celle du Christ—la lettre présente une ecclésiologie d'une richesse théologique impressionnante. C'est particulièrement le cas en 2,4-10. Après avoir appliqué au Christ la métaphore de la « pierre vivante »—le qualificatif « vivant » évoquant ici la résurrection (121)—la métaphore est reportée sur les croyants qui sont dits à leur tour « pierres vivantes, édifiés en maison spirituelle, pour constituer une sainte communauté sacerdotale, pour offrir des sacrifices spirituels agréables à Dieu par Jésus Christ » (2,5). L'attitude attendue du peuple de Dieu est exprimée en termes cultuels, mais en régime chrétien il n'y a plus de place pour des sacrifices offerts au Temple (d'ailleurs disparu sans doute à l'époque où la lettre est écrite) et le commentaire rattache fort bien ces sacrifices spirituels aux « belles oeuvres » de 2,12. Communauté « sacerdotale », mais d'un sacerdoce qui s'exerce au plan éthique : c'est par les « belles oeuvres » que les croyants ont accès à Dieu (124). On retrouverait ici tout à fait, il me semble, la perspective éthique exprimée en He 13,15-16, qu'il eût été heureux, peut-être, de rappeler, où les sacrifices qui plaisent à Dieu sont l'*eupoiia* et la *koinônia*. Par ailleurs, dans son bref *excursus* sur «Le sacerdoce des baptisés» (141-42), JS montre bien que le sacerdoce commun dont il est ici question ne transmet pas aux baptisés les pouvoirs attribués aux ministères ordonnés (142). Aux anciens et aux pasteurs dont il est question en 5,1-4, qui incarnent le ministère de direction dans la communauté, ne sont attribuées aucunes caractéristiques sacerdotales. Sur la base de 1 P, on ne peut donc discuter du sacerdoce des baptisés et du sacerdoce ministériel (142). Il faut encore souligner, dans cette perspective ecclésiologique, la participation des croyants au Christ mort et ressuscité qu'implique le baptême, « qui vous sauve par la résurrection de Jésus Christ » (3,21; p. 219 et 222-23), le tout intimement lié au thème de la renaissance/régénération (1,3.23 ; 2,2 ; p. 110).

Il y aurait bien d'autres richesses à signaler dans ce commentaire qui fait le point sur tout ce qu'on a pu écrire récemment, dans les différentes langues, sur la première épître de Pierre. Il faut féliciter Jacques Schlosser et le remercier d'avoir mené à bien un travail qui devrait rester longtemps, pour ceux et celles qui se préoccupent des origines du christianisme et de la pensée théologique qui y circulait, une référence incontournable.

Reading Second Peter with New Eyes: Methodological Reassessments of the Letter of Second Peter, edited by Robert L. Webb and Duane F. Watson. Library of New Testament Studies 382. New York: T&T Clark, 2010. Pp. 224. Hardcover. $140.00. ISBN 9780567033635.

David K. Burge, Union Bible Theological College, Ulaanbaatar, Mongolia

The value of this volume is its presentation of a variety of methodological approaches to 2 Peter, following 150 years of scholarship that has been predominantly historical-critical in nature. The book is a revised compilation of six papers originally presented at the 2007 Annual Meeting of the Society of Biblical Literature under the theme "Methodological Reassessments of the Letters of James, Peter, and Jude." Alongside similar volumes on James, 1 Peter, and Jude, the present volume represents the fourth and final in this series.

In the introduction, the editors Webb and Watson do a commendable job of showing how the various papers might flow from one study to the next. Reading through the chapters, however, particularly the three chapters that use sociorhetorical interpretation (chs. 2–4), there is a trying redundancy as the three authors begin their chapters by defining the same methodology (spanning four long pages in the case of Callan's chapter). The contributors to this volume do, however, express awareness of the other chapters and make apposite references to them.

Approaching this book with a sense of expectation that the well-worn critical debates will be put aside, it seemed unfortunate that the first three sentences of the introduction begin with the no-longer unanimous and thus contentious view that 2 Peter was written by a pseudonymous author. Indeed, the commentaries of two of the contributors, Ruth Anne Reese and Gene Green (published 2007 and 2008), argue that Peter is a likely candidate for authorship. That said, the entire work is not absorbed by these matters and does push beyond them to a large extent.

In chapter 1, Gene Green argues that 2 Peter's borrowing from Jude (the majority view) can be best explained as an example of the ancient practice of *imitatio* (or μίμησις), in which highly respected sources were integrated into an author's own work. More discussion may have been helpful in Green's analysis about another practice that could equally explain 2 Peter's use of Jude, namely, the practice among the authors of Scripture in both Testaments to cite texts they deemed authoritative. Could it that 2 Peter's use of Jude is not best explained as adhering to Greco-Roman practice, nor necessarily because of Jude's familial relationship to Jesus, but because he simply deemed Jude's letter (or an earlier common source) to bear divine authority (as he clearly did Paul's writings in 3:15–16)? Hence the corollary Green draws about the text being a window into the social status of Jesus' family members is, in my view, not yet as certain as is acknowledged in the chapter. Nevertheless, Green's article is a stimulating read that shows a good aquaintance with extrabiblical sources and generates genuinely original insights.

The next three chapters (chs. 2–4) offer sociorhetorical interpretations (hereafter SRI) of 2 Peter. In chapter 2, Duane Watson provides a description and comparison of rhetorical and sociorhetorical analysis. The attention he then gives to 2 Pet 3:1–13 adequately demonstrates his point about the distinction.

Terrance Callan (ch. 3) shares the interest of Watson, employing SRI for an analysis of the apocalyptic sections of the letter (1:16–2:10a and 3:1–13). He demonstrates that the rhetology of these sections (i.e., their argumentation) is strengthened and nuanced, or, to use his word, is given "discernment" (88) by their rhetography (i.e., the images evoked by the text).

Dennis D. Sylva also adopts SRI to show how the individual images in 2 Pet 1:3–15, from the perspective of conceptual integration theory, "are developed into a coherent larger picture of a journey in ways designed to inspire the reader to undertake the rigors of the moral life rather than sink into self-serving sensuality" (91). His interest is in the powerful use and connection of 2 Peter's vivid images to achieve the purpose of ethical exhortation.

The editors' decision to commit three of the volume's six chapters to the sociorhetorical methodology developed by Vernon Robbins exposes the book in a large degree to the same praise and criticism due to Robbins's approach. SRI's capacity to produce a reading "with new eyes" demands some reflection in this review.

First, the "newness" of the observations made using SRI in these three chapters seems overstated. While the value of SRI appears to be that it examines technically what has been understood intuitively, the results seem little more than highly complex descriptions of that which was already commonly perceived through basic exegetical practices. Interestingly, James C. Miller in a later chapter refers to Neyrey's use of social-rhetorical criticism as leading him to "methodological overkill, detecting what is readily apparent by other, simpler means" (159). The same charge might be laid against the SRI analyses in chapters 2–4 of this volume.

Second, while the many approaches to 2 Peter using SRI generate fresh observations, it must also be recognized that such analysis is far removed from the author's and recipients' perception of the letter. Postmodernists may not be concerned by this, and such concerns need not deter such analyses, but the enormous epistemological gap between modern and ancient mind is in my view inadequately acknowledged. Watson states, for example, that the author's "use of intertexture is also directed by his need to increase the ethos of his argumentation" (36). Did the author really perceive such a need, and did he see "intertexture" as the means by which to fulfill it? When the author is "credited" for complying with the rhetorical formulations of modern observers in these three chapters, the analyses have an anachronistic ring. Elsewhere Watson says, "Rather than simply using the apocalyptic rhetorolect alone and affirming that the Parousia is a reality, the author embeds other rhetorolects in his refutation to create an inner progression, from the intentions of God in creation (apocalyptic), to the redemptive plan of God (priestly), to the ultimate creation of a new household at the consummation (wisdom)" (55). Is this really what the author "did"? In these and other examples the author and the letter seem overwhelmed by the strong arm of this epistemologically foreign methodology.

Offering a change from SRI, Ruth Anne Reese (ch. 5) describes the narrative method as it has been applied to New Testament Gospels and to the less overt narrative of New Testament epistles. She then offers a clearly presented narrative analysis of 2 Peter that focuses on the "events, narrative voice, and time" of 2 Peter.

The final chapter, written by James C. Miller, approaches 2 Peter from the sociological category of "collective identity." Miller's interest is in the way the assumptions of 2 Peter's author about the audience, and the author's instruction to them, served to shape the recipients' self-understanding and behavior. To explore this topic, Miller employs categories such as "norms and identity descriptors," "categorization," and "collective memory." Miller's view that his perspective "differs from many that have gone before" (176) is true, but more in the sense of the (social-scientific) vocabulary and methodology he employs than in any new discovery per se. This does not deny, however, that his observations are well constructed and to some degree new.

Indeed, this is one challenge that comes with the recent and rapid explosion of interpretive approaches and volumes that gather them together. In this volume at least, the originality that is on display is predominantly the terminology and methodology employed rather than any substantial contribution to understanding the *object* of our study: 2 Peter. Readers of this volume who consider methodology to be more a means to an end than an end in itself might find themselves somewhat frustrated by the emphases and conclusions of this study of 2 Peter. This volume does, however, contain substantial as well as what might be called terminological or methodological originality, with Green's chapter in my view offering the most substantial contribution to our knowledge of the letter itself.

In summary, *Reading Second Peter with New Eyes* is a stimulating and welcome addition to 2 Peter scholarship, especially for those with an interest in modern interpretive methods. Indeed, a significant benefit of the book is the introduction it offers readers to the field of hermeneutics. Six competent 2 Peter scholars explain their interpretive approach before putting it to work on the text. By pressing beyond traditional critical concerns and allowing 2 Peter to be interpreted as a unified work written by a competent author, this volume achieves its purpose of bringing to light new features of the letter.

Friendship and Benefaction in James, by Alicia J. Batten. Emory Studies in Early Christianity. Blandford Forum: Deo, 2010. Pp. vi + 222. Paper. $35.95. ISBN 9781905679102.

Oda Wischmeyer, Friedrich-Alexander-Universität Erlangen-Nürnberg, Erlangen, Germany

Alicia J. Batten legt in ‚*Friendship and Benefaction in James*' ihre überarbeitete Dissertation vor, die von John S. Kloppenborg betreut wurde. Alicia Batten, die gegenwärtig an der University of Sudbery/Ont. lehrt, hat 2009 bereits eine Einführung in den Jakobusbrief unter dem Titel: ‚*What are they saying about the Letter of James*' (Mahwah/Minn.: Paulist Press) geschrieben und mehrere Aufsätze zur Sprache von Arm und Reich, zu Gott als Wohltäter oder Patron und zu ideologischen Strategien im Jakobusbrief veröffentlicht. Ihr exegetisches Interesse wird von Fragestellungen der *Context Group* und sozialgeschichtlichen Konzepten wie *patronage* und *benefaction* bestimmt. Ihre Methode ist die des *social-rhetorical criticism*, die sie leicht didaktisch vereinfacht auf S. 7 beschreibt.

In ihrer Dissertation befragt sie zwei antike Konzepte, *friendship* und *benefaction*, auf ihre Leistung für die Interpretation des Jakobusbriefes. Ihre These ist,

Freundschaft sei im Jakobusbrief von *benefaction*, nicht von *patronage* her konzipiert: „Thus the intricate knot in which patronage, friendship and benefaction were entangled must be untied such that James's strategy of invoking friendship and benefaction to undermine patronage can be understood" (4). Batten versteht das Konzept von *patronage* "as one of the rhetorical exigencies that the letter of James addresses", als eines der wichtigen Probleme, mit denen sich der Brief auseinandersetzt: „James exposes the ‚false friendship' of patron-client relations" (8).

Battens Dissertation verbindet gründliche Einführungen in die Themen von Freundschaft, Patronatswesen und Wohltätigkeit mit exegetischen Kapiteln zu Jak 1,2–18; 2,1–13.14–26 und 4,13–4,10. Kap. 1 ist der Freundschaft in der griechisch-römischen Antike, im frühen Judentum und im frühen Christentum gewidmet. Sie zeichnet ein kenntnis- und facettenreiches Bild antiker Freundschaftskonzeptionen (besonders gestützt auf die Arbeiten von D. Konstan). Besonderes Gewicht legt sie u.a. auf die Freundschaftskonzepte von Aristoteles, Cicero und Ben Sira (anhand der Arbeiten von J. Corley und F. Reiterer). Insgesamt findet sie in der gesamten griechisch-römischen Antike ein Freundschaftsverständnis, das von „loyalty, generosity, reliability, equanimity" gekennzeichnet ist und auch das Sterben für den Freund einschließen kann (41). Einige Aspekte beleuchtet sie besonders: (1) das Motiv, Freunde seien ‚ein Herz und eine Seele' (für Batten der Hintergrund für die Kritik am *dípsychos* in Jak), (2) Freunde hätten ‚alles gemeinsam' (der sog. ‚Liebeskommunismus' der Apostelgeschichte), (3) die „fictive kinship language" (46), die statt *philós* lieber *adelphós/adelphé* verwendet (unter Hinweis auf P. Arzt-Grabner und Ph. A. Harland). Ihr Fazit lautet: „We have seen that qualities such as loyalty, faithfulness, being of ‚one mind/one soul', sharing possessions, as well as proving one's friendship through trials, were commonly associated with friendship, appearing in Graeco-Roman, Jewish and Christian sources" (55). Sie weist darauf hin, dass Schriftsteller wie Ben Sira, Philon und Paulus der Freundschaft eine theologische Dimension geben. Allerdings trifft dies meiner Meinung nach vor allem auf die johanneische Schriftengruppe zu, die bei Batten zu kurz kommt (35). Batten teilt L.M. Whites Interpretation des Philipperhymnus, nach der Phil 2,8 Ausdruck höchster Freundschaft ist. Allerdings steht 2,8 unter dem Stichwort des Gehorsams (anders vielleicht Röm 5,6–8, Batten 35, Anm. 141). Außerdem scheint mir auch unabhängig von Phil 2 der Nachweis, dass Phil ein ‚Freundschaftsbrief' sei, nicht erbracht.

Kap. 3 gilt den „distinctions between friendship, benefaction and patronage, as the language of friendship was regularly employed in the latter two forms of relationships" (55). Während Euergetismus vor allem den Göttern bzw. dem Gott Israels und den Königen, dann aber auch den führenden römischen Personenkreisen wie den Senatoren zukomme (vgl. den Art. Euergetes in: RAC 6, Stuttgart 1966, 848–860, B. Kötting) und nach Batten grundsätzlich altruistisch konzipiert ist (anders z.B. die Interpretation des Phänomens bei Paul Veyne, den Batten nicht einbezieht), stellte das Patronats-/Klientenwesen eine wichtige Säule des sozialen Lebens in der antiken Mittelmeerwelt dar. Batten stellt die griechische politische *philos*-Konzeption unter Hinweis auf G. Herman kurz dar. Ausführlich behandelt sie die römische *clientelia* im Gegensatz zur *amicitia* unter ausführlicher Benutzung besonders von Troels Engberg-Pedersens Arbeiten zu Plutarchs Schrift über Freundschaft und Schmeichelei und *parrhesía*. Allerdings werden weder Schmeichelei noch *parrhesía* im Jakobusbrief thematisiert. Das Ergebnis von Kap. 3 ist: „It is easy to understand how ‚friend' is used within the exchange systems of both benefaction and patronage. These two forms of exchange overlap with one another in a variety of ways, but they are also distinct" (88). Die thematischen Einführungen ziehen in sehr besonnener Weise umfangreiche Literatur heran und vermitteln einen ebenso soliden wie aktuellen Einblick in die behandelten Konzepte.

In den Kapiteln 4-6 erprobt Batten die Relevanz ihres sozialhistorischen Konzepts an ausgewählten Texten des Jakobusbriefes. Dabei geht sie stets nach denselben Parametern vor: author to hearers—community members—God (as benefactor or friend). In Kap. 4 untersucht sie nach einleitenden Bemerkungen zu (1) Jak als „'literary letter'" (93), zum (2) *exordium* und (3) zur Bedeutung der Rhetorik für Jak (unter besonderer Bezugnahme auf W.H. Wachob) Jak 1,2-18. Batten findet in diesem Text die wichtigen Aufgaben des *exordium* erfüllt: die Etablierung der Autorität des Schreibenden und die Angabe der Themen. Battens Interesse gilt den Konzepten von Freundschaft und Euergetismus: beides findet sie in 1,2-18. Jak ist zwar kein Freundschaftsbrief, sondern der Typ von „moral exhortation and advice" (108), aber der Verfasser spricht als Lehrer mit *parrhesía* und redet sein Auditorium in freundschaftlicher Weise mit *adelphoí* an. Und: „James encourages qualities in his audience consistent with the friendship tradition" (110). Den *dípsychos* von 1,8; 4,8 interpretiert Batten als negatives Gegenbild zur freundschaftlichen Tugend des ‚Ein Herz und eine Seele'-Motivs. Auch Gott selbst wird im Kontrast zum *dípsychos* als „generous benefactor" (118) dargestellt. Battens Fazit: zwar werden weder Freundschaft noch Euergetismus in 1,2-18 thematisiert, aber sie stellen die Konzepte dar, vor deren Hintergrund der Text erst seine Konsistenz erhält.

Kap. 5 beschäftigt sich mit Jak 2,1-13 und 14-26. Bei der rhetorischen Analyse folgt Batten vor allem D.F. Watson (NTS 39, 1993, 94-121) und versteht die beiden Texte als jeweils vollständige Argumentationsgänge. Im Anschluss an J.S. Kloppenborg interpretiert sie die Szene in 2,1-13 als Kritik am Patronat reicher Gemeindeglieder. Die Textpragmatik liegt für sie in der Warnung vor der Versuchung, das Patron-Client-Verhältnis in den Gemeinden zu übernehmen. 2,6 zeigt deutlich, dass der Verfasser das bekannte und viel verhandelte Ehre-Scham-Konzept, das zu dem Klientelkonzept gehört und auf der Verbindung von Reichtum, Macht, Ehre und u.U. eben Patronat beruht, nicht nur kritisiert, sondern außer Kraft setzt. Garant dieser ‚Umkehrung der Werte' ist Gott (2,5). 2,14-26 liest Batten weniger von dem klassischen Topos ‚Glaube-Werke' her, vielmehr arbeitet sie die der Argumentation unterliegende Struktur von Freundschaft und Euergetismus heraus und betont die Funktion der Beispiele von Rahab und Abraham, den der Verfasser ‚Freund Gottes' nennt. Hier ist in der Tat ein Zusammenhang zwischen dem Gehorsam Abrahams und dem Freundschaftskonzept greifbar:

der Gehorsam macht Abraham zum Freund Gottes (anders in Phil 2, wo—wenn überhaupt—Jesu Tod Ausdruck seiner Freundschaft zu den Menschen ist). So findet Batten in Jak 2 ein dichtes Netz von Freundschaft und Wohltätigkeit einerseits und Warnung vor *patronage* andererseits.

In Kap. 6 stellt Batten die Texteinheit Jak 3,13–4,10 unter das Thema „Friendship with God" (145). Sie plädiert mit P.H. Davids, R.P. Martin und L.T. Johnson für die Einheit von 3,13–4,10 und legt eine eigene plausible rhetorische Analyse vor: 3,13–14 statement of theme, 3,15–18 reason, 4,1–6 argument, 4,7–10 conclusion (149), die auch die Basis ihrer Interpretation darstellt. Ihr Fazit: die Texteinheit ist ein „theme exercise, centred on the idea that true wisdom from above resides in humility and calmnesss in contrast to a life of envy and resultant strife" (176). Batten stellt 4,4 ins Zentrum ihrer Interpretation. Sie hält 4,4 für die Adaption eines Jesuslogions (Mt 6,24/Lk 16,13 und 2 Clem 6,1–5, mit besonderem Bezug auf P.J. Hartin) und für den inhaltlichen Schlüssel der Texteinheit in der literarischen Funktion einer Maxime. In Anlehnung an J.S. Kloppenborg versteht sie die Veränderung des Jesuslogions als Ausdruck bewusster literarischer *aemulatio* (anders als R. Bauckham).

In ihrer Zusammenfassung (Kap. 7) macht Batten abschließend deutlich, dass der Verfasser das Patronat für ein wichtiges „problem that needs correction" (178) hält. Sie macht darauf aufmerksam, dass damit nicht eine bestimmte historische Situation in den Gemeinden, die der Rundbrief (encyclical 179) erreicht oder die in der Gemeinde des Verfassers besteht, vorausgesetzt ist, sondern dass es ihr um die ‚rhetorischeSituation' geht, die Bestandteil der Weltsicht des Verfassers ist. Die Themen, die der Brief explizit anspricht: richtiges Sprechen, Zorn, richtige Behandlung der Armen, wahre Weisheit und tägliche Erfahrungen in den Gemeinden (180), werden durch die implizite Weltsicht des Verfassers gesteuert. Der Verfasser nimmt „patronage as an exigence" wahr (180) und stellt dem die ethische Weltsicht der Freundschaft gegenüber. Dies ethische Konzept wird nicht als solches thematisch entfaltet, sondern stellt das innere Regulativ für die Mahnungen zu den einzelnen genannten Themen dar. Die Pragmatik der von ihr ausgewählten Teiltexte des Jak liegt für Batten darin, dass die Gemeinden der Verlockung, Patrone zu suchen, widerstehen („resistance to patronage" 184) und statt dessen ein Ethos der Freundschaft pflegen („pursuit of friendship, both with God and with the other members oft he community" 184). Am Ende weist Batten darauf hin, dass der Freundschaftstopos aus der elitären griechisch-römischen literarischen Tradition stammt (allerdings auch aus der jüdischen Freundschaftsethik, die aber ihrerseits elitäre Züge trägt, wie Ben Sira zeigt!), aber vom Verfasser des Jakobusbriefes zugunsten der Armen eingesetzt wird.

Die Studie zeichnet sich durch die Tugenden der Klarheit, Kürze und guten Lesbarkeit aus. Die Verfasserin hat dabei in vorbildlicher Weise die stets anschwellende wissenschaftliche Literatur dokumentiert und in ihre Argumentation einbezogen (es fehlt der Kommentar von Ch. Burchard im HNT) und sich dabei keineswegs auf die angelsächsische Literatur beschränkt. Sie macht in ihren Textanalysen deutlich, wie sich die frühchristlichen Texte im Zusammenhang antiker sozialer, politischer und kultureller Konzepte interpretieren lassen, ohne dass ihre eigenen Themen dabei vernachlässigt werden. Erfrischend ist die Selbstverständlichkeit, mit der der Jakobusbrief grundsätzlich von vornherein nicht als christlicher oder jüdischer religiöser Sondertext in den Blick kommt, sondern als griechischer Text der frühen Kaiserzeit gelesen wird, der dann im Lauf der Interpretation seine Eigenarten—für die Verfasserin ist Jak vor allem ein tief theozentrischer Text (165)—entfaltet. Wie viel Neues die Studie im nordamerikanischen exegetischen Kontext beiträgt, möchte Rez. nicht abschätzen. Für die deutschsprachige Exegese sind Beiträge wie diese, die die rhetorische Analyse und die sozialgeschichtliche Kontextualisierung erfolgreich üben, ebenso nützlich wie anregend.

I and II Peter and Jude: A Commentary, by Lewis R. Donelson. New Testament Library. Louisville: Westminster John Knox, 2010. Pp. xxiii + 301. Hardcover. $40.00. ISBN 9780664221386.

Peter H. Davids, Houston Baptist University, Houston, Texas

This work by Lewis R. Donelson is another solid contribution to the New Testament Library series, a piece of good workmanship, even if it has the expected weaknesses of not being one of the larger commentaries on the three letters that it covers.

The work is structured starting with the usual front matter, including a table of abbreviations, followed by a nine-page bibliography that, while far from comprehensive, covers a solid representation of contemporary literature on these three letters. This bibliographical representativeness is true in terms of geographical spread, theological positions of the authors, and literary type, covering commentaries, monographs, and journals. This is important, for since the work is only sparsely footnoted (53 footnotes in 301 pages, so an average of just over one footnote every six pages), the bibliography is the main way one discovers the breadth of literature that Donelson has consulted in producing this commentary.

The bibliography is followed by a brief introduction to the whole commentary in which Donelson clearly points out his reading position, namely, that these works are fascinating voices from the postapostolic period that demonstrate a flowing together of multiple streams of earlier Christian literature. He will eventually date them from the time of Domitian (1 Peter) to as late as 120–150 C.E. (2 Peter).

With his position marked out in the general introduction, what remains is to discuss the three letters in detail in the chronological order of 1 Peter–Jude–2 Peter. Each work has a brief introduction (18 pages for 1 Peter, but only 7 and 6 pages respectively for Jude and 2 Peter), followed by a discussion of the content of the letter, section by section. Each section has an introduction followed by an original translation (with translation notes), after which the content of the section is discussed in one- or two-verse units. Greek words are discussed, although the Greek is transliterated and the discussion is clear enough that knowledge of Greek is not necessary to read this work, even if some acquaintance with grammatical terms would be helpful. The work concludes with thirteen pages of indexes (ancient sources and subjects are indexed; there is no need of a modern author index with so few footnotes and references to other authors in the commentary text).

The content of the comments is, of course, dictated by the content of the three letters and so does not differ significantly from other mainline commentaries that date the works similarly. Donelson is in some ways traditional in that, while conversant with ancient texts, especially 1 Enoch, a necessity if one is to study these letters, he is not trying to immerse the reader in the ancient world, such as Jerome Neyrey does in his *2 Peter, Jude* (Anchor Bible) or Charles Talbert does in his recent *Matthew* (Paideia). Rather than being a sociorhetorical study, this commentary is a clear, relatively straightforward explanation of the text.

There are both strengths and weaknesses with the approach of this work (an approach that was surely influenced by the series guidelines; it is unfortunate that there was no introduction to the series included in this volume). First, the use of transliterated Greek that is explained clearly makes the work far more accessible than a work that uses Greek script, let alone discusses Greek grammar in detail, such as Mark Dubis's *1 Peter* (Baylor Handbook on the Greek New Testament), but it also limits the depth in which Donelson can discuss Greek terms and grammar. That being said, he does an admirable job in working within these limitations and bringing out not just the meaning of vocabulary but also the rhetoric of the various letters. For example, on page 31 Donelson explains the rhetorical force of the repeated *alpha* privatives in 1 Pet 1:4 quite well.

Second, the condensed style of the introduction and sparse use of footnotes allows one to get a quick grasp of the introductory issues of the letter in a writing style that is clear and a relatively easily read (i.e., any seminary graduate should find it a good read). But the lack of detailed interaction with the positions of other scholars can make Donelson's conclusions sound too easy and too secure. For instance, in arguing for pseudepigraphical authorship for Jude (162 and a bit on 163), Richard Bauckham's arguments for considering Jude the brother of James and Jesus the actual author are confined to a reference in a three-line footnote, half of which is spent on supporting Donelson's position. This brevity of his discussion does not do justice to Bauckham's detailed arguments, reducing them, as it were, to a mere negative (that he holds Jude to be the author "simply because there is insufficient evidence not to do so").

Finally, the limited bibliography and limited citation of the bibliography again makes for a clear read in that the commentary text is uncluttered by numerous footnotes or references to other authors, but it also means that issues are missed. For example, in the discussion of Sarah in 1 Pet 3:6 (92), Donelson discusses how the one time Sarah calls Abraham "lord" in Gen 18:12

(LXX) can be construed as 1 Peter construes it (although other commentators seem to struggle with this more than he). However, his bibliography contains an article by Troy W. Martin ("The TestAbr and the Background of 1 Pet 3,6," *ZNW* 90 [1999]: 139–46) that disputes that 1 Peter is citing Genesis at all, but rather argues that the author is citing the Testament of Abraham, in which Sarah, made over into an ideal Hellenistic wife, *always* addresses Abraham as "my lord." Donelson is also aware of the volume Jacques Schlosser edited, *The Catholic Epistles and the Tradition*, for although there is no mention of it in the bibliography, an article from it is cited on page 207; this volume has an article supporting Martin's position. But there is no indication in the commentary text that this position exists. What is more, one would think that Martin's argument would be welcome to Donelson, for it supports his dating and contextualization of the work.

None of these issues mentioned are meant to distract from the value of this work. This is a solid and serviceable commentary, and there is no doubt about that. But these issues with their examples (and the examples could easily be multiplied) clearly indicate both the strengths and weaknesses of this condensed format. On the one hand, one gains clarity. This book is a good read and leads one through the text expeditiously. Donelson is a seasoned scholar, and it is just plain fun (at least to me) to listen to him explaining his take on the text, even at those points where one does not entirely agree with his conclusions. Students and pastors (since Donelson refers to works such as 1 Enoch with some frequency, at least some theological education is needed to appreciate this commentary) will profit from this clarity. They will quickly know how Donelson reads any particular verse, and that will bring them the understanding they seek. Pastors in particular are rarely looking for a full critical discussion of a passage, and they will find Donelson's work far more accessible than many of those in his bibliography. That being said, there is a reason why John H. Elliott could write his massive commentary *1 Peter* (Anchor Bible) after writing other books on the same letter and why Paul J. Achtemeier's *1 Peter* (Hermeneia) is as large as it is (although smaller than Elliott's tome). There is a reason why the *bibliography* to Reinhard Feldmeier's *The First Letter of Peter* (Baylor) is thirty-five pages long (versus Donelson's nine pages for three letters). There is a reason why 300-plus page commentaries are written on 2 Peter and Jude alone: one cannot fully discuss the various options in these works without taking that amount of space. Not every audience is willing to read such full discussions, but if one condenses the discussion that others take 600-plus pages for into 300 pages, leaving out most of the footnotes, something is going to get lost. It cannot be otherwise.

If one reads Donelson's commentary to get Donelson's reading of these letters, one will not be disappointed. If one reads it to get a full critical discussion of these works, sooner or later one will discover that, while this commentary is informed by much of that discussion, that full critical discussion is not its purpose. So this is indeed a solid work, but a carpenter's hammer is not a sledgehammer, although each is a fine tool for its own purposes.

REVELATION

A Feminist Companion to the Apocalypse of John, edited by Amy-Jill Levine with Maria Mayo Robbins. Feminist Companion to the New Testament and Early Christian Writings 13. New York: T&T Clark, 2009. Pp. xi + 262. Paper. $49.95. ISBN 9780826466518.

Renate Viveen Hood, The University of Mary Hardin-Baylor, Belton, Texas

A Feminist Companion to The Apocalypse of John is the thirteenth commentary in the now fourteen-volume series, Feminist Companion to the New Testament and Early Christian Writings, edited by Amy-Jill Levine, E. Rhodes and Leora B. Carpenter Professor of New Testament Studies at Vanderbilt University Divinity School and Graduate Department of Religion and Director of the Carpenter Program in Religion, Gender and Sexuality in Nashville, Tennessee. This particular work is co-edited by Maria Mayo Robbins, a doctoral candidate in religious studies at Vanderbilt University.

In this volume, the reader is invited to read the Apocalypse of John in variegated ways. Standing on the shoulders of those feminist scholars who first broached the Apocalypse either to save it from its presumed misogynistic mark of the womanist beast or to give up on its claim as sacred scripture, a diverse group of contributors engage the text once more by intersecting older theories and fresh methodologies in gynocentric readings of the text. Employing approaches, some of which are more unique than others, the authors provide new insights while digging up an occasional old bone and revisit old dilemmas while voicing new questions. The essays further crystallize the nuances of female imagery in the text while at times leaving the reader more mystified.

Levine herself authored the introduction. Recounting her time as a student taking New Testament courses in the 1970s looking for women commentators, she describes in what manner her journey led her to conclude that female scholarly activity in the field was virtually nonexistent. She notes the few exceptions to that observation by recognizing some initial female scholars of the time regarding the book of Revelation, such as Elisabeth Schüssler Fiorenza and Adela Yarbro Collins. Interestingly, several decades later female scholars still take a succinct interest in studies pertaining to the Apocalypse of John. Aspects of female imagery in Revelation in particular appear to intrigue the scholars.

Next Levine introduces the contributors to this volume. In lieu of a conclusion or epilogue at the end of this collection of essays, she not only presents the argument and outcomes of each study but provides constructive criticism as well. The authors represent a wide spectrum: female and male, American and international, and of differing faith traditions. They use a variety of approaches to the Apocalypse.

The first essay, entitled "Gender and Empire: Sexualized Violence in John's Anti-imperial Apocalypse," written by John W. Marshall, focuses on sexualized violence in Revelation as part of John's worldview. By applying a postcolonial analysis, Marshall determines Babylon as the personification of diabolic Rome, whereas Jezebel may refer to an actual historical woman whom John condemns. Marshall's thesis hinges on a 69 C.E. date for Revelation, since a colonized setting requires a recent diaspora. He views the Roman Empire as a colonial empire. Domination, exploitation, and an ideology of natural domination are recognized as three factors indicative of a colonial Roman empire.

Hanna Stenstrom, in "'They Have Not Defiled Themselves with Women…': Christian Identity according to the Book of Revelation," refrains from asking historical questions. Rather, she investigates John's use of mythopoetic language. Her approach builds on Schüssler Fiorenza's work, the concept that language reaches the reader on a deeper level than the intellectual. Analyzing the text of the Apocalypse globally and Rev 14:1–5 in particular with an eye for Christian identity, Stenstrom views the 144,000 as an anti-image of the beast's followers. Her conclusion is based on examination of purity language in the text. This language is understood as showing that purity is based on a life of virtue. In her final analysis Stenstrom appears to reveal a paradox: the normative, that is, pure, Christian is male; his behavior is modeled after the paradigm of the good woman. However, Stenstrom does not think that a gender analysis of Revelation leads to a reinforcement of stereotypes. Rather, by exposing oppressive patterns, change will be encouraged.

In "Women in Myth and History: Deconstructing John's Characterizations," David L. Barr seeks to analyze the mythological character of the Apocalypse and the degree of intersection with the historical situation, noting that the blending of historical and mythological images is characteristic in Revelation. He deems the female characters in Revelation's social constructs and seeks to determine the correlation between the mythic reality and the historical backdrop. Tracing female characters in Revelation against mythological narratives, Barr finds that John uses women's bodies as symbolic constructs by portraying four mythic queens—two good and two bad. The good, the Queen Mother and the Queen Consort, "correspond only in a general way to the historical reality of the community of the faithful, whether Israel or the church. They have only an accidental gender identity" (62). The bad queens, the Roman Empire and Jezebel, however, are portrayed stereotypically, emphasizing sexual identity. The question posed is how modern readers are to respond to the oppressive nature of the images presented. Barr engages in the ongoing discussion surrounding this question. He concludes that three of the four mythic queens correlate to the historical reality in a manner inclusive of men and women, though dominated by men: Israel, the Roman Empire, and the Johannine community. One of the bad queens, Jezebel, relates to a historical female character. Barr agrees with Schüssler Fiorenza that one should not take the assigning of gender in the text literally. Thus he concludes men were expected to identify with the female images as images only.

The author of the fourth essay, Pamela Thimmes, self-identifies as a resistant reader. Her study of the letter to Thyatira, "'Teaching and Beguiling My Servants': The Letter to Thyatira (Rev. 2.18–29)," consists of two sections: section 1 examines the conflicts between John and the community at Thyatira; section 2 discusses presumed competition for authority in the community between John and Jezebel. A key component for observing this latter conflict in the text is the triad of women, sex, and food. Thimmes concludes that with John as an outsider and Jezebel as an insider of the community the conflict revolved around control over group boundaries.

Next, Jorunn Økland briefly evaluates various contemporary feminist theories as applied to Revelation in "Why Can't the Heavenly Miss Jerusalem Just Shut Up?" She then augments a feminist critical approach with philological biblical criticism so as to explore how, for example, sexual or linguistic difference is expressed through a dominant language. The "mobile places" in Revelation are called "elsewhere," because neither "heaven" nor "earth" are applicable due to the constant motion in the text. Økland designates "elsewhere" as a gendered space, since "a group of males lives on and off the female ground" (105).

Caroline Vander Stichele combines a lexical analysis of the Apocalypse with a postcolonial reading. In considering the portrayal of Babylon as a whore, a disturbing metaphor, Vander Stichele poses the question, "To what extent is gender essential to the metaphor?" (114). In her analysis of the correlation between gender and metaphor, she does not attribute the use of male and female imagery in Revelation to mere cultural influence. Rather, the colonizer is a penetrator and thus is portrayed as male, and the colonized, Babylon, is the violated one and thus portrayed as female. Observing this engendering of metaphors will affect one's response to the text.

Using a history of religions approach, Adela Yarbro Collins evaluates the woman clothed with the sun in Rev 12. Thus, in "Feminine Symbolism in the Book of Revelation" she compares the passage in Rev 12 with texts from the same historical context and culture. Drawing on ancient Near Eastern and Greco-Roman works, Collins concludes that the woman clothed with the sun, as well as Babylon in Rev 17 and the bride in 20, are goddesses. Comparing and contrasting the portrayals of these goddesses in the text and in the historical context, as well as drawing on psychological interpretation of images embedded in culture, the woman clothed with the sun is understood as "the Great Mother" (127). She is a protector in chapter 12 but needs additional protection in the closing chapters of the Apocalypse (129–30); she is utterly dependent on the male God.

Mary Ann Beavis continues the investigation into goddesses in John's Revelation in "Jezebel Speaks: Naming the Goddesses in the Book of Revelation." She views the woman clothed with the sun (Rev 12:1) as an ancient goddess, a synthesis of various goddesses from mythology. She views the earth (12:16), the whore (17:1–6), and the bride (19:7; 21:2, 9; 22:17) likewise as goddesses. The negative portrayals of female images in Revelation, Beavis concludes, are a result of John's intense resentment of Jezebel (2:20–21).

In the subsequent essay, entitled "A Man's Choice: Wealth Imagery and the Two Cities of the Book of Revelation," Greg Carey analyzes female images in light of rhetography. This reading of the text in terms of "the senses" contrasts the wealth of the cities in Rev 17 (Babylon) and 22 (New Jerusalem) by way of focusing on sight, touch, sound, and smell. Carey finds that the difference between the two cities is not the affluence of the cities but the kind of wealth possessed by each. Carey discusses specifically Revelation's two most pronounced female images—the whore and the bride—and draws conclusions that identify those associated with the images as well. The Beast Group (Rome and its allies) forms a stark contrast with the Lamb Group (faithful believers and their heavenly advocates) when observed in the sensory world. In the end, John rejects, "even destroys, the more fully embodied sensuality presented by Babylon in favor of the New Jerusalem's idealized and abstract opulence" (158). Carey concludes that all men are indicated in the Apocalypse as faced with a choice: "a woman of substance and agency or a woman reduced to a passive ideal" (158).

Lynn R. Huber addresses the nuptial themes in Revelation, utilizing Roman nuptial-familial rhetoric. Playing off the opening word of the Apocalypse, which metaphorically shares a semantic domain of "the lifting of a veil," she titles her essay "Unveiling the Bride: Revelation 19:1–8 and Roman Social Discourse." Huber explains the historical setting and the concept of "imperial vision of the '*domus*,'" describing the ideal Roman woman. In Revelation, the divine family of the Lamb and the heavenly Jerusalem form a stark contrast against the prevailing social discourse of the imperial family depicting the ideal family. Observing in the text steps associated with wedding preparation as well as an actual wedding, Huber expounds on the expectations for John's community. Revelation, according to Huber, reflects the ancient "Roman view of idealized feminine gender" (178). Thus, in Revelation John encourages the Christian community to identify with a bride who will become the wife of the Lamb, though this image of a bride is adjusted to satisfy idealistic sensibilities.

"Hypermasculinity and Divinity," written by Stephen D. Moore, takes a unique approach by investigating divine imagery in light of the phenomenon of male bodybuilders and reality television. He aims to use his various reflections to see God. In Revelation, Moore finds, the attributes of the deity carry strong masculine overtones. The "Bea(u)tific Vision in Revelation … is the hyper-idealized male imaged—absolute power residing in a body all but undescribed, but nevertheless coded as male, and beautiful enough, apparently, to merit an eternal, worshipful gaze" (204).

The final essay in this volume is Catherine Keller's "Ms. Calculating the Endtimes: Additions and Conversation." In this essay Keller responds to editorial questions regarding both her original chapter in *God and Power: Counter-apocalyptic Journeys* as well as from other chapters of the same work. Not only does she respond to constructive challenges to *God and Power*, but she also provides a response to various themes offered throughout the essays in this companion volume. Her aim in her discussion, the same as in *God and Power*, is "to counteract the dualism of the apocalyptic as well as its ascetic, heroic and dominating masculinity" (15). The reader is invited to join a counterapocalypse.

This companion volume provides rich and insightful contributions to the study of Revelation. Levine's introduction clarifies the intent of the volume, but the work could have benefited from an epilogue. Levine's criticism, however astute, provided in the introduction perhaps set an unintentional tone for the reader. However, she provides expert criticism and in her apt writing style continually draws the reader to the book's essays and into their rich discussions.

Certain contributions are more persuasive than others, in part depending on the reader's agenda. At times arguments appear open to multiple interpretations, fulfilling the portents of the introduction. Marshall, for example, concludes that John is what he opposes, yet what he opposes is determined by viewing the text as his creation. His thesis is totally dependent on dating Revelation to 69 C.E., providing a feeble stance. Similarly, in some other essays the theses are dependent on particular variables. Such is the case with Stenstrom's contribution. Her thesis solely rests on assumptions that Revelation is influenced by variations in purity/impurity conceptualization in early Judaism and that the Apocalypse is influenced by Judaism alone. However, Robert Parker's *Miasma*, though dealing with pollution and purification in early Greek religion, seems to indicate a trajectory that well may extend into Asia Minor.

The volume contains a collection of challenging and engaging methodologies, both within the field of biblical studies and of an interdisciplinary nature. Perhaps an expressed application of narrative criticism with special emphasis on character formation and gender spacing might have augmented the volume.

Upon finishing the final essay in this volume, the reader is further challenged with a plurality of basic approaches with which to engage female imagery in the Apocalypse. One can read as a resistant reader or with an eye to salvage the text. Vander Stichele, for example, writes in the concluding part of her essay that readers should rejoice in the death of the whore but that resistant readers will not do so. Let the reader decide.

Gynocentric readings of the text are presented amidst a cacophony of engendered voices. Depending on one's point of departure, various approaches aid in illuminating the text. Some essays overlap or complement one another; other essays contradict outcomes. This lack of cohesion may not serve the underlying purpose of feminist criticism. However, neither does a prescripted reading of the text. Perhaps the field of feminist readings has evolved to the point that this mere "umbrella term" has served its time. This volume certainly exposes this development and pushes forward the need for continued dialogue. For anyone interested in gynocentric readings of the Revelation or the state of the feminist discourse as related to Revelation specifically and female imagery in texts in general, this volume is an indispensable companion.

Revelation and the Two Witnesses: The Implications for Understanding John's Depiction of the People of God and His Hortatory Intent, by Rob Dalrymple. Eugene, Ore.: Wipf & Stock, 2011. Pp. vii + 165. Paper. $20.00. ISBN 9781610971386.

Russell Morton, Ashland Theological Seminary, Ashland, Ohio

Dalrymple describes this book as a "study motivated by scholarly objectives," yet focused on the instruction and edification of the Christian church (2). As such, it has a certain bi-focal character that may be confusing to a number of readers within the guild of biblical studies. While there is a certain attempt to provide a reasonable alternative for readers more accustomed to popular millenarianism, at the same time it attempts to advance the understanding of John's Apocalypse.

Following a brief introduction, chapters 3–4 (3–58) focus on the portrayal of the two witnesses in Rev 11. It is assumed that Rev 11:1–2 and 3–13 constitute a unity, against source-critical analyses, which assert that the Seer employed different sources in constructing the vision of chapter 11 (43–44). One reason given for this conclusion is that both Rev 11:2 and 11:4 utilize Daniel's three-and-a-half-year framework (Dan 7:25). Also, the Danielic number of three and a half is employed in 11:9, 11 as the number of days that the two witnesses' bodies lay unburied. Thus, it is assumed that both sections are not only employing the same imagery but are also from the same hand.

In addition to the imagery from Daniel, the description of the two witnesses as olive branches and lampstands is understood, correctly in my opinion, to be a reference to Zech 4. This imagery is also linked to Rev 1:12–20, where the seven churches are described as lampstands. On this basis, John's portrayal of the two witnesses is understood as referring not to individual prophets but as symbolizing the Christian church (34–40). In this respect, Dalrymple is following the tradition of interpretation represented by such figures as G. B. Caird. Where Dalrymple disagrees with Caird, however, is that, while Caird understood the two witnesses to signify only the portion of the church that goes through persecution, Dalrymple asserts that the witnesses are symbolic of the whole church, which is expected to undergo persecution and martyrdom (see 36–37).

If the witnesses of Rev 11:1–13 represent the church as a whole, what is John trying to portray through this imagery? Dalrymple asserts that four main themes may be derived through a close reading of this text (47–58). First, in Rev 11:1–2, the temple is preserved against defilement, although the outer court is trampled by the nations. This imagery portrays divine protection of the people of God. This protection is further asserted in 11:7, where the witnesses are protected until the time period of their witness is completed. Second, the two figures are described as witnesses, a portrayal that demonstrates God's purpose for the church, to be witness of Christ's work. Third, the people of God will suffer persecution, perhaps martyrdom. Finally, the people of God will be vindicated, as demonstrated in the witnesses' resurrection in Rev 11:11–12. These themes fulfill a hortatory purpose of encouraging John's audience to be ready to endure persecution and, perhaps, martyrdom.

Dalrymple understands these four themes to apply not only to Rev 11 but to John's portrayal of the people of God throughout the book. At this point in chapter 5 (59–85), Dalrymple discusses the structure of Revelation and how Rev 11 fits within the context of the book as a whole. This arrangement is somewhat puzzling. The reader might think that Dalrymple's argument would have been strengthened if it had begun with a discussion of the structure of Revelation, how there are four themes about the people of God, and then how a close analysis of Rev 11 confirms this analysis.

The concluding chapters discuss how the four themes found in Rev 11 also apply to other sections of the Apocalypse. In chapter 6 Dalrymple applies the themes to Rev 7. In chapter 8 the relevance of the four themes for understanding Rev 2–3 is discussed. Finally, in chapter 9 three of the themes—witness, persecution, and vindication—are related to the Christology of Revelation as a whole. The final chapter provides a discussion of the relationship of Revelation to the Hebrew Bible, particularly Daniel, and to Second Temple apocalypses. While Dalrymple notes that much of the imagery of Revelation reflects material from the First Testament, he is much more reserved about the relationship of John's imagery to Second Temple material. One wonders here, however, if Dalrymple's sample is too narrow and if a more thorough consideration of Second Temple literature, including 2 and 4 Maccabees may have yielded different results.

Finally, mention must be made of two of the rather unusual aspects of this work. In the first place, Dalrymple chooses some rather odd conversation partners. While he is in dialogue with credible scholars such as Caird, Bauckham, Aune, Schüssler Fiorenza, and Beale, he also cites Walvoord and even Hal Lindsay. While Dalrymple cites the latter two only to make points of disagreement, their inclusion as discussion partners could lead some readers to question his assertion that his is a scholarly rather than popular work. Also, Dalrymple does not employ inclusive language, contrary to current standard scholarly conventions.

In conclusion, on the positive side Dalrymple provides general readers a more reasoned, if not universally accepted, interpretation not only of Rev 11 but of the Apocalypse as a whole. On the other hand, for the guild of scholarship, the choice of some of his conversation partners will be troubling. Also, although he gives a reasoned analysis for both his symbolic interpretation of the two witnesses, those employing source-critical analysis of Rev 11 will likely find the argument unconvincing. The four themes he finds in Rev 11 and that he applies to the Apocalypse as a whole may provide encouragement for churches undergoing persecution, which fits within the purpose of Revelation as a prophetic apocalypse to encourage embattled churches to maintain their Christian faith. For the scholarly guild, however, this reading will not necessarily be persuasive. In short, Dalrymple's book, while providing useful grist for a more popular audience, will not be as productive for those with a greater familiarity with the academic bibliography on John's Revelation.

L'Apocalypse de Jean: Révélation pour le temps de la violence et du désir, by Jean Delorme and Isabelle Donegani. Lectio divina 235–236. Paris: Cerf, 2010. Pp. 255 + 265 (2 vols.). Paper. €43.00. ISBN 9782204092319.

Nils Neumann, Institut für Evangelische Theologie, Universität Kassel, Kassel, Deutschland

Bei dem Kommentar „L'Apocalypse de Jean. Révélation pour le temps de la violence et du désir" handelt es sich um ein Gemeinschaftswerk von Isabelle Donegani und Jean Delorme. Donegani hat in Fribourg (Schweiz) zu einem Thema aus dem Bereich der Johannesoffenbarung promoviert, und Delorme war bis zu seinem Tod im Jahr 2005 Professor für Neues Testament in Lyon. Zusammen haben die beiden katholischen Gelehrten häufig an Themen rund um die Johannesoffenbarung gearbeitet. Aus dieser gemeinsamen Arbeit ist über Jahre hinweg in mehreren Lektüre-Durchgängen der vorliegende Kommentar erwachsen. Er liegt als zweibändiges Werk vor und wurde 2010 in der Reihe Lectio Divina von den Éditions du Cerf veröffentlicht.

Methodisch verpflichtet sich der Kommentar in erster Linie einer semiotischen Herangehensweise (sémiotique biblique), welche die Verfasser aber nicht exklusiv verstanden wissen wollen sondern mit anderen methodischen Einsichten verbinden, wo dies sinnvoll ist (1:15–16). Hinsichtlich des Aufbaus orientiert sich das Werk naturgemäß am Textverlauf der Johannesoffenbarung: Jeder Abschnitt wird zunächst mit einer möglichst exakten Übersetzung eröffnet, woraufhin der Text eine Erläuterung erfährt. Allerdings geschieht dies nicht strikt versweise, sondern die Verfasser widmen sich einzelnen kleinen Sinneinheiten, die wiederum explizit in größere Zusammenhänge eingebettet werden, so dass der vorliegende Kommentar deutlicher als andere Werke des gleichen Genres die Logik im Aufbau des biblischen Texts nachzuzeichnen vermag. Auf diese Weise befasst sich das Werk nacheinander mit der Einleitung der Johannesoffenbarung in Offb 1,1-8 (1:27–50), mit der Beauftragungs-Vision in Offb 1,9-20 (1:51–75), den Botschaften an die sieben Gemeinden in Offb 2–3 (1:77–138), den Visionen vom himmlischen Thron in Offb 4–5 (1:139–82), den sieben Siegeln in Offb 6,1-8,1 (1:183–209), den sieben Posaunen in Offb 8,2-11,19 (1:211–50), dem letzten Kampf in Offb 12,1-14,5 (2:9–42), den Ankündigungen des Gerichts in Offb 14,6-16,21 (2:43–72), dem Gericht selbst in Offb 17,1-19,10 (2:73–112), dem endgültigen Sieg in Offb 19,11-20,15 (2:113–53), den Visionen von der erneuerten Welt in Offb 21,1-22,5 (2:155–94) und schließlich mit dem Schluss der Schrift in Offb 22,6-21 (2:195–223).

Das Schwergewicht der Auslegung liegt dabei auf der Beschreibung von intertextuellen Beziehungen, die einerseits innerhalb der Johannesoffenbarung Sinnlinien ziehen und andererseits auch das letzte Buch der Bibel innerhalb des biblischen Kanons verankern. Auch die Fußnoten widmen sich vorwiegend solchen intertextuellen Zusammenhängen. Diese Schwerpunktsetzung entspricht dem semiotischen Grundinteresse des Kommentars. Sie ermöglicht es den Verfassern, aufzuzeigen, wie in der Johannesoffanbarung Sinnkonstruktion auf der

Basis der Zeichenrelation von Ausdruck und Inhalt geschieht. So nimmt etwa die Beschreibung des Menschensohn-Ähnlichen in Offb 1,13–16 deutlich die Vision des Daniel-Buchs (Dan 7) auf, distanziert sich aber gleichzeitig von dieser, indem die Johannesoffenbarung das Objekt des Sehens eben nicht schlichtweg als „Menschensohn" benennt sondern es durch die Verwendung des Worts „wie" (homoios) vom Menschensohn des Daniel-Buchs unterscheidet (1:131). Nähe und Distanz kennzeichnen somit das Verhältnis zwischen dem Prätext und der Darstellung in der Apokalypse. Ähnliche Beobachtungen ergeben sich im Zusammenhang mit der innertextlichen Intertextualität. Die Verfasser des Kommentars machen deutlich, dass die Vision vom Reiter auf dem weißen Pferd in Offb 19,11–16 durch Entsprechungen des Ausdrucks deutlich mit der Figur des Menschensohn-Ähnlichen aus Offb 1 in einer semantischen Verbindung steht. Im vorliegenden Kontext handelt es sich um die Christus-Figur der Johannesoffenbarung, die vielerorts aber auch als „Lamm" vorgestellt wird (etwa Offb 5). Auch zwischen dem Lamm (Offb 5) und dem Menschensohn-Ähnlichen (Offb 1) sowie zwischen dem Lamm und dem Reiter auf dem weißen Pferd (Offb 19) besteht ein semantischer Zusammenhang. Aber dennoch—so das Votum der Kommentatoren—dürfen Lamm und Reiter nicht vollständig miteinander identifiziert werden. Vielmehr gibt es gute Gründe dafür, dass Christus im Kontext des endgültigen Sieges über die widergöttlichen Mächte gerade nicht als Opferlamm sondern als Reiter präsentiert wird (2:124–15). Nähe und Distanz werden durch die semiotische Auslegungsmethode sichtbar gemacht.

Für methodische Einführungen und hermeneutische Reflexionen werden zahlreiche über den gesamten Kommentar verteilte Exkurse (Repères) genutzt (vgl. 1:16). Dies hat den enormen Vorteil, dass die Verfasser auf diese Weise direkt in die Auslegung des Bibeltexts einsteigen können und die dabei verwendete Methodik immer dann einbringen, wo sich dies sachlich anbietet. Die Leserinnen und Leser werden dadurch unter anderem mit den Theoremen vom „impliziten Leser" (1:37), von verschiedenen „Stimmen" des Textes (1:39–40.48), von der „apokalyptischen Literatur" (1:74) usw. vertraut gemacht. Es entsteht somit ein Kommentar zur Johannesoffenbarung, der für interessierte Laien nachvollziehbar ist und gleichzeitig auch exegetischen Fachleuten aufschlussreiche Einsichten auf der Grundlage einer semiotischen Lektüre beschert.

Ein besonderer Verdienst der semiotischen Herangehensweise an den Bibeltext besteht darin, dass die Verfasser die bildhaften Schilderungen, die in der exegetischen Tradition meist als „Symbole" begriffen werden, zunächst einmal so präzise wie möglich anhand des vorliegenden Texts beschreiben, bevor eine mögliche Übertragung bzw. gar Decodierung erfolgen kann. Paulschalen Identifikationen dieser Beschreibungen mit bestimmten Gegenständen begegnen die Autoren mit Zurückhaltung. Sie vermeiden es dadurch zu Recht, zugunsten einer gängigen „Dechiffrierung" vom Bibeltext abzuweichen. So verwahren sie sich gegen eine einlinige Interpretation des Tieres mit der Zahl 666 in Offb 13 als Kaiser Nero oder Nero Redivivus. Eine solche Identifikation droht nämlich, den Blick dafür zu verstellen, dass das Tier in Offb 13 noch schlimmer ist als ein menschlicher

Kaiser es je sein könnte, da dieses Tier seinen Einfluss von einer transzendenten widergöttlichen Macht bezieht (2:36). Diese Zurückhaltung hinsichtlich der Übertragung von „Symbolen" lässt zwar gewisse Fragen offen—und mag daher auch manche Fachkolleginnen und -kollegen nicht restlos zufrieden stellen—, ist aber gegenüber dem vorliegenden Bibeltext vollkommen angemessen. Der Text wird durch den semiotischen Ansatz gegenüber zu weit führenden Interpretationen in Schutz genommen. Die Zurückhaltung im Hinblick auf einlinige zeitgeschichtliche Interpretationen ermöglicht heutigen Bibelleserinnen und -lesern zudem eine leichtere Anwendbarkeit des Texts auf ihre gegenwärtige Situation.

In Anbetracht der Stellung der Johannesoffenbarung im biblischen Kanon bietet es sich natürlich an, die zahlreichen deutlichen intertextuellen Bezüge auszuwerten, die die Apokalypse insbesondere mit den prophetischen Schriften etwa Jesajas und Hesekiels verbinden, wie es die Autoren in der oben beschriebenen Weise tun. Dieser gute und richtige Ansatz ließe sich noch stärker aber auch auf die Intertextualität zwischen der Johannesoffenbarung und außerbiblischen Texten ausweiten, die in der biblischen Schrift ihren Niederschlag finden. An einigen Stellen des Kommentars nutzen die Verfasser auch die Anmerkungen dazu, um derartige Verbindungen nachzuzeichnen und zu diskutieren (vgl. etwa 1:133–35). Bemühungen in dieser Richtung ließen sich verstärken, um dadurch dem semantischen Universum, das die Johannesoffenbarung voraussetzt, noch besser gerecht zu werden.

Begrüßenswert ist es auch, dass die Autoren sich in ihrer Auslegung fortwährend auf den griechischen Bibeltext beziehen. Dass die griechischen Worte und Wendungen dazu lateinisch transkribiert dargeboten werden, entspricht vermutlich den Vorgaben der Reihe. Jedoch ist eine solche Transkriptionsarbeit ein störanfälliges Verfahren, durch das sich zahlreiche Fehler und vor allem Uneinheitlichkeiten einschleichen können. Für eine zweite Auflage des Kommentars sollten die Transkriptionen darum noch einmal überprüft werden.

Die Auslegung wird gerahmt durch ein Vor- und Nachwort des Lyoner Exegeten Jean Calloud. Ein Literaturverzeichnis rundet das Werk ab. Die sich anschließende Auflistung der eigenen Veröffentlichungen des Autoren-Teams, die das Literaturverzeichnis bei Weitem überragt, wirkt in diesem Verhältnis allerdings etwas überreichlich.

NEW TESTAMENT AND BIBLICAL THEOLOGY

The Sacred Text: Excavating the Texts, Exploring the Interpretations, and Engaging the Theologies of the Christian Scriptures, edited by Michael Bird and Michael Pahl. Gorgias Précis Portfolios 7. Piscataway, N.J.: Gorgias, 2010. Pp. xv + 268. Hardcover. $142.50. ISBN 781607247418.

Sean A. Adams, University of Edinburgh, Edinburgh, Scotland

This work seeks to present an overview of the formation, reception, and interpretation of Christian Scriptures. It is divided into three parts—"The History of the Texts," "The Interpretation of the Texts," and "The Theological Status of the Texts as Scripture"—with each part containing four essays.

Michael F. Bird opens the volume with "Introduction: From Manuscript to MP3." Commencing with a brief overview of the volumes' articles, Bird traces the contours of the collection and maps out its intention to stimulate students, teachers, and ministers to think and reflect on questions of the Bible as a whole (7). Following this, Bird provides a reflection of his own experiences of Christian Scripture, specifically addressing the ideas of the phenomena of Scripture, the relationship between ecclesiology and bibliology, the interconnectedness of ecclesiastical tradition, biblical interpretation, and the Holy Spirit, the role of the author and authorial meaning in interpretation, and the use of "infallibility" and "inerrancy" as terms to describe Scripture.

The first essay in the volume is Karen H. Jobes's "The Septuagint as Scripture in the Early Church." She begins with a brief discussion of the origins of the "Septuagint" and some of the differences between the Hebrew and Greek versions of the Old Testament. Jobes then discusses the different positions of the "inspiration" of the Greek versions as held by Augustine and Jerome. This leads to an investigation of the use of the Greek Old Testament by New Testament writers, focusing on what Jobes regards as the most influential books: Isaiah, Psalms, Genesis, and the Twelve. Jobes's next section, "The Canon of the Greek Old Testament," provides a succinct discussion of the canonical nature of apocryphal works and the role of the Greek New Testament today.

Following this, Tomas Bokedal investigates "Scripture in the Second Century." This is a growing field, with many potentially interesting areas for study. In this short piece Bokedal attempts to address many of them and provides a cursory discussion of the usage, interpretation, text, and canon of Scripture in the second century. With a very wide range of topics (including *nomina sacra*, manuscript production, liturgical function of the Gospels, New Testament citations in the apostolic fathers, orality versus literacy, etc.) this chapter begins to show the breadth of topics for future inquiry.

Next is an interesting essay by Michael Pahl, titled "Scripture and Tradition," which seeks to find a middle path between Protestant *sola Scriptura* and Catholic "Sacred Scripture and Sacred Tradition." Tracing the contours of orality and apostolic witness in the early church, Pahl argues that there are substantial similarities between the Protestant and Catholic views, properly defined. Moreover, Pahl contends that both have gone too far in their perspectives and that there is significant space for dialogue for both groups to share a common path of the relative authority and respective roles of Sacred Scripture and church tradition.

The final essay in this section is John C. Poirier's thought-provoking "Scripture and Canon." Here Poirier challenges current reasoning about Scripture's authority based on "inspiration" and suggests that Scripture's authority is derived from the doctrinal centrality of kerygma. This, Poirier suggests, is closest to the New Testament's view of Scripture. In support of his argument, Poirier provides an alternate reading of 2 Tim 3:16, 2 Pet 1:20–21, and Eph 2:19–20. Moreover, the role of kerygma and the biblical author's relationship with Jesus was one of the pivotal reasons for a work's inclusion in the New Testament.

Part 2, "The Interpretation of the Texts," opens with Jamie A. Grant's "Scripture and Biblical Criticism." This essay outlines the origin and development of literary and historical criticisms in the post-Enlightenment study of the Scriptures and how they have come to us today. Although well-written, there is not too much original contribution here.

Next, Thorsten Moritz's "Scripture and Theological Exegesis" provides an intriguing look at hermeneutics as method, art, and content. Surveying seven approaches to interpreting the text (speech-act theory, hermeneutical geography, implied versus empirical, storied hermeneutic, the role of imagination, open versus closed texts, and community and the social brain), Moritz challenges readers to reevaluate their hermeneutical approaches to allow for a more full reading of the text. This chapter would make a good introductory essay to a hermeneutics course.

Following this, Robert Shillaker's "Scripture and Postmodern Epistemology" outlines the many different contours of postmodern thought. Highlighting the dynamic relationship between modernism and postmodernism, Shillaker argues that postmodern thought is actually the completion and intensification of modernistic methods. Shillaker concludes with a discussion of postmodernism's view of the author and authorial intent.

Jennifer Bird's "Scripture and New Interpretive Approaches: Feminist and Postcolonial" concludes section 2. Here Bird provides a short outline of the sociological impetus for the rise in feminist and postcolonial interpretations. These theories are applied rather briefly to the household code in 1 Pet 2:18–3:6.

The final section, "The Theological Status of the Texts as Scripture," comprises four articles, each providing a perspective on Scripture from a major theological tradition. First is "Catholic Doctrine on Scripture" by Brant Pitre, which draws upon statements from councils, letters, and catechisms of the Catholic Church regarding Scripture. From these documents Pitre articulates the doctrines of inerrancy, inspiration, and interpretation and how their integration informs modern Catholic study of Scripture.

The next theological tradition is Eastern Orthodox, outlined by George Kalantzis. Beginning with an acknowledgement that Eastern Orthodoxy is diverse and not always uniform in its perspectives, Kalantzis defines the Orthodox understanding of theology as the intersection of Scripture and tradition in which both are mutually engaged. The last part of the chapter outlines three different eras of Orthodox interpretation: patristic, traditionalist, and modern.

The penultimate essay advocates a strong evangelical approach to Scripture. In "Still *sola Scriptura*," James M. Hamilton Jr. argues for three points: that the sixty-six books of the Protestant canon are recognized as inspired by the books themselves and that only these books are inspired by the Holy Spirit; that the "Bible itself claims to be inspired by the Holy Spirit, flawless, totally true, and completely trustworthy"; and that the key objections to the doctrine of inerrancy are wrong.

The final essay, "The Word as Event," by David W. Congdon, evaluates Barth's and Bultmann's perspective(s) on Scripture. Commencing with an overview of both scholars' perspective on the nature and interpretation of Scripture, Congdon argues that Barth and Bultmann share substantial common ground in their view of Scripture despite their dissimilarities. Congdon further suggests that the views these scholars were responding against caused their differences to be emphasized rather than their similarities affirmed.

The volume closes with a good subject index, although the work would have benefited from the inclusion of an authors index and an index of scripture cited. After all, the latter is what this work is all about.

Michael Bird claims in the introduction that the purpose of this volume is "to provide a brief introduction to the many complex issues including: (1) the formation of the Christian canon in the context of the ancient church; (2) hermeneutical strategies for interpreting the Christian Scriptures; and (3) the theological status and function of Scripture in various Christian traditions" (1). However, while there are some very good essays directed to those issues, one cannot help but think that essays on any one of these three topics could have sufficiently filled a volume. As a result, the reader is left wanting more. Moreover, though Bird's introductory essay provides some macrosctructure to the work, there is no other essay to provide synthesis or integration of ideas for the reader. Rather, this is left up to the reader, which might have been the intention of the editors, but can potentially leave less experienced readers with questions.

Unlike some other edited volumes, in this volume there is good coherence among the pieces in that no essay seems out of place. This creates a feeling of unity within the work as a whole.

Another positive is that this compilation, particularly part 3, provides a strong ecumenical and ecclesiastical perspective. Containing articles from Catholic, Eastern Orthodox, and American evangelical writers, this work successfully shows the diversity of ways Scripture is and has been theologically interpreted. This is a particular strength of the work, as it affords the reader a variety of perspectives by which Scripture is viewed and used.

Overall, this volume would be of benefit to anyone interested in the role and nature of Scripture. Furthermore, it would be a helpful text for a course on Scripture or hermeneutics.

Jewish and Christian Scriptures: The Function of 'Canonical' and 'Non-canonical' Religious Texts, edited by James H. Charlesworth and Lee Martin McDonald. T&T Clark Jewish and Christian Texts Series 7. New York: T&T Clark, 2010. Pp. xxii + 226. Hardcover. $120.00. ISBN 9780567618702.

Everett Ferguson, Abilene Christian University, Abilene, Texas

This volume collects the papers presented at the section on "The Function of Apocryphal and Pseudepigraphical Literature in Early Judaism and Earliest Christianity" of the 2007 meeting of the Society of Biblical Literature in San Diego. The sessions were co-chaired by the editors of this volume, which is intended to be the first of a series. The corpus of works denominated "Apocrypha" and "Pseudepigrapha" has grown enormously with the discovery of the Dead Sea Scrolls and publication of numerous other works. These writings largely neglected in previous scholarship are now recognized to be important historical sources, and their study has raised questions about their function in the communities that produced and preserved them, for many seem to have been accorded an authority equal to that of writings that came to be generally accepted as "canonical."

After an introductory essay by James A. Sanders, Lee Martin McDonald writes the programmatic contribution, "What Do We Mean by Canon? Ancient and Modern Questions." McDonald and other contributors rightly note that "canonical" and related terms are anachronistic for the centuries immediately surrounding the beginning of Christianity. On specifics MacDonald states that a "universally adopted" twenty-seven book New Testament canon "is first fixed by the Roman Catholic Churches in 1546 at the Council of Trent" (21), but he correctly notes on page 27 that this canon was affirmed at the councils of Hippo (393) and Carthage (397). He comes out for a fourth-century date for the Muratorian Fragment over against a second-century date (35 n. 43) without considering the now-plausible case for its composition by Victorinus of Pettau in the third century. He fails to address my rejection of the characterization of the Muratorian Fragment as a "list" (24). Despite much repetition of what he has previously written, McDonald does not engage other ways of putting the development together than the simplistic paradigm he opposes. Loren L. Johns's response to McDonald helpfully applies "set theory" to canon formation. The church moved in its understanding of the Bible from a "centered set" to a "bounded set" (43).

James Hamilton Charlesworth, in "The Book of the People from the People of the Book: 1QpHab and Its Scribes," argues for the role of the community in shaping and transmitting the sacred scriptures. He takes as his illustration the work of the scribe in the pesher on Habakkuk from Qumran. Charlesworth concludes that 1QpHab was more authoritative for the community than Habakkuk itself (54). Does this confuse a result with an intention?

Andrei A. Orlov's response points out that the scribe was not doing anything different from interpreters after there was a closed canon (61). Indeed, my observation before reading Orlov's response was that the same circumstance of an interpretation becoming functionally more authoritative than the text interpreted happens with received texts in communities of faith today, so the scribal activity at Qumran offers no indication of reduced authority for texts commented on (if anything, the very act of interpreting was an indication of the text's authority). Orlov's comment is that at Qumran there was neither the absence of a canon nor a fully developed canon but a precanon or proto-canon.

Ken M. Penner, on "Citation Formulae as Indices to Canonicity in Early Jewish and Early Christian Literature," shows that how these formulae were used points to divine or authoritative texts. A different method of citation was used for clearly nonscriptural texts. There is no difference in the way Enoch and some other works were cited from the formulae used for "Scripture." This would indicate that the formulae themselves are not a sufficient criterion for how a work was classified.

Casey D. Elledge's "Rewriting the Sacred: Some Problems of Textual Authority in Light of the Rewritten Scriptures from Qumran" offers five criteria for evaluating the authority given to rewritten scriptures before the closure of the canonical process. According to these criteria it appears that Jubilees certainly and probably Psalms of Joshua, Reworked Pentateuch, and the Temple Scroll were regarded by the Qumran community as scriptural (95). These writings were valued by the community, but when that community ceased to exist, so did whatever authority these documents had, unless they were accepted by others. Brent A. Strawn, in "Authority: Textual, Traditional, or Functional? A Response to C. D. Elledge," suggests dependence on authoritative traditions instead of textual sources and observes that functionally authoritative literature is not necessarily the same as Scripture.

Jeremy Hultin's "Jude's Citation of 1 Enoch" considers different responses in ancient authors to Jude's use of 1 Enoch: acceptance of 1 Enoch on the basis of Jude's citation (Tertullian, Priscillian); rejection of Jude because of this quotation (testimony of Origen and Jerome); or acceptance of Jude but rejection of 1 Enoch on the grounds that no scripture existed before Moses (Athanasius) or that Enoch was a prophet but not accepted among the Scriptures preserved in the temple (Augustine) or that the quotation is an occasional citation like Paul's citation of Greek poets (Jerome).

Leslie W. Walck suggests that, in addition to the decline of apocalyptic in early Christianity, there was a theological factor in the rejection of 1 Enoch: human agency in sin assumed more importance than attributing the source of evil to fallen angels (as in 1 Enoch). Another factor was the Jewish rejection of the calendar employed by 1 Enoch.

Craig A. Evans's contribution, "The Pseudepigrapha and the New Testament: The Case of the Acts of the Apostles," has a misleading title, for he deals principally with the influence of Joel on Acts 2. He includes a listing of over four pages of the parallels from the literature of late antiquity with verses in Acts.

Stephen J. Shoemaker's "Apocrypha and Liturgy in the Fourth Century: The Case of the 'Six Books' Dormition Apocryphon" laments the neglect of Marian apocrypha in much of the study of early Christianity and argues for the New Testament Apocrypha not being failed scripture but a component of ecclesiastical tradition. This may apply to the Marian texts he studies, but I suggest a variety of motives were at work in the production of the varied literature. Shoemaker points out that the early and medieval church used apocryphal writings for reading at feast days of saints. The "Six Books" apocryphon was used already in the fourth century for the liturgical commemoration of Mary. He says that "supplementary rather than supplanting" (157) applies to much of the New Testament Apocrypha.

George T. Zervos's response to Shoemaker prefers the term "Christian Apocrypha" over "New Testament Apocrypha" but thinks it better to abolish the term *apocrypha* and use the term *pseudepigrapha* for much of the New Testament as well. He represents the line of thinking that implies that if something was early it has as much claim to credence as what was judged authoritative or "apostolic" by the great church.

Simon Lee contributes "The Transfiguration Remembered, Reinterpreted, and Re-enacted in *Acts of Peter* 20–21: An Exploration of the Dynamic Relationship between the Scriptures, Their Interpretive Traditions, and Their Interpreting Community." The Acts of Peter remembers the transfiguration in the first half of chapter 20 through the reading of the Gospel account, reinterprets it in the second half of the chapter in terms of the incarnation, that Jesus is both divine and human, and in chapter 21 finds it reenacted in the life of the community through the different ways Jesus is experienced. The response to Lee by Henry W. Morisade Rietz suggests Isaiah and Acts as antecedents as well as Mark.

Ten pages of abbreviations indicate the range of texts and modern publications used, but many of the authors appeal to the same works for their presentation.

Readers may find the individual contributions more significant than the overall perspective within which they are put. Several of the authors take as the position to be opposed an older paradigm of canon formation that no longer obtains and indeed is to some extent misrepresented. The book is an appropriate reminder that *apocrypha, pseudepigrapha, canonical, noncanonical*, and related terms are modern classifications that should not be read into the early sources and that early writers (Jewish and Christian) quote works not in their later canons as Scripture, but sometimes the impression is left (McDonald is more careful here) that this situation collapses what canon stands for or that the lack of precise boundaries meant there was no standard. Moreover, in our present circumstances, what other way are we to speak of these books? The plea not to import later terminology into the ancient texts should be accompanied by a similar generosity allowing modern writers to use the terminology of our time. As these papers demonstrate, the process of recognition of the Jewish and Christian canons was messy at the edges, but we should remember that there was little doubt about the center.

EARLY CHRISTIANITY AND EARLY CHRISTIAN LITERATURE

The Paraphrase of Shem (NH VII,1): Introduction, Translation and Commentary, by Michel Roberge. Nag Hammadi and Manichaean Studies 72. Leiden: Brill, 2010. Pp. xii + 192. Hardcover. $122.00. ISBN 9789004182028.

James F. McGrath, Butler University, Indianapolis, Indiana

Michel Roberge's volume in Brill's Nag Hammadi and Manichaean Studies series, *The Paraphrase of Shem (NH VII, 1): Introduction, Translation and Commentary*, is a translation of Roberge's French edition of the Paraphrase of Shem published in 2000. The English version of the book includes the most essential elements one needs from a critical edition of a Nag Hammadi text: an English translation, commentary, an introduction that discusses the text's genre and the relationship of its contents to other ancient works and systems of thought, and bibliography and indexes that facilitate the relating of the Paraphrase of Shem to other texts and the pinpointing of passages where intersections and relationships have already been observed. The English edition apparently removes some elements that were present in the French original, such as the Coptic text and the Coptic and Greek indexes, while adding additional notes.

The Paraphrase of Shem is a highly distinctive and original work, one that has often seemed impenetrably difficult. As a result, it has rarely received the attention it merits. As far as its genre is concerned, the Paraphrase of Shem is an apocalypse (albeit with a paraphrase incorporated into it). It reflects and presents a unique system of thought that foreshadows Manichaeism in certain important respects. Other influences and conversation partners can also be identified confidently, such as Valentinianism and the Chaldean Oracles. But it is important, Roberge emphasizes, not only to compare individual details that may be shared in common—such as terminology, metaphors, or doctrines—but to compare and contrast entire systems of thought and the way details that may be common to two systems are *configured* within each (87). Roberge's book offers precisely this with respect to the Paraphrase of Shem and other ancient works, sometimes presenting the key similarities and differences in chart form (88 and in the appendix on 159). Helpful outlines make it easier for readers to trace the flow of thought in the work. The Paraphrase of Shem offers a relatively coherent account of origins involving three eternal powers: Darkness, Light, and Spirit as an intermediate entity between them. While Hippolytus mentioned several groups and individuals with a system of thought of this sort, Roberge regards the *Sethians* as those whose viewpoint, as described by Hippolytus and others, most closely resembles the system found in the Paraphrase of Shem (33), although in its precise details and configuration the Paraphrase of Shem remains distinct from them in certain key respects.

Based on the contracts that were used in creating the binding for the codex of which the Paraphrase of Shem was a part, the copy found at Nag Hammadi can be dated to the middle of the fourth century (2). Among the distinctive emphases of the work is its strongly antibaptismal polemic. Roberge speculates that the target of such polemic may have been Elchasites at the time of its composition (95, 136). Given the importance of baptism in Mandaism, it is unfortunate that the Mandaeans are not included in the book's indexes.

Roberge regards the Paraphrase of Shem as reflecting a form of *Christian gnosis*. Although there is no explicit mention of Jesus, Roberge is not the first to understand the reference to Soldas, a demon who baptizes, as having Jesus in view. While some scholars have argued for an identification of Soldas with John the Baptist, Roberge is among those who understand him to be the *bodily* Jesus, distinct from the spiritual savior figure Derdekeas, who is also the revealer who addresses Shem over the course of the work. The interpretative crux with respect to this matter is the passage 39.24b–40.3. Roberge renders the passage as follows, with the words in parentheses added to clarify the meaning (122):

> That is why I appeared, being without deficiency: because the clouds are not equal (and) in order that the wickedness of Nature might be brought to completion. For (Nature) wished at that time to seize me. She will (in fact) affix Soldas (to the cross) who is the dark flame, who will stand on the h[eigh]t, (nailed) t[o the wood] of error, that it might seize me. She took care of her faith, being vain.

It will be clear that there is significant ambiguity about whether Jesus and his crucifixion are genuinely in view here. Among the major interpretative considerations relevant to drawing a conclusion are the parallel ideas found in the Paraphrase of Seth and the understanding of the Greek term *pēssein*, which Roberge renders as "affix." Since the Coptic text is not provided, those seeking to evaluate the translation and interpretation offered by Roberge are forced to turn elsewhere for some of the resources needed in order to do so.

Whatever one makes of this single ambiguous passage, the work as a whole cannot be said to have any explicit Christian elements, although there certainly are ideas and phrases that resemble those found in Christian sources. One example is 36.2–15, which depicts the Savior as the revealer who endures the wrath of the world and triumphs, adding, "Not one of them knew me" (120). The reader familiar with early Christian literature will inevitably wonder about connections to Johannine thought and tradition.

Roberge inserts section headings into the translation that clarify instances when certain characters and events from biblical narratives are in view, which it might otherwise be possible to miss, the figure of Abraham in the work's treatment of the people of Sodom being a case in point. As one might expect, typical gnostic reversals of details in Genesis are to be found, so that Abraham is characterized as a demon, whereas the Sodomites are those who "will rest with a pure conscience"—even though Sodom will "be burnt unjustly by perverse Nature" (117). For precisely these reasons, it is said to be important that Shem reveal his teachings to them.

The text as a whole focuses much of its attention on the interaction of the primordial powers. These interactions, which produce the various spiritual and material entities believed to inhabit the cosmos, are described in imagery that, even at its most euphemistic, is overtly sexual. The soteriological focus of the work becomes clear when Derdekeas explains the origin of humanity in general and of Shem and his race in particular, describing the opposition of Nature to the plan of salvation and providing crucial knowledge about the powers that stand opposed to the race of Shem.

On the whole, the English translation does an impressive job of walking the fine line between rendering the text faithfully with all its difficulties and ambiguities and clarifying the meaning wherever possible so as to facilitate comprehension. The commentary is surprisingly sparse (less than ten full pages), but this is compensated for to some extent by the substantial discussion of key passages offered in the introduction. Extended discussion of some of the more important matters of translation and interpretation would have made the volume all the more valuable, as would the inclusion of the Coptic text. Yet even if it is possible to identify shortcomings or wish that other things had been included in the volume, these points do not ultimately change the fact that this is an extremely important book, one that promises to bring about renewed and increased interest in a text that has often seemed at best confusing and at worst incomprehensible and suffered from scholarly neglect as a result. As a result of Roberge's book being published in this English edition, English-speaking scholars who work on a range of subjects, including not only Nag Hammadi texts and Gnosticism but also early Christianity in general, Mandaeism, and Manichaeism, will benefit from improved access to this fascinating ancient work.

Pseudepigraphie und Verfasserfiktion in frühchristlichen Briefen, edited by Jörg Frey, Jens Herzer, Martina Janßen, and Clare K. Rothschild. Wissenschaftliche Untersuchungen zum Neuen Testament 246. Tübingen: Mohr Siebeck, 2009. Pp. xii + 902. Cloth. €139.00. ISBN 9783161500428.

Christoph Stenschke, Forum Wiedenest and University of South Africa, Pretoria, Republic of South Africa

This substantial volume had its origin in an international conference at the University of Munich in June 2007 (the annual Münchener Bibelwissenschaftliches Symposium). The conference papers were later supplemented by other contributions on request. In view of the often vague discussion and the apparent stalemate in the scholarly debate on pseudepigraphy in New Testament studies, the editors conclude:

> Es reicht nicht mehr aus, im Blick auf eine Schrift lediglich die Frage nach ihrer Authentizität oder Pseudonymität aufzuwerfen, vielmehr ist zu diskutieren, wann bzw. unter welchen Voraussetzungen von Pseudepigraphie gesprochen werden kann, welche Typen und Spielarten von pseudonymer Autorenschaft es gibt, wodurch die Anwendung einer solchen Darstellungsweise motiviert und dann bzw. unter welchen Umständen sie als "legitim" oder "illegitim" zu bezeichnen ist. Ist Pseudepigraphie tatsächlich, wie oft behauptet, ein gebräuchliches und allgemein akzeptiertes Darstellungsmittel in einer bestimmten Epoche, Gruppe oder Bildungsschicht? (v)

The answers that have been given to such questions often appear one-sided or lacking in precision in view of the plurality of pseudepigraphic constructions of authors, addressees, situations, opponents, and so on. It is therefore necessary to aim at nuanced descriptions of such individual constructions in the context of a wide range of possibilities of pseudonymous modes of presentation. This will lead to precise assessments of the type, intention and implication of the literary shape of a text. The volume aims at providing a "Bestandsaufnahme wesentlicher Aspekte der gegenwärtigen Pseudepigraphieforschung" (vi).

The "Einführung" (3–24) by M. Janssen and J. Frey provides a fine survey of present research on pseudepigraphy (3–16) and an introduction to the layout and the individual contributions to the volume. The essays appear in three parts. Part 1 addresses *early Jewish contexts*. L. G. Perdue addresses "Pseudonymity and Graeco-Roman Rhetoric Mimesis and the Wisdom of Solomon" (27–59); he shows how the rhetorical technique of *mimesis*, the imitation of older authors, is an essential element of the literary shape of a text, and it is probable that this literary technique was recognized by readers. K. M. Hogan examines "Pseudepigraphy and the Periodization of History in Jewish Apocalypses" (61–83), offering the view that the pseudonymous authors of apocalyptic texts function like "bridges" and represent continuity in transmission; they serve to restore and secure threatened identity. E. Tigchelaar surveys "Forms of Pseudepigraphy in the Dead Sea Scrolls" (85–101); this is a helpful summary of the insights for pseudepigraphy to be gained from the scrolls).

Part 2 addresses the Greco-Roman context of New Testament pseudepigraphy. W. Speyer writes on "Göttliche und menschliche Verfasserschaft im Altertum" (105–24); he draws attention to the religious dimension in the background of pseudepigraphical constructions of authorship. M. Janssen surveys "Antike (Selbst-)Aussagen über Beweggründe zur Pseudepigraphie" (125–79); this is a survey of the various reasons that led to pseudepigraphy. All the categories surveyed are to be applied in a nuanced manner; their application to the phenomena of early Christianity requires careful reflection, if early Christian writings are to be understood adequately and not anachronistically. M. Frenschkowski asks "Erkannte Pseudepigraphie? Ein Essay über Fiktionalität, Antike und Christentum" (181–232); some of Frenschowski's conclusions challenge the popular thesis that early Christian pseudepigraphy would have been easily recognized by the readers. K. Luchner studies "Pseudepigraphie und antike Briefromane" (233–66); she questions the idea that collections of letters are to be interpreted as so-called letter-novels. T. Glaser contributes "Erzählung im Fragment: Ein narratologischer Ansatz zur Auslegung pseudepigrapher Briefbücher" (267–94), in which he applies the idea of an ancient letter-novel to the Pastoral Epistles; if they were understood as a Paul-novel, the creation of a new portrait of Paul by drawing on older tradition would become comprehensible. One may note that the "Paul-novel" in the New Testament is the book of Acts in the form of a *narrative*! Finally, R. M. Calhoun addresses "The Letter of Mithridates: A Neglected Item of Ancient Epistolary Theory" (295–339). He includes a translation and detailed study of the letter, offering an instructive example of the discussion of pseudepigraphical letters and collections of letters in Greco-Roman antiquity.

The third part is devoted to early Christian contexts and examines the New Testament writings that have been considered pseudepigraphical in their canonical sequence. H. Y. Gamble examines "Pseudonymity and the NT Canon" (333–62), discussing the significance of the phenomenon of pseudepigraphy for the development for the canon. E.-M. Becker writes on "Von Paulus zu 'Paulus': Paulinische Pseudepigraphie-Forschung als literaturgeschichtliche Aufgabe"

(363–86). This is a survey of criticism of the authenticity of Pauline letters and discusses the importance of orthonymity in Pauline epistolography and the problem and function of Pauline pseudepigraphy. M. Hüneburg contributes "Paulus versus Paulus: Der Epheserbrief als Korrektur des Kolosserbriefes" (387–409), in which Ephesians is seen as a revision and development of Colossians. N. Frank writes on "Der Kolosserbrief und die 'Philosophia': Pseudepigraphie als Spiegel frühchristlicher Auseinandersetzungen um die Auslegung des paulinischen Erbes" (411–32). Colossians is seen as a paradigm for reconstructing the origin and development of Pauline and wider early Christian pseudepigraphy caused by the necessary interaction with the legacy of Paul.

T. Thompson comments on "A Stone That Still Won't Fit: An Introductory and Editorial Note for Edgar Krentz's 'A Stone that Will Not Fit'" (433–38), giving a short introduction to Krentz's influential 1983 paper, hitherto unpublished, and an assessment in view of the current discussion. This is followed by E. Krentz's "A Stone That Will Not Fit: The Non-Pauline Authorship of Second Thessalonians" (439–70) and T. Thompson's "As If Genuine: Interpreting the Pseudepigraphic Second Thessalonians" (471–88), which discusses of the historical location of 2 Thessalonians. Thompson seeks a method that does justice to the complexity of the pseudonymous construction and the double personality of the author of a pseudonymous letter.

J. Herzer asks "Fiktion oder Täuschung? Zur Diskussion über die Pseudepigraphie der Pastoralbriefe" (489–536); it is an excellent survey of research, identifying a number of unresolved problems and arguing that one should allow for different authors and situations addressed by the three letters. C. K. Rothschild examines "Hebrews as a Guide to Reading Romans" (537–73). She attempts to add Hebrews to a growing list of early Christian writings understood as guides to early Pauline letter collections: "Hebrews, although probably informed by other letters of Paul as well as by Acts, offered to readers of an early *Corpus Paulinum* context clarification and/or development of key ideas in Romans. Its author regarded several areas of Romans as requiring elaboration and/or correction and thus furnishes a tool designed to impact its interpretation" (572). See also her *Hebrews as Pseudepigraphon: The History and Significance of the Pauline Attribution of Hebrews* (WUNT 235; Tübingen: Mohr Siebeck, 2009).

M. Konradt addresses "'Jakobus, der Gerechte': Erwägungen zur Verfasserfiktion des Jakobusbriefes" (575–97), arguing once more for the pseudepigraphical nature of the letter in view of the positions of the historical James as they are reflected in other New Testament writings. M. Jackson-McCabe examines "The Politics of Pseudepigraphy and the Letter of James" (599–623), an instructive survey of the underlying loyalties and convictions of the proponents of different positions.

K. M. Schmidt contributes "Die Stimme des Apostels erheben: Pragmatische Leistungen der Autorenfiktion in den Petrusbriefen" (625–44); this deals with the paradigmatic function of both letters in the context of the churches that are addressed. L. Doering devotes himself to "Apostle, Co-Elder, and Witness of Suffering: Author Construction and Peter Image in First Peter" (645–81). He states: "the image of Peter developed in the letter is in several aspects significantly shaped toward 'reaching' the predominantly Gentile Christian addressees in their situation of 'dispersion' and suffering, including their intra-communal relations. It refers to a foundational 'integrative' apostle of uncontested authority in the areas explicitly addressed. 'Peter' stands (similar to 'James') for a different type of letter writing, not uninfluenced by Paul but distinct in its connection with the Jewish encyclical letter tradition" (681).

J. Frey turns to "Autorfiktion und Gegnerbild im Judasbrief und im Zweiten Petrusbrief" (683–732). Frey concludes: "Erst aufgrund einer möglichst sorgfältigen und differenzierten Klärung und Einordnung der pseudonymen Strukturen von Autor *und* Gegnern kann dann auch nach ihrer leitenden Intention, ihrem argumentativen Wert und ihrer ethischen und kanontheologischen Legitimität gefragt werden" (732). J. Leonhardt-Balzer surveys "Pseudepigraphie und Gemeinde in den Johannesbriefen" (733–63); the circumstances of writing 1–3 John and the various author attributions are particularly complex. In closing, S. Krauter raises the question "Was ist 'schlechte' Pseudepigraphie? Mittel, Wirkung und Intention von Pseudepigraphie in den *Epistolae Senecae ad Paulum et Pauli ad Senecam*" (765–85), in which he asks: What are the criteria for bad pseudepigraphy? For various reasons such as bad style and meager content, the *Epistolae* are an example of a simplistic, bad pseudepigraphy in literary and theological matters.

Of particular interest is the final essay, by D. E. Aune, "Reconceptualizing the Phenomenon of Ancient Pseudepigraphy: An Epilogue" (789–82). Aune masterfully summarizes the contributions of the volume, sets them in the larger framework of past and present research, and draws some conclusions for further research. His discussion documents the recent interest in pseudepigraphy and describes its complexities and the implications for the New Testament canon. Aune further addresses the social and cultural contexts of pseudepigraphy (the Dead Sea Scrolls, divine and human authorship in antiquity, types of fictional discourse in antiquity), the degrees of systematic fictional elaboration in pseudepigraphic letters, and the theological and ethical problem of canonical pseudepigrapha. Aune also comments on the specific reasons for choosing a particular pseudonym and the function of pseudepigraphical letters as introductions to collections of letters. He closes with a survey of how the essays in this volume address the individual New Testament books identified as epistolary pseudepigrapha (810–21) and offers concluding observations. He notes that the application of the term "pseudepigraphy" to Jewish, Greco-Roman, and Christian literature of antiquity is both complex and problematic and comments that future research should involve the continued exploration of the fictional elements, that is, the fictional author, the fictional recipients, and the fictional rhetorical situation, each of which must not only be considered individually but must also be recognized as a structural feature of a fictional communication situation. "Each of the three elements constitutes a fictional 'image' within each letter that has associations external to each letter that together help us understand how the letter might have been understood as authentic by Christians in the late first and early second centuries (and beyond)" (823).

One wishes to add to these quests an openness to reconsidering fictionality, if indeed authenticity makes better sense of the evidence gained from nuanced study of the letter. In view of the historical plausibility of some of the reconstructions offered in this volume (and elsewhere!), one need not be particularly conservative to wonder if the traditional ascriptions of authorship and authenticity are not at least as credible as some of the solutions to some of the home-made problems of the pseudepigraphy debate in its more or less nuanced forms, if not more so.

The list of contributors (825–27) and various indexes (829–902) round off this well-produced volume. Unfortunately, the volume does not provide German or English abstracts for the essays.

Many of the essays raise new questions, apply new or more refined methodology, and offer fresh insights. The essays address by and large what to make of pseudonymity, its implications, its intention, and its function in view of ancient literature. Not sufficiently discussed are the criteria (and their validity) by which pseudonymity may be discovered and proven in New Testament letters that mention authors. This would mean addressing once more the role of secretaries and co-authors, the validity and hard criteria in discussions of the alleged differences in style and of theological "differences," the impact of the intended reader(s) on the nature of writing, and the influence that the use of early Christian tradition may have had on the nature of a writing. Some of these issues have recently been addressed by K. Haacker, "Rezeptionsgeschichte und Literarkritik: Anfragen an die *communis opinio* zum Corpus Paulinum," *ThZ* 65 (2009): 209–28.

While several essays interact with the recent contributions of A. D. Baum (*Pseudepigraphie und literarische Fälschung im frühen Christentum: Mit ausgewählten Quellentexten samt deutscher Übersetzung* [WUNT 2/138; Tübingen: Mohr Siebeck, 2001]; see my review in *NovT* 47 [2005]: 91–93) and T. L. Wilder (*Pseudonymity, the New Testament and Deception: An Inquiry into Intention and Reception* [Lanham, Md.: University Press of America, 2004]; see my review in *Neot* forthcoming), neither of these authors contributes from his research to this volume.

The last words belong to J. Frey: "Es ist zu hoffen, dass die hier gebotenen Überlegungen im Ganzen zu einer differenzierteren Wahrnehmung der in den einzelnen Texten vorliegenden Autor-, Situations- und Gegnerkonstruktionen führen, die dann erst ein präzisiertes Urteil über den Typus, die Intention und die Implikationen der jeweiligen literarischen Ausgestaltung ermöglicht" (24).

Paradise Reconsidered in Gnostic Mythmaking: Rethinking Sethianism in Light of the Ophite Evidence, by Tuomas Rasimus. Nag Hammadi and Manichaean Studies 68. Leiden: Brill, 2009. Pp. xx + 355. Hardcover. $169.00. ISBN 9789004173231.

Gesine Schenke Robinson, Episcopal Theological School of Claremont, Claremont, California

Ever since Hans-Martin Schenke constructed his typological model of Sethian mythology, critiques and advocates alike have been fascinated by the phenomenon of Sethianism. Schenke's concept has inspired a great deal of scholarly research and generated countless essays and books dealing with that phenomenon. The volume at hand, the latest product in this field, is a revised version of a doctoral dissertation that its author completed jointly at the Université Laval, Québec, Canada, and the University of Helsinki, Finland. He had already published several articles on which some chapters of this present work are based. This volume represents his intensive engagement with Ophitism, Sethianism, and the Nag Hammadi texts.

The book starts from the premise that Schenke's model is insufficient in so far as the group of texts from which it derived excludes important documents that display features to which Irenaeus and later heresiologists attached the label "Ophite." Thus the model would only "reveal part of a larger whole to which the Ophite evidence belongs as an important and organic component." Moreover, without the Ophite mythology, viewed as Christian-Gnostic, "Sethianism and its origins cannot be properly understood." While in the nineteenth century, Rasimus maintains, Ophitism was regarded as the earliest and classic form of Gnosticism, it was replaced by Sethianism due to the Nag Hammadi findings and the general acceptance of Schenke's theory. Its dominance resulted in a scholarly bias and the neglect of important sources that deserved to be studied. The declared purpose of this book, therefore, is to deconstruct the Sethian concept and replace it with a new model by reorganizing and extending the Sethian corpus in order to provide a suitable "framework and justification for the study of the Ophite evidence." Since Seth would no longer be the focal point of this new concept, Rasimus proposes to name it "Classic Gnostic."

The volume is divided into four parts and subdivided into nine chapters. Part 1 presents the "Introduction," consisting of a prologue and chapter 1, entitled "Rethinking Sethianism." Here Rasimus starts out to examine the pertinent heresiological reports and related accounts on which previous research on Ophites had drawn. He then explores those Nag Hammadi texts that betray Ophite mythology and compares his results with the findings in the documents commonly considered Sethian. Since certain features that he deems part of the Ophite mythology, such as narrative material about the events in the Genesis story, can be detected in Sethian as well as non-Sethian texts, whereas some Sethian texts lack one or another typical Sethian element, he declares Sethianism to be a "problematic category" and introduces his attempt to provide a wider category that also includes the Ophite material.

When dealing with the similar attestations of mythological themes and elements in both types of gnosis, Rasimus often comes to the conclusion that some of those features belong to the Ophite rather than Sethian mythology. Thus key texts hitherto considered typical Sethian are now claimed for what he has established as "his Ophite corpus," set against Schenke's Sethian corpus. Moreover, since the name Seth does not occur in every Sethian text and Sophia is sometimes called Barbelo, he is harking back to a view prevalent before the Nag Hammadi findings and regards the Sethian material as a combination of two different types of mythological speculation. He rejects the common synonymous use of the terms Sethian and Barbeloite and thus truncates the Sethian corpus even further by dividing it into a Barbeloite and a Sethite category. The latter is not represented by any gnostic text other than heresiological accounts, but is installed in order to prepare the way for his assertion of a secondary Sethianization of earlier gnostic materials, as some scholars have occasionally suggested. After having sketched the criteria for his new category of "Classic Gnosticism," on which he will elaborate further in the upcoming chapters, he rightfully makes clear that such terms as Ophite, Sethian, and Barbeloite are merely convenient reference tools employed to "denote typologically constructed categories." Yet this definition already renders his division attempt obsolete, since the term "Barbelo-Gnostic" derives solely from Irenaeus, who does not use the term Sethian at all, whereas later heresiologists use the term "Sethian" when referring to one and the same issues.

Part 2, "Myth and Innovation," comprises chapters 2–6, which make up the principal part of the book, where major mythological themes are investigated in the relevant sources containing Ophite material. Beginning with the snake speculations examined in chapter 2, which assesses the role the serpent plays in the paradise story, chapter 3 looks at the demonic creator and its archons, particularly focusing on their theriomorphic depictions in the Ophite diagram. While chapter 4 deals with the Sophia myth in connection with Jewish wisdom speculations and discusses the link to 1 Corinthians, chapter 5 attends to the Ophite rewriting of the creation story and explores the correlation between the heavenly Adam and Christ in relation to Philo and 1 Cor 15. Finally, chapter 6 focuses on the role of Seth and the purported secondary Sethianization of both the Barbeloite and Ophite myth.

Rasimus again evaluates each of those themes against their uses in the remaining Sethian texts. As the conclusions following each chapter indicate, however, the investigations appear to be directed mainly toward excluding as many of the features similarly found in both contexts as possible from the established Sethian myth and attributing them to Ophite mythology. Yet in doing so, Rasimus deprives the Sethian mythology of almost all of its cosmological and anthropological aspects, leaving more or less only its theogony, with the godhead distinct from the Ophite one and the events taking place in the supra-celestial realm, in what he now calls the Barbeloite category. The altered distribution of the texts enables him to show that the elements of his Ophite corpus agree rather well with each other on a given theme, whereas the texts in the now abridged Sethian corpus offer a quite different version of the same themes. Interestingly enough, the heresiological reports included in his corpus are put on equal footing with primary gnostic documents when it comes to surveying the mythological elements in question and to classify them as Ophite. Rasimus appears to be hung up on names and figures such as Sophia, Yaldabaoth, and Seth in a statistical sense, without taking into account their role and function in a given narrative, even though the name itself may not occur, or vice versa, a name may be added, such as Barbelo or Christ, without changing the function of the figure identified with it.

This second part strives to explore also the social reality behind the Ophite mythology and looks for the types of social situations out of which key concepts or elements here examined could have emerged. Being aware of the fact that the results will be rather hypothetical in nature, Rasimus rightly points to the difference between a typological construction and a historical entity. Yet since source material can yield valuable clues as to the origin of gnostic thought still shrouded in conjectural clouds, the book investigates particular rhetorical claims, self-designations, and polemical statements in search of sociological information regarding the creation of the Ophite myth.

Chapters 7–9 constitute part 3, "Ritual." Here the search for clues to sociological information continues, particularly probing the veracity of claims made in heresiological accounts with regard to Ophite rituals such as snake worship, which is examined in chapter 7; Origen's claim about the cursing of Jesus is appraised in chapter 8; and the Ophite seal, in connection with the practice of anointing, baptism, and virtual ascension, is evaluated in chapter 9. Since the heresiological reports are known to have their own malevolent agenda, Rasimus also studies a variety of pertinent Nag Hammadi texts in search for corroborating evidence. While reports about Ophite snake worship and the information about the diagram and its ritual use are attributed to heresiological exaggeration and tendentious misunderstanding of Ophite scriptural exegesis, Celsius's reference to an anointment ritual called the "seal" is considered a more reliable information—against Origen's judgment. Though one can only conjecture what the lost work of Celsius had in mind, considering this ritual to be Ophite allows Rasimus to ascertain that the Sethian rituals of baptism and ascension are dependent on Ophite theology. Special attention is also given to the relationship between those baptismal practices and the Johannine prologue, where the tradition history is steered in the same direction of dependence.

The "Conclusion," part 4, contains an epilogue, an imposing bibliography, and very helpful indices that bear witness to the breadth of researched sources. In addition to five charts and three tables dispersed throughout the volume, the book rounds off with twenty appended plates. Nine of those show different reconstructions of the Ophite diagram, whereas others are depictions connected to snake mythology. While they provide visual aide especially to part 3, the epilogue revisits the presuppositions and assumptions explicit in this volume and summarizes the results of a study that covered this remarkable wide variety of ancient texts.

Although admiring the impressive analyses in this outstanding scholarly work, the reviewer can agree with neither the premises nor the conclusions of its author. Rasimus declares up front that, due to Schenke's influential concept, scholarship became prejudiced toward Sethianism at the expense of the Ophite material. Yet if there was indeed a shift in interest from the Ophite to the Sethian Gnosis, it was after the Nag Hammadi texts revealed a coherent group of texts that were essentially non-Christian. Sethianism rightly came to be regarded as the earliest form of gnosis, manifest in a probably pre-Christian, but at least non-Christian Jewish-oriented baptismal movement whose members understood themselves as the "seed of Seth," that is, his progeny. It became obvious that the literary witnesses produced and used by this group whose rites include a sealing after baptism and a contemplative heavenly ascent of the soul were secondarily Christianized, often merely in appearance, but apparently never morphed into a full-blown Christian gnosis—which would entail its texts being a affirmative reinterpretation of Christian concepts from a gnostic point of view. Ophitism, on the other hand, has a completely different background, so that its material could not have been included in the same corpus in spite of some shared names and mythological features. Unfortunately, Schenke's exegetical criteria underlying his prevalent hypothesis were never fully discussed in this book; Rasimus rather states briefly Schenke's results but repudiates them in great detail.

Following trends in gnostic research that tend to rely more on heresiological accounts than on the primary gnostic texts, Rasimus perceives Gnosticism only as a Christian phenomenon without even considering a non-Christian provenance or a possible Christianization of its texts. Ophite mythology is claimed to represent an earlier form than "Schenke's Sethian" one and is said to have emerged from a Platonic interpretation of Genesis through Christian lenses and developed further in a debate with Jews over Christ's divinity as well as the correct interpretation of monotheism. Yet it is not at all evident why the Jewish God had to be demonized and rejected in the process. The Barbeloite type, according to Rasimus, did not derive from a controversy but developed in the attempt to express the Christian concept of the Trinity in philosophically acceptable terms. Yet though some of its later texts show a tendency toward philosophy, this view does not take into account the particularly deep-rooted religious mythology and even devotion to magic of this particular type of gnosis, where the ultimate subject is invocation, not emanation, and the ultimate character is liturgical and dualistic, not monistic. Rasimus, then, sees the secondary Sethianization of both types in connection with a dispute between Jews and Christians, questioning the authority of Moses regarding the paradise story; the focus shifted to Seth as a better guarantor for the right interpretation, because he has a closer connection to what happened in paradise. Yet this assessment does not explain why gnostic Christians would regard Seth as the savior and transmitter of salvific knowledge after a Christology with Jesus as the Christ and savior was already in place. The identification of the heavenly Seth with Christ only makes sense when a religious group, be it called Sethian or otherwise, recognized its own revealer figure (Seth) in Christ. As striking as the chain of events outlined in the book may appear, whether it will carry the day remains to be seen. Rasimus's theory of a "Classic Gnosticism," however, may be untenable in its given form, not least because the Nag Hammadi texts were taken in their present state and only subjected to literary-critical analysis without employing all the other exegetical methods at interpreters' disposal. Allowing for text-critical and redaction-history considerations, for instance, could have proven fruitful for showing the literary stages within those texts themselves.

No matter what one thinks of its thesis, the volume is definitely one of the more interesting and creative books on the origin and development of gnostic mythology. A reading of this book will be worthwhile precisely for the challenges it poses and also for the stimulus it provides scholars with different points of view. It is also worth consulting for the broad variety of sources studied and the works employed. The systematic and comprehensive analysis of the Ophite mythology is highly appreciated, no matter if one shares the explicit assumptions or not. The study is well-presented and makes a valuable contribution to important topics. I gladly recommend the book to everyone interested in those issues, but particularly to the specialists in the field who might be urged to go beyond statistical allocations and ponder the results of this book in connection with questions as to the worldview and motivation that could have led to such a phenomenon as gnostic mythology in the first place and to the way in which this ideology and existential stance came to manifest itself in distinct concepts. Despite the reservations expressed above, this book will be indispensable for and have a vital place in the future research on Gnosticism.

The Gnostics: Myth, Ritual, and Diversity in Early Christianity, by David Brakke. Cambridge: Harvard University Press, 2010. Pp. xii + 164. Hardcover. $29.95. ISBN 9780674046849.

James F. McGrath, Butler University, Indianapolis, Indiana

David Brakke's *The Gnostics* represents an important contribution to the ongoing discussion of the applicability of terms such as "gnostic" and "Gnosticism" and the appropriate definition for those terms if it is felt that they should be used at all. Brakke steers a middle course between the extremes of avoiding the label "gnostic" altogether and using it broadly for a wide range of different texts and viewpoints.

The first chapter presents the key methodological issues and some background to the subject. After a brief mention of recent discoveries, such as the Gospel of Judas, Brakke quickly turns his attention to Irenaeus, the ancient Christian author whose use of the term "gnostics" has shaped subsequent usage. While the information Irenaeus provides will be the focus of attention in chapter 2, in the first chapter the primary concern is methodological, surveying and evaluating scholars' use of terminology and models. After a long period in which the field was dominated by the church fathers' own model of orthodoxy and unity preceding heresy and division, Brakke points out the major change brought about by Walter Bauer's classic 1934 study. Although nearly every precise detail of Bauer's specific reconstructions have been called into question, his model continues to be influential in leading scholars to presuppose initial diversity rather than unity. Brakke uses an analogy offered by Philip Rousseau, likening the study of early Christianity from this perspective to watching a rerun of a horse race. We will tend to keep our eye on the horse that we know will win, even when it is not in the lead (7). Yet Brakke notes that, unlike a horse race, early Christian groups did not have the clear boundaries separating one from another that horses have. Further, while the latter model is preferable to the older one, it is not without its shortcomings. Brakke proposes that the perspective of postcolonial studies, especially regarding hybridity, rhetoric, and ethnicity, can help us improve upon it. "Our goal should be to see neither how a single Christianity expressed itself in diverse ways, nor how one group of Christians emerged as the winner in a struggle, but how multiple Christian identities and communities were continually created and transformed" (15).

Brakke suggests that some of the confusion about terminology in relation to "Christianity" and "Gnosticism" is due to confusion about which of two types of categories these are. Heuristic categories are ones that help modern scholars make sense of data, speaking, for instance, of "apocalyptic Judaism" even though members of the Qumran group and Paul the apostle would probably not either have self-identified as such or have considered themselves part of "the same movement." Social categories, on the other hand, seek to describe, however imperfectly, "how ancient people actually saw and organized themselves" (16). Although the two can overlap, the distinction remains important, and Brakke writes that Gnosticism "is an outstanding example of a scholarly category that, thanks to confusion about what it is supposed to do, has lost its utility and must be either abandoned or reformed" (19).

Henry More coined the term "Gnosticism" (as well as the term "monotheism") in the seventeenth century as a designation for the array of views that Irenaeus and other ancient heresiologists wrote about. Brakke indicates, on the one hand, the need not to treat Irenaeus uncritically and to strive to get behind and beyond the face value of his use of the term "gnostic." On the other hand, Brakke emphasizes that Irenaeus is clearly not completely wrong nor simply making everything that he says up, so a complete dismissal of the information from Irenaeus is unjustified. Thus in chapter 2 Brakke returns his attention to Irenaeus and makes the case that one particular group, which scholars have frequently designated "Sethians," are in fact the original group that referred to itself as "gnostics." While most ancient thinkers emphasized gnosis, knowledge of some particular sort, the use of *gnostikoi* in reference to people was unusual. The term itself was also a positive one. So Brakke makes the case that Irenaeus would not have volunteered a positive designation of this sort for those with whom he disagreed. Therefore the moniker *gnostikoi* most likely reflects the group's own usage. Irenaeus's broader application of the term sometimes hints that it is being used by extension in those instances or that the other groups are offshoots or borrowers from that primal form of Gnosticism. Porphyry's independent testimony to the group and its status as a *hairesis* or "school of thought" is also important evidence.

Brakke argues that, since ideas and characters are frequently shared between otherwise divergent groups, the best way to search for the distinctive identity of the original gnostics is by describing their mythological system.

> The myth-oriented method of collecting works that originated among the Gnostics differs significantly ... from the typological approach. It does not extract ideas, characters, or motifs from their mythic contexts and then study them in isolation, nor does it rely on general concepts or spiritual attitudes that may flow from any number of different sacred narratives (for example, an emphasis on *gnōsis* rather than faith). Rather, it looks for a shared myth of origins, fall, and salvation (and, we shall see, a shared ritual as well), which could serve to establish and to maintain the unique identity of a distinct religious movement over time. (44)

So Brakke proceeds using those works that Irenaeus and Porphyry explicitly connect with the gnostics and then by extension other works that share the same mythical elements. While this still does not leave a body of literature that fits together without discrepancies, it does provide a core that can be associated with a single movement or group, to the same extent that the works included in the New Testament can. The gnostic school of thought, like the broader phenomenon of Christianity, was characterized by unity as well as diversity, as is to be expected.

Chapter 3 then proceeds to describe the myth set forth in the relevant works. In the process, Brakke highlights the fact that some elements, such as creation by a demiurge, were not unique to gnostics. Genuine distinctive features include the sheer number and complexity of their system of mediating principles and the ignorant/malicious character of their craftsman god (61). Important details are pointed out in the process of presenting the gnostic myth, such as the importance of gender in their stories and the fact that, contrary to what is often asserted, gnostic texts do not consistently view Jesus in a Docetic fashion. On the contrary, the flesh may be something negative, and a temporary abode of the Christ, but still be considered real and important.

Although Brakke notes that the identity of the incarnate redeemer is often not specified in gnostic texts, he nevertheless views Gnosticism as a fundamentally Christian phenomenon (68). This is in keeping with his focus on the gnostics as known to Irenaeus, who clearly represented what we would recognize as a form of Christianity. Later in the chapter (83–85) he considers and rejects the view that Gnosticism first appeared in non-Christian Judaism. The chapter also includes discussion of evidence related to distinctive gnostic rites, in particular baptism.

In chapter 4 Brakke's begins with the New Testament evidence for debates over circumcision and uses this as a stepping-off point for a discussion of unity and diversity in the church in second-century Rome, where we know that Gnosticism was among the available religious options. Three examples of the diversity in that time and place are offered: Marcion, Valentinus, and Justin, each of whom is to be distinguished from, and viewed as reacting and responding to, the gnostic school of thought. Brakke argues that not only lumping Marcion and Valentinus with gnostics but also categorizing Justin as proto-orthodox is problematic. "The vehemence with which Justin denounced Marcion and Valentinus as 'heretics' is an indication of their similarity to him as much as their distance" (111).

Chapter 5 focuses on how Christians differentiated themselves from others and from one another. Brakke points out that familiar ways of speaking, such as "why the church rejected Gnosticism," are problematic, because there was no unified entity such as "the church" that could accept or reject anything, and "the dynamics of self-differentiation and boundary formation in which the Gnostics and their opponents participated was far more complex than simple 'rejection' of one party by another" (113). In this chapter Brakke's attention focuses on the examples of the Valentinian school, Irenaeus, Clement of Alexandria, and Origen. Those who participated in a Christian group with a Valentinian teacher probably had no sense that the views they were being exposed to were outside "the mainstream" (115–16). While the gnostics often rewrote Scripture in their retellings, Valentinians, on the other hand, were pioneers in exegesis of Jewish and Christian sacred texts and in the production of commentaries (118). All the individuals discussed in this chapter, and the communities of which they were a part, used many of the same strategies, such as claims to apostolic tradition, allegorical interpretation of the emerging canon, and withdrawal of communion (132).

Although it seems somewhat ironic that more direct attention is given here to individuals and groups that Brakke does *not* consider gnostics, he uses the evidence from the second and third centuries to make the case that the emergence of more explicitly Christian teachings of a variety of sorts, on the one hand, and the appearance of gnostics on the radar of the Platonists, on the other, during this same period, suggests that the gnostics may have been losing ground to others in the process of Christian mutual self-definition (133). But the process whereby this occurred was not the simple one that envisages a proto-orthodoxy, on the one hand, and views that were gnostic or indebted to the gnostics, on the other. The structures and networks that were forged in this period were crucial in the emergence of a "universal" church in the longer term. But even then attempts to forge and enforce unity and uniformity were not entirely successful.

In concluding, Brakke notes that, if Christians today are not Marcionites and Valentinians, neither are they Origenists or Justinians. "No forms of Christianity that existed in the second and third centuries have survived intact today; rather, they have all contributed, in greater and lesser ways, to the ongoing development of Christianities" (136).

Brakke manages to provide both a broad introduction to past scholarship and some creative suggestions for new directions in a relatively slender volume. But certainly there are arguments that could have done with further expansion and detail. For instance, it might be asked whether, in limiting the term "gnostics" to the group scholars refer to by the designation "Sethians," Brakke is not in danger of re-essentializing the phenomenon, in a manner not entirely unlike what defenders of "orthodoxy" have done with respect to Christianity. Can the term "Christian" be denied to later wearers of the label, simply because they are later offshoots of the original movement and do not entirely maintain its beliefs and practices? The orthodox Christianity of the fourth century might have to surrender the label, if that is the standard. In the case of Gnosticism, however, the situation differs, since we do not know that any later group embraced the term "gnostics," although one proposed etymology of the term "Mandaean" is that it means precisely that.

On the question of whether Gnosticism had Jewish origins, Brakke's case may also be found unpersuasive by some. While Brakke regards the fact that parallels between Jewish and gnostic literature and ideas often have in mind significantly later Jewish sources, some may see this as an argument *in favor of* rather than against a Jewish origin for Gnosticism. Is it more likely that later Jewish authors borrowed from a specifically Christian movement or that Jewish Gnosticism influenced both Christian and non-Christian forms of Judaism? At the very least, those who find the case for Jewish Gnosticism compelling will probably not find reason to change their mind in Brakke's brief treatment of this topic, although they will certainly find much stimulating food for thought.

Be that as it may, as an overview of what we know about gnostics from insider and outsider sources, and of the methodological issues related to the scholarly study of this ancient religious phenomenon, Brakke's book provides both an excellent introduction as well as some innovative proposals that are bound to stimulate further discussion. The volume is certainly one that students and scholars are going to need to familiarize themselves with and engage in the years to come.

Irenaeus and Genesis: A Study of Competition in Early Christian Hermeneutics, by Thomas Holsinger-Friesen. Journal of Theological Interpretation Supplements 1. Winona Lake, Ind.: Eisenbrauns, 2009. Pp. xv + 250. Paper. $34.95. ISBN 9781575067001.

Thomas Andrew Bennett, Fuller Theological Seminary, Pasadena, California

Recent years have shown a renewed scholarly interest in Irenaeus primarily on account of his explanation and development of the "rule of faith" or "rule of truth" (*regula fidei, regula veritatis*). There are multiple reasons for this, not the least of which involves a concern for identifying the mark of decidedly *Christian* interpretation(s) of Scripture. That is, with both the linguistic turn in philosophy and the postmodern foundering of faith in historical-critical methods to deliver the "real" meaning of texts, researchers have begun looking back to Irenaeus's rule of faith (and patristic interpretation in general) to shore up Christian readings over and against merely academic handlings of Scripture. It may be a surprise, then, that very little work has actually been done on Irenaeus's working method. Very few commentators have tried to *exegete* how he handled texts.

There are two reasons for this; taken together, they form the thematic core of this publication of Thomas Holsinger-Friesen's dissertation, which was directed by Francis Watson at the University of Aberdeen. First, under the extended influence of Harnack, Irenaean studies have been locked into the assumption that some doctrine, usually recapitulation, lurks behind and undergirds all of Irenaeus's textual and argumentative work. On this view, the center of Irenaeus's thought revolves around recapitulation. All other considerations—be they apologetic, philosophical, speculative, or otherwise—hover in orbit around a doctrinal sun. Thus hermeneutics is seen to be incidental to a larger theological enterprise. For this reason, a majority of scholarship has embraced a second position, that Irenaeus's treatment of Scripture is haphazard and undisciplined. A number of studies have attempted to mitigate or overthrow this charge, but theirs is a concern for developing a hermeneutics that will explain the hidden consistency behind Irenaeus's various interpretive moves.

Holsinger-Friesen's contribution rather boldly attempts to change the trajectory of more than a century of scholarship. As to the first issue, Holsinger-Friesen treats recapitulation as a sort of theological fallout of hermeneutical practice. Thus, recapitulation enters the monograph late and only in apologetic response to the positions of the Ophites and Valentinians as Irenaeus has construed them. At the same time, he eschews any attempt to develop an "Irenaean hermeneutic," insisting rather on describing individual exegetical moves that Irenaeus makes, averring that these are all hermeneutical "tools" that Irenaeus "puts to work" in the service of reading Scripture under the rule of faith.

In terms of structure, *Irenaeus and Genesis* is a dissertation through and through. A general introduction explains and sets in context Holsinger-Friesen's two main concerns. This is followed by an exhaustive review of the literature. He begins with Harnack, progresses through his followers and critics (Bousset, Brunner, Wingren, Nygren; also attending to the outlier Aulén, who subsumes Irenaeus under a reappropriation of *Christus victor*), detours through the biblical theology movement (Lawson), revisits post-Harnackian analysis (Potter, Kelly, Pelikan, Torrance), and reviews some of the more recent proposals that have focused on Irenaeus's potential contributions to contemporary discourse on the atonement (Osborn and Boersma). The section mostly highlights the dominance of recapitulation theory in the literature. In an effort to turn the scholarly tide, Holsinger-Friesen then reframes the argument in terms of hermeneutics, citing the relative paucity of uses of the word recapitulation in *Adversus haereses* compared to the frequent, almost continuous references to Gen 1–3. Rather than analyze a concept to see how it is imposed on texts, Holsinger-Friesen would rather work from the ground up, as it were, investigating individual instances of Irenaean interpretation.

To set the stage for this task, Holsinger-Friesen next develops an extensive and impressively detailed account of Irenaeus's representation of Ophite and Valentinian beliefs as they relate to the Genesis narrative. He frames these gnostic beliefs as presenting two types of challenges that Irenaeus must overcome. First, the Ophites bring a premodern "hermeneutic of suspicion" to the Genesis texts. By supplying an alternate back story to Mosaic authorship, they suggest that Moses is merely a pawn of Ialdabaoth ("God" in the creation stories), airbrushing events to conceal how Sophia (a rival wisdom goddess) bested Ialdabaoth's plans in the garden by convincing Eve to eat from the tree. By couching this telling in terms of a "hermeneutic of suspicion," Holsinger-Friesen hopes to emphasize how whatever Irenaeus does with Gen 1–2 must convincingly reestablish the trustworthiness of the creation accounts as such. As for the Valentinians, he shows how Irenaeus's portrayal of their gnostic account does not so much invalidate the Genesis story as supply an alternate "meta-narrative" that locates human origin and destiny in an otherworldly, nonbodily existence. Against this, Irenaeus must offer an alternate, thoroughly embodied account out of the Genesis narrative. Though this goes beyond Holsinger-Friesen's language, it sums up his point: Irenaeus's arguments against the Ophites and the Valentinians were not so much a battle over speculative theology as a battle for the Bible.

With this in mind, we turn to the central feature of Holsinger-Friesen's study, the theological use of Gen 1:26 and 2:7. Meriting a chapter each, extensive analysis of what Irenaeus does with these texts and how he does it is described in this way: "So richly fertile and exceedingly flexible, [Gen 1:26 and 2:7] could be marshaled at a moment's notice to enable Irenaeus to say almost anything necessary about Christian doctrine" (107). Elsewhere these texts are "peerless because of two characteristic features: extraordinary *flexibility* and suitability for *wide typological readings*" (40, emphasis original). What Holsinger-Friesen almost says, but never quite manages, is that Irenaeus *does not hold to a specific, consistent meaning* for, say, "the image of God." Rather, he uses any and all possibilities as instruments to make various theological cases. This is undoubtedly a fascinating contention and flies directly in the face of both the Harnackian recapitulation-rules-all and the consistent-and-coherent-interpretation strands of Irenaean scholarship. If Holsinger-Friesen is right, then Scripture is eminently *deployable*. When faced with what he takes to be heresy, Irenaeus meets enemy doctrines on their own scriptural turf, as it were, and is happy to win in their court and on their terms. This is why Irenaeus demonstrates what Holsinger-Friesen calls a "protological orientation" (i.e., an interest in texts of origin, namely, Gen 1–3). The Ophites and the Valentinians want to undermine and co-opt the texts respectively; Irenaeus vindicates those texts under the rule of faith. Thus, against the Ophites Irenaeus shows how the image of God is truly present in Genesis and truly restored in Christ. There is therefore no reason to be unduly suspicious of the Genesis text. Against the Valentinians, Gen 2:7 projects an intimately involved Creator fashioning truly and thoroughly embodied humans. Since human destiny begins "from dust," it is fitting that Christ, too, should come—and remain—in the flesh. While demonstrating no consistent reading of *imago Dei* or "dust" or "breath," Irenaeus does manage to hold the Old and New Testaments together, simultaneously countering the specific challenges of the Ophites and the Valentinians.

The rule of faith proscribes certain readings of Genesis—especially those where the Creator God is *not* the Father of Jesus Christ. From Irenaeus's perspective, then, having or not having a consistent and coherent reckoning of what it is to bear the image of God is just not the point. What matters is preserving a ruled reading of the texts. This is a bracing argument, to be sure, and the value of Holsinger-Friesen's work would have been significantly strengthened were he to fashion it in this way. Nevertheless, the whispers and intimations are present; the attentive reader will no doubt recognize their import.

A few critical remarks. Given the argumentative turn Holsinger-Friesen seeks to make, I suspect that readers would have benefited from more direct refutation of the longstanding Harnackian/anti-Harnackian assumptions. How does the Scripture-is-deployable thesis better reckon Irenaeus's overall practice than what is argued by Harnack and others? Moreover, if it is the case that Irenaeus is either inconsistent or simply ambiguous in his thinking about "the breath of life" or Adam being "formed from the dust," and it is the case that Holsinger-Friesen is explicitly recommending that postmodern theological hermeneuts follow his example, would it not be appropriate to consider some of the implications of this stance for orthodox postmodern theology? On Holsinger-Friesen's view, what makes a reading "wrong" is primarily the extent to which it tears the Old and New Testaments apart, since the texts of Genesis are "flexible" and open to a diversity of "typological readings." How exactly ought contemporary theological hermeneuts follow or diverge from Irenaeus's practice, if at all?

In one sense, these remarks indicate the extent to which Holsinger-Friesen is directing the conversation in the right directions. The vast potential for this work is precisely the reason that I wish he had gone a bit further. Moreover, his work signals perhaps a new kind of interest in patristic hermeneutics—one less concerned with consistency, coherence, and grand ideas and more concerned with rediscovering the value of interpretive moves that, on first glance, look jarring, alien, or hopelessly naïve to us.

Cyprian and Roman Carthage, by Allen Brent. Cambridge: Cambridge University Press, 2010. Pp. xv + 365. Paper. $99.00. ISBN 9780521515474.

J. Jayakiran Sebastian, Lutheran Theological Seminary at Philadelphia, Philadelphia, Pennsylvania

This comprehensive work by Allen Brent will take a prominent place in the study of the enduring contributions of the mid-third century martyr-bishop of Carthage, Cyprian, in the first part of the twenty-first century, as the massive work by the archbishop of Canterbury, E. W. Benson, *Cyprian: His Life, His Times, His Work* (London: Macmillan, 1897), did for the first part of the twentieth century. No doubt there are other recent works that provide an overarching view of Cyprian's life, including J. Patout Burns, *Cyprian the Bishop* (London: Routledge, 2002), but this volume will provide the touchstone for all future work and research.

The opening one-page introduction makes the important point that the Cyprianic corpus is crucial to understanding events in the Roman Empire, as well as in the church, in the middle of the third century, since other available sources are scattered and fragmentary. Chapter 1 offers a compact overview of the man and the issues that he dealt with during his decade-long episcopate. This also sets the tone for what follows, in that we do not meet Cyprian standing isolated from the broader currents and philosophical, religious, cultural, and social realities of that time but as someone firmly located within, and also reacting to, this ethos and worldview. By intertwining analysis of Roman history, imperial coinage, funerary and public monuments, philosophical writings (especially Stoicism), and available Christian sources throughout the book, Brent shows us how this shaped all that Cyprian was and did—as an upper-class Roman and Christian patron who used his position both in church and society to react to the situations that he had to confront, including the Decian and Valerian persecutions and the turmoil that this led to within the church.

Further depth analysis is provided in chapter 2, which deals with Cyprian's background in the city that had had a complex relationship with Rome: Carthage. Apart from obvious sources such as Cyprian's account of his conversion and the biography written by his deacon, Pontius, Brent delves extensively into the convoluted history of Carthage, including its destruction and reconstruction following the wars with Rome and how the city known to Cyprian had evolved around the defining of sacred space and buildings associated with governance and public entertainment. All this had a bearing on how Cyprian saw himself as the one duly appointed to uphold certain norms and principles within the space of the church and how, when someone like the presbyter Novatian, questioned the role of Cyprian (who had, with what he saw as legitimate grounds, left the city during the time of the Decian persecution), his understandable reaction, also shaped by his drawing from a Stoic worldview, was to reassert his authority over against someone whom he saw as having invaded his domain and tried to usurp his legitimate authority.

This meticulous analysis of what was happening when Decius ordered all those within the empire to offer sacrifice continues in chapter 3, where Brent considers historiography. Again, given that popular versions of Stoicism speak about a cyclic reality of decline and renewal, and recognizing that Rome had just celebrated its millennia, Brent draws on the expectations prevalent in Roman society regarding how the present could be transformed and unity achieved by the various components that went into the making of society sticking together in a cohesive manner. This was reflected by Cyprian's understanding of ecclesiology, which led him to uphold the status of Cornelius as the bishop of Rome and by not distinguishing between those whom he saw as schismatics and heretics, since both rebelled against the principle of unity. This stance regarding authority and unity was also reflected in Cyprian's dealings with those confessors who had suffered during the Decian persecution and were now claiming the right to ask Cyprian to readmit the lapsed to full fellowship in the church. One question still needs to be pushed: that of the certainty of salvation that those clamoring to be readmitted sensed was the exclusive prerogative of those who belonged. Given the wares available in the religious marketplace at that time, what aspects of Christology were deemed crucial and why?

Chapter 4, dealing with political rhetoric and the religious policy put in place during the relatively brief reign of Decius, a time when the world was seen to be entering old age with all that this entailed, *senectus mundi*, indicates how the measures put in place were not specifically aimed against the Christians as such but were more on the lines of calling the people of the realm to come together and reaffirm what bound them as a people as citizens under the rule of the emperor. How could an emperor function as the *restitutor* of the *nouum saeculum*? Brent analyzes the understanding of *supplicatio*, something led by the emperor with the participation of all his subjects, in the edict of Decius, which called for a public affirmation and sign of the unity of the empire's subjects through religious sacrifice, an act by which he sought the return of *pax* throughout the land. A massive and universal public demonstration of unity is one thing, but what about the underlying factors that wanted to place so much emphasis on the role of the emperor within the cult? The scrappy sources do not allow us to get into what ultimately motivated Decius, but the question still remains.

This leads to chapter 5, about the Decian persecution, how this was implemented, and the consequences for the church. How could Cyprian deal with the various categories of people who were impacted by what Decius ordered—those who willingly, even eagerly, offered sacrifice? those who bribed magistrates to obtain a certificate to say that they had sacrificed? those who got a substitute to sacrifice for them? those who fled rather than sacrifice? and those who refused and paid the price? Again, Brent does not remain with the Christian sources and report what they reveal but probes the religious and sociological outlook of that time, including examining cases of religious syncretism in art and literature. Were some of those who offered sacrifice doing so out of the conviction that they were participating in a civic duty, which they considered had no bearing on their religious preference? But what about those who were firmly convinced that doing this would violate their theological convictions?

Chapter 6 deals with the church of the martyrs, those confessors who had survived the consequences of their actions in refusing to offer sacrifice. Even when some of these were in prison, they had written certificates of peace (*libellus pacis*) where they asked for leniency for the lapsed by invoking the authority that they claimed was derived through suffering. Was this a request or a command? Taking this in the latter sense, Cyprian was faced with the dilemma of, one the one hand, not being seen as confronting those who had earned the respect of the wider community and, on the other, to uphold his authority and reassert his conviction that he would be the one to decide on the question of penance and readmittance. Brent shows how this dilemma led him to come up with a new understanding and redefinition of martyrdom, where confessors could not be seen to undermine church order. This had consequences not only in Carthage but also in Rome, where those promoting leniency, others affirming an unyielding rigorist position, and yet others talking about an appropriate penitential model all had to be dealt with. To top it all, just when the laxists under Felicissimus had been ruled to undermine the possibility of maintaining church discipline, the deaths caused by the plague, as well as rumors of yet another assault on the church, this time under Valerian, forced Cyprian to make concessions. But this was not a blanket amnesty: on the question of the recognition of baptism offered by those whom he considered outside the boundaries of the church, Cyprian was resolutely unyielding, and this led to the great debate with Stephen, the bishop of Rome, which is the subject of the last major chapter.

Chapter 7 extensively documents the course of the baptismal controversy with Stephen. Brent examines this under the rubric of *sacramentum unitatis*—asking as to how something that seemed so obvious to Cyprian, namely, that those baptized "outside" the church needed to be baptized, not rebaptized, since according to him what was claimed to be baptism was no baptism at all. Brent retraces the events in Cyprian's episcopate, including the conflict with the Novatians, and examines Letters 69–75 and the anonymous treatise *De rebaptismate*, which he sees as an accurate representation of Stephen's position. My own work on this controversy, *"...baptisma unum in sancta ecclesia...": A Theological Appraisal of the Baptismal Controversy in the Work and Writings of Cyprian of Carthage* (Ammesbek bei Hamburg: Verlag an der Lottbek [Peter Jensen], 1997), judged that this document, part of the vigorous pamphleteering of that time, led to an untidy and messy theory regarding baptism and the role of the bishop in the receiving of the Holy Spirit.

In scrutinizing the decisions taken at the councils held in Carthage during the years 254–256, Brent examines the enduring issue of the emergence of the "primacy" of Rome through the claims of an episcopal monarchy (and Cyprian's earlier role in fostering the grounds for such a claim) and looks at the visual representation of various ecclesiastical leaders in the cemetery of Callistus in Rome, where we find a painting of Cyprian next to that of Cornelius. The acrimonious baptismal controversy ended without resolution with the death of Stephen in 257 and the martyrdom of Cyprian in September 258.

The unresolved and unanswered questions left behind have impacted many aspects of Christian doctrine down the centuries. While this is not a topic addressed in the book, the final one-and-a-half page chapter in the form of a postscript highlights Cyprian's legacy—a legacy that, Brent notes, failed "abysmally" and "spectacularly" not only in the context in which Cyprian lived, wrote, and died but also in the centuries following. Is this too harsh? Are these judgments too hasty? These questions will linger long after one interacts with the superb analysis and important insights found in this book.

HISTORY OF INTERPRETATION

History of Biblical Interpretation, Vol. 3: Renaissance, Reformation, Humanism, by Henning Graf Reventlow. Translated by James O. Duke. Society of Biblical Literature Resources for Biblical Study 62. Atlanta: Society of Biblical Literature, 2010. Pp. viii + 278. Paper. $32.95. ISBN 9781589834590.

A. K. M. Adam, University of Glasgow, Glasgow, Scotland

With this volume, eminent historian of interpretation Henning Graf Reventlow brought his survey of biblical interpretation from the fourteenth century (where he closed volume 2 of this series with John Wyclif and Nichlas of Lyra) to the fifteenth and on into the seventeenth century, where this volume closes with Grotius and Calov. The exposition follows individual scholars one by one, outlining their lives first and subsequently citing characteristics of their interpretive practice. Reventlow focuses on "decisive developments" (2) of his exemplary figures rather than surveys of the broad currents of history; thus he intends to reveal the truest characteristics of a particular cultural moment's appropriation of the Bible.

Reventlow begins by recounting the lives and work of Renaissance and early humanist interpreters. He selects Gianozzo Manetti, Lorenzo Valla, Marsilio Ficino, Johannes Reuchlin, Jean Lefèvre, John Colet, and Erasmus as his exemplars of Renaissance and humanism. Manetti merits attention for his commitment to studying the Old Testament in Hebrew, with guidance from rabbinic literature. Valla most famously applied his critical scholarship to exposing the forged "Donation of Constantine"; he also, however, produced a commentary on the New Testament of the Vulgate, in which he introduced discussion of text-critical issues and opened some of the Vulgate's translations to question by comparing them carefully to the Greek texts. Ficino's fragmentary commentary on Romans introduces a humanist Platonic spin to traditional interpretation of Paul. Reuchlin, the renowned Hebraist, advanced Renaissance humanism by translating classical and theological works into German, by studying Judaic texts carefully (though still with Christian biases), and by producing the textbook that taught European scholars how to understand Hebrew. Lefèvre produced an annotated Psalter that compared five early versions, wrote commentaries on the Gospels and Pauline Epistles, and translated the Bible into French. Colet offered Neoplatonizing lectures on the Pauline Epistles, and Erasmus collated the critical edition of and annotations on the Greek New Testament and advocated an interpretive practice that valued patristic sources over the testimony of scholasticism.

The second division of this volume highlights Reformation interpreters, beginning with Martin Luther and including Melanchthon, Zwingli, Calvin, Müntzer, the Zurich Baptists, Sebastian Franck, the Münster revolutionaries, and Pilgram Marpeck. Although Luther's greatest contribution as a biblical scholar may be his translation of the Bible into German, his numerous works of biblical interpretation display his development from a thoroughly medieval interpreter in his first lectures on the Psalms to an exegesis fully informed by his clear emphasis on the characteristic keynotes of the Reformation. Melanchthon's *Commonplaces* constitute a unique synthesis of biblical and dogmatic interpretation, and Zwingli mediates Erasmian influences to the Reformation through his extensive teaching, preaching, and commentaries. Calvin displays various traits of "precritical" (129) interpreters, including an insensitivity to literary-critical considerations, although he shares a humanist's awareness of rhetorical devices. Calvin's wide-ranging interpretive practices are united mostly by his interests in securing the biblical foundations of doctrine and in the practical applicability of the Bible to the believer's daily life.

Of the more radical Reformers, Reventlow presents a perspective on Müntzer as anticlerical agitator (rather than as a general revolutionary) moved by his prophetic judgment against ordained ministers both Catholic and Protestant. The Zürich brethren who produced the Schlechtheim Articles construe Scripture as a definitive guide to Christian life, to an extent that took too many texts too literally. Franck propounds a mystical, spiritual understanding of God that guides readers beyond Scripture to a truth that transcends even the Bible. The Münster Baptists imagined themselves to be completing the Reformation by moving beyond the Reformers and actually implementing the way of life that the Bible instituted. Finally, Pilgram Marpeck developed an interpretation of the New Testament that relegated the Old Testament to a secondary status, as the hints and prophecies that would only actually be fulfilled in the teachings of Jesus and his followers.

The third portion of the book touches on the Catholic Reformation with a summary of Joannes Maldonatus's interpretation, the late humanism of Hugo Grotius, and the beginnings of Protestant Orthodoxy in Abraham Calov's writings. Maldonatus followed Cajetan's example by meeting the Reformers on their own ground, foregrounding the biblical basis of Catholic teaching; his exegesis bore the grammatical and semantic marks of his humanist milieu, in service of his scholastic theology. Grotius resolved many interpretive problems with reference to the historical background of the author (excepting the prophets, whose divine inspiration overrode their historical limitations) and advanced the work of textual criticism. Abraham Calov sought to ground all the Reformation's great theological principles in a consistent exposition of the literal sense of the Bible—to the detriment of his exegesis.

If the preceding summary seems a staccato series of disjointed observations, that impression reflects the experience of reading this volume. Where one might look forward to an eminent scholar's assessment of how the various streams of interpretive practice converge and diverge in themes or in relation to particular broader economic and political circumstances, we receive instead a collection of biographical sketches followed by observations on each scholar's interpretations. Reventlow indicates that this is deliberate: "only a reduction of the materials to the most decisive developments permits us insights into the motives behind the understanding of the Bible for the epoch" (2). Unfortunately, the reasoning that justifies concluding that something constitutes a decisive development"—and the relation of these developments to one another or to their broader cultural conditions—remains insufficiently clear. Such topics as Platonism and Neoplatonism, the standing of spiritual interpretation, the authority of the Vulgate and of vernacular translations, and the basis of an interpreter's authority affect all of the figures Reventlow discusses (and he usually mentions them), but Reventlow does little to connect the dots among these themes, their imbrication in political movements, and the interpreters who debate them. As this work seems to aim at articulating an intellectual history, the specific streams of influence and *Wirkungsgeschichte* deserve greater prominence (as do the conditions of interpretive production).

Though the general exposition adopts an impartial tone, Reventlow occasionally assesses interpreters by the extent to which they measure up to the Reformation's perspective. Lefèvre "paved the way for the Reformation" (45); "The Reformation message was foreign to [John Colet]" (47); Erasmus "could not come to the Reformation understanding [of fallen humanity]" (58); Melanchthon attained interpretation consonant with "Reformation theology in its main points in accordance with Luther's understanding" (94); Zwingli sometimes differs from Luther, but in other areas he "unambiguously shows himself to be a Reformation thinker" (112); and so on. The Lutheran flavor this lends to the narration will impress some readers more than others, but it would have strengthened the book if Reventlow had brought this premise to the foreground and (pardon the expression) justified it more extensively.

Finally, the translation and editing fall short of what readers should expect of the publishing arm of a scholarly organization. The translation—often leaden, sometimes outright baffling—ill befits James O. Duke, who has translated numerous works so gracefully over a distinguished career. Had the editors even employed just a spell-checker, they would have caught "lthey ed" (for "they led," 98), "dhurch" for "church" (104), "repudiaiton" (114), and so on, even if they had not caught "canon" instead of "canton" (95)—all from a relatively short span of pages.

Reventlow knew more about biblical interpreters and their works than all but a very few scholars, and his erudition shows on page after page. The radiance of his learning, however, is clouded by many of the most prominent aspects of this volume. A researcher may here find useful nuggets of information relative to particular interpreters of interest, and a determined reader will benefit especially from Reventlow's treatment of less-famous figures. Still, this volume has to be reckoned a missed opportunity: the author, the translator, and the press promise much more than the book delivers.

History of Biblical Interpretation, Volume 4: From the Englightenment to the Twentieth Century, by Henning Graf Reventlow. Translated by Leo G. Perdue. Society of Biblical Literature Resources for Biblical Study 63. Atlanta: Society of Biblical Literature, 2010. Pp. x + 471. Paper. $49.95. ISBN 9781589834606.

Jeffrey L. Morrow, Seton Hall University, South Orange, New Jersey

Over three decades ago, Henning Graf Reventlow established himself as a giant among scholars of the history of modern biblical criticism with his groundbreaking work *The Authority of the Bible and the Rise of the Modern World* (1980).[1] In that important work, Reventlow demonstrated that German biblical scholarship was a late-comer to the field, a thesis that went contrary to the received scholarly opinion, which often locates eighteenth- or nineteenth-century German scholarship as modern biblical criticism's birthplace. Reventlow showed, however, how modern biblical criticism entered German lands from England (especially by way of the English Deists), where it had already a long history of development. As he writes in the present volume, "German biblical scholarship, in comparison with that of Western Europe, had to be viewed at the time of Semler [early to mid-eighteenth century] almost as a straggler" (182). Apart from this work, Reventlow has produced significant shorter studies in the form of articles and essays on important figures within this history, including Richard Simon (1980), Bernhard Duhm (1988), and Eberhard Gottlieb Paulus (1993). His chapter on Thomas Hobbes in *Authority of the Bible*, remains, in my opinion, one of the finest treatments of Hobbes's biblical criticism in print.[2]

The four volumes of his massive (over 1,300 pages) *Epochen der Bibelauslegung* (*History of Biblical Interpretation*), originally published in German between 1990 and 2001, have proved themselves to be indispensible resources for scholars interested in the history of exegesis. The first volume of that series, *From the Old Testament to Origen*, addressed such issues as innerbiblical interpretation, early pre-Christian Jewish interpretation, issues of interpretation involved in translation, the use of the Old Testament in the New Testament, early Christian and related interpretation (apostolic fathers, Justin Martyr, Marcion, Irenaeus, Origen), as well as early rabbinic interpretation. His second volume, *From Late Antiquity to the End of the Middle Ages*, included a discussion of a wide range of biblical interpreters during this time period, including Theodore of Mopsues-

---

1. Unfortunately, the English translation omitted the subtitle: *Die bedeutung des Bibelverständnisses für die geistesgeschichtliche und politische Entwicklung in England von der Reformation bis zur Aufklärung* (*The Significance of the Biblical Understanding for the Intellectual History and Political Development in England from the Reformation to the Enlightenment*). See Henning Graf Reventlow, *The Authority of the Bible and the Rise of the Modern World* (trans. John Bowden; Philadelphia: Fortress, 1985).

2. "Thomas Hobbes: The Philosophical Presuppositions of his Biblical Criticism," 194–222 and endnotes on 524–38.

tia, Jerome, Ambrose of Milan, Augustine, Gregory the Great, Isidore of Seville, Venerable Bede, the *Glossa Ordinaria*, Peter Abelard, Hugh of St. Victor, Joachim de Fiore, Aquinas, Bonaventure, Rashi, Ibn Ezra, Nicholas of Lyra, and John Wyclif, among others. His third volume, *Renaissance, Reformation, Humanism*, dealt with a number of significant figures important for understanding the roots of modern biblical criticism, including Lorenzo Valla, Marsilio Ficino, Johannes Reuchlin, Erasmus, Luther, Melanchthon, Zwingli, Calvin, Thomas Müntzer, and Hugo Grotius.

The English translation of his final volume should be received with great joy. This final volume brings Reventlow's history into the twentieth century. After a brief introduction (1–2), Reventlow begins his first chapter, "Lutheran Hermeneutics in Germany" (3–22), in which he examines the historical context of exegetes Matthias Flacius Illyricus (3–13) and Johann Gerhard (13–22). Reventlow's second chapter, "The Bible in England from the Sixteenth to the Eighteenth Centuries" (23–72) contains important background material to the biblical interpretive work of Thomas Cartwright (23–32), Thomas Hobbes (32–51), John Locke (51–65), and John Toland (65–72). His third chapter, "The Battle for the Text of the Bible" (73–81) discusses a number of important figures within the history of modern biblical interpretation: Elias Levita (73–74), Johannes Buxtorf (74–75), Louis Cappel (75–77), Johannes Buxtorf II (76), John Mill (78–79), Johann Albrecht Bengel (79), and Johann Jakob Wettstein (79–81). Next comes one of his shortest and yet most important chapters for laying the groundwork for later biblical criticism, chapter 4, "France and the Netherlands in the Seventeenth and Eighteenth Centuries" (83–122), in which he examines the lives and work of Richard Simon (83–89), Baruch de Spinoza (89–110), and Pierre-Daniel Huet (110–22).

His fifth chapter, "The Bible in Pietism and the German Enlightenment" (123–229), the longest chapter in the book, examines the pivotal seventeenth- and eighteenth-century works of Philipp Jakob Spener (123–32), August Hermann Francke (133–44), Johann Christian Edelmann (144–55), Hermann Samuel Reimarus (155–65), Gotthold Ephraim Lessing (165–75), Johann Salomo Semler (175–90), Johann Gottfried Herder (190–202), Johann Jakob Griesbach (202–4), Heinrich Eberhard Gottlob Paulus (204–10), Johann Gottfried Eichhorn (211–19, 221–28), and Johann Philipp Gabler (212–15, 217–21, 228–29). In his sixth chapter, "Biblical Studies as a Science in the Nineteenth Century" (231–334), Reventlow takes a look at some very significant figures for this history: Wilhelm Martin Leberecht de Wette (231–45), David Friedrich Strauss (245–62), Wilhelm Vatke (262–76), Ferdinand Christian Baur (276–85), Ernst Wilhelm Hengstenberg (286–98), Heinrich Ewald (298–303), Heinrich Julius Holtzmann (303–10), Julius Wellhausen (311–25), and Bernhard Duhm (326–34). Many of these scholars (e.g., de Wette, Holtzmann, and Wellhausen) are, in the standard histories of scholarship, more commonly associated with modern biblical criticism than are some of the figures in Reventlow's earlier chapters.

His seventh chapter, "The History of Religion School" (335–77), explores the work of Hermann Gunkel (337–58), Wilhelm Bousset (358–72), and Johannes Weiss (372–77). The eighth and final chapter, "New Directions in the Twentieth Century" (379–411), focuses on two twentieth-century exegetes, Karl Barth (379–94) and Rudolf Bultmann (394–405). In this final chapter, Reventlow attempts, over a span of about five pages, to survey the field from Bultmann to the end of the twentieth century, a task that he concedes "is difficult to outline" in such short space (405). In the back material he includes a useful but very thin "Selected Resources and Readings" (413–48), followed by three short indices.

Reventlow opens his final volume by restating his intention for the entire four-volume set: "to trace in the life's work of selected theologians and laity their developing understanding of the Bible in the context of the particular periods in which they lived" (1). In this regard, he has done a masterful job in all four volumes, but especially in this final installment. Indeed, one of the greatest strengths of this final volume is the way in which Reventlow pays careful attention, not only to the main overtures of a specific exegete's scholarly work, but also how exegetes fit within their broader lived contexts. In histories of scholarship, it is typical to focus so exclusively on the scholarly works of particular exegetes that readers are left with the impression that the scholarship of these biblical interpreters is simply the result of stoic individuals heroically pursuing the worthy goals of *Wissenschaft* in complete isolation at their desks and hidden in libraries. Reventlow helps place these scholars in their broader lived contexts, showing their connections with one another, bringing out details of their family life, of their theological and philosophical outlooks, and often of their active participation in the politics of their day. For example, Griesbach not only studied under Semler but lived in his house as well and became very close friends with Goethe and Schiller. Or consider Locke's role as secretary for an English "diplomatic legation," secretary to the Earl of Shaftesbury, and his many political activities in Whig politics. Other examples of this sort abound.

Later figures such as de Wette, Holtzmann, and Wellhausen provide further examples. De Wette was very close to the philosopher Herder. Herder not only gave de Wette his examinations at the gymnasium, but de Wette attended Herder's sermons and traveled with him on a winter trip to Geneva. De Wette also attended Griesbach's lectures and, after his move to the University of Berlin, came into close contact with Schleiermacher. Holtzmann was one of Vatke's students, and his teacher influenced him greatly. Along with Ewald, Holtzmann was one of the founding members of the Protestant Association. One of Holtzmann's more famous students was Schweitzer. Wellhausen's most influential teacher was Ewald, with whom he eventually had personal conflict over political differences. Wellhausen visited Vatke as well as Kuenen, he befriended Ritschl, and he became a very close friend of the classicist Wilamowitz.

Reventlow's discussion of the scholars' roles in the great political movements of their days is also quite illuminating. Reventlow's volume underscores the often inextricable links between German and Prussian politics and the scholars working at their state-supported institutions. Semler was elected the official rector of the University of Halle and thus became the king's representative. De Wette was sympathetic to the student movement that attempted to increase democracy and move toward a unified Germany. De Wette was eventually discharged from the University of Berlin because the government intercepted a private letter of his to a grieving mother whose son had been executed. It was only outside of Prussia, in Basel, that de Wette was able to work in peace. Ewald provides yet another example. Ewald was among seven faculty members of the University of Göttingen who were fired because they refused to acknowledge the revocation of the Kingdom of Hanover's state charter and its attendant releasing of civil servants from the oaths they had sworn to that constitution. At the request of the king of Württemberg, Ewald moved to the University of Tübingen. Later, when Prussia absorbed the Kingdom of Hanover, Ewald was dismissed again upon his refusal to swear an oath of allegiance to the new ruler, Bismarck—which accounts for his later dispute with Wellhausen, who (along with Wilamowitz) was a staunch Bismarck supporter.

Reventlow's final volume in this series includes a rich array of details that often are omitted in such works. It is so easy to simply place scholars in their history without actually addressing their work directly, yet Reventlow does an impressive job of explaining the main points of each figure's *oeuvre* showing concrete examples with numerous quotations and citations throughout. Reventlow likewise includes a lot of historical background material that is often forgotten in the standard histories. An important example is the fact that written Bibles were often unavailable to the wider public before the invention of the printing press at the end of the fifteenth century. This is true, but as Reventlow points out, even by the seventeenth century Bibles were still prohibitively expensive for most people to own (130). Another important insight Reventlow continually brings up throughout his work is the antipathy to priesthood, sacrifice, and cult (and often attendant denigration of Judaism) evidenced in much of the seventeenth-, eighteenth-, and nineteenth-century biblical scholarship of scholars such as Toland, Semler, Eichhorn, de Wette, Wellhausen, and Duhm (65, 184–85, 222, 242–43, 275, 317–18, 321, 324–25, 327), which he sees as an inheritance of the Enlightenment.

In light of some of the figures he includes, it might have been appropriate to include a few others, if only in brief subsections. A few come to mind off the bat, most of whom Reventlow mentions in passing in various places throughout his volume: Isaac La Peyrère, Lodewijk Meyer, Johann David Michaelis, Hermann Hupfeld, Karl Heinrich Graf, and Abraham Kuenen. The longest section (nearly twenty-two pages) deals with Baruch de Spinoza (89–110). This seems appropriate because of how important a role Spinoza's framework played in later discussions, as has become increasingly recognized.[3]

---

3. E.g., the recent study by Nicolai Sinai, "Spinoza and Beyond: Some Reflections on Historical-Critical Method," in *Kritische Religionsphilosophie: Eine Gedenkschrift für Fried-*

There are some minor typographical errors throughout: for example, in the selected readings section, under Griesbach, there is a citation error for David Dungan's book on the Synoptic problem. Reventlow has Lee as Dungan's middle name, but the actual volume in question correctly has Laird as his middle name. Moreover, contrary to the citation in his book, Dungan's work was not published by Eisenbrauns.[1] I have not been able to double-check whether or not this is the fault of the German original or simply of the English translation. Overall, Reventlow has produced a very important work on the history of modern biblical scholarship. This will prove to be an essential reference for English-reading students and scholars alike, as the German original has already proven to be.

L'invention critique de la Bible, XVe–XVIIIe Siècle: L'invention moderne de la critique du texte biblique, by Pierre Gibert. Paris: Éditions Gallimard, 2010. Pp. 377. Paper. €27.50. ISBN 9782070786534.

Jeffrey L. Morrow, Seton Hall University, South Orange, New Jersey

Pierre Gibert's work is well known by scholars of the history of modern biblical criticism. His work on Jean Astruc, as well as his annotations and introductions to the modern scholarly editions of Astruc's *Conjectures sur la Genèse* (1999) and Richard Simon's *Histoire critique du Vieux Testament* (2008), are important contributions to this growing field of study. Gibert's *L'invention critique de la Bible* will prove to be an important study of the history of modern biblical criticism. The task he sets out for himself is an ambitious one, yet he does a marvelous job. He traces the emergence of modern historical biblical criticism from the fifteenth century to the eighteenth century. Gibert shows how modern biblical criticism developed from the Renaissance, through the Reformation and Enlightenment periods, culminating in the nineteenth and twentieth centuries.

The Renaissance developed philological tools and historical analyses that became essential for later historical biblical criticism. The Protestant Reformation, with its insistence on *sola Scriptura*, brought with it a critique of traditional patristic and medieval exegesis as well as a methodological shift wherein the Bible was to be studied in light of itself and cut free—at least theoretically—from the moorings of church tradition. An important part of the debate within this period was the role and nature of reason in interpretation, as well as the differing receptions of Renaissance humanism. The remainder of the sixteenth and seventeenth centuries brought with them debates about apparent errors and contradictions

---

rich Niewöhner (ed. Wilhelm Schmidt-Biggemann and Georges Tamer; Berlin: de Grutyer, 2010), 193–214. I owe Nicolai Sinai thanks for providing me a copy of his essay.

1. David Laird Dungan, *A History of the Synoptic Problem: The Canon, the Text, the Composition, and the Interpretation of the Gospels* (New Haven: Yale University Press; originally New York: Doubleday, 1999).

in the biblical texts, with a number of significant figures emerging within this historical continuum, for example, Lodewijk Meyer, Baruch Spinoza, and Richard Simon. It is especially in the seventeenth century that Cartesian philosophical skepticism and concerns about the nature of historical methodology entered this story. In many regards, the reception and further development of biblical criticism in England and Germany in the eighteenth century was a response to and in many instances a continuation of the criticism that was forged at the end of the seventeenth century.

Gibert covers a number of very important figures within his history, including such a diverse group as Ibn Ezra, Lorenzo Valla, Elia Levita, Desiderius Erasmus, Martin Luther, Sebastian Castellion, Joseph Scaliger, Isaac La Peyrère, Meyer, Spinoza, Simon, Henning Bernard Witter, Jean Astruc, Johann Gottfried Eichhorn, and so many others—nearly fifty in all. He focuses most of his attention on Spinoza and especially on Simon (discussing the latter in various places totaling a span of about 150 pages!). In light of the many figures he brings up, there are some quite significant omissions. Curiously, Gibert makes not even a single mention of Johann David Michaelis, who was a towering figure within the history of eighteenth-century biblical criticism and was the individual who introduced Eichhorn (Michaelis's student at Göttingen)—and the rest of the German-speaking world—to Astruc's *Conjectures*. The fact that Gibert spends nearly six pages on Witter's work, which does not appear to have had much influence on later scholarship, coupled with the fact that Gibert correctly makes much of Eichhorn's appropriation and modification of Astruc's work, makes his omission of Michaelis rather glaring. Another figure one would have expected to see in these pages was Johann Salomo Semler, who is particularly significant in the dissemination of Simon's work in the German-speaking world.

A final critique pertains to two topical omissions. In light of the growing consensus of scholars from diverse backgrounds (Michael Gillespie, John Milbank, and Charles Taylor) to the important role William of Ockham and Nominalism played in the development of the modern Western intellectual tradition, and the role of Ockham specifically in the development of trends that led to modern biblical criticism (A. J. Minnis, Michael Waldstein, and Matthew Levering), it would have been beneficial to mention some of the ways this Nominalist tradition influenced the history Gibert discusses, particularly with the Reformation. Second, the role of medieval Muslim engagement with Jewish and Christian Scriptures, as well as medieval Muslim philosophical trends, has been increasingly recognized as an important factor giving rise to modern biblical criticism in Western Europe (especially in the works of Roger Arnaldez and Hava Lazarus-Yafeh). These omissions admittedly fall outside of the range of his study, which is from the fifteenth through the eighteenth centuries. However, Gibert includes quite a bit of material that falls well beyond his proposed time frame. He discusses the modernist crisis within the Catholic world as it relates to Catholic engagement with modern historical biblical criticism (e.g., Alfred Loisy), from the late nineteenth to early twentieth centuries, and even includes more recent Catholic discussions such as

Pope Pius XII's encyclical *Divino Afflante Spiritu*. On the earlier end, he includes an entire chapter devoted to the medieval work (twelfth century) of Abraham Ibn Ezra. My comments here should not be seen as detracting from Gibert's fine work. His book makes a substantial contribution to the field and represents an amazing ability to synthesize an enormous body of literature, tracing the influence each intellectual exerted within this history. This book is a must read for anyone interested in the history of modern biblical criticism. One of the significant points he brings out is the importance of the question of the Mosaic authorship of the Pentateuch in the rise of modern historical biblical criticism. He explains this theme in more detail in his important volume *L'invention de l'exégèse moderne: Les "Livres de Moïse" de 1650 à 1750* (2003).

The book under review here is divided into three parts and includes thirty-two major chapters as well an epilogue that spans over twenty pages. The book's first part is called "Criticism before Criticism." Chapter 1, "A Precursor: Lorenzo Valla," highlights the important role of the textual-critical work of Renaissance thinkers such as Valla. Chapter 2, "Erasmus' 'Reason,'" shows how Erasmus's work continued the textual-critical trends of Renaissance humanism. Chapter 3, "The 'Diatribe': Erasmus and Luther," introduces the reader to the role of the Reformation within this history. Chapter 4, "The 'Difficulties' of Sebastian Castellion," focuses on Calvinist developments within the history of modern biblical criticism. Chapter 5, "The Entrance into the 17th Century: 'Scholarly Libertinism,'" sets the stage for Gibert's lengthy discussion of seventeenth-century biblical criticism, which spans twenty three chapters and about two hundred pages of text. Chapter 6, "Of 'Pre-Adamites': The Implications of Cartesianism," emphasizes the influence of Descartes' philosophy, as well as the foundational biblical exegesis of La Peyrère. Chapter 7, "When Criticism Appears," hones in on the textual-critical work of Louis Cappel. Chapter 8, "The 'Prolegomena' of Walton," discusses the exegetical work of Brian Walton. Chapter 9, "In the Beginning was Moses: Criticism without the Name," specifies how the question of Mosaic authorship of the Pentateuch became such a focal point within the rise of modern biblical criticism. Chapter 10, "A Question of History? Jean Morin," examines Morin's work on the Bible.

The second part is entitled, "Criticism in Search of Itself." Chapter 11, "When Philosophy Gets Involved…," is primarily about Meyer's work and the important role of philosophy. Chapter 12, "The Demonstration of Lodewijk Meyer," takes a more focused look at Meyer's development of a philosophical methodology for analyzing the Bible. Chapter 13, "Spinoza or the Philosopher Grammarian," situates Spinoza, Meyer's mentor, within this history, emphasizing Spinoza's pivotal role. Chapter 14, "On the Interpretation of Scripture," lays out Spinoza's attempt at developing a scientific methodology for studying the Bible in his *Tractatus theologico-politicus*. Chapter 15, "Inevitable History," explores the question of Mosaic authorship and biblical history within Spinoza's work. Chapter 16, "The 'Historian' Simon," introduces Gibert's focused discussion of Simon's work over the next five chapters. Chapter 17, "Of Criticism or of History?" discusses Simon's role in the debates concerning the compositional history of the Pentateuch, in his *Histoire critique du Vieux Testament*. Chapter 18, "Receive and Translate the Bible," examines Simon's methodological principles.

The third part is entitled "When Criticism is Invented." Chapter 19, "An Original Sin," discusses the broader historical background to the controversy over Simon's work. Chapter 20, "The Invention of a History," examines Simon's engagement with his contemporaries. Chapter 21, "At the Beginning of a European Enterprise: Ibn Ezra," underscores the influence of Ibn Ezra on modern biblical criticism. Chapter 22, "Jewish Humanism: Elia Levita," focuses on Levita's influence on modern biblical criticism. Chapter 23, "Of Interpretation," takes a look at Simon's engagement with Jewish biblical interpretation. Chapter 24, "A Misunderstanding: The Inspiration of Scripture," discusses Simon's views concerning biblical inspiration. Chapter 25, "On the Nature of Prophecy," discusses Simon's critique of Spinoza on prophecy. Chapter 26, "A Critical Europe," looks back over the history of biblical criticism in Europe thus far covered. Chapter 27, "The European Destiny of Richard Simon," examines the reception of Simon's work. Chapter 28, "And the New Testament?" focuses on Simon's *Histoire critique du texte du Nouveau Testament* and *Histoire critique des versions du Nouveau Testament* and their role within the development of biblical criticism of the New Testament and of later studies of the historical Jesus. Chapter 29, "Of Strange Lights," discusses the reception of seventeenth-century biblical criticism (especially Spinoza and Simon) among eighteenth-century Enlightenment thinkers (especially Voltaire and Diderot). Chapter 30, "Contradictions of a Century: Jean Astruc," takes a look at Astruc's work, especially the ways it attempts to respond to La Peyrère, Spinoza, and Simon, but also how it appropriates some of their methodologies. It is here that Gibert mentions the importance of Astruc's work for the development of the Documentary Hypothesis, first with Eichhorn, and the role that it played in furthering modern biblical criticism. Chapter 31, "The Shift to Germany," explores the development of modern biblical criticism in Germany, which, contrary to conventional scholarly opinion, was a relative late-comer to the scene. Chapter 32, "To the 19th Century," takes a closer look at eighteenth-century exegetes—Ilgen, Eichhorn, Geddes, and Vater—and especially the significance of the German translation and reception of Simon's oeuvre. The epilogue, "Criticism Criticized," brings Gibert's book to a close, delving into the nineteenth century and even the twentieth century with the modernist crisis in the Catholic world. Gibert's book concludes with a very useful nine-page chronology and a map of the main centers (e.g., universities and presses) of biblical criticism within Europe.

As one would expect from Gibert, *L'invention critique de la Bible* is masterfully written. The author is to be commended on handling so complex a topic with such a diverse group of exegetes spanning over three centuries. It is to be hoped that this work will be translated into English to facilitate a broader reading audience. Despite the topic, the book is written in such a way that it would be accessible to nonspecialists and, indeed, would likely be of interest to anyone wishing to read more about the development of modern biblical interpretation.

HERMANEUTICS AND METHODS

Wrestling the Word: The Hebrew Scriptures and the Christian Believer, by Carolyn J. Sharp. Louisville: Westminster John Knox, 2010. Pp. xvii + 154. Paper. $20.00. ISBN 9780664230678.

Phillip G. Camp, Lipscomb University, Nashville, Tennessee

In *Wrestling the Word: The Hebrew Scriptures and the Christian Believer*, Carolyn J. Sharp, Associate Professor of Hebrew Scriptures at Yale Divinity School, invites seminary students, pastors, and laity to consider the relevance of the Old Testament for today. She also offers helpful guidance for those who teach introductory Old Testament courses in theological schools.

Sharp does not intend to provide an exhaustive introduction to Old Testament interpretive methods, and she says that no one method provides the only correct understanding of the text. In fact, she argues that insisting on a single method or interpretation can be harmful. Thus, she encourages readers of the Old Testament to see how various approaches lead to hearing the texts in a variety of legitimate ways, and she stresses the need for Christians to read in community.

The perspective from which Sharp writes is decidedly and unapologetically Christian, though she expresses hope that non-Christians will benefit from her work as well. She notes her own life of faith in the context of the Episcopal Church, expresses her belief that the Holy Spirit works through the Old Testament text, and asserts that Christians "read in the presence of the One who calls us continually to renewed relationship with the Holy and with one another" (xvii).

Chapter 1 addresses how what we bring to the text shapes our reading of the text and how our reading of the text shapes us. Awareness of these aspects of reading matter because reading is not a neutral act; it has power for good or ill. To illustrate how presuppositions affect interpretation and the effects those interpretations can have, Sharpe contrasts the historical-critical method with literary and postmodern readings of the Old Testament. She presents a rather lengthy treatment of the strengths and weaknesses often found in historical-critical readings of the text. She then highlights aspects of the literary approach but is less systematic and thorough in discussing its limitations. She clearly has a strong appreciation for the value of the literary approach, though she is unwilling to give up the necessity of taking authorial intent into account.

Sharp ends the first chapter with an overview of the work of Julia Kristeva on "intertexuality" and "foreignness" and Emmanuel Lévinas on "the other." These concepts provide the ethical foundations for her discussion on how to approach and apply the Old Testament texts.

In chapter 2 Sharp calls upon readers to recognize and honor the multiple "voices" within the biblical text. To illustrate the presence of multiple voices, Sharp turns to the Pentateuch and the Documentary Hypothesis. While strongly critiquing the reasoning that stands behind the Documentary Hypothesis, she also highlights the value and ethical importance of attending to the various voices preserved in the final form of the Pentateuch. She then discusses the work of Walter Brueggemann and Mikhail Bakhtin as helpful guides for attending to the various voices in Scripture.

Chapter 3 discusses the issues surrounding historical representations within the Old Testament text and historical reconstructions of Israel's history based on the biblical text and other data. As Sharp engages these matters, she gives her "governing convictions": (1) "Memory is powerful"; (2) "Creativity and bias are intrinsic to cultural production"; (3) "God is real" (80). She then calls upon the readers to be self-reflective about the convictions that guide their understanding of history and its impact on their faith.

Sharp presents the difficulties of historical reconstruction when it comes to ancient Israel and then addresses challenges that confront many Christian readers when they encounter critical discussions of history in the Old Testament. The first challenge is the cultural similarities of ancient Israel to the ancient Near East, including the use of similar "genres and motifs." The second challenge is the question of the historicity of the exodus and conquest traditions. Here she introduces and contrasts the positions of the so-called "minimalists" and "maximalists." The final challenge for Christian readers is the biblical portrayal of David, particularly his historical significance and the varying portrayals of him in the Bible itself.

In answer to these challenges, Sharp invites the reader to hear and appreciate the differing voices in the complex historical traditions of the Old Testament, understanding that each reveals something true. History, she argues, includes but is more than simply the past act. She is unwilling to give up all factual bases for the history represented in the exodus/ conquest narratives and the Old Testament presentations of David, but history is also the imaginative and creative retellings of the past in differing contexts. Each of these retellings reveals something of truth about God, and struggling with the various retellings becomes a means for strengthening one's faith.

In chapter 4 Sharp addresses the role of the interpreter directly. She argues that individuals and communities must be self-aware of what they bring to a text as they interpret. The presuppositions they bring to biblical texts and the methods of interpretation they use have consequences for how they then employ those texts in relation to other people and groups. Such self-awareness is an ethical issue because, she argues, "every act of interpretation is an act of power" (113), and every interpretive act serves "ideological goals" (114).

Sharp also calls for awareness that stories within the Bible have had a detrimental effect on readers because the stories draw lines between insiders and outsiders, and interpreters either see themselves among the outsiders in the biblical text or biblical texts have been used to marginalize them. She specifically addresses the debates in biblical studies over matters of "gender, sexuality, and imperialist rhetoric" (116) by highlighting four groups of interpretive approaches: (1) feminist and womanist readings; (2) African and African American biblical hermeneutics; (3) queer readings; (4) postcolonial criticism.

The brief final chapter calls for collaborative and interdisciplinary studies of the Old Testament. Such joint efforts are important, Sharp says, because they remind us of the complexity of the biblical text, prevent the privileging of one reading, and invite us to learn from one another. She offers her students' descriptions of the kinds of interpreters of Scripture they want to be, showing the different ways of viewing Scripture and the variety of interpretive goals. She ends with an invitation to the reader to wrestle with Scripture, in community, and through that struggle to perhaps "glimpse the face of God" (140).

Sharp's book is a helpful guide to reading the Old Testament for a number of reasons. First, she demonstrates that critical and scholarly readings of the Bible do not have to be at odds with reading from a faith perspective, a matter of no small importance to many seminary students. Second, she rightly calls for self-awareness and awareness of others as one interprets and makes use of Old Testament texts, pointing out the dangers of reading without such awareness and the harm that can be and has been done by it. She does a nice job of revealing how that lack of self-awareness affects not only the student or lay reader but also biblical scholars. Third, she practices what she preaches by confessing her own faith background and commitments and how these affect her reading of the Old Testament. Fourth, and consistent with her call for recognition of the "other," she recognizes the different background and faith commitments of the readers of her book. Thus, she understands that not all readers will accept her claims and interpretations. Rather than attempting to coerce the reader to accept her views, Sharp invites readers to consider them honestly from within the framework of their own traditions but with an awareness of how those traditions affect their responses. Fifth, to illustrate the various approaches to the Old Testament that she discusses, Sharp uses the story of Jael and Sisera from Judg 5. This gives the reader the advantage of understanding how different methods bring to light different hearings of a single text.

The book, however, does have a few problems, in my opinion. First, given that her intended audience is primarily Christian, I found it a bit surprising that Sharp grounds the ethical foundation of her presentation so heavily on the works of Kristeva and Lévinas. Their works certainly resonate with ethical themes of the Bible. But a call to Christians to read their authoritative Scripture ethically might be better accomplished by rooting the ethics primarily in Scripture or by showing how the views of Kristeva and Lévinas are consistent with biblical ethics. Second, in her examples of different kinds of readings in chapter 4, I was a little surprised to see her join feminist and womanist readings and African American and African readings under the same headings. She does so because there are great areas of overlap in the experiences and aims of these methods. Yet given her call to give attention to different voices and interpretations, it seems to me that combining the methods can serve to mute voices by blurring the distinctions. Third, for a book that calls for giving heed to different interpretations and perspectives, there is little recognition of evangelical or conservative scholarship in the footnotes and quotation boxes, other than in her contrast of historical minimalists and maximalists.

Wrestling the Word would make a good supplementary text for an Old Testament introduction or exegesis course. If used in an introductory course, it should probably be assigned for the end of the term because the author assumes the reader has familiarity with some aspects of critical scholarship.

A Handbook of New Testament Exegesis, by Craig L. Blomberg with Jennifer Foutz Markley. Grand Rapids: Baker, 2010. Pp. 304. Paper. $22.99. ISBN 9780801031779.

Jan G. van der Watt, Radboud University, Nijmegen, The Netherlands

Blomberg and Markley's book aims at providing a textbook that they hope can be widely used by both specialists and nonspecialists alike, whether they have studied Greek or not. At the outset they argue that there are only a "fairly small number of unvarying rules or principles with which one needs to acquaint oneself; the rest of the skill comes from repeated practice and from the evaluation of the work of other practitioners" (xiii). It is therefore necessary to guide "the student step by step through the full exegetical process" by discussing methodology to the extent necessary in order "to get the introductory theological student under way in the process." Examples are provided in each case. It is claimed that they will proceed in a "sequential fashion according to the logic of the exegetical task itself" (xiii). The book is divided into ten chapters that are more or less equal in length. Thus some of the basic aims and presuppositions with which this book is written are given. Simply looking at these points of departure already creates some uneasiness: for instance, to satisfy the beginner and the specialist, to deal with Greek and not with Greek, and so forth could prove to be problematic. One is immediately confronted with questions such as: How, for instance, does one translate without having knowledge of the source language, or how does one make text-critical judgments if one is unable to read the Greek text?

The book starts with an introduction and then moves on to textual criticism as the first of ten chapters. The second chapter deals with translation and translations and is followed by chapters on the historical-cultural context, literary context, word studies, grammar, interpretative problems, outlining, and theology, ending with a chapter on application, assuming that this sequence corresponds with the "logic of the exegetical process itself" (xiii). A summary of each chapter then follows with a checklist for doing biblical exegesis as an appendix. A select bibliography, scripture index, and subject index conclude the book.

In chapter 1, on textual criticism, the aim is not to give a comprehensive explanation of the entire field but "to introduce the topic in a way that will allow students and pastors to engage in the practice" (2). The question is answered: What is textual criticism? Some terms are defined; a brief historical overview is given followed by a discussion of some of the characteristics of these texts. Then an explanation is given on how textual criticism is practiced. Perhaps the expectations are a bit high that beginners will be able to *practice* textual criticism, but at least they will be able to understand certain choices after mastering this chapter.

The aim of chapter 2 ("Translation and Translations") is to help students to get a "rough-and-ready" translation, also helping them to understand why translations differ. They should be able to assess the relative merits of different translations. Different translation theories are discussed as well as some delicate issues such as translating metaphors, reproducing style, and the issue of inclusive language.

Then the authors turn to discussions of historical-cultural issues in chapter 3, distinguishing between what they call "historical-context analysis" (history behind the text, i.e., of the author or the receivers or historical events that affected the writing = diachronic) and "social-scientific analysis" (i.e., history at the same time as the text = synchronic; 66ff.). The distinction between these two aspects of historical-cultural research could be confusing. Could categories like the author or the receivers and their historical situation at the moment of writing not also be classified as "at the same time as the text" (= synchronic)? Malina, the doyen of the social-scientific approach, wrote material on, for instance, Paul as author. Both diachronic and synchronic elements are involved. There would obviously also be questions from representatives of certain social approaches whether they could be classified as "social-scientific" and not rather as social-historical or just as social approaches to the text; the authors try to include all of these approaches under the description "social-scientific criticism" (86–90).

The relevance of the literary context for interpreting the text is discussed in chapter 4. The literary contexts of books are described as well as the significance of literary forms and genres. Important figures of speech also receive attention, while rhetorical analysis and narrative criticism are briefly mentioned. Chapter 5 explains how "word studies" should be approached that will result in an "original, context-specific meaning of the word under study" (118). Different scholarly resources such as lexica, concordances, and theological dictionaries also receive due attention.

The issue of "grammar" is discussed in chapter 6. I am not so sure that the few remarks on grammar in this chapter are all that enlightening; trying to summarize Greek grammar, its complexities, and its significance takes more than a few pages; the majority of the chapter is devoted to examples. Chapter 7 is set aside to deal with "interpretative problems." It explains that one knows one has "interpretative problems" when there are different forms of tensions in the text or interpretation of the text, resulting in complex debates, disagreements between different sections or books in the Bible, and the like. Examples are then given to show how one should "fix" the problem (174ff.). Obviously, in this instance one could ask whether these types of problems will not also become apparent during the other phases, while analyzing the grammar, the historical or social aspects, and so forth.

Outlining is the topic of chapter 8, that is, diagramming Greek sentences. The question is: How can this be the last step in the process before one starts to theologize? How one could understand any Greek sentence without paying close attention to the syntax, in other words, how the different elements of a Greek sentence should be interrelated is not clear. This assumes that this phase should be dealt with earlier—a translation of a text is not possible without paying close attention to the syntax. Chapter 9 deals with "theology," inter alia, looking at issues such as the relationship between exegesis and theology as well as systematic theology. "Application" is dealt with in chapter 10. Certain pitfalls are noted, and the nature of communication is highlighted. A "method for bringing the Bible to our own world" is also proposed (249ff.).

Although the book is well-written with clear examples of what is expected, there are some basic problems regarding the presuppositions of the book that should be considered. The authors claim to follow the logic of the exegetical process. Is the logic of the process and the actual application of the process the same? Is it, for instance, possible to make a translation of a text before you have dealt with the grammar or syntax (grammar is discussed in chapter 6, syntax in chapter 8, while translation should apparently logically be done at the beginning—chapter 2)? It also seems more logical to me (since the authors speak of a logical process) to first try to see what the text itself says (grammar and word meaning is needed for this) before one moves to considering all types of scenarios about the social-scientific background.

Importantly, does this question not point to a larger issue, namely, that exegesis implies a circular movement rather than a sequence where one step follows on the other, without denying that there is a measure of sequence? That is, one must first choose a text and start to read and interpret the language. But sociolinguistics has made us aware of the fact that language is a social phenomenon and cannot be evaluated without taking the sociohistorical framework into account; in trying to determine the meaning of words, one has to deal with their social embeddedness. Recent semantic studies have understood that, in order to establish the meaning of a word, the literary context needs be taken into account, which means that both grammar and syntax play a role. Genre studies emphasize that understanding is strongly influenced by the identification of the literary types (if one starts to read a "yoke" literally, there might be some interesting consequences). These are not steps that should, or could, only be put on a list and ticked off as one goes along reading the text. The point is that exegesis is only a linear process to an extent. It is a more integrated (circular or spiral?) process where there is a constant movement between the different aspects of the process using and interrelating the information from the different processes to come to a better understanding of the whole.

It is often stated in books on methodology that exegesis is to some extent an "art," implying, inter alia, that the exegete should be able to enrich the interpretation by integrating and interrelating the information gained from the process as a whole (nearly like a painter integrates colors in a painting). I guess that the authors would not disagree with me on the point that exegesis is not simply going through a checklist sequentially. I know that in Professor Blomberg's work this is not the case. It is a pity, however, that this point is not enlightened in the book to a larger extent. I have observed many beginners trying to follow such a "step-by-step" process, resulting in an unbalanced and often a rather sterile process where the student sits with a lot of material (able to tell all about the background or the meaning of a word) but does not know what to do with the information in the actual process of interpretation.

A last and perhaps the most critical point is the treatment of hermeneutics in the book. The issue of the theory and problems of understanding is treated in the last chapter (10) under the heading "Application." Obviously, application of the biblical material to current-day situations is a major hermeneutical issue involving a vast array of problems as well as possibilities. Some of these problems are discussed in this chapter, as was shown above. But the basic question is crucial: Why is it necessary to go through all these often-complicated steps or spend all this time on exegesis? Why should we look at the social or historical background or try to establish the ancient literary form? Why can we not simply trust the Spirit or ask the leadership of the church to tell us what the Bible says, as some Christian groups seem to do? Is the Bible, some could ask, not the Word of God that communicates directly to us today as the unfailing Word of God? Further, what about postmodern insights that all interpretation is relative and the meaning of the text is restricted to what it means to me? Do I really need hours and hours behind a desk with heaps of books to try to determine what the texts means? Moreover, is determining the meaning of a text even possible? These and many other hermeneutical questions influence the way we treat the biblical text, some even before we pick up and read the Bible. What the Bible is for the reader and what one wants to know and how one should approach the Bible are all theoretical (hermeneutical) questions that must be answered before a decision can be made on the methodology to be followed in interpreting the text. Methodology is based on hermeneutics as practice is based in theory. I missed a solid consideration of these theoretical issues in the book. For instance, in chapter 3, on the historical-cultural context, it is mentioned that we should "eavesdrop" on the Bible to overcome the obstacle of the cultural difference that poses a threat to good biblical interpretation (63). This is a basic remark when dealing with exegetical work, but why is this necessary? The necessity is based on hermeneutical considerations that are not treated adequately. Based on the theory of communication, it is assumed that the Bible wants to *communicate* a message to us and that communication requires that the cultural framework of the receiver should be in synchronization with that of the sender, lest misunderstanding result. A proper theory of communication should therefore support such methodological actions. The rationale for trying to establish, for instance, the historical-cultural background, the specific meaning of words, the impact of ancient literary features, and so forth all lies within such deeper hermeneutical considerations.

There are many similar books on methodology available that treat similar material, and the list seems to grow by the year. This book provides solid information with good examples but leaves me with some very specific questions, as indicated above. I do not envisage that it will become a standard book on this topic, but the book does provide good, usable information for anyone interested in New Testament exegesis.

Biblical Metaphor Reconsidered: A Cognitive Approach to Poetic Prophecy in Jeremiah 1–24, by Job Y. Jindo. Harvard Semitic Monographs 64. Winona Lake, Ind.: Eisenbrauns, 2010. Pp. xv + 343. Hardcover. $39.95. ISBN 9781575069364.

Colin Toffelmire, McMaster Divinity College, Hamilton, Ontario, Canada

In *Biblical Metaphor Reconsidered: A Cognitive Approach to Prophecy in Jeremiah 1–24*, Job Jindo provides a helpful contribution to the growing scholarship related to metaphors in the Bible and provides a strong examination of Jer 1–24 in light of the insights of a cognitive approach to metaphor. Though the presentation of cognitive linguistics is somewhat sparse, and though there are some points of difficulty in Jindo's argument, the engagement with the text of Jeremiah is particularly good and will certainly be of use to interpreters working in Jeremiah. Jindo's principle argument, that metaphor can be seen as a world-creating or "orientational" and not merely rhetorical or decorative, is defended well and certainly produces exegetical fruit in his examination of Jer 1–24.

A reworked version of Jindo's 2006 doctoral dissertation, *Biblical Metaphor Reconsidered* is well-written and well-organized. It is divided into two major portions. Chapters 1–3 provide an introduction to the work as a whole, an introduction to a cognitive approach to metaphor, and a short introduction to Jindo's understanding of the basic structure of Jer 1–24. After these introductory chapters, Jindo moves on to his examination of the metaphors of Jer 1–24, which is presented in a chapter on the global metaphor of destruction and a chapter on local metaphors (particularly plant metaphors) in Jer 1–24. These two chapters make up the bulk of the work and are followed by a short concluding chapter. Jindo's writing is excellent and the organization of the book is easy to follow, but it is notable that there is a typographical error on the page header of every right-hand page in chapter 5.

Jindo's understanding of metaphor is grounded in the work of cognitive linguistics and cognitive poetics (particularly thinkers such as Lakoff, Gibbs, Johnson, and Kövecses; Fauconnier is very notably absent), but he tends to spare the reader from long, terminologically laden discussions of the linguistic underpinnings of the theory. He subscribes to a qualified version of the standard view of metaphor in cognitive linguistics, holding back somewhat in his unwillingness to suggest that all conceptual systems are fundamentally metaphorical, though metaphor does play a hugely important role in all conceptual systems (29–30 n. 11). He focuses on the primary distinction between "orientational" and "propositional" views of metaphor. The "propositional" view suggests that metaphor can be accurately paraphrased or translated and consequently implies that metaphor serves a mostly aesthetic or rhetorical purpose. The "orientational" view suggests that, far from being only ornamental, metaphors actually evince a self-contained reality that cannot be paraphrased. The metaphor consequently "orients our perspective to the object it describes" (45).

Jindo's assessment of the value of the cognitive approach is good, and he describes its benefits and possibilities very ably. That said, Jindo's opposition between "propositional" and "orientational" approaches to metaphor gives the impression that only cognitive approaches, or approaches grounded in cognitive linguistics, do justice to the orientational nature of metaphorical language and that other approaches consign metaphor to "mere ornament" (43–44). This is something of a straw man, as there are a great many works on metaphor that move well beyond the "propositional" approach and yet make no particular use of cognitive linguistic categories or concerns (e.g., Black and Ricoeur, both of whom Jindo references at other points in the book). My complaint is not that Jindo is mistaken here, simply that he has overstated both his case against ornamental metaphor and the centrality of a cognitive approach for moving beyond a propositional understanding of metaphor.

In his conceptual scheme, Jindo presents two different models: "*global* models, which give structure to the conceptual framework of that prophecy, and *local* metaphorical models, which present the inner experiences of characters—their emotional development in the narrated drama, as well as their inner orientation toward whatever they are describing" (49). This distinction is reflected in the organization and presentation of Jindo's work in Jeremiah, as he devotes a major chapter each to global and local metaphors in Jer 1–24. The global metaphor that Jindo explores is described in terms of "the royal model of lawsuit and consequent destruction" (49) and is expressed in terms of the fundamental metaphorical concept that "the cosmos is a state."

Much of this portion of his analysis is deeply grounded in a comparative approach that begins with the assumption that the biblical authors and the creators of Mesopotamian lament literature "share the same conceptual framework" (73). It is difficult to see how one could truly substantiate this claim. Certainly there is a likelihood that cultures in the same geographical and temporal environment would experience overlap in what Jindo refers to as "conceptual framework," but it is difficult to believe that this overlap would be complete. Indeed, it is difficult to believe that the overlap of conceptual framework for individuals within the same cultural and linguistic cohort would be total, let alone that between two different cultural and linguistic cohorts.

A more conscious differentiation between sameness, similarity, and difference would have been very helpful in all of Jindo's examinations of cognate literature. For example, Jindo suggests that "[biblical] authors incorporated and appropriated the literary and cultural conventions they, or their culture, had inherited from their surrounding societies, and transformed those conventions according to their own value system; hence, resemblances between biblical and other ancient Near Eastern sources" (75). This seems an imbalanced, mono-directional notion of cultural relationships. Also problematic is Jindo's emphasis, noted immediately following this quotation, that he will be focusing on the synchronic over the diachronic. If this is a synchronic study, then it seems that what matters more is the semiotic system of the culture in which Jeremiah was produced, not other cultures removed by geographical or temporal distance. Interpretation based on parallels from other cultures should, in this kind of approach, be secondary to analyses of the meaning making system of exilic and postexilic Israelite culture (note that Jindo is explicitly interested in the Hebrew version of Jeremiah, which he deems to have been produced for the exilic or early postexilic community in the sixth/fifth century B.C.E.).

The practical outcome of all of this has to do with how evidence is weighed. At various points Jindo gives the impression that one can draw conclusions about Israelite social and conceptual structures by observing evidence from other cultures or that examples of a particular phenomenon in the conceptual structure of another culture somehow validate or prove the existence of that structure in ancient Israelite culture (e.g., election language in relation to Mesopotamian kings and Israel, 108ff.). I am not suggesting that some relationship does not exist between these cultures; however, claims should be validated primarily based on internal and not external evidence.

One very positive note regarding Jindo's comparative work is that he engages the various parallels not only on formal grounds but also on conceptual or semantic grounds. Thus he is interested not only in surface structures that are similar or the same but on areas of conceptual overlap (143). Though this kind of analysis poses its own dangers, it is a step in the right direction for both comparative studies and studies of genre. For instance, Jindo's examination of the function of the prophet within the global metaphor of destruction is intriguing and has much to recommend it. Particularly interesting is Jindo's presentation of the prophet not only as emissary from YHWH to the people but also as royal confidant or advisor, acting as an intercessor to YHWH on behalf of the people (122–23). Thus the prophet's role is not mono-directional; he stands within the breach between YHWH and the people, speaking to both parties in the dispute. Here Jindo's emphasis on the global metaphors as orientational is powerful, and his attention to the metaphorical value of participant relationships (as opposed to focusing simply on metaphorical words) is particularly insightful.

Jindo also spends a great deal of time discussing horticultural imagery, in relation to both global and local metaphors. This discussion is interesting and highly instructive at many points. He does seem to be correct that imagery tied to gardens or growing things operates as an important metaphorical concept in Jer 1–24. Having said this, there are some places where his particular analyses are questionable. For instance, note his discussion of horticultural imagery as tied to the notion of divine election. When discussing the destruction of foreign powers in terms of garden/tree imagery, Jindo suggests that horticultural "imagery shows the deeper truth of the historical event: the collapse of these emperors as the result of the divine deprivation of their elected status in the universe" (115). But this begs the question that these foreign powers or their rulers were ever among the elect within the conceptual structure of the Hebrew Bible/Old Testament. Though this may in some instances be the case (e.g., the king of Tyre in Ezek 28, one of Jindo's examples), it is less clear that it must be so in others (e.g., Assyria in Isa 10, also an example used by Jindo). The lack of clarity on this issue cannot, in my view, be adequately adjudicated by reference to the conceptual or semantic systems of other cultures but must be examined based upon extant evidence from ancient Hebrew. In such a situation a reappraisal of the legitimacy of Jindo's "election" language is warranted.

Another issue arises in Jindo's examination of the horticultural imagery of Jer 1–24 in the chapter on local metaphors. Here he continues to flesh out his initial global metaphor "the promised land is YHWH's estate" (111) and the more specific discussion of the people as "YHWH's 'royal garden'" (185) with an examination of harvesting language (205). The difficulty, however, is that he does not differentiate between the conceptual structure of a royal garden and the conceptual structure of Israelite agriculture. In the various instances where we find royal gardens in the Hebrew Bible, there is no particular sense that the garden is ever harvested, as a field or orchard would be in standard agriculture. This suggests that what we have here may not be a single conceptual domain but two related domains (the people as YHWH's garden and Israel as YHWH's agricultural land, or some such) that are being blended.[1] It is not that Jindo's observations regarding Jeremiah are invalid (on the contrary, they are very interesting), but the precise nature of how these metaphors overlap is more complex than he suggests, and his work may have benefited from engagement in more recent cognitive linguistic theory on metaphorical blending.

Jindo closes his study with a set of conclusions and suggestions for further study. Among his interesting proposals here is the suggestion, following Newsome, that cognitive theory may be a fruitful method for the study of genres in biblical literature. Jindo's suggestions that genre-based analysis should be conceptual as well as "verbal" (by which he means oriented toward surface structure) and that it should be holistic and not atomistic are very welcome (though I might amend the second point to suggest that genre analysis should be *both* holistic *and* atomistic). Indeed, readers interested in the value of cognitive linguistics for genre analysis may benefit from reading Jindo's concluding discussion on the subject before engaging his arguments regarding genre in Jer 1–24, found in chapter 4.

Biblical Metaphor Reconsidered is a strong work both at the level of theory and at the level of specific textual analysis. Scholars and graduate students interested in metaphor, cognitive linguistics and poetics, and Jeremiah studies would certainly benefit from Jindo's hard work and particularly from his examination of the text of Jeremiah.

---

1. For an example of discussions of cognitive metaphor that explore blended domains, see Gilles Fauconnier and Mark Turner, "Rethinking Metaphor" (29 September 2008), online at: http://ssrn.com/abstract= 1275662. For an extensive bibliography related to conceptual blending, see Mark Turner's website at: http://markturner.org/blending.html.

Exploring Postcolonial Biblical Criticism: History, Method, Practice, by R. S. Sugirtharajah. Chichester: Wiley-Blackwell, 2012. Pp. vii + 211. Paper. $34.95. ISBN 9781405158572.

Jean Louis Ska, Pontifical Biblical Institute, Rome, Italy

This is a difficult book to read and to review, not only because of its content, but also because of the tone adopted by its author. Several readers will probably stop reading it after a few pages, others will be tempted to brush it aside just because of its title, and a third group may consider it as biased as the kind of exegesis it criticizes. I read it carefully and patiently until the end, however, and I did not regret it. These are my reasons. First, this publication is less a book than the expression of long suffering because of oppression and injustice. One cannot ask people who suffered to be always nuanced and well-balanced. Second, the professional (Western) exegete will perhaps not be able to discover many new insights on known biblical texts or exegetical conundrums, nor will he or she fill bibliographies with many new titles. The worth of this book lies elsewhere, in its exposing a very different point of view on the Bible or, better said, the use of the Bible and the role of Christianity in the so-called Third-World or in the former colonies. Third, it challenges some of the more established conventions of Western exegesis and calls for a more critical attitude, to self-criticism, which will surely lead to a more conscious, less prejudiced, and, one hopes, more fruitful exegetical work.

As for the book itself, it comprises an introduction, six short chapters, an afterword, a bibliography, an index of scriptural references, and an index of names and subjects. The footnotes follow the chapters (endnotes), which makes the book less user-friendly than one would wish it to be.

The introduction defines the purpose of the publication: "Essentially, postcolonial biblical criticism is about exploring who is entitled to tell stories and who has the authority to interpret them" (3). After this, we find a short overview of the content of the volume.

Chapter 1, "Postcolonialism: Hermeneutical Journey through a Contentious Discourse," offers a short history of how this new hermeneutic emerged among other biblical and theological methodologies and disciplines. It also speaks of what colonialism is, in the past and more recently, of the evolution of postcolonial studies, and about its merits and limits. The reader will find some definitions, as, for instance, that of "contrapuntal reading."

Chapter 2, "The Late Arrival of the 'Post': Postcolonialism and Biblical Studies," grapples with two main topics. First, the author endeavors to pinpoint the main historical factors that lead to the emergence of postcolonial biblical criticism. Second, he also analyzes the Bible itself and denounces some colonial and imperialistic tendencies enshrined in the Scriptures.

Chapter 3, "Postcolonial Biblical Studies in Action: Origins and Trajectories," is written by Ralph Broadbent. This is a kind of bibliographical survey of the major works in the field and their interaction with other similar tendencies in the intellectual world, for example, feminism and studies on notions such as "empire" and "imperialism."

Chapter 4, "Enduring Orientalism: Biblical Studies and the Repackaging of Colonial Practice," treats a vast topic from two very different points of view. First, the author affirms that the study of the Bible should be part of the study of all the cultures of the Orient. This sounds rather obvious, but the chapter has more to do with the idea of Orient generated by Western authors. The source of inspiration of this part is Edward Said, *Orientalism* (London: Penguin, 2003), who severely criticizes the way Western culture represents the "other," even with sympathy, but to affirm eventually the superiority of one's own culture. The second part is a scathing critique of the sociocultural work by J. J. Pilch and B. J. Malina on the differences between North American and Mediterranean cultures. It would have been better, it seems to me, to mention a work such as Oded Borowski, *Daily Life in Biblical Times* (SBLABS 5; Atlanta: Society of Biblical Literature, 2003), which is surely less one-sided.

Chapter 5, "Postcolonial Moments: Decentering of the Bible and Christianity," refers to two important events that took place in the nineteenth century and prepared for a postcolonial mindset: the publication of the *Sacred Books of the East* under the direction of Max Müller (1879–1910) and the Parliament of Religions held in Chicago in 1893. The publication is hailed as a positive effort to view in a different light the religious traditions of the East and to challenge some commonplace opinions such as, "The West is rational, scientific, and the East is spiritual and instinctive" (135). Nevertheless, this work still bears the marks of a Western sense of superiority. In the second case, some of the participants radically challenged several Western claims, such as its cultural supremacy, the superiority of biblical revelation, and the uniqueness of Christianity. The author takes this opportunity to denounce the evils of neo-colonialism. The content of this chapter could be encapsulated in one of the typically trenchant sentences of this book: "In the highly bureaucratized and theologically conservative atmosphere that prevails in these religions, Buddha would have found it difficult to be a Buddhist, and Jesus a Christian" (152). We also find here a definition of the so-called "contrapuntal method": "What the contrapuntal method does is to bring various textual worlds together and to enable us to picture and perhaps better yet, envisage an alternative world which may not be accessible if one is confined to one text" (152); or: "[contrapuntal reading is a reading] in which all texts are constantly impelled by a desire for connection and conversation" (143). In other words, our author recommends a more systematic use of a comparative method, something similar, but not fully, to what the *Religionsgeschichtliche Schule* proposed some time ago.

Chapter 6, "The Empire Exegetes Back: Postcolonial Reading Practices," offers some examples of postcolonial exegesis. Personally, I found this chapter more attractive. The examples chosen are taken from the New Testament: the birth narratives of Buddha and Jesus; the so-called "late style" (E. Said) of Paul and John; the parable of the Rich Man and Lazarus (Luke 16:19–31). The first example is, in my opinion a good illustration of a fair comparison between two very similar religious texts and could be compared with Eugen Drewermann's *Dein Name ist wie der Geschmack des Lebens: Tiefenpsychologische Deutung der Kindheitsgeschichte nach dem Lukasevangelium* (Freiburg im Breisgau: Herder, 1986). The second applies to Paul and John the idea that authors often change their minds at the end of their lives (E. Said). Paul becomes mellower and more loyal to civil authorities, whereas John, on the opposite, becomes very negative and critical toward the Roman Empire. This supposes, for instance, that the Letter to the Romans is a later writing of the apostle and that the book of Revelation can be attributed to John. Not everyone, to my knowledge, will agree with these assumptions. The third example will probably be hotly discussed by Luke's specialists, but it is surely challenging and thought-provoking. Does the parable foster a positive vision of the rich and a negative vision of the poor? There is room for different answers to this question, it seems to me. See, for instance, George Soares Prabhu, "Good News to the Poor: The Social Implications of the Message of Jesus," *Bible Bhashyam* 4 (1978): 200–210.

The afterword, "Postcolonial Biblical Criticism: The Unfinished Journey," spells out some major tasks for a postcolonial biblical criticism. The Bible, we are told, is a contested and ambiguous book (172) or, as it is said before, the Bible is itself the problem (69). Moreover, and this is a kind of bitter statement, "the reality is that our world will never be post-imperial" (179). Therefore, postcolonial criticism will always be in order. Eventually, the three main evils of the Bible—conquest, conversion, and election—are not confined to only one religion (180–82).

To sum up this review, it seems to me that the author insists on two major points. First, postcolonial criticism should inoculate intellectual elites with some basic notions so that imperialism, neo-colonialism, and Western chauvinism will disappear sooner or later, and better sooner than later (52–53). Second, dialogue is indispensible. He speaks in this respect of "interfaith cross-fertilization" (72).

This short summary does not render justice to the wealth of reflections packed into these pages. Unable to discuss the many affirmations it contains, I limit myself to a few points that deserve, in my opinion, further study. First, as one says in Italian, "Non dobbiamo fare di ogni erba un fascio," which corresponds more or less to the English saying, "Don't throw the baby out with the bathwater." Western exegesis is perhaps somewhat more variegated that what is described in this book. I do not think, for instance, that the works of H. Gunkel or M. Noth in biblical exegesis or that of M. Eliade in "comparative religions," just to quote a few names, are tarnished by all the flaws listed by our author in his study. Second, several important personalities denounced and condemned the evils of colonialism. Some are mentioned (Bartolomé de la Casas, John William Colenso). Let me quote another voice, not mentioned in this volume: "Who can describe the injustice and cruelties that in the course of centuries they [the coloured peoples] have suffered at the hands of Europeans? … If a record could be compiled of all that has happened between the white and the coloured races, it would make a book containing numbers of pages which the reader would have to turn over unread because their contents would be too horrible." This was written by Albert Schweitzer, a New Testament scholar and the founder of a famous hospital in Lambaréné (now in Gabon) in his book *On the Edge of the Primeval Forest* ([New York: Macmillan, 1931], 115). Third, I would say with Umberto Eco that it is indispensable to distinguish between the interpretation of a text and its use. I would add, between the interpretation or misinterpretation, the use or misuse or abuse, of a text. A (biblical) text misused is not necessarily dangerous or contestable in itself. Eventually, it seems to me that the author puts us again—and with strong arguments for which we must thank him—before our task that I would summarize with a free quotation from Julius Wellhausen: we always have to interpret biblical texts; the only choice we have is to interpret rightly or wrongly.

Ancient Laws and Contemporary Controversies: The Need for Inclusive Biblical Interpretation, by Cheryl B. Anderson. Oxford: Oxford University Press, 2009. Pp. ix + 240. Hardcover. $25.00. ISBN 9780195305500.

William R. G. Loader, Murdoch University, Murdoch, Australia

Cheryl Anderson, Associate Professor of Old Testament at Garrett Evangelical Theological Seminary, presents us with a book squarely focused on hermeneutics. Her opening chapter identifies the need: both within Scripture itself and especially among its interpreters there are values that she sees as contradicting who she believes "God is and how God is at work in the world" (3). Accordingly, her subtitle uses the word "inclusive," by which she means not an imperialism that encompasses and subordinates all but a respect and valuing of all, especially those who do not fit the stereotype of the white, Western, heterosexual, well-off, Christian male. As she puts it, "to me, what is eternal, absolute, and unchanging is the divine commitment to justice" (28). Thus, "the voice of God emerges from Scripture in the context of dialogue within faith communities" (8), where such theology is affirmed. I would have liked to have seen more in this chapter about these core values that clearly govern her analysis. Perhaps she saw no need to defend them, but when we pit them against competing claims, as this reviewer would also do, we have to make a positive case for them and show that they are deeply rooted in biblical tradition, where they grow alongside tendencies with which they are in tension and which, in turn, inspire other values.

Her affirmation of inclusivity comes to expression primarily in the way she portrays its opposite: exclusivity. Within scripture she initially cites Judg 19 and laws about rape and slaves as examples where an inclusive interpretation must therefore engage in critical evaluation. For "whether we recognize it or not, however, such laws and their underlying values shape how we think of our own lives of faith and the parameters of the Christian community" (4). Most of the opening chapter focuses on such influence and the way it in turn has shaped biblical interpretation, leading to exclusion of women and disadvantage and discrimination against the "other." Anderson then sets out the controlling interests typical of patriarchy, making connections between its various manifestations: male, "white (race), Christian (religion), heterosexual (sexuality), and Western (a colonial power. Under a system of domination and subordination, all who are different from that 'ideal male' are marginalized" (12). These interests, she argues, are masked in claims to objective interpretation and in assertions of biblical inerrancy, but also in historical stances. She notes, for instance, Luther's statements about Jews and his allegations about Rome as a source of homosexuality. Anderson chooses to work with binary construction (male-female, etc.) in her critique of patriarchy and abuse of power, though she acknowledges that many resist its simplifications. One might argue that whatever excludes and demeans others fails her core criteria of compassion and justice. Such injustice finds a way of jumping around among the binary categories and can assume multiple identities, as she later notes (136–37). The chapter sets the scene well for what follows.

Turning to problematic biblical laws, Anderson again notes the inequalities and injustices implicit in the laws about so-called rape and also considers the prohibition of same-sex relations. The latter reflects concern both with procreation and with men taking passive (female) roles that would demean their maleness, an implicit diminution of women. She takes this also as the primary rationale in Paul's comments in Romans, although there, I would argue, we also see concern with the divine order established in Genesis and condemnation of both partners, not just the passive ones. More examples follow. Not all laws to protect the poor are good news for them; some are clearly unjust. Similarly, beside laws urging respect for foreigners are accounts urging annihilation, which apologists seek to explain away. The Decalogue addresses well-off males, marginalizing others, and does not address women. The chapter then ends with critical discussion of scholars who use Old Testament models for ethics without adequately addressing the implications they have for others. Rationalizations of treatment of Canaanites on grounds of their being especially wicked are exposed for their inadequacy. "Engaging biblical texts and discerning ethical principles are markedly different enterprises when the perspectives of the marginalized groups are taken into account" (55). Indeed, one might argue that instead of faith functioning as a distortion through defensive reading to protect the divine, it might inspire openness to sense difference and distance and better perceive what might or might not cohere with fundamental criteria of justice and humaneness. Anderson finds encouragement in the observation that already within the biblical tradition we see revision and correction going on (56–57).

In chapter 3 Anderson exposes the reader to a wide range of readings of Ruth and Esther from different contemporary social contexts. Thus Ruth is a model of empowerment for some, for others a symbol of assimilation. Esther is a hero of liberation for some, for others a servant of nationalist interests and counterviolence. Anderson proposes that such texts be approached "thematically, intertextually, and contextually" (71). This amounts to a critically selective identification of positive elements, in particular, the theme of redemption or liberation. Intertextual reading connects them to this theme in other texts. Contextual reading has interpreters identifying analogous experiences of their own, whether as oppressors or as oppressed, including, where it fits, perhaps at times a greater identification with Orpah than Ruth or with Vashti than Esther.

Turning to the New Testament, Anderson affirms that the dispute between Jesus and the Pharisees was not over whether to keep the law but about how to do so and that this dispute finds echoes in attacks by fundamentalists today against those who argue for the more inclusive approach of Jesus (84). She notes the need to recognize development and difference among the Gospels, reflecting their different contexts, but these "should not restrict our ability to live out a more comprehensive love commandment today that includes our enemies" (93). However, much in the Gospel tradition that is relevant to her theme is missing. For instance, one might have expected more about attitudes toward Gentiles such as the Syro-Phoenician woman and the distance kept from them. More significantly, the Gospel traditions reflect engagement with issues of patriarchy and power, not least in Mark's exchanges between Jesus and the disciples about the suffering Son of Man and their alternative vision of greatness. Issues of violence are also not absent, so that the same critical engagement called for on Old Testament texts needs also to apply here.

The discussion of Paul similarly lacks a sustained critical perspective, so that of offending texts Anderson tells us that they may be interpreted positively. "On the whole, the Pauline tradition has been interpreted in ways that are not helpful to any liberationist struggle" (99). The issue may lie not only in the interpretations but in the texts themselves. She sees this in Paul's comments on sexuality, though with overemphasis on negativity in 1 Cor 7, on the active-passive model for interpreting Rom 1, and with a misreading of the place of passion in both. Further, 1 Cor 11:2–16 and 14:33–36 are too lightly explained away. I also missed discussion of Paul's hermeneutic in engaging biblical tradition, not just in dispensing with circumcision, but in declaring believers no longer wedded to the law, from which valuable conclusions could have been drawn that would strengthen the argument for a hermeneutics of inclusivity. Hermeneutical issues are at the heart of Paul's disputes with fellow believers just as much as they were between Jesus and the Pharisees and are similarly relevant today.

A chapter on Luther, Calvin, and Wesley argues that they shared an affirmation of God's grace but adapted their approaches to biblical law in the light of their different settings and over against existing tradition. In this way they set a precedent for similar adaptation today that calls us to address inclusivity. None of the three was fundamentalist. Each operated with a christological hermeneutic, though in slightly different ways, and with an understanding of Christian life to which the law contributed from within that perspective. "Collectively, these reformers affirm the joy of faith in an eternal God who loves us as we are, the corresponding call to love others as we have been loved, the need to express that love in our treatment of those around us, and the effectiveness of the divine power that enables us to express such love" (127). We may, Anderson suggests, embrace these values, even though history tells us that these reformers did not always act in accordance with them, especially over against minorities and opponents. They do, however, inspire an emphasis on Christ as the Word, canonical scripture as a means of grace, and differentiation and intertextuality within it as a means of focus, so that inclusivity might override texts of exclusivity, for instance, about homosexuality.

Anderson proposes an approach to biblical authority that does not assume the Bible as dominant power but as partner, so that the community of faith engages it openly and critically, taking seriously its cultural contexts. Ethical biblical interpreters seek to be aware of their own agendas and engage with the readings of others. She sees unethical interpretation in attempts to explain away Jesus' prohibition of divorce in the interests of modern needs and in interpretations of Rom 1 that fail to acknowledge Paul's presuppositions about homosexuality as divine punishment, "natural" as male-active/female-passive, and sexual passion as undifferentiated. On both issues, divorce and homosexuality, this is bad history, one to appease, the other to establish distance. When, however, Anderson writes that "the condemnation of homosexuality is a plausible reading of the Bible, but it is also an ethically invalid reading" (152), two processes are being confused: what the text might have meant then and how people might want to apply it (where it functions as authority) now. It seems to me that a better way is to embrace the critical engagement on which Anderson wrote earlier and to choose on the basis of more basic values to takes one's distance from the text or otherwise. Throughout Anderson uses inclusivity to address two different but related aspects: what it might lead one to see within the text and how one might responsibly relate the text to situations today.

The final chapter sets hermeneutical issues in relation to dealing with America's constitution, where amendments had to be made to ensure inclusivity in what was originally exclusive of women and slaves. While amending the biblical text is not feasible, the challenge for faith communities is similarly to engage it "through a sense of 'evolving standards' that reflect the needs of all members" (159). Anderson has addressed a central issue of our day in a well-written, well-documented work. Regrettably, the publisher inconveniences the reader by endnotes, but with few other flaws (10:17–20 should be 5:17–20 on page 80 and the formatting of indented text on page 88 is wrong). This is a fine exposition of the hermeneutical issues with a few significant gaps and a convincing challenge to engage in inclusive interpretation, at the level both of seeing what is in the text and of saying what significance it might have for today.

TEXTUAL CRITICISM AND TRANSLATION

Early Christian Books in Egypt, by Roger S. Bagnall. Princeton: Princeton University Press, 2009. Pp. xiii + 109. Hardcover. $29.95. ISBN 9780691140261.

Allen Kerkeslager, Saint Joseph's University, Philadelphia, Pennsylvania

This slim volume originated from lectures in which one of the world's leading papyrologists explores the early copying of Christian literature. It merits more attention than lengthier treatments by specialists in this literature, who betray limited facility in papyri not produced by Jews or Christians. Bagnall offers a critique of the methodology in these studies and examples of a more rigorous alternative.

Chapter 1 introduces the focus on methodology by citing discomfort with the "excessively self-enclosed character and absence of self-awareness" in research on early Christian literature. Bagnall suggests these generate conclusions "profoundly at odds with fundamental social realities of the ancient world and with basic probability" (1). This chapter's example is the tendency to date Christian papyri too early. Paleography, growth of the Christian population, distribution of book ownership by social class, and other factors suggest that most of the earliest Christian papyri should be assigned to the third century or later. Bagnall rejects the classical view that orthodox Christianity experienced triumphant growth in Egypt in the first two centuries. He also rejects the contrasting thesis of Walter Bauer, which is often cited to justify the speculative source criticism of later texts in quests for early "gnostic" communities. Instead, Bagnall argues that the paucity of Christian papyri from Egypt in the first two centuries provides a reliable indicator of the paucity of Christians of any kind in Egypt in this period, especially outside Alexandria. Bagnall only mentions the Jewish revolt of 116–117 in passing, but his arguments are complemented by recent studies suggesting that this had a much more devastating impact on Judaism and Christianity in Egypt than previously supposed. Bagnall concludes, "there is far less evidence for Christian books before the late second century than is usually claimed" (24).

Chapter 2 provides two case studies demonstrating the tendency of specialists in early Christian literature to subjugate inferences verifiable through tangible paleographic evidence to a priori confidence in unverifiable statements made by ancient Christian authors. At one extreme are Carsten Thiede's sensationalist arguments that a Magdalen papyrus of Matthew (P64) should be dated early enough to rehabilitate the reliability of Matthew itself. Bagnall adduces Thiede's "parody" (48) of scholarship to highlight similarities with methods used in more respectable studies of the Shepherd of Hermas. Bagnall recommends that tendentiousness in dating manuscripts be controlled by requiring a broad consensus and more numerous and precise paleographic parallels (49).

Anyone who has benefited from Bagnall's applications of quantitative methods to census returns, tax documents, and onomastics will appreciate the similar approach to the economics of book production in chapter 3. Even if adjustments in the figures were required, Bagnall convincingly demonstrates that books were so expensive that only elites and high-ranking clergy could have purchased them frequently in the fourth century. This buttresses his claim that the number of Christian books must have been very low in earlier centuries. More tentative is Bagnall's proposal to explain the considerable numbers of Christian books that date from the third century. Observing that they follow the recruitment of Hellenized Egyptian elites into the city councils formed early in this century, he cautiously suggests that the struggles of these individuals to form a new social identity may have increased their susceptibility to Christian conversion. They at least provide a likely group with the wealth and education needed to own Christian books and develop Coptic.

Chapter 4 adduces quantitative data to show that the spread of the codex was not uniquely Christian. Even the Christian preference for using the codex for copies of Scripture was paralleled by a shift from roll to codex in sources not dependent on Christian influence. Numerous comparisons add cogency to Bagnall's final argument that the codex attests the Romanization of reading practices, not Christianization.

This greatest contribution of Bagnall's book is its demonstration of a methodology that owes more to the sciences than is typical of approaches used by most scholars of early Christian literature. Bagnall advocates prioritizing concrete artifacts over the self-authenticating claims found in this literature, assigning more confidence to conclusions that can be articulated quantitatively than to untestable inferences from literary criticism, and placing ancient Christian practices in a comparative context rather than treating them as a unique species.

Bagnall's charge that even Thiede's idiosyncrasies can be used to illustrate methodological flaws endemic to the field of early Christian literature is hardly unique. But the impact of similar criticisms has been minimal. Too many scholars have built careers on applying forms of literary criticism to promote untestable speculation about how early Christian literature preserves remnants of "oral traditions" and "lost sources" generated by imaginary "communities." It is almost routine to assign these imaginative constructs to dates as early as possible before the actual documents from which they are inferred. As in the case of Thiede, this habit is typically motivated by a wish to find support for a preferred view of the origins of Christianity. This motive is not easily resisted because the intangibility of hypothetical documents invites self-authenticating circularity. This conditions practitioners to extend this compartmentalized approach to the dating of more tangible papyrus remains of early Christian literature.

Bagnall suggests that this habit can be broken only if these artifacts are treated on their own terms as concrete evidence of the time of their production rather than as mere accidents of the original composition. This requires that they be counted, sorted, assigned a relative chronology, and used to generate statistics. These statistics can then provide a guide to probabilities and a restraint on distorting ideologies. Bagnall's recommendations are indebted to scientific methods ancient historians have adopted from archaeology. The disparity between these recommendations and the practices he criticizes epitomizes the fact that the growth of scientific rigor in the training of archaeologists has no parallel in graduate programs in early Christianity. Most do not require even basic training in probability and statistics. It will be unfortunate if, as with the use of archaeology by most specialists in early Christianity, Bagnall's book is plundered for isolated data while its central methodological contribution is ignored.

Text and Canon of the Hebrew Bible, by Shemaryahu Talmon. Winona Lake, Ind.: Eisenbrauns, 2010. Pp. x + 549. Hardcover. $54.50. ISBN 9781575061924.

August H. Konkel, Providence Theological Seminary, Otterburne, Manitoba, Canada

It is not possible to understand a text apart from a comprehensive knowledge of its history, from its origins until the form in which the reader receives it. In the case of the Hebrew Bible, it is also not possible to reconstruct such a comprehensive history for its vast diversity of texts. It is scarcely even possible to actually compile the evidence to facilitate complete textual analysis. No one understood that better than the late Shemaryahu Talmon, who served as editor of the Ezekiel volume of the Hebrew University Bible (2004). When I asked him about that project, he once told me that God would need to grant him the lifetime of Moses for the task.

Given the complexity of the task, it is ever more critically important to understand correctly the fundamental processes at work in the history of the text. In the past, commentators have tended to follow the proposition most often associated with P. de Lagarde that manuscripts of the largely uniform text created by the masoretes derived from a single archetype of that recension of the compositions. This claim was also applied to the manuscripts of the Greek. The uniformity of this original text dissolved into a pluriformity or multiformity (used interchangeably by Talmon) of the transmitted text as a result of various accidental scribal, linguistic, and literary factors (*lapsus calami*), as well as premeditated linguistic and conceptual changes. Variations in the received texts then are examined to discover how these variations came about in order to reconstruct the original from which they came to deviate.

The first essay in this collection of eighteen articles on text and canon challenges the assumption of an original archetype. Originally published in a volume entitled *Qumran and the History of the Bible Text* (1975), it was the impetus to a paradigm shift in evaluating the textual diversity of the Dead Sea Scrolls. That article was required reading in all my courses on Old Testament introduction at the time. It demonstrated that "professional scribes were not merely slavish copyists of the material which they handled, but rather minor partners in the variegated aspects of the literary process" (84). These practitioners applied on the reproductive level norms and techniques that informed the authors who went before them. Texts must not be analyzed by classification against a limited plurality of text types (as in the thesis proposed by Cross), but rather the loss of other presumably more numerous textual traditions. This study produced much evidence to show that questions of interpretation involving history of composition (higher criticism) cannot be separated from questions of scribal activity in transmitting the text (lower criticism).

Talmon's understanding of the origin of the text follows the thesis of Paul Kahle, who proposed a *textus receptus* and "vulgar texts." The latter were variant versions of the text; according to Kahle, texts developed from a plurality into a unity. Kahle based his opinions on much fuller textual information available to him more than a generation later than Lagarde. Talmon continues in that tradition, with his own definition of the "revolutionary" impact of the Qumran scrolls. This hoard of scrolls and fragments from the late Second Temple period provides a compact replica of the features, data, and problems that can be discerned in the incomparably larger and more diversified corpus of sources that bear witness to the biblical text and the formation of the biblical canon. The phenomena of these texts can be submitted to an analysis in witnesses from the turn of the era, the very earliest attainable stage of textual transmission.

The collection of essays in this volume provides copious examples of the phenomena present in scribal activity in both creating and preserving texts. The formation of a standard text was not a matter of reproducing the best exemplar of a particular composition. Talmon shows that the Masoretic Text is "shot through with evident scribal mistakes" (7); it cannot from the beginning have been based on the most reliable manuscripts available at the time. The variants of textual witnesses cannot be construed as evidence of particular textual traditions and evaluated as deviations from an original exemplar. Variants of the various versions of the biblical texts (Greek, Targums, Qumran, and parallels within the Masoretic Text) can be classified under common categories that are not exclusive to any particular textual tradition.

In a lengthy piece entitled "The Paleo-Hebrew Alphabet and Biblical Text Criticism" (125–70) Talmon provides some ninety variant readings that resulted from the confusion of letters in the Paleo-Hebrew script, often setting off a chain reaction that resulted in strange readings in later versions or compositions. An article entitled "Synonymous Readings in the Mastoretic Text" (171–216) examines ancient traditions established by scribes in distinct social groups, sometimes establishing patterns that crossed into another social group, resulting in a similar reading of dissident groups. The book of Chronicles may preserve a reading from the Samaritan Pentateuch rather than the Pentateuch of the Masoretic Text. "Double Readings in the Masoretic Text" (217–66) examines various categories of doublets that occur, whose development can often be traced through various translations or compositions. These essays demonstrate Talmon's central thesis of how a multiplicity of text forms was produced and how these came to be unified in a very imperfect standard form. Textual critics must engage in a synopsis of all manuscript readings and cannot limit themselves to comparing manuscripts individually in seeking the archetype from which they derived.

The compilation of essays includes more than Hebrew manuscript comparisons. A study entitled "Emendation of Biblical Texts of the Basis of Ugaritic Parallels" examines corrections made on the basis of similar phrases found in Ugaritic texts rather than any comparison with other Hebrew textual evidence. Often Talmon is able to point out how the scribal failure came about from the emended word, which would not be evident from comparison with other versions.

Other essays deal with particular phenomena in understanding the Hebrew text: "The Town Lists of the Tribe of Simeon" (299–314); "*AMEN* as an Introductory Oath Formula" (315–22); "An Apparently Redundant Reading in the Masoretic Text (Jer 1:18)" (323–27). Two articles deal with rabbinic traditions regarding the text: "The Three Scrolls of the Law Found in the Temple Court" (329–46); "Prolegomenon to *The Ten Nequdoth of the Torah*" (347–67). One deals with the liturgical functions of the large Qumran Psalms scroll published by Sanders (11QPs[a]), using some of its features to examine the phenomena of divisions in the middle of a verse.

A comparatively recent article (2000) summarizes Talmon's mature thinking on his lifetime work: "Textual Criticism: The Ancient Versions" (383–418). He states his conviction of textual plurality unequivocally. "The multiformity of the biblical text in antiquity, evinced by the most ancient witnesses attainable, namely the Qumran scrolls and fragments, causes scholars to proceed more cautiously with conjectural emendation of seemingly corrupt readings. One more readily views parallel passages … as possibly exhibiting valid 'genuine' traditions, rather than as variously contaminated emanations of one common prototype" (418). This more prudent approach constructively informs translators and commentators of biblical books.

The final essay, on "The Crystallization of the 'Canon of Hebrew Scriptures' in the Light of Biblical Scrolls from Qumran" (419–42), has been more helpful for me in understanding the formation of canon than any other treatise on the subject. Since it appeared, it has been required reading in my introduction courses. Talmon clarifies not only the development of the term *canon* as it applies to the Scriptures but also the process by which an exclusive list of books came to be formulated, in both Jewish and Christian circles. The "Great Divide," namely, the fall of Judah to the Romans and the destruction of the Second Temple, were decisive for the crystallization of Hebrew Scriptures. These events did not affect the covenanters at Qumran, who had long abandoned city and temple. Their views of Scripture are not directly relevant to the later rabbinical discussions questioning books already in the collection (לגנוז בקשו) and those outside the collection (הידים [את] אינו מטמא). The Christian process of an exclusive list of books was not formally concluded until the Festal Letter of Athanasius in 367.

No book of this size is without its typographical flaws. An example may be found in the LXX citations of Judg 20:15 (224), in which the readings of A and B are reversed. The longer pleonastic reading (ἄνδρες νεανίσκοι ἐκλεκτοί) is found in A, and the shorter reading (ἄνδρες ἐκλεκτοί) is found in B, as might be expected, given the character of the two manuscripts.

While there is consistency in Talmon's thinking, there is also progression and further confirmation of the phenomena observed. The essays are arranged topically, requiring the reader to give attention to the time of each study in relation to the conclusions drawn. Some go back to the earliest periods of the study of the scrolls, while others are written with the availability of the most recent research.

The discussion of text history and interpretation has developed significantly with the complete official publication of the scrolls.

This collection of extensive and erudite studies presents an opportunity to produce a study that would enable interpreters to understand developments of a text, evaluate its variants, and interpret it more precisely. Such a handbook would be of great value for both students and scholars. In each individual biblical composition, it is important to discern when the distinction between formation and transmission becomes clear.

The Social Universe of the English Bible: Scripture, Society, and Culture in Early Modern England, by Naomi Tadmor. Cambridge: Cambridge University Press, 2010. Pp. xvi + 208. Hardcover. $95.00. ISBN 9780521769716.

Lena-Sofia Tiemeyer, University of Aberdeen, Aberdeen, Scotland, United Kingdom

This relatively slim gem of a book explores the social background that has influenced and is also reflected in the different English translations of the Hebrew Bible leading up to the Authorized Version/KJV. Tadmor explores the translations with careful attention to their historical and linguistic details. She claims that one reason for the immense popularity of the English Bible was its "Anglification." In fact, in early modern English one synonym of the verb "to translate" was the now obsolete verb "to English." In many ways, both conscious and unconscious choices of translation rendered the language and the concepts of the Hebrew Bible congenial to the English readers. The translators "Englished" the social relations between the different character in the Bible to fit with the social relations in early modern England and to make them relevant for their English audience.

The book falls into five sections. The introduction provides a succinct survey of the different English translations leading up to and culminating in the KJV. Tadmor touches upon the lives and works of William Tyndale, Miles Coverdale, and John Rogers, as well as on the political events, from Henry VIII to the ascension of James VI of Scotland to the English throne, that paved the way for the creation of the KJV. Tadmor further discusses general aspects of the translation process from Hebrew to English.

The first chapter focuses on *interpersonal relations*. It traces how the Hebrew notions of "loving your friend" or "loving your fellow man" became "loving your neighbor." Tadmor begins by noting that the semantic range of the Hebrew term רעה covers "friend," "companion," "fellow man," and even "every man," which can include an enemy. At the same time, it does not denote a person living nearby (for which Hebrew uses the root שכן). How, then, did רעה come to be translated as "neighbor"? Tadmor argues that this translation was in part motivated by the desire to locate the commandment in Lev 19:18 and Deut 6:4–5, made central to Christian faith by Matt 22:36–39, within the social universe of the local community.

Tadmor traces the semantic development of the term רעה in translations. She notes that the LXX translates the term in various ways, depending on its literary context. For instance, it is translated as *philos* ("friend") in Exod 33:11 and as *plēsion* ("compatriot," "neighbor") in Lev 19:18. This division in meaning was retained when the Greek-speaking Christian church adopted the LXX as its Scripture and as Jerome used it, together with the Hebrew, when he produced the Vulgate. At the time of Wycliffe's translation of the Vulgate into English, Tadmor demonstrates that the English term "neighbor" had come to mean both "fellow man" and a person living nearby in the same community. In subsequent English translations, the two words "friend" and "neighbor" were used to render the Hebrew רעה. The distinction between the two terms gradually became blurred. Also, the use of the term "neighbor" increased at the expense of the term "friend." By the time of Tyndale's translation, Lev 19:18 had become "love your neighbor."

In the latter half of the chapter, Tadmor turns to the historical situation in Tudor and Stuart England. She notes that, although many communities suffered from polarization and social restructuring, for most people the local communities remained the center. In this context, norms for neighborliness were crucial for a functioning society. Early modern catechisms and sermons testify to the emphasis on neighborliness. Tadmor further shows that the biblical language of neighborliness influenced popular culture, as evidenced by writings in parish records and prayer books.

The second chapter explores *gender relations*. Tadmor demonstrates how English conceptions of matrimony influenced the English translations. In particular, English translations of the Hebrew Bible tended to introduce the notion of marriage in contexts where the Hebrew text either lacked it or attested to it in a manner that did not conform to the Christian notion of marriage (founded upon the much clearer notions of monogamy in the New Testament). Tadmor focuses her discussion on the Hebrew terms איש and אשה, which have a wide semantic range, including but not limited to "husband" and "wife." Tadmor also notes that, although the Hebrew Bible refers to a large variety of unions between men and women, the term חתנה ('wedding') is attested only once (Song of Songs 3:11).

As in the previous chapter, Tadmor traces the translations of Hebrew idioms related to marriage. She discusses the semantic range of the five Hebrew verbs that denote the formation of a union between a man and a woman (לקח, נתן, נשא, בעל, and קנה) and the ways in which they are translated into English. For instance, she notes that Wycliffe translates the term פלגש as "secondary wife" or even just "wife" (e.g., Judg 19:1). Looking at statistics, the very term "marriage" appears 19 times in KJV. Further, out of the 569 times that the term אשה appears in singular form in the Hebrew text, KJV renders 312 of those as "wife." A similar tendency to introduce the notion of matrimony into the text exists when it comes to the term "husband." The two Hebrew terms איש and בעל have semantic ranges beyond the English term "husband," yet many English translations rendered them indiscriminately as "husband."

Tadmor further looks at the social situation in early modern England. Mediaeval English marriage laws were not changed until 1753, and the church played a surprisingly small role in the formation of marriage in much of Tudor England. At the same time, processes were in place that sought to make marriage more formal and within the bounds of the church. In this manner, the English translations of the Hebrew Bible worked hand-in-hand with the social processes. While a translation was influenced by social factors, the same translation became a source of influence as it consolidated the same social factors in which it had its genesis. For many people, the Bible was the point of reference in their thinking. A Bible that proscribed marriage was therefore a powerful incentive to marriage.

The third chapter looks at *work relations*. Tadmor notes the intriguing fact that the Hebrew עבד and its female counterpart שפחה or אמה are translated as "servant" rather than as "slave." The translations thus render unfree labor as a contractual and short-term form of free labor. Tadmor argues that this shift was necessary, as the very negative connotations of the English term "slave" often rendered it unsuitable in biblical contexts. Tadmor traces the translation of the above-mentioned terms throughout the LXX, the Vulgate, and the various English translations leading up to the KJV. Among other things, she highlights the importance of Tyndale's translation. In addition to Tyndale's frequent use of the terms "servant," he introduced the term "bondage" to describe labor relationships in which the key aspect was loss of human freedom. Notably, the Israelites were "in bondage" in Egypt (in contrast to Wycliffe's translations, according to which the Israelites were "servants").

Turning to the social reality in Tudor and Stuart England, Tadmor argues that labor was often understood in terms of "service." Most people spent years of their lives as either servants or apprentices. Moreover, service relationships were important to people and determined their position in society. Society was seen as a divinely ordained chain of commands that ensured the social structure and its preservation. It was therefore of utmost importance to anchor the current social structure within the Bible. Tadmor also explores the difficulty in terminology that arose in England shortly after the completion of the KJV with the growing English slave trade between Africa and the colonies in the Americas. In particular, it brought back in force the distinction between "servant" and "slave."

The fourth chapter discusses *relations related to office*, with focus on status and power. Tadmor highlights that fourteen different Hebrew terms denoting rulers and leaders are compressed into a small number of English terms (e.g., "prince" and "captain"). This, in turn, flattened the differences in status and rule between local and central, and between formal and informal, types of governments. For instance, the heads of the Israelite clans came to be on par with the Persian imperial monarchs. Likewise, the English term "captain" came to translate a large array of Hebrew terms, which flattened the social, administrative, and military structures of ancient Israel.

In parallel, other Hebrew terms were singled out and equated with a specific English expression. These expressions—duke, lord, sheriff, lieutenants, chamberlains—enabled the English readers to depict for themselves the ancient Israelite society as a society similar to their own, thus making its politics and events near and relevant. Conversely, it enabled the English order of state to be understood as a social and political order ordained by the Bible.

Tadmor ends the chapter by a discussion of the ways in which the politics of seventeenth-century England used the Bible in order to claim divine favor of a particular way of rule and to support their own political agendas. Just as Charles I used biblical language to challenge those opposing his rule, so Oliver Cromwell appealed to the Bible in support of his brand of republicanism.

Tadmor's book is well-researched and sheds new light on the translations of the English Bible. It is also beautifully produced with thick white paper and a wealth of illustrations. My critique is minor and should not refract anyone from enjoying this delightful book.

First, I found the book at times to be somewhat repetitive. Tadmor tells the reader on several occasions that Tyndale translated the Hebrew Bible from the Hebrew text. Once would probably have been enough of most readers. Second, and more important, it would have been useful if the third chapter had contained a discussion of unfree labor in the ancient world and the forms it took in particular societies at particular times. Given the fluidity between free and unfree labor in ancient Israel, as well as the fact that many aspects that defined slavery in ancient Israel would have defined servants in early modern England, it is possible that English term "servant" actually reflects the meaning of עבד as understood in ancient Israel better than the English term "slave." Tadmor hints at this issue but does not discuss it in any depth.

The Story of the New Testament Text: Movers, Materials, Motives, Methods, and Models, by Robert F. Hull Jr. Society of Bblical Literature Resources for Biblical Study 58. Atlanta: Society of Biblical Literature, 2010. Pp. xiv + 229. Paper. $29.95. ISBN 9789004187078.

Larry W. Hurtado, University of Edinburgh, Edinburgh, United Kingdom

This readable and well-informed book should be on required-readings lists for all serious students of New Testament (and for a good many New Testament scholars as well). There are several respected introductions to New Testament textual criticism, all of them directed more to conveying "how to" matters, so that readers are enabled to begin engaging textual variants intelligently. Hull's study, however, is wholly given over to relating the development of New Testament textual criticism from ancient figures such as Origen on to the early twenty-first century. It is more an introduction to the history and nature of the discipline. But, commendably, Hull's aim is not simply to relate the past; he also points to "rich possibilities" for further developments in New Testament textual criticism (186) and the "excitement and vigor" of the field today, urging (rightly) that there is "no shortage of opportunities for younger scholars" to make their own further contributions (189). Along with its other positive features, Hull's book is particularly commendable in presenting what many assume to be an arid and uninteresting field as the lively and growing area of scholarly research that is New Testament textual criticism today.

In a brief introduction, Hull relates how he became aware of the field in his undergraduate studies and describes his book as "a response to the resurgence of interest in New Testament textual criticism" (3). Not aiming at "working text critics," he instead seeks to address "nonspecialists" (who include students and New Testament scholars) with a narrative that will convey "the birth, growth, and fortunes of textual criticism" (4).

The following chapters form a chronological sequence from ancient to current time, and in each chapter Hull organizes his discussion with the headings mentioned in his subtitle. The "movers" are "the major players" over the centuries who have contributed to the field. The discussion of the "materials" addresses "the collecting, collating, and evaluating of witnesses to the text," which include Greek manuscripts, ancient versions, and quotations of the New Testament in early Christian writers. "Motives" is his label for discussion of the questions pursued by textual critics, and Hull helpfully highlights how in recent decades the questions have multiplied well beyond simply how to arrive at the "original" text of New Testament writings. "Methods" designates developments in the criteria used to weigh variant readings and the approaches to coping with the considerable amount of data involved. By "models" Hull refers to what he regards as "watershed publications" that have advanced the discipline significantly, from earlier ones (e.g., Lachmann, Westcott and Hort) down to recent ones (e.g., David Parker's detailed study of Codex Bezae and Bart Ehrman's attention-grabbing volume, *The Orthodox Corruption of Scripture*).

In chapter 1, "Paul and Luke Become Published Authors," Hull first briefly conveys the processes involved in the composition, sending, reading, and further distribution of Paul's Epistle to the Romans and Luke's Gospel. He then notes the need for New Testament textual criticism arising from the copying of these and other New Testament writings, which inevitably introduced variants, both "unconscious" (accidental) and "conscious" (deliberate).

Chapter 2, "The Precritical Age," includes a brief review of the categories of witnesses to the New Testament (Greek manuscripts, vernacular translations, quotations in early church "fathers") and a concise discussion of key figures (e.g., Origen, Jerome, Erasmus) and their motives and methods employed in addressing textual variation. My only quibble is with his reference to "the almost exclusive use of the codex format for Christian texts" (25). To be sure, early Christians overwhelmingly preferred the codex for writings that they treated as scripture, but, as I have shown elsewhere, they were somewhat less firmly committed to the codex for other religious texts. By my reckoning, about one-third of second- and third-century copies of extracanonical Christian writings (e.g., theological treatises, liturgical texts) are on rolls (see L. W. Hurtado, *The Earliest Christian Artifacts: Manuscripts and Christian Origins*, 43–93).

"The Age of Collecting" (ch. 3) focuses on the period from the first printed Greek New Testaments (sixteenth century) on through the contributions of subsequent figures (e.g., John Mill, Richard Bentley, J. A. Bengel, J. J. Wettstein, J. S. Semler), and "the collection, collating and cataloguing of hundreds of Greek manuscripts and versional witnesses" (52) in the seventeenth and eighteenth centuries. Some of what remain key witnesses (e.g., Codex Alexandrinus, Codex Vaticanus, Codex Bezae) came to notice then, and in figures such as Bengel we have impressive early articulations of criteria and principles to use in assessing textual evidence.

Chapters 4–5 deal with "The Age of Optimism," the period from Griesbach (1745–1812) to the truly landmark work of Westcott and Hort, their edition of the Greek New Testament that appeared in 1881–1882. Chapter 4 presents lively sketches of the major figures of this period, such as Griesbach, Lachmann, von Tischendorf, Tregelles, and Westcott and Hort.

In chapter 5 Hull discusses their key contributions, in terms of their discovery and analysis of key evidence (e.g., Tischendorf and Codex Sinaiticus, Ferrar and Family 13) and underscores the key concern to move beyond the "Textus Receptus" to a critically based edition of the Greek New Testament. In a list of great men, it is unfortunate that Hull did not include reference to the remarkable twin sisters from Scotland, Agnes Smith Lewis and Margaret Dunlop Gibson, who discovered the Syriac Gospels manuscript in St. Catherine's Monastery (see Janet Soskice, *The Sisters of Sinai: How Two Lady Adventurers Discovered the Hidden Gospels*, Knopf, 2009). Also, a couple of errors mar an otherwise fine discussion. The title of Westcott and Hort's work is wrongly given on page 97. The description of textual "mixture" (101) is not quite right either. "Block mixture" happened when a copyist used one exemplar for part of a writing and then switched to another (with a somewhat different textual character) for the rest of it. But it is unlikely that copyists otherwise consulted more than one exemplar. So, other kinds of textual "mixture" likely arose through various other processes, for example, readers amending copies by comparison with other copies.

Chapter 6, "The Age of the Papyri," focuses wholly on the wonderful increase in textual witnesses that characterized the twentieth century, among which early papyri copies of New Testament writings are particularly important. These include many items unearthed in Oxyrhynchus, the major cache of biblical papyri acquired by Chester Beatty, and also the remarkable Bodmer biblical papyri. Hull also includes brief information on a number of other witnesses, including important majuscule and minuscule manuscripts, lectionaries, and versional manuscripts.

In chapter 7, "The Age of Consensus, the Age of Doubt," Hull continues his review of twentieth-century developments, focusing here on the key "movers, methods, and models." These include von Soden's massive project to map the "Byzantine/medieval" text of the New Testament, now commonly regarded as a noble failure, and the proposed "Caesarean text" and Streeter's "local text" theory, which likewise have suffered severe critique. Hull rightly devotes attention here to

Colwell, who in several important essays probed and pushed for methodological refinement in how manuscripts are categorized and how their evidence should be assessed. Hull also discusses debates about "thorough-going eclecticism" (in which emphasis in placed on judging variant readings on the basis of such factors as author's style and without attention to the manuscripts that support variants). He even includes a brief description of "majority text" advocacy (i.e., the idea that the kind of text represented in the mass of late manuscripts is more likely "original").

Chapter 8, "New Directions: Expanding the Goals of Textual Criticism," takes us into the very recent and current scenes, in which fascinating new lines of inquiry and analysis have opened up. As Hull observes, "One of the most distinctive developments in New Testament textual criticism in the postmodern era and beyond is a broadening of its focus beyond the recovery of the original text to the history, motives, and effects of textual variation" (152). Citing Ehrman's "groundbreaking study" mentioned earlier, Hull notes how today's textual critics are more inclined to consider all variants as interesting and indicative of the historical forces that have affected the transmission of New Testament writings. He also considers recent questioning of the whole notion of "original" text (especially by Eldon Epp and David Parker), noting the preference of some now for aiming to recover the *Ausgangtext*, that is, the "initial text" that influenced subsequent copies. Hull discusses major text-critical projects of the twentieth century, prominent among which are the Bible Societies Greek New Testament, the International Greek New Testament Project, and the remarkable output and aims of the Institute for New Testament Textual Research in Münster. It is, however, unfortunate that Hull does not discuss the recent methodological proposal from the Münster Institute, the "Coherence-Based Genealogical Method," which involves use of computer-technology to reconstruct the putative "textual flow" of New Testament writings (see further: http://www.uni-muenster.de/INTF/Genealogical_method.html).

The final chapter, "Reassessing the Discipline," opens by noting what Hull describes as "a rebirth of interest" in New Testament textual criticism in the last several decades. This period has also seen the publication of further textual evidence (including a number of New Testament manuscripts in the Oxyrhynchus series). But Hull's discussion is mainly given to developments in the ways that textual critics do their work now and some major contributions of this period. "One of the most promising" of these is attention given to "the production of manuscripts and the transmission of their texts within the social contexts of early Christianity," citing Kim Haines-Eitzen's *Guardians of Letters* (2009) as a pioneering work. Hull also right notes that others recently have questioned the assumption that deliberate changes should be attributed to scribes/copyists and that readers/users of texts are more likely to have introduced such changes. Hull describes James Royse's massive study, *Scribal Habits in Early Greek New Testament Papyri* (2008), as a work that provides a wealth of data and that requires adjustment in criteria used to assess variants.

In a section of this chapter on "Manuscripts as Artifacts," Hull reviews how recent work has opened up "windows into the world of early Christianity" (179).

The early Christian preference for the codex, the scribal practice called "*nomina sacra*," the "staurogram" (the fascinating device formed by the combination of the Greek *tau* and *rho*), and a number of other physical features of early New Testament manuscripts make these items artifacts of early Christian reading and transmission of their sacred texts. One correction: the *tau-rho* device is not "uniquely Christian" (185) but is a pre-Christian device adopted by Christians and used in a distinctive manner, correctly described by Hull as likely a pictographic reference to the crucified Jesus.

In the final pages Hull helpfully list ten "suggestions for research" that might be engaged by future researchers. As he observes, there is "no shortage of opportunities for younger scholars" (189). A twenty-three-page bibliography and indexes of biblical citations, persons, and subjects completes this very useful volume.

Biblia Coptica: Die koptischen Bibeltexte. Vollständiges Verzeichnis mit Standorten [Band 4, Lfg 3], edited by Karlheinz Schüssler. Wiesbaden: Harrassowitz, 2010. Pp. vii + 192 + 12. Paper. €72.00. ISBN 9783447064170.

Stephan Witetschek, Ludwig-Maximilians-Universität München,
Munich, Germany

Biblical scholars starting to learn Coptic may be in search of a Coptic (Sahidic) Bible. However, the work under review is hardly what they are looking for! To be sure, there is an edition of the Sahidic New Testament (nothing comparable for the Old Testament): G. W. Horner, *Coptic Version of the New Testament in the Southern Dialect Otherwise Called Sahidic and Thebaic* (7 vols.; Oxford: Clarendon, 1911–1924). But this edition, apart from being almost a century old, is based only on a limited number of manuscripts, and its critical qualities, too, are not undisputed, to say the least. An up-to-date critical edition remains a desideratum. This is where Karlheinz Schüssler's newly pioneering work enters.

Schüssler's project Biblia Coptica aims at nothing less than a catalogue of all available Coptic manuscripts of the Old and New Testaments—the necessary prerequisite for establishing a truly critical edition of the Coptic Bible (first in Sahidic). The basic idea (and main criticism of Horner's edition) is that the critical value of the individual manuscripts can only be assessed when they are (re)contextualized in the codices to which they originally belonged. This allows a more reasoned judgment of the date and (implicitly) the value of each codex. In many cases, indeed, Schüssler had to reconstruct the remains of individual codices, leaves of which have made their ways into quite different collections and libraries in Egypt, Europe, and North America (more on this below). This project has been going on for years, and some fascicles have already been reviewed in *RBL*: 1/3 by Melvin K.H. Peters (http://bookreviews.org/pdf/495_283.pdf), 3/1 by Elizabeth Penland (http://www.bookreviews.org/pdf/2022_2768.pdf), and 3/2 by Robert Paul Seesengood (http://www.bookreviews.org/pdf/3830_3787.pdf). I may also refer to Sarah Clackson's review of vol. 1/1 in *BASP* 35 (1998): 229–33.

Meanwhile, the project has advanced considerably; some results are already publicly accessible. An outline of the project (in German) can be found at http://www.k-schuessler.com/bibcop.php. Some New Testament manuscripts have been reestablished and can be consulted electronically at http://www.biblia-coptica.com/: sa (= Sahidic) 505, sa 506, sa 507, sa 508 (all described in 3/1), sa 561 (described in 3/4). These manuscripts (among others) form the basis for the most advanced part of the project, a critical reconstruction of the Gospel of John in Sahidic (see http://www.k-schuessler.com/ john.php). Thus, text-critical work with the Sahidic New Testament is already greatly facilitated.

The fascicle under review comprises forty-eight Sahidic manuscripts from the fourth–thirteenth centuries, mostly with New Testament texts. There are only three lectionaries that include Old Testament passages, namely, from Psalms (sa 694^L, sa 719^L) and from Ezekiel (sa 702^L). Most of the manuscripts are on parchment, only six (sa 687, sa 692, sa 701, sa 703, sa 704, sa 708) on papyrus.

One particularly instructive example (108–20) is sa 699, a fairly large (max. 31.5 x 26.5 cm) and artfully written and decorated parchment codex from the White Monastery (sixth/seventh century) that contains the Gospels of Matthew and John. Twenty-six sheets from nine quires are preserved. These sheets are partly preserved as entire pages, partly as fragments, partly only as scraps ("Schnipsel"). They are scattered over a half-dozen libraries and museums: The British Library (London), the Bodleian Library (Oxford), the Bibliothèque Nationale (Paris), the Louvre (Paris), the Biblioteca Vaticana (Rome), and the Österreichische Nationalbibliothek (Vienna). Based partly on the extant pagination, partly on calculation, the sheets are assigned to their respective places in the (partly numbered) quires. From the survey (109–10) one gets a good idea of what the codex must have looked like before it was torn apart—and one gets an even better idea of how much is missing. The first preserved sheet, sa 699.1 (pp. 33/34, containing Matt 9:9–23), has been brought together from two fragments, sa 699.1.1 from the Bodleian Library, MS Copt. D.271 (P), and sa 699.1.2 from the Louvre, E 10092.j. Another sheet, sa 699.24 (pp. 189/190, containing John 10:12?–29), consists of three fragments that are already catalogued in the Bibliothèque Nationale as parts of one and the same manuscript (Copte 129^{10} fol. 129, 130, 143). On the other hand, the fifteen sheets of sa 699 that are owned by the Bibliothèque Nationale appear under four different catalog numbers. An impression of the writing is given on table 7, where the fragment sa 699.21 is reproduced. With Schüssler's work at hand, it has become much easier to assess the significance of those many fragments and scraps for reconstructing "the" Sahidic translation of the New Testament—and it is an attempt to undo (as far as this is at all possible) the gold-rush-like treatment that many Coptic manuscripts suffered from their excavators and traders.

The main part of this volume with its detailed descriptions of the forty-eight manuscripts is followed by several indices (173–92); noteworthy are the concordances with other editions of the manuscripts presented in the fascicle (186–91). Appended are twelve tables with pictures of selected manuscript pages. Unfortunately, these are printed on ordinary paper and downsized to a measure of 7.5 x

11.5 cm each. Thus, they can convey only an impression of the different types of writing. Some are close to being illegible.

This minor disappointment notwithstanding, Schüssler has once again done an admirable job, one more step toward a critical edition of the Sahidic translation of the New Testament. The meticulous work takes its time, but there is some hope that, in the not so distant future, there may be a handy and reliable reference for the occasional "sa" in the critical apparatus of the *Nestle-Aland/Novum Testamentum Graece*.

The Earliest Advocates of the English Bible: The Texts of the Medieval Debate, edited by Mary Dove. Exeter Medieval Texts and Studies. Exeter: University of Exeter Press, 2010. Pp. lxvii + 236. Hardcover. $100.00. ISBN 9780859898522.

David G. Burke, Nida Institute for Biblical Scholarship, New York, New York

The era between 1300 and much of the 1500s in England witnessed an intense and frequently dangerous debate over the issue of whether or not the Bible should be translated into English, a debate that affected not only religious history in England but also literary and cultural history as well. The aim of *The Earliest Advocates* is to gather into a single volume the key Middle English (ME) texts that advocate for an English Bible translation. In essence, these lay the groundwork for the process that would eventually produce the KJB, by way of its several predecessor translations done from original-language texts (Tyndale, Coverdale, Great Bible, Geneva Bible, Douai-Rheims, and Bishops' Bible), which David Norton views as "early drafts" of the KJB (*KJB: A Short History* [Cambridge: Cambridge University Press, 2011]).

This collection of ME texts in *The Earliest Advocates* has been brilliantly organized, annotated, and contexted by the late Mary Dove, who at the time of her tragically early and sudden death was Professor in English at the University of Sussex. Since so many of these ME documents are not accessible in other editions, this book is a most significant boon for medievalists and all whose work touches on this material. All of the assembled texts argue, to varying degrees of intensity, on the side of the debate that a Bible in English is necessary. Significantly, because they also articulate many of the opposing arguments in order to refute them, we are able to see how hackneyed and misguided these opposing contentions were.

Prior to her general introduction, Dove provides helpful lists of the sources referenced (with their abbreviations), the manuscript sigla, and the locations where the manuscripts may be consulted (ix–xvii). A carefully detailed introduction (xix–lxvii) follows, describing and characterizing each of the eight medieval texts assembled in the main body of the book (1–187) in terms of content, context, authorship, and extant manuscripts. Detailed annotations for each of the texts are supplied as endnotes following the medieval texts (188–224), and these endnotes are then followed by a most helpful (selective) glossary of ME terms, briefly defined and referenced to the texts (225–29). An index of biblical citations made in the texts (230–36) concludes the book.

Dove's introduction first provides the user with general contextual information on the movement associated with the Oxford scholar John Wyclif and his associates, since many of these texts are connected to Wyclif, though not all of them. The so-called Wyclif "Later Version" was completed by his associates around 1390, only a few years after his death in 1384. Wyclif was a vigorous proto-Reformer and a notorious critic of churchly corruption and laxity, who wrote extensively on the need for reform and the return to the authority of Scripture. It was to facilitate these concerns that Wyclif translated the Latin *Vulgata* into English. Less than two decades later, the "Constitutions of Oxford" promulgated under the authority of the Archbishop of Canterbury, Thomas Arundel, in 1408, outlawed the Wyclif Bible as heretical, as well as any public or private reading of Scripture in English. Yet despite the ensuing dangers to anyone possessing a Wyclif Bible, they seem to have been widely distributed, and almost two hundred copies survive today. Dove notes that the Arundel legislation was issued in the heat of this debate about the legitimacy of vernacular Bible translation. Arundel reported to the Vatican that the Wyclif Bible translation was part of this arch-heretic's broad-scale project to attack the faith and doctrine of Holy Church. By gathering together all these pertinent medieval texts, both Wycliffite and not, Dove has enabled all who work with this material to have these sources brought together, but also made clear that the Wycliffite texts were only one source for this spreading advocacy. Some of these advocate texts were not connected at all with Lollardy (e.g., the Cambridge Tracts, 89–142), yet were pressing just as intently for vernacular Bible translation in this era.

Dove's introduction then characterizes the eight texts that are presented in the main body of the book. The first and longest is the *Prologue to the Wycliffite Bible* (PWB), a text of nearly forty thousand words covering such matters as the biblical canon, an Old Testament synopsis, biblical book summaries, and the senses of Scripture (*per* Augustine and Nicholas of Lyra). Its last chapter reviews the process of producing the Wyclif Bible, contending for its approval by the English Church, and refuting the contention that only men as holy as Jerome can do Bible translation by saying that Jerome was less holy than the apostles and evangelists and that the LXX translators were less holy than the writers of the Hebrew Scriptures. Dove notes that the authorship of PWB is unknown, but attribution to John Purvey was already being made in the 1700s. PWB can be dated to 1387–early 1388, but it failed to become the standard Wyclif Bible preface because of its very sharp polemics, which could easily draw the ire of hostile authorities. There are five extant manuscripts with the complete PWB text and eleven others with partial texts or fragments. Dove provides a listing of these with detailed characterizations and locations (xxv–xxx).

Second is the *Prologue to Isaiah and the Prophets* (PIP), the only such prologue written for an individual Old Testament book. It stresses the typical Wycliffite tenet of accessibility of Scripture for ordinary readers. Its base manuscript and twenty others are described and their locations given. Third is the collection of the *Twelve Cambridge Tracts* (CT I–XII), anonymous tracts that in most cases have headings advocating Scripture in English (e.g., *Tract II*, "þis preueþ þat þhei ben blessed þat louen Goddis lawe in þere owen langage," 103). *Tract I*, the longest, at circa 6,800 words, likely was written in response to the Arundel prohibition. *Tract VI* makes the curious point that Christ would not even prevent the devil from speaking Scripture, so it is absurd to prevent laity from reading and discussing it. *Tract XI* presents the analogy that "Holy writ haþ þe lyknesse of a tree þat beriþ fruyt" (126) and concludes that, as a fruit tree must be shaken to get the fruit, so must Scripture be "shaken" (i.e., translated) into a person's own language. Dove provides summary introductions for each tract, and for each the manuscript data is documented in detail.

Fourth is *First seiþ Bois* (FSB), a rendering of sections from a university *determinacio* on Bible translation into English by Richard Ullerston (ca. 1360–1423). Ullerston was orthodox, but this determination strongly favors translation. FSB is organized as a debate between two learned doctors, with one presenting thirty arguments against translation, but the second given six times the space for refutations. As in any book with this amount of complex detail, typos may be inevitable; thus on page xlix "the Council of Council (1414–1418)" should obviously be "the Council of Constance." Again, Dove supplies a full review of the extant manuscripts, as also for all the remaining texts. Fifth is *The Holi Prophete Dauid* (HPD), in which the writer responds to objections from "proud clerkis" against the uneducated reading Scripture, noting that God's commands occur all through the Old Testament that God's word be made known. Sixth is *Pater Noster II* (PN II), whose unique feature is to use the Lord's Prayer's petitions to teach and advocate for English translation. The seventh text is the *Glossed Gospel Prologues and Epilogue* (GG I–V). Each of these accompany glossed Latin Gospels, each seeking to explain the text and help English readers make profitable use of the Latin. A recurring theme is criticism of translation opponents; for example, the prologue to Intermediate Matthew condemns those who "letten [ME "let" means "hinder"] christen peple to knowe, here, rede, write and speke holy writ in Englisch" (178). Dove notes that *GG I–V* were completed between 1400 and 1407 and done by scholars sympathetic to Wyclif who had access to academic resources, probably at Oxford. The eighth text is a very brief prologue titled *In þe Biginnyng* (IB), which contrasts the writer's situation with that of the early church, lamenting that priests no longer ensure that people understand Scripture because they do not understand it themselves.

Dove states in her introduction to the glossary (225) that "[i]t is assumed that users of this book will be familiar with the normal language of Chaucerian English and with the usual grammatical abbreviations found in editions of the medieval vernacular." For such scholars this book will be a delight, with all these "earliest advocates" brought together here and thoroughly annotated. For those less familiar with the older ME alphabetic characters (e.g., yogh, thorn, wynn), using it will present more of a challenge, and it may have been useful to include that alphabet as an appendix.

The Restored New Testament: A New Translation with Commentary, Including the Gnostic Gospels Thomas, Mary, and Judas, by Willis Barnstone. New York: Norton, 2009. Pp. xviii + 1485. Hardcover. $59.95. ISBN 039306493X.

Marvin J. Hudson, Norman, Oklahoma

The title of this excellent work is a crucial clue to the emphases that it follows in presenting a fresh reading of the historic texts of Christianity. In broad terms, Willis Barnstone seeks to represent the New Testament and select extracanonical volumes in such a way as to permit the reader to hear them within the distinctly first- and second-century Jewish ethos. While he seeks to provide a fresh translation that speaks to the contemporary reader through a "Chaste(ly), modern, literary version of a major world text," he does so with clear guiding principles in mind.

These guiding principles are three with addenda. First, he works to restore the Jewish identity inherent within the Christian Scriptures that he perceives to be lost through previous translation efforts. Barnstone affirms that when we hear the Greek names Mark and Andrew in connection with activities, it distances us from their context in Judea and transports them to Grecian soil (14). By rendering such names and similar terminology in more literal Judean vernacular, Barnstone enables readers to hear the story with a fresh and geographically relocated sense of perception. The second guiding emphasis is the effort to recast the text so as to "Clarify the origin of Christianity as one of the Jewish Messianic sects" (14). The idea is to broaden the reader's understanding of primitive Christianity as one of a number of messianic movements that were in play during the era of the early church. Finally, the translator works out of an extensive expertise in poetic studies to reclaim the lyrical movements of the Christian texts. Through his skill, large portions of the text that had been previously rendered (sometimes cumbersomely) as prose in a variety of familiar translations are reclaimed as poetic verse or lyric.

By "addenda" above is meant that other important concerns also motivate Barnstone's work. The first of these is that he intentionally remains neutral on issues of faith within the text. Theological matters are commented upon as needed in annotations within footnotes. This is clearly an effort to separate as much as possible the preconceptions of the translator from a reading of the text. Second, he works with a clear understanding of what he terms a "grand identity theft" that has been perpetuated upon the biblical text by some translational traditions. By theft, Barnstone is alluding to the occasional translational practice of removing perceived pejorative terms such as "Jews" and similar identity vernacular and replacing them with more neutral and unfortunately sanitized expressions. However well-intentioned, such lexical choices have had the effect of robbing the text of its essential Jewishness and lent to the distancing of Jesus and the early church from the culture of Judea. Third, and in perhaps a related manner, the translator also sees his project as addressing the issue of anti-Semitism. A historic issue, many of the realities already mentioned contributed to an implicit call to "hate the villainous Jew." This attitude was exacerbated by translational choices that ultimately fostered a Christian mindset that Jesus and the disciples, and certainly the first Christians, were somehow less than Jewish, and the "New Testament" could be readily seen as a volume apart from any viable connection to historic Judaism.

Perhaps the most significant contribution of this work lies not in the translational product per se. Indeed, a reader with linguistic exegetical skills may frequently take issue with some of the choices made within particular texts, such as treating μηποτε in Matt 7:6b as "They will probably..." or ζηλουτε in 1 Cor 12:31a as an indicative rather than an imperative. However, such matters will occur with any work and actually serve to make the reading more engaging. A more profound contribution is the total impact of the literary style of the text as presented by Barnstone. The character of the text as expressed through the choice of terms, systematic transliteration of Hebrew and Aramaic expressions, and the reclamation of lyric flow make for a text that reads like no other of which this writer is aware. In teaching hermeneutics or exegesis, I am given to describing some elements of the process as a virtual time machine in which one seeks to journey to the *Sitz im Leben* of the text. This New Testament translation will aid both Greek students and certainly English Bible students in their efforts toward this end, at a minimum, on the level of the cultural appreciation of the text. It drives home that the Christian Scripture is not a product of our Western commitment to terse, concrete, and specific compositional prose but flows with a soul that we have perhaps not seen regularly since the early twentieth century and the prose traditions that produced writers of great eloquence in many fields. Any student of Scripture who employs the practice of considering an array of translations across literal to free translational styles would benefit by laying a copy of this text on the desktop.

Many readers will appreciate the annotations, as they both inform of significant details and do so without condescension or too obvious agenda. Where Barnstone speaks to potentially controversial issues, he does so gracefully, I think, in separate essays and appendices. These opinions do not appear to overtly bias his work with the text, and that is to be appreciated by anyone who wishes to come to the text in the absence of predeterminations.

Having said these things, it presents what for me would be my principle critique. The reader will quickly pick up on the fact that for the author the issue of anti-Semitism is of great moment, both historically and within the redactional and translational history of the text. Both in essays and appendices, Barnstone speaks to the issue, lamenting a legacy of negativity and even hatred toward the Jewish nation. Translational work has too often passively facilitated such attitudes by stripping away the Jewishness of Jesus and others of the early church. Much careful reflection is given to both the attitudes toward Jews expressed by historical persons in church history, such as John Donne, and also some of the Gospel writers such as "John," who tend to "demonize" the Jews as culpable for the death of Christ. Some of this is a given; some of this is controversial. However, the critique is simply this. Regarding the anti-Semitic effects of the loss of Jesus' Jewish identity, Barnstone affirms: "Contemporary scholars and some readers know better, but the anachronistic portrayal of Yeshua and his circle as Christians among enemy Jews permits an unquestioned hatred of the Jew, and is a logical, understandable, and inevitable reading of the New Testament as we have it" (18). Barnstone then points to the undoubted consternation that first-century Jews would feel when four decades after Jesus' death a "Jewish Jesus with a Gentile voice" (within the Gospel text) speaks of the destruction of Jerusalem as a terrible punishment (divine?). He sees this as a textual anomaly to be corrected by scholars such as Marcus Borg, whom he cites subsequently as correcting such textual misspeaks. My critique is twofold. First, such a reading that directs enmity toward the Jews as a people-group is scarcely inevitable. The imagery of the New Testament is crystal clear that Jesus loved and was loved by the Jewish people in significant degree. That certain individuals held animosity toward Jesus due to jealousy or resentment over perceived theological claims diminishes in no way the clear message that there is an unbroken thread of continuity between the Hebrew covenant and the Christian covenant. In the Gospel, poor people hear Jesus gladly, women find him to be amazingly egalitarian against the backdrop of the culture, and the outreach to the Jewish community within the early church is so normative as to hardly prompt remark.

Second, without doubt, Barnstone is correct that persons throughout history have shaped the text to fit an anti-Semitic agenda. However, I wonder if the language of the above citation exaggerates the scope of this danger within any given setting, including our own? In thirty years of teaching, pastoral duty, and collegial work, I have not encountered many attitudes from persons that would reflect such. On the contrary, my experience has been that the vast majority of persons are quick to affirm Jesus' Jewishness as well as that of his disciples. They readily affirm that the Jewish people are persons of sacred worth rather than objects of repudiation. Granted, I teach in an institution with an evangelical ethos, and characteristically there has been there a more positive outlook in such matters.

Overall, I enthusiastically recommend this volume as a valuable investment for academic as well as personal collections.

BIBLE AND CULTURE

Ecological Hermeneutics: Biblical, Historical and Theological Perspectives, edited by David G. Horrell, Cherryl Hunt, Christopher Southgate, and Francesca Stavrakopoulou. New York: T&T Clark, 2010. Pp. xii + 333. Paper. $44.95. ISBN 9780567033048.

Russell Pregeant, Curry College, Milton Massachusetts

Ecological Hermeneutics is an important book on an important subject. It is a collection of twenty essays resulting "from a collaborative research project at the University of Exeter, UK, on 'Uses of the Bible in Environmental Ethics'" (vii). Following a general introduction by David Horrell, the book is divided into three sections (indicated by the subtitle), each of which is introduced by one of the other editors. Part 1 consists of eight essays on specific biblical texts, equally divided between the two Testaments; part 2 includes eight articles on figures in the history of Christian interpretation from the patristic period to the present; and part 3 is devoted to four examinations of contemporary hermeneutical possibilities. The result is a unique and useful contribution to the growing literature on ecology and the Bible. The editors have not imposed a specific methodology on the contributors, but the volume reflects in a general way the intention of the Exeter project "to develop a position somewhere between the stance of 'recovery' represented in some evangelical writing and in *The Green Bible* on the one hand, and the critical ecojustice hermeneutic developed by The Earth Bible Team on the other" (8). The individual essays draw in positive ways on both these perspectives (and some members of the Earth Bible Team are among the contributors) but also critique them at some points. The approach of this volume is distinctive as "an attempt to construct an ecological theology which, while innovative, is nonetheless coherent (and in dialogue) with a scripturally shaped Christian orthodoxy," even while acknowledging the difficulty in delineating what is orthodox (8–9). In this reviewer's opinion, the volume is highly successful in walking that treacherous tightrope, and therein lies one of its most attractive features.

The first article in part 1 is a treatment of the creation stories by John Rogerson, who criticizes attempts to soften the implications of the subjugation-terminology in Gen 1:26–28 but argues that a reading in the broader context of Gen 1–9 puts the relationship between human beings and the rest of creation into a different perspective. In an essay on the ritual of sacrifice in Leviticus, Jonathan Morgan stresses the cultural divide between the world of the text and that of the contemporary reader, questions "traditional assumptions regarding the substitutionary function, passivity and victimhood of the sacrificial animal" (33), and interprets sacrifice (in light of Gen 1–11) as an act of humility born of an awareness of human responsibility for violence and corruption. John Barton finds only minimal contributions, such as an awareness of the natural order, in the authentic words of the prophets but points to helpful passages, dating from later times, that reflect a "cosmic covenant." Among the more promising biblical texts, according to Katharine Dell, are the wisdom writings. Focusing on Proverbs, Job, and Ecclesiastes, she finds anthropocentric tendencies but also a strong sense of the inherent value of the natural world apart from human beings as well as of the "complex web of life" that includes all creatures. In an article on the Synoptic Gospels, Richard Bauckham finds significant signs of the creation theology familiar from the Hebrew Bible in Jesus' teachings and argues that the coming of the kingdom both renews creation as a whole and institutes a kind of ecotopia in which human beings and the wild are reconciled and chaotic forces are pacified. Brendan Byrne, in a discussion of Rom 8:19–22, contends that the "groaning of creation" signifies the nonhuman creation's "outward manifestation of hope" (89) and that the restoration/transformation of human beings is intimately linked to that of the rest of the created order. Reading Colossians in light of the Hellenistic cosmology it presupposes, Vicky Balabanski finds a strong affirmation of the interconnectedness of the human and nonhuman components of creation and the articulation of a cosmic Christology that can foster dialogue with current scientific cosmology and challenges the dualism that has pervaded Western thought. Edward Adams tackles 2 Pet 3:5–13, a text with seemingly little positive potential for eco-friendly interpretation, and begins by denying that its image of the earth's destruction can be interpreted as transformation. He argues, however, that the author envisions a renewal beyond the destruction that remains "in continuity with what has gone before" (117).

In part 2, Francis Watson examines Irenaeus's use of the creation motif in the Gospel of John in refuting Valentinian theology. The result is both a challenge to the "anthropomonism" inherent in the construal of the Christian faith in terms of the fall-redemption model and an emphasis on the salvific character of the incarnation. Morwenna Ludlow critiques the assertion of human domination in the writings of Origen, Basil, Gregory of Nyssa, and Augustine—an emphasis continuous with the philosophical and cultural climate of the day. However, she identifies positive elements in the distinctively Christian aspects of their biblical interpretation, such as "the goodness of God's material creation" and "the continuity between humans and other animals" (152). Although many interpreters find a strong anthropocentrism in Aquinas's thought, Mark Wynn uncovers contrary elements rooted in the concept of God as *being*, rather than mind or intelligence, and notes that for Aquinas nonhuman creatures have their own aims and that "the universe as a whole ... images God better in some respects than does any individual creature" (162). Recognizing what he terms a "the-anthropocentric" dimension of Luther's theology, Paul Santmire argues that Luther's mature thought—with its strong sense of God's presence in all things—can be characterized as "a theology of the Word of God *in nature*" (167). Could it therefore, Santmire asks, "be construed both in terms of God and humanity and in terms of God and nature, that is, both the-anthropocentrically ... and the-cosmocentrically?" (178). To many critics, Karl Barth's stringent opposition to natural theology might seem to preclude any positive contribution to eco-friendly biblical interpretation, but Geoff Thompson finds an overlap between Barth and eco-theologians in their shared "critique of and resistance to anthropocentrism" (181), which plays itself out, for example, in the denial of "unlimited human lordship over the earth" (192). David Moss, while acknowledging that Hans Urs von Balthasar had virtually nothing direct to say regarding the environmental crisis, finds an important point of contact in his hermeneutics of beauty, which points beyond particular beings to the whole as well as to a *sympatheia* between human beings and the cosmos. The two final essays in this section, on Eastern Orthodoxy and Jürgen Moltmann, respectively, explore theologians who make more direct contributions to ecological theology. Andrew Louth shows that from early times Eastern thought has placed the fall-redemption arc within the broader arc of creation-deification and goes on to argue that the crucial contribution of this thought lies in its "faithfulness to a sense of the holiness of the created order, and a sense of the holiness of the human being" (222). Moltmann's thought, according to Jeremy Law, "has long been an ecological theology" (223). More specifically, Moltmann develops a Trinitarian hermeneutics designed to bring the biblical texts to bear on current issues as well as a Trinitarian panentheism that recognizes "the presence of God *in* the world as well as the presence of the world *in* God" (232).

Part 3 begins with Harry Maier's examination of a wide range of ways in which American evangelicals have viewed the environment through the lens of the book of Revelation, ranging from hostility toward the environmental movement to forms of "green millennialism" that embrace social activism in one form or another. In an essay on New Testament eschatology informed by postmodern concerns and scientific observations on the fate of the universe, Stephen Barton identifies three tasks involved in the search for wisdom related to the ecological crisis—the biblical-exegetical, the theological-hermeneutical, and the personal-ascetical—and assesses contributions made from each of these perspectives. Tim Gorringe takes up the issue of the sustainability of the countryside, drawing upon the texts for Rogation Sundays in the Revised Common Lectionary to critique oppressive economies and land usage. He stresses the biblical understanding of divine ownership of the land, which implies "common ownership of the means of production" (291), and the spiritual roots of the ecological crisis. In the volume's final essay, Ernst Conradie lays out "broad parameters" for an ecological hermeneutic, defining hermeneutics as a specifically theoretical discipline and its task as "continuously re-appropriating and responding to the significance of signs in everyday life" (298). He discusses various interpretive strategies employed in the task of reappropriating biblical materials as well as the role of specific doctrinal constructs that help the interpreter form "links between the text and contemporary context" (300). In the end, he searches for doctrinal constructs suited to meet the ecological challenge and argues that "an ecological biblical hermeneutics should go hand in hand with a reformulation of Christian doctrine" (311).

The shadow of Lynn White's classic article laying much of the blame for the ecological crisis at the doorstep of the Bible and its interpreters through the centuries looms large in this volume, as indeed it does over the entire contemporary effort to make positive use of the Jewish and Christian scriptures in the face of that crisis. Emphasizing eco-friendly passages in these scriptures can help, but the weight of problematic material is far too great for this approach to be adequate in itself. On the other hand, to consign the Bible to the trash heap would ignore the enormous influence of biblical faith in contemporary society and deprive ecological activists of an important ally. One postmodern alternative is to recognize the inherently perspectival character of all interpretation and simply choose an eco-friendly hermeneutical strategy for garnering meaning. As Conradie points out, however, such an approach deprives scripture of its own distinctive voice, and for the believing reader this means that "[t]he text itself can yield no surprises, no challenges, no shock or amazement, no revelation; God's Word can no longer be heard anew" (304). This collection of essays, in my estimation, avoids the pitfalls of each of these approaches, taken by themselves, in its creative combination of healthy suspicion, a desire for retrieval, and sophisticated modes of rereading.

The fresh and invigorating articles in this volume are all worthy of serious consideration, and the book as a whole merits use in a variety of courses on the graduate and advanced undergraduate levels. By bringing together highly competent essays in the fields of biblical exegesis, the history of interpretation, and theology, the editors offer us an invaluable set of resources for the ongoing task of reshaping Christian thought in light of the environmental crisis.

The Bible in/and Popular Culture: A Creative Encounter, edited by Philip Culbertson, and Elaine M. Wainwright. Semeia Studies 65. Atlanta: Society of Biblical Literature, 2010. Pp. vi + 210. Paper. $26.95. ISBN 9781589834934.

Claudia Setzer, Manhattan College, Riverdale, New York

This volume of essays was inspired by a course taught by the editors on the Bible and popular culture at the University of Auckland, New Zealand. Elaine Wainwright introduces the collection, explaining that no one has systematically unpacked the relationship between the Bible and popular culture, despite biblical scholars sampling liberally from popular culture's adaptations of the Bible and cultural theorists embracing theology and pop culture. To provide more theoretical sophistication, the tools and insights of a diverse group of theoreticians are brought to the unpacking process, including those of Michel de Certeau, Pierre Bourdieu, Mikhail Bakhtin, Judith Butler, and James Scott. A varied group of biblical scholars also make appearances within these pages, including Richard Elliott Friedman, Robert Alter, James Kugel, and J. Louis Martyn.

Michael Gilmour provides an opening image for the volume from Salman Rushdie. All the stories of the world are ever-swirling in a vast sea, and anyone may dip in her cup. Biblical narratives are currents within that sea, infiltrating and colored by other stories. Citing Homi Bhabha and Robert Alter, Gilmour emphasizes an unfixed canon, constant flux, and the Bible as one set of stories among many ("Some Novel Remarks about Popular Culture and Religion: Salman Rushdie and the Adaptation of Sacred Texts").

The body of the book presents essays examining individual artists and their uses of biblical materials, as well as experimenting with method. Mark McEntire parallels the withdrawal of God as active character across the Hebrew Bible, identified by narrative critics such as Friedman and Jack Miles, with the increasingly elusive God invoked by Emmylou Harris in her album *Red Dirt Girl*. Harris seems to be helping her listeners learn to live with God's silence while navigating life's struggles ("Red Dirt God: Divine Silence and the Search for Transcendent Beauty in the Music of Emmylou Harris"). Dan W. Clanton argues that Jesus in popular American culture functions as "an empty shell into which various meanings or significations can be poured" (57). He cites the multiplicities of Jesus figures promoted in American culture, from Henry Ward Beecher through Cecil

B. DeMille and Mel Gibson to graphic novels, arguing that the reception history, or "afterlife," of the Bible has been far more influential than its original contexts. Culbertson's essay makes a similar case, showing that the image of Mary Magdalene as a penitent whore remains compelling to his students, even after they learn its postbiblical provenance. He suggests that the fallen and redeemed woman is a more useful symbol for today's young people, its patriarchy and sexual activity more familiar and consonant with their experience ("'Tis a Pity She's (Still) a Whore: Popular Music's Ambivalent Resistance to the Reclamation of Mary Magdalene").

Jim Perkinson adopts a hip-hop style to tap the resistant and liberating possibilities of several biblical texts ("Spittin', Cursin', and Outin': Hip-Hop Apocalypse in the Imperial Necropolis"). The power of the Bible to shape an alternative identity is also on display in Bob Marley's music, his famous album *Exodus* making him something of a modern Moses, declaring liberation for his people. Noel Leo Erskine shows the ubiquity of the Bible in Jamaica and how Rastafarians equate Jamaica with Babylon and Ethiopia with Zion, Israel's exile the story of Ethiopians and their subsequent exile in Jamaica ("The Bible and Reggae: Liberation or Subjugation").

Tex Sample considers everyday forms of resistance to domination as developed by several theorists, including Certeau, Bakhtin, and Scott ("'Help Me Make It through the Night': Narrating Class and Country Music in the Theology of Paul"). He examines the enduring popularity of two songs among working-class Americans, "Help Me Make It through the Night" and "Me and Bobby McGee," both of which articulate a loss of dignity and autonomy and visualize a precarious future. Sample narrates this struggle for dignity into Paul's theology in Galatians, where enslavement to the "elemental spirits of the universe" is overcome by a new freedom brought about by Christ's death. Paul's antinomies find parallel in today's oppositions based on race, class, and gender. Roland Boer traces a change in the work of songwriter Nick Cave around 1990, when he turned to more introspective, less raucous music, including many references to Jesus ("'Jesus of the Moon': Nick Cave's Christology"). Boer describes this as indicating Cave's working out of his own heretical (because entirely individualistic) Christology.

Terry Ray Clark examines apocalyptic themes in two graphic novels, *Kingdom Come* and *Watchmen*. Despite their comic tone, both offer prophetic calls to action, taking on elements of sacred text as traditional religiosity wanes ("Prophetic Voices in Graphic Novels: The 'Comic and Tragic Vision' of Apocalyptic Rhetoric in *Kingdom Come* and *Watchmen*"). Steve Taylor looks at the New Zealand cartoon series *bro'Town*, which represents the concerns of second-generation Pacific Island migrants, an ethnic minority in New Zealand ("'Pop-Wise': The Very Fine Art of 'Making Do' When Reading the Bible in *bro'Town*"). Clark invokes Certeau's "practical science of the singular" (162) and Scott's "hidden transcripts," looking at the subversive strategies of the everyday by which people "make do." *Bro'Town* presents God as an active agent and ethical teacher, even as it critiques traditional forms of Bible reading.

Tina Pippin's essay is a closing frame to the book's theme of texts and their afterlives ("Daemons and Angels: The End of the World according to Philip Pullman"). She considers the weight of traditional apocalyptic scenarios like those in Revelation or modern-day versions like the Left Behind series or Tribulation Trail in Stockbridge, Georgia. In contrast, the fantasy visions in Philip Pullman's trilogy, *His Dark Materials*, present, for Pippin, a healthy alternative where "we (readers) are pulled into possibilities of life, our own maturity, a rejection of the mad apocalyptic deity" (181). A final section includes a review of the volume by Laura Copier, Jaap Kooijman, and Caroline Vander Stichele ("Close Encounters: The Bible as Pre-Text in Popular Culture") and a reflection by Erin Runions on the implications of pop culture's rewriting of the Bible as a nudge toward social change ("Pop Scripture: Creating Small Spaces for Social Change"). Copier, Kooijman, and Vander Stichele make the case for the value of examining the Bible–pop culture nexus as its own phenomenon, arguing the Bible is not a master text but a "pre-text," a source that generates but does not predetermine what it helps to bring forth.

This volume is a welcome invitation to all biblical scholars to reflect and theorize on the Bible's place in contemporary culture. The Bible is omnipresent, it demonstrates, but has lost much of its authoritative status. It makes the case for taking pop culture seriously as the place where most people, especially the young, spend much of their time. If anything, it uncovers the powerful generative force of texts, even if they no longer exert control over how they are used (if they ever did). The breadth of the contributions is quite amazing, in media, methods, and geography. Subsequent projects may wish to separate the strands a bit, say, distinguishing use of the Bible in the United States from use in New Zealand or Jamaica.

The more compelling essays tried to draw together scholarly insights and pop culture, considering the relation of current adaptations, playful and serious, to the continuing process of interpretation. Even while presenting alternatives, McEntire, Clanton, Sample, Clark, and Pippin engage with "traditional" readings. More irritating are the scholars who assume that they and their subjects are doing something entirely new, that the Bible was an inert, frozen thing, or a domineering "master text" until it was translated into a popular medium. A look at rabbinic midrash shows a playful and creative approach, hardly bound by the literal meaning of the biblical text. Furthermore, Christian theologians such as Serene Jones or Elizabeth Johnson do not treat scripture as a "master text" so much as a rich resource from which to draw.

Three issues arise. First, the evanescent quality of the subject matter is part of its nature. Gospel themes in graphic novels make a good paper topic today, but who cares about "The Gospel according to Peanuts?" Does the short-lived quality of the subject matter present a problem? Second, these examinations also reveal the essential conservatism of popular culture. "The Bible" in this work is the Christian one and is thoroughly canonical. McEntire's essay, for example, requires a canon to make his case for the development of a certain image of God. One author mentions the cliché of the "spiteful God" of the Old Testament versus the "quiet, sad Christ of the New (131)." Culbertson shows that the Mary Magdalene of culture resists even biblical analysis itself. As knowledge of the Bible wanes, does pop culture tend toward caricature? Last, I could not help but think about the surprising esotericism and exclusivism of pop culture, as I, a middle-aged professor, worked my way through the hip-hop interpretation in one author or the slang of New Zealand teenagers in another. By definition, pop culture is audience-specific, often limited to one gender or generation. Humor, especially, rarely transcends generations, as I discovered showing *Annie Hall* to my undergraduates. Thus pop culture excludes as much as any stuffy academic work.

The volume presents us with the expansiveness and nearly unlimited possibility of examining popular culture's hermeneutic. Thus it opens an ambitious, global, and delightful chapter in the interpretation of the Bible as part of the human quest for meaning.

The Bible in/and Popular Culture: A Creative Encounter, edited by Philip Culbertson, and Elaine M. Wainwright. Semeia Studies 65. Atlanta: Society of Biblical Literature, 2010. Pp. vi + 210. Paper. $26.95. ISBN 9781589834934.

Anthony Swindell, Saint Saviour's Rectory, Jersey, United Kingdom

This important collection of essays brings together some widely diverse studies of the Bible's impact on contemporary culture, represented here by material originating from the United States, New Zealand, Jamaica, and Britain.

The aim, as Elaine Wainwright explains in the introduction is, in deliberate contrast to some previous exercises, to go beyond an almost exclusive concentration on film studies and also to provide more engagement with the work of cultural theorists. For example, the ideas of Michel de Certeau about "places" and "spaces" as, respectively, the dominating discourse of the powerful and the resistant discourse of the powerless are brought to bear extensively. In the end, we are offered a multiplicity of possible frameworks rather than one key one, doing justice to the wide variety of material that the constituent essays of this volume cover. However, if one could sum up the overall tendency of the contributors, it is to uncover resistance to the enlistment of the Bible by hegemonic discourse.

The essays begin with Michael Gilmour on Salman Rushdie's *The Satanic Verses* as (in part) a parody of the Oriental Other conceived as the satan of such biblical texts as the Job prologue, the wilderness fasting of Jesus in Matt 4:1–11, and the fall of the devil from heaven in Rev 12:9, with further biblical material borrowed from its refraction in Milton's *Paradise Lost* and mixed with other nonbiblical, including qur'anic, intertexts. Gilmour argues that the monstrous metamorphosis of Saladin Chamcha in the novel is the central conceit for the headlong collision of two previously individuated cultures.

Mark McEntire traces the progress of God as a character in the songs of Emmylou Harris, finding a parallel in the decentralization or veiling of the divine persona that Jack Miles identifies as a central feature of the Hebrew Bible in his book *God: A Biography*. Dan W. Clanton explores aspects of the representation of Jesus in American popular culture, ranging from the inculcation of piety in Mel Gibson's *Passion* through *Jesus Christ Vampire Hunter* to the episodic appearance of the serio-comical Jesus figure in *South Park*. He concludes that Jesus becomes in American popular culture a pliable myth for reinforcing cultural identity. Philip Culbertson's essay on Mary Magdalene then documents the insistently regressive treatment of her as a whore in a range of popular lyrics, concluding that students should be weaned away from binaries and encouraged to appreciate the complexities of Mary Magdalene as a composite representational response to a slender textual witness.

Thereafter several of the essays detect a more immediately optimistic strain in popular appropriation of biblical material. Jim Perkinson argues for hip-hop reading of Scripture as a medium of urban revolt against racism and poverty. Noel Erskine finds in the Jamaican reggae of Bob Marley the liberationist use of biblical themes such as God as creator and the conflated trope of the exodus/the escape from Babylon as a trope for throwing off the colonialist subjugatory use of biblical texts, though it will be left to women like Lilian Allen to cleanse the liberation movement itself of misogyny. Tex Sample adventurously identifies the theology of Paul as an intertext for country music, in particular Kris Kristofferson's "Help Me Make It through the Night." Roland Boer discusses the heretical Christology of Nick Cave's rock music as an engagement with the intensity of Christ's struggle against the mundane and his sorrow. Terry Ray Clark examines the presence of the prophetic voice in the graphic novels *Kingdom Come* and *Watchmen*, though this turns out be more the apocalyptic voice read as a warning against civilization's self-destructive lurch toward nuclear war. Steve Brown utilizes the theories of Certau to interpret the New Zealand TV cartoon series *bro'Town* as a form of resistance to hegemonic discourse, in particular as it affects immigrants from the Pacific Islands. Finally, Tina Pippin presents Philip Pullman's trilogy of children's novel *The Dark Materials* as a salutary counter to the patriarchal and doom-laden discourse of "apocalypseland."

The volume concludes with two "responses" to the foregoing essays. The first, by Laura Copier, Jaap Kooijman, and Caroline Vander Stichele, seeks to draw together the variegated threads, noting that the "Bible" under discussion is already a part of culture and a very particular selection from the totality of the combined Hebrew Bible and Christian New Testament. This short essay also highlights the wide range of interpretive strategies and methodologies used by the earlier authors, arguing that the strength of popular culture lies in its inclusiveness, with its weakness lying in its vulnerability to manipulative use. At their best, the Bible and popular culture can be mutually transformative in an era in which the Bible informs but does not determine the popular use of its themes. The second response, by Erin Runions, looks at "Pop Scripture" as a prescription for social change, observing the push and pull between progressive and regressive uses of biblical material in this arena. She suggests that a central feature of pop scripture is a renegotiation of the nature of the divine in which (in Pippin's terms) the kingdom of heaven gives way to the republic of heaven.

Inevitably, the scale of this project gives rise to a number of questions that the book itself does not address. (1) Why does "popular culture" seem to refer only to *contemporary* popular culture? In the authors' effort to address issues arising from the "teaching the Bible" project, they seem to have disregarded the vast reserves of folkloric tradition in the treatment of biblical material, though this is something that the authors of the penultimate response imply when they state that "there is a long reception history between 'then' and now which cannot be ignored" (192).

(2) In Michael Gilmour's essay, Salman Rushdie's *The Satanic Verses* is treated in an undifferentiated way as part of popular culture. But is it right to lump what many regard as high fiction together with pop culture? The issues raised by the undoubted existence of a Western literary canon cannot simply be bypassed. There is a difference between formulaic or even mass-market fiction and the sort of nuanced, intertextualized fiction of authors like Rushdie. It might also be worth observing that Rushdie's notion of the sea of stories (which the writer of the essay applauds) may suggest less "a seemingly endless mix of voices" from religions across the globe and "high and low art" and more specifically the Kathasaritsagara, the great compendium of Indian folktales and myths dating from what we designate as the eleventh century, the first English translation of which was T. H. Tawney's ten-volume edition of 1880, *The Ocean of Story*. To put it another way, irrespective of what may be imputed to be authorial intention, this is the specific freight that the phrase "ocean/sea of stories" carries in reception history.

(3) Although there is a very searching attempt to distinguish in (for example) Noel Erskine's essay on Reggae between "liberation" and "subjugation," we are not invited in the volume as a whole to consider examples in which popular appropriation of biblical themes might be even more problematic than that which is subjugatory. One thinks of the treatment historically of the figure of Judas in European popular culture.

Overall, despite these minor reservations, the book is a bold and invaluable foray into whole areas in the popular (contemporary) reception of the Bible that have hitherto been neglected. It is also an invitation to other scholars to expand the range of coverage to geographical regions not touched in this sample (South America, Eastern Europe, Asia) and to yet further popular genres in which biblical material is reworked.

In a curious way, this book also reignites rather urgently the debate over the place of realized eschatology in the teaching of Jesus, if the world inhabited by the largely Christian or quasi-Christian popular culture described here finds itself addressed separately by biblically motivated liberationists and those who, mystically or otherwise, await the return of the king.

Secularism and Biblical Studies, edited by Roland Boer. BibleWorld. London: Equinox, 2010. Pp. vi + 219. Paper. $26.95. ISBN 9781845533755.

Brent Landau, University of Oklahoma, Norman, Oklahoma

Does a secular biblical studies exist? What might its hermeneutical principles be? Does it demand strict atheism/agnosticism on the part of its practitioners, or is there some place for religious adherence in it? What deficiencies in the discipline as currently practiced does it attempt to correct? These are some of the thought-provoking questions that run through this collection of essays. The volume, unfortunately, spends perhaps too much time debating the meaning(s) of the contentious term "secularism" and fails to examine in any substantial fashion the state of affairs that has, I suspect, encouraged most of these scholars to contribute to this volume in the first place. I speak of the recent encroachment (or enduring presence, depending on one's perspective) into professional biblical studies of what one contributor refers to as "faith-based academic scholarship" (15). Moreover, there are some questionable editorial decisions about which pieces have received extended discussion. Despite these shortcomings, several of the contributions are truly outstanding, challenging pieces, and numerous insights are also scattered throughout the less-effective chapters.

Roland Boer's introduction to the collection starts by discussing the various ways of defining secularism, as well as noting some of the striking paradoxes found in implementations of secularism (such as the controversy over the headscarf ban in France). Boer then describes how, among the various methodological fissures in biblical studies, there is the increasing visibility of "a struggle between those who rely on a transcendent category in order to interpret the Bible and those who draw their terms purely from this world" (9). An outline of the book's four major sections follows.

The first section consists of two of the pieces arguably most responsible for the renewed interest in this topic: those of Michael V. Fox and Jacques Berlinerblau posted on the *SBL Forum* website in 2006.[1] Fox's short piece makes several points. First, he states that "claims … for the legitimacy of faith-based academic scholarship" have become much more prevalent in recent years (15). Although he mentions two such examples at the end of his essay (18), a much more substantial inventorying of faith-based approaches to biblical studies would be extremely useful. Among the possible culprits for this trend, he blames a mindset, "loosely associated with postmodernism, that tolerates and even encourages ideology in scholarship and advocacy in instruction" (16). In contrast to such faith-based reasoning, he instead calls for a "secular, academic, religiously-neutral hermeneutic" that understands both the best and worst parts of the Bible "as products of human

---

1. The links to Fox's and Berlinerblau's pieces on the *SBL Forum* are: http://www.sbl-site.org/publications/ article.aspx?ArticleId=490 and http://www.sbl-site.org/publications/article.aspx?ArticleId=503.

imperfection and imagination in an ancient historical context" (16). Fox closes with a parting shot at those institutions that "base their scholarship on premises of faith and require conclusions consonant with those premises" (18).

In the title of Berlinerblau's essay, what he refers to as "The Unspeakable in Biblical Scholarship" is the simple fact that most professional biblical scholars came to this career because of their personal faith as Christians or Jews (20). In contrast to Fox, it is not the overtly faith-based scholars who trouble Berlinerblau so much as all those "researchers who in every facet of their private lives are practicing Jews or Christians, but who—somehow—deny that this may influence their professional scholarly work" (21). It is unclear, though, how much overlap he would see between this category of scholars and those who, say, simply attend church or synagogue on a semi-regular basis. In other words, just how involved does someone have to be in a religious community to lose his or her objectivity?

Despite his pessimism concerning the objectivity of biblical researchers, Berlinerblau's essay contains an intriguing, almost throwaway, parenthetical remark that would merit further reflection. While observing the strong tendency of biblical studies to attract the already religious, he notes: "(True, they sometimes exit as something else, but that's another story altogether.)" (22). Actually, I am not sure that it is beside the point: my anecdotal impression is that many people who enter biblical studies become less religiously conservative—or even less religious—over their careers, not more so. But such a supposition would require considerably more research, just as would Berlinerblau's impression of the very conservative specialist in ancient Near Eastern studies (21).

Even though the essays of Fox and Berlinerblau attracted a large number of responses after they were posted on the SBL Forum website, they stand alone in the present volume. The second major section of the book consists of Roland Boer's "A Manifesto for Biblical Studies," followed by four responses. Boer's manifesto consists of five theses to counter the "exploitation and oppression carried out in the name of the Bible" (27) by right-wing church and state institutions. Thus, his essay is expressly political in a way that those of Fox and Berlinerblau are not.

Boer's first thesis is that "an unruly and fractious Bible has been colonized by church, theology, and theological programmes," (38) so scholars must seek to remove themselves from these spheres of influence. I do question, however, whether Boer's claim that the "disciplinary home of biblical studies" (28) is still widely assumed to be in theological schools accurately reflects the situation in the United States, where the major Ph.D.-producing programs in biblical studies are either in the religion departments of state and private, nonsectarian universities or in university-affiliated divinity schools whose confessional identity is practically nonexistent.

Theses two and three are not especially controversial: that scholars need to adopt "a healthy theological suspicion," (38) both for the ideologies of the texts themselves and those of later interpreters; and that biblical studies must become more conversant with other academic disciplines, such as literary, cultural, anthropological, and social-scientific studies (38). All of these other fields are, in fact, derivatives of theology/biblical studies, yet biblical studies has "for too long hidden from the consequences of the methods it unwittingly unleashed" (33).

Given Boer's harsh indictment of church institutions, his fourth thesis is somewhat surprising: secular biblical scholars should use their expertise to assist the religious left in its struggles against the "biblically-based" agendas of the religious and political right (38). Here Boer seems to simply assume that the Bible is friendlier (or at least as friendly) to liberal causes than conservative ones, a point that is certainly contestable, even by those whose sympathies lie with the religious left. His fifth thesis asserts that this sort of alliance may produce more of the revolutionary readings of the Bible that are found in liberation theologies and political reform movements (38).

In the first of four responses, Hanna Stenström points out that Boer's manifesto universalizes the situation of biblical scholarship and does not accurately reflect the situation of an already largely secular discipline in Sweden (42–45). She also suggests that histories of the discipline in specific countries are needed, along with studies of the ways in which biblical scholarship has been received by people outside the academy (46–47). Niels Peter Lemche's piece is, regrettably, quite disjointed and astonishingly simplistic in its depiction of religious adherents (e.g., "There are true believers and the godless. The religious mind knows of no more human categories," 52).

Mark Brett's is the most critical of the four, suggesting that a secular biblical criticism would not necessarily lead to more political activism, since "[p]olitical reading of the Bible tends to motivate people who are disposed to take the Bible seriously in the first place" (60). Todd Penner's response is the most insightful; among his best observations are that "secularism is an ideology that is every bit as disciplining of its subjects as is religious belief proper" (70) and that biblical scholars have been largely complacent as the commodification and commercialization of higher education has taken place right under our feet (73–74).

My own reaction was that, as manifestos go, it was actually quite bland. Most of Boer's theses are not substantially different from the sort of disciplinary changes that Elisabeth Schüssler Fiorenza has been urging for more than thirty years. Furthermore, it seemed tame in comparison to the sorts of radical appraisals of the discipline found in the pieces by Berlinerblau and especially Avalos.

"The End of Biblical Studies as a Moral Obligation" is the contribution of Hector Avalos to the volume, and it also is the first of four essays in the section entitled "The End of Biblical Studies?" It is a distillation of his 2007 monograph *The End of Biblical Studies* and is easily the most "manifesto-like" (in the sense of stating a problem and its solution in the most provocative manner possible) of the book's essays. His first point is that the most important contribution of historical-critical study of the Bible has been to demonstrate how *alien* its thought processes are to the contemporary world. The task of scholars should be to impress this point as strongly as possible upon the general public (85–88). His second point is that, when biblical scholars refuse to do this through softening their translations of "hard sayings," emphasizing the Bible's unsurpassed literary brilliance, recontextualizing ethically problematic content, or through other apologetic strategies, their work is morally equivalent to "rehabilitating" a text like *Mein Kampf* (89–96).

To fully assess Avalos's arguments would require far more space than a review of an edited volume affords,[2] so I will only make two observations. First, Avalos is not calling for the end of *all* biblical studies but rather for the end of scholarship that implicitly or explicitly privileges the Bible at the expense of the multitude of important but overlooked texts outside of the canon (96–97). As a scholar who specializes in the Christian Apocrypha, I can certainly agree with this sentiment.

Second, as part of his evidence that the Bible is irrelevant to contemporary life, Avalos cites statistical data indicating that most Americans have very little concrete knowledge of what is in the Bible (87), yet I think that this point needs further clarification: in vast swaths of the United States, the Bible is *enormously* relevant to social, cultural, and political life, even if this relevance does not translate into high levels of biblical literacy. Therefore scholars may need to consider models of relevance and influence that do not include knowledge of the names of biblical books, the differences between the four Gospels, and so forth.

Although the title of this third section clearly references the work of Avalos, the remaining three contributions do not constitute "responses" to his piece, as did those that followed Boer's manifesto. Instead, they reference Avalos only briefly and then present quite different ways of refashioning traditional biblical studies. In the most developed of these, Joseph Marchal argues that scholars should concentrate their efforts on the analysis of "biblical or biblical-sounding arguments" (102), since appealing to Scripture for specific policies or courses of action is the most potent—and often damaging—way in which the Bible is utilized today.

The essays of Heike Omerzu and Philip Chia are rather disappointing. Omerzu assesses the state of New Testament scholarship in Germany, which he argues has significantly weakened since its heyday in the late nineteenth and early twentieth century (116–18). He observes that German scholars have been far more resistant to postmodern and poststructural biblical interpretation than their counterparts in the United States, Britain, and France—although he never speculates about why such resistance exists. Chia's essay intends to address biblical studies as it is practiced in China and its environs. Boer already called attention to China in his manifesto, noting that the Chinese government had commissioned a "scholars' translation" of the Bible, done without the involvement of ecclesiastical authorities (31). Chia, however, does not mention this intriguing case or any other specifics about the situation in China. He briefly suggests that the Bible could aspire to the sort of status that the Chinese classics have, as repositories for societal wisdom (135), but this receives no elaboration.

---

2. As regards Avalos's monograph, the *Review of Biblical Literature* has published one review of it—in German (http://bookreviews.org/pdf/6354_6835.pdf). Only a handful of other scholarly journals have reviewed it.

The fourth and final section, entitled "The Paradoxes of Secularism," discusses several instances of the interplay between religious and secular approaches to the Bible. The first of these essays is Ward Blanton's, which does not fit the "case study" approach of the others. Blanton's main point apparently is that "the religious" and "the secular" do not actually exist as independent entities but only become meaningful through juxtaposition to one another. I say that this is "apparently" his point because it was the only part of his jargon-laden essay that I understood.

The other four essays do contain the sort of specificity that much of the volume has lacked, though it comes quite late in the conversation. Edgar Conrad observes that the recent proliferation of "Ten Commandments monuments" throughout the Bible Belt of the United States is not that different from Thomas Jefferson's removal of miraculous elements from the life of Jesus. Most of these monuments delete significant portions of the texts of the Decalogue—perhaps because they do not seem especially relevant to contemporary life (172–74). Athalya Brenner examines the book of Ruth with reference to the plight of foreign workers in the modern state of Israel, suggesting that knowledge of their situation would make interpreters less likely to romanticize Ruth's accompaniment of her mother-in-law Naomi. Yairah Amit presents the recent case of an Israeli biblical scholar who was consulted about whether or not Samaritans should be considered eligible for Jewish immigrant status on the basis of the evidence for Samaritan origins found in the Bible; that the scholar decided in the affirmative had more to do with ethical and political considerations than with an accurate reconstruction of biblical history. The final essay, by Philip Davies, contends that a mandate for secularism can indeed be found in the Bible—primarily in the wisdom literature of Proverbs and Qoheleth and in a few New Testament passages.

In conclusion, the volume contains several important contributions, but the overall difficulties with the collection undermine their effectiveness. Since most edited volumes suffer from some degree of unevenness of quality among the essays, it is not unusual that this would also be the case here. Unfortunately, however, the problems with the framing of the volume's subject matter and the dearth of attention paid to Avalos's, Berlinerblau's, and Fox's provocative pieces have contributed significantly to the collection's shortcomings.

Love, Lust, and Lunacy: The Stories of Saul and David in Music, by Helen Leneman. Bible in the Modern World 29. Sheffield: Sheffield Phoenix, 2010. Pp. xii + 399. Hardcover. $95.00. ISBN 9781907534065.

Christina Landman, University of South Africa, Pretoria, South Africa

This study shows how the biblical narratives of David and Saul were used as intertexts in operas and oratorios during the nineteenth and twentieth centuries. Special emphasis is on the ability of music to add mood and emotion to the retelling of a known narrative through volume, duration, pitch, and tone.

Apart from George Friedrich Handel's eighteenth-century oratorio *Saul* (1738), fifteen nineteenth- and twentieth-century works have been selected for analysis on the grounds of originality, quality, and accessibility. Oratorios from the nineteenth century include Carl Reissiger's *David* (1852), Ferdinand Hiller's *Saul* (1858), Friedrich Nuhn's *Die Könige in Israel* (1867), Sir George Macfarren's *King David* (1883), and C. H. H. Parry's *King Saul* (1893). One nineteenth-century opera is analyzed: Antonio Buzzi's *Saul* (1852). The twentieth-century oratorios discussed are Charles H. Gabriel's *Saul* (1901), Arthur Honegger's *Le Roi David* (1921), and Christopher Brown's *David* (1970). Finally, the largest group of works presented are six operas from the twentieth century: *Saul og David*, by Carl Nielsen (1902); *David*, by Darius Milhaud (1954); *Shaul b'Endor* (1957) and *Amnon and Tamar*, by Josef Tal (1957); *And David Wept*, by Ezra Laderman (1971); and Flavio Testi's *Saül* (1991). In terms of time and language, these works encompass a vast variety.

The book is well-structured, covering the lives of Saul and David in eight periods as they are described in 1 and 2 Samuel and 1 Kgs 1–2. Each chapter retells the specific period in summary. In this section Leneman points primarily to "gaps" and ambiguities in the biblical story as she experiences it. Leneman is, for instance, amazed at the fact that Saul did not know the young David who was offering to slay Goliath when David had previously delighted him by playing the lyre (64). She also finds a gap in the story in that Michal and Jonathan, who were both Saul's children, did not share a sibling relationship (6). Leneman's retelling of the story is simply based on a surface reading of the text. Some of the "facts" surfacing from a surface reading are, of course, quite interesting, although they do not really bear on the intertextuality of the biblical story as libretto. For example, the conversation between David and Abigail is the lengthiest between a man and a woman in the Bible (8). Also, "David takes up more narrative space … than any other character in the Hebrew Bible" (11). David and the man in the Song of Songs provide the only two instances of the description of male beauty in the Hebrew Bible (13).

In the second sector of each chapter, Leneman provides commentary on the part of the story under discussion. She places the story in historical-critical perspective and exposes it to ideological critique, often supplying a feminist reading of the text. Leneman is not a skilled theologian, and the "commentary" is taken at random from secondary sources without a specific focus or method in mind. Leneman, however, grows in confidence in introducing theological works into her commentary toward the end of the book.

Third, the main section of each chapter consists of an analysis of the setting to music of the storyline under discussion. It is here that Leneman excels in leading readers through the brilliance of the music and librettos and how they "mood"ify the story. Here again Leneman concentrates on how far the librettos and music have deviated from the "original" biblical story, thereby applying a method that mixes a surface reading of the text with historical and ideological readings that are haphazardly applied. Nevertheless, this section makes interesting reading, although it is not to be read at leisure because of the amount of information given and the comprehensiveness of the musical analysis. One interesting feature of the stories of David and Saul put to music is the role that Michal plays in the oratorios and operas. This is quite an extensive role, in spite of the fact that Michal is not well known in lay and even theological circles, excluding, of course, feminist scholarship. The latter does not concentrate on the love between David and Michal but on David abusing her to obtain royal kinship, an interpretation not mentioned in this work. Leneman points out that love duets between David and Michal occurred in all the works studied. In Parry's oratorio David sings to Michal in words from the Song of Songs (119). This appears to be a clear example of how Leneman detects deviations between the musical and biblical versions of the story, without being able to see the differences in ideology and theology.

Each chapter, then, closes with a conclusion that summarizes some findings of the research analysis at random without relating them to the focus of the book, which, as a point of criticism, is never really and clearly defined in the book.

In sum, then, this book is, on the one hand, thin in theology and, on the other, so thick in musical analyses that the average theologian will not be able to grasp the book's implications and depth. However, it is not to be missed by theologians. Not a book that can be read for the fun of it, it nevertheless surprises theologians with interesting interpretations of well-known biblical narratives when these stories fall into the hands of musicians and librettists.

The theological interpretations of the David and Saul operas and oratorios, then, are slim and mainly based on deviations between the biblical text and the librettos. This is a pity, because there is a whole world of interpretation to be done between the lived worlds of the biblical text and the lived worlds of the musical renderings. Between the two lie thousands of years. Obviously the music was written for "biblically literate" audiences, but audiences whose perception of the music was colored by the nineteenth or twentieth century. Leneman would have done well not only to explore the differences in rendering the biblical stories in music but also to explain these differences in terms of the different life-worlds of those for whom the librettos were written in later centuries. Why, for instance, is the patriarchy endemic in the biblical text repeated without criticism in librettos of the nineteenth and twentieth century?

In spite of these few shortcomings, the book is recommended for libraries and students in this field of study. It is well-researched and unique in its contribution.

Index

AUTHORS AND EDITORS

Altmann, Peter	91	Dalrymple, Rob	407
Anderson, Cheryl B.	465	Dearman, J. Andrew	137
Anderson, Paul N.	319	Dell, Katharine	193
Annus, Amar	36	Delorme, Jean	409
Ascough, Richard S.	247	Donegani, Isabelle	409
Assmann, Jan	31	Donelson, Lewis R.	399
Aus, Roger David	284	Dove, Mary	483
Bagnall, Roger S.	468	Dow, Lois K. Fuller	16
Bakirtzis, Charalambos	56	Dozeman, Thomas B.	83, 99
Barnstone, Willis	486	Dubis, Mark	382
Bartor, Assnat	102	Dunn, James D. G.	350
Batten, Alicia J.	395	Duran, Nicole Wilkinson	303
Bers, David	165	Ellens, J. Harold	324
Binder, Donald D.	199	Ellington, Scott A.	19
Bird, Michael	411	Elmer, Ian J.	375
Bock, Darrell L.	272	Fernández, Miguel Pérez	312
Bodi, Daniel	112	Fisk, Bruce N.	275
Boer, Roland	498	Frey, Jörg	420
Botta, Alejandro F.	27	Friesen, Steven J.	56
Brakke, David	429	Gibert, Pierre	447
Brent, Allen	436	Görg, Manfred	21
Brown, William P.	154	Grabbe, Lester L.	60
Burns, Jeffrey	165	Greer, Rowan A.	355
Callaham, Scott N.	39	Hamori, Esther J.	95
Cameron, Ron	347	Hardin, James W.	53
Carter, Christopher L.	364	Heacock, Anthony	116
Charlesworth, James H.	414	Heil, John Paul	372
Choi, Young Sook	352	Herzer, Jens	420
Christensen, Duane L.	147	Hiebert, Robert J. V.	186
Collins, John J.	3	Holsinger-Friesen, Thomas	433
Conklin, Blane	48	Horrell, David G.	488
Corley, Jeremy	300	Horsley, Richard A.	278
Corley, Kathleen E.	265	Hull, Robert F., Jr.	477
Creangă, Ovidiu	72	Hunt, Cherryl	488
Culbertson, Philip	492, 495	Hutton, Jeremy M.	104
Culy, Martin M.	321	Instone-Brewer, David	223

Jaffé, Dan	240	Parry, Robin A.	149
Janßen, Martina	420	Patte, Daniel	1, 303
Jindo, Job Y.	458	Pippin, Tina	13
Kartzow, Marianne Bjelland	369	Portier-Young, Anathea E.	178
Kazen, Thomas	205	Powell, Mark Allan	287
Kelle, Brad E.	64	Radine, Jason	141
Kim, Hyun Chul Paul	129	Rasimus, Tuomas	425
Kirk-Duggan, Cheryl A.	13	Reventlow, Henning Graf	440, 443
Kloppenborg, John S.	247	Reymond, Eric D.	213
Knobloch, Harald	126	Reynolds, Kent Aaron	161
Koltun-Fromm, Naomi	7	Rindos, Jaroslav	293
Kolyada, Yelena	68	Robbins, Maria Mayo	402
Koosed, Jennifer L.	157	Roberge, Michel	417
Kwon, Oh-Young	342	Robertson, C. K.	258
LaCocque, André	89	Rollston, Christopher	50
Lee, Jae Hyun	360	Rothschild, Clare K.	420
LeMon, Joel M.	172	Roukema, Riemer	268
Leneman, Helen	502	Rubenstein, Jeffrey L.	227
Lenzi, Alan	36	Runesson, Anders	199
Levine, Amy-Jill	402	Salmeier, Michael A.	327
Livesey, Nina E.	10	Sandnes, Karl Olav	250
Lyons, Michael A.	132	Schiffman, Lawrence H.	208
Markley, Jennifer Foutz	454	Schlosser, Jacques	388
Matthews, Shelly	334	Schremer, Adiel	219
McCruden, Kevin B.	385	Schüssler, Karlheinz	481
McDonald, Lee Martin	414	Scolnic, Benjamin Edidin	183
McNamara, Martin	234	Scott, Ian W.	358
Miano, David	75	Sharp, Carolyn J.	451
Miller, Merrill P.	347	Short, J. Randall	109, 118
Miller, Robert D., II	196	Sleeman, Matthew	329
Mitchell, Margaret M.	378	Smith, Richard G.	121
Mohrmann, Douglas C.	258	Southgate, Christopher	488
Mol, Jurrien	144	Stavrakopoulou, Francesca	488
Moo, Jonathan A.	180	Steinmann, Andrew E.	168
Moore, Megan Bishop	64	Stone, Michael E.	202
Morales, Rodrigo J.	340	Stulman, Louis	129
Myers, E. A.	244	Sugirtharajah, R. S.	462
Nasrallah, Laura	56	Tadmor, Naomi	474
Oakes, Peter	254, 337	Tait, Michael	254
Okure, Teresa	303	Talmon, Shemaryahu	471
Olsson, Birger	199	Taussig, Hal	261
Oropeza, B. J.	258	Tawil, Hayim	44
Pahl, Michael	411	Thomas, Matthew A.	86
Park, Yoon-Man	306	Thomas, Samuel I.	217

Tjen, Anwar	189	Webb, Robert L.	272, 392
Tooman, William A.	132	Wechsler, byMichael G.	232
Tree, Stephen	165	Weigl, Michael	24
Wagner, Andreas	81	Wire, Antoinette Clark	296
Wahlde, Urban C. von	315	Witherington, Ben, III	256
Wainwright, Elaine M.	492, 495	Xeravits, Géza G.	176
Watson, David F.	282, 309	Zoccali, Christopher	345
Watson, Duane F.	392	Zsengellér, József	176

REVIEWERS

Adam, A. K. M.	440	Engle, John	213
Adams, Sean A.	411	Esler, Philip F.	364
Allen, David M.	358	Eynikel, Erik	176
Allen, Spencer L.	75	Fadden, John W.	205
Angel, Joseph L.	202	Ferguson, Everett	414
Batten, Alicia J.	247	Firth, David G.	109
Becker, Eve-Marie	360	Ford, David E. C.	312
Becking, Bob	64	Gauthier, Randall X.	189
Bennema, Cornelis	319, 324	Grindheim, Sigurd	340
Bennett, Thomas Andrew	433	Grundeken, Mark R. C.	300
Bhayro, Siam	3	Hamilton, Mark W.	21, 24, 81
Botha, Pieter J. J.	261	Hayward, Nicola	265
Brawley, Robert	334	Hoffmeier, James K.	31
Briggs, Richard S.	89	Hogan, Karina Martin	180
Brueggemann, Walter	193	Hood, Renate Viveen	402
Burge, David K.	392	Horsley, Richard	272
Burke, David G.	483	Howard, Melanie	13
Burns, John Barclay	116	Howell, Timothy D.	275
Burns, Joshua Ezra	234	Hudson, Marvin J.	486
Camp, Phillip G.	451	Hundley, Michael B.	95
Chancey, Mark A.	244	Hurtado, Larry W.	296, 477
Collins, Matthew A.	208	Hutton, Jeremy	112
Collins, Raymond F.	350	Hutton, Jeremy M.	39, 172
Crossley, James	284	Jobes, Karen H.	186
Davidson, Steed Vernyl	129	Kaltner, John	232
Davids, Peter H.	399	Kerkeslager, Allen	468
Deppe, Dean	291	Kierspel, Lars	352
Dietrich, Walter	104, 121	Kletter, Raz	53
Donfried, Karl P.	56	Koester, Craig R.	385
Dozeman, Thomas B.	102	Koller, Aaron	27
Draper, Jonathan A.	282	Konkel, August H.	471
Dunn, James D. G.	1, 306, 345	Labahn, Antje	168
Dunn, Steven	161	Landau, Brent	498
Elliott, John H.	382	Landman, Christina	502

Lee, Yongbom	342	Rothschild, Clare K.	293
Leneman, Helen	68, 157	Rubin, Aaron D.	44
Loader, William	254	Russell, Brian D.	99
Loader, William R. G.	465	Satlow, Michael L.	7
Lopez, Davina C.	375	Satterthwaite, Philip E.	19
MacDonald, Dennis R.	250	Scaiola, Donatella	147
Macwilliam, Stuart	72	Schipper, Friedrich	60
Maier, Christl M.	126	Schmeller, Thomas	378
Mathews, Danny	83	Schöpflin, Karin	144
McCruden, Kevin B.	278	Schwartz, Daniel R.	183
McEntire, Mark	86	Schwartz, Joshua	223, 227
McGrath, James F.	268, 417, 429	Sebastian, J. Jayakiran	436
McKenzie, Steven L.	118	Setzer, Claudia	492
McLeod, Frederick G.	355	Ska, Jean Louis	462
Michaud, Jean-Paul	388	Smith, Daniel A.	287
Mitchell, Matthew W.	165	Smith, Steve	303
Morales, Rodrigo J.	372	Stenschke, Christoph	420
Morrow, Jeffrey L.	443, 447	Stone, Timothy J.	149
Morton, Russell	407	Swindell, Anthony	495
Nasuti, Harry P.	154	Thiessen, Matthew	10
Neef, Heinz-Dieter	137	Tiemeyer, Lena-Sofia	474
Neumann, Nils	16, 409	Timmer, Daniel C.	141
Newsom, Carol A.	217	Toffelmire, Colin	458
O'Leary, Anne M.	321	Tomson, Peter J.	219, 240
Osborne, William R.	132	Ukwuegbu, Bernard	258
Parsenios, George L.	315	Walton, Steve	329
Person, Raymond F.	196	Watt, Jan G. van der	454
Pervo, Richard I.	327	Winn, Adam	309
Pregeant, Russell	488	Wire, Antoinette Clark	347
Reed, Stephen A.	91	Wischmeyer, Oda	395
Reinhartz, Adele	199	Witetschek, Stephan	481
Reynolds, Benjamin E.	178	Wright, Richard A.	337
Robinson, Gesine Schenke	425	Young, Ian	50
Rohrbaugh, Richard L.	256	Zamfir, Korinna	369
Rollston, Christopher A.	36	Ziegler, Yael	48

PUBLISHERS

Abingdon	129, 154	Cascade	89, 196, 296
Baker	275, 358, 454	Cerf	388, 409
Baylor University Press	256, 382	Concordia	168
Brill	144, 161, 176, 199, 232, 240, 250, 306, 360, 417, 425	de Gruyter	24, 91, 95, 104, 247, 369, 385
Cambridge University Press	1, 83, 99, 244, 287, 329, 378, 436, 474	Deo	395
		Éditions Gallimard	447

Index of Publishers

Editorial Verbo Divino 312
Eerdmans 3, 64, 137, 149, 178, 202, 208, 223, 234, 272, 315, 350
Eisenbrauns 48, 53, 205, 433, 458, 471
Equinox 68, 498
Fortress 261, 265, 278, 282, 303, 309, 319, 337
Francke 352
Gorgias 411
Gütersloher Verlagshaus 81
Harrassowitz 21, 39, 126, 165, 481
Harvard University Press 56, 109, 118, 429
Johns Hopkins University Press 227
Ktav 44
Lang 293
Mohr Siebeck 10, 141, 340, 375, 420
Neo-Assyrian Text Corpus Project 36
Norton 486
Oxford University Press 7, 219, 334, 465
Pickwick 19, 132, 291, 327, 345
Princeton University Press 468
Sheffield Phoenix 16, 72, 112, 116, 321, 324, 502
Society of Biblical Literature 13, 50, 75, 102, 186, 213, 217, 347, 355, 372, 440, 443, 477, 492, 495
T&T Clark 27, 60, 86, 121, 189, 193, 254, 258, 268, 300, 364, 392, 402, 414, 488
University of Exeter Press 483
University of South Carolina Press 157
University of Wisconsin Press 31
University Press of America 183, 284
Vandenhoeck & Ruprecht 172, 180
Westminster John Knox 399, 451
Wiley-Blackwell 462
Wipf & Stock 342, 407
Yale University Press 147

New and Recent Titles

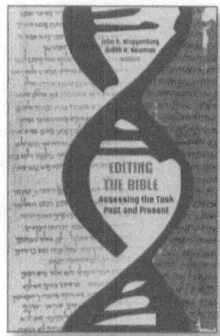

EDITING THE BIBLE
Assessing the Task Past and Present
John S. Kloppenborg and Judith H. Newman, editors

This volume, representing experts in the editing of the Hebrew Bible and the New Testament, discusses both current achievements and future challenges in creating modern editions of the biblical texts in their original languages.
Paper $32.95   978-1-58983-648-8   238 pages, 2012   Code: 060369P
Resources for Biblical Study 69   Hardcover edition www.brill.nl

SOCIAL THEORY AND THE STUDY OF ISRAELITE RELIGION
Essays in Retrospect and Prospect
Saul M. Olyan, editor

This volume assesses past, theoretically engaged work on Israelite religion and presents new approaches to particular problems and larger interpretive and methodological questions, engaging theory from social and cultural anthropology, sociology, postcolonial studies, and ritual studies.
Paper $29.95   978-1-58983-688-4   230 pages, 2012   Code: 060371P
Resources for Biblical Study 71   Hardcover edition www.brill.nl

TEXT, IMAGE, AND OTHERNESS IN CHILDREN'S BIBLES
What Is in the Picture?
Caroline Vander Stichele and Hugh S. Pyper, editors

These essays highlight the complex and sometimes tense relationship between text and image in children's Bibles. Their shared focus is on the representation of "others"—foreigners, enemies, women, even children themselves—in predominantly Hebrew Bible stories.
Paper $31.95   978-1-58983-661-7   378 pages, 2012   Code: 060656P
Semeia Studies 56   Hardcover edition www.brill.nl

Society of Biblical Literature • P.O. Box 2243 • Williston, VT 05495-2243
Phone: 877-725-3334 (toll-free) or 802-864-6185 • Fax: 802-864-7626
Order online at www.sbl-site.org

www.ingramcontent.com/pod-product-compliance
Lightning Source LLC
Chambersburg PA
CBHW020300010526
44108CB00037B/170